Literary Criticisms of Law

Literary Criticisms of Law

GUYORA BINDER AND ROBERT WEISBERG

PRINCETON UNIVERSITY PRESS

PRINCETON, NEW JERSEY

Library of Congress Cataloging-in-Publication Data

Binder, Guyora.
Literary criticisms of law / Guyora Binder and Robert Weisberg.
p.   cm.
Includes bibliographical references and index.
ISBN 0-691-00723-3 (cloth : alk. paper)—ISBN 0-691-00724-1 (pbk. : alk. paper)
1. Law and literature. 2. Culture and law. 3. Law—Interpretation and construction.
4. Literature—History and criticism. I. Weisberg, Robert, 1946– II. Title.
K487.C8B56   2000
340—dc21   99-037484

This book has been composed in Times Roman typeface

The paper used in this publication meets the minimum requirements
of ANSI / NISO Z39.48-1992 (R1997) (*Permanence of Paper*)

http://pup.princeton.edu

Printed in the United States of America
1 2 3 4 5 6 7 8 9 10

TO

ARIEL JOSEPH BINDER,

GALIA OLIN BINDER,

ELIZABETH SARAH PAULINE WEISBERG,

AND OLIVER PAUL WEISBERG

CONTENTS

PREFACE

THIS BOOK examines the many ways we can view law as a kind of literary or cultural activity. It represents law as a practice of making various kinds of literary artifacts: interpretations, narratives, characters, rhetorical performances, linguistic signs, figurative tropes, and representations of the social world. It treats law as a process of meaning making and as a crucial dimension of modern cultural life.

Such a work is possible today only because of the efforts and innovations of scores of scholars in law, literature, and other fields over the last two decades. Thus, in presenting law as a kind of literature, this book also summarizes and builds on many of the achievements of a new interdisciplinary movement devoted to the study of "Law and Literature." This movement embraces both the study of legal themes in imaginative literature—law *in* literature—and the use of the methods of literary criticisms in understanding and evaluating laws, legal institutions, and legal processes—law *as* literature. It is this latter endeavor, the study of law *as* literature, that is the subject of this book.

While we agree that law is usefully seen as a practice of literary creation, we remain mindful that to depict law is in itself to perform a kind of literary trope, to create a literary artifact. A central aim of this book is to turn the critical tools of literary theory back on the Law and Literature movement and to evaluate it as a cultural phenomenon.

For whom is this book written? The principal audience for this book will likely be students and scholars of law and literature, but it is designed to satisfy the curiosity of scholars in other fields, and of educated general readers as well.

For students and scholars of law and government, this book offers an introduction and comprehensive guide to an important contemporary movement in legal scholarship. It collects evidence and arguments that the values at stake in legal disputes and decisions are not merely economic or instrumental, but also aesthetic and expressive. Accordingly, this book may also interest practicing lawyers who reflect on the social role and cultural significance of their profession.

This book should be of equal interest to students, teachers, and scholars of literature. In recent decades, literary studies have transcended their traditional focus on imaginative literature and have begun to examine literary aspects of a broad range of social phenomena. Literary studies have become "Cultural Studies," applying the methods of the humanities to the subject matter of the social sciences to reveal and interpret a "social text." The literary criticism of law examined in this book should be seen as part of this larger development within literary studies. Indeed, the Law and Literature movement may represent the most extensive effort to date to apply literary methods outside the traditional literary sphere. If, as we argue, law is a crucial dimension of modern culture, the literary criticism of law should be central to the new conception of literary studies as cultural studies, and part of any contemporary education in literature.

Students and scholars of other fields will also find stimulation here. Many claims for the usefulness of literary method in understanding law are epistemological or ethical claims, and many of the "literary" theories that have most influenced legal thought are also contributions to philosophy. Our efforts to explain the cultural significance of the Law and Literature movement depend on an interpretation of the intellectual history of American legal thought that we develop in chapter 1 and refer to throughout the book.

A broadly interdisciplinary topic like ours, though it may be intriguing to many readers, may also be daunting to all. Few readers will bring to this book great facility in both legal and literary theory. Thus, we have tried to write this book in such a way as to presume little formal background in these fields. This book's first chapter provides most of the background in the history of American legal thought that the lay reader will need in order to follow debates about law and literature. The next five chapters review different forms or "genres" of literary criticism of law, each depicting law as a different kind of literary activity (interpretation, narration, rhetoric, signification, and representation). Each of these chapters begins with a summary of the literary theories and methods used in the genre discussed. Thus, the book should be accessible to the literary critic with no particular knowledge of law, to the lawyer unfamiliar with literary theory, and to the generally educated reader with little exposure to law or literary theory.

A great many debts have been incurred in preparing this book. The greatest of them are owed not to any one individual, but to two extraordinary intellectual communities, the State University of New York at Buffalo School of Law and the Stanford Law School. Both of these institutions have long sustained traditions of intellectual seriousness, eclectic interdisciplinarity, and rigorous irreverence. We hope that this work bears witness to the similar virtues of the two places where it was nurtured. More concretely, this book has benefited from the encouragement, both material and collegial, of Deans Barry Boyer and Nils Olsen at Buffalo and Dean Paul Brest at Stanford. Research for this book was supported by the Magavern Fellows Fund at Buffalo, and the Stella and Ira S. Lillick Research Fund and the Edwin E. Huddleson, Jr. Professorship endowment at Stanford.

Many colleagues and friends read and commented on portions of the manuscript, talked through ideas with us, or supplied useful bibliographical leads. Thanks are owed to Jack Balkin, Leonard Binder, Linda Bosniak, Gregg Crane, Pablo De Greiff, Markus Dubber, Sara Faherty, Terry Fisher, Barbara Fried, Donald Gjerdingen, David Golove, Robert Gordon, Thomas Grey, Janet Halley, Lynne Henderson, Royce Kallerud, George Kannar, Leo Katz, Duncan Kennedy, Steven Knapp, Estelle Lau, Klaus Luederssen, Patrick Martin, Toni Massaro, Martha McCluskey, Errol Meidinger, Elizabeth Mensch, Michael Meurer, William Ian Miller, Neil Netanel, Dennis Patterson, Stephanie Phillips, Robert Post, Margaret Jane Radin, Carol Sanger, John Henry Schlegel, Reva Siegel, William Simon, Avi Soifer, Nancy Staudt, Robert Steinfeld, Simon Stern, Henry Sussman, Brook Thomas, Michael Vorenberg, Jeremy Waldron, James Wooten, and Robin West. None is responsible for errors.

The book has also benefited from the responses of workshop and conference audiences at the law schools of the State University of New York at Buffalo, Stanford, Yale, the University of London, the University of Frankfurt, Berkeley, Rutgers-Camden, Arizona, UCLA, and Indiana, and the English Department at Berkeley.

For outstanding research assistance, we thank two students at Buffalo, Douglas Sylvester and Nicholas Smith, and two at Stanford, William Hapiuk Jr. and Marta Miyar.

The authors' spouses, Judith Olin and Susan Weisberg, are owed deep thanks for their unstinting encouragement and patience in the long preparation of this book. And our children, to whom this book is dedicated, were good.

Brief portions of chapters 1 and 2 appeared in Guyora Binder, "Institutions and Linguistic Conventions: The Pragmatism of Lieber's Hermeneutic," *Cardozo Law Review* 16 (1995): 2169. Portions of chapter 3 appeared in Robert Weisberg, "Proclaiming Trials as Narratives: Premises and Pretenses," *In Law's Stories: Narrative and Rhetoric in the Law*, ed. Peter Brooks and Paul Gewirtz (New Haven: Yale Univ. Press, 1996), and in Weisberg, The Law-Literature Enterprise, *Yale Journal of Law and the Humanities* 1 (1988): 1. Portions of chapter 5 Appeared in Guyora Binder, "Representing Nazism: Advocacy and Identity at the Trial of Klaus Barbie," *Yale Law Journal* 98 (1989): 1321, and in "What's Left?" *Texas Law Review* 1985 (1991). Chapter 6 appeared in slightly different form as Guyora Binder and Robert Weisberg, "Cultural Criticism of Law," *Stanford Law Review* 49 (1997): 1149.

Literary Criticisms of Law

INTRODUCTION

THIS BOOK EXPLORES the uses of literary criticism in understanding and evaluating laws, legal institutions, legal arguments, and the decisions of legal actors. It identifies the sources and aspirations of this growing field of scholarship, explicates and evaluates its achievements, and recommends the most fruitful directions for future literary criticisms of law.

The Law and Literature movement emerged in the 1970s around the time that the rival Law and Economics movement was achieving notoriety. The early Law and Literature scholars set themselves the twin tasks of defending judicial discretion and informing its exercise with Kantian liberal values. They anticipated that both goals could be advanced by more closely linking law to literature. First, they characterized legal argument and judgment as interpretive activities necessarily affording their practitioners wide latitude for creativity, but nonetheless constrained by craft values that were ultimately aesthetic. Second, they identified these aesthetic concerns with an empathetic sensibility that could alert the good lawyer or judge to the effect of legal decisions on the personhood or dignity of parties. They offered this literary sensibility as a restraint on and reproach to what they saw as the heartless utilitarianism of the new legal economists.

The Law and Literature movement embraces two distinct forms of scholarship. What is often called Law *in* Literature scholarship is a species of conventional literary criticism and history that treats works of imaginative literature that contain legal themes or depict legal practice. This category of scholarship might seem at first to fall within the coverage of this book's title—after all, Dickens's *Bleak House*, in its searing portrayal of the British legal system, might be described as a "literary criticism of law." But our book is solely about the second category of Law and Literature scholarship, often called Law *as* Literature. This scholarship employs the techniques and principles of literary criticism, theory, and interpretation to better understand the writing, thought, and social practice that constitute legal systems and offers these techniques and principles as tools for reforming those legal systems. Though only the latter body of work is the subject of this book, we will sometimes advert to the former, first because Law *in* Literature offers some general guidance about the intellectual impulses motivating the Law *as* Literature work we study here, and second because it illuminates the views of particular scholars who have contributed to both enterprises.

Many scholars have contended that reading great literature addressing legal problems can expand and enhance the moral sensibility with which we approach questions of justice. Some have applauded literature's freedom, its independent vantage point to criticize authority, and its ethical value in inculcating a capacity for empathy. Arguably, the literary imagination can help us not only to conceive a new and better legal regime, but also to imagine what living under alternative regimes might feel like. Literature can offer a complex, multilayered experience that transcends rigid categories, alerting us to the plurality and dynamism of the meanings we attach to social life. And a literary perspective could thereby encourage the lawgiver to eschew mechanistic regulation in favor of an open-minded pluralism, to become an empathetic, inclusive, and imaginative architect of the common good. These kinds of claims are plausible and, in the hands of scholars like Thomas Grey,[1] have sometimes been developed with considerable insight and persuasive power.

But when the value of a literary sensibility to law is expressed in terms of the profit to be derived from reading imaginative literature, it is too easily inferred that the literary imagination can have no place in the actual practice, critique, and reform of law. The result can be a reductive view of law and an uncritical acceptance of imaginative literature's hardly impartial self-portrayals. Consider two alternative formulations of the relationship between fiction and the criminal law in the nineteenth century, both offered by literary scholars. According to Wai Chee Dimock, the nineteenth century witnessed "something like a division of signifying labor: on the one hand, the impulse toward precision in the criminal law gave it an ever diminishing range of reference; on the other hand, the impulse toward amplitude in the novel gave it a continuing (or perhaps expanding) capacity for symbolization."[2] Novels, concludes Dimock, offer an alternative scheme of justice; they provide "an echo chamber with a far more complex series of resonances than do their counterparts in the criminal law."[3]

Perhaps the law is indeed myopic while literature is subtly perceptive; but according to Tony Sharpe, literature has not always demonstrated this subtlety of perception in its portrayal of the law,

> which sometimes borders on travesty. Here I am . . . concerned . . . with texts in which legal methodology is implicitly compared to literature's ways of working: a comparison which tends to construct law as an inflexible system, largely incapable of the

---

[1] See Thomas Grey, *The Wallace Stevens Case: Law and the Practice of Poetry* (Cambridge: Harvard Univ. Press, 1991). Grey takes on the daunting task of finding connections between law and literature in the work of a great poet who happened to be a lawyer-businessman, and who tended to deny, and rarely explicitly manifested, any connection whatsoever between his poetic imagination and his mundane work of legal and business analysis. Grey discovers in Stevens's poetry a lesson for lawyers about the value of a resilient pragmatism. Rather than sentimentally offering literature as a corrective to law, Grey sees poetry as a medium to help lawyers build a bridge between rule-of-law legal classicism and equity-favoring Romanticism. He argues that literature can teach lawyers the crucial art of keeping antithetical premises in mind and recognizing the limits of one's necessarily reductionist conclusions. He sees in Stevens's poetry a dialog between realism and idealism, with intimations of, but not the vain hope of finally achieving, what Grey calls an "integrative perspectivism."

[2] Wai Chee Dimock, "Criminal Law, Female Virtue, and the Rise of Liberalism," *Yale Journal of Law and the Humanities* 4 (1992): 209, 215–16; see Wai Chee Dimock, *Residues of Justice: Literature, Law, and Philosophy* (Berkeley: Univ. of California Press, 1996), 11–27.

[3] Dimock, "Criminal Law, Female Virtue," 217.

subtle or even magical discriminations possible in fiction. . . . Law is thus constituted as a process by which meanings are excluded, and literature as one by which they may be licensed.[4]

Sharpe invites us to see law and the novel as rival professional discourses in the nineteenth century, and to greet the latter's testimony about the former skeptically. He hypothesizes that "when literature deals with law, it does so to confirm its own advantage as a means of dealing with reality . . . by taking a partial or distorted view of law's premises, operations and consequences."[5] The more we credit the possibly self-serving claims of imaginative writers to a monopoly on insight, the less we may learn about the insights to be derived from the use of literary methods and sensibilities *in* legal thought and practice.

Sharpe presents imaginative literature as a professional discourse, reminding us that literature is not only a kind of language, but also an institution with its own interests and jurisdictional turf. In treating literature as a kind of regime, Sharpe provokes us to see law not only as a rival *to* literature, but also as a dimension or aspect *of* literature itself. While we ordinarily think of law as the work of a particular profession, we may conceive law more broadly as an ordering function, a process of identifying, allocating, and contesting authority, that pervades all spheres of social life. In the same way, we may identify "the literary" narrowly with the work of a particular profession, or more broadly with imagination, complexity of perception, density of meaning, and the qualities of dramatic and aesthetic interest. If we conceive "the literary" in these broader terms, it becomes a meaning-making function that pervades social life. It is when we take law and literature in these broad senses that the relation between them becomes the richest and most interesting. Throughout this book, we will be asking the reader to keep in view these dual meanings of law and literature—as historically specific disciplines, and as the indispensable and inextricable cultural functions of defining authority and making meaning that these disciplines respectively strive, but fail, to monopolize.

The Law and Literature movement encompasses both efforts to break these monopolies and efforts to extend the domain of either one at the expense of the other. It is part of a larger profusion of interdisciplinary studies of society, particularly applying the methods of the humanities to subjects studied by the social sciences. All such interdisciplinary importations share an implicit logic. The host and guest disciplines are in one sense interchangeable—each can illuminate the same phenomena. Yet their powers of illumination differ in quality or quantity. The guest discipline can correct the host's deficiencies, either improving it or displacing it altogether. To import literature into law is therefore to see the two enterprises as potential collaborators or competitors in the same enterprise. What assumptions are common to the diverse disciplines of the humanities and

---

[4] Tony Sharpe, "(Per)versions of Law in Literature," forthcoming *in Law and Literature*, ed. Michael Freeman and Andrew Lewis (Oxford: Oxford Univ. Press, 1999).

[5] Ibid.

social sciences that allow them to compete against one another? What assumptions do we make about society when we view it as the common object of all these disciplines?

We probably follow Weber—or, more fashionably, Foucault—in assuming that there is some connection between the emergence of these disciplines of inquiry and the emergence of a "modern" bureaucratic and commercial society. In this spirit, our account of the Law and Literature movement proceeds on the basis of four premises, the usefulness of which we hope to demonstrate in the chapters that follow. We assume, first, that the disciplines that had achieved professional status by the end of the nineteenth century offered themselves as competing modes of apprehending modern society, or—insofar as they interested themselves in the ancient or the "primitive"—society's evolution towards modernity. Second, that part of what is meant by "modernity" is the experience of social life as presented by these disciplines—the experience of work as economic activity, the experience of child rearing and of relationships as psychological processes, and so on. Third, that these disciplines, and the portrait of society they paint, play a role in social order or control. In other words, the disciplines ease the bureaucratic and managerial functions of the state and other institutions both by informing these institutions about the populations they regulate and by encouraging these populations to perceive themselves as institutions perceive them. Fourth, that the disciplines perform this dual function of disciplining both social investigators and the objects of social investigation, insofar as they are modes of apprehending subjectivity.

This at any rate is how lawyers and legal scholars see the disciplines they appropriate. Legal decisions turn on diverse representations of the *will* of legal actors: injunctions, intentions, consents, interests, meanings, needs, expectations and purposes, as well as rights, privileges, and competences. To lawyers, at least, the disciplines of the humanities and social sciences represent techniques for determining, representing, measuring, and summing desire. The "modern" society revealed by these disciplines is a field of competing and transacting subjects.

What does it mean to represent or experience this social field in a more literary way? To approach this question we need to locate literature and literary criticism within the broader enterprise of apprehending a society composed of such modern characters as citizens, bureaucrats, experts, merchants, consumers, investors, inventors, employees, members, partners, patients, spouses, gangsters, professionals and clients, debtors and creditors, immigrants, tourists, journalists, and candidates.

Placing literature within modern society will require us to investigate how literature came to be conceived as a distinct discipline during the nineteenth and early twentieth centuries—when terms like "society," "culture," and "modernity" became important analytic categories, and when intellectual life organized itself into distinct academic disciplines. Accordingly, we will briefly examine the appearance in the Romantic period, in England and America, of a new conception of imaginative writing as a discrete professional discourse and of the literary author as a distinct character or social type. We will then proceed to consider how this Romantic conception of literature was amended as literature became an academic subject in Victorian England and Progressive America. This will give us an impression of the received cultural associations of the "literary," and so of the broad connotations of urging the introduction of literature into another discipline like law. These connotations in turn will alert the reader to some of the intellectual risks implicit in the Law as Literature trope. After identifying these risks, this introduction will also identify the more promising possibilities of this trope. The introduction will conclude with a summary of the themes, the strengths, and the weaknesses of the particular genres of literary criticism of law examined in this book.

FROM LETTERS TO LITERATURE

A precondition to the application of literary theory to legal interpretation is their initial separation. Yet before the nineteenth century, literature was less the discrete enterprise it is today. Fiction, poetry, and drama were continuous with philosophy, history, and other learned discourses, including the more intellectually ambitious legal writing, and these discursive forms were all different genres of "letters." An autonomous category of literature, available for appreciation and criticism, may be said to have developed only with the salience of two conceptual distinctions that now seem self-evident.

The first was a distinction between universal and personal perspectives that enabled a division between scientific discourse on the one hand, and expressive discourse on the other. The second was a functional division of letters into the instrumental and the aesthetic, the prosaic and the poetic, the quotidian and the quotable. Taken together, these two distinctions enabled the emergence of a conception of literature as the presentation for aesthetic appreciation of self-expressions.

This new expressive conception of literature replaced a classically rooted mimetic conception of literature,[6] by which art found its content in the facts of nature or the truths of reason and revelation, and artistry lay in the skillful rendering of a given subject matter. Typical of this view was Sydney's defense of poetry as morally educative and Pope's argument that poetry is scientifically valuable because it imitates nature.[7] On these accounts, poetry was neither an invention of the creative imagination nor an expression of the artistic soul. Understanding any writing was a matter of understanding the subject represented rather than the intentions or sensibility of the writer. Even the classical tradition's interest in rhetorical tactics is better characterized as a craftsmanlike concern with the instru-

---

[6] M. H. Abrams, *The Mirror and the Lamp* (New York: Oxford Univ. Press, 1953).

[7] Sir Philip Sydney, "An Apology for Poetry," in *Critical Theory Since Plato*, ed. Hazard Adams (New York: Harcourt Brace Jovanovich, 1992), 155–77.

mental link between generic purposes and techniques than any interest in the author's unique vision and style.

None of this is to deny that Renaissance and Neoclassical writing can *now* be read as expressive literature—any lyric poetry lends itself to this kind of reading. It is simply to say that in these periods portrayals of personality more likely would have been read as depicting virtues and vices, or aspects of the human soul, or the sentiments appropriate to the speaker's situation. If classical philosophy prescribed self-knowledge, if Christianity exalted the soul, if stoicism valued personal independence, these traditions still affirmed subjective experience as a window on universal truths. The idea that inner experience was an independent reality, valuable in itself, is a distinctively modern one.

Nevertheless, the expressive conception of literature did build on themes of classical and Enlightenment thought. In legitimating scientific practice, empiricist epistemology appeared to root the authority of knowledge in individual sense experience. Moreover, seventeenth- and eighteenth-century writers conceived the mind as an active synthesizer of all it saw. Following Aristotle and Plotinus, Neoclassical aesthetics assumed that the poetic imagination could not only imitate but even surpass nature. By grasping and recombining nature's forms, the imagination copied the divine process of creation.[8] The British empiricists acknowledged a role for the imagination in associating sense experiences; and yet in condemning imaginative writing as mendacious rhetoric, they invented the chimerical ideal of a pure language of sense experience that we now associate with logical positivism.[9] Finally, Romanticism could claim one classical precursor in Longinus, who introduced the concept of "the sublime" into aesthetic discourse. An awe-inspiring quality of dramatic contrast, the sublime was achievable in literature by virtue of the artist's qualities of soul.[10]

Like expressive writing, aesthetic appreciation by readers was by no means unknown before the nineteenth century. But provoking aesthetic appreciation was seldom seen as the central or defining purpose of a work. Appreciating writing was a matter of appreciating the author's mimetic skill. Even poetry was seen as an instrument, a form of rhetoric designed to persuade, entertain, ridicule, or

---

[8] Samuel Henry Butcher, *Aristotle's Theory of Poetry and Fine Art*, 4th ed. (New York: Dover Publications, 1951), 13–20; Plotinus, *The Six Enneads*, trans. Stephen MacKenna (London: Faber & Faber, 1966); Sydney, "An Apology for Poetry"; Joseph Addison, "On the Pleasures of the Imagination" in Adams, *Critical Theory since Plato*, 288–92.

[9] See John Locke, *An Essay Concerning Human Understanding* (Menston: Scholar Press, 1970); Edmund Burke, *A Philosophical Inquiry into the Origin of Our Ideas of the Sublime and Beautiful*, ed. J. Boulton (Oxford: Basil Blackwell, 1987); David Hume, "Of the Standard of Taste," in Adams, *Critical Theory since Plato*, 314–23. For a discussion of pure language of observation see Richard Rorty, *Philosophy and the Mirror of Nature* (Princeton: Princeton Univ. Press, 1979).

[10] W. Rhys Roberts, ed. and trans., *Longinus on the Sublime* (Cambridge: Cambridge Univ. Press, 1933), 23–40. In what is generally considered a precocious anticipation of Romanticism, the early-eighteenth-century writer Edward Young urged the spirit, taste, and genius of past authors as the poet's proper object of study and imitation. Edward Young, *Conjectures on Original Composition* (Leeds: Scholar Press, 1966).

instruct. Critical writing about poetry often took the form of how-to advice or commercial endorsement.[11]

While neoclassical criticism did investigate rhetorical techniques for evoking a variety of sentiments such as catharsis[12] and delight,[13] rhetoric's purpose was not to evoke emotion as such. Rhetoric typically involved deploying familiar generic conventions to reinforce institutions by ritually evoking appropriate sentiments. Indeed, eighteenth-century authors began to complain that the conventions of rhetoric were restricting their emotional palette.[14] On the other hand, empiricists attacked rhetoric from a different direction, identifying its generally conservative function with irrationality. To them, rhetoric's emotional colors were altogether too vivid. Hume denied that aesthetic appreciation permitted the actual experience, as opposed to the detached contemplation, of emotions.[15] To have an aesthetic experience of language was to be insulated against its persuasive, manipulative power. By the end of the eighteenth century, rhetoric was widely seen as cluttering the minds of readers with sentimental platitudes.

The Wordsworthian ideal of literature as emotion recollected in tranquillity synthesized these curiously inconsistent critiques of rhetoric as insufficiently and excessively emotional. Literature would now express the passion of the author in all its idiosyncrasy and originality, yet this passion would be presented for *contemplation* rather than evoked in readers. Mediated but authentic passion, rather than unmediated but conventional sentiment, was the true poet's product. Hence Romantic criticism envisioned a social world populated by individual characters, distinguished by their unique emotional lives; it repudiated the neoclassical vision of society as a chorus harmonized by common manners and conventional attitudes.

The very category of literature—writing presented as art—was a creature of Romanticism, and insofar as we continue to view literature as an autonomous category of writing or experience, we moderns remain committed to Romantic aesthetics. For that reason it is useful to review some of the basic assumptions of Romantic aesthetics, the package of associations evoked whenever we hear the term *literary* outside of the academic field of literature.

First, Romanticism celebrated the *imagination* as a form of knowledge.[16] Imagination was knowledge of the particular, the faculty of mind by which the will, the

---

[11] Jane P. Tompkins, "The Reader in History: The Changing Shape of Literary Response," in *Reader-Response Criticism: From Formalism to Post-Structuralism*, ed. Jane P. Tompkins (Baltimore: Johns Hopkins Univ. Press, 1980), 201–32.

[12] *Aristotle's Poetics*, ed. Stephen Halliwell (London: Duckworth Press, 1986).

[13] John Dryden, *An Essay of Dramatic Poesy*, ed. T. Arnold (Oxford: Clarendon, 1964).

[14] Pierre Corneille, "Of the Three Unities of Action, Time, and Place," trans. Donald Schier, in *The Continental Model: Selected French Critical Essays of the Seventeenth Century*, rev. ed., ed. Scott Elledge and Donald Schier (Ithaca: Cornell Univ. Press, 1970), 101–15; Dryden, *An Essay of Dramatic Poesy*.

[15] Hume, "Of the Standard of Taste."

[16] Immanuel Kant, *Kant's Critique of Aesthetic Judgement*, trans. J. C. Meredith (Oxford: Clarendon, 1911), 30–34, 58–60, 86–89; Percy Bysshe Shelley, "A Defense of Poetry," in Adams, *Critical Theory since Plato*, 499–513.

subjectivity, or the personality of individuals could be known.[17] Since imaginative knowledge was unmediated by concepts or categories, it was a faculty of mind both opposed and superior to reason.[18] For Keats, imagination was associated with a critical sensibility that opposed all logic: "negative capability," the capacity to accept uncertainty and contradiction.[19]

Second, artistic production was identical to imagination, art being an *ideal* product of the mind, rather than a material product of the hand. Some interpreters of Romanticism have understood the identity of artistic production with imagination to imply that the "real" work of art is the one the artist intended to produce not the one she actually produced, and that a literary work is identical with the meanings intended by the author.[20] Others have denied that Romantic aesthetics posited disembodied meanings.[21] In any case, the identity of art with imagination meant that all human beings were artists, while professional artists were professional imaginers, expert examples of a basic faculty of mind.

Third, imagination entailed *innovation*. Imaginative works had to be original, not just skillful renderings of familiar themes.[22] As experts in innovation, artists extended the boundaries of human thought. In refurbishing language, for example, poets became "the unacknowledged legislators of the world," according to Shelley's influential formulation.[23]

Fourth, the imagination was a distinctively *individual* faculty. Art therefore expressed something unique about the creator: his or her personality or style. Imaginative works had to be authentic to the author.[24]

Fifth, great works of art therefore manifested the *genius* of their creators, the extraordinary capacities for innovation inherent in their unique personalities.[25]

---

[17] See Arthur Schopenhauer, *The World as Will and Idea*, trans. Richard Burdon Haldane and John Kemp, vol. 1 (New York: Humanities Press, 1964).

[18] See Harold Bloom, Commentary to *The Complete Poetry and Prose of William Blake*, ed. David V. Erdman and Harold Bloom, new rev. ed. (New York: Anchor-Doubleday, 1988), 894–970; Samuel Taylor Coleridge, *Biographia Literaria*, ed. John Shawcross (London: Oxford Univ. Press, 1954), 1:66–73; Friedrich Wilhelm von Schelling, "On the Relation of the Plastic Arts to Nature," in Adams, *Critical Theory since Plato*, 446–58.

[19] John Keats, "Letter to Georgia Keats and Thomas Keats," in *Selected Letters of John Keats*, ed. Lionel Trilling (New York: Farrar, Straus, and Young, 1951), 91–92.

[20] William K. Wimsatt and Monroe C. Beardsley, "The Intentional Fallacy," in Adams, *Critical Theory since Plato*, 1005–21 (attributing these implications to Romanticism.)

[21] Benedetto Croce, *Aesthetic as Science of Expression and General Linguistic*, trans. Douglas Ainslie (New York: Noonday, 1963).

[22] Georg Wilhelm Friedrich Hegel, vol. 1, "The Philosophy of Fine Art," ed. and trans. F. B. Osmaston (London: G. Bell and Sons, 1920), 394–405.

[23] Shelley, "A Defence of Poetry," 513; see also Ralph Waldo Emerson, "The Poet," in Adams, *Critical Theory since Plato*, 545–54.

[24] See Coleridge, *Biographia Literaria*; Schelling, "On the Relation of the Plastic Arts"; Emerson, "The Poet."

[25] See Kant, *Critique of Judgment*, 168–83, 191, 226; on art as embodiment of the artist's spirit see Hegel, "Philosophy of Fine Art," 1:380–91.

Sixth, great art exemplified the aesthetic quality of *sublimity*—evoking awe at the infinite, generally through dramatic contrast.[26] Sublime effects were often associated with the depiction or evocation of strong emotion—the juxtaposition of euphoria and despair.[27] It was the extraordinary sensibility of the artist, her capacity for unprecedented depths of feeling, that enabled her artistic genius. For Wordsworth the poet was one "endowed with more lively sensibility, more enthusiasm and tenderness, who has a greater knowledge of human nature, and a more comprehensive soul, than are supposed to be common among mankind." Poetry was a "spontaneous overflow of powerful feelings."[28]

Seventh, aesthetic experience was nevertheless *contemplative*; it entailed perceiving but not feeling emotion.[29] Wordsworth's "spontaneous overflow" was "captured in tranquillity."[30]

Eighth, artistic expression was therefore a form of *sublimation*, involving the mastering of great passion and its fashioning into an object for contemplation. In thus disciplining her passions, the artist mastered and re-created herself.[31]

Ninth, in thus simultaneously determining and expressing herself the artist realized her full human freedom and threw off the restraints of necessity. The faculty of imagination was thus central to the Romantic conception of *freedom as self-realization*.[32]

Finally, tenth, because aesthetic experience presupposed detachment from the passions, and creativity entailed the sublimation and control of the passions, Romanticism celebrated art as *a realm apart* from the utilitarian pursuit and gratification of desire.[33] For example, Kant distinguished aesthetic judgment, which concerned ends, from teleological judgment, which evaluated means by reference to ends.[34] Moreover, because art involved the mastery of passion, aesthetic pursuits were seen as nobler, as morally superior to utilitarian pursuits. Works of art, almost regardless of content, stood as indictments of an increasingly commercial and industrial society.

Indeed, the very idea of literature depended on the emergence of a purely aesthetic sensibility for receiving writing, defined by contrast to a merely instrumen-

---

[26] Kant, *Critique of Judgment*, 90–134.

[27] See M. Royce Kallerud, "Rousseau's Ambivalent Sublime," *The Wittenberg Review* (spring 1991): 34; Thomas Weiskel, *The Romantic Sublime* (Baltimore: Johns Hopkins Univ. Press, 1976).

[28] William Wordsworth, Preface to *Lyrical Ballads*, ed. Michael Mason (London: Longman, 1992), 82.

[29] See Kant, *Critique of Judgment*, 123–26.

[30] Wordsworth, Preface to *Lyrical Ballads*, 32.

[31] See Friedrich Schiller, *Letters on the Aesthetic Education of Man*, ed. and trans. Elizabeth M. Wilkinson and L. A. Willoughby (Oxford: Clarendon, 1967), 21, 79, 83, 93. 103, 119, 125–27, 141, 153, 167, 189.

[32] Ibid., 17–21, 95, 117, 147, 161, 183–88, 205, 213, 219.

[33] See Hegel, "Philosophy of Fine Art," 65–87; John Stuart Mill, "What Is Poetry?" in *Mill's Essays on Literature and Society*, ed. J. B. Schneewind (New York: Columbia Univ. Press, 1965), 102, 106–7, 109–10.

[34] Kant, *Critique of Judgment*, 19–35.

tal sensibility. In the modern era, as Jane Tompkins writes, "The imputation that a poem might break out of its self-containment and perform a service would disqualify it immediately from consideration as a work of art. The first requirement of art in the twentieth century is that it should *do* nothing."[35] Literature requires a literary public, and just as importantly a philistine public as well. The aesthetic sensibility of Romanticism was at once opposed to and bound up with the calculating, instrumental sensibility of commercial capitalism, and the calculating instrumental discourse of the utilitarian, the classical liberal, or the legal positivist. If, in the discursive world that emerged in the nineteenth century, literature was an aesthetic discourse of subjectivity, law was an instrumental discourse of subjectivity. A common concern of lawyers and literary critics with interpretation followed from the common function of legal and literary language as media for representing subjectivity. To interpret a literary text was to identify the sensibility it expressed, while to interpret a legal instrument was to identify the will it represented.

While Romanticism exalted the artistic sensibility as the antithesis of the commercial sensibility, some literary historians have ironically seen the Romantic image of the artistic creator as the embodiment of the commercial self-interest of producers in an emergent market for intellectual property. As Neil Netanel (skeptically) summarizes this story,

> early Romantic notions of "genius," "originality" and "art" [emerged in] the struggle of eighteenth century publishers and writers to gain political and juridical recognition of a natural property' right in writings. . . . On one hand, writers attained the status of holders of proprietary rights only because they came to be seen as originators. On the other, the Romantic persona of the author could not reach fruition until the writer held title to his work. In sum Romantic authorship necessarily carries with it the "possessive individualism" of nascent capitalism.[36]

From this viewpoint, the emergent Romantic author was identical with the new rights-bearing, utility-maximizing liberal subject. And though Netanel gives the Romantic author a less central role in the emergence of capitalism,[37] it is fair to say that Romantic idealism and the persona of the Romantic author would not have emerged without capitalism; and that the Romantic author was an enterprising self-promoter. Yet Romanticism did not endorse capitalism as such, and the self it promoted was not the rational utility maximizer. The Romantic author

[35] Tompkins, "The Reader in History," 210.

[36] Neal Netanel, "The Law Literature Critique of the Law of Literature" (unpublished ms., 1993) (summarizing the arguments of Peter Jaszi, "Toward a Theory of Copyright: The Metamorphoses of Authorship," *Duke Law Journal* (1991): 455; Mark Rose, "The Author as Proprietor: *Donaldson v. Becket* and the Genealogy of Modern Authorship," *Representations* 23 (1988): 51; Martha Woodmansee, "The Genius and the Copyright: Economic and Legal Conditions for the Emergence of the "Author," *Eighteenth Century Studies* 17 (1984): 425, 429–31.

[37] Netanel argues that the emergence of markets in commercial instruments and investment securities enabled the recognition of other forms of intangible, including intellectual, property. "The Law Literature Critique."

assumed the role of the dissenter from all that was crass and utilitarian, the architect of a sanctuary from commercial society to which sensitive souls could repair, albeit for a fee.

LITERARY CANONS AND ACADEMIES

In late-nineteenth-century England and America, literature became a subject of instruction in secondary schools, colleges, and research universities. This development reflected a judgment that the Romantic aesthetic ideas on which the very category of literature depended were personally edifying and socially useful. Yet as literature became an academic subject, the idea of literature and the practice of literary criticism were also reshaped by the purposes of literary education.

Literary instruction, like the marketing of literature, paradoxically involved the standardization and mass distribution of individuality. Thus, the role of literary instruction within a general education in Victorian England and Progressive America tended to suppress the subversive and individualist themes in literary thought and to highlight literature's meliorative, "humanizing" import. Rather than protesting the alienation attendant upon modernization, literature would alleviate it by providing a common discourse to unite an atomized society, and by providing an inner world of imagination and sensibility to substitute for the lost world of nature and village. In this way literary instruction promised to grease rather than gum the gears of commerce.

According to a familiar argument, literary canons were part of the nineteenth-century project of inventing national cultures for dissemination to the soldiers and bureaucrats of the new nation-states.[38] Thus, the industrialization of commodity and weapons production, transportation, and communication encouraged polities to organize masses of people into a geographically dispersed commercial economy and state apparatus. Mobilizing and coordinating masses of people entailed inculcating a common language, shared habits and norms, and literacy. It also meant inculcating a common identity to replace local attachments and take the edge off anomie. And if it was difficult to arm masses of men without enfranchising them, it then became necessary to fit them for orderly political participation. All this required primary education on an unprecedented scale, cadres of civil servants and teachers with secondary and even university training, and the assembly of a national cultural canon to be appreciated in new institutional spaces like museums, libraries, opera houses, and secondary schools.[39] Indeed, the first modern literary curricula in Britain appeared not in the universities, but in the local mechanics' institutes.

---

[38] Raymond Williams, *Culture and Society, 1780–1950* (New York: Columbia Univ. Press, 1983); Ernest Gellner, *Nations and Nationalism* (Oxford: Blackwell, 1983).

[39] Guyora Binder, "The Case for Self-determination," *Stanford Journal of International Law* 29 (1993): 223, 232–33; Guyora Binder, "Post-totalitarian Politics," *Michigan Law Review* 91 (1993): 1491, 1503.

As literature and the other arts became subjects of academic instruction, the Romantic sensibility became a unifying as well as an individuating characteristic. Conceived as culture and curriculum, literature became a medium of socialization and the literary sensibility a discipline of decorum. In nineteenth-century England, readers were taught to *appreciate* rather than analyze literature, to reexperience in the poem's organic unity the lost harmony of country life.[40] Literary appreciation was a model for tasteful consumption more generally. Reading literature at once taught and conferred civility, as novels offered a world in which gentility was available on the slim budget of a parson's daughter. While posturing as a protest against the heartlessness and vulgarity of commerce, literature assured readers that their dignity could survive the vagaries of the market, that a cultivated moral sensibility proved as worthy as, and might be rewarded by, a legacy from a prosperous relative.

As the British critic Terry Eagleton notes, literature was in several ways a suitable candidate for this enterprise. As a liberal, "humanizing" pursuit, it could check political bigotry and extremism. It dealt with "universal human values" and thus could absorb and dilute the particular demands of working people. It induced respect for the moral riches of bourgeois civilization and taught the virtues of solitary contemplation rather than collective action, absorbing and transforming the energy of nineteenth-century religious movements.

While nineteenth-century English literature remained morally edifying, it now depicted morality as a matter of independent conscience rather than common moral sense.[41] To the utilitarian vision of subjectivity as sensuality, literature opposed a vision of subjectivity as sensibility. Yet the two were mutually complicitous. If majoritarian democracy was to make utility-maximizing decisions, participants must be taught not only to vote their preferences, but to deliberate the general good.[42] The problem was to get the new middle class to think like shopkeepers on behalf of the nation, not just themselves or their class. Victorian humanists like Matthew Arnold saw literature as a salve for cleavages in the body politic, offering the newly enfranchised a status of cultural dignity in exchange for political docility.[43]

In America, transcendentalist philosophy and religious evangelism paralleled some of the themes of English Romanticism, and the likes of Cooper, Poe, and Hawthorne initiated an American Romantic literature. Yet letters remained more classical than Romantic, and more civic than aesthetic until the Civil War. Still continuous with scientific, political, and legal writing, imaginative writing was part of the task of the self-effacing citizen of a republic. While American classicism emphasized the unity and utility of all intellectual effort, the dominant art

[40] Terry Eagleton, *Literary Theory* (Minneapolis: Univ. of Minnesota Press, 1983), 17–53.

[41] Ibid., 27.

[42] Mill, "Considerations on Representative Government," in *Essays on Politics and Society*, vol. 19 of *Collected Works of John Stuart Mill*, ed. J. D. Robson (Toronto: Univ. of Toronto Press, 1977), 371, 435–81.

[43] See generally Matthew Arnold, *Culture and Anarchy* (New York: Norton, 1972); see also Walter Horatio Pater, *Studies in the History of the Renaissance* (London: Macmillan, 1922).

form was oratory, which called its audience to a common civic identity in the face of geographic mobility and sectional strife. The model of achievement for American intellectuals was Cicero.

Law was intimately associated with literature in the post-Revolutionary period, as perhaps half of the editors of and contributors to literary periodicals were educated in the law.[44] Lawyers' courtroom oratory, steeped in classical learning and literary allusion, was a popular form of entertainment. There was also a practical nexus between letters and law: the republican attitude of disinterested citizenship meant that writing could not be a paying proposition, so that the writer needed an income. Then too, the Ciceronian imperative of civic engagement, with its attendant contempt for idle learning, provided ideological support to the material, imperatives of the middle-class litteratus.[45] In the American context, it was more religion than literature that functioned as the Romantic critique of classical values,[46] the evangelical sermon that provided the counterpoint to the Ciceronian oration.[47] Only after the Transcendentalists had fully developed the idea of a private life of self-cultivation as a religious vocation, and only in the face of the civic crisis over slavery, did literature become appealing as a calling rather than as part of a civic life.[48]

In America's Progressive Era, English literature instruction was promoted as an instrument of maintaining solidarity among divergent social classes.[49] Within the new graduate institutions modeled on the German university, the American English professor of the late nineteenth century might present himself as some kind of philologist. But as a teacher of undergraduates and on ceremonial occasions, he would present himself as a generalist seeking to disseminate an edifying and unifying culture of moral uplift. Perhaps as a result of the apocalyptic experience of civil war, the civilizing mission of literature in Progressive America owed more to the evangelical than the Ciceronian tradition. According to Gerald Graff, the "aim was essentially to adapt the old college ideal of liberal culture to the challenge of modern times," that is, to the emergence of a philistine elite and a disgruntled proletariat, and to the declining political and economic importance of the cultured class. Generalists "channeled into literature emotions that, a half-century earlier, would likely have been expressed in evangelical Christianity, Unitarianism, or Transcendentalism, investing the experience of literature with . . . redemptive influence."[50] During World War I, the socializing mission of higher

[44] Robert A. Ferguson, *Law and Letters in American Culture* (Cambridge: Harvard Univ. Press, 1984), 92 (discussing Theophilus Parsons and Gulian Verplanck).

[45] Ibid., 73–75.

[46] See Perry Miller, *The Life of the Mind in America: From the Revolution to the Civil War* (New York: Harcourt, Brace & World, 1965), 3–35.

[47] See John P. Diggins, *The Lost Soul of American Politics: Virtue, Self-interest, and the Foundations of Liberalism* (New York: Basic Books, 1984).

[48] George Fredrickson, *The Inner Civil War: Northern Intellectuals and the Crisis of the Union* (1965), 7–12, 19–21. An exception who underscored the rule was Longfellow, whose 1839 *Hyperion* lamented America's inhospitability for poetry.

[49] See Gerald Graff, *Professing Literature* (Chicago: Univ. of Chicago Press, 1987).

[50] Ibid., 85.

education in literature became even more explicit, as college textbooks presented American literature, duly selected and anthologized, as "a powerful adjunct to training for citizenship" or "a training in the ideals that underlie our faith" and "our democratic institutions."[51]

In short, by comparison to the British, Americans proceeded from classicism to academicism with barely a Romantic interlude between. When antebellum poets wanted to identify their work with Romanticism they often set it in Europe or wrote from a European point of view. To this day literary Romanticism, with its slightly subversive associations, tends not to be identified as genuinely American. It is not that literature lacks Romantic connotations in the American context, but that by virtue of these exotic connotations, to identify with the literary is to become a figurative expatriate.

THE RISKS AND POSSIBILITIES OF LAW AND LITERATURE

The contemporary significance of the category of "literature" is conditioned by the meanings it acquired in its Romantic and academic periods when it was bounded off as a separate category of discourse and research. While the nineteenth-century ideas about literature reviewed here tell us little about the recent literary theory most directly influential on the Law and Literature movement, they do suggest the associations evoked when we are exhorted to experience law in a more literary way. We are urged to express our authentic selves and escape alienating roles and to value passion—especially empathy, mercy, love—over reason and rule. Yet we are also urged to be detached rather than engaged, decorous rather than vulgar, gracious rather than grasping, and to value each other aesthetically rather than instrumentally. We must be prepared to decry big institutions as heartless and small ones as petty and provincial. We are encouraged to be inventive, eloquent, and refined. These exhortations may be delivered in the form of a lecture or address, to a "generalist" audience—lawyers rather than professional literary critics—in a milieu like a law review or law school auditorium often devoted to constitutional debate. If so, the context will emphasize the civilizing and morally edifying functions of literature over its message of personal liberation. On occasions commanding piety—graduations, memorial lectures, bicentennials—paeans to the power of imagination may amount to little more than entreaties to suspend disbelief in received truths and tired institutions. Yet the Law as Literature trope may announce an equally ritualized irreverence, a predictable disillusionment with the merely human origins of human arrangements.

Hence, the characteristic risks of the Law as Literature trope that we refer to throughout this book: First, a *sentimentalism* in which passion is never cruel or self-indulgent or muddle-headed, invention is never destructive or dishonest, and civility is always inclusive and never elitist. Second, a facile sophistication that mistakes *skepticism* for criticism and dishonors good causes with bad arguments.

---

[51] Ibid., 131.

Third, a genteel *authoritarianism* that restricts the aesthetic to the role of ornamenting institutionalized power and becalming the spirit of discontent.

What do we mean by "sentimentalism"? The "sentimental" is a second-order experience of pleasure in, or attitude of appreciation for, the experience of emotion—even of unpleasant emotion. Sentimentality is therefore a kind of pleasure or interest or motive. By "sentimentalism" we mean the indulgence of that pleasure, its pursuit without regard to, or its valuing to the exclusion of, other values. Sentimentalism may motivate one to treat politics, morals, art, or personal relationships as occasions for the experience of the sentimental, to the detriment of other values. Sentimentalism may also motivate one to insulate the experience of sentimentality, or of the emotion that enables it, from critical reflection—to idealize or simplify it. Thus, the pursuit of the sentimental can induce self-deception about the nature of one's own experience. Finally, sentimentalism can become a standard of judgment that condemns critical reflection as a threat to the experience of the sentimental.

While there may be appropriate settings for the pursuit of the sentimental, sentimentalism is obviously a vice in discursive practices like literary or social "criticism" that presuppose an attitude of critical reflection. A discourse may be sentimentalist either in the sense that it gratifies the sentimental motives of the author, or in the sense that it seeks to win affection or admiration by gratifying the sentimental motives of its audience. The epithet "self-indulgent" accuses the sentimentalist writer of both: of indulging his own sentimentality so as to then congratulate himself for being so sensitive.[52] Much writing about Law and Literature models a sentimentalist persona for the reader to admire and adopt. Signatures of sentimentalism in the field of Law and Literature include applauding certain attitudes or values as natural or authentic, while condemning others as artificial or alienated; attacking reason as incompatible with passion; protesting the inevitable reductiveness of all representations of persons in social thought; and pretending that social life could proceed without institutions, arbitrariness, coercion, and trade-offs among social goods.

What do we mean by "skepticism"? Skepticism is the disposition to view practices as illegitimate unless they can be shown to rest on some justificatory foundation independent of human purposes. In legal thought, skepticism usually demands that legal thought or practice justify itself by reference to some kind of objective knowledge—of moral truth, linguistic meaning, or popular will. Skeptical criticism of law tends to vastly overestimate the role of metaphysics and epistemology in justifying the authority of political institutions and thereby evades political argument and grapples with strawmen. In the field of Law and Literature, skeptical criticism often involves the additional vice of equating the literary with the merely subjective, thereby reducing it to a pejorative epithet.

What do we mean by a "genteel" authoritarianism? In the field of Law and Literature, we will rarely encounter a crude authoritarianism that would automati-

---

[52] This sort of gratification in being capable of sentimentality is actually a third-order experience of emotion.

cally align ruling elites with truth, natural right, or good order. But we will en-counter subtler forms of authoritarianism that identify elites with aesthetic value. In essence, these strategies seek to preempt a skeptical critique of institutions by sentimentalizing them. Fearing that the subjectivity of value threatens society with intractable conflict and denies legitimacy to governing institutions, scholars of Law and Literature may endow officials with charismatic authority by ascribing to them special aesthetic qualities or powers of aesthetic perception. Or they may encourage an aesthetic appreciation of the legal process as an artistic representa-tion of an idealized democratic politics. In this way, Law and Literature can mar-shall the aesthetic in the service of political quiescence and thereby degenerate into a cult of good taste.

In sum, the field of Law and Literature is beset by the temptations of sentimen-talism, skepticism, and a soft authoritarianism. In the face of these temptations, it tends to fluctuate between fearing subjectivity as an avaricious threat to social peace and exalting it as a fount of authenticity and humane feeling. This antino-mian view of the self is bound up with equally dichotomous and reductive charac-terizations of law as mere Letter—dry, abstract, rigid, cynical, calculating, conten-tious, profane—and literature as a redemptive Spirit that can humanize, subvert, or ornament the law.

Although Law and Literature scholarship is in constant danger of blundering down one of these impasses, this is not the whole story. While Law and Litera-ture's failures tend to fall into predictable, even hackneyed patterns, its suc-cesses—in illuminating the meanings of a particular legal dispute, fashioning a normative argument adapted to a particular cultural context, or grasping and transcending the limits of a point of view—often elude generalization. To illus-trate the uses of literary methods in apprehending and criticizing law, we will have to immerse the reader in the particularities of a diverse array of works.

In addition to illustrating these accomplishments, we will also identify promis-ing possibilities that the Law and Literature movement has yet to fully exploit. Realizing these possibilities will require moving beyond Law and Literature's traditional projects of justifying legal interpretation and exalting Kantian over utilitarian ethics. We must also be prepared to abandon a view of "the literary" as something extrinsic to law that corrects or redeems or ornaments it. We should recognize that the literary is intrinsic to law insofar as law fashions the characters, personas, sensibilities, identities, myths, and traditions that compose our social world.

The most promising literary criticisms of law are not particularly aimed at defending legal interpretation against majoritarian politics or defending human dignity against utilitarian rationality. Instead they interpret law as a cultural datum and analyze legal processes as arenas for generating cultural meaning. In such "cultural studies" of law, the fixed preferences of economic analysis and the stable self-sufficient persons of Kantian ethics give way to a more complex and contin-gent picture of the self. Our desires are not simply our own, given in advance of the political, economic, and legal institutions that recognize them or the cultural media available for expressing them. Instead our preferences and interests depend upon the identities socially and culturally available to us. Although socially recognized, these identities are not simply dictated by class or gender or any other invariant social structure. They are often temporary settlements of continuing struggles and negotiations among social actors engaged in projects that are at once strategic and aesthetic, instrumental and expressive. And often these struggles over meaning are legal struggles waged in legal forums.

Cultural criticism of law has rich implications for descriptive and normative legal theory. While much Law and Literature scholarship has opposed the literary to the instrumental analysis that dominates contemporary legal discourse, cultural criticism of law rejects this dichotomy. Instead, it implies that far from excluding aesthetic or expressive considerations, such instrumental policy analysis has a constitutively important expressive dimension that literary reading can illuminate. The best cultural studies of law reveal how policy decisions may reshape the expressive possibilities and social identities available to individuals, thereby conditioning the preferences considered by conventional policy analysis. For example, in contrast to the early Law and Literature scholarship, the newer cultural criticism implies that civil libertarian policies cannot be adequately delineated or defended by reference to the natural rights of individuals to personal autonomy or integrity. If identity is the contingent outcome of socially conditioned choices, it is neither natural nor, in the traditional sense, "personal." Cultural criticism of law demands that normative argument defend institutions on the basis of the kind of identities they will cultivate rather than their ability to protect or accurately represent existing personalities.

In short, we will encourage a legal scholarship that explores and enhances the expressive and compositional power of legal thought and practice in the specific political and economic worlds in which they operate. Such a scholarship recognizes the literary as a constitutive dimension of law rather than a redemptive supplement. If law is inevitably literary, the call to make it so is not just pointless but deceptive: it implies that if only law becomes more literary, criticism of law will no longer be necessary. To recognize the constitutively literary dimension of law is not to commend law as inevitably humane or redemptive, however. Law's creations may starve the poor or demean the weak; they may arise out of struggle, strategy, and violence. They demand critical evaluation. Nevertheless, laws, legal judgments, legal arguments, and legal transactions all have expressive meaning, and to miss law's meaning is to miss a part of what needs criticism. Thus, there is no reason why the literary reading of law must be laudatory. To say that law is literary is also to admit that literature is, like law, an arena of strategic conflict. Indeed, some of the most illuminating contemporary criticism of imaginative literature recognizes that literature is a social practice conditioned by institutional conventions, social power, and practical aims. Literature may be a realm of artifice and invention, but so is the confidence game; not every expression of creativity exalts the human spirit. Whether any particular literary work is redemptive or humane must be an open question if reading is to qualify as honest inquiry. Similarly, the redeeming qualities of any legal institution must remain in question if literary criticism of law is to be an honest job.

GENRES OF CRITICISM

In his *Economic Analysis of Law*,[53] Richard Posner showcased the many applications to law of a single theory, reduceable to the axioms that people pursue self-interest, that price is a function of supply and demand, and that transactions put goods to their most valued uses. Ours is a different kind of book devoted to a different kind of inquiry.

First, it is not a brief for Law and Literature scholarship. Such works abound, and the reader will see their arguments considered critically here. But neither is it—like Posner's *Law and Literature: A Misunderstood Relation*[54]—a polemic against such scholarship. It is an interpretive and critical work, using some of the very methods it reflects upon, to understand and refine the Law and Literature enterprise.

Second, unlike the economic analysis of law, the literary criticism of law is not a single theory. Many different kinds of scholarship animated by different conceptions of literature are considered here. Nor is literary criticism "theoretical" in the same way that economic analysis is—as is commonly said, the humanities are distinguished from the sciences by their concern with the particular. A practice of literary criticism cannot be reduced to a set of axioms or abstracted from the texts it reads. Insightful reading is a sensibility rather than a technique, developed more by immersion than instruction. Thus, "learning" the field of Law and Literature means abiding with the many authors who have made it their own, grasping their intellectual projects and absorbing their aesthetic sensibilities. Accordingly, this book will expose you to many styles of reading, each of course filtered through our own.

For this book is not merely an endorsement of the newer, "cultural" criticism of law and legal thought described earlier—it is also an example of it. We have endeavored to place the works of legal and literary scholarship we explicate in relevant cultural and intellectual historical contexts. While the literary criticism of law is not a single theory, it can be understood as a series of *genres*—discrete, historically specific social practices of criticism, organized by recurrent purposes and interests, canonical texts, problems and themes, and characteristic rhetorical tropes, voices, and forensic strategies. The different "literary criticisms" of law explicated and critiqued here all share the single, fertile rhetorical figure of the Law as Literature trope. Yet each genre hinges this law-literature analogy on a different image of literary activity and so promotes a different variant of the Law as Literature trope.

The first genre we take up is the *hermeneutic criticism of law*, which treats interpretation as the basic mode of literary action. Within this genre, the Law as Literature claim becomes a claim that law is most fundamentally a practice of interpretation. This was the first and remains the most familiar genre of Law and

[53] Richard Posner, *Economic Analysis of Law* (Boston: Little, Brown, 1973).

[54] Richard Posner, *Law and Literature: A Misunderstood Relation* (Cambridge: Harvard Univ. Press, 1988).

Literature scholarship. To understand why this genre developed is to understand how legal scholars came to see literary criticism and literary theory as relevant to law.

Chapter 1 of this book, "Interpretive Crises in American Legal Thought," offers such an explanatory account of the origins of the Law and Literature movement. This account explains how, and with what assumptions, antebellum American lawyers developed a sophisticated view of law as an interpretive activity that retained some relation to the Ciceronian ideal. It recounts the increasing stresses on that hermeneutic model of lawyering as the Civil War approached, and the cultural changes that later encouraged Progressive Era lawyers to see themselves more as scientific observers of American society than as authoritative interpreters of American political institutions. It reveals that Progressive lawyers increasingly identified a creative and aesthetic dimension to the judicial tasks of observing and representing society. Yet their firm sense that law properly served prevailing social custom and consensus prevented any great anxiety about the legitimacy of the judicial imagination. Indeed, they were more likely to criticize conservative judicial decisions as unimaginative than as overly inventive.

Throughout this period, legal interpretation was seen either as a fairly conventional exercise or as a matter of putting texts to discernible social purposes. Interpretation might require skill, but it was not an impossible matter of determining inherently indeterminate meanings. Chapter 1 argues that only with the civil rights revolution did reformist lawyers lose their confidence that legal interpretation—particularly constitutional interpretation—could be grounded in social custom or majority opinion. If the judicial guardian of minority rights could not be a social scientist, she needed some other identity—a void that the idea of the judge as artist might fill. And if the meaning of the Constitution's vague civil rights clauses could no longer be supplied by social consensus, it would have to be invented. A residual majoritarianism suggested that judges, like artists, could have only persuasive rather than coercive power over the public. Lacking final power, judges could only engage the public and its political representatives in a process of dialogue and hope to win their way by charm.

In the meantime, American literary criticism, partly under the sway of continental influences, had evolved in the direction of celebrating the reader as the true creative source of literary meaning. Chapter 2, "Hermeneutic Criticism of Law," summarizes these developments and shows how they were appropriated by legal scholars. It shows how continental "hermeneutics" and American "Reader-Response" theory seemed suited to explain the new practice of countermajoritarian constitutional interpretation as a noble and necessary act of literary invention. In his or her role as constitutional interpreter, the judge became an example of a previously unrecognized type of literary artist: the literary critic. The judge as literary critic metaphor was the central trope of the hermeneutic criticism of law, around which was organized a largely epistemological debate about the legitimacy of legal interpretation. How, if interpretation was unconstrained by text or authorial intent, could it be objective? If not objective, how could interpretation be impartial; and if not impartial, how could it be fair? Yet if constrained by social convention, how could interpretation be fair to the marginalized and despised?

Chapter 2 expresses our doubt that debate about the validity or justice of legal interpretation can be usefully conducted at this level of generality: most legal interpretation does not raise the fundamental questions about American society that interpretations of the Civil War Amendments must address. We suggest that a shared sense of interpretive crisis is itself an internal interpretive judgment about discord in a particular institutional tradition. As an interpretive judgment, such a sense of crisis cannot be taken as evidence that interpretive judgments are inherently baseless. We will conclude that the debate over the objectivity of legal interpretation is therefore an example of the skeptical misuse of literary theory. A genuinely "hermeneutic" criticism of legal institutions would have to criticize them from within the particular traditions, history, and culture of an actual society.

By reconstructing the tradition of American legal thought about interpretation (in chapter 1), and locating the Law and Literature movement in relation to that tradition (in chapter 2), we provide an example of such internal criticism. We argue that the American legal tradition has been philosophically sophisticated in its appreciation of the role of custom and convention in the development of legal meaning, although ethically blind in its accommodation of the racism in American custom and culture. By contrast, recent scholarship on legal interpretation has often made "language" and "meaning" into philosophical pseudo-problems and thereby obscured the specific political and cultural sources of incoherence in the American constitution. But the fault, we suggest, lies not in language, which is ordinarily a tolerably useful tool. Instead, the resistance of the Civil War Amendments to interpretation results from the painful fact that the American polity is constituted as much by its history of racial hierarchy and exclusion as by the textual promise of racial equality. In the face of these painful contradictions, it may be that no morally satisfying interpretation of the American polity is possible. If so, this is no idle methodological quibble, but an urgent challenge to the authority of American law and to our personal identity and political obligation as Americans. In the context of this interpretive crisis, scholarly assertions of the inscrutability of language in general serve to excuse the incoherence of the American Constitution in particular, and so to insulate our identification as Americans from critical reflection. Thus, the interpretation debate may have, ironically, used skeptical arguments to sentimental ends.

A second genre of literary criticism of law, reviewed in chapter 3, treats the paradigmatic literary activity as the telling of stories. Hence, the Law as Literature trope takes the more specific form of law as narrative. In the narrative criticism of law, "narrative" tends to connote particularity rather than abstraction, emotional involvement rather than detached rationality, creativity rather than technicality, and fluidity rather than rigidity. Often the Law as Narrative trope contrasts a redemptive vision of law as life-giving spirit with an indictment of law's actuality as desiccated letter. In this line of writing, law's redemptive function is to bear witness to the pathos of human suffering. On the other hand, the Law as Narrative trope may play a debunking role, embarrassing law's aspirations to rationality and regularity with an exposure of lawyers' trickery or judges' inconsistency. Rather than connoting the concrete truth of human suffering, story telling may stand for the skillful distortion of reality and the emotional manipulation of an audience. A third alternative presents narratives as neither authentic self-expressions nor deceptive stratagems, but as unauthored myths or stereotypes that circulate through a culture like currency or contagion, shaping the consciousness of all who are not immune. Law may be portrayed narratively as a story of progress or corruption, of learning or of falling away from timeless verities and original understandings.

Narrative scholarship is largely a debate over the cognitive worth and political significance of narrative in law. Does it reveal or distort? Is it reliable? Does it lull us into acceptance of oppression or awaken us to resistance? Does it promote self-deception or self-understanding? One assumption found on all sides of this debate is that narrative—whether redeeming or corrupting—is an alien element in law.

Chapter 3 will conclude with a critical examination of this assumption. We will consider a variety of claims that law and narrative are intrinsically related: that legal reasoning has an inherently narrative structure, for example, or that such paradigmatic narrative forms as the novel and the history presuppose the legal institutions of the modern state. In particular, we will explore an argument that legal claims involve implicit assertions of the authority of some legal system; and that such claims to sovereign authority entail the invocation of an historical narrative. This argument reprises a theme from chapters 1 and 2: that to assert or recognize the authority of law, to identify as the agent or citizen of a sovereign state, entails an act of literary imagination. Like interpretation, narration is inherent in justifying political obligation and so is intrinsic to law. Both social orders and personal identities are anchored by narratives, and linked through narratives, to one another. Narratives therefore do not stand outside social authority—they are part of it. So the value of the narrative criticism of law lies not in invoking some abstract idea of narrative to challenge law, but in examining, critiquing, and revising the particular narratives embedded in law, and the identities and institutions these narratives enable.

Chapter 4 considers a genre that we call rhetorical criticism of law. Such rhetorical criticism presents the literary aspect of law as the activity of persuasion, or focusing more on the hearer rather than the speaker, the activity of deliberation. Its recurrent tropes then are Law as Persuasion, Law as Deliberation, and Law as Dialogue. More than any other genre, rhetorical criticism draws its inspiration from classical literature and philosophy. It is closely tied to the ideal of a civic republic in which politics engages all citizens but in a disinterested way. The virtuous citizen experiences politics as an intellectual debate or dialogue rather than a contest of opposing interest groups. The organizing question for rhetorical criticism of law is how the civic attitude is to be encouraged in a modern society premised on the subjectivity of value. Rhetorical criticism of law draws from the classical rhetorical tradition a concern with how language affects the emotions of the hearer, and an identification of the good with the maintenance of virtuous character rather than achievement of good results or enforcement of just rules.

Yet rhetorical criticism combines these ancient concerns with certain modern ones. First, if modern society sees politics as a realm of self-interest ungovernable by reason, it sees art as a realm of disinterested contemplation. If we can no longer credibly ask citizens to adopt an attitude of rational detachment in politics, perhaps we can replicate classical virtue by encouraging aesthetic detachment in politics. Second, while classical philosophy valued the deliberative character as a substantive good, some variants of modern liberalism value the deliberative process as a just procedure for reconciling opposed interests. Thus, classical ideas of the good can be justified to modern audiences as instruments for achieving the right. Third, the rhetorical tradition's interest in audience sentiment and classical philosophy's concern with the development of character both resonate with reader-response theory's interest in the experience of the reader over time. Finally, the classical tradition's moral interest in personality and emotion can be presented to modern audiences as a therapeutic concern with emotional health.

The problem confronting this project of rhetorical revival is the loss of the organic political culture of shared values and virtues that classical rhetoric presupposed. The more conservative proponents of rhetorical revival treat it as an elite project of cultural preservation—conserving classical wisdom in a licentious age and attempting to quietly maintain its influence over rulers. But many enthusiasts of rhetoric in law are liberal pluralists, who see the orator statesman not as the exponent of an organic culture or of eternal verities, but as a kind of literary creation—a character who models an ethos for the edification of an audience.

The values proffered by the liberal rhetorician may be the liberal process values of tolerance and open-mindedness, or the Romantic values of creativity and independence of mind. In either case, there will be a tension between the liberal content of these values and their rhetorical presentation as virtues for emulation. Thus, the efforts of some liberal rhetoricians to model vague virtues like judiciousness and impartiality, without favoring any particular conception of the good, can produce a hollow shell of rhetoric, principled in tone without particular principles.

But the classical model of eloquence would seem to require the speaker to identify with some conception of the good. To present one's self as a model of virtue is to accept the risks of normative commitment. These include submitting one's own character for judgment and claiming the authority to stand in judgment of others. The rhetorician admonishes her audience to govern itself according to definable virtues, not just to express creative impulses or authentic desires. In so doing the rhetorician implies that the values her audience adopts, and the character it develops, are matters of public and political concern. By treating character and culture as political questions, the rhetorical tradition points to a more profound conception of politics than that commonly associated with liberal pluralism, but one potentially threatening to cherished freedoms. By extending the domain of the political to culture and character, the rhetorical criticism of law points to the possibility of a more complete cultural criticism of law, which evaluates not just the rhetorical personae lawyers adopt, but the legal institutions, legal decisions, and legal forms that shape character and identity in our society.

Chapter 5 examines a genre we call "deconstructive criticism of law." This genre of literary criticism of law takes its inspiration from the work of literary critic and philosopher Jacques Derrida, who in recent years has turned his attention to law. Most practitioners of deconstruction in law are on the left wing of the legal academy, either "critical legal scholars" or feminist scholars. Deconstructive criticism treats law as no more and no less literary than any other use of language. One of its recurrent tropes is Law as Language. However, it draws an additional trope from Derridean deconstruction: Language as Literature. Deconstructive critics treat all language use, or "signification," as figurative rather than literal. In sum, deconstructive criticism represents law as an inherently literary practice of signification. In deconstructive criticism of law, the fact that signification is figurative is often treated as an indictment: language distorts or obscures what it represents. Above all it reduces the richness and complexity of the experienced world. Law, as a form of signification—as the letter—is therefore inherently reductive. This criticism generally takes two forms, one epistemological and one ethical.

The epistemological version usually appears as part of an argument that legal rules do not have clear or determinate implications for future cases. Legal standards condition results on "subjective" mental states, but these can only be known through inherently reductive "objective" indicia. The law's inevitable gap between rule and purpose, letter and spirit, is a recurrent source of (presumably undesirable) flexibility. Chapter 5 suggests that much of this criticism amounts to facile skepticism. Because it applies equally to all legal standards and institutions, such epistemological deconstruction cannot effectively criticize any particular institutions. Moreover, because it portrays legal language as always equally conflicted and incoherent, such deconstruction cannot explain why legal actors sometimes experience legal language as in crisis and sometimes do not.

Ethical deconstruction finds different implications in the reductiveness of legal language: first, that representations of the public interest or of society in legal settings will always be partial and partisan; second, that the groups or "voices" excluded from representation will often be the weakest and most oppressed. Deconstruction can be used to show that such voices have been excluded and to challenge such exclusion as itself oppressive "violence." The difficulty is that deconstructive premises imply that such "exclusion" or partiality is inevitable in any use of language, so that there can be no ethical imperative to be all inclusive. Deconstruction appears to be at best an ornament if not an actual impediment to arguments for greater political participation by the underprivileged. Indeed, the principal target of Derrida's own polemics has been the ideal of participatory democracy, which he sees as dangerously populist.

But, that deconstruction adds little to the work of its exponents in the field of law does not drain their work of interest. Much of this work builds on other sources—cultural feminism, pragmatist epistemology, the Frankfurt School, Foucault—to mount illuminating accounts of the cultural place of law.

Chapter 6 explicates the cultural criticism of law discussed earlier in this introduction. This genre of criticism treats legal disputing and transacting as occasions for the representation of self, others, and society. It equates the literary with the depiction of character and the delineation of a social landscape. In this way, the cultural criticism of law metaphorically extends the concept of literature from the presentation of such depictions for aesthetic consumption to the everyday practical activity of staking claims to desirable roles and identities or interpreting those roles in advantageous ways. Law, then, is literary insofar as it involves claiming, exchanging, and distributing not just resources, but also cultural meanings. Law as Representation is this genre's constitutive trope. Chapter 6 reviews some of the intellectual sources of this genre in the structuralism of Michel Foucault, the pragmatic cultural sociology of Pierre Bourdieu, the normative aestheticism of Nietzsche, and the recent Cultural Studies and New Historicism movements in literary studies. It then considers examples of cultural representation in two sorts of legal settings. First, it reviews scholarship "reading" the representations of parties in disputes—trials, but also appellate litigation, feuds, and street confrontations. Second, it considers examples of the representation of character, credit, and value in commercial and financial law. It concludes not only that cultural meaning is a dimension of law to which legal and policy analysts should attend, but also that law is an arena for contesting, negotiating, and fashioning meaning that should be of interest to any student of culture.

While chapter 6 explicates the cultural criticism of law, the entire book illustrates it, beginning with this introduction. And the entire book's success in explicating and evaluating the cultural meaning of the various literary criticisms of law will provide our strongest argument for the efficacy of this approach.

This introduction has for the most part stressed the differences among the various genres of literary criticism of law, and particularly between cultural criticism and all the others. Yet as the chapters to follow show, there are important similarities as well. All five genres of criticism discussed in this book portray law as a practice of composing a kind of literary artifact—a reading, a story, a performance, a sign, or a representation. Since each of these portrayals is really a simile or metaphor or trope, none is necessarily inconsistent with any other. That making a legal argument is like telling a story need not entail or imply that it is unlike interpreting a novel or performing a dramatic role. While the different genres of criticism portray law as the composition of different kinds of artifacts, each portrays law as a practice of composition; and the different accounts they give of the practice of literary composition exhibit a certain family resemblance: each can be described as a process of appropriating and reshaping old materials.

This is perhaps most obviously true of the Law as Interpretation trope on which the Hermeneutic criticism of law relies. An interpretation presupposes a text, or some other object of interpretation, to be understood, applied, appreciated, and brought to life.

The derivative character of narration is less obvious than the derivative character of interpretation, since we sometimes think of narrative fiction as pure invention, as the creation of an imaginary world out of whole cloth. Yet as the chapter on narrative criticism underscores, narration works on and modifies many kinds of received materials, including both actual experience and generic conventions. Thus, to portray law as narration is also to portray it as a process of reusing what is already at hand.

The same is true of the Law as Rhetoric trope, which treats law as an extension of classical oratory. Classical rhetoric expected orators to persuade and inspire by modeling an exemplary character. In this sense, the practice of rhetoric involves the dramatic performance of a conventional role. Sometimes the rhetorical criticism of law focuses on a different process of appropriation and transformation—the process of modifying opinion, reconciling antagonism, or transcending self-interest through deliberative dialogue.

Deconstructive criticism portrays law as a practice of signification. This activity also is conceived in dual terms. From a deconstructive perspective, any speech act relies on, but also modifies and shows the instability of, the preexisting network of significance we call a language. By analogy, the practice of legal argument "deconstructs" any pretense that law is a static or self-contained code of norms.

Finally, the cultural criticism of law portrays law as an arena within which participants contest how persons, groups, institutions, and values are to be represented. In so doing, they interpret texts, retell and reframe narratives, perform characters, and use and reshape languages. But cultural criticism of law emphasizes that legal actors do all of these and more. The medium in which law composes and is composed is not limited to authoritative legal texts, or even to language. It includes characters, identities, traditions, institutions, and markets. And the composers are not autonomous Romantic artists. Composition is a collective political process, a kind of negotiation.

In sum, the five genres of criticism discussed in this book share a view of law as a compositional process that involves appropriating and reconfiguring available cultural materials. The hermeneutic, narrative, rhetorical, and deconstructive criticisms of law portray this process in ways that are limited, and potentially limiting, if any of them is taken as an exhaustive portrayal of law's composition. Our aim is not to repudiate these genres of criticism, but to incorporate them into a more flexible and eclectic understanding of law as a practice that constantly appropriates, reproduces, and reshapes a culture.

Interpretive Crises in American Legal Thought

INTRODUCTION

The principal case for the relevance of literary theory to law casts literary theorists as experts on interpretation. Thus, the claim that law is literary most often precedes an argument that interpretation is the central activity of legal actors, that interpretation is nevertheless a lawless enterprise in need of legitimation or critique, and that literary theory, habituated to the wilder thickets of the human mind, can gently hedge legal interpretation, or free it to realize its potential. Literary theory, in short, can supply criteria for a hermeneutic criticism of law.

In identifying interpretation as a contestable enterprise, Law and Literature scholars have frequently articulated a sense of disillusionment, a "loss of the sense of doing and speaking in the name of someone or something recognizable and unquestionably valid,"[1] a "crisis of legitimacy."[2] Law and Literature scholars witness to their crisis of faith by ritually exposing language as unreliable and meaning as unstable or controversial.

This skeptical form of argument presumes that the legitimacy of legal decision making has traditionally depended upon the ability of lawyers to ground it in legal texts of demonstrably definite meaning, and that lawyers have traditionally believed—or at least asserted—that legal texts have demonstrably definite meanings. These assumptions are in part historical assumptions. Thus, the recurrent motif of disillusionment in Law and Literature scholarship presumes something like the following lapsarian narrative.

With the coming of religious liberty and political democracy, enlightened skepticism replaced innocent faith in natural law. Unable to claim that law was divinely willed or objectively just, lawyers were now compelled to defend law as an objectively accurate transcription of democratic will. And so, since the advent of modernity, lawyers have been obliged to pretend that the meaning of legal texts can be transparently discerned without any discretion or subjective judgment. Yet the sophisticated accounts of language offered by pragmatist philosophy and poststructuralist literary theory reveal that the meaning of laws cannot be fixed by their language or the intentions of their authors. Hence, discretion is inevitable,

---

[1] Sanford Levinson, "Law as Literature," in *Interpreting Law and Literature: A Hermeneutic Reader*, ed. Stanford Levinson and Steven Mailloux (Evanston, Ill: Northwestern Univ. Press, 1988), 158.

[2] Mark Tushnet, *Red, White and Blue: A Critical Analysis of Constitutional Law* (Cambridge: Harvard Univ. Press, 1988), 3.

objectivity is a pretense, and epistemological crisis is an ever-present threat. The history of modern legal thought has been nothing but a series of fig leaves disguising the laws' semantic indeterminacy and epistemological bankruptcy.

Many look to the advent of law as a subject of university instruction and academic research, after the Civil War, as the moment in American history when the law assumed its pretense of objectivity. The early-twentieth-century Supreme Court is presumed to have donned this mantle of objectivity in defending its competence to review progressive economic and labor legislation under the Commerce Clause and the Due Process Clause of the Fourteenth Amendment. The controversial decision in *Lochner v. New York*, striking down a limitation on the working hours of able-bodied competent adults as a violation of their liberty of contract, is read as a climactic event.[3] The ensuing debate over judicial implementation of laissez-faire economic policy becomes a debate over the objectivity of legal interpretation. From this perspective, the policies at issue were of only superficial interest: the *real* issue was the epistemological status of adjudication, especially interpretation.

This chapter offers a history of American legal thought about interpretation that (1) shows the lapsarian narrative presumed by the interpretation debate to be misleading, (2) accounts for the sense of epistemological crisis animating this debate, and (3) helps explain why legal scholars turned to literary theory to articulate or resolve this sense of crisis. By our account, modernization did initiate a view of law that gave new emphasis to interpretation. But this hermeneutic view of law did *not* require faith in the objectivity of interpretation or the determinacy of meaning. American legal thought did pass through a traumatic and transformative period around the time of the Civil War, and Americans did lose faith in legal interpretation. But the crisis was temporary, and it was not primarily epistemological.

In the history we offer here, antebellum American lawyers developed a conception of legal interpretation as a rhetorical art of mediating between a volatile popular will and the need for institutional stability. They placed this rhetorical art at the center of what they hoped would be a coherent republican culture. The slavery crisis and Civil War discredited this vision of an integrated civic culture and with it the notion of law as a literate and humane practice of cultural creation and conservation.

For the next century, law and literature largely went their separate ways. Lawyers reconceived their interpretive function in a fashion that aligned them more closely to the new sciences of society. Legal interpretation was a search not so much for verbal meaning as for knowledge of societal interests and purposes.

---

[3] *Lochner v. New York*, 198 U.S. 45 (1905); Gary Peller, "The Metaphysics of American Law," *California Law Review* 73 (1985): 1151; Morton Horwitz, *The Transformation of American Law 1870–1960: The Crisis of Legal Orthodoxy* (New York: Oxford Univ. Press, 1992); Elizabeth Mensch, "The History of Mainstream Legal Thought," in *The Politics of Law*, rev. ed., ed. David Kairys (New York: Pantheon Books, 1990), 13–37.

Legal opinion divided on the nature of these interests and how they could best be acertained and served, but that society was ultimately intelligible was the common ground of this debate. The conventional division of the post–Civil War period into formalist and realist eras is misleading. The better view is that these were different strands of a single Progressive discourse, characterized by scientism, evolutionism, and a competitive struggle to legitimize governmental institutions as professionally disciplined. Progressive critics of laissez-faire regretted that courts were doing a poor job of representing society but did not consider them incapable of so doing. Progressives acknowledged a creative and sometimes even aesthetic dimension to the task of representing societal interests, but they saw the legal decision maker as properly a servant of popular will.

The contemporary sense of epistemological crisis is a very recent event. Only when the post–World War II courts confronted racial segregation and discrimination did the notion of adjudication as fundamentally and appropriately countermajoritarian prevail. After the war liberal legal scholars had, for the first time, to confront a problem to which Progressive legal thought offered no solution: justifying the countermajoritarian expression of judicial subjectivity. This was the situation that made judicial subjectivity presumptively illegitimate and provoked the second hermeneutic crisis of American legal thought. What it shared with the first was its origin in the contradiction between the American public's egalitarian ideals and its deep-rooted commitment to racial exclusion. Neither crisis reveals anything of interest about the nature of language or meaning generally. Both crises are reminders of the tragic incoherence of the constitutive texts and traditions of American political life in particular.

One response to the second hermeneutic crisis was to revive the ideal of the lawyer as a rhetorical artist that had been discredited by the first hermeneutic crisis. The judicial task was no longer to represent political majorities, but to engage them in a dialogic legal process with the aim of provoking, teaching, and transforming popular opinion. Constitutional scholars began to write or deliver models of duly inspiring rhetorical performance for judicial emulation. Conditions were ripe for the emergence of a Romantic vision of the constitutional interpeter as alienated social critic and imaginative artist, and for a reinterpretation of the countermajoritarian difficulty as a problem of literary theory.

Part 1.1 of this chapter, "The Crisis of Whig Hermeneutics," describes the flexible, adaptive model of legal interpretation developed by antebellum American lawyers, particularly those associated with the Whig Party. It lays out the cultural assumptions on which that model of interpretation was premised and the process by which the dispute over slavery discredited those assumptions. Part 1.2, "Progressive Interpretation," lays out the shared ideas of science, professionalism, and evolutionary social change from which Progressive Era lawyers derived a variety of competing accounts of legal interpretation. Part 1.3, "The Crisis of Progressive Interpretation," describes the dilemma posed for progressive jurisprudence by the civil rights movement and depicts the postwar ideas of "process" and "dialogue" and the new character-type of the judicial artist as responses to that dilemma.

1.1 The Crisis of Whig Hermeneutics

Interpretation in Premodern Legal Thought

The idea that interpretation is the principal activity of lawyers depends upon a model of law and society that came to prevail during the nineteenth century. According to this model, society is made up of competing interests, and law is an expression of the wills of those interests as articulated by their representatives or agents. Thus, law is a text with an instrumental meaning, and the task of lawyers is to interpret that text in order to know its meaning. There is a great deal of play in this model, permitting interpreters to look for subjective preferences, objective interests, formal expressions, reasonable expectations, conventional meanings, or institutional functions; to view actors as repositories of will or as representatives of the will of others; to measure preference or interest at the time of a transaction, at the time of adjudication, or over some longer interval of time. On this model, legal argument can accommodate a good deal of disagreement about who has lawmaking authority and how their wills are to be determined; but it remains fundamental that law is always an interpretation of the will of some competent authority.

This model of law as interpreted will is distinctively modern. For most of the history of Western jurisprudence law was more often conceived as custom than as the will of an identifiable sovereign.[4] Adjudication and advocacy in a customary regime could not simply be described as interpreting the will of the lawmaker.

In medieval Europe, customary law was generally a question of fact, provable by the testimony of local witnesses in assembly. In the early modern period, however, as populations became more mobile and legal disputes lost their local character, custom tended to become unprovable or incapable of resolving disputes. Custom had to be supplemented by written records of judicial decisions and testimony of use in other locales, extended by analogy and the practical reason of experienced lawyers, perhaps even replaced by Roman, canon, or natural law, retaining all the while its rhetorical pride of place. By the eighteenth century, custom had lost its character as a procedure for identifying the law and had become, like natural law and sovereignty, a vague source of authority for the legitimation or critique of legal institutions.[5]

Along the way, custom tended also to lose its association with the local and the oral. Written records of diverse local customs, rationalized, reconciled, and

---

[4] An identification of positivism with a conception of law as the will of a lawmaker has a better pedigree than popular misconception might allow. Even before Austin, Bentham defined law as a volitional act, and he did so in order to identify law with statute and to disqualify custom and nature as sources of law. See David Lieberman, *The Province of Legislation Determined* (Cambridge: Cambridge Univ. Press, 1989). The more sophisticated theories of Kelsen and Hart, by accounting for the legal authority of custom, religion, and the like, arguably abandon the chief feature of legal positivism that made it attractive to its originators.

[5] James Q. Whitman, "Why Did the Revolutionary Lawyers Confuse Custom and Reason?" *University of Chicago Law Review* 58 (1991): 1321.

supplemented by principles of Roman and natural law, became sources for learned treatises on national custom. These treatises became an important source of the related ideas of national culture and fundamental law that informed modern notions of popular sovereignty and constitutionalism, respectively.[6] The modern idea of a sovereign people or nation emerged out of the early modern idea that any group obedient to a common customary regime was a distinct people.[7] Since national identity depended upon common customary law, the fundamental law that we now see as a limitation on popular sovereignty was originally the condition of popular sovereignty's very intelligibility.

While it is clear that custom was authoritative in the medieval world, the medieval world had no single cogent account of why custom was authoritative. Instead, custom was variously associated with a number of often inconsistent conceptions of authority. That authoritative practices dated from time out of mind accorded with the Platonic and Augustinian notions that truth was static and eternal. Alternatively, custom could be seen as the accumulated wisdom of the ages, a species of Aristotelian practical reason.[8] Thus, in William Dugdale's ambivalent formulation, common law was both pure and tried reason.[9] But then the Digest of Justinian identifies custom with tacit agreement—will rather than reason.[10] According to the fourteenth-century Romanist Baldus, custom's material cause was frequent use, its formal cause was consensus, its efficient cause was duration, and its final cause was utility.[11] Later enthusiasts of Gothic liberty identified custom with popular consent, assuming that customary rights were not simply attested to but constituted and preserved by popular action.[12] According to the fifteenth-century common law commentator Sir John Fortescue, custom was a "second nature" founded by "common consent" and serviceable to "common interest."[13]

---

[6] Ibid.; J. G. A. Pocock, *The Ancient Constitution and the Feudal Law: A Study of English Historical Thought in the Seventeenth Century: A Reissue with a Retrospect* (Cambridge: Cambridge Univ. Press, 1987).

[7] Donald R. Kelley, *The Human Measure: Social Thought in the Western Legal Tradition* (Cambridge: Harvard Univ. Press, 1990), 106.

[8] Thus Hale: "The Lawes . . . are the production of the long and iterated Experience wch tho' itt be commonly called the mistrisse of Fooles, yett certainly itt is the wisest Expedient among mankind, and discovers those defects and Supplys wch no witt of Man could either at once forsee or aptly remedye"; Matthew Hale, *Criticisms on Hobbess Dialogue of the Common Laws* (British Library, Harleian MS 711, fols. 418–39), in Kelley, *Human Measure*, 182.

[9] William Dugdale, *Origines juridiciales* (London: Newcomb, 1671), 3.

[10] Kelley, *Human Measure*, 115.

[11] Ian Maclean, *Interpretation and Meaning in the Renaissance: The Case of Law* (Cambridge: Cambridge Univ. Press, 1992), 174.

[12] Pocock, *Ancient Constitution and the Feudal Law*; James Q. Whitman, *The Legacy of Roman Law in the German Romantic Era* (Princeton: Princeton Univ. Press, 1990); Guyora Binder, "Angels and Infidels: Hierarchy and Historicism in Medieval Legal History," *Buffalo Law Review* 35 (1986): 527. For a thirteenth-century discussion illustrating the confused state of thinking on custom's authority see *Dissensiones dominorum sive controversiae veterum iuris romani interpretum qui glossatores vocantur*, ed. Gustav Haenel (Leipzig, 1834), 129–30.

[13] Kelley, *Human Measure*, 168–69.

Perhaps we moderns can best reconcile these divergent accounts of custom's authority by conceiving the sources of medieval law as corporations chartered for some virtuous purpose, composed not only of contemporary witnesses to past use, but of past and future generations as well.[14] Thus conceived, custom reflected not the majority will of contemporary witnesses, but the majority *judgment* of all the generations within contemporary memory—judgment as to how best to worship God, organize the manufacture and trade in leather goods, or cultivate and divide the fruit of the earth in a given locale. In this model, the corporate purpose represents the abiding Platonic aspect of custom, and the accumulated judgment of generations represents the empirical, Aristotelian aspect of custom, while the participation of multigenerational majorities in enacting and revising law represents the democratic aspect of custom. Because, according to this model, contemporary majorities are restrained by deference to corporate purpose and past popular judgment, customary law can simultaneously be a product of popular consent and a constitutional constraint on popular will.

Because the idea of customary law effaces the process of legislation, it permits no clear distinction between customary legislation and customary adjudication. Lawmaking and law applying involve the same process of making judgments. If modern legal thought populates society with wills contracting, voting, bequeathing, legislating, and otherwise placing the stamp of their legal personality on their surroundings, custom evokes a company of roles, lots, appointments, benefices, pulpits, and crowns—fiduciaries bound to fulfill trusts. The key is that the inhabitant of custom's commonwealth exercises *judgment* rather than choice. Thus, in premodern discussions rights were often portrayed not as liberties, but as posts or offices, conferring inalienable responsibilities.[15] Where the modern outlook contrasts judicial restraint with the freedom of the legislator, the customary outlook confers both legislative power and judicial responsibility on every legal actor.

While custom was the dominant model of law in the Middle Ages and Renaissance, it was not the only model. Medieval and Renaissance lawyers were familiar with statutes, saw interpretation as an important problem in their application, and saw legislative intention as an important object of interpretive inquiry.[16] Intentionalist techniques included "extensive" and "restrictive" interpretation in which legislative intent was deemed to encompass more or less than statutory language.[17] Even equitable interpretation was sometimes explained, following Aristotle, as a hypothetical inquiry into how the legislator would have resolved an unforeseen

[14] Ernst H. Kantorowicz, *The King's Two Bodies: A Study in Mediaeval Political Theology* (Princeton: Princeton Univ. Press, 1957).

[15] Richard Tuck, *Natural Rights Theories: Their Origin and Development* (Cambridge: Cambridge University Press, 1979); Garry Wills, *Inventing America: Jefferson's Declaration of Independence* (Garden City, N.Y.: Doubleday, 1978); Peter N. Riesenberg, *Inalienability of Sovereignty in Medieval Political Thought* (New York: Columbia Univ. Press, 1955); Kantorowicz, *King's Two Bodies.*

[16] Kelley, *Human Measure,* 134–35.

[17] Maclean, *Interpretation and Meaning,* 119–20.

case.[18] Yet inquiry into the intention of the legislator was premised on a notion of the legislator as an official entrusted only with judgment rather than sovereign will: the legislator's aim is always conceived to be the *"utilitas reipublicae."*[19] While "intention" had many meanings to Renaissance legal scholars,[20] the intention that most governed interpretation was the law's manifest "reason," its life-giving spirit as opposed to its deathly letter.[21] The law's reason embraced the mischief necessitating it, its purpose, and its conformity to natural or eternal reason.[22] Thus, the intention that mattered for interpretation was conventional rather than psychological. The paradigm for authoritative language remained religious scripture, the will of whose author was inaccessible by definition.

Medieval and Renaissance jurists developed a plethora of textualist interpretive techniques. Many approaches focused on correctly glossing terms.[23] Some developed elaborate schemes for distinguishing and classifying legal terms, and for identifying and reconciling contradictions within legal texts.[24] Others urged historical investigation into the original use of the law's terms, or even etymological speculation.[25] But the most important of the nonintentionalist techniques of interpretation was indicated by an oft-cited maxim from Justinian's *Digest*: "Custom is the best interpreter of law."[26] The early Renaissance jurist Bartolus placed custom above even a law's reason as an interpretive guide.[27] Custom was by no means the only source of law in premodern Europe, but it was so central to the lawyer's conception of authority as to color all of his methods, interpretation included.

Interpretation in the Common Law

The common law tradition, of course, influenced early American ideas about fundamental law. The idea of the common law as a national customary law, developed by learned adjudication, was one early modern revision of the medieval customary idea. According to Hale and Blackstone, judicial precedent was authoritative evidence of custom, even though written rather than oral, and esoteric rather than common.[28] Strangely, in the century following Parliament's coronation as sovereign, legislation became increasingly disreputable, while the common law was increasingly praised, not only as a repository of ancient wisdom, but as an engine of progress and reform. Where Parliamentary legislation was myopic, chaotic, venal, and harsh, common law adjudication was farsighted, conformable to

[18] Ibid., 22, 175.
[19] Ibid., 94.
[20] Ibid., 147.
[21] Ibid., 152.
[22] Ibid., 153.
[23] Ibid., 104–14.
[24] Ibid., 111–14, 123.
[25] Kelley, *Human Measure*, 132–37.
[26] Ibid., 91, 154 (referring to Digest 1.3.37).
[27] Maclean, *Interpretation and Meaning*, 174.
[28] Whitman, "Why Did the Revolutionary Lawyers?" 1360–65.

reason, conscientious, and equitable. Indeed, legislation's faults were frequently blamed on its departures from the common law, even as such common law judges as Mansfield were praised for their innovations, for example, in conforming commercial law to evolving mercantile custom.[29]

Common law was paradoxically praised as both older and newer than statute, since statute could fall into desuetude yet remain on the books as an invitation to confusion and oppressive enforcement. As a form of custom or "consuetude," common law was renewed by use. Common law innovation proceeded on the understanding that judges did not legislate social change, but rather conformed the law to existing, albeit evolving, custom.[30] Behind the oft-voiced platitude that judges found rather than made the law stood the seldom articulated idea that common law judges found rather than made social change. The eighteenth-century conception of the common law closely paralleled Montesquieu's contemporaneous notion of "The Spirit of the Laws" with its "lesson . . . that manners and customs could not be changed by laws but rather had to undergo change themselves; and then, through experience and learning as well as pure reason, the laws and institutions of a nation might be accommodated to them."[31]

Thus, many common law enthusiasts voiced no objection to legal change, so long as change was a product of judgment rather than legislative will, social observation rather than social engineering. While this hostility to social engineering may be given a conservative interpretation, it also lends itself to a democratic reading: change should percolate from below, manifesting itself in the customs of the people rather than the follies of their governors. The American Revolutionaries joined in this pattern of thinking by praising the common law as a fount of liberty, and an inspiration for revolution, while excoriating Parliamentary legislation as a new Norman yoke.[32] Revolutionary polemicists conceived republics as corporate institutions devoted to the general welfare and to preserving the ancient liberties necessary for popular self-government against the threat of corruption. Within this rhetoric, custom, natural law, and popular will are compatible and even mutually entailed sources of legal authority.[33] To the American Revolutionaries, custom was partly constitutive of sovereignty, partly enacted by sovereignty, and partly ordained by a Wisdom or Power superior to sovereignty.[34] James Wilson praised "the blessings of the common law springing

[29] Lieberman, *Province of Legislation Determined*, 142–43.

[30] An instructive example is *Keeble v. Hickeringhill, Queens Bench*, 11 East 574, 103 Eng Rep. 1127 (1707).

[31] Kelley, *Human Measure*, 222. For the claim that judges in a republic should follow the letter of the law, see Montesquieu, *The Spirit of the Laws*, trans. Thomas Nugent (New York: Hafner, 1949), 75.

[32] Pocock, *Ancient Constitution and the Feudal Law*.

[33] For preambles of revolutionary constitutions see Francis Newton Thorpe, *The Federal and State Constitutions, Colonial Charters, and Other Organic Laws of the State, Territories, and Colonies Now or Heretofore Forming the United States of America* (Washington, D.C.: GPO, 1909).

[34] For a polemical argument that by contemporary standards the revolutionary lawyers were jurisprudentially confused because historically ignorant, see Whitman, "Why Did the Revolutionary Lawyers?"

warm and spontaneous from the manners of the people."[35] Indeed, insofar as judicial discretion came under attack in America, it was the judicial construction of statute, not common law adjudication, that was perceived as potentially dangerous.[36]

Common law ideas about statutory interpretation were premised on the tightly circumscribed role of legislation in a customary law system. The 1584 decision in *Heydon's Case* presumed that all statutes were designed to remedy a "mischief and defect for which the common law did not provide," so that "the office of all judges is always to make such construction as shall suppress the mischief and advance the remedy."[37] Statutes, in short, were themselves interpretive judgments, extending the common law principles to unprovided-for cases, not revisions or repudiations of the common law.

Accordingly, an interpreter of legislation could ignore the actual motives or expectations of the legislator and interpret the legislation by direct reference to its function as an instrument of the policies implicit in the common law. This narrow legislative function could be understood to dictate the complete subordination of legislative to judicial judgment, as in Coke's 1609 dictum in *Dr. Bonham's Case* that statutes contrary to common right and reason were void.[38] Yet the deference owed custom by all institutions charged with declaring the law did not imply any necessary hierarchy among those institutions, because all were, in this key sense, judicial in function. Because legislation was an exercise in judgment it could be erroneous, and when manifestly so could be corrected. Hence legislation could be ineptly drafted so as to fail in its presumed aim of remedying an unprovided-for mischief, or worse still drafted in ignorance of the remedies provided by the common law or preexisting legislation.[39]

Thus, the first step in interpreting a statute was to identify a gap in the texture of the common law—an unremedied mischief analogous in some fashion to those already remedied by the common law. This gap in the regime for enforcing the common law's implicit goals or values would serve as the statute's "reason" or "intent." Coke's dictum in *Dr. Bonham's Case* implied that a statute for which no such reason could be found could not be applied; in practice, however, reasons could always be found for legislation, and legislation could be construed not to reach results incompatible with their reasons.[40] It was because these reasons were

[35] James Wilson, *Lectures on Law*, Lecture 1, in *The Works of James Wilson*, ed. Robert G. McCloskey (Cambridge: Harvard Univ. Press, Belknap Press, 1967), 1:70.

[36] Morton Horwitz, *The Tranformation of American Law 1780–1860* (Cambridge: Harvard Univ. Press, 1977), 5.

[37] H. Jefferson Powell, "The Original Understanding of Original Intent," *Harvard Law Review* 98 (1985): 885, 898–99, citing *Heydon's Case*, 3 Co. Rep. 7a, 76 Eng. Rep 637 (1584).

[38] Coke wrote, "And it appears in our books that in many cases the common law will controul acts of parliament, and sometimes adjudge them to be utterly void: for when an act of parliament is against common right and reason, or repugnant, or impossible to be performed, the common law will controul it, and adjudge such act to be void." *Dr. Bonham's Case*, 78 Eng. Rep. 646, 652 (K.B. 1610).

[39] Lieberman, *Province of Legislation Determined*, 185–89.

[40] William Blatt, "A History of Statutory Interpretation: A Study in Form and Substance," *Cardozo Law Review* 6 (1985): 799, 804–5.

to be found, not in nature, but in the texture of the common law that common law adjudication was said to involve "artificial reason."[41]

In general, concludes Jefferson Powell, "the late eighteenth century common lawyer conceived an instrument's 'intent'—and therefore its meaning—not as what the drafters meant by their words, but rather what judges, employing the 'artificial reason and judgment of law,' understood 'the reasonable and legal meaning' of those words to be."[42] Judical interpreters would examine not only the statute's relationship to earlier case law, but also its preambular language and its later application:[43] "Judicial precedent served as the most important source of information about an act's meaning beyond its actual text. This followed almost by definition from the basic notion of 'intent' as a product of the interpretive process rather than something locked into the text by its author."[44]

Much of the above also applies to the common law's interpretation of legal instruments other than statutes. Deeds, wills, and contracts were all seen as the exercise of powers created and conditioned by the common law. Contractual interpretation, for example, paid little heed to the intentions of the parties, who were deemed familiar with common law maxims of construction. These emphasized attention to the ordinary meaning of words, the nature of the contract and its parties, and substantive fairness. Regardless of intent, parties to a contract were presumed not to enter into agreements detrimental to their own survival. In any event, contract interpretation was more a theoretical than a practical problem in Colonial America. The legal system more often analyzed unconsummated trans-actions as the wrongful receipt of a benefit rather than the failure to fulfill a promise.[45] Juries in transactional disputes received no instructions on the legal meaning of contracts, and their attention probably focused on the compensation the plaintiff had earned rather than the performance that contractual language had authorized him to expect.[46]

Eighteenth-century ideas about constitutional interpretation were even less formed, because written constitutions were novel and stood in an uncertain rela-tionship to the customary model of law that shaped legal method. On the one hand, custom was clearly a source of fundamental law that could authorize not

[41] *Prohibitions del Roy*, 12 Co. Rep. 63, 65, 77 Eng. Rep. 1342, 1343 (1608).

[42] Powell, "Original Understanding of Original Intent," 896.

[43] Ibid., 899.

[44] Ibid.

[45] Contractual obligations were created by the receipt of consideration for a promise rather than the acceptance of an offer, although promised performance could in theory suffice for consideration. Kevin M. Teeven, *A History of the Anglo-American Common Law of Contract*, Contributions in Legal Studies 59, ed. Paul L. Murphy (Westport, Conn: Greenwood Press, 1990), 166, 177; A. W. B. Simp-son, "The Horwitz Thesis and the History of Contracts," *University of Chicago Law Review* 46 (1979): 533, 543. While Morton Horwitz's characterization of eighteenth-century American contract law as premised on a standard of just price now seems exaggerated, American courts were more likely than English courts to examine the fairness of bargains and the fitness of goods. Compare Horwitz, *Trans-formation of American Law 1780–1860*, 160–73; Teeven, *Anglo-American Common Law of Contract*, 157–67.

[46] Teeven, *Anglo-American Common Law of Contract*, 166; Horwitz, *Transformation of American Law 1780–1860*, 166.

only judicial review of, but also popular resistance to, legislation.[47] On the other hand, the eighteenth century witnessed a movement throughout Europe to codify custom. Hence, the mounting enthusiasm for written constitutions may be seen as part of an impulse to codify rather than repudiate custom,[48] and thus it was not clear whether the new written constitutions were to be construed against a background of customary norms or as substitutes for custom, exhausting its authority.

Americans of the Revolutionary generation probably assumed that their constitutions would be construed as the common law construed other written instruments. Debates over framing and ratifying the federal constitution seem to have presumed that much of its meaning would be determined by later judicial and legislative construction, that interpreters would rely on the express language supplemented by structural reasoning and, where possible, would reconcile the text with common law liberties. Nevertheless, the Federalist view that a constitution was a statute passed by the people inspired traditional worries about the dangers of statutory innovation.

Federalists responded that judicial interpretation of the Constitution would be disciplined by the expectations and customs of the people. In the event of judicial subversion of popular expectations, the people could reassert their authority through the Article V Amendment Process,[49] or revolutionary action.[50] Yet this response evaded the point of the antifederalist critique, which feared faithful quite as much as faithless interpretation of the Constitution. The federal power was a novelty: by bringing it into being, the people were exercising will rather than simply defending their customary rights, as they supposedly had done in revolting against England and establishing state governments.[51] Where revolutionary state constitutions were justified as responses to English violations of custom, the federal Constitution was an inventive solution to new problems. It was not and did not pretend to be an elaboration of the common law. Accordingly, in the antifederalist view, the Constitution was different in function from a statute, and its enactment and interpretation would represent dangerous departures from the conception of fundamental law that had inspired the revolution.

The Emergence of a Hermeneutic Conception of Law

Between the Revolution and the Civil War, American lawyers came to conceive of themselves as interpreters of laws. In broad terms, this development reflected the replacement of a customary conception of law with a positivist conception

---

[47] J. W. Gough, *Fundamental Law in English Constitutional History* (Oxford: Clarendon, 1955); Thomas Grey, "Do We Have an Unwritten Constitution?" *Stanford Law Review* 27 (1975): 703.

[48] Kelley, *Human Measure.*

[49] Powell, "The Original Understanding of Original Intent," 907.

[50] Or perhaps, as Akhil Amar has recently suggested, through an ad hoc majoritarian process replicating the revolutionary process of constituting the state and federal governments. Akhil Amar, "The Consent of the Governed," *Columbia Law Review* 94 (1994): 457.

[51] Thomas Grey, "Origins of the Unwritten Constitution in American Revolutionary Thought," *Stanford Law Review* 30 (1978): 843, 890–93.

that distinguished legislative will from legal judgment. Lawyers came to see legal judgment as a matter of identifying and applying the will embodied in written legal instruments. Yet they also saw the mediation of legal judgment as indispensable to the realization of will.

If there was one legal proposition commanding universal assent in early-nineteenth-century America, it was that application of a legal instrument was an effort to realize its "intent." Yet there was controversy and confusion about whether the "intent" of an instrument meant the desires of its author or the law's purpose in giving such an instrument legal effect. Since "intent" was roughly synonymous with "meaning" or "purpose," the new interest in "intent" bespoke nothing more specific than a new identification of adjudication with interpretation. In post-Revolutionary America, this new hermeneutic conception of law by no means reflected wholehearted embrace of popular sovereignty by the legal profession: a written fundamental law, although celebrated as the institutional embodiment of revolutionary action, tended to give popular will a remote and abstract character and legal interpretation an authoritative status.

Public men of the antebellum period were acutely aware of their belated place in history as heirs to the founding fathers and custodians of their handiwork; in this sense, all participants in public life saw themselves as interpreters and conservers of an authoritative tradition.[52] American high culture in the first few decades of the nineteenth century was dominated by this conservative project, in marked contrast to the restless discontent of European Romanticism. American literature remained didactically aimed at inspiring public virtue, steeped in classical references, and ordered by the aesthetic values of balance and unity. The authors and editors of this belatedly classical oeuvre, as shown by Robert Ferguson, were typically lawyers.[53] These men saw learned Ciceronian oratory as the salvation of a republic inevitably threatened by the corruptions of time, whether embodied by untutored mobs or unlanded arrivistes. They also retained and perpetuated veneration for the common law, with its attendant scope for judicial creativity: John Marshall embodied their vision of the judge as lawmaker. Alongside the Constitution, and Cicero, antebellum lawyers with pretentions to learning revered Blackstone, whose ordered explication was believed to have rendered the common law as "scientific" as Roman law. The dominant legal authors of the antebellum era, Chancellor Kent and Justice Story, saw themselves as American Blackstones.[54]

The neoclassical conservatism of many of America's antebellum lawyers was challenged and reshaped by two native forms of Romanticism: the passion of

---

[52] Abraham Lincoln, "The Perpetuation of Our Political Institutions: Address before the Young Men's Lyceum of Springfield, Illinois, January 27, 1838," in *Abraham Lincoln: His Speeches and Writings*, ed. Roy Basler (Cleveland: World Publishing, 1946), 76–85; Peter C. Hoffer, *Revolution and Regeneration: Life-Cycle and the Historical Vision of the Generation of 1776* (Athens: Univ. of Georgia Press, 1983); Paul W. Kahn, *Legitimacy and History: Self-Government in American Constitutional Theory* (New Haven: Yale Univ. Press, 1992).

[53] Robert Ferguson, *Law and Letters in American Culture* (Cambridge: Harvard Univ. Press, 1984).

[54] R. Kent Newmyer, *Supreme Court Justice Joseph Story* (Chapel Hill: Univ. of North Carolina Press, 1985), 137, 181, 191, 243, 244.

evangelical religion and the populism of Jefferson and Jackson. Charismatic religion had more ambivalent implications for legal interpretation than has been commonly recognized. Granted, it fostered suspicion of the mediation of sacred texts by institutional or academic interpreters. But insofar as it condemned expert interpretation as pharisaical and overly technical, revivalism implied the legitimacy of interpretation that favored spirit over letter and invoked sentiments accessible to all. Hence, evangelical religion may have inspired legal interpreters to compete for common assent by liberally invoking the law's spirit; certainly, classical rhetorical ideas encouraged the learned to thus disarm and accommodate rather than provoke the public.[55] Even more than evangelism, Jeffersonian Republicanism and Jacksonian Democracy were too successful to be ignored. From the outset, the conservative project of institutionalizing the Revolution in law was challenged by Jefferson's view that a republican polity must be refashioned by the people in each generation. Perhaps in response, judges claimed to harmonize their interpretations with the progressive spirit of the age.

In fact, the Federalist account of the Constitution as popular statute proved almost as short-lived as the Federalist party. Jefferson's "second revolution" of 1800 swept into power a new party and a new conception of the Constitution as a contract among sovereign states. In line with principles of natural and international law governing treaties between sovereign states, the American republics were presumed not to have jeopardized their own survival by alienating their sovereignty.[56] With the electoral triumph of Jackson, this view of the Constitution's "original intent" achieved popular acceptance. John Calhoun voiced it in the Senate;[57] and with John Marshall's replacement by Roger Brooke Taney, it triumphed on the Supreme Court.

The best-known example of Taney's originalism was his *Dred Scott* opinion rejecting a slave's claim that he was free by virtue of his sojourn in federal territory. Taney portrayed the federal government as an abstract agency of the real sovereign communities of America, the states. Wisely, reasoned Taney, the states had never authorized the federal government to exercise the inherently local functions of defining property rights and regulating master-servant relations; accordingly the Missouri Compromise barring the institution of slavery from certain federal territories was a taking of property without due process of law. Taney added that, even if free, African-Americans were not U.S. citizens capable of suing in federal court. Stressing antimiscegenation laws in force upon the framing of the compact of states, Taney argued that blacks were then and forever excluded from the American political family. He concluded that "the duty of the court is to interpret the instrument they have framed . . . and to administer it as we find

[55] For discussion of conflict between legal reason and religious passion in antebellum culture, see Perry Miller, *The Life of the Mind in America: From Revolution to Civil War* (New York: Harcourt, Brace & World, 1965).

[56] Powell, "The Original Understanding of Original Intent," 927.

[57] See John C. Calhoun, *A Disquisition on Government and a Discourse on the Constitution and Government*, ed. R. Cralle (Columbia, S.C.: A. S. Johnston, 1851), 254.

it, according to its true intent and meaning when it was adopted."[58] By the 1850s, then, many Democrats saw the original compact of states as a racially exclusive community and the Constitution as a charter of white supremacy.

Other enduringly influential tenets of the Democratic creed conceived legislation as a product of popular will rather than customary judgment, and economic development as a product of individual initiative rather than institutional prudence. Jacksonian populism fed the codification movement by lauding legislation as more democratically legitimate and accessible than common law rules. Democrats' ideas about statutory interpretation shared certain features with their approach to constitutional interpretation. Statutory meaning was fixed by original intent, but original intent was usually the purpose of a statute manifest in its language. Where the language was unclear, the statute would be fit into the fabric of statutory law. Where absolutely necessary, the generally apparent historical conditions might be consulted. But legislative motives were irrelevant, and esoteric records of legislative debate, unknown to the people, could not be law. In the 1845 case of *Aldridge v. Williams*, Justice Taney forcefully distinguished the search for the intent of a statute from any inquiry into the motives of legislators:

> In expounding [a] law, the judgment of the court cannot, in any degree be influenced by the construction placed upon it by individual members of Congress in the debate which took place on its passage, or by the motives or reasons assigned by them for supporting or opposing amendments that were offered. The law as it passed is the will of the majority of both houses, and the only mode in which that will is spoken is the act itself; and we must gather their intention from the language there used, comparing it, when any ambiguity exists, with the laws upon the same subject, and looking, if necessary to the public history of the times in which it was passed.[59]

The Democrats' conception of law as publicly accessible required that, where employed in interpretation, history be plainly legible. Despite their originalism, Democrats were therefore reluctant to use historical argument. History played a much more important role in the legal thought of their Federalist and, later, Whig opponents. In Federalist and Whig jurisprudence, history was neither static nor public; it was evolving custom, and its interpretation was a matter of expert legal judgment.

Federalist views survived on the Supreme Court until Taney's takeover in the 1830s. Thereafter, they survived within the legal elite, particularly in New England where Justice Story founded the Harvard Law School as a fount of Federalist legal thought, and within the Whig Party; but Federalist ideology was reshaped

---

[58] *Dred Scott v. Sandford*, 60 U.S. (19 How.) 393, 405–7 (1857). Extending Taney's trope of the political family to the relations among states, the Mississippi Supreme Court barred a former slave manumitted under Ohio law from inheriting from her White father and former master. *Mitchell v. Well*, 37 Miss. 235 (1859).

[59] *Aldridge v. Williams*, 44 U.S. (3 How.) 9, 24 (1845).

by the challenge of mass politics and religion.[60] With the electoral and cultural triumphs of Jefferson and Jackson, adherents to the Federalist persuasion lost their taste for the rhetoric of popular sovereignty, even as competitive electioneering compelled them to mouth it. Fundamentally, the nationalism of the Whigs was a nationalism of elites and institutions; their nation was constituted by law, into which popular will had been exhausted.[61] Their positivism was more concerned with identifying authoritative law than with identifying the sovereign. Typical of this institutional positivism was Whig leader Daniel Webster's response in *Luther v. Borden*[62] to claims that a popularly organized referendum had dissolved Rhode Island's malapportioned legislature and broadened its restrictive franchise:

> The people of a state is the *political body—the corporate unit*—in which are vested . . . the ultimate powers of sovereignty; not its inhabitants or population, considered as individuals. . . . Except as an *organized body*, that is, *except when acting by its recognized organs*, the entire population of a state already constituted, were it assembled on some vast plain, could not constitutionally pass a law or try an offender.[63]

Webster's institutionalist argument thus anticipated the posture toward Southern secession of erstwhile Whig Abraham Lincoln.

Legal interpretation lay at the heart of the institutional positivism that Whig lawyers developed in response to the populist challenges of the antebellum period. Interpretation would enable far-seeing stewards of America's institutions to preserve them from periodic overthrow by adapting them to changing circumstances and social needs. Successful accommodation of social change would insulate prudent stewards against demagogic mobilization of the populace; while institutional preservation would ensure commercial development by providing a stable and predictable environment for investment. Justice Story articulated this conservative hermeneutic program in his 1833 *Commentaries on the Constitution of the United States*, where he called for a "science of law that can distinguish the permanent from the transitory."[64]

Story's view of interpretation as adaptation did not prevent his embrace of the antebellum commonplace that "the first and fundamental rule in the interpretation of all instruments is, to construe them according to the sense of the terms and the intentions of the parties."[65] Yet he insisted that the only discernible intent of legal authors was to adopt the language chosen: "Nothing but the text itself was adopted by the people."[66] The vagueness of constitutional language and its function in

[60] For an argument that the Whigs so far accommodated and emulated the dominant Democratic policies and politics that they were barely distinguishable from their adversaries, see Rush Welter, *The Mind of America 1820–1860* (New York: Columbia Univ. Press, 1975), 165–249.

[61] Kahn, *Legitimacy and History*, 38.

[62] *Luther v. Borden*, 48 U.S. (7 How.) 1 (1849).

[63] John Alexander Jameson, *The Constitutional Convention* (New York: Scribner's, 1867), 232.

[64] Kahn, *Legitimacy and History*, 41, quoting Joseph Story, *Commentaries on the Constitution of the United States*, ed. Ronald Rotunda and John Nowak, 3d ed. (Durham: Carolina Academic Press, 1987), 1:143.

[65] Story, *Commentaries on the Constitution*, 1:400.

[66] Ibid., 287–88.

framing a government for the ages left interpreters a wide latitude to develop its meaning over time. Rather than resorting to contemporaneous interpretations of constitutional language, interpreters were better guided by subsequent judicial glosses, especially if acquiesced in by other governmental authorities. If the people objected to their judicially elaborated constitutional law, they could amend the Constitution through these other political organs of government.[67]

If adaptive interpretation of the Constitution could preempt the Jeffersonian program of recurrent revolution, adaptive interpretation of common law precedent could similarly preclude Sisyphean cycles of codification and recodification. Whig jurists argued that the codifiers' dream of circumscribing the future in legislative language clear and accessible to the common man was chimerical and self-defeating: codes would inevitably be overly rigid and insufficiently complete; once consulted, popular majorities could be counted upon to neither keep silent nor keep a steady course. But if fickle majorities were incompetent to improve upon the common law's fusty technicality, prudent interpreters like Kent and Story were confident they could meet the challenge. As Robert Gordon explains, their common law treatises and decisions assumed that

> The corrective for the occasional irrationality of custom was to submit its principles to a critical and creative control technique, a complex amalgam of . . . (1) The . . . theory . . . that history had direction, especially in the American republic, away from hierarchy, superstition, technicality, and restraints on disposition of property and labor and towards political equality, rationality, free disposition, and liberality in rights definition . . . (2) . . . A comparative method [that] consisted of looking to the practices of other civilized nations—especially, in matters of commercial law, to international commercial custom and European civilian writers on it. (3) . . . A highly educated reason steeped in classical and historical studies, political theory, and the law of nations. There were also metarules about when to apply the technique liberally (when one was trying to facilitate commercial convenience) and when to hold strictly to precedent (when one was trying to protect vested rights).[68]

This fusion of custom and positive law was permitted by the Whigs' peculiarly institutional conception of custom itself as experience digested by learned legal thought. Commercial law reflected general rather than local custom, modeled on the stable and boundary-traversing customs collected in the Law Merchant. Where Jacksonians identified development with unrestricted individual opportunity, Whig lawyers identified development with the public nurturance of established trades, in part so as to ensure continuity of political leadership. Because development involved merely the proliferation of familiar enterprises, the legal and social conditions for development could be distilled from accumulated experience.

---

[67] Robert M. Cover, *Justice Accused: Antislavery and the Judicial Process* (New Haven: Yale Univ. Press, 1975), 136–37; Kahn, *Legitimacy and History*, 41.

[68] Robert W. Gordon, "Legal Thought and Legal Practice in the Age of American Enterprise 1870–1920," in *Professions and Professional Ideologies in America*, ed. Gerald L. Geison (Chapel Hill: Univ. of North Carolina Press, 1983), 84.

Contract interpretation became important to lawyers once transactions were more commonly conceived as enforceable bilateral promises, initiated by the acceptance of an offer, the meanings of which were questions of law. Whig contract interpretation thus focused on the intentions of the parties, but through the prism of trade custom. John Powell's 1790 treatise on contract, the first to appear in England, borrowed the doctrine of offer and acceptance from the French civilian writer Pothier, who opined that an offer became enforceable when its acceptance created a "concurrence of intention."[69] But Powell clearly meant the intent of the instrument rather than the intent of its authors, and he advised interpreters to consult "men's general motives, conduct and actions," rather than the statements or actions of the parties themselves.[70]

American Whig writers on contract interpretation would develop a slightly more psychological version of contractual intent and combine it with the interpretive liberality advocated by Kent and Story. Thus, intention was said to prevail over the letter. Kent proclaimed that "To reach and carry . . . the mutual intentions of the parties . . . into effect, the law, when it becomes necessary, will control even the literal terms of the contract if they manifestly contravene the purpose."[71] Yet intentionalism was reconciled with an obligation of good faith that deflected attention from the expectations of the author to those of the typical reader of contractual language. Rather than holding each party to his own intended commitments, antebellum writers held each party to his own *beliefs* about the other party's expectations. According to William Story, the Justice's nephew, "The undertaking of each must be construed in that sense, in which he supposed it to be understood by the other."[72] Accordingly, "terms, which are doubtful or ambiguous, are to be taken most strongly against the person engaging."[73]

Thus, antebellum interpreters attributed to contractual signatories the intentions with which honest men would use the language employed. But a presumption of honesty in promising was not a presumption of openness in bargaining or fairness in exchange. Gulian Verplanck, author of the first American treatise on contract, scorned the notion that "before I deal with my indolent neighbour, I shall communicate to him . . . all the results of that knowledge and address which have been

---

[69] John J. Powell, *Essay upon the Law of Contracts and Agreements*, 6th ed. (New York: G. Lamson, 1825), 334; Robert Joseph Pothier, *A Treatise on the Law Obligations or Contracts*, trans. W. Evan, (Philadelphia: R. H. Small, 1826), 4. Whig private law treatises and opinions were "full of what we would call obligations implied by law, inhering in good custom, precedent, and general considerations of public policy concerning persons of different status in their relations with one another." Gordon, "Legal Thought and Legal Practice," 88.

[70] Powell, *Essay upon the Law of Contracts and Agreements*.

[71] James Kent, *Commentaries on American Law*, 2d ed. (New York: O. Halsted, 1832), 2:554.

[72] William W. Story, *A Treatise on the Law of Contracts Not under Seal* (1844; reprint, New York: Arno, 1972), §232.

[73] Ibid., §258; accord Joseph Chitty, *A Practical Treatise on the Law of Contracts Not under Seal; and upon the Usual Defences to Actions Thereon*, 4th Amer. ed. (Springfield, Mass.: G. and C. Merriam, 1839), 62.

the hard-earned acquisitions of my own industry and activity."[74] Verplanck concluded that "a price agreed upon honestly . . . is always a fair price between the parties; however excessive or inadequate it may appear to others."[75] Thus, the appeal of contractual intentionalism was its promise to vindicate party autonomy, especially to insulate merchant communities from the moral judgment of juries. Yet the irony was that conditioning the meaning of the contract on the actual intentions of the parties made it entirely a question of fact within the discretion of the jury.[76] Theophilus Parsons Jr., Story's successor as Dane Professor of Law at Harvard, proposed an answer to this problem of jury discretion in what became the dominant contracts treatise of the late nineteenth century:

> If any one contract is properly construed, justice is done to the parties directly interested therein. But the rectitude, consistency, and uniformity of all construction enables all parties to do justice to themselves. For then all parties, before they enter into contracts, or make or accept instruments, may know the force and effect of the words they employ, of the precautions they use, and of the provisions which they make in their own behalf, or permit to be made by other parties. It is obvious that this consistency and uniformity of construction can exist only so far as construction is governed by fixed principles, or, in other words, *is a matter of law.*[77]

Yet the promised predictability of judicial construction of contracts could not be achieved were judges to investigate the idiosyncrasies and unarticulated hopes of contractual parties. Accordingly, Parsons subordinated intent to contractual language and conventions of use:

> The rule of law is not that the court will always construe a contract to mean that which the parties to it meant; but rather, that the court will give to the contract the construction which will bring it as near to the actual meaning to the parties as the words they saw fit to employ when properly construed, and the rules of law, will permit.[78]

These "rules of law" were the judicially recognized uses associated with a particular trade or relationship.[79] Parson's contractual interpretation on the basis of implied intent embodied a sophisticated view of legal meaning as a conventional construct, but it rested on the increasingly anachronistic assumption that economic development implied the proliferation rather than the obsolescence of

---

[74] Gulian Verplanck, *An Essay on the Doctrine of Contract* (New York: G. and C. Carvil, 1825), 8–9. When he wrote this treatise, Verplanck was a Democratic congressman from New York, but he began his career a Federalist and ended it a Whig.

[75] Ibid., 225.

[76] Horwitz, *Transformation of American Law 1780–1860*, 197.

[77] Theophilus Parsons, *The Law of Contracts*, 2d ed. (Boston: Little, Brown, 1862), 2:4 (emphasis supplied); see also Duncan Kennedy, "The Rise and Fall of Classical Legal Thought, 1850–1940," part 4 (unpub. ms.)

[78] Parsons, *Law of Contracts*, 4–7.

[79] Ibid., 49–50. In this Parsons followed in the footsteps of his father, Theophilus Parson Sr., who as Chief Judge of the Massachusetts Judicial Court sought to ground commercial decisions in trade usage. See 14 *Dict. Am. Bio.* 272 (1934), s.v. "Theophilus Parsons."

familiar trades. After the Civil War, industrialization would belie this economic axiom of Whig legal thought. Parson's delicate reconciliation of intentionalism and textualism depended upon an economic context that was fast disappearing.

Whig statutory interpetation adapted the common law tradition to Jacksonian popular sovereignty. In deference to the new reality, Whig jurisprudence treated statutes as binding sources of law rather than as mere evidence of evolving common law principle. But it preserved a sphere of judicial action by emphasizing the judge's interpretive function.

As in contract cases, early-nineteenth-century statutory cases made increasing reference to intent: "A thing which is within the intention of the makers of the statute is as much within the statute as if it were within the letter; and a thing which is within the letter of the statute, is not within the statute, unless it be within the intention of the statute."[80] But as in contracts cases, intent was more a matter of language, convention, and context than of authorial psychology. Thus, the above opinion adds that "intention is to be collected from the act itself and other acts" on the same subject and that "intention is sometimes to be collected from the cause or necessity of making the statute."[81] A frequently cited passage from Bacon's Abridgment repeated the Aristotelian notion that equity involved inquiry into the hypothetical intent of a rational legislator:

> In order to form a right judgment whether a case be within the equity of a statute, it is a good way to suppose the lawmaker present, and that you have asked him this question, did you intend to comprehend this case? Then you must give yourself such answer as you imagine he, being an upright and reasonable man, would have given.[82]

Indeed, for some early-nineteenth-century courts, legislative intent was the spirit of the law or "equity of statute," which a compassionate Christian interpreter would seek to realize.[83]

Since "equity" denoted a body of principle that pervaded and unified the law, early-nineteenth-century invocations of legislative intent did not always preclude efforts to subordinate statute law to natural right or the customary values of the common law.[84] Nevertheless, Whig statutory interpretation generally recognized that a written constitution demoted the common law from the status of fundamental law and thereby changed the statutory interpreter's task. No longer must a statute's reason be found in the overall purposes and principles of the common law. No longer could the absence of such a "reason" justify a court in ignoring a statute. Instead, Whig jurisprudence reduced common law principles to justifications for interpreting statutes "extensively" or "restrictively." Extensive interpretation was appropriate for remedial statutes and statutes exempting property from

---

[80] *People v. Utica Insurance Co.*, 15 Johns 358, 381 (N.Y. 1818) (Thompson, J.).

[81] Ibid.

[82] Matthew Bacon, "Statute," in *A New Abridgement of the Law*, 7th ed., ed. Henry Gwyllim (Philadelphia: Thomas Davis, 1846), 9:248.

[83] See *Bridgeport v. Hubbell*, 5 Conn. 237, 244 (1824).

[84] Blatt, "A History of Statutory Interpretation," 810, 821.

execution.[85] Restrictive interpretation was applied to statutes derogating from the common law, statutes against "common right" (such as those imposing slavery), and statutes defining crimes, imposing liability, imposing taxes, exempting from taxes, interfering with legitimate industries, or granting government power.[86]

A Hermeneutic Philosophy of Law

The Whig conception of law as the hermeneutic perpetuation of institutions achieved its most general statement in Francis Lieber's treatise *Legal and Political Hermeneutics* (1839). A remarkable and unjustly overlooked figure in American legal history, Lieber was born in turn-of-the-century Prussia to a family of ardent nationalists, fought Napoleon, and later studied at Jena, Halle, and Berlin during the tenure there of Schleiermacher, Hegel, and Savigny. Involved in various intellectual and political movements in Europe, Lieber arrived in the United States an author and lecturer on many subjects and became a professor of politics and law (at the University of South Carolina and Columbia) and a contributor of belletristic essays to literary reviews.

Like many German liberals of his generation, Lieber opposed natural law theory on the grounds that democracy must be mediated by historically evolved institutions.[87] He identified common law with the historical jurisprudence advocated by Romantic German jurists like Savigny, and the complex American constitutional structure with the mediating institutions advocated by Hegel. In his *Civil Liberty and Self-government* (1853), the leading American political science textbook of the nineteenth century, Lieber argued that participation mediated by institutions could discipline, educate, and ennoble the citizen—transforming democratic self-government into government of, as well as by, the self. In his *Manual of Political Ethics* (1838–39), Lieber conceived a pluralistic polity in which the diffusion of sovereignty among multiple institutions would develop law organically. Story praised the *Manual* as "one of the best Theoretical treatises on . . . government which has been produced in modern times . . . when so many . . . disturbing doctrines are promulgated," while Kent enthused to Lieber, "I love you; you are so sound, so conservative . . . so very safe."[88]

Originally intended as part of the *Manual*, Lieber's treatise on legal hermeneutics was "the definitive defense"[89] of the interpretive discretion favored by Whigs. Lieber conceded to Jacksonian opinion that the meaning of legal instruments depended on authorial intent,[90] that compacts should be strictly interpreted to

---

[85] Ibid., 807.

[86] Ibid., 807–8.

[87] Indeed, Vernon Parrington held him responsible for the demise of natural law thought in America. Vernon Parrington, *Main Currents in American Thought*, vol. 1, *The Beginnings of Critical Realism in America* (New York: Harcourt, Brace, 1927), 119–21.

[88] Frank Freidel, *Francis Lieber, Nineteenth-Century Liberal* (Baton Rouge: Louisiana State University Press, 1947) 164–65.

[89] Cover, *Justice Accused*, 137.

[90] Francis Lieber, *Legal and Political Hermeneutics*, 3d ed. (St. Louis: F. H. Thomas, 1880), 19.

reflect the will of the parties, and even that constitutions could be regarded as compacts.[91] But Lieber rejected the Democratic characterization of the Constitution as a compact of states; an enthusiast of national union in his adopted as in his original country, Lieber was a leading proponent of American nationalism[92] and later wrote pro-Unionist propaganda and advised Lincoln's War Department.[93] Yet Lieber's legal hermeneutics did not take Calhounian originalism straight on; rather than debating whose intent should govern constitutional interpretation, Lieber exposed the very aspiration to strict intentionalist interpretation as incoherent.

His argument proceeded from an expressive conception of meaning reminiscent of Hegel's and probably influenced by the linguistic ideas of Schleiermacher, Lieber's spiritual mentor and founder of the intellectual movement of hermeneutics. We will have occasion to review Schlieiermacher's ideas in greater detail in chapter 2 when we explicate this movement's contributions to literary theory. But, briefly stated, Schleiermacher conceived of the interpretation of a text as a dialectical process of reconciling (1) the author's subjectivity with her cultural context, and (2) the conditions under which the text was written with the conditions under which it is read. For Schleiermacher, the author's subjectivity comprised not only her intended meanings but her intended *audience* as well. The text's cultural context consisted in the language in which it was written, and the social conditions that could interest the intended audience in such a text. Schleiermacher saw languages as living practices of social interaction, so that linguistic meaning was in constant flux. He conceived texts as scriptural and presumed that all authors intended to be read within a tradition and wanted a community of readers to perpetuate the conditions of their work's relevance. Yet he assumed that patterns of language and social concerns would change, and that authors were presumed to accept adaptive interpretation as the condition of their work's retaining vitality and meaning.[94]

For Lieber, all linguistic expression is linked to religious and aesthetic feeling and aims to articulate the self in a concrete, sensuous, and inherently social medium.[95] Thus, meaning is not conferred on language by private intentions that preexist their articulation; instead, meaning inheres in language's use by groups of language users, especially institutions.

Lieber's expressive conception of meaning enabled him to qualify his assent to the prevailing intentionalism. Thus, he insisted that textual language was the best evidence of authorial motives[96]—indeed, that the presumed authorial motive was to project the self by using the language employed. His insistence on textual

[91] Ibid., 172–77, 184.

[92] Merle E. Curti, "Francis Lieber and Nationalism," *Huntington Library Quarterly* 4 (1941): 263.

[93] Phillip S. Paludan, *A Covenant with Death: The Constitution, Law and Equality in the Civil War Era* (Urbana: Univ. of Illinois Press, 1975), 23.

[94] Friedrich Schleiermacher, *Hermeneutics: The Handwritten Manuscripts*, ed. Heinz Kimmerle, trans. James O. Duke and Jack Forstman (Missoula, Mon.: Scholars Press, 1977), 95–121, 147–51.

[95] Lieber, *Legal and Political Hermeneutics*, 13–17.

[96] Ibid., 113–14, 128.

indeterminacy meant that his reduction of intent to language was merely a stratagem to justify an active interpreter. In the end, he approved intentionalist interpretation, itself reinterpreted as the expansive interpretation of instruments in light of their institutional purpose rather than the motives of their authors.[97] He favored the legislative articulation of goals in preambular language and the publication of legislative debates to aid, though not to control, interpretation.[98] He mocked the aspiration to "strict" or "literal" interpretation as resting on a naive, even illiterate, dichotomy between literal and metaphoric meaning. Following idealist philosophers, he insisted that the physical objects to which language refers are distinguished from the flux of experience only by the constructive activity of mind.[99] Accordingly, Lieber argued that all meaning is figurative or "tropic," so that the Luddite aspiration to purify language of rhetoric could only succeed at the cost of purifying language of meaning.[100]

In Lieber's view, new metaphoric meaning constantly regenerates itself; depending on the context, concepts become more or less specific, acquiring and shedding connotations and implications. Because "these processes are going on at the same time, with many different people,"[101] the meaning of a text is unstable and uncertain even at the very moment it is written. Even the simplest instruction depends on infinitely many contextual assumptions and can be reduced to nonsense by a perverse literalism.[102] The more complex an injunction the more easily it can be traduced. Thus, "nothing is gained by trying to speak with absolute clearness and endless specifications. . . . The more we strive in a document to go beyond plain clearness and perspicuity, the more we do increase, in fact, the chances of sinister interpretation."[103] Sophisticated language users realize this historicity and contextuality of language and so frame their injunctions to the future broadly, inviting future interpreters to use their good sense.[104] Lieber argued that the impulse to control future interpreters through elaborate and precise instructions bespeaks dictatorial egoism and foolish naïveté. Over time, he predicted, such superfluous instructions become contradictory, hobbling well-meaning interpreters with arbitrary absurdities, or licensing unforeseen mischief.[105]

Lieber added that a static conception of meaning was inconsistent with the very legislative supremacy its proponents desired, since legislatures claim the power to authoritatively interpret earlier legislation.[106] That successive legislatures composed of multiple members may be fictively viewed as a single author underscores Lieber's larger point that legal authors are institutions, whose identity over time

[97] Ibid., 135, 139–40, 186.
[98] Ibid., 41–42.
[99] Ibid., 33.
[100] Ibid., 33–34, 66–69.
[101] Ibid., 26.
[102] Ibid., 29.
[103] Ibid., 30–32.
[104] Ibid., 37.
[105] Ibid., 44, 97.
[106] Ibid., 74.

depends upon the very process of interpretation that naive intentionalists fear: "It is one of the most efficient agencies in the civil progress of a nation, that, certain principles being established, they should be left to unfold themselves gradually, and to be expanded, modified, and limited, by the civil action of the nation itself, by the practical political intercourse of society."[107] Because interpreters are properly devoted to the perpetuation of institutions, Lieber argues, they must set aside not only the original but even the contemporary meaning of a legal text when unforeseen circumstances arise that the text does not sensibly address.[108] Lieber called this process "construction" rather than "interpretation":

> Construction is unavoidable . . . relations change with the progress of time, so that, after a long lapse of time, we must give up either the letter of the law, or its intent, since both owing to a change in circumstances, do not any longer agree. . . . Interpretation, seeking but for the true sense, forsakes us when the text is no longer directly applicable; because the utterer, not foreseeing this case, did not mean it, therefore it has no true sense in this particular case.[109]

Modern readers will misconstrue Lieber if they take his distinction between the interpretive pursuit of true sense and the constructive pursuit of advantageous results to imply that true meaning is stably determined by authorial intent. Rather, a text has a true sense only where the author has framed it flexibly enough to permit adaptation to social change. Hence, legally meaningful texts invite discretionary interpretation: if legislatures will not provide interpretable texts, judicial interpreters must construct them.

Having established the inevitability of legal interpretation, Lieber consoled his readers that it posed no threat to democracy. Because interpretation is the condition of institutional survival, it is broadly participatory in a pluralistic polity like America, permeated by institutions. In Lieber's vision of an "organic" republic, legal interpretation is an edifying process of deliberation, a universal civic duty.[110] Arguing that freedom from tyranny depends upon an ever-vigilant people rather than written rules,[111] Lieber concluded that the educative benefits of popular participation in the interpretive process far outweighed the threat of judicial usurpation.

Whig jurisprudence supplied the antebellum lawyer with a professional identity as an interpreter of laws; but though resistant to the broader cultural trends of the Jacksonian Era, Whig legal jurisprudence lived less by challenging, than by accommodating and interpreting, the positivism and populism of its time. In this respect, Whig tactics mirrored Whig ideology: the legal hermeneutic impulse was also the spirit of compromise, and so the Whigs' political leaders are remembered for accommodating slavery to preserve the Union; indeed, Lieber spent the bulk of

---

[107] Ibid., 44.
[108] Ibid., 56–58, 112.
[109] Ibid., 121–22.
[110] Ibid., 76.
[111] Ibid., 179–80.

his academic career as a South Carolinian on cordial terms with John C. Calhoun, prudently suppressing the antislavery and nationalist sentiments he penned in private letters to Charles Sumner.[112]

The Whigs' willingness to deal could not, in the long run, buy them political success. But their institutional positivism did persuade many Democrats, whose hostility to government could accommodate them to checks on popular sovereignty.[113] The inroads Whig institutionalism made in democratic thought would later help mobilize Northern Democrats to the Union cause.[114] In the end, however, the failure of compromise in the sectional crisis would demoralize the Whigs and doom their vision of an institutional polity unified by hermeneutic discourse. The Kansas-Nebraska Act and the caning of Charles Sumner on the Senate floor proved that reason and rhetoric could no longer govern the forum of politics. The *Dred Scott* decision, in rending their carefully crafted compromise, also shredded their faith in judicial interpretation as the preserver of union, while Francis Lieber sadly learned the efficacy of his theories when he saw his own students lead the charge into secession. Hermeneutic ingenuity could no longer paper over cracks in the house.

Legal Hermeneutics in the House Divided

The culmination and transcendence of Ciceronian legal and literary culture came with Lincoln's interpretation of the sectional crisis. The intellectual roots of Lincoln's political thought in the Whig Party have long been established, but he was a Whig in jurisprudence as well. From the time of Lincoln's first important speech, the Lyceum address, he characterized the Constitution as an evolving institution, requiring at least as much energy and virtue to preserve as to found.[115] But where Kent and Story devoted the hermeneutic activity of preservation to a professional elite, Lincoln from the first defined constitutional interpretation as a necessarily popular project.[116] This followed from his egalitarianism: "No man is good enough

---

[112] Freidel, *Francis Leiber*, 233–58. Lieber actually went so far as to hire a Black servant to accompany him on his job interview to reassure his hosts of his taste for slavery, and he soon acquired slaves. The price of his hypocrisy was high: twenty years of suppressing his opinions could not overcome the suspicions that ultimately denied him the presidency of the University of South Carolina, but when he resigned his position and moved North, he left behind a son who died in a Confederate uniform.

[113] See George Sidney Camp, *Democracy* (New York: Harper & Brothers, 1842), 214, where the democratic publicist wrote, "The people do not any less govern, by thus governing in a certain mode which they themselves prescribe." The Yankee Democrat Theodore Sedgwick, though an opponent of judicial discretion, agreed that "the constitutional check [on tyranny and corruption] is the only one which people voluntarily assume, and is the only one known, that is based upon a liberal representation of the popular will." Theodore Sedgwick, "Constitutional Reform," in *A Series of Articles Contributed to the Democratic Review upon Constitutional Guarantees in Political Government*, ed. Thomas Prentice Kettell (1846), 2b.

[114] Welter, *Mind of America*, 371–91.

[115] Kahn, *Legitimacy and History*, 32–35.

[116] Don Fehrenbacher, *Lincoln in Text and Context* (Stanford: Stanford Univ. Press, 1987), 126; see also Welter, *The Mind of America*, 387–91.

to govern another man without that other's consent . . . this is the leading principle—the sheet anchor—of American republicanism."[117] Preserving the Constitution meant preserving popular allegiance through public education and deliberative politics, not just adjudication. Devotion to the Constitution had to be a "political religion";[118] the annual celebration of the Declaration of Independence must
embody all the passion of a religious revival.[119]

Lincoln embraced the antebellum truism that the spirit controlled the letter of
the Constitution, but for him that spirit was historically specific in origin and
historically dynamic in effect: "Our republican robe is soiled, and trailed in the
dust. Let us repurify it. Let us turn and wash it white in the spirit, if not the blood,
of the revolution. . . . Let us readopt the Declaration of Independence."[120] Like so
much of Lincoln's rhetoric, this image of a redeeming spirit of revolution combines the Whig vision of progress, the millenarian imagery of revivalist Christianity, and the radical and egalitarian strains in Jefferson's thought, all held in check
by the nostalgia common to Whig conservatism and Democratic originalism. Lincoln's synthesis of elite Ciceronian culture with Bible Belt populism in a prophetic
nationalism marked the emergence in American culture of a Romantic sensibility
also discernible in the melancholic vision of Melville and the vernacular language
of Whitman and Twain.[121] Garry Wills has persuasively interpreted Lincoln's spiritual conception of the Union as a reflection of Transcendentalist ideas[122] and has
traced some of his ideas about progress to the Schleiermacher-trained Transcendentalist George Bancroft.[123] To Taney's "political family," Lincoln opposed a
Union "dedicated to a proposition," a "mystic" chorus "of memory,"[124] united by
"the electric cord in [the] Declaration that links the hearts of patriotic and liberty-
loving men everywhere."[125]

Lincoln's constitutional theory was less an interpretation of the Constitution
than an interpretation of America's history and destiny: the revolutionary spirit
that should inform popular interpretation of the Constitution was itself inscribed
in the egalitarian propositions of the Declaration of Independence. In a famous
fragment, Lincoln confessed his faith that

> All this is not the result of accident . . . the primary cause of our great prosperity . . . is
> the principle of "Liberty to all"—The expression of that principle in our Declaration of

[117] *The Collected Works of Abraham Lincoln*, ed. Roy P. Basler and Christian O. Basler (New
Brunswick, N.J.: Rutgers Univ. Press, 1990), 266.

[118] Ibid., "Lyceum Speech," 112.

[119] Ibid., "Speech at Chicago," 401–2.

[120] Ibid., 276.

[121] For comparison of Lincoln and Melville see John P. Diggins, *The Lost Soul of American Politics:
Virtue, Self-Interest, and the Foundations of Liberalism* (New York: Basic Books, 1984), 277–333.
For comparison of Lincoln and Twain see Garry Wills, *Lincoln at Gettysburg* (New York: Simon &
Schuster, 1992), 148.

[122] Wills, *Lincoln at Gettysburg*, 90–120.

[123] Ibid., 46, 105.

[124] Don Fehrenbacher, ed., *Abraham Lincoln: A Documentary Portrait through His Speeches and
Writings* (Stanford: Stanford Univ. Press, 1977), 224.

[125] Ibid., 456.

Independence, was most happy, and fortunate. Without this as well as with it, we could have declared our independence . . . ; but without it, we could not, I think, have secured our free government, and consequent prosperity. . . . The assertion of that principle, at that time, was the word "fitly spoken" which has proved an "apple of gold" to us. The Union, and the Constitution, are the picture of silver, subsequently framed around it. The picture was made, not to conceal or destroy the apple; but to adorn and preserve it. The picture was made for the apple—not the apple for the picture.[126]

Lincoln's belief that the constitution of the republic depended on popular fidelity to the Declaration explains his "House Divided" doctrine. A synthesis of republican political economy with antislavery constitutionalism, this doctrine held that "either the opponents of slavery will arrest the further spread of it, and place it where the public mind shall rest in the belief that it is in the course of ultimate extinction; or its advocates will push it forward till it shall become alike lawful in all the states."[127] Because slave society failed to reward the aspirations of the laborer, it could never compete with republican society. Lincoln believed that the profitability of slave ownership accrued entirely from the sale of slaves,[128] so that slavery was an impoverishing vice that survived by the constant corruption of others. Accordingly, supporters of republican government could not afford indifference on the slavery question, and so the argument that slavery was permanently entrenched in the very Constitution it threatened was a pernicious attempt to corrupt the public mind.[129]

While Lincoln always opposed abolition by unconstitutional means, he insisted that slave society's inherent decadence rendered such means unnecessary. Simply by impeding its expansion, the authors of the Constitution had set slavery upon the course of ultimate extinction: "Why did those old men, about the time of the adoption of the Constitution, decree that slavery should not go into the new territory, where it had not already gone? Why declare that within twenty years the African slave trade, by which slaves are supplied, might be cut off by Congress?"[130] In promulgating the Declaration of Independence, these men "did not mean to assert the obvious untruth that all men were enjoying . . . equality, nor yet that they were about to confer it immediately upon them. In fact they had no power to confer such a boon. They meant simply to declare the *right* so that enforcement of it might follow as fast as circumstances should permit."[131]

Like Taney, Lincoln grounded his constitutional interpretation in part on the original intent of the framers—for Lincoln, their intention to set slavery upon the path of "ultimate extinction." But like other Whig lawyers, Lincoln conceived intent as the manifest design of an instrument rather than the psychological mo-

[126] Roy P. Basler and Christian O. Basler, eds., *Collected Works of Abraham Lincoln*, 513.

[127] *The Life and Writings of Abraham Lincoln*, ed. Philip Van Doren Stern (New York: Modern Library, 1940), 429.

[128] Harry Jaffa, *Crisis of the House Divided* (Garden City, N.Y.: Doubleday, 1959), 395–407.

[129] David Brion Davis, *The Slave Power Conspiracy and the Paranoid Style* (Baton Rouge: Lousiana State Univ. Press, 1970), 62–86.

[130] Stern, ed., *Life and Writings of Abraham Lincoln*, 442–43.

[131] Jaffa, *Crisis of the House Divided*, 316.

tives of its author. In his 1838 Lyceum speech, Lincoln argued that the revolutionary achievement of the founders was motivated by ambition rather than virtue.[132] Interpretation required a pious, self-abnegating commitment to republican principles the founders may have embraced as mere means to their self-aggrandizement. Accordingly, the founders do not provide appropriate psychological models for properly self-restrained interpreters. "Towering genius . . . thirsts and burns for distinction; and if possible, it will have it, whether at the expense of emancipating slaves or enslaving freemen."[133]

Emancipation, when it came, should arise from the unfolding in history of the founders' institutional design, not an act of will. Certainly, interpreters should not emulate the founders' ambition. Hence, as Lincoln would later argue in the Lincoln-Douglas debates, popular sovereignty was self-defeating unless the people could embody and preserve their will in institutions that depended in turn upon good-faith interpretation.[134] But if interpreters should not substitute their own will for that of the founders, neither should they passively defer to the founders' equally undisciplined will. That the founders themselves held slaves, for example, was irrelevant. Interpreters are properly devoted not to the personality of the founders but to the institutions they founded; rather than standing in awe of the founders, interpreters must complete their "unfinished work."[135]

From Lincoln's perspective, the whole design of the federal Constitution, by protecting the right of any state to exclude slavery and thereby nurture republican prosperity, forced the crisis of the House Divided. Slowly garrotted by the expansion of republican government, slave society would either die a quiet death or cross swords with the Constitution.[136] One way or another, slavery's fundamental incompatibility with republican government would work God's will "in God's own good time."[137] Of his Emancipation Proclamation, Lincoln wrote, "I claim not to have controlled events, but confess plainly that events have controlled me."[138] And it was not because of any great virtue that the North would free the slaves. "God," he said in 1862, "will compel us to do right, . . . not so much because we desire [it], but because [it] accords with his plans for dealing with this nation."[139]

Confessing faith in an American people tested by war, the Gettysburg Address conceded that the preservation of the American republic could no longer be left to courts and commentators; whether America was destined to transcend its divi-

---

[132] Roy P. Basler and Christian O. Basler, eds., *Collected Works of Abraham Lincoln*, 82.

[133] Ibid.

[134] Jaffa, *Crisis of the House Divided*.

[135] Roy P. Basler and Christian O. Basler, eds., *Collected Works of Abraham Lincoln*, 734.

[136] Don Fehrenbacher, *Prelude to Greatness* (Stanford: Stanford Univ. Press, 1962), 95.

[137] Ibid., 77.

[138] David Donald, *Lincoln Reconsidered: Essays on the Civil War Era*, 2d ed. (New York: Vintage Books, 1956), 138.

[139] David Hein, "Lincoln's Theological and Political Ethics," in *Essays on Lincoln's Faith and Politics*, ed. Kenneth Thompson (Lanham, Md.: University Press of America, 1983), 135.

sions would thenceforth be for the people to determine.[140] This, Lincoln charged them, was their "unfinished work."[141] Directly addressing the people in the Gettysburg Address and Second Inaugural Address, Lincoln enacted his interpretation of American constitutional history and "prepar[ed] the public mind"[142] for the amendments to follow. These speeches stood to the imminent constitutional changes as Lincoln claimed the Declaration of Independence stood to the original Constitution—authoritative interpretations of the "course of human events" giving birth to new institutions.

Historians have recently argued that "Lincoln won the war with metaphors" and that his "words . . . remade America."[143] But Lincoln has proven an impossible act for any lawyer to follow. He recognized and affirmed that the nation was constituted by its history, not its frame of government, so that constitutional interpretation would thenceforth become a popular contest over the meaning of the Civil War. The war's monstrous carnage and bitter legacy exploded any optimism that a spiritual union would soon evolve. Lincoln's homilies ensured only that the battle over national identity would be bounded by the abstract propositions that the war had been fought to preserve the Constitution and to abolish slavery. Since many Americans continued to conceive the Constitution as a compact of autonomous and racially exclusive communities, abolition and constitutional preservation remained antithetical goals; the great issues of the Civil War remained to be decided, and the House Divided was divided still.

Lincoln's hermeneutic constitution was obsoleted by the same economic changes that condemned Whig private law. The Jeffersonian free labor society, the "apple of gold" that Lincoln believed would outlast slavery, was a republic of independent producers—self-employed farmers and artisans. By the 1850s, however, industrialization was driving urban artisans into poverty and unemployment,[144] and the hope that they could start fresh as farmers in the West proved quixotic.[145] The independent artisan or yeoman farmer was destined to become the dependent wage worker that republican tradition scorned as little more honorable or free than a slave.[146] And so the people on whom Lincoln relied for a "new

[140] For argument that Lincoln successfully appropriated the Democratic values of popular sovereignty, national expansionism, and economic opportunity for the union cause, see Welter, *The Mind of America*, 371–79, 387–91.

[141] Wills, *Lincoln at Gettysburg*, 263.

[142] Don Fehrenbacher, *Abraham Lincoln: A Documentary Portrait through His Speeches and Writings* (Stanford: Stanford Univ. Press, 1977), 717–18.

[143] See the essay by James M. McPherson, "How Lincoln Won the War with Metaphors," in *Abraham Lincoln and the Second American Revolution* (New York: Oxford Univ. Press, 1990), 93–112; see also Wills, *Lincoln at Gettysburg*.

[144] Robert Fogel, *Without Consent or Contract: The Rise and Fall of American Slavery* (New York: Norton, 1989), 354–62.

[145] Eric Foner, *Free Soil, Free Labor, Free Men: The Ideology of the Republican Party before the Civil War* (New York: Oxford Univ. Press, 1970), 32.

[146] *The Oceana of James Harrington and his Other Works*, 3d ed., ed. J. Toland (London: A. Millar, 1737), 496–97; Edmund S. Morgan, *American Slavery, American Freedom: The Ordeal of Colonial Virginia* (New York: Norton, 1975), 295–383; Foner, *Free Soil, Free Labor*, 16–30.

birth of freedom" would be less capable of deliberation, interpretation, and self-government than he supposed. Lincoln left a house divided not only between abolition and union, but also between the increasingly antithetical ideals of individual independence and material equality.

The Whig hope that the lawyer's craft could cabin these fundamental conflicts was doomed before the Civil War's first shot, as was the promise of a coherent republican culture integrated by legal interpretation. Lawyers have mourned their loss of cultural authority ever since. Useful they might be in an unheroic, parasitic sort of way; but as cultural icons they have had only their stuffy propriety—that desiccated husk of their aspiration to civility—to offer a nation yearning for redemption.[147] Lincoln, it is said, exuded a funereal gloom that impressed his contemporaries as nobly tragic.[148] By contrast, his ghoulish epigones at the bar bestir all the affection and authority accorded undertakers: formally attired, feigning sympathy, complimenting the corpse, and counting the fee.

1.2 PROGRESSIVE INTERPRETATION

The Idea of Legal Science

The Civil War and Reconstruction left Americans with the lingering belief that political conflict—particularly over race—was irresolvable and potentially catastrophic. The claim of governmental institutions to shape and smooth national history was discredited. Instead, crisis would be avoided only by confining conflict to the fluid, ameliorative sphere of civil society. The role of governmental institutions would be to reflect and respond to change naturally occurring within that sphere, a role at odds with the legal transformation of society seemingly demanded by the Reconstruction Amendments.[149]

American legal thought now conceived a society distinct from government and acknowledged the legal profession's displacement from the center of civic and cultural life. Where antebellum lawyers saw society as an organic constitution of laws and institutions, Progressive Era lawyers saw it as a civil society constituted by desire, interest, and need, a natural entity with an ontogeny of its own. Law could now be set off from society as alien or artificial. Whether society was merely a market evolving towards productivity or a marketplace of ideas evolving towards rationality, it was a self-improving organism. Law could only be legitimate as an instrument rather than a constituent of society.

The crisis of the Civil War discredited the authority of lawyers and all three branches of government that they occupied.[150] Policymaking by lawyers was sub-

---

[147] Ferguson, *Law and Letters in American Culture*, 305–18; Diggins, *Lost Soul of American Politics*, 296–333.

[148] Wills, *Lincoln at Gettysburg*, 75.

[149] For a similar account of the frustration of emancipation by conservative constitutional theory, see Paludan, *Covenant with Death* (see especially 214–17, 225–26).

[150] On the reaction to the Supreme Court decisions *Dred Scott* and *Ex Parte Milligan*, see Paludan, *Covenant with Death*, 121–23, 226–31.

ject to more severe scrutiny, and the capacity of lawyers to interpret the law was no longer sufficient warrant for their political authority. A newly scientific conception of law would allow lawyers to take their place in Progressive society—but as scientific experts rather than exemplars of civic literacy. This new legal science would play a role in the Progressive project of professionalizing all three branches of government. Application of the new legal science would render courts politically neutral, scientific, and progressive—by contrast to Taney's tendentious and reactionary performance in *Dred Scott*. Legislators would become, or rely on, scientific experts on social problems—by contrast to the partisan and corrupt Congress of Reconstruction. And executive officials would become merit-qualified, educationally certified civil servants rather than patronage hacks.

The new legal scientists sought to limit judicial discretion as part of the larger project of disciplining all government decision makers. According to Robert Gordon,

> The postwar legal elite, by contrast [to the Whig-Federalist lawyers], disclaimed any special competence on the part of legal scholars or judges to prescribe behavior in particular situations. The function of legal science was rather to draw as clearly and sharply as possible the boundary lines beyond which the conduct of social actors would be sanctioned and behind which it would not. Legal science would thus create, as it were, combat zones of free conduct in which individuals might do as they willed without fear of legal reprisal, and it would specify the precise legal consequences of infringing on someone else's zone.[151]

On Gordon's account, legal "scientists" hoped to realize this liberal vision of autonomy by persuading courts and legislatures to base all liability on the objectively manifest consent, intent, or negligence of juridically equal actors. Juridical equality implied that employees, debtors, consumers, and tenants deserved no rights or protections they did not bargain for. Requiring that legal actors objectively manifest their wills was supposed to limit judicial discretion to impose liability based on uncertain interpretations of actors' unexpressed intentions.[152] Thus, legal science discouraged interpreters from seeking the spirit rather than the letter of legal texts.

Judicial discretion was only one concern. The new legal scientists also sought to develop an orderly and standardized curriculum on which they could stake their claim to license admission to the profession, and a program and method of research that could justify their place in the new graduate universities. Lawyers had a variety of successful models of "science" to emulate. To be sure, one was the German legal science, which attempted to ground liberal legal principles in analysis of Roman Law texts. Another was the analytic jurisprudence of Bentham and Austin. But lawyers were also likely to think of the natural science of biology,

---

[151] Gordon, "Legal Thought and Legal Practice," 88.

[152] For further exploration of spheres of autonomy in nineteenth-century Anglo-American legal thought, see Joseph William Singer, "The Legal Rights Debate in Analytical Jurisprudence from Bentham to Hohfeld," *Wisconsin Law Review* (1982): 975.

which provided the new social sciences with evolutionary models, and the human science of philology, the natural history of those languages that identified distinct cultures and societies. Harvard Law School Dean Christopher Langdell's manifesto for the case method of instruction invoked all these models indiscriminately, in support of a curriculum chiefly attractive for its ready reproducibility.[153]

Nor was the ideology of legal science always as cogent as Gordon's summary. Scholarly legal writing of this era combined classical liberalism with such other currents of thought as the historicism of Burke, Savigny, Frederick Pollock, and Henry Maine;[154] the Scottish Enlightenment's political economy and its celebration of commerce as an arena of sociability;[155] Social Darwinist ideas of economic, cultural, and racial evolution, articulated by such sociologists as Herbert Spencer and William Graham Sumner; and a "naturalistic" conception of human agency as the expression of deterministic drives and instincts. The will so important in late-nineteenth-century thought was not always the free will suggested by the label "liberal."[156] The product of this pastiche of influences was a vision of the common law of the Anglo-American race, evolving toward a laissez-faire market, which in turn would select in favor of the enterprising and biologically fit.

While legal scientists absorbed the claims of Austin that judges should be restrained by clear rules, they were more impressed with Austin's analytic rigor than with his hostility to judicial lawmaking. For the "liberal" legal thinkers Gordon invokes, discretion-minimizing rules were to be enacted by the very judges in need of constraint. Some hoped the necessary constraint could come from the discipline of legal science itself, but others placed their faith in the invisible hand of natural selection. Holmes, for example, wrote that

> lawyers, like other men, frequently see well enough how they ought to decide on a given state of facts without being very clear as to the ratio decidendi. . . . It is only after a series of determinations on the same subject matter that it becomes necessary to reconcile the cases, as it is said, that is, by a true induction to state the principle which until then has been obscurely felt. . . . A well settled legal doctrine embodies the work of many minds, and has been tested in form as well as substance by trained critics whose practical interest it is to resist it at every step.[157]

[153] Christopher Columbus Langdell, *A Selection of Cases on the Law of Contracts* (Boston: Little, Brown, 1871), vi–vii.

[154] James E. Herget, *American Jurisprudence: 1870–1970* (Houston: Rice Univ. Press, 1990); Kahn, *Legitimacy and History.*

[155] Herbert Hovenkamp, *Enterprise and American Law 1836–1937* (Cambridge: Harvard Univ. Press, 1991). For the influence of Scottish moral thought on Progressive reformers, see William R. Brock, *Investigation and Responsibility: Public Responsibility in the United States, 1865–1900* (Cambridge: Cambridge Univ. Press, 1984), 27–31.

[156] See David A. Hollinger, "The 'Tough-Minded' Justice Holmes, Jewish Intellectuals, and the Making of an American Icon," in *The Legacy of Oliver Wendell Holmes, Jr.,* ed. Robert Gordon (Stanford: Stanford Univ. Press, 1992), 216, 218–22.

[157] Oliver Wendell Holmes, "Codes, and the Arrangement of the Law," *American Law Review* 5 (1870): 1.

Still others praised the common law not as naturally rational or efficient, but simply as culturally authentic—a better representation of society than could be provided by elected officials. Emulating the German Romantic jurist Savigny, some American lawyers argued that legislative codification would impede the law's customary development. They agreed with Blackstone that "it is one of the characteristic marks of English *liberty*, that our common law depends upon custom; which ... was probably introduced by the *voluntary consent* of the people."[158] James Coolidge Carter urged that "in free popular states, the law springs from and is made by the people; ... the process of building it up consists in applying, from time to time, to human actions the popular ideal or standard of justice."[159] By focusing on popular standards of justice rather than popular will, Carter could oppose adjudication to legislation as more just rather than less democratic. For Carter, strained statutory interpretation was the inevitable result of the mistake of enacting legislation in the first place.[160] In opposition to Austin, Carter insisted that law is

> not a body of commands imposed upon society from without. . . . It exists in all times as one of the elements of society springing directly from habit and custom. It is therefore the unconscious creation of society, or in other words, a growth. For the most part it needs no interpreter or vindicator. The members of society are familiar with its customs and follow them; and in following custom they follow the law.[161]

Here Carter finds no tension whatsoever between the laissez-faire *policies* associated with liberalism and the sociological *jurisprudence* later associated with Progressive critics of laissez-faire. Judicial decisions are properly guided by societal interests, which are already immanent within the common law. But because society spontaneously governs itself in this way, legislative regulation is unnecessary. Adjudication is legitimate not because it avoids interpretive discretion, but because it interprets society more discerningly than the political process. Laissez-faire legal doctrine recommends itself as an experimental science of society.

Professionalizing Interpretation . . . and Legislation

The argument that "formalist" interpretation facilitated private autonomy was most influential in the area of contract law. In the later nineteenth century, the implication of contractual intent from custom gave way to a more complete formalism. Commercial and industrial innovation rendered Parsons's classification of trades archaic, while the system of status relations that figured in his analysis

---

[158] William Blackstone, *Commentaries on the Laws of England* (Chicago: Univ. of Chicago Press 1979), 74.

[159] James C. Carter, "The Proposed Codification of Our Common Law," paper published by the Bar Association of the City of New York (New York: Evening Post Printing Office 1884), 6.

[160] James C. Carter, "The Provinces of the Written and Unwritten Law," speech to the Virginia State Bar Association (New York: Bank and Bros., 1889), 39.

[161] Ibid., 21.

came under ideological attack. Austin's increasingly influential *Lectures on Jurisprudence* argued that the concept of personal status was superfluous in analyzing a system of entitlements,[162] while Henry Sumner Maine identified modernity with the movement from relations determined by status to relations determined by voluntary contract.[163] After the Civil War, these arguments were enthusiastically received by educated American lawyers as rationalizations of the South's defeat and slavery's dissolution.[164] The creative, modernizing function of contracting precluded the invocation of custom in contractual interpretation. To contract was to choose the future and escape the past.

Paradoxically, the apotheosis of contracts as emblems of voluntariness sparked no renewed interest in the actual intentions of contractual parties. Holmes devoted his *Common Law* to the thesis that modernization entailed movement not only from status to contract, but from subjective to objective standards of liability.[165] The will enforced by courts would be the will manifested in the language of the contract, and the only "meeting of the minds" that need be proved would be the common assent to that language.[166] Williston, whose contract treatise supplanted Parsons's, defined contract interpretation as "the process of determining from the expressions of the parties what external acts must happen or be performed in order to conform to *what the law considers* their will. . . . Where [the parties] . . . incorporate their agreement into a writing they have attempted more than to assent by means of symbols to certain things, they have assented to the writing as the adequate expression of the things to which they agree."[167] Thus, Williston concluded, "it is not the real intent but the intent expressed or apparent in the writing which is sought."[168]

The problem of statutory interpretation placed liberal legal scientists in a dilemma. On the one hand, literal interpretation could foster a predictable environment for private action; on the other hand, legislatures might corruptly or arbitrarily enact statutes that, read literally, infringed private autonomy. Should judges discipline unscientific legislatures through discretionary interpretation? Or in an effort to preserve their own interpretive discipline, should judges exercise the greater power of invalidating legislation that, read literally, infringed unwritten constitutional principle? Should they permit legislative discretion, curb it through discretionary statutory interpretation, or curb it through discretionary constitutional interpretation? The dilemmas posed by Progressive legislation precluded any easy identification of liberalism or scientific rationality with formalist interpretation.

---

[162] John Austin, *Lectures on Jurisprudence*, 4th ed. (London: J. Murray, 1873), 718–47.

[163] Henry S. Maine, *Ancient Law* (London: J. M. Dent, 1972), 164–65.

[164] Kennedy, "The Rise and Fall of Classical Legal Thought," part 4, 22, 42.

[165] Oliver Wendell Holmes, *The Common Law* (Cambridge: Harvard Univ. Press, Belknap Press, 1963), 241–42.

[166] Ibid., 243–44 (quoting Langdell); Samuel Williston, "Mutual Assent in the Formation of Contracts," *Illinois Law Review* 14 (1920): 527.

[167] Samuel Williston, *The Law of Contracts* (New York: Baker, Voorhis, 1920) 2: §§606, 610.

[168] Ibid., §§610.

Post–Civil War support for formalist statutory interpretation was encouraged by the posthumous influence of two antebellum proponents of legislative supremacy—the British legal positivist John Austin (1790–1859) and the Democratic lawyer-journalist Theodore Sedgwick (1811–59).

Austin agreed with his contemporaries that statutory interpretation was a search for intent, but he used "intent" to mean the intent ascribable to an author by virtue of the common meaning of the author's words.[169] If statutory language was ambiguous, the overall purpose of the law might serve as evidence of the sense a legislator attached to its language, but this purpose should not prevail over the intended sense. Moreover, the purpose of the law was the purpose actually entertained by the legislature, not those purposes of the common law to which the statute could be put: sovereign lawmakers needed no authorization from customary law to legislate, and they had no duty to serve its aims. In Austin's eyes, "equitable" interpretation wrongly subordinated legislative intent to judicial will. Austin condemned as "bastard interpretation" efforts to extend the coverage of a law to cases falling within its reason or "general design although . . . not embraced by the actual and unequivocal provisions."[170]

A Democrat but no populist, Sedgwick opposed both judicial legislation and popular election of judges. His influential treatise on statutory interpretation condemned equitable interpretation as judicial legislation and favored the "plain meaning" rule: "If the statute is plain and unambiguous, there is no room for construction or interpretation. The legislature has spoken; their intention is free from doubt and their will must be obeyed."[171] For "the construction of doubtful provisions," Sedgwick conceded, "the only object of judicial investigation . . . *is to ascertain the intention of the legislature which framed the statute.*"[172] This legislative intent was a question of fact rather than a legal question or a matter within the discretion of the judge.[173] Yet Sedgwick approved the statement of a Pennsylvania court that legislative "journals are not evidence of the meaning of the statute; because this must be ascertained from the language of the act itself, and the facts connected with the subject on which it is to operate."[174] Sedgwick concluded that "no extrinsic fact, prior to passage of the bill, which is not itself a rule of law or an act of legislation, can be inquired into or in any way taken into view."[175] Instead of consulting legislative history, Sedgwick suggested that interpreters determine the purpose of a "doubtful" statutory provision by looking to the overall object of the statute enunciated in the preamble.[176] Yet "the idea that

---

[169] Austin, *Lectures on Jurisprudence*, §§1023–24.

[170] Ibid., 596–97.

[171] Theodore Sedgwick, *A Treatise on the Rules Which Govern the Interpretation and Construction of Statutory and Constitutional Law* (New York: Baker, Voorhis & Co., 1874), 194–95.

[172] Ibid., 194.

[173] Ibid., 193.

[174] Ibid., 203, quoting *The Southwark Bank v. The Commonwealth*, 26 Penn. State Review 446 (1856) (Lewis, C.J.).

[175] Ibid., 208–9.

[176] Ibid., 201.

any regard is to be paid to the consequences that may flow from a given construction, has been rejected."[177] A second approach involved the maxim "that, in the construction of a statute, effect is to be given, if possible to every clause and section of it."[178] Third, all statutes on the same subject matter should read together, in an effort to render them all consistent and to render each effectual.[179]

Sedgwick's insistence that legislative intent be determined by reference to statutory text alone was repeated in the first edition of Sutherland, still the leading statutory interpretation treatise today.[180] Yet for Sutherland, the process of cashing meaning out of the text was much more convention-bound. Going much farther than Sedgwick's general admonitions to read particular statutory provisions in light of the whole, Sutherland included extensive discussions of canons of construction requiring that particular words be known by terms associated with them in the text,[181] that general classifications preceded by specific enumerations be confined to particulars similar to those enumerated (the rule of *ejusdem generis*),[182] and that the expression of one alternative excluded others (the rule of *expressio unius*).[183] He also included such nontextualist canons as the rule that statutes in derogation of the common law be strictly construed.[184] Taken together, these and other discussions give Sutherland's textualism a very different flavor from Sedgwick's. In Sutherland's hands, textualism is not so much a bulwark against the threat of judicial interpretation as a set of conventions ensuring that judicial interpretation would be disciplined and professional.

While some Progressive Era courts accepted the plain meaning rule, the more popular alternative to equitable interpretation of statutes was the "golden rule," applying the statutory language unless it yielded manifestly absurd results. On this view, general equitable principles operated only to restrict, but never to extend, the application of the statute.[185] Henry Black's influential turn-of-the-century treatise on statutory construction purported to limit judicial discretion by applying statutory language even where irrational or self-defeating, consulting legislative intent only where statutory language was ambiguous, and condemning application of the judiciary's "own ideas as to the justice, expediency, or policy of the law."[186]

---

[177] Ibid., 264.

[178] Ibid., 201.

[179] Ibid., 211.

[180] John Gridley Sutherland, *Statutes and Statutory Construction* (Chicago: Callaghan, 1891).

[181] Ibid., §§262–66.

[182] Ibid., §§268–81.

[183] Ibid., §§325–29.

[184] Ibid., §§289–91. This canon of construction was particularly the target of progressive critics of laissez-faire jurisprudence, who assigned it a leading role in the judicial frustration of the will of Progressive legislatures. See Roscoe Pound, "Common Law and Legislation," *Harvard Law Review* 21 (1908): 383. But while the canon was sometimes deployed to preclude implication from regulatory statutes of tort remedies unknown to the common law, it was also used to narrow reform legislation that advanced the classical liberal agenda, such as laws enhancing married women's legal personality. The canon was also used to frustrate legislative innovations in lien law, whether favoring laborers or employers. See cases cited by Sutherland, §§289–91.

[185] Blatt, "A History of Statutory Interpretation," 813–14.

[186] Henry Black, *Handbook on the Construction and Interpretation of the Laws* (St. Paul: West, 1896), iii–iv, 35–36.

Yet without acknowledging any contradiction in his position, Black also embraced the golden rule, on the ground that "a case which falls within the letter of a statute is not governed by the statute . . . if it is not within the spirit and reason of the law and the plain intention of the legislature."[187]

By the turn of the nineteenth century, legislative intent was less frequently equated with general equity, although it still could refer to the manifest design, policy, or purpose of the particular law. Although courts increasingly emphasized the rationale for the particular law rather than the principles of the legal system as a whole, they did not yet inquire into the motives of legislators as revealed in floor debates, private letters, public speeches, or even committee reports.[188] In an 1875 case, the Supreme Court considered the likely effect of military exigency on congressional intentions in chartering and capitalizing the Union Pacific Railroad during the Civil War.[189] Yet the Court distinguished this from any inquiry into the opinions of legislators, quoting Taney's dictum in *Aldridge v. Williams*.[190]

The first cases inquiring into legislative deliberations involved the interpretation of the Civil Rights Act of 1866 as part of an interpretation of the Civil War Amendments[191] or review of legislation for discriminatory motive under the Civil War Amendments.[192] During the same period, judges began to express suspicions that Progressive legislation reflected redistributive rather than health or safety motives, although usually unsupported by evidence from legislative debates.[193] Partly in the face of this sort of skepticism, legislatures began to develop more systematic factual records to support their decisions. Increasingly, some form of hearing was seen as a condition of due process, warranting the reasonableness of regulation.[194] The period between the Civil War and the turn of the century witnessed a proliferation of investigative commissions and boards, whose responsibilities involved proposing as well as implementing state legislation on

---

[187] Ibid., 48.

[188] The nearest example is *The Walter A. Wood Mowing & Reaping Co. v. Caldwell*, 54 Ind. 270, 281 (1876), in which the Indiana Supreme Court construed that state's foreign corporation act in light not only of the amendments and deletions recorded in the legislative journal, but also of a marginal comment on a section of the statute in the revised statutes prepared by one "Judge Hester, who was a prominent member of" the legislature that passed the statute.

[189] *United States v. Union Pacific Railroad*, 91 U.S. 72 (1875).

[190] Many late-nineteenth-century courts followed Taney's emphatic repudiation of the probative value of legislative debates. *Stewart v. Atlanta Beef Co.*, 18 S.E. 981, 986 (Geo. 1893); *City of Richmond v. Supervisors of Henrico County*, 2 S.E. 26 (Va. 1887); *District of Columbia v. Washington Market Co.*, 108 U.S. 243, 254 (1883).

[191] *Slaughter-House Cases*, 83 U.S. (16 Wall.) 36, 91–92 (1872) (Field, J., dissenting).

[192] "The statements of supervisors in debate on the passage of the ordinance cannot, it is true, be resorted to for the purpose of explaining the meaning of the terms used; but they can be resorted to for the purpose of ascertaining the general object of the legislation proposed, and the mischiefs sought to be remedied." *Ho Ah Kow v. Nunan*, 12 F.Cas. 252, 255 (D. California, 1879) (Field, J.).

[193] Hovenkamp, *Enterprise and American Law*, 193–204; Horwitz, *Transformation of American Law 1870–1960*, 26, 29–30.

[194] David Currie, "The Constitution in the Supreme Court: The Protection of Economic Interests 1889–1910," *University of Chicago Law Review* 52 (1985): 324, 371–74; *Davidson v. New Orleans*, 96 U.S. 97, 105 (1877); *Chicago, Milwaukee and St. Paul Railway v. Minnesota*, 134 U.S. 418, 457 (1890).

such matters as railroads, insurance, corrections, charities, education, agriculture, and health.[195]

Janet Lindgren has shown how judicial review of regulatory legislation in New York state between 1870 and 1920 was more a matter of *informing* the legislative process than of frustrating or nullifying it.[196] Judicial enforcement of constitutional strictures on the form of special legislation pushed the legislature to seek more comprehensive and arguably fairer policy solutions to the various problems that attended industrialization.[197] Due process review of legislation gave voice to interests that had been unheard in the initial legislative process; when these interests proved insubstantial, the legislation typically would be repassed, with some minor improvements in procedural fairness.[198] But where litigation revealed that licensing laws arbitrarily excluded qualified participants from a trade, the legislature gave in.[199] In the highly contested arena of labor relations, due process invalidation of protective labor legislation provoked constitutional amendments that chastened the New York Court of Appeals. At the same time, the threat of judicial review inspired the legislature to support its legislation with data. Thus, one New York statute prohibiting women's night work was declared unconstitutional in 1907 on the basis of largely abstract arguments about denials of privileges and freedom of contract. But a second one, passed in 1913 at the behest of the legislatively appointed Factory Investigating Commission, was upheld on the basis of the commission's detailed study of women working the night shift in a cordage factory.[200]

Historian William Brock notes a tremendous expansion of state regulation outside of New York and a few other states in the later decades of the nineteenth century, unimpeded by constitutional requirements of reasonableness and generality: "Judges sometimes expressed fears, but time and again they came back to the principle that only the law-making body could judge what means best served the public good."[201] They did so because legislation was now supported by the efforts of inspectors and statisticians investigating mines, prisons, and poorhouses. Thus, due process review became one mechanism in a broad movement toward the professionalizing of legislation in the decades after the Civil War. Reforms in congressional procedure aimed at reducing the power of parties divided decision-making authority by subject matter among committees; electoral reforms facilitated longer careers for effective and popular legislators and so promoted the development of expertise on those committees.[202] The result was a seniority sys-

---

[195] Brock, *Investigation and Responsibility*, 5, quoting *Journal, of the House of Representatives of the State of Michigan* (1883): 68.

[196] Janet S. Lindgren, "Beyond Cases: Reconsidering Judicial Review," *Wisconsin Law Review* 1983 (1983): 513, 583.

[197] Ibid., 594–95.

[198] Ibid., 599–604.

[199] Ibid., 626–29.

[200] Ibid., 612–14

[201] Brock, *Investigation and Responsibility*, 61. See 62–85 for case law survey.

[202] William E. Nelson, *The Roots of American Bureaucracy 1830–1900* (Cambridge: Harvard Univ. Press, 1982), 114–19. Steven S. Smith and Christopher J. Deering, *Committees in Congress* (Washing-

tem and a new self-image for the legislator as a career policy expert.[203] Due process review combined with such reforms to cast legislation as a much more rational and deliberative process than in the Jacksonian Era. In defending Progressive legislation against the presumption that common law adjudication brought to bear greater accumulated experience, Roscoe Pound argued that

> there is coming to be a science of legislation. . . . Modern statutes are not to be disposed of lightly as off-hand products of a crude desire to do something, but represent long and patient study by experts, careful consideration by conferences or congresses or associations, press discussions in which public opinion is focussed upon all important details, and hearings before legislative committees.[204]

Accordingly, courts began to grant legislative history a role in statutory interpretation. The watershed case for federal law was the 1892 decision in *Rector of Holy Trinity Church v. United States*,[205] in which the Supreme Court ruled that a statutory prohibition on employers "assist[ing] or encourag[ing] the importation . . . of any alien . . . under contract . . . to perform labor or service of any kind in the United States" did not apply to the hiring of a minister. In the old "equitable" style, the court found that inconveniencing a church must violate the "spirit" of any law enacted by "a religious people." But the court also discerned the "intention of [the statute's] makers" by looking at "contemporaneous events, the situation as it existed, and"—here departing from Taney's dictum—"as it was pressed upon the intentions of the legislative body." In concluding that Congress intended "labor or service" to refer only to low-paid menial work, for which competition might depress the wages or employment opportunities of the poor, the Court referred to petitions to Congress[206] and testimony before congressional hearings, and gave special credence to committee reports.[207] Though hornbook law remained to the contrary for quite some time, by the 1920s resort to federal legislative historical materials was frequent[208] and was urged by commentators as a way to lessen judicial legislation.[209]

---

ton, D.C.: CQ Press, 1984), 33. Jonathan N. Katz and Brian R. Sala, "Careerism, Committee Assignments, and the Electoral Connection," *American Political Science Review* 90 (1996): 21–33.

[203] Smith and Deering, *Committees in Congress*, 35.

[204] Pound, "Common Law and Legislation," 384.

[205] *Church of the Holy Trinity v. United States*, 143 U.S. 457 (1892).

[206] For an early instance of consulting petitions in assessing congressional intent, before the Civil War, see *Ogden v. Strong*, 18 F.Cas. 616, no. 10460 (circa 1800) (Curtis, C.J.).

[207] An earlier case uses a committee report, but merely to show the drafting history of a bill, not the expression of legislative opinions about the bill's purposes or proper construction. See *Blake v. National Banks*, 90 U.S. (23 Wall.) 307 (1875).

[208] *New York & Cuba Mail S.S. Co v. United States*, 297 F. 158 (2d Cir. N.Y., 1924); *United States ex rel. Patton v. Tod*, 297 F. 385 (2d Cir., N.Y., 1923); *Binns v. United States*, 194 U.S. 486 (1904); *Bate Refrigerating Co v. Sulzberger*, 157 U.S. 1 (1895); *Marshall Field & Co. v. Clark*, 143 U.S. 649 (1892); *United States v. Burr*, 159 U.S. 78 (1895); *United States v. St. Paul, Minneapolis & Manitoba Railway Co.*, 247 U.S. 310 (1918).

[209] Charles A. Miller, "The Value of Legislative History of Federal Statutes," *University of Pennsylvania Law Review* 73 (1925): 158; Frederic P. Lee, review of *The Transportation Act, 1920—Its*

   If formalist interpretation triumphed, it was only in state courts, and only for a brief season, before giving way to the new conception of legislative intent. For example, until 1910 courts were divided as to whether murderous heirs had to be awarded the estates of their victims under inheritance statutes that did not provide otherwise. Some courts refused to apply inheritance statutes to the benefit of murderers, reasoning that legislatures could not have intended to vio-late the common law principle that wrongdoers should not profit from their wrongs.[210] Over the next decade, however, many courts repudiated this view as unwarranted judicial legislation and applied what they considered the plain meaning of the statute.[211] Yet after 1920, momentum swung just as dramatically in the opposite direction, with most courts invoking public policy or the hypo-thetical intent of a rational legislature to prevent the murderous heir from inheriting.[212]

   The long-run effect of the formalist attack on equitable interpretation was not the triumph of formalism in statutory interpretation, but the emergence of a new pattern of judicial ascription of legislative intent—call it "policy rationalism." The courts began to look for certain kinds of legislative reasons in both reviewing and interpreting statutes, and legislatures endeavored to supply them. Where judges found such reasons they implemented them, with increasing sympathy and creativity as time went by. Rather than seeing post-Reconstruction courts simply as antagonists to Progressive legislatures, we can count courts among the condi-tions for the emergence of legislative Progressivism. On this view, Progressive

---

Sources. History, and Text, by Rogers MacVeagh (New York: H. Holt, 1923), *Columbia Law Review* 24 (1924): 214–15.

[210] *Riggs v. Palmer*, 22 N.E. 188 (N.Y. 1889); *Box v. Lanier*, 79 S.W. 1042 (Tenn. 1904); *Perry v. Strawbridge*, 198 S.W. 641 (Mo. 1908); cf. *Shellenberger v. Ransom*, 59 N.W. 935 (Neb. 1894); *Deem v. Milliken*, 44 N.E. 1134 (Ohio 1895); *In re Carpenter's Estate*, 32 A. 637 (1895); *McAllister v. Fair*, 84 P. 112 (Kan. 1906); see *De Graffenreid v. Iowa Land & Trust Company*, 95 P. 624 (Okla. 1908) (applying plain meaning rule to permit inheritance by murderous heir).

[211] *Gollnik v. Mengel*, 128 N.W. 292 (Minn. 1910); *Hill v. Noland*, 149 S. W. 288 (Tex. Civ. App. 1912); *Wall v. Pfanschmidt*, 106 N.E. 785 (Ill. 1914); *Eversole v. Eversole*, 185 S.W. 487 (Ky. 1916); *Hagan v. Cone*, 94 S.E. 602 (Ga. 1917); *Johnston v. Metropolitan Life Insurance Co.*, 100 S.E. 865 (W.Va. 1919).

[212] *Slocum v. Metropolitan Life Insurance Co.*, 139 N.E. 816 (Mass. 1923); *In re Tyler's Estate*, 250 P. 456 (Wash. 1926); *In re Wilkins' Estate*, 211 N.W. 652 (Wis. 1926); *Garwols v. Bankers Trust Co.*, 232 N.W. 239 (Mich. 1930); *De Zotell v. Mutual Life Insurance Co. of New York*, 245 N.W. 58 (S.D. 1932); cf. *Price v. Hitaffer*, 165 A. 470 (Md. 1933) (applying the golden rule and citing Black-stone to reach the same result); *Bryant v. Bryant*, 137 S.E. 188 (N.C. 1927); *Sherman v. Weber*, 167 A. 517 (N.J. 1933) (applying constructive trust doctrine to achieve similar effect). The New York courts developed an ingenious solution approved by commentators but not by other courts, according to which the murderer inherited in accord with the statute, but only as a trustee for the testator's next of kin. *Ellerson v. Westcott*, 142 N.E. 540 (N.Y. 1896). See Benjamin Cardozo, *The Nature of the Judicial Process* (New Haven: Yale Univ. Press, 1921), 40–43; see also James B. Ames, *Lectures on Legal History and Miscellaneous Legal Essays* (Cambridge: Harvard Univ. Press, 1913); G. P. Costi-gan, "Comment: Constructive Trusts—Is One Who Murders His Ancestor in Order to Secure by Descent the Latter's Property to Be Deemed a Constructive Trustee?" *Illinois Law Review* 9 (1915): 505; "Note: Constructive Trust Theory as Applied to Property Acquired by Crime," *Harvard Law Review* 30 (1917): 622.

Era courts and legislatures were engaged in a partly competitive and partly cooperative dialectic, challenging one another to embody scientific rationality. Judicial interference with legislation became less legitimate as the public became convinced not that *courts* were making policy *incompetently*, but that *legislatures* were making policy *competently*.

Interpreting the Evolving Constitution

This dialogue between court and legislature in interpreting society remains evident in the scholarly justifications for laissez-faire constitutionalism. Such key figures as Thomas Cooley (1824–98) and Christopher Tiedeman (1857–1903) betrayed little anxiety about judicial frustration of democratic will, because they saw courts as representatives of democratic will. Along with the astonishingly prolific treatise writer Francis Wharton (1820–89), less famous but in his day equally influential, these figures were participants in a tradition of constitutional theorizing that identified constitutional law with evolving social custom. Participants in this tradition divided over which governmental institutions were most competent to give voice to society, but all agreed that society was knowable and that such social knowledge was supreme law.[213]

A common theme in this tradition was that democratic sovereignty lay with neither the courts nor the legislature, but in civil society. This accorded with Social Darwinist notions that society was properly governed not by its political rulers, but by economic and biological imperatives immanent in civil society. Wharton, citing Savigny, Burke, Darwin, and Spencer,[214] made this naturalistic conception of customary law explicit: "The law should be allowed to grow by itself; . . . the unconscious tendencies of a Christian nation . . . are more wise and healthy than the conscious policy of its legislators, or rulers, or even its own component members meeting for popular deliberation."[215] Law should be "the silent and spontaneous emanation of the nation, past as well as present, adapting itself to the conditions in which, in each decade, it is placed."[216]

Cooley's influential treatise on the Fourteenth Amendment[217] identified constitutional law with the common law, which defined individual rights and inherent limitations on state powers.[218] Cooley equated due process of law with the protection of "vested rights":

> The whole community is . . . entitled at all times to demand the protection of those ancient principles which shield private rights against arbitrary interference, even though

---

[213] Kahn, *Legtimacy and History*, 65–96.

[214] Ibid., 82.

[215] Francis Wharton, *Commentaries on Law, Embracing Chapters on the Nature, the Source, and the History of Law; on International Law, Public and Private; and on Constitutional and Statutory Law* (Philadelphia: Kay & Brothers, 1884), 61.

[216] Ibid., iii–iv.

[217] Thomas Cooley, *A Treatise on the Law of Constitutional Limitations Which Rest upon the Legislative Power of the States of the American Union*, 6th ed. (Boston: Little, Brown, 1890).

[218] Ibid., 174.

such interference may be under a rule impartial in its applications. It is not the partial character of the rule, so much as its . . . unusual nature, which condemns it as unknown to the law of the land.[219]

For Cooley, property was a creature of custom, not natural right.[220] Far from seeing customary limits on state power as a check on majority will, Cooley saw custom "when voluntary, [as] the conclusive proof of the final and settled conviction of the people as to what the rule of right and conduct should be on the subject to which it relates."[221]

A German-American, Tiedeman was exposed to Savigny's historical jurisprudence and Jhering's sociological jurisprudence in legal study at Göttingen; he later taught in St. Louis during the ascendancy there of a Hegelian movement.[222] Like Cooley, Tiedeman identified constitutional law with continuing custom, rather than any text or original enacting will. Constitutions are not made, he held, "they grow."[223] The longevity and success of the American constitution derived from "the complete harmony of its principles with the political evolution of the nation . . . and not the political acumen of the conventions which promulgated it."[224] American government would flourish to the extent it adapted to the Darwinian law that "society . . . can attain its highest development by being left free from governmental control, as far as this is possible."[225]

"Evolutionary constitutionalism" is only barely a metaphor, since it contained an explicitly eugenic theme. Liberal market society was seen as both cause and culmination of an evolutionary process that favored the European ethnic groups who were supposedly genetically adaptable to the flexibility of contractual society.[226] According to Wharton, "Laws are the instinctive and unconscious outgrowth of the nation . . . [which] comprises that people as wrought up in one continuous body with those who preceded it as part of a common race. . . . The people of the United States, as primary lawmakers, form one with the people of England."[227] The racialist and historicist undertones of laissez-faire constitutional thought found confirmation in the turn-of-century social science of Columbia political scientist John W. Burgess, Johns Hopkins historian Herbert Baxter

[219] Ibid., 355.

[220] Gerald Berk, *Alternative Tracks: The Constitution of American Industrial Order 1865–1917* (Baltimore: Johns Hopkins Univ. Press, 1994), 102–3.

[221] Thomas Cooley, "Labor and Capital before the Law," *North American Review* 139 (Dec. 1884): 503.

[222] Kahn, *Legitimacy and History*, 236; *Dictionary of American Biography*, s.v. "Tiedeman, Christopher Gustavus."

[223] Christopher Gustavus Tiedeman, *The Unwritten Constitution of the United States* (New York: G. P. Putnam's Sons, 1890), 19.

[224] Ibid., 21.

[225] Ibid., 78.

[226] John Fiske, "The Laws of History," *North American Review* 119 (1869): 197; see Guyora Binder, "The Slavery of Emancipation," *Cardozo Law Review* 17 (1996): 2063.

[227] Francis Wharton, *Commentaries on Law*, iii–iv.

Adams,[228] and Yale sociologist William Graham Sumner.[229] The conception of the Constitution as the naturally evolved customs of the Anglo-American race implied a traditionalism inconsistent with any use of the Civil War Amendments to restructure society. Indeed, in in *Plessy v. Ferguson*, Justice Brown asserted that the constitutionality of segregated railway cars rested on the state's "liberty to act with reference to the established usages, customs, and traditions of the people, and with a view to the promotion of their comfort and the preservation of the public peace and good order." He added ominously that "if the two races are to meet upon terms of social equality, it must be the result of natural affinities. . . . [Legislation] is powerless to eradicate racial instincts."[230]

In the end, Legal Science is best understood as an opportunistic project of professionalization rather than a systematic philosophy of language. The Legal Scientists' interpretive methods were various: they were fiercely formalist in private law, feebly so in the statutory milieu, and contextualist when interpreting constitutions or precedent. If there was any common denominator in this eclectic body of thought, it was an epistemologically optimistic vision of the common law as a laboratory of social knowledge.

Progressive Constitutional Interpretation

Just as laissez-faire jurisprudence was more a sociology than a metaphysics, Progressive criticism of laissez-faire jurisprudence reflected more sociological than epistemological disagreement. The credibility of the Supreme Court's claim to scientific expertise broke down, not because the principle of rational governance was questioned, but because it was relocated.[231] The new locus of rationality was the legislature, which could develop knowledge of society, in place of courts, and which could rationally order society, in place of the unregulated market. Yet the legislature did not entirely displace courts as social observers, and progressive arguments for legislative priority in developing policy conceded the intellectual competence of courts.

James Bradley Thayer, Holmes's colleague at Harvard Law School, is chiefly remembered today for his criticism of judicial review. He is seen as the intellectual progenitor of the New Deal Supreme Court's deferential rationality standard, and the articulate defender of that posture of "Olympian" detachment that enabled Holmes to uphold the rights of legislatures to pass, and dissidents to urge, left-wing policies he considered foolish. Thayer called for the Court to validate all legislation that any rational person might view as constitutional.[232] He asserted that

---

[228] Alfred S. Konefsky, "Men of Great and Little Faith: Generations of Constitutional Scholars," *Buffalo Law Review* 30 (1981): 365, 369.

[229] Richard Hofstadter, *Social Darwinism in American Thought* (New York: G. Braziller, 1959), 36–37.

[230] *Plessy v. Ferguson*, 163 U.S. 537 (1896).

[231] Kahn, *Legitimacy and History*, 117.

[232] James B. Thayer, "The Origin and Scope of the American Doctrine of Judicial Review," *Harvard Law Review* 7 (1893): 129, 144.

it is the legislature to whom this power is given,—this power not merely of enacting laws, but of putting an interpretation on the constitution which shall deeply affect the whole country, enter into, vitally change, even revolutionize the most serious affairs, except as some individual may find it for his private interest to carry the matter into court.[233]

On constitutional questions, Thayer reasoned, the legislature stands to courts as civil society stands to courts on questions of private law. Accordingly, Thayer likened the courts' judgment of the reasonableness of legislation to the jury's judgment of the reasonableness of care in negligence—both interpret conduct to determine whether it accords with custom.[234]

Thayer did not object to the exercise of ethical and constitutional judgment in constitutional interpretation, but only to its exercise by courts in place of the people and their elected representatives. Thus, he opposed judicial review on the ground that it impeded the moral and political development of the people: "Not being thrown back on themselves, on the responsible exercise of their own prudence, moral sense and honor, [the people] lose much of what is best in the political experience of any nation."[235] Thayer insisted that "the safe and permanent road towards reform is that of impressing upon our people a stronger sense . . . of the great range of harm and evil that our system leaves open, and must leave open, to the legislatures, and of the clear limits of judicial power; so that responsibility may be brought sharply home where it belongs."[236] Thayer shared his contemporaries' idea that law should not impede natural processes of social struggle and consequent development. He also shared his contemporaries contempt for legislatures as undisciplined, but he proposed that they be improved by natural evolution rather than judicial intervention.

Hence, where the turn-of-the-century Supreme Court saw custom as a constraint on the activism of legislatures, Thayer saw it as a constraint on the activism of courts. He did not regard constitutional objections to legislation as ordinary policy objections in disguise—otherwise he would not have feared that judicial review would preclude constitutional deliberation by legislatures. Nor did he regard these objections as beyond the intellectual capacity of courts to judge. He simply thought it was not their place. So even Thayer, the sternest critic of activist judicial review, regarded constitutional interpretation as possible, desirable, and within the intellectual, if not the jurisdictional, competence of the courts. Indeed, he fairly clearly considered courts better interpreters of the Constitution than legislatures, and less needful of practice.

A parallel strand of Progressive constitutional theory came from the political scientist and President Woodrow Wilson. A partisan of progressive regulation and an opponent of nativism, Wilson nevertheless was no less a social Darwinist than his conservative opponents. But in his view, evolution required constitutional

---

[233] Ibid., 136.
[234] Ibid., 147.
[235] Ibid., 129.
[236] Ibid., 155–56.

innovation rather than bondage to tradition: "The trouble with the [framers' political] theory is that government is not a machine but a living thing. It falls, not under the theory of the universe, but under the theory of organic life. It is accountable to Darwin, not Newton."[237] For Wilson, as for Thayer, any people could be improved by the responsibilities of self-government; but such responsibilities were imposed any time a governing institution showed itself responsive to popular opinion. Wilson saw Congress as the branch of government most responsive to public opinion, and he saw the Executive as the branch best able to display its responsiveness and thereby engage public opinion in dialogue.[238] Yet Wilson also accorded courts both a representative and an interpretive role. Courts would adapt the Constitution, by measuring but also by refining public opinion to reflect "the enlightened judgment of men of thought and good conscience," rather than "the opinion of desire, of self-interest, of impulse and impatience."[239] Wilson's Progressive constitutionalism depended upon all three branches of government investigating and helping to formulate public opinion.

Wilson's protégé, political scientist Edward Corwin, did become one of the bitterest critics of judicial enforcement of laissez-faire constitutionalism. But the problem for Corwin and his contemporaries was not judicial activism, so much as judicial rigidity and unresponsiveness to popular will. As Fred Konefsky comments;

> It would . . . be missing the point to characterize the focus of these men's scholarship as the legitimacy of judicial review. The major intellectual problem for all of these constitutional scholars, the one which obsessed them, was the scope and viability of American democracy. How to ensure that the people's will was expressed and regarded, how to guarantee that power was not usurped, especially in the face of what they conceived to be static constitutional interpretation based on outdated principles—that was the question.[240]

Not an excess of interpretation, but a paucity of good interpretation—of imaginative apprehension and application of the public will—was the difficulty. Thus, the Progressive objection to the evolving constitution of laissez-faire legal science was that it did not evolve fast and creatively enough.

This impatience is evident in Jacobus tenBroek's 1939 analysis of the Supreme Court's use of original history in constitutional interpretation. TenBroek did lodge very modern-sounding epistemological objections to the search for original intent, arguing that the concerns expressed in debates and speeches were too parochial to resolve the disputes of a later era, while modern reconstructions of the framers' general values would inevitably be influenced by modern concerns.[241] But he did

---

[237] Woodrow Wilson, *Constitutional Government in the United States* (New York: Columbia Univ. Press, 1911), 56.

[238] Kahn, *Legitimacy and History*, 91–95.

[239] Wilson, *Constitutional Government in the United States*, 102; Kahn, *Legitimacy and History*, 157–58.

[240] Konefsky, "Men of Great and Little Faith," 373.

[241] Jacobus tenBroek, "Use by the United States Supreme Court of Extrinsic Aids in Constitutional Construction: The Intent Theory of Constitituonal Construction," *California Law Review* 27 (1939):

not object that the indeterminacy of original intent gave constitutional interpreters too much discretion. Indeed, discretionary interpretive judgment was needed to keep the Constitution in tune with the times. Thus tenBroek argued that the aim of *fixing* constitutional meaning was futile and counter-productive: "the Constitution, too, must change or its stability as the organ of a living society will turn into the landmark of a soon forgotten past."[242] tenBroek criticized originalism for impeding the the progressive evolution of judicial rather than legislative policy. He offered as a model of Progressive constitutional interpretation Justice Brandeis's opinion in *Erie R.R. v. Tompkins*,[243] in which the "policy" of applying a general common law was disapproved because, after experience in applying it, the Court found that its expected benefits had not accrued and that it had resulted in confusion, lack of uniformity, and unjust discrimination. It was "the facts of its operation," rather than its judicial origin, that discredited a general common law and thereby "changed the meaning of the Constitution."[244]

Progressive Jurisprudence as the Interpretation of Society

Progressive jurisprudential writing styled the judge as social observer and policy scientist. But we can also see in this literature the beginnings of the modern conception of judge as *artist*. In making policy the judge represents society's mute sense of justice; so this model of judging inevitably involves an imaginative, constructive component, revealing a modernist consciousness of the inevitability of mediation. The judicial reconstruction of the popular conscience depends, for its popular acceptance, on such aesthetic qualities as vividness and grace. And if the scientific function of the progressive judge is evident in the jurisprudence of Roscoe Pound, the identification of that function with artistic craft is evident in the jurisprudential writings of Learned Hand, Benjamin Cardozo, and Lon Fuller. Yet, their view of interpretation as art and craft did not entail skeptical doubts about its validity.

Pound (1870–1964) saw judicial lawmaking as inevitable but denied that this lawmaking was interpretive in character. He complained that the Supreme Court's "mechanical jurisprudence"

> conceives of application of law as involving nothing but a mechanical fitting of the case with strait jacket of rule or remedy. The inevitable adjustments and extendings and limitations, which an attempt to administer justice in this way must involve, are covered up by a fiction of interpretation in order to maintain the general security. . . . The greater part of what goes by the name of interpretation in this way of thinking is really a lawmaking process, a supplying of new law where no rule or no sufficient rule is at hand.[245]

399, 405. Earlier installments of this work appear at *California Law Review* 26 (1938): 287, 437, 664 and *California Law Review* 27 (1939): 157.

[242] Ibid., 412–13.

[243] 304 U.S. 604 (1938).

[244] tenBroek, "Use by the United States Supreme Court of Extrinsic Aids," 409–10.

[245] Roscoe Pound, *An Introduction to the Philosophy of Law*, rev. ed. (New Haven: Yale Univ. Press, 1954), 49–50 (based on lectures delivered during 1921–22).

Pound characterized the judicial contribution to lawmaking as sociological, but his sociology involved an element of construction as well as observation. Following Progressive trends in the German jurisprudential literature,[246] Pound asked judges not only to identify the consequences of available policy choices, but also to evaluate those consequences by balancing societal interests. These interests were not simply the desires of individuals—they were desires that were legally recognizable because representative of some socially important institution, or because socially approved. To identify the interests to be balanced therefore required normative judgment and interpretive construction. Pound's objection to laissez-faire jurisprudence was that it rested on bad economics and sociology. Like the New York legislature, Pound challenged any court that purported to discipline legislative policymaking to ratchet up the scientific legitimacy of its own policymaking.[247]

Embracing a similarly sociological conception of the judicial function, Judge Learned Hand (1872–1961) stressed the constructive and literary aspect of sociological jurisprudence. In a 1916 essay,[248] Hand reverted to the hermeneutic characterization of judicial policymaking:

> The judge has, by custom, his own proper representative function as an organ of the social will, and in so far as conservative sentiment, in the excess of caution that he shall be obedient, frustrates his free power by interpretation to manifest the half-framed purposes of his time, it misconceives the historical significance of his position and will in the end render him incompetent to perform the very duties upon which it lays so much emphasis.[249]

To identify social customs or interests was to give articulate form to the inchoate desires of the masses. The legal profession's tenuous claim to elite status depended, Hand implied by the very cadences of his rhetoric, on its *literacy*, its ability at once to represent and to ennoble popular will with pith and style. Courts had endangered their inherited authority by woodenly resisting rather than creatively embellishing popular will: "Only as an articulate organ of the half-understood aspirations of living men, constantly recasting and adapting existing forms, bringing to the high light of expression the dumb impulses of the present, can [the successors of past lawmakers] continue in the course of the ancestors whom they revere."[250] For Hand, the balance of interests sought by sociological jurisprudence was an aesthetic quality, affiliated with such Burkean aesthetic values as social harmony and historical continuity. Discretion was not a license, but a duty to exercise authority with delicacy and tact, thereby conserving it:

> The profession is still drawn and . . . will always be drawn from the propertied class, but other classes have awakened to conscious control of their fate, their demands are

---

[246] Herget, *American Jurisprudence: 1870–1970*, 164–65.

[247] Kahn, *Legitimacy and History*, 124.

[248] Learned Hand, "The Speech of Justice," *Harvard Law Review* 29 (1916): 617, reprinted in *The Spirit of Liberty*, 3d ed. (Chicago: Univ. of Chicago Press, 1977), 13–20.

[249] Ibid., 14.

[250] Ibid., 16.

vocal which before were dumb, and they will no longer be disregarded. If justice be a passable accommodation between the vital and self-conscious interests of society, it has taken on a meaning not known before. But the profession has not yet learned to adapt itself to the change; that most difficult of adjustments has not been made, an understanding of and sympathy with the purposes and ideals of those parts of the common society whose interests are discordant with its own. Yet nothing can be more certain than that its authority . . . must in the end depend upon its power to learn precisely that adaptation. As mediator it must grasp from within the meaning of each phase of social will; it must divine the form of what lies confused and unexpressed. . . . To adjust and to compromise, to balance and to value, one must first of all learn to know, not from the outside, but as the will knows.[251]

Attention to popular will was not merely, as for Pound, a matter of utility and instrumental rationality. Nor was it merely a matter of prudently maintaining the political legitimacy of an embattled elite: it was crucial for maintaining the *cultural vitality* of a ruling class in danger of decadence. "The profession of the law . . . is charged with the articulation and final incidence of the successive efforts towards justice; it must feel the circulation of the communal blood or it will wither and drop off, a useless member."[252] Legal elites must respond to the challenge of social change to keep fit. Their refinement and eloquence must be put to public use or lapse into an empty and alienated aestheticism.

Like Hand, Justice Benjamin Cardozo (1870–1938) conceived the judge as at once policymaker, popular representative, and poet. The judge's job was to gauge the evolving public sense of justice, formulate policy accordingly, and persuade the public to support, and the bar to accept, that policy.

In *The Nature of the Judicial Process*,[253] Cardozo embraced the sociological jurisprudence of Pound, and the European progressives that had influenced Pound: "Law springs from the relations of fact which exist between things. . . . The source of law . . . is in social utility." Cardozo argued that judicial policymaking was necessary because "the legislator has only a fragmentary consciousness" of the requirements of social utility. "He translates it by the rules which he prescribes. When the question is one of fixing the meaning of those rules, where ought we to search? Manifestly at their source; that is to say in the exigencies of social life."[254]

Like Pound, Cardozo identified a normative element in social utility: social welfare included not only "expediency or prudence" but also "the mores of the community . . . the social sense of justice."[255] While the articulation of that social sense involved creativity and aesthetic judgment, judges were not "free to substitute their own ideas of reason and justice for those of the men and women whom they serve. . . . In such matters, the thing that counts is not what I believe to be right. It is what I may reasonably believe that some other man of normal intellect

---

[251] Ibid., 17.
[252] Ibid., 14–15.
[253] Cardozo, *Nature of the Judicial Process.*
[254] Ibid., 122.
[255] Ibid., 72.

and conscience might reasonably look upon as right."[256] Hence, "the judge's . . . duty to declare the law in accordance with reason and justice is . . . a phase of his duty to declare it in accordance with custom."[257] Cardozo agreed with the evolutionists claim that "law is . . . an historical growth" and "the expression of customary morality." Precedents "that cannot prove their worth and strength by the test of experience are sacrificed mercilessly and thrown into the void."[258] Yet he also stressed that legal adaptation was a conscious achievement, not a natural process: "The standards or patterns of utility and morals will be found by the judge in the life of the community. They will be found in the same way by the legislator. That does not mean, however, that the work of the one any more than that of the other is a replica of nature's forms."[259]

Cardozo consistently characterized the articulation of customary morality as doubly creative: it transformed preexisting law,[260] and it reflected the expressive sensibility of the judge.[261] For Cardozo, then, sociological jurisprudence was more "art" than science. Indeed, sociology, history, and legal science were simply rhetorical tools that could be deployed together in crafting a creative decision.[262] Citing the European "free lawyers" Eugen Ehrlich and Francois Gény, Cardozo declared that the "judge as interpreter for the community of its sense of law and order must . . . harmonize results with justice through a method of free decision" and that ultimately "there is no guarantee of justice except the personality of the judge."[263]

Cardozo saw this amalgam of historical and sociological jurisprudence as particularly appropriate for constitutional interpretation, because of the vagueness and historicity of constitutional concepts. By contrast to the arguments of Maine and Holmes that liberal individualism was the telos of legal evolution, Cardozo insisted that cultural history revealed a movement from individualist to collectivist conceptions of freedom, which movement should be reflected in judicial interpretation of the due process clause.[264] Cardozo offered the expansion of the concept of "property affected with public interest" (and therefore subject to regulation) as an example of the appropriately evolving meaning of constitutional language: "Men are saying today that property, like every other social institution, has a social function to fulfill."[265]

While critical of laissez-faire constitutionalism, then, Cardozo objected to neither judicial discretion nor substantive judicial review of legislation. By contrast to Thayer, Cardozo argued that judicial review based on evolving social values makes legislative judgment more rather than less responsible:

---

[256] Ibid., 89.

[257] Ibid., 106.

[258] Ibid., 22–23.

[259] Ibid., 104–5.

[260] Ibid., 62.

[261] Ibid., 15.

[262] Ibid., 36.

[263] Ibid., 16–17, quoting Eugen Ehrlich, "Freie Rechtsfindung and Freie Rechtswissenschaft," *Modern Legal Philosophy Series*, vol. 9, 65; Cardozo, *The Nature of the Judicial Process*, 45.

[264] Cardozo, *Nature of the Judicial Process*, 83–85.

[265] Ibid., 87.

The great ideals of liberty and equality are preserved against the assaults of opportunism, the expediency of the passing hour . . . by enshrining them in constitutions, and consecrating to the task of their protection a body of defenders. By conscious or subconscious influence, the presence of this restraining power, aloof in the background, but nonetheless always in reserve, tends to stabilize and rationalize the legislative judgment, to infuse it with the glow of principle, to hold the standard aloft and visible for those who must run the race and keep the faith. . . . The restraining power of the judiciary does not manifest its chief worth in the few cases in which the legislature has gone beyond the lines that mark the limits of discretion. Rather shall we find its chief worth in making vocal and audible the ideals that might otherwise be silenced, in giving them continuity of life and expression, in guiding and directing choice within the limits where choice ranges.[266]

Having conformed legal policy to the evolving public sense of justice, the judge was obliged to defend that policy on two rhetorical fronts. First, the judge should protect popular principles of justice against the depredations of lawyers by anchoring them in the fabric of judicial precedent, thereby constantly reinterpreting judicial doctrine to accord with changing popular conceptions of justice. In an oft-quoted passage, Grant Gilmore remarks that "the more innovative the decision to which [Cardozo] had persuaded his brethren on the court, the more his opinion strained to prove that no novelty—not the slightest departure from prior law— was involved."[267] Thus, for Cardozo, judicial artistry consisted in part, in cleverly concealed innovation, a sort of legal *trompe l'oeil*.

Second, the judge should explain the outcome of a case in the accents of customary morality, to mobilize popular support for the new principle, and, again, to protect it against subsequent surreptitious reversal as a result of the clever, technical interpretations of advocates for the private interests of particular litigants. Thus, Cardozo saw judicial rhetoric as crucial for determining the later course of interpretation of precedent. A properly spun opinion should involve the public as a participant in the evolution of precedent, ensuring that the law changed only when change occurred in the popular sense of justice, or prevailing social conditions. For Cardozo, the interaction between judiciary and public opinion was a dialogue. The progressive judge should not merely observe, articulate, and apply public opinion. He should also mobilize it by addressing the public, thereby bringing the judicial process under public scrutiny, and ensuring its future responsiveness to popular will.

In an essay entitled "Law as Literature," Cardozo stressed the importance of writing style to effective judicial lawmaking.[268] Clarity is important to foster com-

---

[266] Ibid., 92–99.

[267] Grant Gilmore, *The Ages of American Law* (New Haven: Yale Univ. Press, 1977), 75, cited in Richard Posner, *Cardozo: A Study in Judicial Reputation* (Chicago: Univ. of Chicago Press: 1990), 12; Alfred F. Konefsky, "How to Read, or at Least Not Misread, Cardozo in *The Allegheny College Case*," *Buffalo Law Reviev* 36 (1987): 645.

[268] Benjamin Cardozo, "Law and Literature," in *The Law as Literature*, ed. Louis Blom-Cooper (London: Bodley Head, 1961), 182.

pliance by precluding inadvertent or artful misinterpretation; but clarity itself involves artifice. Clear rules necessitate abstraction—hence, discretion. So clarity is an aesthetic quality, communicating a *feeling* of precision purchased at the price of *actual* precision: "The picture cannot be painted if the significant and the insignificant are given equal prominence."[269] Thus, judicial power paradoxically involves commanding deference to an imperfectly communicated judicial will, and the judge must combat misreading by courting it. The judge is a kind of high-pressure salesman, pitching a new nostrum: "The opinion will need persuasive force, or the impressive virtue of sincerity and fire, or the mnemonic power of alliteration and antithesis, or the terseness and tang of the proverb and the maxim. Neglect the help of these allies and it will never win its way."[270] Yet the rhetorical task facing the progressive judge is made still more delicate by his obligation of deference to popular will, custom, and a wiser future: "The development of law is conceived of, more and more, as a process of adaptation and adjustment. The pronouncements of its ministers are timid and tentative approximations, to be judged through their workings, by some pragmatic test of truth."[271] As a solution to these difficulties, Cardozo especially recommended the homely illustration that links a proposed rule to customary morality:

> How impossible to fight against it when the judge brings it down to earth and makes it walk the ground, the brother of some dictate of decency or of prudence we have followed all our lives. . . . We glide into acquiescence when negation seems to question our kinship with the crowd. Something must be set down also to the sense of fellowship awakened when judges talk in ways that seem to make us partners in the deliberative process.[272]

Making a virtue of necessity, Cardozo strove to quiet the obstreperous lawyers with a display of humble deference to the crowd. By seeking popular support for judicial innovation in an essentially informal, customary lawmaking process, Cardozo hoped to render sociological jurisprudence responsive to, not merely representative of, the people. Cardozo's judicial "process" was a dialogical aesthetic project of *representing* society and *presenting* that representation for society's judgment.

These were Cardozo's ambitions as a judicial rhetorician, not necessarily his accomplishments. It has been suggested that Cardozo's first purpose, hiding his legal innovations from the lawyers in a thicket of convoluted common law reasoning, frustrated his second purpose, that of addressing, winning, and mobilizing the public.[273]

In a series of articles from the early 1930s, Lon Fuller joined Cardozo in presenting common law adjudication as an inherently deceptive process of rein-

---

[269] Ibid., 184.

[270] Ibid.

[271] Ibid., 186–87.

[272] Ibid., 188.

[273] For discussion of criticisms of Cardozo's writing style as stilted and unclear, see Posner, *Cardozo*, 10–12.

venting the law without appearing to do so. Fuller stressed that this process involved a double process of creation—the creation of new law, and the creation of new meanings for old legal rules and concepts. Fuller argued that law adapts through figurative construction. Thus, the "legal fictions" so maligned by Bentham and Austin are an inevitable feature of law's growth and change. New standards arise through the metaphoric extension of existing standards, their figurative status signaled by such modifiers as "constructive" or "implied," and eventually are no longer seen as metaphors.[274] Fuller styled this figurative inventiveness as an expression of pragmatism and flexibility—a willingness to use whatever linguistic tools were ready to hand. At the same time, Fuller challenged the tough-minded pose taken by critics of legal fictions, accusing them of a semantic fastidiousness pushed beyond the point of practicality, a kind of preciosity masquerading as precision:

> A wholesale rejection of fictions . . . is *inadvisable* because to reject all of our fictions would be to put legal terminology in a straitjacket—fictions are, to a certain extent, simply the growing pains of the language of the law. It is *impossible* because fiction, in the sense of a strained use of old linguistic material, is an inevitable accompaniment of progress in the law itself and this progress can scarcely be expected to wait out of deference for the tastes of those who experience an unpleasant sensation at the sight of words browsing beyond their traditional pastures.[275]

Fuller generalized his claim about the utility of invention, fiction, and figuration in acquiring and assimilating new information. Scattering references to American pragmatism,[276] Gestalt psychology,[277] and especially the German hermeneutic philosopher Hans Vaihinger,[278] Fuller argued that

> Our minds are not passive reflectors of the external world; they are instruments for enabling us to deal with that world. As instruments is it any wonder that they *alter* reality? . . . If the alteration that reality undergoes in our minds is called falsification, it is because we have been proceeding upon an erroneous theory of truth, a theory we may call the picture theory of truth. If we regard the matter in its true light, this alteration of reality is a sign not of the weakness of the human intellect but rather of its strength. If we dealt with reality as it is, in its crude, unorganized form, we should be helpless. Instead of that our minds have the capacity for altering, simplifying, rearranging reality.[279]

---

[274] Lon Fuller, *Legal Fictions* (Stanford: Stanford Univ. Press, 1967), 113–16.

[275] Ibid., 22.

[276] Ibid., 96, 107.

[277] Ibid., 111, 134.

[278] Ibid., 94–137. A somewhat similar but much more skeptical account of legal fictions (as neurotic wish fulfillment), also making extensive use of Vaihinger, may be found in Jerome Frank, *Law and the Modern Mind* (New York: Brentano's, 1930), 160–69, 312–22.

[279] Fuller, *Legal Fictions*, 103–4, quoting Hans Vaihinger, *Die Philosophie des Als Ob* (Berlin: Reuther and Reichard, 1911), 3.

Fuller's fusion of the ideals of practicality and aesthetic vitality exhibits none of the philosophical skepticism we will see in contemporary scholars of legal interpretation.

Fuller's account of legal fictions illustrates a typically Progressive strategy of "misreading." The Progressive interpreter of precedent begins with a doctrinal concept—say, offer in contract, or negligence in tort—that legal scientists viewed as the embodiment of a private legal actor's will. The Progressive interpreter then reinterprets the concept as a tool to achieve some social purpose—a tool perhaps ill-suited for its task, but jerry-rigged to meet some emergency. In this way a concept once seen as a real feature of a social landscape is reinterpreted as a symptom of a hidden feature. The legal judgment applying the concept may purport to be an interpretation of private will but is "really" an interpretation of public need.

We can see such an interpretive strategy at work in the Progressive critique and reform of Willistonian contract doctrine. Progressive contract theory rejected the ideal of civil society as a sphere of unregulated contractual choice. Hence, it urged movement from laissez-faire to greater paternalism, while rejecting the claim that such paternalism could be justified only by the incompetence or degraded status of its beneficiaries. Accordingly, Progressive contract theory was largely concerned with developing theories of liability and defenses arising out of the necessarily unequal interactions of the parties, whether or not these were formally integrated in an agreement. For example, one might be liable because her unfulfilled promise induced detrimental reliance, even though she was promised nothing in return; or one might be liable for bargaining in bad faith, though the negotiations never led to an agreement.

In making agreements less important, Progressive contract theory appeared to diminish the importance of their interpretation. Yet the new noncontractual theories of recovery required the interpretation of contextual circumstances—including language not agreed to—which might also inform interpretation of an agreement. The most influential exponent of Progressive contract interpretation was Arthur Corbin. Corbin insisted that contractual meaning was always a question of historical fact concerning the beliefs of actual persons, or the beliefs likely among classes of actual persons.[280] In answering this historical question, courts could and should consult any probative evidence. Corbin dismissed the "plain meaning" rule in contract by arguing that "some of the surrounding circumstances always must be known before the meaning of the words can be plain and clear; and proof of the circumstances may make a meaning plain and clear when in the absence of such proof some other meaning may also have seemed plain and clear."[281] Corbin offered a similar criticism of the parole evidence rule that

> purports to exclude testimony only when it is offered for the purpose of "varying or contradicting" the terms of an "integrated" contract; [but] . . . does not purport to ex-

---

[280] Arthur L. Corbin, *Corbin on Contracts*, 2d ed. (St. Paul: West Publishing, 1950), §554.
[281] Ibid., §542.

clude evidence offered for the purpose of interpreting and giving a meaning to those terms. The terms of any contract must be given a meaning by interpretation before it can be determined whether an attempt is being made to "vary or contradict" them.[282]

While meaning was always an historical question about the beliefs of persons, the matter of which person's beliefs were controlling was a normative or legal question for Corbin.[283] He argued that cases in which courts purported to apply "objective" standards were simply cases in which they had decided as a matter of law that Smith *should* be bound by the meaning Brown ascribed to him, if Smith had reason to know of it.[284] Under such circumstances, Smith would be precluded from testifying about his actual meaning because that was not the meaning he culpably induced Brown to agree to.[285] The purportedly "objective" and intrinsic interpretation of an agreement actually involved the subjective and contextual interpretation of language, which, although reasonably relied on by one party, was recognized not to express an agreement at all. Public policy masqueraded as the enforcement of a fictional private agreement.

Purposivist Statutory Interpretation

Like Progressive interpreters of precedent and contracts, statutory interpreters looked beyond language to context and conceived even context as an artifact of interpretation, a formulation of otherwise inchoate social purposes. They "deferred" to a legislative will defined at a high level of abstraction, and dependent upon judical imagination for its adaptation to unforeseeable events. As courts moved from the role of disciplining and rationalizing legislative will to that of applying legislative policy to changing circumstances, the method of "policy rationalism" tended to evolve into the method of "purposivism."[286] The object of the statutory interpreter was to construct the policy goal for which a statute stood, and to advance that goal. The Progressive judge was to think of a regulatory statute as the charter of an institution and to identify that institution's overall purpose. According to Learned Hand,

> laws need but one canon of interpretation, to understand what the real [legislative] accord was. The duty of ascertaining its meaning is difficult enough at best, and one certain way of missing it is by reading it literally, for words are such temperamental beings that the surest way to lose their essence is to take them at their face. Courts must reconstruct the past solution imaginatively in its setting and project the purposes which inspired it

[282] Ibid., §543.
[283] Ibid., §536.
[284] Ibid., §560.
[285] Ibid., §§538–39.
[286] But see Felix Frankfurter, "Some Reflections on the Reading of Statutes," *Columbia Law Review* 47 (1947): 527, 545–46. Frankfurter interprets the statutory opinions of Holmes, Brandeis, and Cardozo. He tempers his purposivism with an emphasis on judicial restraint in supplementing statutes, so as to discipline legislatures.

upon the concrete occasions which arise for their decision. . . . [This is] the only means by which [the popular will] . . . can become articulate and be made effective.[287]

As the legislative process became more professionalized, and courts became more sympathetic to Progressive policy, courts and legislatures increasingly shared a common discourse of instrumental policy analysis and a convergent set of aims. In this emerging era of interbranch understanding and complicity, skeptical critiques of statutory interpretation assumed the new significance of deflating judicial pretenses to technical rigor as unnecessary and incompatible with the team spirit required to meet national crises like depression and war. Statutory interpretation was not rocket science, but a craft; a statute was an organic unity, not a machine analyzable into component parts, each with a discrete semantic function. The various techniques of statutory interpretation—formalist canons, legislative historical research, conventionalist or consequentialist analysis—all were merely tools that, like Cardozo's disparate "methods" of common law adjudication, could be combined or dispensed with, so long as the legislature's broad policy aims were advanced. In the arena of statutory interpretation, Progressive legal thought conceived judges less as court painters, rendering flattering portraits of the sovereign public; statutory interpreters were more in the nature of musicians or thespians, bringing the legislature's design to life by performing an interpretation.

Thus, the apparently skeptical critiques of statutory interpretation offered by some exponents of "Legal Realism"[288] are best seen as rhetorical defenses of a craft aesthetic and can-do pragmatism, or even primitivism, that was sanguine and credulous at the core.[289] This tension between a rhetoric of tough-minded

---

[287] Learned Hand, "The Contribution of an Independent Judiciary to Civilization," reprinted in Hand, *The Spirit of Liberty*, 157.

[288] The advent of Realist Jurisprudence or Legal Realism was announced in works by Karl Llewellyn and Jerome Frank in 1930. Karl Llewellyn, "A Realistic Jurisprudence—The Next Step," *Columbia Law Review* 30 (1930): 431; Frank, *Law and the Modern Mind*. We will sidestep the quagmire of defining Legal Realism. See John Henry Schlegel, "A Tasty Tid-bit," *Buffalo Law Review* 41 (1993): 1045 (reviewing Horwitz, *The Transformation of American Law 1870–1960*). In two recent works, Morton Horwitz has defined Legal Realism broadly as including any attack on legal science (variously characterized as legal orthodoxy or classical legal thought) in the name of Progressive social policy. Horwitz,*Transformation of American Law 1870–1960*, 169–212; *American Legal Realism*, ed. William W. Fisher III, Morton Horwitz, and Thomas A. Reed (New York: Oxford Univ. Press, 1993), xii–xiv). Since we see legal science as an aspect of, or at most a dialectical moment in, the evolution of Progressive legal thought, we find this definition ultimately unhelpful. It amounts to building an ideologically and epistemologically purified Progressivism by projecting much of its conservative, technocratic, and elitist currents onto a fictively coherent opponent. This evades the challenge of understanding how ideas that today seem antithetical could have coexisted in the same discourses, the same social circles, and the same minds. We think it better to treat Legal Science and Legal Realism as necessarily marginal academic movements, illuminating sideshows to and rhetorical hypertrophies of mainstream legal thought.

[289] Indeed, Horwitz argues—convincingly—that what separated the self-proclaimed realists Llewellyn and Frank from Cardozo was their commitment to skeptical, irreverent, and hyperbolic rhetoric. For Horwitz, this marks Cardozo as essentially a proto-realist. For us it marks the realists as

skepticism regarding technique, and a rhetoric of rhapsodic mysticism regarding craft, is evident in well-known works on statutory interpretation by Max Radin, James Landis, Frank Horack, Karl Llewellyn, and Jerome Frank.

Radin's 1930 polemic "Statutory Interpretation"[290] is best known for its caustic dismissal of the newly regnant intentionalism. One of his arguments was the now familiar point that legislation has no single author:

> The most approved method [of interpretation] is to discover the intent of the legislator. Did the legislator in establishing this determinable have a series of pictures in mind, one of which was this particular determinate? . . . This transparent and absurd fiction . . . is . . . an illegitimate transference to law of concepts proper enough in literature and theology. The . . . law maker . . . does not exist, and only worse confusion follows when in his place there are substituted the members of the legislature as a body. A legislature certainly has no intention whatever in connection with words which some two or three men drafted, which a considerable number rejected, and in regard to which many of the approving majority might have had, and often demonstrably did have, different ideas and beliefs.[291]

Radin's skepticism extended to other techniques of statutory interpretation besides intentionalism, including the purposivism he would later endorse. Judges were constrained, not by technique, but only by psychological and sociological determinants of personality and perspective. The indeterminacy of all the recommended techniques of interpretation implied that "a judge is impelled to make his selection . . . by those psychical elements which make him the kind of person that he is."[292]

Radin portrayed legislators and judges as participants in a process, although it was more like an assembly line than a communicative or dialogic process. Legislators and judges were both craftsmen, engaged in practical, constructive action. Radin's view was that legislators make tools, and judges use them to make all kinds of things that legislators need not, should not, and cannot anticipate:

> The specific individuals who make up the legislature are men to whom a specialized function has been temporarily assigned. That function is not to impose their will . . . but to pass statutes, which is a fairly precise operation. That is, they make statements in general terms of undesirable and desirable situations, from which flow certain results. . . . And once the words are out, recorded, engrossed, registered, proclaimed, inscribed in bronze, they in turn become instrumentalities which administrators and courts must use in performing their own specialized functions.[293]

Radin was immediately reprimanded by his fellow realist, James Landis, who pointed out the inconsistency between Radin's skeptical treatment of legislative

---

a strand of Progressive legal thought, distinguished largely by its rhetorical strategems. Horwitz, *Transformation of American Law 1870–1960*, 185–92.

[290] Max Radin, "Statutory Interpretation," *Harvard Law Review* 43 (1930): 863.

[291] Ibid., 870.

[292] Ibid., 881–82.

[293] Ibid., 871–72.

intent as a fictional mental entity and his characterization of legislation as a useful reality.[294] Landis argued that just as what constitutes a statute and how it can be used are matters of convention, the same is true of legislative intent. The making of legislative intent is no more the thinking of a thought than is the making of statutes. Both are events in the world from which consequences result. Rules of statutory interpretation are conventions for making use of textual and extratextual evidence, which render the process of interpretation predictable to the legislature: "The so-called rules of interpretation are not rules that automatically reach results, but ways of attuning the mind to a vision comparable to that possessed by the legislature."[295] Thus, while Landis conceded that legislatures neither could nor should *control* interpreters, they could and increasingly did *provide* interpreters with evidence of their general purposes and policies, and it would be perverse and undemocratic for interpreters not to use the tools so provided:

> Barbaric rules of interpretation [that] . . . exclude the opportunity to get at legislative meaning in a realistic fashion, originating at a time when records of legislative assemblies were not in existence, deserve no adherence in these days of carefully kept journals, debates and reports. . . . To ignore legislative processes and legislative history in the processes of interpretation, is to turn one's back on whatever history may reveal as to the direction of the political and economic forces of our time.[296]

In response to this criticism and what he apparently felt was the improving performance of courts after the Supreme Court's abandonment of laissez-faire jurisprudence, Radin abandoned his skepticism in favor of interpretation in light of "objective purpose."[297] Presenting technique as a falling away from the primitive purposivism of *Heydon's Case*,[298] Radin expressed satisfaction that "the court today explores the mischief in order to discover, first, the nature of the structure which the administrators are to erect and, second, how much of the existing social structure is to be saved in the process."[299] Radin now conceded Landis's commonsense proposition that "within its constitutional powers, the legislature does in fact issue directives to the court and . . . a court that refused to accept them would be openly violating its duties."[300] His polemical criticisms of legislative intent "were undoubtedly somewhat too sweeping."[301]

Radin mocked as "solemn nonsense" the skeptical notion that "there is no middle course between . . . automatic action and wild and irregular caprice,"[302] but he objected to *any* "method" or technique designed to render interpretation automatic, whether formalist or intentionalist. Citing "New Critics" I. A. Richards,

---

[294] James M. Landis, "A Note on 'Statutory Interpretation,'" *Harvard Law Review* 43 (1930): 886.

[295] Ibid., 892.

[296] Ibid., 890–92.

[297] Max Radin, "A Short Way with Statutes," *Harvard Law Review* 56 (1942): 388.

[298] Ibid., 388–89.

[299] Ibid., 421.

[300] Ibid., 396.

[301] Ibid., 410–11.

[302] Ibid., 410.

and C. K. Ogden, Radin insisted that the judicial function "is not to determine exactly and precisely what the words of the statute 'meant.' This notion is based on the doctrine that words singly and in combination contain some secretion called a 'meaning' and that this secretion can be removed from the words and applied . . . to acts."[303] Similarly,

> Since our legislature is no more and no less sovereign than administrators or judges, and since all constitutional officials have a prescribed function . . . [a] statute is better described as an instruction to administrators and courts to accomplish a definite result, usually the securing or maintaining of recognized social, political, or economic values.[304]

Radin now held that by contrast to the technical and fictional concept of legislative intent, "the purpose, program, or policy of the statute is generally apparent. If the preamble does not tell us, the legislative report that accompanies the statute often will."[305] Finally, Radin concluded the court must decide, "Is this statutory purpose . . . good? We need not trouble ourselves about the statement that the court must not legislate. . . . They cannot help doing so by the mere act of 'enforcing' or 'applying' laws or carrying out the legislative purpose."[306]

Frank Horack's revision of Sutherland's treatise[307] adopted a similar purposivism, but rather than *contrasting* purpose to intent, Horack deferred to the expectations of practicing lawyers by *identifying* purpose with intent.[308] Like Radin, Horack approvingly cited *Heydon's Case* in support of purposivism and Ogden and Richards against the plain meaning rule[309] and other relics of "the now discarded idea that words 'mean' something in themselves."[310] The statute, as applied in a practical context, was an organic unity, not a collection of words and clauses.[311]

Since interpretive discretion was inevitable and desirable, Horack rejected the doctrine that a statute can be constitutionally void for vagueness.[312] Where earlier Progressives might have seen this doctrine as useful in professionalizing legislative drafting, Horack saw it as a mere pretext for overruling legislative policy judgments. Where the first edition of Sutherland was notable chiefly for its formulation of canons of construction, Horack's revision repudiated any effort to mechanize or even professionalize interpretation:

---

[303] Ibid., 406. Radin cites Charles Kay Ogden and I. A. Richards, *The Meaning of Meaning: A Study of the Influence of Language upon Thought and the Science of Symbolism* (New York: Harcourt & Brace, 1923); Ogden and Richards are also cited approvingly by Frank, *Law and the Modern Mind*, 84.

[304] Radin, "A Short Way with Statutes," 406–7.

[305] Ibid., 423.

[306] Ibid., 422.

[307] John Gridley Sutherland, *Statutes and Statutory Construction*, 5th ed., ed. Norman Singer (Deerfield, Ill.: Clark, Boardman & Callaghan, 1943).

[308] Ibid., §4701.

[309] Ibid., §§4501–2.

[310] Ibid., §4504.

[311] Ibid., §4801.

[312] Ibid., §§4808, 4920.

None of these methods or the numerous subsidiary canons of interpretation can be criticized if they in fact reflect the intent of the legislature, but none can be supported when they result in a finding of legislative intent which did not in fact exist with the legislature. No single canon of interpretation can purport to give a certain and unerring answer to the question. The question of meaning lies deeper than the law. It involves questions of judgment too subtle for articulation and issues of the transference of knowledge as yet unprobed by lawyers, scientists or psychologists.[313]

Horack's style of argument is well illustrated by his treatment of the rule of *ejusdem generis*. Horack explains this formal rule as a misguided effort to overcome the absurdities and contradictions generated by other, equally misguided formal rules. Horack argued that the resulting insistence on reading enumerated cases as limiting a general category yielded systematic misunderstanding and frustration of the legislative purpose:

> Usually the legislative intent is directly contrary to the result obtained by the *ejusdem generis* rule. The legislative intent is to enumerate specific objects or conditions which have come to their attention, but this enumeration is not intended to limit the operation of the statute to the specific objects set forth. They provide express examples of the problem; the legislative intent is to regulate *the problem* and not the *enumeration*.[314]

While denying that technique could render interpretation automatic, Horack insisted that legislative purpose or "intent" was discoverable.[315] But where earlier Progressives would have attributed this to the legislature's professional competence and scientific rationality, Horack attributed it to the legislature's immersion in custom and unschooled craft. A judge sufficiently well informed about the history of legislative regulation of a subject could fit a statute into evolving tradition in exactly the way he could fit precedent into the evolving common law.[316] The judge was no more concerned with the will of legislators than with the will of common law judges. Since legislation was a continuous effort, by trial and error, to respond to persistent social problems, there were bound to be many more statutes than there were legislative purposes. Lawyers and judges should worry less about the legislative history of particular statutes; they instead should steep themselves in the history of legislation.

A good example of antitechnical argument masquerading as skepticism is an essay by Llewellyn that appears to dismiss legal doctrine as fatally indeterminate.[317] The piece is best known for Llewellyn's arrangement of more than fifty

---

[313] Ibid.

[314] Ibid., §4910.

[315] Ibid., §4506.

[316] Ibid., §4507.

[317] Karl N. Llewellyn, "Remarks on the Theory of Appellate Decision and the Rules or Canons about How Statutes Are to Be Construed," *Vanderbilt Law Review* 3 (1949): 395. This chart looks very much like diagrams of the antithetical structure of legal argument in Jack Balkin, "The Crystalline Structure of Legal Thought," *Rutgers Law Review* 39 (1986): 1, discussed in chapter 5.

canons of construction into neatly opposed pairs, showing that for every textualist rule like the plain meaning rule, there is a consequentialist or purposivist counterpart like the golden rule, setting aside plain meaning when it requires absurd results.[318] Yet for Llewellyn, this dazzling display of doctrinal indeterminacy in no way implied judicial illegitimacy. Like Horack, Llewellyn compared statutory interpretation to the craft of common law adjudication so as to lend the latter's presumptive legitimacy to the former. Llewellyn begins the essay with a demonstration of the indeterminacy of precedent, *and an insistence on the propriety of this situation.* Indeterminacy does not preclude the court from reaching any legitimate result, but instead produces a surfeit of legitimate results that judges may choose among: "In the work of a single opinion-day I have observed 26 different, describable ways in which one of our best state courts handled its own prior cases. . . . What is important is that *all* 26 ways . . . are correct. They represent not evasion, but sound use, application and development of precedent."[319] The various ways of handling precedent are not techniques for determining the one correct result, but tools enabling the court to reach any result that accords with "the current tradition of the court or . . . the current temper of the court or . . . the sense of the situation as the court sees that sense"[320] or "uprightness, or conscience, [or] . . . responsibility."[321]

The canons of statutory construction are like these "ways of handling" precedent:

> The accepted convention still unhappily requires discussion as if only one single correct meaning could exist. Hence there are two opposing canons on almost every point. Plainly, to make any canon take hold in a particular instance, the construction contended for must be sold, essentially, by means other than the use of the canon: The good sense of the situation and a *simple* construction of the available language to achieve that sense, *by tenable means, out of the statutory language.*[322]

The proliferation of opposing canons is no embarrassment to judicial interpretation if they are seen in their proper light: as mere conventions of legal argument, rules of etiquette in brief writing and opinion writing, *not* techniques of actual persuasion or decision.

The most expressly aesthetic articulation of purposivist interpretation comes from Jerome Frank.[323] In his postwar essay "Words and Music," he argued for the organic unity of statutory meaning, and the dependence of that unity on the subjectivity of the interpreter.[324] Frank praised Hand as chief exemplar of the

---

[318] Llewellyn, "Remarks," 403.

[319] Ibid., 395–96.

[320] Ibid., 396.

[321] Ibid., 398.

[322] Ibid., 401.

[323] Frank has an earlier, more skeptical discussion in which he argues that the inevitable adaptation of statutes to unforeseen circumstances is not interpretation at all, but judicial legislation. Viewing this as inevitable, he argued judges should candidly assume responsibility for making new law. Frank, *Law and the Modern Mind*, 186–95.

[324] Jerome Frank, "Words and Music: Some Remarks on Statutory Interpretation," *Columbia Law Review* 47 (1947): 1259.

requisite "brilliant sympathetic imagination"[325] and hinged his argument on Hand's epigram that "the meaning of a sentence may be more than that of the separate words, as a melody is more than the notes."[326] Frank thought he detected in Hand's emphasis on the experiential unity of melodies and sentences "echoes" of phenomenological or Gestalt theories of perception.[327] Frank argued that statutes depend for their realization on interpretation in much the same way that music depends on performance, and that just as a metronomically correct rendition of a piece leads to a wooden performance, a literalist interpretation frustrates rather than realizes legislative will: "Some judges . . . sabotaged legislative purposes by sticking to the exact words of statutes. When judges . . . use their imagination in trying to get at and apply what a legislature really meant, but imperfectly said, they cooperate with the legislature."[328]

Frank argued not only that "the personal element in statutory construction is unavoidable,"[329] but that democracy was best served by encouraging interpretive creativity, for four reasons. First, Frank thought interpretive discretion enabled judges to realize legislative purposes. Second, a candid acknowledgment that judges must exercise policymaking discretion would alert the people to the need to monitor judicial policymaking.[330] Third, Frank thought acknowledging the co-equal lawmaking function of legislature and judiciary would remind all concerned that both were subordinate to the people. But finally, Frank suggested that tolerance of judicial discretion accorded with a cultural nonconformity and psychological freedom. Frank had long argued that the belief that judges could or should follow rules or precedent was the manifestation of a neurotic fear of adult responsibility.[331] But now, drawing on fashionable postwar psychoanalysis and psychology, he presented the impulse to control legal interpretation as fascistic, a manifestation of the "authoritarian personality."[332]

1.3 THE CRISIS OF PROGRESSIVE INTERPRETATION

From Progress to "Process": How the House Divided Again

Progressive legal thought cast the courts as interpreters of society, translating evolving popular morality into principles of justice and reinterpreting both common law rules and legislation as policies serving important social purposes. Hence, it saw "society" as an intelligible process of development towards a social or corporatist democracy. But of course the blind spot in this Progressive vision

---

[325] Ibid., 1267.

[326] *Helvering v. Gregory*, 69 F.2d 809, 810–11 (2d Cir. 1934) (Hand, J.).

[327] Frank, "Words and Music," 1267.

[328] Ibid., 1263.

[329] Ibid., 1264, citing Ernst Krenek, "The Composer and the Interpreter," *Black Mountain Coll. Bull.* 3 (1944) (arguing against work-fidelity and authentic interpretation).

[330] Frank, "Words and Music," 1271.

[331] Frank, *Law and the Modern Mind.*

[332] Frank, "Words and Music," 1268.

of American society was the legacy of slavery. The political triumph of Progressivism in the 1930s depended upon an alliance with Southern Democrats that forced Progressive jurisprudence to defer to majority will rather than refine popular conscience into principles of justice.

This alliance complicated the dilemma facing the Supreme Court when it considered abandoning laissez-faire jurisprudence in the face of mounting popular support for the New Deal. At this juncture, federal regulation of labor was impeded not only by the Supreme Court's interpretation of the due process clause, but also by the federalist doctrine that labor relations were a local police matter that the federal government was not empowered to regulate under the Commerce Clause.[333]

The Court had two available paths to upholding federal labor regulation. First, maintaining its claim to enforce due process in the deprivation of liberty, the Court could have acknowledged that identifying liberty as the right to enter into exploitative labor contracts no longer accorded with the popular sense of justice. To the contrary, Progressive regulation of wages, hours, and working conditions protected the liberty of workers proclaimed by the Thirteenth and Fourteenth Amendments.[334] Hence, Progressive federal labor legislation violated no civil rights and, moreover, was authorized by virtue of the federal government's responsibility to enforce civil rights.[335]

Second, abandoning its claim to enforce due process in the deprivation of liberty, *and* its federalism, the Supreme Court could hold that Congress could infringe liberty whenever it thought it necessary to do so to achieve any policy objective. By expanding the commerce power to embrace any subject having a remote or speculative effect on interstate commerce, and by holding that due process for the legislative infringement of liberty required only instrumental rationality, the Court chose this second path.

Both strategies would have flouted *stare decisis*. The second strategy involved a striking abdication of judicial power *in no way demanded by Progressive legal theory*. But the first strategy, treating labor regulation as civil rights legislation, would have raised the issue of race and continued to pit the court against Congress. Legal historian Marc Linder has pointed out the constitutive effect on New Deal labor legislation of slavery's legacy in the South. Linder argues that, by design, the Fair Labor Standards Act excluded from its benefits the two classes of workers who would be the most compelling claimants to the protection of antislavery legislation—agricultural and domestic workers. The only region in the country where farmers paid their workers substantially below FLSA standards was the South, where those workers were overwhelmingly Black. Moreover,

---

[333] *Carter v. Carter Coal Co.*, 298 U.S. 238 (1936).

[334] James Gray Pope, "Labor's Constitution of Freedom," *Yale Law Journal* 106 (1997): 941, 942–43, 962–63, 979–82 (discussing the Labor Movement's invocation of the Thirteenth Amendment in critiquing antistrike legislation and inequality of employee-employer bargaining relationship.)

[335] There is language compatible with this understanding of progressive labor legislation in the Supreme Court's pathbreaking decision to uphold state wage regulation under the Due Process Clause in *West Coast Hotel Co. v. Parrish*, 300 U.S. 379 (1937).

Linder and others have argued, the exclusion of fieldhands and maids from the FLSA was part of a pattern of ensuring passage of New Deal legislation with the support of Southern Democratic congressional committee chairs, by endeavoring to exclude Blacks from any social welfare benefits that might reduce their availability to employers.[336] Had the Court determined that Congress could legislate to protect workers only under its power to abolish slavery and secure civil rights, it might not have been able to uphold any labor legislation Congress would have then been willing to pass.

Yet recognizing protective labor regulation as civil rights legislation would have drawn the Court even deeper into political controversy. In acknowledging that the liberty of all workers depended on public protection from private power, the Court would have acknowledged that the liberty of Black workers, consumers, tenants, and homebuyers could also depend on public protection from private power; it would also have acknowledged that such protection implied no different or degraded civic status for Blacks, since all contracting by all legal persons was subject to protective public regulation. Thus, recognizing protective labor regulation as civil rights legislation would have overturned laissez-faire in race relations as well as labor relations. It would have challenged the "state action" limitation in civil rights law and authorized, perhaps even required, sweeping legislative or judicial efforts to control or redistribute private power between the races.[337]

In short, the Supreme Court could not easily maintain its claim to impose the discipline of constitutional principle on legislatures, and also approve popular labor legislation, without challenging customary regimes of racial hierarchy. The legacy of slavery was the Achilles' heel in Progressive constitutionalism, rendering judicial power to interpret the Civil War amendments potentially countermajoritarian. This accounts for a development that Morton Horwitz considers surprising: that on the Supreme Court, at least, the

> Progressive elaboration of a theory of the changing constitution . . . ground to a halt after 1937. We see no more of the progressive assertion that constitutional meaning changes over time until the Warren Court. . . . The new majority justified overruling the *Lochner* court precedents not because a living constitution inevitably required periodic reinterpretation and adaptation to a changing world, but rather on the ground that the *Lochner* majority had itself departed from the timeless truths of constitutional legitimacy. Suddenly, democracy was put forth as the fundamental source of constitutional principle. . . . The major appeal to democracy after the New Deal majority formed was to advocate or to justify radical limitations on judicial power. . . . The ideal of democracy

---

[336] Marc Linder, "Farm Workers and the Fair Labor Standards Act: Racial Discrimination in the New Deal," *Texas Law Review* 65 (1987): 1335; see also Ira Katznelson, Kim Geiger, and David Kryder, "Limiting Liberalism: The Southern Veto in Congress, 1933–1950," *Political Science Quarterly* 108 (1993): 283, 289, 297.

[337] Bruce Ackerman offers a similar argument that the New Deal—interpreted as a vision of public responsibility to positively secure the conditions of human freedom—implied public responsibility to at least avoid race discrimination. Bruce Ackerman, *We the People* (Cambridge: Belknap Press, 1991), 142–50.

itself came to be understood to have nothing to say about the protection of minorities. In fact, in order to limit judicial review, New Deal ideologues narrowly and mechanically defined democracy simply to entail majority rule.[338]

Reversing the causal relationship Horwitz asserts in this last sentence makes the development he notes less surprising. In deference to the fragile Democratic coalition, the Court equated democracy with majority rule by largely abandoning judicial review.

Progressive jurisprudence offered two disparate strategies for coming to terms with the withdrawal of the judiciary from constitutional policymaking that would influence its confrontation of racial injustice in the postwar period: a strategy of deferential engagement with public opinion that we may associate with Cardozo, Edward Levi, and later Alexander Bickel, and a strategy of Olympian and skeptical disengagement that we may associate with Thayer, Holmes, and Hand.

The first attitude was articulated in some of the proregulation opinions of Cardozo and Charles Evans Hughes during the mid-1930s.[339] But after 1940 maintaining this attitude involved denying the extent of the Court's surrender of power. We can see this evasive maneuver in Edward Levi's 1948 book *Introduction to Legal Reasoning*. Like Fuller, Levi sets out to vindicate legal reasoning's shifting, inconsistent deployment of categories and rules as pragmatic. Levi concedes that "the rules change as the rules are applied," and that "this kind of reasoning is open to the charge that it is classifying things as equal when they are . . . different, justifying the classification by rules made up as the . . . classification proceeds." Yet he insists, citing Dewey, that "in a sense, all reasoning is of this type."[340] Every concept, he implies, is defined by evolving use rather than any essential characteristic. Levi endeavors to show that legal reasoning works by analogy, deploying flexible concepts that it continuously redefines by example, in the face of changing social conditions and purposes. This, he suggests, with frequent citation to Cardozo, allows law to adapt to social change passively, and so without the imposition of judicial will. His key examples are the concepts of inherently dangerous goods in tort, transporting persons for immoral purposes under the Mann Act, and inherently dangerous goods under the commerce power:

> The history of the gradual growth of the inherently dangerous or evil category is a history of expansion through reasoning by example until previously innocuous items are included. The growth is a reflection of a period in which increasing government

[338] Morton Horwitz, "Foreword to Supreme Court, 1992 Term—The Constitution of Change," *Harvard Law Review* 107 (1993): 30, 56–57, 62–63.

[339] See *Home Building and Loan Association v. Blaisdell*, 290 U.S. 398 (1934) (Hughes, C.J. and unpublished concurring opinion of Cardozo, J.); Paul Brest and Sanford Levinson, *Processes of Constitutional Decisionmaking: Cases and Materials*, 2d ed. (Boston: Little, Brown, 1983), 296; see discussion of Cardozo's influence on Hughes's opinion in Horwitz, "Foreword to Supreme Court," 54–57; see also *West Coast Hotel Co. v. Parrish* (Hughes, C. J.); *Carter v. Carter Coal*, 324 (Cardozo, J. dissenting).

[340] Edward H. Levi, *An Introduction to Legal Reasoning* (Chicago: Univ. of Chicago Press, 1949), 3–4, citing John Dewey, *Logic, the Theory of Inquiry* (New York: Henry Holt, 1938).

control and responsibility for the individual were thought to be proper. No one economic or social theory was responsible although, as changes came about in the manner of living, the social theory moved ahead to explain and persuade. . . . It could not have been planned; it happened. . . . The liability of a seller of a previously innocuous article was not enlarged because some economic theory said this would be appropriate. Rather the growth of inventions made it hard to distinguish, when reasoniong by example was used, between steam engines thought unusual and dangerous in an early day, and engines that moved and now were commonplace. . . . And similarly in the development of a constitution, increased transactions and communication made activities previously re-mote and local now a matter of national concern. When a wage earner in New York thought his pay was dependent upon the standard of living in Georgia, whether it was or not, a fundamental change had taken place. . . . The contrast between logic and the actual legal method is a disservice to both. Legal reasoning has a logic of its own. Its structure fits it to give meaning to ambiguity and to test constantly whether the society has come to see new differences or similarities.[341]

Levi argues that the Supreme Court's dramatic abandonment of its objections to Progressive labor legislation should be seen as an example of the ordinary evolu-tion of the law through analogic reasoning. Following Cardozo, he claims that the seeds of a conception of labor as subject to national legislation under the commerce power had been laid in earlier cases. He ignores the additional barrier that liberty of contract appeared to place in front of these statutes, but his implicit argument is that labor regulation was always possible by the states where it in-volved property affected with a public interest. Nationalization of the economy made federal legislation in support of the state police power gradually appear more necessary and hence more permissible under the Commerce Clause, just as the Depression appeared to affect all industry and business with a public interest. Thus, Levi could argue that the Progressive conception of courts as popularly responsive and legitimate lawmakers survived the Court-packing crisis intact.[342]

The second attitude is expressed in a speech by Hand on judicial independence given in 1942, a few years after the Court-packing crisis and the Court's sudden acceptance of the New Deal.[343] Of the Constitution's "general principles" of jus-tice he writes,

Nothing which by the utmost liberality can be called interpretation describes the process by which they must be applied. Indeed if law be a command for specific conduct, they are not law at all; they are cautionary warnings against the intemperance of faction and the first approaches of despotism. The answers to the questions which they raise demand the appraisal and balancing of human values which there are no scales to weigh. . . . It is true that . . . cases can arise where courts might intervene, not indeed because the

[341] Ibid., 102–4.

[342] Frankfurter also sought to preserve the dignity of the Court by insisting that Justice Roberts changed his position prior to the Court-packing crisis. Felix Frankfurter, "Mr. Justice Roberts," *University of Pennsylvania Law Review* 104 (1955): 311.

[343] Learned Hand, "The Contribution of an Independent Judiciary to Civilization," in *The Spirit of Liberty*, 155–65.

legislature has appraised the values wrongly . . . but . . . because its action has been nothing but the patent exploitation of one group whose interests it has altogether disregarded. But the dangers are always very great. What seems to the losers mere spoliation appears to the gainers nothing less than a reasonable relief from manifest injustice. . . . So long as law remains a profession . . . judges must be drawn from a professional class with the special interests and special hierarchy of values which that implies. And even if they were as detached as Rhadamanthus himself, it would not serve unless people believed that they were.[344]

Hand equivocates between a genuine skepticism based on the subjectivity of values, and a suggestion that popular ignorance precludes the masses from appreciating and respecting the superior wisdom of the educated classes. When elites protect hated minorities, he warns, they risk sharing their fate. In addition, Hand argues against courts assuming the power to judge the constitutionality of legislation for fear that they will be politically compelled to legitimate popular folly as principled; and invokes Thayer's argument that the legislature will become less principled if it can rely on the prospect of judicial review:

If an independent judiciary seeks to fill [these empty vessels] . . . from its own bosom, in the end it will cease to be independent. . . . There are two ways in which the judges may forfeit their independence if they do not abstain. If they are intransgent but honest, they will be curbed. But a worse fate will befall them if they learn to trim their sails to the prevailing winds. A society whose judges have taught it to expect complaisance will exact complaisance; and complaisance under the pretense of interpretation is rottenness. If judges are to kill this thing they love, let them do it, not like cowards with a kiss, but like brave men with a sword. . . . And so . . . judges . . . should not have the last word in . . . basic conflicts of "right and wrong." . . . You may ask then what will become of the fundamental principles of equity and fair play which our constitutions enshrine. . . . I do not think anyone can say what will be left of those principles; I do not know whether they will serve only as counsels; but this much I think I do know—that a society so riven that the spirit of moderation is gone, no court can save; that a society where that spirit flourishes, no court need save; that in a society which evades responsibility, by thrusting upon the courts, the nurture of that spirit, that spirit in the end will perish.[345]

By the rhythms of his rhetoric, Hand invokes Lincoln's authority[346] in recommending a stance of aesthetic detachment before the spectacle of passion, politics, and human folly.

Aided by such evasions, Progressive jurisprudence survived into the postwar period to confront the challenge of minority rights posed by Nuremberg and Little Rock. In the areas of contractual and statutory interpretation, judicial function

[344] Ibid., 160–62.

[345] Ibid., 163–64.

[346] See Wills, *Lincoln at Gettysburg*, 171–72 (Gettysburg Address: "shall not perish;" repetition of phrases beginning with "that" and triads, unseparated by "and's"; 1862 message to Congress: "nobly save or meanly lose the last best hope of earth" and many other speeches about preservation of threatened republic).

remained largely unchanged and uncontroversial. Legal theory continued to laud pragmatic adaptation to evolving social need, to criticize literalism or conceptualism, and to imagine the court in dialogue with other decision makers. But the judicial function in constitutional law became the focus of controversy, centering on the Supreme Court's decision in *Brown v. Board of Education*.[347] For the first time, liberal reformers were calling on the courts to make policy without ascribing that policy to popular will. This required a new conception of constitutional law and a new justification for constitutional interpretation by judges. The solutions assayed by legal theorists involved emphasizing and recasting two previously subordinate elements of Progressive legal thought: the idea of process, and the metaphor of the judge as literary artist.

"Process"—Cardozo's term for discreet judicial lawmaking—had a double significance in postwar parlance. First, it stood for a new conception of constitutional law as a set of procedural ground rules for social choice rather than society's evolving substantive values. Defending racial equality as procedural justice had a number of advantages in the Cold War Era. It presented America to the world as constitutionally tolerant and egalitarian notwithstanding the manifest racism of the American public; and by associating equality with civil rights and liberties rather than material redistribution, it implicitly lumped communism with fascism as equally totalitarian opponents of the rule of law. But while "process" now connoted the rule of law, it retained the Cardozian connotation of rules subject to renegotiation. The implication was that courts did not really render decisions or make law, but simply contributed to an endless "legal process," digesting and passing on information from one institution to another. Law was a discursive process in which no institution had the last word, in which, win or lose, every interest could be heard and heard and, with toleration, heard again.

A second adaptation of Progressive legal thought in the Civil Rights Era was an increasing emphasis on the judge's artistic sensibility as a justification for the exercise of *moral* discretion. To the extent that judicial review could no longer be defended as the necessary craft of articulating society's inchoate sense of justice, it became the persuasive and performative process of inspiring society with a sense of justice. The judge, like the modern literary author, was expected to provide charismatic moral leadership—not only to be institutionally independent, but also to embody personal independence of thought and incorruptible principle in an age of conformity and complicity.

The "Process" of Statutory Interpretation

In the arena of statutory interpretation, "process" stood for a pragmatic antiliteralism constrained by iterated interbranch dialogue. The most influential exposition of this perspective was the "Legal Process" course developed by Henry Hart and Albert Sacks at Harvard. Fundamentally, Hart and Sacks embraced the purposivism typical of New Deal Progressives. Interpretation was a search for the

---

[347] *Brown v. Board of Education*, 347 U.S. 483 (1954), supplemented by 349 U.S. 294 (1955).

broad aim of legislation, rather than the specific applications intended by legislators. The whole thrust of their textbook[348] was that legislators were just as much
professionals as judges, constrained by their role to exercise judgment rather than
will about policy choices, after gathering facts, and playing an inherently limited
role in policy design. Legislators were competent only to speak in generalities,
delegating the implementation of policy to the judgment of other professionals.
The interpreter

> should assume, unless the contrary unmistakably appears, that the legislature was made
> up of reasonable persons pursuing reasonable purposes reasonably. It should presume
> conclusively that these persons . . . were trying responsibly and in good faith to dis-
> charge their constitutional powers and duties. The court should then proceed to do, in
> substance, just what Lord Coke said it should do in *Heydon's Case*. . . . The gist of this
> approach is to infer purpose by comparing the new law with the old. Why would reason-
> able men, confronted with the law as it was, have enacted this new law to replace it?
> . . . The whole context of a statute may be examined in aid of its interpretation. . . . The
> court may draw on general public knowledge of what was considered to be the mischief
> that needed remedying. The internal legislative history of the measure . . . may be exam-
> ined, . . . but . . . the history should be examined for the light it throws on *general
> purpose*. Evidence of specific intention with respect to particular applications is compe-
> tent only to the extent that the particular applications illuminate the general purpose and
> are consistent with other evidence of it.[349]

What Hart and Sacks added to Progressivism was primarily an enhanced concern with procedural fairness. Language was more of a constraint for Hart and
Sacks then for Radin or Horack, not because meaning inhered in language, but
because emphasizing language was good policy. Thus, the traditional canons of
construction retained utility for them as "policies of clear statement." Where Horack saw the void-for-vagueness doctrine as an irrational constraint on legislative
flexibility and judicial discretion, Hart and Sacks insisted that the public have
notice of the way statutes might be applied so as to avoid the arbitrariness and
secrecy of totalitarian regimes.[350] This concern with notice required interpreters
to plausibly reconcile statutory purpose with the publicly available statutory language,[351] and to justify attributions of purpose exclusively by reference to public
statements or publicly available facts:[352] "Language is a social institution. Humpty
Dumpty was wrong when he said that you can make words mean whatever you
want them to mean. The language belongs to the whole society and not to the
legislature in office for the time being."[353] In addition, the effort to render legislative meaning public meant that "purpose" was not only more general and flexible

---

[348] Henry Hart and Albert Sacks, *The Legal Process: Basic Problems in the Making and Application
of Law* (tentative ed., Cambridge, Mass, 1957).

[349] Ibid., 1341–42.

[350] Ibid., 1339.

[351] Ibid., 1337.

[352] Ibid., 1341–42.

[353] Ibid., 1338.

than intent; it was also *conventional*. Regardless of their actual motives, legislators were presumed interested in maximizing utility or ameliorating problems traditionally subject to legislative regulation or common law remediation. This was essentially a measured movement back in the direction of policy rationalism.

A philosophically sophisticated variant of the legal process approach was offered in a remarkable essay by the attorney Charles Curtis in 1950.[354] Curtis was less concerned with publicity or procedural fairness than were Hart and Sacks; the process theme in his thinking consisted in the reduction of meaning itself to procedure, by analyzing interpretation as the allocation of decision-making authority. Requirements of reasonableness functioned not to discipline decision making, but merely to reallocate decision-making authority.

Curtis's core proposal was that in interpreting statutes, judges should estimate and realize the will of future rather than past legislatures: "Better that the courts should set their decisions up against the possibility of correction than make them under the shadow of a fiction which amounts to a denial of any responsibility for the result."[355] Like Horack, then, he implicitly lumped together the judiciary and the legislature as fungible participants in a single process of evolutionary policymaking.

Like Fuller and Levi, Curtis set out to vindicate conventional legal reasoning as pragmatic. Curtis turned to pragmatist philosophy of language to explain why both literalism and intentionalism depended upon metaphysical beliefs that enchanted few practicing lawyers. The practical demands of promulgating and applying standards inevitably involved *generalization*, Curtis reasoned, but not *abstraction*. Like Levi, Curtis reasoned that legal categories were not defined by any essential characteristic, but could grow and change through analogical extension and unforeseen application. This linkage of specific past applications to an indeterminate future allowed legal categories to combine concreteness and generality:

> We talk about negligence or about fraud. These are abstract terms. They name a property which is shared by those acts which we call negligent or fraudulent. These are general terms, not abstract. . . . A lawyer does not have a case of fraud or a case of negligence. He is presented with and he is engaged to deal with certain particular acts and events . . . which someone has called negligent or fraudulent in one aspect. . . . Quine says that as soon as we elevate general terms to the status of singular abstract terms, as we do when we think in terms of "negligence" instead of "negligent acts," we run into the question whether there are any such abstract entities. Quine wants to keep logic and logicians clear of this metaphysical question.[356]

---

[354] Charles P. Curtis, "A Better Theory of Legal Interpretation," *Vanderbilt Law Review* 3 (1950): 407, 407–37. Curtis's style—flippant rather than earnest—associates him more with realism than with the legal process tradition. It should be clear that we think that little more than tone distinguished the realists on the one hand and the legal process scholars on the other from the mainstream of Progressive legal thought.

[355] Ibid., 414–15.

[356] Ibid., 420.

Curtis goes on to argue that literalism supposes abstract qualities to inhere in statutory words, and intentionalism supposes them to be supplied by legislative intent.[357] Yet legislators provide for unforeseen cases not by identifying qualities to be sought by future decision makers, but by allocating decison-making author-ity—by deciding procedure rather than substance:

> The meaning of words is to be sought, not in their author, but in the person addressed, in the other party to the contract; not in the grantor but in the grantee; not in the testator but in the executor or the legatee. . . . Words are but delegations of the right to interpret them, in the first instance by the person addressed, in the second and ultimate instance by the courts who determine whether the person addressed has interpreted them within their authority.[358]

In making this argument, Curtis draws both an analogy between law and litera-ture and a contrast. Both are properly concerned with the concrete, but the literary work of art is also specific and sufficient unto itself. Legal writing, by contrast, always implicitly presents the particular as an example of the general.[359] Skillful legal drafting may involve leaving room for future argument and negotiation through the strategic use of generalities of a kind that literary skill may eschew.[360] For Curtis, the embeddedness of legislator, lawyer, and judge in a legal process prevents them from impressing their personality very deeply into the law. Law is a craft, not an art; by virtue of its generality legal language is irredeemably prosaic:

> Once we have got over our prejudice for the precise, and are willing to recognize the equally admirable properties of selective and adjustable inexactitude . . . we shall be free to substitute for what the orthodox theory of interpretation calls . . . intention of the [author] . . . , the particular thing to which the word is applied by the person . . . to whom the words were addressed and to whom the power of applying them was delegated. The vaguer they are, the more imprecise they are, the greater the delegation. . . . The question is not whether the doubted, denied, controverted, and now litigated application is or is not to be taken as what the word means. It is whether the person to whom the word was addressed acted reasonably in choosing and acting on the one of many meanings which he did choose and did act on.[361]

In Curtis's conception of law as process, the legal meaning of language consists simply in its allocation of decision-making competence. Secrets of the heart, the law need not know.

Constitutional Interpretation as Process and Performance

The critical battleground in postwar American jurisprudence was the problem of justifying countermajoritarian judicial protection of minorities, in light of the New

---

[357] Ibid., 421.
[358] Ibid., 424.
[359] Ibid., 422–23.
[360] Ibid., 421.
[361] Ibid., 422.

Deal Courts' repudiation of judicial review. This debate was framed by the confrontation of the two attitudes earlier associated with Cardozo and Hand: denial and withdrawal.

The Supreme Court's controversial decision in *Brown v. Board of Education* was closer to the first. As some have recently observed, Chief Justice Warren's opinion represented a return to the Progressive idea of a judicially discernible evolving Constitution.[362] Although decision in the case had been delayed to permit briefing on the intent of Congress in framing and passing the Fourteenth Amendment, Warren brushed aside all such inquiries as inconclusive. Statements in floor debates should be discounted as partisan and strategic, he said, and any thoughts legislators had on the subject of school segregation were outmoded by the modern role of public education in socializing citizens. A study of the historical problem confronting the Court by Justice Frankfurter's law clerk Alexander Bickel suggests that the Court abandoned the quest for original intent in favor of a broad purposivism, implicitly authorized by Congress's adoption of vague language "capable of growth."[363] Avoiding any explicit condemnation of segregation as invidiously intended, or of *Plessy* as wrongly decided, Warren justified overruling earlier interpretation of the Fourteenth Amendment by pointing to the increased importance of public education, and to previously unavailable social science data purporting to show segregation's detrimental educational effects on Black children.

From the perspective of a Thayer or Hand, however, the Court had no business making policy in this area anyway. In the 1958 Holmes Lecture, *The Bill of Rights*, Hand articulated the attitude of judicial disengagement from constitutional policymaking, arguing that judicial review was neither explicitly authorized nor foreclosed by the Constitution's text. Nevertheless, invoking Progressive ideas about statutory interpretation, he conceded that courts customarily and legitimately interpret instruments so as not to defeat their objects.[364] Because it was necessary to have some means of resolving Legislative-Executive conflict, he continued, judicial review—although itself an infringement of separation of powers—appeared regrettably necessary to maintain the Constitution's scheme of coequal branches. Because this justification for judicial review was merely prudential, Hand concluded, the power of judicial review should be exercised only so far as necessary to preserve the separation of powers.[365] Invoking the same procedure-substance distinction adverted to by Curtis, Hand insisted that judicial review was available only to determine who should make a policy choice, never to make a policy choice of its own.[366]

Hand conceded that delineating the boundary between governmental authority and individual liberty might be seen as such a procedural allocation of decision-making authority, but he objected that the Constitution gives courts too little

---

[362] Kahn, *Legitimacy and History*, 152–53; Horwitz, "Foreword to Supreme Court," 63–64, 89–90.

[363] Alexander Bickel, "The Original Understanding and the Segregation Decision," *Harvard Law Review* 69 (1955): 1, 62–63.

[364] Learned Hand, *The Bill of Rights* (Cambridge: Harvard Univ. Press, 1958), 18–23.

[365] Ibid., 10–11, 14–25.

[366] Ibid., 37.

guidance in making that allocation. Courts may apply recent statutes to unforeseen circumstances, because they can grasp the problem the statute aims to solve, and the amount and kind of trouble the legislature was willing to impose on society to solve it. But such terms as "equality," "liberty," and "due process" framed a century or two ago have too little to say about contemporary disputes: "It would be fatuous to attempt imaginatively to concoct how the Founding Fathers would have applied them to the regulation of a modern society."[367] Inevitably then, judicial enforcement of the due process or equal protection clauses makes the Court "a third legislative chamber."[368] Hand concludes that in attending to the changing function of public education and to the psychological effects of segregation, the *Brown* Court made contingent policy judgments of a kind appropriate to legislatures. This contingent, circumstantial reasoning belied "the notion that racial equality is a paramount value that state legislatures are not to appraise."[369]

In the next Holmes lecture, Herbert Wechsler accepted Hand's premise that progressive judicial policymaking was no longer legitimate in constitutional law.[370] But to Wechsler, Hand's characterization of the *Brown* opinion as legislative in character because ad hoc and consequentialist suggested the presumptive legitimacy of judicial enforcement of "principle." Wechsler, who had worked with Justice Robert Jackson on the Nuremberg prosecutions, explained the legitimacy of judicial review by quoting Jackson on the virtues of the rule of law: "Liberty is not the mere absence of restraint, it is not the spontaneous product of majority rule, it is not achieved merely by lifting underprivileged classes to power, nor is it the inevitable by-product of technological expansion. It is achieved only by a rule of law."[371] Asserting a judicial duty founded in the constitutional text to review legislation, even under the vague language of the Fourteenth Amendment and Bill of Rights, Wechsler conceded that such review entailed judicial value judgment. Yet he insisted that judicial value judgment was categorically different from legislative value judgment. Judicial value judgment was "principled," by which he meant (1) articulately defended (2) by reference to reasons independent of the identity of the parties affected by the dispute before the court: "When no sufficient reason of this kind can be assigned for overturning the value choices of the other branches of the Government, or of a state, those choices must . . . survive."[372]

As long as courts made policy in a judicial rather than a legislative *manner*, Wechsler contended, they were within their competence and so were playing their legitimate role within the legal process. Many have criticized Wechsler's notions

[367] Ibid., 34.

[368] Ibid., 42.

[369] Ibid., 54.

[370] Herbert Wechsler, "Toward Neutral Principles of Constitutional Law," *Harvard Law Review* 73 (1959): 1.

[371] Ibid., 16 (quoting Robert Jackson, *The Supreme Court in the American System of Government* [Cambridge: Harvard Univ. Press, 1955], 76).

[372] Ibid., 19.

of generality and neutrality as vacuous.[373] Since Wechsler acknowledged that his principles were to be adapted and adjusted to changing circumstances, it is hard to see what separates "result-oriented" decision making from the use of flexible "purposive" standards that most of Wechsler's contemporaries saw as the essence of legal method. But the key to Wechsler's characterization of judicial policymaking as principled lay in his emphasis on the judicial obligation to offer reasons in a written opinion. "Neutrality" was chiefly a judiciousness of style and tone, of the sort that Hand exemplified, and therefore an aesthetic matter. For Wechsler, Hand's doubts about the defensibility of desegregation on grounds of principle exemplified the *aspiration* to impartiality and impulse-restraint, which—far more than any success in *achieving* neutrality—justified judges in assuming the power of review. The "rule of law" was not only a societal but also a personal discipline; it was a moral art.

In order to performatively illustrate this judicial quality of moral anxiety, Wechsler concluded by disingenuously posing the question whether an adequately neutral rationale for desegregation might be found. He admitted that for him "the problem lies strictly in the reasoning of the opinion . . . which . . . did not declare, as many wish it had, that *the Fourteenth Amendment forbids all racial lines in legislation.*"[374] Two pages after thus resolving the segregation controversy in a sentence, he restored dramatic suspense by opposing racial integration with the strawman of freedom of association. The point of this designedly bad argument was not to condemn desegregation, but to justify it as the outcome of a process of open-minded moral deliberation:

> If the freedom of association is denied by segregation, integration forces an association upon those for whom it is unpleasant or repugnant. Is this not the heart of the issue involved, a conflict in human claims of high dimension, not unlike many others that involve the highest freedoms . . . ? Given a situation where the state must practically choose between denying the association to those individuals who wish it or imposing it on those individuals who would avoid it, is there a basis in neutral principles for holding that the Constitution demands that the claims of association should prevail? I should like to think there is, but I confess that I have not yet written the opinion. To write it is for me the challenge of the school-segregation cases.[375]

This was the challenge taken up by an entire generation of scholars.[376] To the Legal Process generation, "writing the opinion" was a Sisyphean process, a matter of maintaining the mood of moral earnestness that both justified and constituted the "rule of law." This required confessing that the opinion remained to be written

[373] See Mark Tushnet, "Following the Rules Laid Down," *Harvard Law Review* 96 (1983): 781.

[374] Wechsler, "Toward Neutral Principles," 32 (emphasis added).

[375] Ibid., 34.

[376] Wechsler's remains the most cited law review article on a constitutional law subject of all time. See Fred Shapiro, "The Most-Cited Law Review Articles Revisited," *Chicago-Kent Law Review* 71 (1997): 751, 767. But the urgency of the challenge did not depend on Wechsler's rhetorical skills. Bickel and Fuller were among the many scholars who took up the question even before Hand and Wechsler wrote.

notwithstanding that one had, in the very act of confession, already written it. We will focus on three participants in the Legal Process debate over *Brown*: Lon Fuller, Charles Black, and Alexander Bickel. All three became important precursors to the contemporary Law and Literature movement.

For Fuller, the problem of *Brown* was the problem of Nuremberg. In each case, the problem was how to command obedience for legal change that was unquestionably just, but neither popularly accepted nor technically authorized. Fuller drew the connection between *Brown* and Nuremberg in a reply to the English philosopher H. L. A. Hart. Hart had urged distinguishing between law and morals. On the basis of this distinction, he classified Nazi law as immoral but law nonetheless, and he argued that where judges exercise discretion in interpreting ambiguous legal rules, they are unconstrained by law. Fuller objected that these claims undermined the legitimacy of controversial judicial decisions by denying that judges could exercise discretion in a way that was faithful to law; these claims also implied that citizens had no moral obligation to obey laws with which they disagreed: "To be effective a written constitution must be accepted, at least provisionally, not just as law, but as good law."[377] Fuller added that

> Confirmation for this observation may be found in the slight rumbling of constitutional crisis to be heard in this country today. During the past year readers of newspapers have been writing to their editors urging solemnly, and apparently with sincerity, that we should abolish the supreme court as a first step toward a restoration of the rule of law. . . . If all the positivist school has to offer in such times is the observation that, however you may choose to define law, it is always something different from morals, its teachings are not of much use to us.[378]

Fuller did not go so far as to say that immoral rules can have no status as law. He made four narrower claims:

First, he held that Nazi law was immoral in a particular way that deprived it of status as law; that is, it lacked the characteristic moral virtues associated with the rule of law—publicity, specificity, prospectivity, impartiality, procedural regularity, and procedural fairness.[379] This "internal morality of the law" included also a procedural obligation of rational discourse of the sort Wechsler preached: "I shall have to rest on [the] assertion . . . that coherence and goodness have more coherence than coherence and evil. . . . I also believe that when men are compelled to explain and justify their decisions, the effect will generally be to pull those decisions toward goodness."[380]

Second, drawing on Progressive and Realist accounts of legal interpretation, as well as the later Wittgenstein,[381] Fuller argued that the application of any rule required the ascription of a purpose to it; thus, legal rules were incomplete without

---

[377] Lon Fuller, "Positivism and Fidelity to Law," *Harvard Law Review* 71 (1958): 630, 642.

[378] Ibid., 634–35.

[379] Ibid., 646–61.

[380] Ibid., 636.

[381] Ibid., 669; see Ludwig Wittgenstein, *Philosophical Investigations*, 3d ed., trans. Gertrude E. M. Anscombe (New York: Macmillan, 1968).

constructive choice by their interpreters. In other words, moral discretion was not an extralegal source of norms for deciding hard or unprovided for cases only; it inhered in the application of law even in those easy cases in which all plausible purposes dictated the same result. To argue, as Hart did, that easy cases resulted from clear rules rather than circumstantially convergent purposes was to commit the fallacy of presuming that meaning inhered in words.[382]

Third, Fuller noted that Hart conceived legal validity as depending on the existence of a legal system accepted by its subjects as legitimate.[383] The more a system's rules offend morality, Fuller reasoned, the less obligation its subjects have to accept the system as legitimate, and so to accept its rules as law. When a political order is as pervasively immoral as the Nazi regime, it becomes immoral to recognize any of its norms as law. Conversely, when a regime is sufficiently moral to deserve legitimacy, it is immoral to deny the status of law to unavoidably discretionary decisions by officials charged with interpreting and applying that law.

Finally, because the discretionary ascription to legal rules of moral purposes enhances the (normative) legitimacy of the legal system as a whole, it is an expression of fidelity to that legal system. Conversely, to choose worse over better purposes is to betray the legal system by undermining its legitimacy. The legal decision maker has not just a moral but a legal obligation to morally improve the law.[384]

Fuller's argument supported the Court's decision in *Brown* in three ways. First, the mere fact that the decision involved a discretionary interpretation of the vague equal protection clause reduced neither its status as law nor the obligation of its opponents to obey it. Second, insofar as the *Brown* Court ascribed to the equal protection clause the purpose of making legislation more impartial, it vindicated what Fuller called the "inner morality of the law." Third, Fuller's purposive theory of statutory meaning implied that no court could apply and enforce a segregation statute without reaching a judgment as to its purpose. To say that the meaning of a segregation statute is clear is to admit that its purpose is clear. From Fuller's perspective then, there was no burden on the Court to prove the invidious purpose of segregation, because the Justices could not enforce or even read a segregation statute until they had used their common sense to understand its purpose. Even *Plessy* had conceded that if "separate but equal" facilities were invidiously intended, they violated equal protection. Thus, a justification for overturning segregation emerged out of Fuller's conception of the judicial craft of statutory rather than constitutional interpretation.

Fuller's "opinion" in a sense argued that the *Brown* Court had simply acted as good Progressive judges. The fundamental difficulty with this argument was that Progressive judges had traditionally seen their task of improving the law as a

---

[382] Fuller, "Positivism," 661–69; see also Lon Fuller, *The Morality of Law*, rev. ed. (New Haven: Yale Univ. Press, 1969), 84–87, 228.

[383] Fuller, "Positivism ," 639, 656.

[384] Ibid., 647.

matter of conforming it to public opinion or prevailing social norms, not transcendent morality. Yet the Nuremberg model cut Progressive interpretation from its epistemological anchor in conventional morality and cast it adrift on the swells of conscience. In a later work, Fuller distinguished the morality of law, which reproduces itself through reasoned justification, from an "aspirational morality" of "virtue," which inspires by example and "shows its affinity in this respect with aesthetics."[385] But if fidelity to law now meant fidelity to conscience, then institutional legitimacy appeared to depend upon judicial virtue. It followed that judicial legitimacy could only be performatively demonstrated rather than rationally defended, so that judicial reasoning could only be apprehended and evaluated aesthetically, as the performance of a role.

Charles Black coauthored an NAACP brief to the Supreme Court in *Brown*. His answer to the challenge of "writing the opinion" appeared in 1960 in two parts: a book defending judicial review, and an article defending the *Brown* decision.[386] His theory of judicial review depended upon applying the "Realist" account of statutory interpretation to the Constitution. In other words, the Constitution was to be interpreted organically in light of the broad purposes of the institution it established, rather than parsed word by word. In a later work, *Structure and Relationship in Constitutional Law*, Black argued for such a functionalist interpretation of the institutional relationships implied by the Constitution:

> Suppose there were no Fourteenth Amendment. Could a state make it a crime to file suit in a federal court? Could a state provide that lifelong disqualification from voting or holding property was to result from even a short service in the United States Army? Could a state prohibit marriages by federal officials, so long as they remained in office? Could a state disqualify voters who would not take an oath to vote for the Republican candidate for Congress? As matters stand, we would prefer, I think, to point to texts, mostly in the Fourteenth Amendment, to establish the unconstitutionality of such extreme actions. But is it not clear that, if those texts were not there, we would point to other texts, so long as we adhered to the textual style? And is it not further clear, that our real reasons would not be textual, and that if we had no text . . . we would still decide these, and a host of other similarly extreme cases, in the same way, on the substantial ground that such state measures interfere with and impede relations which the national government has set up for its purposes?[387]

Reasoning in this extratextual way, Hand had established the constitutionality of judicial review as a necessary guarantor of the constitutionally mandated separation of powers. Black made a similarly functionalist argument for judicial review as necessary to give meaning to the individual rights Hand thought judicially unenforceable. Black argued that America was essentially and peculiarly a limited

[385] Fuller, *Morality of Law*, 14–15.

[386] Charles Black, *The People and the Court: Judicial Review and Democracy* (New York: Macmillan, 1960); Charles Black, "The Lawfulness of the Segregation Decisions," *Yale Law Journal* 69 (1960): 421.

[387] Charles Black, *Structure and Relationship in Constitutional Law* (Baton Rouge: Louisiana State Univ. Press, 1969), 12.

government rather than a pure democracy, and he noted, like Fuller, that legal systems need to maintain systemic legitimacy in order to elicit obedience from those who disagree with particular laws. And if this legitimating function was crucial even in societies committed to majority will, it was even more important in a society committed to limited government. *Some* institution was needed, independent of the political branches, that could legitimate their decisions as within their power. The Supreme Court served that legitimating function, through its infrequently exercised power to overturn government action for usurping powers not granted by the people. Black continued that the theory of limited government can be given no determinate content apart from its institutional embodiment in judicial review, that judicial review was accepted from the outset and had become an integral and traditional part of a working constitutional order, and that practically efficacious institutions should not be scrapped for theoretical reasons. By thus appealing to the Jacksonian conception of government as limited, and to antebellum tradition, Black carefully aimed his argument for the Court's power to impose racial equality at Southerners like himself.

Black's functional defense of judicial review had a *literary* aspect: from the structure and context of the institution of judicial review, Black inferred its expressive significance, its social meaning. He claimed not that judicial review ensured the legitimacy of government by limiting it—but that judicial review legitimated American government by expressing its character as limited. Judicial review did not *achieve* limited government but *stood for it*. In Black's hands, purposivist interpretation becomes a search not for the goals served by a law, but for the values expressed.

The legibility of law's expressive meaning is the basis of Black's moving revision of the *Brown* opinion, which attends to the structure and context of segregation:

> I was raised in the South, in a Texas city where the pattern of segregation was firmly fixed. I am sure it never occurred to anyone, white or colored, to question its meaning. . . . Segregation in the South comes down in apostolic succession from slavery. . . . [It] grew up and is kept going because and only because the white race has wanted it that way. . . . This fact, perhaps more than any other, confirms the picture which a casual or deep observer is likely to form of the life of a Southern community—a picture not of mutual separation of whites and Negroes, but of one in-group enjoying full normal communal life and one out-group that is barred from this life and forced into an inferior life of its own. . . . Segregation is historically and contemporaneously associated in a functioning complex with practices that are grossly and indisputably discriminatory. . . . Generally speaking, segregation is the pattern of law in communities where the extralegal patterns of discrimination are the tightest, where Negroes are subjected to the strictest codes of unwritten law as to job opportunities, social intercourse, patterns of housing, going to the back door, being called by the first name, saying "Sir," and all the rest of the whole sorry business. . . . "Separate but equal" facilities are almost never really equal. . . . Attention is usually focused on these inequalities as things in themselves, correctable by detailed decrees. I am more interested in their very clear character as

evidence of what segregation means to the people who impose it and to the people who are subjected to it. . . . We have here to do with the most conspicuous characteristic of a whole regional culture. It is actionable defamation in the South to call a white man a Negro. A small proportion of Negro "blood" puts one in the inferior race for segregation purposes; this is the way in which one deals with a taint, such as a carcinogen in cranberries. . . . A court may advise itself of [these points] as it advises itself of the facts that we are a "religious people," that the country is more industrialized than in Jefferson's day, that children are the natural objects of fathers' bounty, that criminal sanctions are commonly thought to deter, that steel is a basic commodity in our economy, that the imputation of unchastity is harmful to a woman. Such judgments, made on such a basis, are in the foundations of all law, decisional as well as statutory; it would be the most unneutral of principles . . . to require that a court faced with the present problem refuse to note a plain fact about the society of the United States—the fact that the social meaning of segregation is the putting of the Negro in a position of walled off inferiority—or the other equally plain fact that such treatment is hurtful to human beings.[388]

Black acknowledges that this stirring passage is an implicit indictment of the *Brown* opinion: "It seems to me that the venial fault of the opinion consists in its not spelling out that segregation, for reasons of the kind I have brought forward in this Article, is perceptibly a means of ghettoizing the imputedly inferior race."[389] Yet it is also an explicit reprimand to Wechsler's claim to have improved upon the opinion by enhancing its already regrettable timidity and deliberative ambivalence. Black's "opinion," though not delivered from a rostrum, was clearly also a performance that sought to confront the reader experientially, with the simple justice of desegregation: "I am not really apologetic for the simplicity of my ideas on the segregation cases. The decisions call for mighty diastrophic change. We ought to call for such change only in the name of a solid reasoned simplicity that takes law out of artfulness into art."[390]

As Frankfurter's law clerk, Alexander Bickel had developed a purposivist defense of *Brown*'s compatibility with the original intent of the Reconstruction Congress. In 1962 he published a widely acclaimed defense of judicial review. In *The Least Dangerous Branch* Bickel confronted the crisis civil rights posed for the Progressive conception of the judge as popular representative.

Bickel embraced the Progressive vision of an evolving Constitution. Building on his previous work, he argued that the close study of debates attending the framing of constitutional language tends to dispel the assumption that framers' intent can warrant or preclude any particular policy: "No answer is what the wrong question begets."[391] But from the mere fact of creating a Constitution with broad language, an intent to delegate decisions to future interpreters may be in-

---

[388] Black, "Lawfulness of the Segregation Decisions," 424–27.

[389] Ibid., 430.

[390] Ibid., 429.

[391] Alexander Bickel, *The Least Dangerous Branch: The Supreme Court at the Bar of Politics*, 2d ed. (New Haven: Yale Univ. Press, 1986), 103.

ferred. Invoking nineteenth-century German historiography, Bickel argued that we are legitimately

> guided in our search for the past by our own aspirations and evolving principles, which were in part formed by that very past. When we find in history, immanent or expressed, principles that we can adopt or adapt, or ideals and aspirations that speak with contemporary relevance, we find at the same time evidence of inconsistent conduct. But we reason from the former, not from the frailties of men who, like ourselves, did not always live up to all they professed or aspired to. Lincoln reasoned, not from the Framers' resignation to the fact of slavery, but from the abolition of the slave trade and numerous manumissions.[392]

Adapting the Constitution to modern conditions required leaving text and original history behind: "Anything that might be called 'construction' of the written Constitution has come to suffice less and less."[393] For Bickel's postwar generation, the "text" requiring purposive construction was Progressive constitutional theory itself.

While endorsing the creative, adaptive function of the Progressive judge, Bickel saw it as antithetical to the Progressive's commitment to majoritarian democracy. "The root difficulty," he admitted, "is that judicial review is a counter-majoritarian force in our system."[394] By contrast to Black, Bickel saw the United States not in Jacksonian terms as a limited government, but in Lincolnian terms as a self-government, in which the constraints on popular rule must ultimately be internal. The United States was neither a limited government nor a direct democracy but a "deliberative democracy." This deliberation was an essentially judicial function, involving the reconciliation of policy with "principle."[395] "Principles" were, for Bickel, the historically received "enduring values" of a nation. Although historically contingent, they nevertheless exerted a constraint on current majority will, for two reasons: first, because they reflected the popular sense of justice rather than mere public opinion, and second, because fidelity to enduring ideals was the price of claiming an American identity and ancestry. While immune from simple repeal by current majorities, principles could be affected, eroded, reinforced, or reinterpreted by government action. These value implications add a second dimension of meaning to policy choices that might otherwise be evaluated on the basis of instrumental considerations alone.[396]

Because governmental actions could have meaning as well material effects, it was possible for an institution like the Court to have a function yet still lack any decisive effect. Bickel agreed with Black that the Court's function was not to *enforce* principle, which it lacked the power to do, but to *stand for* principle. For

---

[392] Ibid., 109–10.
[393] Ibid., 39.
[394] Ibid., 16.
[395] Ibid., 27.
[396] Ibid., 24.

Bickel, the Court was the "least dangerous branch" because it could not enforce its decisions without popular support.[397] But it could promote and preserve principle by giving a principled interpretation to policy decisions the public was prepared to accept. Its function was interpretive and educative rather than legislative. As imagined by Bickel, the Court differed very little in vocation from the academy. Justices were obliged to "follow the ways of the scholar in pursuing the ends of government" and were "inevitably teachers in a vital national seminar."[398]

Yet the Court differed from the academy in one crucial respect: Like Black, Bickel saw the Court's acquiescence as uniquely legitimating. In the tradition of Thayer,[399] Bickel saw the legitimating potential of the Court as a danger; following Hand, he saw that danger exacerbated by the political weakness of the Court. The Court stood in danger of being coerced or inveigled into legitimating unprincipled popular action, or, in the alternative, into discrediting principle and destabilizing the polity by flouting popular will in principle's name. These dangers were acutely raised by the desegregation decision, which reopened the wound in the nation's "moral unity, seriously broken only once, over the extension of slavery."[400] On the one hand, the Court lacked the power, and the authority, to impose the principle of racial equality on a recalcitrant public. On the other hand, for the Court to legitimate racial inequality as principled would be even more irresponsible: "Is it not clear that our nation would be severely damaged . . . if in the second half of the twentieth century it believed that segregation of the races was neither right nor wrong; if it were committed to no principle in the matter, one way or the other?"[401] This was the previously noted fatal flaw of Progressive jurisprudence—its willingness to flatter and indulge majority will left it helpless to resist hatred and atrocity. To avoid such a disaster, Bickel argued, Progressive jurisprudence needed to recover the Ciceronian ideal of the republican lawyer-poet.

Bickel sought to stand to the Progressive tradition in jurisprudence as Lincoln stood to the Ciceronian tradition—to bind up a constitutional discourse divided between principle and popular will by refiguring legal principle as the cause rather than the effect of social evolution: "The segregation crisis has its roots . . . in the slavery crisis of a hundred years before. And it plays back faithfully an earlier tension between principle and expediency, which was reconciled in the person of Lincoln. . . . Only in the continuity of this reconciliation can the Supreme Court fulfill its function."[402] The Supreme Court's function was to pursue principle, not by enacting it, but by teaching it:

> The hard fact of an existing evil institution such as slavery and the hard practical difficulties that stood in the way of its sudden abolition justified myriad compromises short of abandoning the goal. The goal itself—the principle—made sense only as an absolute,

---

[397] Ibid., 258–59.
[398] Ibid., 26.
[399] Ibid., 35.
[400] Ibid., 30.
[401] Ibid., 65.
[402] Ibid., 65.

and as such it was to be maintained. As such it had its vast educational value, as such it exerted its crucial influence on the tendency of prudential policy. But expedient compromises remained necessary also, chiefly because a radically principled solution would collide with widespread prejudices, which no government resting on consent could disregard.[403]

Segregation challenged the Court to maintain its ability to guide and educate the public in the direction of principle: to stand for principle, without insisting upon it. This the Court could do through the exercise of the "passive virtue"[404] of deciding not to decide:

> The essentially important fact, so often missed, is that the Court wields a threefold power. It may strike down legislation as inconsistent with principle. It may . . . in Charles L. Black's . . . word, legitimate legislation as consistent with principle. *Or it may do neither.* It may do neither, and therein lies the secret of its ability to maintain itself in the tension between principle and expediency. . . . When the Court . . . stays its hand and makes clear that it is staying its hand and not legitimating, then the political processes are given relatively free play.[405]

Bickel argued that the *Plessy* Court had erred, not in failing to strike down segregated public education, but in prematurely and unnecessarily deciding the constitutionality of all segregation, thereby enshrining it as principled. Bickel implied that the Court had done right in avoiding further provocation of Southern prejudice by not immediately applying *Brown* to strike down antimiscegenation statutes, and he urged that the Court approach "benevolent quotas" with similar caution: "They may well be for the 1960s the equivalent of segregated schooling a century ago."[406]

An important "passive" strategy involved simultaneously avoiding final decision and denying the finality of decision by the political branches. By prolonging the decision-making process the Court could avoid legitimating unprincipled majority will and avoid flouting it. Bickel described this strategy as the method of "colloquy" or interbranch dialogue. By "withholding constitutional judgment," the Court does not "forsake an educational function, nor does it abandon principle." Instead it poses "prudential questions that, in such a society as Lincoln conceived, lie in the path of ultimate issues of principle. . . . All the while the issue of principle remains in abeyance and ripens."[407] An example of such a technique was the strategy of striking down a statute as defective in form—excessively vague, for example—rather than in the substance of its policy aim. The Court thereby returned the legislative decision to the legislature with an invitation to reconsider its policy.[408] A second example was the technique of withholding

[403] Ibid., 67–68.
[404] Ibid., 111.
[405] Ibid., 69–70.
[406] Ibid., 71–72.
[407] Ibid., 70–71.
[408] Ibid., 156.

unsavory applications of a statute clearly intended but not stated by the legislature. By ascribing a fictively benign motive to the legislature a court could again force the legislature to reconsider the unsavory policy.[409]

Thus, Bickel's judge, like Cardozo's, must be *artful* as well as artistic. The artfulness inhered in a quality of restraint, evasion, even manipulation, but also faith. Like the rational legislator described by Lieber and Frank, the artful judge should not presume to control the future. Bickel points to the Supreme Court's order that school boards develop plans to desegregate with "all deliberate speed," a phrase that Bickel traces to devotional poetry and the traditions of equity practice:

> A phrase, then, that resembles poetry and resembles equity techniques of discretionary accommodation between principle and expediency, but that fits precisely one thing only, namely, the unique function of judicial review in the American system. The formula does not signify that the process of judicial review will involve itself in finding expedient compromises for a difficult situation. It means only that the Court, having announced its principle, and having required a measure of initial compliance, resumed its posture of passive receptiveness to the complaints of the litigants. The political institutions might work out their compromises. The Court placed itself in a position to engage in a continual colloquy with the political institutions, leaving it to them to tell the Court what expedients of compromise and accommodation they deemed necessary.[410]

As for the artistry, Bickel agreed with Black that principles were virtues proven to the public *aesthetically*—that conviction is the product of experience rather than ratiocination:

> What standards, [Dwight MacDonald] asked, should apply to literary judgments? How does one prove that Faulkner was an important artist and J. P. Marquand was not? . . . "Faulkner's" superiority Mr. MacDonald answered "cannot be proved, [but] it can be demonstrated, a quite different operation involving an appeal—by reason, analysis, illustration, and rhetoric—to cultural values which critic and reader have in common." I would assert the rightfulness of the Segregation Decisions can be demonstrated in like fashion.[411]

Yet what Black would have had the Court prove with rhetoric, Bickel suggested might only be proven by the struggles of ordinary people, and the cinematic concreteness of events themselves:

> Segregation . . . is an abstraction, and to a good many people a neutral or sympathetic one. . . . [The riots in Little Rock] which were brought instantly, dramatically, and literally home to the American people, showed what it means concretely. Here were grown men and women furiously confronting their enemy: two, three, a half dozen scrubbed, starched, scared and incredibly brave colored children. The moral bankruptcy, the shame of the thing, was evident.[412]

[409] Ibid., 216.
[410] Ibid., 253–54.
[411] Ibid., 237–38.
[412] Ibid., 267.

Bickel closed on a note of optimism, relieved that the national conscience had risen to the occasion and resolved the crisis, oblivious of the grim reality the future would reveal: that Northern Whites, despite their scorn for the vulgarity of Southern racism, would prove no less committed to segregation. For all his attention to civil rights law's countermajoritarian difficulty, Bickel greatly underestimated it. Eventually, Nixon's Supreme Court would draw back from the brink,[413] and the election of Ronald Reagan would signal an altogether unexpected denouement to the quarter century we call the Sixties. Legal reformers would recollect the passions of the civil rights movement in the tranquility of their studies, sublimating their frustrations in the literary criticism of an unredeemed reality, or imagining a better one, ruled by interpreter-kings.

CONCLUSION

Much contemporary Law and Literature scholarship presupposes a lapsarian narrative of American legal thought, a fall from innocent faith in what Bentham called the "nonsense on stilts" of natural law. According to this narrative, positivism exposed adjudication as naked will and then proceeded to disguise the shameful truth with the fig leaf of interpretation—the claim that the will enforced by judges was not their own, but that of an authoritative lawmaker captured by written rules. But insofar as this mechanical model of interpretation presumed that legal language has definite meaning inhering either in its words or in the intent of its authors, it merely replaced one naive metaphysics with another, trading the "nonsense on stilts" of natural law for what we might call "sense on stilts." Law and Literature scholarship completes the narrative by knocking the stilts of literal meaning and original intent from under legal interpretation.

This chapter has told a different story of interpretation in American legal thought, one in which foundationalist metaphysics figures less, both before and after the advent of modernity. American lawyers were not simple-minded naturalists before the start of the nineteenth century. They were not simple-minded literalists or originalists after. Legal interpretation is an institutionally situated practical activity and has often been so understood even by legal theorists. The bitter legacy of slavery has twice provoked profound hermeneutic crises in American legal thought. But crisis has neither been continuous nor rooted in philosophic error. Indeed, to seek philosophic solutions to American legal thought's interpretive crisis is to evade its political sources.

Before the development of a modern conception of subjectivity as desire, legal discourse and literary discourse were subsumed within an undifferentiated activity of literate reflection. Law had institutional embodiments, but because of its customary source of legitimacy, it transcended those embodiments; and literature did not yet exist as a separate category of letters. Interpretation played an uninteresting role in premodernist legal thought. Identifying and applying the law were

[413] See Alan D. Freeman, "Legitimizing Discrimination through Anti-Discrimination Law," *Minnesota Law Review* 62 (1978): 1049.

commonly experienced as processes of customary judgment, not as the interpretation of sovereign will. Accordingly, legal judgment was not seen as remote from, or in a semiotic relation to, virtue.

The separation of law and literature became possible with a new conception of language as the representation of desire: law was reconceived as an instrumental discourse, in which language functioned as a means to realize desire; literature was bounded off as intrinsically worthy discourse, the production of language for consumption. Yet the experience literature offered for consumption was an aesthetic contemplation of desire, or its sublimation. As law was conceived in positivist terms, literature was conceived in Romantic terms. Law and literature were each understood as representations of desire, but they represented desire by means of different tropes, the tropes of realization and sublimation, respectively.

A view of language as the representation of desire was the precondition to the centrality and controversiality of interpretation. The modern view of language as the representation of subjectivity challenged traditional intellectual operations to relegitimate themselves as objective mirrors of subjectivity. In antebellum America Jacksonian positivism posed a challenge to legal judgment, while religious Romanticism challenged reason as pharisaical. Whig Legal Hermeneutics answered and accommodated both Jacksonian positivism and charismatic religion by promoting adherence to the "spirit" of law, as a form of deference to legislative intent. Although a defense of legal judgment against these subjectivist challenges, Legal Hermeneutics was an expression of Romanticism. In fact, it mobilized Romantic aestheticism against positivism, offering to ennoble interpreters by setting them at an aesthetic remove from interest and faction.

Legal Hermeneutics proved a reasonably effective response to the centripetal forces of Jacksonian democracy and evangelical religion, supplying lawyers with a shared professional identity, in the period of their ascendancy. Legal Hermeneutics was also an impressive intellectual achievement. Although naive about the extent of social dislocation industrialization would bring, and wedded to a conservative and elitist politics, Legal Hermeneutics reflected remarkably sophisticated and modern views of language as a social practice, and of meaning as an institutional product. Its critique of "strict" originalist interpretation is as sophisticated as any developed by contemporary legal scholars and without the puerile despair about the meaninglessness of language and the resulting illegitimacy of normative judgment. Legal Hermeneutics foundered not on the inherent contingency of meaning, which it acknowledged, but on the political contradictions of American society, which it sought to repress. It was ultimately the conflict over slavery that proved too divisive for Legal Hermeneutics to overcome, and that brought lawyers into cultural disrepute. However, that disrepute extended to all of the institutions of government led by lawyers, not only the courts. It also marked the collapse of the ideal of a common republican citizenship.

After the Civil War, elites built a new professional identity around a conception of legal reasoning as a process of adapting legal rules to evolving social custom. Adherents to this school disagreed about what, to them, were important issues: the content of evolving custom, the institutions best suited to discern it, and the arena in which social custom evolved. By and large, the supporters and critics of laissez-faire agreed that policy choices should be based on the interpretation of tradition and evolving social need, and most agreed that judges should play a prominent role in thus forming policy. The critics of judicially imposed laissez-faire objected to judicial review *when* it was countermajoritarian, not *because* it was *inherently* countermajoritarian. Even insofar as some thinkers objected to courts as incompetent interpreters of the Constitution, they saw constitutional interpretation as a necessary and possible activity—for other institutions. Thus, their objection to judicial review was not based on epistemological skepticism about the possibility of interpretation.

The conventional division of the post–Civil War period in legal thought into two eras, one liberal-formalist and the other progressive-realist, is misleading. The better view is that these were different strands of a single Progressive discourse, characterized by scientism, evolutionism, and a competitive struggle to legitimize governmental institutions as professionally disciplined. Thus, in the decades before the constitutional crisis of the New Deal, criticism of the Court mostly argued that its social theory was outmoded, not that it should have no social theory. Progressive critics did not anticipate, and did not at first recognize, that laissez-faire judicial policy would be replaced by the Court's abdication of any policymaking role. Many assumed that courts had an important role to play in identifying, formulating, and realizing majority will.

Not until the postwar Court confronted the problem of race did a conception of the Court as fundamentally countermajoritarian prevail. Only at this point was the legitimacy of judical policymaking as such broadly questioned. The reason is that desegregation could not be defended within the Progressive paradigm—it was neither supported by majority will nor conservative of tradition. Indeed, to ask seriously what the constitutional eradication of slavery required was to confront—in the wake of Nuremberg—Progressivism's complicity with customs, prejudices, an entire culture condemned by world opinion.[414]

The challenge confronting postwar reformers was to justify for the first time the countermajoritarian and countercultural expression of judicial subjectivity. The result was the emergence of an image of the judge as moral artist—as alienated critic of society rather than tribune of the people, exemplifying the artistic virtues of nonconformity, independence, and integrity. Legal scholars endeavored to inspire and justify judicial enforcement of civil rights by offering exemplary performances of the role of moral artist. In the wake of the civil rights revolution, legal scholars would turn to literary theory to explain and justify their new conception of constitutional interpretation as moral artistry.

---

[414] Mary Dudziak, "Desegregation as a Cold War Imperative," *Law and History Review* 41 (1988): 61.

CHAPTER TWO

Hermeneutic Criticism of Law

INTRODUCTION

The Civil Rights era precipitated an interpretive crisis in Progressive jurisprudence by setting Progressive judicial activism against the social custom on which Progressive jurisprudence had long based legal interpretation. Legal theorists could no longer think of legal interpretation as a mirror of society. Legal interpretation was part of a "process" of "dialogue" with society, a stimulus to provoke majority deliberation on matters of "principle." The role of the judge in this dialogic process was a demanding one, requiring incisive social criticism, inspiring vision, and rhetorical charm. The "legal process" seemed to require a judicial artist with the skills of a literary critic.

The evolution of legal process scholarship into literary criticism of law was not immediate, however. In the 1970s legal theorists explored the possibility that Kantian moral philosophy could serve as a source of legal "principle" independent of majority will. The most prominent exponent of "principle" was Ronald Dworkin, who set out to answer the democratic objection to unconstrained judicial discretion that had earlier troubled Bickel and Fuller.[1] For Dworkin adjudication was not a technique of applying rules but rather a creative practice of developing principles that could reconcile and justify precedent. It was from principles, rather than the precedent reflecting them, that decisions derived their authority. Dworkin presented "hard cases" as questions of principle, not meant for majoritarian resolution.

Dworkin first identified principle with John Rawls's account of justice as the distribution of entitlements rational agents would consent to if ignorant of their own place in society. In deriving constraints on majority will from hypothetical consent, Rawls seemed to meet the countermajoritarian objection to minority rights. But by the early 1980s Rawls had been effectively attacked by communitarian critics as psychologically unrealistic. Communitarians insisted that moral norms could only emerge from reflection on the obligations and dilemmas of situated social actors in particular communities. But this made "principle" seem indistinguishable from prevailing custom and prejudice. Like Progressive jurisprudence, the jurisprudence of principle seemed more likely to mimic than to challenge society.

Seeking a nonmimetic model of interpretation, legal scholars turned to literary theory, then dominated by one or another form of Reader-Response criticism. Some invoked Reader-Response and allied movements—usually deconstruc-

[1] Ronald Dworkin, *Taking Rights Seriously* (Cambridge: Harvard Univ. Press, 1977), 84.

tion—to articulate the continuing crisis of progressive jurisprudence in alarmist tones. Others enlisted Reader-Response and allied movements—usually hermeneutics—in efforts to allay it. Thus, legal scholars responded to the crisis of Progressive jurisprudence by developing what we might call a "Hermeneutic Criticism of Law." They identified law as a kind of interpretation and interpretation as a kind of literary invention. This chapter will assess their efforts.

We will first critically review the literary theories of interpretation available to legal scholars in the 1970s and 1980s. Reader-Response criticism, which viewed the interpreter as the source of literary meaning, was by and large the literary criticism that legal theorists viewed as a model for legal interpretation. Yet Reader-Response was an eclectic synthesis of competing traditions, including the formalist "New Criticism" developed in the United States and England and its European structuralist cousin, and the historicist and phenomenological hermeneutics developed in Germany. These traditions also spawned formalist and intentionalist competitors to Reader-Response criticism, and legal scholars have invoked these competing hermeneutic theories as well.

Having explicated the literary theories of interpretation on which legal scholars have drawn, we will review and assess the influence of these sources in recent constitutional and statutory scholarship. While the hermeneutic turn in legal theory is an intriguing episode in intellectual history, our conclusion is that this type of scholarship has more past than future. Legal hermeneutics makes two claims about legal language that are sensible but no longer surprising.

First, much of it repeats the now familiar objections to empiricist conceptions of linguistic meaning developed by Wittgenstein, Quine, and other pragmatist philosophers: that all thought is mediated by language, that language is conventional, that there can be no private language of sensation, that there can be no theory-free description of sense-data, that meaning is use. Generally these ideas are deployed to ritually slaughter imaginary proponents of the view that the meaning of legal texts can be authoritatively fixed by reference to the intentions or other mental states of their authors.

Second, much of the recent legal hermeneutics also repeats the pragmatist attack on rationalist conceptions of linguistic meaning. Thus, from the maxim that all thought is in language it follows that concepts are always conventional categories, to be used and interpreted in light of the experiences and expectations of communities of language users, that the contents of such conventional categories may be linked by historical association rather than any shared characteristic, and that the domains of concepts are therefore inherently unstable and their boundaries indeterminate. Generally legal hermeneutic scholarship applies these points in ritually slaughtering imaginary proponents of the view that the meaning of legal texts is fixed by their language.

From these sensible claims about the indeterminacy of legal meaning, legal hermeneutic scholars frequently derive a third claim that we find dubious: that the indeterminacy of legal texts undermines the legitimacy of legal interpretation. In our view, when legal hermeneuticists equate indeterminacy with illegitimacy they forget the lessons of their own pragmatism. Linguistic meaning is indeterminate only in the sense that it is conventional, and so contingent on the evolving practice of a community of language users. Legal interpretation similarly is a conventional practice. And we see no reason why the admission that interpretation is conventional implies its illegitimacy. Even granting that the conventions of legal argument include the invocation of "legislative intent" and "plain meaning," lawyers can and do perform these conventions while recognizing them to be nothing more.

The crisis of judicial legitimacy to which legal hermeneutics responds is real enough. But, as chapter 1 revealed, the sources of that crisis are not philosophical, and so neither are its solutions. The legitimacy crisis with which American legal scholarship has struggled for the better part of a century is not occasioned by the resistance of language in general to interpretation. It is occasioned by the resistance to interpretation of the Civil War Amendments in particular. Its roots are in enduring cleavages in American society and politics, and its challenges are political rather than technical. If literary theory is to help us meet these challenges, it must do so in, not in place of, politics.

2.1 LITERARY THEORIES OF INTERPRETATION

Modernist Literature, Formalist Criticism

The twentieth century witnessed the emergence of a number of formalist movements in literary criticism: Russian formalism in the 1920s, Anglo-American New Criticism in the interwar and postwar periods, structuralist criticism in prewar Czechoslovakia and postwar France. All of these movements shared with Romanticism a commitment to bounding literature off from instrumental discourse. All of them treated reading as a search for meaning. Yet all of them rejected Romanticism's psychologistic concern with the sensibility of the author. For structuralism and Russian formalism, meaning was an effect of form; for New Criticism, form was an effect of meaning. But for all these movements, interpretation was primarily an inquiry into language, not into the experience of authors or readers.

Russian Formalism may be thought of as an aestheticist protest against turn-of-the-century moral criticism, and against the philistine demands for politically didactic art ascendant in postrevolutionary Russia. Like Shelley, Victor Shklovsky saw poetry as dynamic and revolutionary in form rather than content. The place of the poet was to intensify lived experience by "defamiliarizing" it:

> as perception becomes habitual, it becomes automatic . . . "if the whole complex lives of many people go on unconsciously, then such lives are as if they had never been." And art exists that one may recover the sensation of life; it exists to make one feel things, to make the stone stony. . . . The technique of art is . . . to increase the difficulty and length of perception because the process of perception is an aesthetic end in itself and must be prolonged.[2]

[2] Victor Shklovsky, "Art as Technique," in *Critical Theory since Plato*, ed. Hazard Adams (New York: Harcourt, Brace, Jovanovich, 1992), 751, 753–54.

This odd, counterintuitive faith that abstracting from the content of experience would yield a more "vital" because less mediated experience was perhaps the central idea of modernist aesthetics. Abstract art would focus our attention past the conventions that mediate and organize our sensory experience. Stripped of their formal wrappers, raw sense data would scandalize the viewing public. In an intriguing essay, Nathaniel Berman has suggested that modernist thought is paradoxically characterized by simultaneous enthusiasms for the primitive and the technically advanced.[3] Even more than Russian formalism, Anglo-American New Criticism exhibited this paradox. As Gerald Graff puts it, the New Criticism was divided between a technocratic-professional "effort to purge literature of social and moral impurities" and a Romantic-nostalgic impulse "to promote it as a form of knowledge that could save the world from science and industrialism."[4]

The New Criticism emerged in England and America between the wars as a movement of writers, poets especially, defending the autonomy of literature and demanding that it be judged by purely aesthetic rather than moral or political standards. At its inception, then, the New Criticism was anti-academic, attacking both the moralism and the antiquarianism of the professors. The New Criticism styled itself as vital, sinewy, aesthetically pure, and uncorrupted by cant, sedentary comfort, and institutional conservatism. Ironically, the New Criticism became the academic orthodoxy after the war, when its claim to apply content neutral standards of excellence fit the postwar academy's identification with scientific neutrality.

While asserting literature's autonomy from the exigencies of modern society, many New Critics evinced nostalgia for a premodern union of art and society.[5] New Critics tended to admire the unity of feeling and rationality of Elizabethan consciousness and to lament the individualism of Romanticism and capitalism alike. Great literature was possible in an organic society or, failing that, an organic tradition—meaning was created by the enabling constraint of generic form, which modeled the enabling constraint of social order and moral consensus. Agreement on the generic conventions and normative assumptions against which texts would be read permitted a community of close readers to find a common meaning in a text. Disciplined reading involved submission to a moral and aesthetic order. New Criticism's aesthetic was organic and parsimonious, demanding that every aspect of sound and sense fit together into a structural unity.

The New Criticism's treatment of the text as nonreferential was not only a negative program, expressing skepticism about the accuracy of representation. It was also a positive program, implying enthusiasm for the sensuous concreteness of language. As such, it shared with the modern movement in art an association between abstraction and the ornamental, expressive, naive, or enchanted qualities

---

[3] Nathaniel Berman, "Modernism, Nationalism and the Rhetoric of Reconstruction," *Yale Journal of Law and the Humanities* 4 (1992): 351, 354–62.

[4] Gerald Graff, *Professing Literature: An Institutional History* (Chicago: Univ. of Chicago Press, 1987), 128.

[5] Ibid., 148–50, 15–56.

ascribed to folk or "primitive" art. To see "the verbal icon" as an abstraction was to see it as potentially an embodiment of the favored aesthetic quality of "vitality." The critique of representation was also a critique of sentimentalism. The work of literature was supposed neither to represent the author's feeling nor to manipulatively evoke feelings. Instead, the work directly *presented* feeling. The New Critics decried sentimentality while sentimentalizing what they took to be the spontaneity of the primitive.

In *Science and Poetry*, I. A. Richards offered an account of writing and reading as sensual experiences, occasions for expressing and mysteriously communicating "impulses" rather than formulating and considering propositions. If the literary experience is nonpropositional, it follows that a concern for cogency of thought in reading literature is boorish, like expecting representational accuracy in modern art. On Richards's view, literature exemplifies and teaches that reason is deadening and repressive while desire is vital: "The best life . . . which we can wish for our friend is one in which as much as possible of himself is engaged (as many of his impulses as possible). The more he lives and the less he thwarts himself the better. . . . And if it is asked, what does such life feel like . . . the answer is that it feels like and is the experience of poetry."[6]

Alongside their fascination with the primitive, modernist movements displayed a simultaneous celebration of technology. Vitality inhered not only in the primitive that preceded convention but in the new that repudiated convention. The machine was the primitive craftwork of modern times. New Criticism, with its emphasis on techniques of close reading, exemplifies the technical, scientific aspect of modernist movements. In its emphasis on accounting for every detail of a single text as part of an integrated whole, New Criticism can be seen as a form of scientific observation. It bounds off a data set, the text, from any surrounding context that might distort the results of investigation. It then minutely inspects all the data within the boundary, attempting to account for every datum. By following this standardized method an investigator may hope to achieve reproducible and hence impersonal results.

New Criticism's technocratic aspect was increasingly apparent after World War II, when it was embraced by the very mandarins it once polemicized against. It has been suggested that New Criticism appealed to the pragmatic, technocratic, unsentimental, and apolitical culture of the postwar universities.[7]

A classic examplar of this technical tendency in postwar New Criticism is the influential pair of essays by William Wimsatt and Monroe Beardsley, "The Intentional Fallacy" and the "Affective Fallacy." In these two essays, the authors attack Romantic and Victorian criticism for attending to the sensibility of the author and the reader, respectively, rather than "the poem itself." According to Wimsatt and Beardsley each of these approaches involves a "fallacy" about the object of interpretation:

---

[6] I. A. Richards, *Science and Poetry*, 2d ed. (London: K. Paul, Trench, Trubner, 1935), 33.

[7] Terry Eagleton, *Literary Theory: An Introduction*, 2d ed. (Minneapolis: Univ. of Minnesota Press, 1983), 43.

The intentional fallacy is a confusion between the poem and its origins, a special case of what is known to philosophers as the genetic fallacy. It begins by trying to derive the standard of criticism from the psychological causes of the poem and ends in biography and relativism. The affective fallacy is a confusion between the poem and its results (what it is and what it does), a special case of epistemological skepticism. . . . It begins by trying to derive the standard of criticism from the psychological effects of the poem and ends in impressionism and relativism. The outcome of either fallacy, the intentional or the affective, is that the poem itself tends to disappear.[8]

What is this "poem itself" if it is not a thought in the minds of authors or readers? According to Wimsatt and Beardsley the poem consists in the conventional or public meanings of its language: "The poem is not the critic's own and not the author's (it is detached from the author at birth and goes about the world beyond his power to intend about it or control it). The poem belongs to the public. It is embodied in language, the peculiar possession of the public."[9]

Significantly, for our purposes, Wimsatt and Beardsley allow that intentionalist and affective interpretation may be appropriate for nonliterary language; but "poetry differs from practical messages which are successful if and only if we correctly infer the intention."[10] Thus, Wimsatt and Beardsley limit their claim about the publicity of meaning to literary language. To what extent do their arguments for formalist interpretation of literature recommend formalist interpretation in law?

Some of their arguments against psychologistic accounts of literary meaning turn on epistemological skepticism about the interpreter's access to the privileged psychological states of authors and readers. These arguments recommend formalist interpretation of any discourse, even instrumental discourse, as more accurate than psychologistic interpretation.

Both essays argue that psychological claims are neither verifiable nor falsifiable; and that the best historical evidence for the intentions of a text's authors and the text's emotional impact on its original readers is the text itself. In "The Intentional Fallacy," the authors ask "how the critic expects to . . . find out what the poet tried to do? If the poet succeeded in doing it, then the poem itself shows what he was trying to do."[11] Critics should use contextual evidence of meaning only if it can be confirmed by textual evidence. Wimsatt and Beardsley acknowledge that "a poem [may] express a personality or state of soul," but argue that it is naive to confuse the poem's personality with the poet's: "We ought to impute the thoughts and attitudes directly to the dramatic speaker . . . [rather than] the author."[12] "The Affective Fallacy" includes a similar argument that the psychological states of readers are unverifiable: "The more specific the account of

---

[8] William K. Wimsatt Jr. and Monroe Beardsley, "The Affective Fallacy," in *The Verbal Icon*, ed. William K. Wimsatt Jr. (Lexington: Univ. of Kentucky Press, 1954), 21.

[9] Ibid., 5.

[10] Ibid.

[11] Ibid., 4.

[12] Ibid., 5.

the emotion induced by a poem, the more nearly it will be an account of the reasons for emotion, the poem itself."[13] These epistemological doubts about the mental states of authors and readers would seem generally applicable to all psychological accounts of linguistic meaning, whether the language in question is literary or not.

The New Criticism's detractors have argued that there can be no such thing as a purely formal interpretation, that ostensibly formal interpretations of "public" meaning depend upon hidden psychologistic assumptions about likely authorial intent or reader response. For example, "New Historicist" critic Walter Benn Michaels argues that contextual evidence cannot be checked against a text because no text can be read apart from context.[14] He illustrates the point with a discussion of the parol evidence rule excluding extrinsic evidence to the meaning of a written contract. Arguing that a literal application of this rule is impossible, Arthur Corbin insisted that extrinsic evidence should always be admissible for the purpose of interpreting but not contradicting or replacing the text of a contract. Corbin argued that "when a judge refuses to consider relevant extrinsic evidence on the ground that the meaning of the words is to him plain and clear, his decision is formed by and wholly based upon the completely extrinsic evidence of his own personal education and experience."[15] In *Frigaliment v. B.N.S.,*[16] plaintiff sought to show that defendant had breached a contract to supply "chickens" by delivering tough old "stewing" chickens rather than the tender young "fryers" implied by the term "chickens" in trade usage. The judge concluded that "chicken" is intrinsically ambiguous so that resort to "extrinsic" evidence of trade usage is unavoidable. As Corbin pointed out, however, there is nothing intrinsic about the ambiguity of chicken—it is the context of the dispute[17] that renders "chicken" ambiguous. Accordingly, resort to external evidence is inevitably part of the process of interpretation; but, according to Corbin, "contradiction, deletion, substitution; these are not interpretation."[18] The difficulty, Michaels argues, is that we cannot decide whether external evidence contradicts the writing until we know what the writing means, and "our decision about what the writing means is itself dependent on some form of extrinsic evidence if only that of our own experience."[19]

But perhaps the extrinsic, circumstantial basis of legal ambiguity is a function of legal language, which is drafted to be as precise as possible. Formalism suggests that literary language is designedly ambiguous, in order to draw attention to language's constructive, mediating role in our experience. Here Michaels ar-

---

[13] Ibid., 34.

[14] Walter Benn Michaels, "Against Formalism: Chickens and Rocks," in *Interpreting Law and Literature: A Hermeneutic Reader*, ed. Sanford Levinson and Steven Mailloux (Evanston, Ill.: Northwestern Univ. Press, 1988), 221.

[15] Arthur L. Corbin, "Interpretation of Words and the Parol Evidence Rule," *Cornell Law Quarterly* 50 (1965): 164.

[16] 190 F. Supp. 116 (S.D.N.Y. 1960).

[17] Michaels, "Against Formalism," 218.

[18] Corbin, "Interpretation of Words," 171.

[19] Michaels, "Against Formalism," 219.

gues that literary ambiguity is also a product of extrinsic evidence. At the end of Wordsworth's "A Slumber Did My Spirit Seal," the speaker's departed lover, or his slumbering spirit, is "Rolled round in earth's diurnal course with rocks and stones and trees." This final simile may suggest a chilling vision of inert necessity to an existentialist, or a warm vision of womblike reintegration with nature to a pantheist.[20] While evidence of Wordsworth's views might be probative in resolving the ambiguity, Michaels argues that the ambiguity is the product of critical disagreement, rather than its cause. Thus, the conventions of literary criticism make available a third reading of "rocks" as designedly and admirably ambiguous. By contrast, the conventions of legal interpretation preclude a reading of a contract as aiming at this sort of aesthetic suspense.[21] Of course, a judge could read a constitutional clause as designedly vague to allow for evolution, or interpret a judicial opinion as an effort to decide a controversy on narrow grounds, leaving further definition of a law's meaning to future controversies. Yet none of this undercuts Michaels's point that ambiguity is a feature of *conventions* of reading rather than the *text* read.

In sum, the epistemological case for formalism rests on an argument generally applicable to all discourse including law: the inaccessibility of psychological states. If persuasive, Michaels's argument for the inevitability of psychological claims in interpretation refutes the epistemological case for formalist interpretation not only in law, but in literature as well.

Some of Wimsatt and Beardsley's arguments are normative rather than epistemological: they argue that formalist interpretation fits a normative conception of aesthetic judgment as rational and impartial. Thus, "The Intentional Fallacy" suggests that in ascribing aesthetic emotions to the author rather than the text, Romantic criticism transformed critical judgment of literary works into ad hominem moral judgments.[22] To judge work on the basis of authorship rather than authors on the basis of their work struck them as simply corrupt and authoritarian. The "Affective Fallacy" charged that affective critics report their emotional responses because they are unwilling to subject their reasons to the critical judgment of readers. Such criticism seemed to exalt the charisma and sensibility of the critic at the expense of the text.

The anti-authoritarian critique of affective criticism is readily transferrable to the legal context, where judges are expected to rationally justify their conclusions. But the anti-authoritarian critique of intentionalist criticism is less obviously transportable, since there are grounds for thinking that democratically elected legislatures *ought* to be treated as authoritative. The analogous critique of intentionalism in the legal context would be the legal process argument that the liberty interests of those subject to laws are compromised if they can be liable for violating the unexpressed intentions of legislative authors.

---

[20] Ibid., 221.

[21] Ibid., 224.

[22] William K. Wimsatt Jr. and Monroe Beardsley, "The Intentional Fallacy," in Wimsatt, *The Verbal Icon*, 7–9.

There was one innovation of New Criticism of great importance for the subsequent development of Reader-Response criticism: the discovery of "voice." New Criticism treated characters as formal elements in fiction. From here it was but a short step to identifying the authorial voice or voices in any text as characters or rhetorical figures. Next the reader addressed by the author could be reconstructed from textual evidence. These steps were attractive for two reasons: first, because these "characters" or "figures" were only implicit, they took close reading to discover—they were uniquely products of critical technique of the sort that New Critics placed at the center of the critical enterprise. Second, by absorbing the subjectivities thought to donate meaning to the text, the reconstruction of narrative speakers and ideal readers freed the critic from any obligation to study its context.

The New Criticism prepared the ground for Reader-Response in another way as well. Its organic aesthetic made density of meaning a desirable aesthetic property, so that the value of literature seemed increasingly to depend upon the creativity of critics in accumulating diverse readings.[23] Paradoxically, the very success of New Criticism in proliferating interesting readings belied New Criticism's promise that attention to the text alone would constrain interpretation. As Stanley Fish concluded, such anti-objectivist theories as Reader-Response and deconstruction would have been "literally unthinkable were it not already an article of faith that literary texts are characterized by a plurality of meanings and were it not already the established methodology of literary studies to produce for a supposedly 'great text' as many meanings as possible."[24] Graff reports that by the mid-1970s "under the influence of continental theory" theoretical inquiry had shifted "from the authority of literature to the authority of criticism."[25]

One important development in continental theory that helped shift authority away from the isolated text was the emergence of structuralist literary criticism in postwar France. Structuralist criticism was an outgrowth of structuralist linguistics, first developed in the early-twentieth-century by Fernand de Saussure. Saussure rejected philology's historical focus on word origins: the important thing to know about a word was its location or function within a language rather than its history.[26]

The premise of Saussure's method was that the relationship between signs and meanings was arbitrary or conventional. As Jonathan Culler explains, the structuralist's "domain is that of conventional signs, where there is no intrinsic or 'natural' reason why a particular [signifier] and [signified] should be linked. In the absence of intrinsic one-to-one connections, he . . . must account for [signs] by revealing

---

[23] Graff, *Professing Literature*, 238.

[24] Stanley Fish, *Doing What Comes Naturally: Change, Rhetoric, and the Practice of Theory in Literary and Legal Studies* (Durham: Duke Univ. Press, 1989), 155.

[25] Graff, *Professing Literature*, 237

[26] Ferdinand de Saussure, *General Course of Linguistics*, ed. Charles Bally and Albert Riedlinger, trans. Wade Baskin (New York: McGraw-Hill, 1959).

the internally coherent system from which they derive."[27] In order for something to function as a sign, then, it must be differentiable from other signs within a linguistic system.

How does the conventionality of signs dictate their systematicity? Imagine that two previously unacquainted people arrange to meet at a public place, each wearing a yellow carnation. The carnation is an arbitrary or conventional sign of their respective identities. Yet they cannot convey the agreed meaning of the sign to one another except through language. Whether explicitly or tacitly, meanings can only be agreed to by reference to other signs.[28]

Meaning then is a feature of entire systems rather than individual signs; and the meaning of a given sign depends on and affects the meaning of every other sign in the system. Structural linguistics attempts to understand the linguistic system, rather than to interpret the linguistic acts the system enables. Understanding a linguistic system means describing its "generative grammar," or the rules by which all its utterances can be generated. Usually this will consist of rules governing what elements can be combined with what others and in what sequences.

Drawing on Saussure's structural linguistics, the Russian formalist Roman Jakobson developed a conception of "the poetic" as one basic function of language. Poetic language is language drawing attention to the linguistic medium itself; poetic reading is intrinsically rather than instrumentally motivated. In Jakobson's view, literary study should concern poetics, the formal conditions for language serving the poetic function, rather than hermeneutics, the interpretation of literary works.[29]

In postwar France structuralism influenced a broad range of disciplines and traditions. Claude Lévi-Strauss's structural anthropology was particularly significant for literary critics. By developing a structural account of myth, Levi-Strauss showed that narrative fiction could be read as a cultural artifact rather than an expression of authorial imagination.[30] The semiotic psychoanalysis of Lacan[31] and the structural Marxism of Althusser[32] similarly impressed literary critics because they involved persuasive structuralist interpretations of the writings of Freud and Marx, respectively. At the same time, Lacan and Althusser reinterpreted the interiority of the subject as an effect of language.

---

[27] Jonathan Culler, *Structuralist Poetics: Structuralism, Linguistics and the Study of Literature* (Ithaca, N.Y.: Cornell Univ. Press, 1975), 18.

[28] Ibid., 19–20.

[29] Roman Jakobson, *Language in Literature*, ed. Krystyna Pomorska and Stephen Rudy (Cambridge: Harvard Univ. Press, Belknap Press, 1987).

[30] Claude Lévi-Strauss, *The Savage Mind* (Chicago: Univ. of Chicago Press, 1966); *Structural Anthropology*, trans. Claire Jacobson and Brook Grundfest Schoepf (New York: Basic Books, 1963).

[31] Jacques Lacan, *The Language of the Self: The Function of Language in Psychoanalysis*, trans. Anthony Wilden (Baltimore: Johns Hopkins Univ. Press, 1968).

[32] Louis Althusser, *For Marx*, trans. Ben Brewster (New York: Pantheon Books, 1969).

Such literary critics as Roland Barthes,[33] Gérard Genette,[34] and Tzvetan To-dorov[35] elaborated on Jakobson's project. A major development of structuralist criticism was the revival of interest in such classical rhetorical figures or "tropes" as metaphor, metonymy, and synecdoche. In a departure from Russian formalism, literary structuralists focused not only on the "defamiliarizing" effects of literary style, but also on the refamiliarizing or recuperative activity of the reader in mak-ing sense of literature. The reader knew how to decode rhetorical tropes, translat-ing "crowns" into kings and "storms" into turbulent emotions. She knew how to translate narrative sequence into chronological time. The reader was familiar with the defamiliarizing properties of literature; in reproducing these properties, the literary author was not inventing, but following, rules.

Literary structuralism shared with New Criticism a formalist method and a disinterest in psychological events. Yet it rejected the New Criticism's aesthetic and methodological commitment to the integrity of the particular literary text. Where the New Criticism organized itself around the production of "readings" of particular works, structuralist criticism sought an "understanding of the conven-tions and operations of an institution, a mode of discourse."[36] In a sense, the literary work was authored by the language rather than the imagination of the author. While structuralist interpretation reduced the dignity of the author, it en-hanced the dignity of the critic by expanding her domain to encompass the linguis-tic and cultural frames of consciousness.

Structuralism met with a warm reception in North America in the 1960s and 1970s. Northrop Frye had already broadened the focus of Anglo-American for-malism in the "archetypal" criticism outlined in his influential *Anatomy of Criti-cism*.[37] According to Frye's conception, Western literary history is unified by re-current mythic motifs and narrative forms that reflect basic attitudes toward desire. Hence, the analogy of literary criticism to cultural anthropology was al-ready familiar. Structuralism also resonated with American critics' increasing in-terest in the implied reader. Jonathan Culler would eventually assimilate structur-alism into the new Reader-Response criticism by reinterpreting structuralist descriptions of literary language as accounts of the expectations and activities of "competent" readers of literature.[38]

One controversial feature of the Saussurian conception of the sign system as a discrete body of rules is that it gives the system a definite boundary. In *Philosophi-cal Investigations*, however, the pragmatist philosopher Ludwig Wittgenstein ar-gues for the instability of sign systems, which he calls "language games." Since

---

[33] Roland Barthes, *Elements of Semiology*, trans. Annette Lavers and Colin Smith (London: Jona-than Cape, 1967).

[34] Gérard Genette, *Narrative Discourse: An Essay in Method*, trans. Jane E. Lewin (Ithaca: Cornell Univ. Press, 1980).

[35] Tzvetan Todorov, *The Poetics of Prose*, trans. Richard Howard (Oxford: Basil Blackwell, 1977).

[36] Jonathan Culler, *The Pursuit of Signs: Semiotics, Literature, Deconstruction* (Ithaca: Cornell Univ. Press, 1981), 5.

[37] Northrop Frye, *Anatomy of Criticism: Four Essays* (Princeton: Princeton Univ. Press, 1957).

[38] Culler, *Structuralist Poetics*, 113–60.

meaning is use in his pragmatist scheme, understanding a sign means competence in using it in a discourse. Such discourses do not have hard boundaries—the range of moves that may be recognized as going on with a linguistic practice, as "within the rules," cannot be exhaustively specified in advance and is contingent on the responses of other participants in the game. There is no common feature, for example, that all correct uses of a word must have. Correct uses are unified only by a "family resemblance," a set of "overlapping" characteristics not specifiable in advance. Wittgenstein concludes that "the extension of [any given] concept is not closed by a frontier."[39]

Pragmatist objections to the structuralist effort to define sign systems by reference to generative rules of grammar have provoked "poststructuralist" criticism, which typically uses structuralist analysis to subvert structuralism's assumptions that sign systems are discrete and static. Reader-Response critics like Culler also assimilated pragmatist philosophy of language, redefining discrete genres or rhetorics as historically contingent practices of reading rather than sign systems identified by formal regularities.[40]

The Hermeneutic Tradition

A psychologically oriented Romantic criticism also remained a formidable challenge to formalism throughout the latter's career. Psychological criticism flourished primarily in Germany, under the rubric of "hermeneutics." Hermeneutics conceived of the interpretation of literary texts as part of the broader enterprise of understanding the cultural experience and mental activity of human beings. Scholars trained in this tradition were disinclined to treat either particular texts or literature generally as autonomous from historical context. One strand of this tradition, phenomenology, was particularly concerned with modeling the subjective experience of language users. Hermeneutic thinkers showed an equal interest in the subjectivity of authors and readers. Hermeneutic tradition is a source not only of contemporary Reader-Response theory, but also of its intentionalist critics.

From its inception, hermeneutics was a practical discipline, taking as its optimistic premise the possibility of rendering objects of interpretation intelligible. Yet the history of hermeneutic thought displays a recurring temptation to offer metaphysical explanations for the fact of intelligibility. The explanations have taken roughly three forms: authors and interpreters are participants in an historically contingent common *language*, authors and interpreters are capable of experiencing identical *consciousness*, or authorship and interpretation are manifestations of a unifying spirit or *lifeworld*.

Hermeneutics influenced American literary thought in two periods: between 1870 and 1914 when American universities were reorganized on the German

---

[39] Ludwig Wittgenstein, *Philosophical Investigations*, trans. Gertrude E. M. Anscombe (New York: Macmillan, 1968) part 1, s. 67, 2e.

[40] Jonathan Culler, "Prolegomena to a Theory of Reading," in *The Reader in the Text: Essays on Audience and Interpretation*, ed. Susan Suleiman and Inge Crosman (Princeton: Princeton Univ. Press, 1980), 49.

model and German achievements in history and philology set the standard for rigorous scholarship in the humanities, and again after World War II, when the European exodus converged with the great expansion of the American university system to bring many European-trained scholars into the American academy.

Modern hermeneutics describes interpretation as a conversation between text and reader, in which the meaning of the text is its transformative impact on a reader. Hermeneutic theorists tend to portray interpretation as a "circular" movement or dialogue between a reader and text, since the reader must find what in the text is meaningful to her concerns, while being open to persuasion and learning from the text. In this way, hermeneutics suggests an ethic and epistemology of openness to persuasion by other points of view, and an aesthetic of openness to experience, or spontaneity.

The term *hermeneutics* derives from Hermes, messenger of the Gods, and it referred primarily to the interpretation of religious Scripture until the nineteenth century.[41] The eighteenth century saw the emergence of a market among increasingly rationalist Protestant ministers in Germany for manuals of scriptural interpretation to use in preparing sermons. These manuals strove to justify biblical texts as historically conditioned expressions of invariant truths of reason.

Friedrich Schleiermacher (1768–1834), generally considered the originator of secular hermeneutics, was also the leading Protestant theologian of the nineteenth century and a major figure of German Romanticism. Schleiermacher redefined hermeneutics as a general science of understanding all writings, with the implication that religious and secular texts were of a common kind. He argued that hermeneutics was not about exposing the rational content of texts for inspection, but of experiencing them in a more fully human or affective way. The spirit or mind immanent in texts of all kinds was not universal reason but a historically situated, subjective, particular human spirit. To understand a text was to experience the emotion it expressed. By thus replacing metaphysics with emotional experience, Schleiermacher initiated modern theology's psychological turn and anticipated many of the themes of existentialist philosophy. He also preserved the eighteenth-century notion that religion was an innate human capacity. Schleiermacher's call for a general hermeneutics stemmed from his view that this capacity to emotionally apprehend spirit was the fount of all culture and communication. Religious sensibility therefore enabled the appreciation of art and literature.

Schleiermacher's account of interpretation made meaning a function of both individual subjectivity and cultural convention.[42] While interpretation was an effort at empathetic and respectful understanding of the author, to understand an author was to ascribe conventional meanings to her actions in a known cultural

---

[41] Kurt Mueller-Vollmer, "Introduction," in *The Hermeneutics Reader: Texts of the German Tradition from the Enlightenment to the Present*, ed. Kurt Mueller-Vollmer (New York: Continuum, 1985), 2.

[42] Friedrich Schleiermacher, "The Compendium of 1819 and The Marginal Notes of 1828," in *Hermeneutics: The Handwritten Manuscripts*, ed. Heinz Kimmerle, trans. James Duke and Jack Forstmann (Missoula, Mon.: Scholars Press, 1977).

context rather than to identify her interior psychological states: "That we must consciously grasp the author's linguistic sphere . . . implies that we understand the author better than he understood himself."[43] Knowing which audience was being addressed and what effect the work was to have on them, "the interpreter knows everything that is necessary."[44]

For Schleiermacher, interpretation was not a search for a mental or metaphysical entity, the author's or the text's "true" meaning. Instead, interpretation was a conventional practice of constructing meaning, disciplined by two assumptions: first, that to write a text is to intend whatever meanings are ascribed to it by future readers; second, that to read is to ascribe to the text whatever someone in the author's position would likely have meant by such language to the people that then appeared likely to read it. In short, interpretation assumes that writers and readers participate in a shared convention.

Schleiermacher used two influential metaphors in describing this practice of interpretation. First, he described the author's cultural context—the linguistic conventions familiar to the author, the audiences available and known to the author, the purposes, projects, and commitments available to a person of the author's social position—as the author's "sphere" or "circle."[45] Interpretation should begin by "determining the sphere common to the author and the readers"[46] and identifying "the whole circle of literature to which a writing belongs."[47] Later contributors to the hermeneutic tradition employed such related metaphors as "horizon," "worldview," and "lifeworld."

A second and related metaphor describes the interpreter's movement between linguistic and psychological interpretation, and between the perspectives of original and contemporary readers as "circular." Each of these perspectives is unstable by itself: the text's conventional meaning depends upon the meaning ascribed to the text by future readers, which depends upon their perceptions of the author's intentions, which depends in turn upon the conventional meanings likely available to the text's original readers, and so on. The context for each contingent interpretive judgment is supplied by other equally contingent interpretive judgments; "Complete knowledge always involves an apparent circle, that each part can only be understood out of the whole to which it belongs, and vice versa. . . . Also within each given text, its part can only be understood in terms of the whole. . . . Here, too, there seems to be a circle."[48] These circular metaphors connote that interpretive judgments are validated by coherence rather than correspondence: interpretive arguments are inevitably circular, in the sense of being without foundations, and they are to be judged by aesthetic criteria of harmony among

[43] Ibid., 118.
[44] Ibid., 151.
[45] Ibid., 115, 118.
[46] Ibid., 118.
[47] Ibid., 115.
[48] Ibid., 113.

judgments all of which involve creative construction or invention.[49] Finally, the hermeneutic circle is like a circle of friends. None of the judgments on which a comprehensive interpretation depends can withstand skeptical critique. Each must support the other. Communication depends on community, and understanding on sympathy.

Hermeneutic thinkers of the late nineteenth century developed Schleiermacher's characterization of interpretation as an empathic and aesthetic activity distinct from science. Particularly important were the "philosophers of life" Wilhelm Dilthey and Friedrich Nietzsche, often seen as links between Romanticism and existentialism.

Dilthey is one of several figures credited with formulating a distinction between interpretive understanding and causal explanation.[50] To understand a legal decision in Dilthey's sense is to identify the reasons justifying it rather than the interests motivating it. Understanding a normative argument implies an internal perspective that accepts the relevance of some system of norms to the validity of the argument.

For Dilthey, successful communication and understanding were fundamental facts of spiritual experience. The ultimate unity of Spirit was demonstrated by the fact of understanding. Dilthey asserts that when taking up a text a reader already has a partial pre-understanding of it. Where Schleiermacher explained the interpreter's immediate affinity with an unfamiliar text largely as a consequence of shared linguistic conventions, Dilthey presented hermeneutic understanding as primarily psychologistic, turning on empathetically reexperiencing the author's subjectivity. Dilthey argued that the capacity to understand was a feature of "life situations" rather than a matter of linguistic competence as such.

Dilthey developed a perspectivist description of life experience as organized by the backgrounds, projects, and commitments of individuals—their lifeworld. Dilthey saw all life activity, whether aesthetic or instrumental, as expressive. The self externalized or expressed in life activity is the only self available to understanding by others and by one's self. There can be, in short, no unexpressed subjectivity and so no inner life inaccessible to common understanding.[51] Hence, like Schleiermacher, Dilthey stressed that it was possible for the discerning interpreter to understand an author better than the author understood herself.[52] For Dilthey, the aim of understanding is the empathic reexperiencing of expressed

---

[49] Ibid., 112.

[50] Some observers view him as a source of the interpretive sociology of Weber and Simmel. (Compare Rudolf Makkreel, *Dilthey: Philosopher of the Human Studies* [Princeton: Princeton Univ. Press, 1975], 320, n. 68, and H. P. Rickman, "Wilhelm Dilthey," in *Encyclopedia of Philosophy*, ed. Paul Edwards [New York: Macmillan, 1967], 2:403, 406; with Georg Iggers, *The German Conception of History: The National Tradition of Historical Thought from Herder to the Present* [Middletown, Conn.: Wesleyan Univ. Press, 1983], 133–34. (Simmel and Weber influenced by two rival, neo-Kantian theorists of the *Geisteswissenschaften*, Heinrich Rickert and Wilhelm Windelband.) Vico is also credited with an early formulation of the distinction.

[51] Wilhelm Dilthey, *Der Aufbau der Geschichtlichen Welt in den Geisteswissenschaften, Gesammelte Schriften* 7, ed. Bernard Groethuysen (Stuttgart: B. G. Teubner, 1961), 146.

[52] Wilhelm Dilthey, "The Understanding of Other Persons and Their Life-Expressions," in Mueller-Vollmer, *The Hermenutics Reader*, 159.

feeling.[53] This reexperiencing is possible because of the common structure of experience that unifies all "spirit."[54] Thus, subjects organize experience into "worldviews" that are dominated by sensation, will, or reason, animated by optimistic or pessimistic "moods," and driven by such recognizable emotions as anger, envy, love, hope. Disparate individuals, groups, and cultures are therefore all linked by a common repertoire of spiritual attitudes.

Contemporary cultural critics are much more likely to see not only cosmologies but even emotions as culturally determined.[55] Hence, they are likely to reject any cross-cultural taxonomy of mental outlooks as metaphysics. Dilthey's answer to all such objections is that no culture is autonomous. Conflicting worldviews are all truthful reflections of "the many-sidedness of aliveness. . . . The contradictions arise because the . . . world pictures become autonomous in the consciousness of scientists. By becoming autonomous, a system becomes metaphysics."[56] Cosmological closed-mindedness, Dilthey suggests, is itself a culturally determined characteristic of the scientific age. Although they may describe the world differently, different cultures inhabit the same world, and it is in the nature of any culture that it can understand any other culture's alternative description of that world.

While the world of life experience was desirably unified for Dilthey, it was fragmented for Nietzsche, containing as many different worlds as there were perspectives.[57] All perspectives were real in the sense that each perspective would yield a view of all the others, and that the more informed one was about other perspectives with which one interacted the more self-aware one would be.[58] Yet the relationship between perspectives was ultimately antagonistic, and each perspective was fragile:[59]

> "Everything is subjective" you say, but even this is interpretation. The "subject" is not something given, it is something added and invented and projected beyond what there is.—Finally, is it necessary to posit an interpreter behind the interpretation? Even this is invention, hypothesis. In so far as the word "knowledge" has any meaning, the world is knowable; but it is interpretable otherwise. It has no meaning behind it, but countless

---

[53] Ibid.; cf. Makkreel, *Dilthey*, 6: "He hardly ever makes use of the term . . . empathy . . . and certainly not to equate it with *Verstehen*."

[54] Dilthey, "The Understanding," 159.

[55] William Ian Miller, *Humiliation and Other Essays on Honor, Social Discomfort, and Violence* (Ithaca: Cornell Univ. Press, 1993), 93–130.

[56] Wilhelm Dilthey, "Das Geschichtliche Bewusstsein und die Weltanschauungen," *in Gesammelte Schriften* 8, 8.

[57] Friedrich Nietzsche, *Thus Spake Zarathustra*, in *The Viking Portable Nietzsche*, ed. and trans. Walter Kaufmann (New York: Viking Press, 1968), 198; *Genealogy of Morals*, in *Basic Writings of Nietzsche*, ed. and trans. Walter Kaufmann (New York: Modern Library, 1968), 555.

[58] Nietzsche, *Zarathustra*, 198 (identifying "our 'objectivity' " with awareness of other perspectives).

[59] Arthur C. Danto, *Nietzsche as Philosopher* (New York: Macmillan, 1965), 80; cf. Brian Leiter, "Perspectivism in Nietzsche's Geneology of Morals" in *Nietzsche, Genealogy, Morality: Essays on Nietzsche's Genealogy of Morals*, ed. Richard Schacht (Berkeley: Univ. of California Press, 1994), 334, 352n. (attacking Danto's understanding of Nietzsche's perspectivism but acknowledging that it is shared or followed by most Nietzsche interpreters).

meanings.—"Perspectivism." It is our needs that interpret the world; our drives and their For and Against. Every drive is a kind of lust to rule; each one has its perspective that it would like to compel all the other drives to accept as a norm.[60]

Achieving a distinctive perspective and organizing a world around one's projects and purposes seemed to Nietzsche increasingly difficult in the bureaucratic mass society of fin-de-siècle Europe. While all perception was interpretive, not all interpretations reflected the perspective of the perceiver. Thus, the goal of interpretation for Nietzsche was not empathic understanding of others, but the achievement of autonomy by self-consciously shaping one's own perceptions. Because of the self-discipline and self-awareness requisite for "strong" subjectivity, Nietzsche viewed such "power" over one's self as the functional equivalent in his perspectivist epistemology of "objectivity" in foundationalist epistemologies.[61] In the inevitably interpretive process of perception described by Nietzsche one is either a creative agent or a passive instrument of reigning perspectives.

Indeed, for Nietzsche the sameness of perspective characterizing modern mass society was a symptom of spiritual impoverishment. Nostalgic for the pre-Christian virtues of heroic society, Nietzsche saw artistic creation—the invention of new perspectives—as the modern equivalent of the heroic commitment to honor. A professor of classical philology, Nietzsche saw the interpretation of literature as an appropriate field for the display of artistic virtue. Indeed, one implication of Nietzsche's perspectivism was that interpretation was a matter of giving a text meaning within one's own lifeworld, not finding the meaning inherent within it. "Power" entailed the ability to create value, and the exercise of such power was the ultimate aim of reading.

In a crucial passage in one of his epigrammatic works, *The Gay Science*, Nietzsche summarizes his aesthetic reinterpretation of classical virtue:

One thing is needful—to "give style" to one's character—a great and rare art! It is practiced by those who survey all the strengths and weaknesses of their nature and then fit them into an artistic plan until every one of them appears as art and reason and even weakness delights the eye. . . .

It will be the strong and domineering natures that enjoy their finest gaiety in such constraint and perfection under a law of their own . . . conversely it is the weak characters without power over themselves that hate the constraint of style . . . for one thing is needful: that a human being should attain satisfaction with himself whether by means of this or that poetry, or art; only then is a human being at all tolerable to behold.[62]

[60] Friedrich Nietzsche, *The Will to Power*, ed. Walter Kaufman, trans. Walter Kaufmann and R. J. Hollingdale (New York: Random House, 1968). Because this, like other of Niezsche's most skeptical passages, is from Nietzsche's late, posthumously published writings, its place in Nietzsche interpretation is controversial, see Leiter, "Perspectivism," 335–36 (views expressed in the posthumous notes should be attributed to the "mature" Nietzsche only if confirmed by passages from his last six published works).

[61] Nietzsche, *Genealogy of Morals*, 555.

[62] Friedrich Nietzsche, *The Gay Science*, trans. Walter Kaufmann (New York: Random House, 1974), 290.

Here we see the rejection of any utilitarian validation for perspectives in favor of aesthetic criteria. Nietzsche's perspectivism does not take the interpreter's desires as given in advance of self-interpretation. The subject itself must be created, and succumbing to creature needs involves a craven flight from aesthetic responsibility: "Every art, every philosophy may be viewed as a remedy and an aid in the services of growing and struggling life; . . . Regarding all aesthetic values I now avail myself of this main distinction: I ask in every instance 'is it hunger or superabundance that has here become creative.' "[63] "Life" then does not refer to practical concerns and commitments, but to a process of personal growth and self-transformation. In *The Use and Abuse of History* Nietzsche suggested that the spontaneous creativity requisite for "Life" might be stifled by a self-conscious concern with innovation. Nietzsche thus revealed that the pursuit of originality might have a paradoxically self-defeating aspect.

The "phenomenology" developed by Edmund Husserl (1859–1938) and applied to the activity of reading by his student Roman Ingarden (1893–1970) takes our experiences of intending and understanding meaning as a given "phenomenon" to be accounted for. As with the philosophers of life, the experience interesting Husserl was not simply sense perception, but the organization of sensation into the furniture of a lived world.[64] But unlike the philosophers of life, Husserl focused not on the practical contexts that shaped life experience, but the mental acts by which life experience was constituted.

In attempting to work out the acts of consciousness implicit in the understanding of language, Husserl drew attention for the first time to the mental activity of the reader. For Husserl, communication presupposed the possibility of perceiving the intentional acts of other consciousnesses.[65] Language use implied intentions to associate signs with certain "intentional objects" and to convey those associations to the hearer addressed. Understanding entailed perceiving the intended associations and the speaker's communicative intentions.[66] Communication therefore entailed that speaker and hearer engage in correlative intentional acts. These acts were inherently reproduceable, so that any two readers accurately understanding the same text would perceive the same acts of authorial intention and so perform the same intentional acts. Moreover all persons have in common a form of mental experience in that the perception of a world of meaningful objects presupposes the categories of language, which presupposes in turn intentionality and a world of intentional actors or subjects.[67]

This "phenomenological" account of communication and understanding has been criticized as unnecessarily metaphysical because it posits an ideal realm of mental objects and acts for which we have no evidence. Nevertheless Husserl's influence on literary theory has been widespread—through the hermeneuticists

---

[63] Nietzsche, *Gay Science*, 380; see Danto, *Nietzsche as Philosopher*, 64–65, for parallel passage from the posthumous notes.

[64] Edmund Husserl, "Logical Investigations," in Mueller-Vollmer, *The Hermeneutics Reader*, 185.

[65] Ibid., 17.

[66] Ibid., 173.

[67] Ibid., 185.

Dilthey, whose last works Husserl influenced, and Martin Heidegger (1889–1976), the German Reader-Response theorists Roman Ingarden and Wolfgang Iser (b. 1926), and the American intentionalist E. D. Hirsch (b. 1928).

Ingarden set out to understand cognition of literary works through a phenomenological description of reading.[68] According to Ingarden, a constant verbal meaning is necessary to explain communication because if meaning is purely subjective or psychological, no one can ever know if they use words as others do.[69] Understanding is a matter of having the mental experience or phenomenological "intention" indicated by the text. Thus, to understand a text is to have in mind "an intention identical with the word or sentence intention of the text."[70]

The experience of reading described by Ingarden is a comfortable one, a "flow."[71] Texts are accessible to us, and we read with an expectation of understanding. Each word we encounter provokes expectations in the form of an array of possible sentence meanings, to be fulfilled by the words remaining in the sentence. Each sentence in turn generates expectations for what is to follow.[72] Ingarden describes the violation of expectations as an "obstacle" that must be "overcome."

Reading, in short, is made possible by the expectations and prejudgments of the reader, her advance familiarity with what is to come. A phenomenology of reading would therefore chart this process of projecting and realizing expectations. Expectations may have to be modified by future experience, and even the meanings of words and sentences already read may be revised as a result of what follows.[73] All this the properly "active" reader expects and assimilates into the flow of reading. If the reader is to understand at all, she must always be there in advance of the text, blithely ready to resolve its anomalies, fit everything into place, and imagine what comes next. In this sense, Ingarden's blasé reader is "cocreator of the literary work of art."[74]

Like Ingarden, Heidegger stressed the interpreter's necessary foreknowledge and presented reading as a flowing, expectation-confirming experience. But instead of a phenomenological inspection of linguistic understanding, Heidegger called for an engaged interpretation of life experience. Heidegger saw life experience as a unity, so that knowledge of reality was self-knowledge. We are always already inside the hermeneutic circle. Accordingly, Heidegger treated skepticism[75] and abstraction or "thematization" alike as symptoms of self-alienation or "inauthenticity." Authentic understanding, for Heidegger, was active rather than reflective, practical rather than theoretical, intuitive rather than methodical, instinctual rather than deliberate. Heideggerian self-knowledge was not self-consciousness.

---

[68] Roman Ingarden, *The Cognition of the Literary Work of Art*, trans. Ruth Ann Crowley and Kenneth R. Olson (Evanston, Ill.: Northwestern Univ. Press, 1973), 8–12.

[69] Ibid., 25–27.

[70] Ibid., 32.

[71] Ibid., 33.

[72] Ibid., 34.

[73] Ibid. 33–34.

[74] Ibid., 41.

[75] Martin Heidegger, *Being and Time*, trans. John Macquarrie and Edward Robinson (New York: Harper, 1962), 194.

Heideggerian interpretation simply articulated an inchoate self-understanding, "working out" the practical possibilities inherent in some situation in their relation to some project.[76] What is interpreted is largely supplied by the interpreter: "An interpretation is never a presuppositionless apprehending of something presented to us. If, when one is engaged in . . . textual interpretation, one likes to appeal to what 'stands there,' then one finds that what 'stands there' . . . is nothing other than the obvious undiscussed assumption of the person who does the interpreting."[77] These interpretive assumptions flow from a reader's projects. For two readers to have the same mental experience would therefore entail that they have the same projects.

This kind of intersubjectivity need not require shared desires. When a group of undergraduates sit down together in a literature class to discuss a novel they may be trying to one-up each other; they may wish to be elsewhere. But they all understand that the situation calls for them to talk about a particular text, as an example of important literature, in ways intelligible to the teacher and one another. Heidegger saw such shared conventions as the precondition to understanding, and while we might question particular conventions, others must be in place for understanding to proceed.[78]

Troubling questions about the political implications of Heidegger's hermeneutics are raised by his initial enthusiasm for Nazism and his service to the Nazi regime as Rector of the University of Freiburg.[79] The relationship between Heidegger's Nazi sympathies in the 1930s and the ideas expressed in his 1927 magnum opus *Being and Time* is the focus of increasing controversy.[80] Nevertheless, Heidegger's impact on the thought of both literary critics and literary authors has been significant. He was a major influence on existentialist writers, and poststructuralist Jacques Derrida. His notion of unconscious interpretive assumptions is reflected in Stanley Fish's Reader-Response theory. Finally, he was the teacher and primary influence on the most important continental hermeneutic theorist, Hans-Georg Gadamer.

Contemporary Hermeneutics

Gadamer returned the hermeneutic tradition from metaphysics and philosophy of mind to the problems of interpreting cultural artifacts. Following Heidegger, Gadamer saw the interpreter's understanding of the past as necessarily and desirably dependent on the interpreter's prejudices. Interpretations are always "interested" rather than objective, because it is only our own projects that interest us

---

[76] Ibid., 188–91.

[77] Ibid., 191–92.

[78] Ibid., 203.

[79] Victor Farías, *Heidegger and Nazism*, ed. Joseph Margolis and Tom Rockmore, trans. Paul Burrell and Gabriel R. Ricci (Philadelphia: Temple Univ. Press, 1989, 4–6, 41, 75, 102–8, 119.

[80] Farías, *Heidegger and Nazism*; Jacques Derrida, *Of Spirit: Heidegger and the Question*, trans. Geoffrey Bennington and Rachel Bowlby (Chicago: Univ. of Chicago Press, 1989); Jean-François Lyotard, *Heidegger and "the Jews,"* trans. Andreas Michel and Mark S. Roberts (Minneapolis: Univ. of Minnesota Press, 1990).

in the past at all.[81] In this sense, we have already constructed the past before we investigate it, and even after the most thorough investigation the past must remain for us different than it was for its participants.[82] Thus, the antebellum period will always remain for us the prologue to emancipation, constitutional reconstruction, and the contemporary problem of "race relations," regardless of whether antebellum Americans could have anticipated any of these events with any precision.

While our understanding of the past is shaped by our current projects, we do not choose our projects in a historical vacuum. For Gadamer, any contemporary project claims, constructs, and gives meaning to some past: "History does not belong to us, but we belong to it. Long before we understand ourselves through the process of self-examination, we understand ourselves in a self-evident way in the family, society, and state in which we live. That is why the prejudices of the individual, far more than his judgments, constitute the historical reality of his being."[83] Because we are historically situated in this way, Gadamer sees all our practical activity, even literary creation, as "within tradition"[84]—provoked, if not necessarily circumscribed, by conventions, of genre, by issues and struggles of past and ongoing concern to a literary public, by canonical works or historical events of central and therefore contested significance in a culture, and so on. For Gadamer it is an historically contingent tradition rather than spirit, consciousness, or a "lifeworld" that links the interpreter and the object of interpretation and enables understanding. Interpretation is a mutually constituting dialogue between past and present, evoked by the metaphor of the hermeneutic circle, a spiraling movement of mutual transformation.[85]

Following Nietzsche and Husserl, Gadamer describes the historically situated perspectives of interpreter and text as their "horizons."[86] For interpretation even to begin, there must be some overlap between these horizons. Interpretive dialogue is a matter of fusing the horizons of text and interpreter. Clearly the interpreter's horizon can shift by learning information about the past—but how can the horizon of a past text move or expand? The Gadamerian answer is that the past we interpret consists not of authors, but of artifacts that command our attention only as contributions to a continuing tradition. It is the nature of textual meaning to shift over time, as the concerns that motivate reading the text change: "Gadamer's hermeneutics insists that the effect, or *Wirkung*, of a text is an important constituent of its meaning. Since this *Wirkung* differs for different ages, it has a history and tradition."[87] Gadamer treats all texts as canonical for some institution, dedicated as much to the preservation of its future viability as to the

    [81] Hans-Georg Gadamer, *Truth and Method* (New York: Seabury Press, 1975).

    [82] Kurt Mueller-Vollmer, "Introduction," in Mueller-Vollmer, *The Hermeneutics Reader*, 38–39; David Couzens Hoy, *The Critical Circle: Literature, History, and Philosophical Hermeneutics* (Berkeley: Univ. of California Press, 1978), 41.

    [83] Gadamer, *Truth and Method*, 245.

    [84] Ibid., 250.

    [85] Ibid., 235–40, 258–67.

    [86] Ibid., 269.

    [87] Hoy, *Critical Circle*, 42.

conservation of its past values. In this way Gadamer treats the legal text as the paradigm for all texts. The meaning of any text ultimately consists in its contemporary application to problems unforeseen when the text was generated.[88] Nothing could be further from the view that textual meaning is fixed by authorial intent.

Gadamer's emphasis on tradition and prejudice, and his intellectual debt to Heidegger, have prompted accusations that his thought is similarly reactionary.[89] Yet by stressing that both text and interpreter are altered by the interpretive encounter, Gadamer breaks out of the complacent, unified world of Husserl and Heidegger, in which everything intelligible is already understood in advance, and evokes some of the alienation of Nietzsche's fragmented world:[90] "Every encounter with tradition that takes place within historical consciousness involves the experience of the tension between past and present. The hermeneutic task consists in not covering up this tension by attempting a naive assimilation but consciously bringing it out."[91] Gadamer insists that because his hermeneutics both implicates and depends upon the interpreter, it should not be seen as a *method*. Instead, it is a challenging process of *Bildung* or self-cultivation.

Gadamer's influence in America has been considerable. By 1979 René Wellek would defend the New Criticism against intentionalism, not by arguing that historical context was irrelevant to interpretation, but by arguing that intentionalism "excluded a proper dialogue between past and present and postulates a concept of history divorced from presents interests and concerns."[92] Beyond the boundaries of literature, hermeneutics has had its greatest American impact in philosophy and the behavioral sciences.

David Hoy, the leading partisan of hermeneutics in American philosophy, sees Gadamer's tendency to anthropomorphize the text as a useful alternative to the scholastic proliferation of mental entities required by phenomenology: "Speaking about the intention of the text" rather than the author or reader "has the potential theoretical advantage of avoiding . . . the antinomies of subject-object language."[93] Having thus anthropomorphized the text, Hoy endorses "the hermeneutic theory of Gadamer, who argues that the text takes part in an interpretive dialogue."[94]

Another American philosopher much read by literary critics is Richard Rorty. Although chiefly identified with the pragmatic philosophers Dewey, Wittgenstein, Quine, and Kuhn, Rorty also claims intellectual inheritance from Gadamer. As a critic of efforts to anchor knowledge in metaphysical foundations, Rorty is chiefly

---

[88] Gadamer, *Truth and Method*, 273–74, 289–305; Hoy, *Critical Circle*, 53–54.

[89] David Couzens Hoy, "Interpreting the Law: Hermeneutical and Poststructuralist Perspectives," in *Interpreting Law and Literature*, 319, 323–22; for other views on this controversy see generally David Rasmussen, ed., *Universalism vs. Communitarianism: Contemporary Debates in Ethics* (Cambidge: MIT Press, 1990).

[90] Hoy, *The Critical Circle*, 6.

[91] Gadamer, *Truth and Method*, 273.

[92] René Wellek, "A Rejoinder to Gerald Graff," *Critical Inquiry* 5 (1979): 577.

[93] Hoy, *Critical Circle*, 40.

[94] Ibid.

interested in Gadamer's abandonment of the quest for objective knowledge in favor of the frankly relativist project of self-cultivation or, in Rorty's terms, "edification." In a widely quoted passage, Rorty links the pragmatist critique of epistemology to the hermeneutic tradition:

> I think the view that epistemology . . . is necessary to culture confuses two roles which the philosopher might play. The first is that of the informed dilettante. . . . In his salon, so to speak, hermetic thinkers are charmed out of their self-enclosed practices. Disagreements between disciplines and discourses are compromised or transcended in the course of the conversation. The second role is that of . . . the Platonic philosopher king who knows what everybody else is really doing . . . because he knows about the ultimate context (the Forms, the Mind, Language) within which they are doing it. The first role is appropriate to hermeneutics, the second to epistemology. Hermeneutics sees the relations between various discourses as those of strands in a possible conversation, a conversation which presupposes no disciplinary matrix which unites the speakers, but where the hope of agreement is never lost so long as the conversation lasts.[95]

For Rorty, then, Gadamer's contribution is to free hermeneutic understanding from the philosopher's stone of consciousness or spirit or being: "The importance of Gadamer's [*Truth and Method*] is that he manages to separate off . . . spirit as romantic self-transcending creativity" from spirit as that which is "distinctively human" and also from spirit as the faculty of organizing sense-impressions into phenomenal experience.[96] In disentangling these three senses of spirit, Gadamer enables a cultural rather than a metaphysical or psychological description of creativity and substitutes "the notion of *Bildung* . . . for that of knowledge as the goal of thinking."[97] Hermeneutics can "keep space open for the sense of wonder which poets can sometimes cause."[98] As Rorty would have it, "the cultural role of [such] edifying philosophy is to help us avoid the self-deception which comes from believing that we know ourselves by knowing an objective set of facts."[99] By reminding us of culture's capacity to change and to change us, by reminding us of the unpredictability of our future, hermeneutics paradoxically gives us a more accurate self-portrait and confronts us with our responsibility to make ourselves.[100] Hermeneutics has taken on the role of the cultural generalist in Rorty's thought: it represents all that is eclectic, urbane, unmethodical, edifying, and morally uplifting. Rorty's hermeneutics is Nietzschean in its antinomian perspectivism and its ethic of self-creation, yet Arnoldian in the civility and tolerance of its vision of a larger cultural conversation, braced rather than subverted by the challenge of the Nietzschean iconoclast.

[95] Richard Rorty, *Philosophy and the Mirror of Nature* (Princeton: Princeton Univ. Press, 1979), 318.

[96] Ibid., 343, 358.

[97] Ibid., 359.

[98] Ibid., 370.

[99] Ibid., 373.

[100] Ibid., 373–79.

The most influential contemporary exponent of hermeneutic methods in the social sciences is anthropologist Clifford Geertz. In "Notes on the Balinese Cockfight,"[101] Geertz offered a memorable argument for the epistemological payoff of a frankly subjective and interested investigative posture in understanding an unfamiliar culture.

Geertz was engaged in fieldwork in a Balinese village, where he had great difficulty winning the confidence or even recognition of the villagers. One day he stood in a crowd watching a cockfight. Cockfighting was forbidden by the authorities, and when police arrived, the villagers ran in fear, and Geertz, who had been engrossed in the fight, instinctively ran with them. This event transformed Geertz's status in the village; having identified himself with the villagers rather than the authorities in a moment of confrontation, Geertz suddenly found himself the object of greetings, smiles, and affectionate ribbing. He was welcomed into the world of the cockfighters and soon learned that the cockfight was the key to the social structure and belief system of the villagers. Beyond this, Geertz found that the resources of his own culture, far from proving an impediment to understanding the Balinese cockfight, illuminated certain aspects of it. For example, the double meaning of "cock" in English helped Geertz intuit similarly sexual connotations in this Balinese ritual of male rivalry. Finally, by unfolding his interpretation of the cockfight in the form of a first-person narrative rather than a structural analysis, Geertz performed as well as defended his hermeneutics. Geertz invited the reader to identify with him in an engaging drama of alienation overcome by communal acceptance and thereby to experience rather than observe hermeneutic investigation. By the time the critical reader wonders whether an investigator can recover others' experience by sympathizing with them, she has already done so in her very act of reading.

Reception Theory

In Germany Reader-Response criticism emerged as an outgrowth of phenomenological and historicist hermeneutics. The resulting "Reception Theory" treats texts as contributions to a tradition of reading. The two major exponents of Reception Theory are Wolfgang Iser and Hans Robert Jauss. Each mines a different vein of the hermeneutic tradition: Iser develops the phenomenology of Husserl and Ingarden, while Jauss is primarily concerned with the historical issues that preoccupied Dilthey and Gadamer.

Iser's best-known theoretical formulation appears in an essay entitled "The Reading Process: A Phenomenological Approach."[102] He sets out to account within the phenomenology of Husserl and Ingarden for the capacity of readers to learn from texts, rather than simply to reexperience their expectations. Thus, he

---

[101] Clifford Geertz, "Deep Play: Notes on the Balinese Cockfight," in Clifford Geertz, *Interpretation of Cultures* (New York: Basic Books, 1973), 412–53.

[102] Wolfgang Iser, *The Implied Reader: Patterns of Communication in Prose Fiction from Bunyan to Beckett* (Baltimore: Johns Hopkins Univ. Press, 1974), 274–94.

aims to reconcile two contradictory legacies of Romanticism. On the one hand, the Kantian tradition of explaining understanding by reference to the capacities already inherent in consciousness portrays reading as an experience that leaves the reader little affected. On the other hand, the tradition of seeing aesthetic experience as a process of "defamiliarization" presents reading as a turbulent transformation of consciousness.[103] Iser synthesizes these conflicting portrayals of reading by characterizing it as a "dialectic"[104] between reader and text.

Accordingly, Iser revises the phenomenological description of the reading experience developed by Husserl and Ingarden to incorporate the idea of literature as a challenge to the reader's preconceptions. Commenting on Husserl's claim that interpretation depends upon "bringing to fruition" the interpreter's expectations, Iser argues that

> for this bringing to fruition, the literary text needs the readers' imagination. . . . Expectations are scarcely ever fulfilled in truly literary texts. . . . Strangely enough, we feel that any confirmative effect—such as we implicitly demand of expository texts . . .—is a defect in a literary text. . . . The very clarity of such texts will make us want to free ourselves from their clutches. But . . . literary texts do not develop in this way for the expectations they evoke tend to encroach on one another in such a manner that they are continually modified as one reads. . . . The subsequent modification . . . will also have a retrospective effect on what has already been read. This may now take on a different significance from that which it had at the moment of reading.[105]

For Iser, reading is not simply a linear experience, in which the reader rides the track determined by the text. Instead, it is a constant movement forward and backward, revising past conclusions and projecting new expectations. What Iser has done here is to combine the formalist conception of the literary work as a complex system of meaning, every part of which depends on every other with the phenomenological account of reading as a process that unfolds in time. On the one hand, the phenomenologist wrongly portrays reading as a kind of passive entertainment—it involves the hard intellectual work of the tough-minded New Critic or structuralist. On the other hand, these technicians wrongly portray reading as an objective scientific investigation in which the reader can suspend judgment until all the data is assembled. The literary work is experienced as a complete system from its first word, because the reader completes it—supplements it—with her own experience and expectations. The systematic or structural aspect of the work, which the reader is obliged to construct to give meaning to each newly encountered element, is the work's "virtual dimension." This is the vertical dimension that enables the active reader to hop about, free of the horizontal linear flow of the text: "It will always be the process of anticipation and retrospection that leads to the formation of the virtual dimension, which in turn transforms the text into an experience for the reader."[106]

---

[103] Ibid., 288.
[104] Ibid., 293.
[105] Ibid., 277–78.
[106] Ibid., 281.

Far from a detached and patient observer, the reader is constantly hazarding premature conclusions in which her own assumptions are implicated.[107] As the reader's assumptions are challenged by the twists and turns of the text, the reader revises not only her conception of the work, but her conception of her self, just as she is compelled to do by real-life experience. Life experience, too, has a virtual dimension, and the self is an ever-shifting interpretive construct, constantly reconfiguring all of its past experience and future expectations into a coherent whole in light of new information. In reading,

> text and reader no longer confront each other as object and subject, but instead the "division" takes place within the reader himself. In thinking the thoughts of another, his own individuality temporarily recedes into the background, since it is supplanted by these alien thoughts. . . . In reading, . . . these two levels—the alien "me" and the virtual "me"—. . . are never completely cut off from each other. . . . Every text we read draws a different boundary within our personality, so that the virtual background (the real "me") will take on a different form, according to the theme of the text concerned.[108]

The reader or "virtual" self is not only different for each work or "alien" self that it reads, but is continuously altered throughout the reading experience.

If the reader cannot remain autonomous from the reading experience, neither can the text. The text is not a static structure but, like the reader, has a dynamic identity. It is different for each reader and with each rereading. Also like the reader, the literary work acquires its dynamic character from its encounter with something outside of itself. The dialectical context on which the work depends is the reader, without whose experiences, expectations, and constructive activity the text cannot exist as a literary work. For Iser, the aesthetic integrity and identity of the read work and the reader's personality are both illusory. The dialectical encounter with the reader completes the work, just as it is only in the dialectical encounter with other personalities—through reading and other media—that the personality of the reader has its life and growth.

While Iser offers a phenomenology of literary reading inspired by Husserl, Hans Robert Jauss calls for a history of literary reading inspired by Gadamer's hermeneutics. Following Gadamer, Jauss attacks the ideal of "objective" history and literary interpretation, since historical understanding is always a matter of grasping the difference between past artifact and the interpreter's particular present.[109] Jauss defends this proposition with an argument first offered by Schleiermacher: that the status of a work as literature, Scripture, or legal authority depends upon its continuing reception as such by a tradition of readers.[110] Jauss's reader is not an empirical individual but a tradition or institution that accepts a given text as canonical. Individuals count as readers insofar as they identify themselves with this tradition.

[107] Ibid., 281–82.

[108] Ibid., 293.

[109] Hans Robert Jauss, *Toward an Aesthetic of Reception*, trans. Timothy Bahti (Minneapolis: Univ. of Minnesota Press, 1982), 21–22.

[110] Ibid., 22.

One plausible rationale for such methodological wholism could be that it respects the actual expectations of ambitious authors, who offer their work to an audience of indeterminate membership and longevity, knowing that the larger and more enduring the audience they achieve the less they can anticipate how that audience will read their work. Jauss eschews this rationale, however, rejecting inquiry into the actual mental states of authors and readers alike. The unreasonable expectations of a particular author or the idiosyncratic responses of a particular reader are irrelevant to literary history, which is the history of conventions of reading. The subject of literary history is "the objectifiable system of expectations that arises for each work in the historical moment of its appearance, from a pre-understanding of the genre, from the form and themes of already familiar works, and from the opposition between poetic and practical language."[111]

One danger in this line of argument is that if the conventions of reading chronicled by "literary history" become too independent of the actual expectations of empirical authors and readers, they may cease to be rooted in history at all. A case in point is Jauss's methodological commitment to "the opposition between poetic and practical language," an opposition that did not become conventional before the advent of Romanticism. Like Iser, Jauss identifies literary experience with surprise and transformation, while dismissing the confirmation of expectations as "culinary" or "entertainment" writing.[112] Because historical change renders familiar and banal the classic art that once was "horizon-shifting," the genuinely artistic or literary appreciation of a work requires reconstructing a historical context in which its effect would have been disruptive. This need not be the "original" context: "there are works that at the moment of their appearance . . . break through the horizon of literary expectations so completely that an audience can only gradually develop for them."[113]

What this suggests is that one could also experience contemporary kitsch as artistic by reconstructing a past in which its modernity would have seemed subversive—which is to say that the study of a sufficiently alien past is itself an aesthetic experience, permitting the investigator to see her entire milieu anew, filling her mundane surroundings with aesthetic import. For the mere analysis of literary influence Jauss would substitute "a literary history of readers," an inventory of alien worldviews. The stated function of this enterprise is to equip the reader to appreciate the otherwise inaccessible defamiliarizing power of certain literary works. But insofar as *unfamiliar* past perspectives permit a *defamiliarized* view of the present, reception history promises an aesthetic experience of defamiliarization, without the unnecessary detour of reading literary works.

Confirming this inversion of the functions of literary creation and criticism, Jauss concludes that literary history reveals "a process in which the passive recep-

[111] Ibid.
[112] Ibid., 25.
[113] Ibid.

tion is on the part of authors."[114] Creativity is dictated by the literary public, not the literary artist; and it is the reception theorist, not the "passive" literary author, who brings the reading public to self-consciousness:

> The reconstruction of the horizon of expectations in the face of which a work was created and received in the past . . . brings to view the hermeneutic difference between the former and the current understanding of a work; it raises to consciousness the history of its reception, . . . and it thereby calls into question as a platonizing dogma . . . the apparently self-evident claims that in the literary text, literature is eternally present.[115]

That the literary quality of the work depends on the context in which it is read raises the question of whether the identification of the literary with the defamiliarizing is not itself historically contingent. If literary defamiliarization is a characteristically modern aspiration, then reading past texts as literary may make them records of expectations that their original readers never had. Because Jauss identifies "literature" with the aesthetic appreciation of writing, his "literary history" cannot be a history of the myriad purposes of writing and reading. Instead, it is an aesthetic appreciation of the past, more literary than historical.

American Reader-Response

In the United States, Reader-Response criticism arose not only out of the influence of hermeneutic thought but also out of increasing attention to the implied reader as a rhetorical figure of interest to New Criticism. American Reader-Response criticism has read its European sources, both hermeneutics and structuralism, through the lens of pragmatist epistemology. Hence, Reader-Response critics such as Jonathan Culler and Stanley Fish often assimilate literary traditions and linguistic structures to conventions or institutional practices of reading. Finally, the theme of influence in the production of literature is also an important constituent of response theory, as it blurs the boundaries between creating literature and interpreting literary tradition.

The most widely recognized practitioner and theorist of Reader-Response criticism in America has been Stanley Fish. Fish has promoted his method as a way of apprehending the uses of legal and other nonliterary texts and attacked the formalist distinction between literary and nonliterary language.[116] Fish's overall project has been to move the implied reader outside of the text. This project has been plagued by uncertainty as to whether this newly liberated reader is a descriptive or a prescriptive concept and whether it is individual or collective. In other words, it has not always been clear whether Fish is claiming to report the actual reading experiences of most readers, his views on how readers should read, his own reading experience, or his own aspirations for reading. He has moved from

---

[114] Ibid., 32.

[115] Ibid., 2.

[116] Stanley Fish, *Is There a Text in This Class?* (Cambridge: Harvard Univ. Press, 1980), 50.

descriptions of reader experience, like Iser's, to more sociological accounts of the institutional setting of reading, like those proposed by Jauss. But his readings seem too idiosyncratic to be taken as descriptions of how people read, and too formulaic to be taken as descriptions of his own actual experience. As prescriptions, however, they seem curiously futile given his deterministic account of reading as an unself-conscious conventional practice.

A consistent theme throughout Fish's evolution is the view that the meanings of signs are conventional—arbitrarily but collectively ascribed. Only by virtue of some group practice are marks recognizable as words, which is to say similarly meaningful for all members of the practice. Similarly, literature "is a conventional category. What will, at any time, be recognized as literature is a function of a communal decision as to what will count as literature."[117]

Fish initially set out to establish reader-centered criticism as a more objective rival to the text-centered New Criticism. Thus, his initial response to the proliferation of conflicting "close readings" was not to celebrate the creativity of the interpreter, but to seek to better constrain the interpreter. His method of so doing was to follow Ingarden in focusing on the role of reader expectations in structuring the reading experience.

Since the inanimate text itself could not constrain the reader, Fish reasoned, it had no inherent formal properties. On the other hand, the social practice of reading had the very definite formal properties of ordinality and temporality. By beginning at the beginning and proceeding to the end, assimilating the information in the text not just sentence by sentence but word by word, one gave the text formal definition it would not otherwise have. In order to give the literary reading experience a finely articulated structure, however, Fish rejected Ingarden's characterization of the reading experience as a trancelike flow. In his two early works on seventeenth-century devotional poetry "Surprised by Sin"[118] and "Self-consuming Artifacts,"[119] Fish joined Iser in characterizing reading as an intriguing puzzle, a tease sustained by the repeated frustration of readerly expectations. In Fish's hands, the familiar identification of literature with discomfiture transformed every text into an ordered sequence of moments of discomfiture produced by an alternating rhythm of premature conclusion and surprised second thought. Hence, literary works had formal properties, but they were in the experience of the reader and products of the literary way of reading.

Explicating his method in the influential essay "Literature in the Reader: Affective Stylistics,"[120] Fish acknowledged that no two readers respond identically to a given work. Nevertheless, he speculated that "if the speakers of a language share a system of rules that each of them has somehow internalized, understanding

---

[117] Fish, *Text*, 10; see also 59–60, 97–111, 322–37.

[118] Stanley Fish, *Surprised by Sin: The Reader in Paradise Lost*, 2d ed. (London: Macmillan, 1967).

[119] Stanley E. Fish, *Self-consuming Artifacts: The Experience of Seventeenth-Century Literature* (Berkeley: Univ. of California Press, 1972).

[120] Fish, *Text* , 21–67.

will, in some sense, be uniform," and that every reader has "a backlog of language experience which determines probability of [authorial] choice and therefore of [reader] response."[121] As a reader unusually experienced in the reading of literature, Fish was unusually "competent" to read it. Thus, Fish purported to describe the reading experience of any linguistically and literarily competent reader.[122] But if Fish's readings were authoritative because better informed than that of most readers, he edged away from his claim to ground interpretation in an intersubjective reading experience.

An alternate account of Fish's authority would emphasize that reading is conditioned by participation in a language as well as in the conventions of some more specialized practice. Yet because language is nothing more than a web of specialized discourses, the better informed one is about such specialized discourses the more generally competent one is in the language. It would follow that the best-informed reading would be the most intersubjective in the sense that it would include the perspectives of the most readers. On this view literary critics could enhance intersubjective understanding by teaching their readers and students a higher level of linguistic competence—that is, fluency in a range of specialized codes and facility in moving among them. Thus, Fish might be read as proposing for literary criticism an edifying function akin to that proposed for hermeneutic philosophy by Richard Rorty.

On either interpretation of "Literature in the Reader," one would expect a fair amount of convergence among the readings of such similarly experienced readers as professional literary critics. How then did Fish explain the proliferation of conflicting critical readings? Fish resorted to a distinction between interpretation and evaluation. The true meaning of the work for Fish was not the intention of the author but the experience of the properly literary reader. Critical *evaluations* of this meaning could legitimately diverge, but the wildly divergent *interpretations* produced by Fish's contemporaries were the unfortunate consequence of textual formalism's invitation to critics to ignore their own reading experiences.[123]

The tensions in Fish's defense of Reader-Response criticism provoked objections that engendered a series of reformulations. A recurring objection was that Fish's readings were paradoxically too original and controversial to be taken seriously as a description of the actual reading experience of most people or even most critics. Indeed, Fish's readings seemed too artfully contrived and too mechanically consistent to be accepted as descriptions of even his own reading experience. As Jonathan Culler argued:

> Fish's reader never learns anything from his experience. Time after time he is discomfited to see the second half of the sentence take away what the first half had seemed to assert. Time after time he is bewildered to see the self-consuming artifact he is reading

[121] Ibid.
[122] Ibid., 48.
[123] Ibid., 52.

consume itself. What distinguishes Fish's reader is this propensity to fall into the same traps over and over again. . . . The conclusion seems inescapable: what Fish reports is not Stanley Fish reading, but Stanley Fish imagining reading as a Fishian reader.[124]

Fish's response to skepticism about his empirical claims was to alter his description of literary reading and to change the status of his claim for his method from a descriptive to a prescriptive claim. Admitting the existence of a plurality of ways of literary reading, he claimed his own was better. Yet he did not wish to give up his view that reading was a conventional practice and that these conventions were responsible for the reader's familiar sense of being acted upon by the "formal features" of the text. His solution was to explain interpretive disagreement as a clash of "interpretive communities" whose members were committed to different "interpretive assumptions." Within such communities there was a shared reading experience, so that interpretive claims could still be unreflectively true for a particular "interpretive community." The determinate text was still "written" by the conventions of reading, but a plurality of conventions could "write" different texts.[125]

The concept of interpretive community marked a subtle shift in Fish's account of the effect of linguistic experience. In "Literature in the Reader," the more specialized conventions one encountered, the more generally competent one became. This emphasis on general linguistic competence implied that each specialized discourse was enmeshed in the language as a whole and that the terms in general circulation carried with them legible traces of their specialized uses. But in his later essays, the sheltering sea of language recedes, leaving each specialized community of interpreters stranded to evolve alone in the isolation of its own mudhole. Different communities of interpretation cannot even understand, let alone persuade, one another.

This new account, announced in in his seminal work "Is There a Text in This Class," had two related problems. First, while the new image of literary reading as a Babel of incommensurable discourses explained disagreement and agreement, it failed to account for the equally familiar experiences of debate and persuasion.[126] Fish seemed to drastically underestimate the capacity of speakers of the same language, let alone such similarly socialized and situated speakers as literary scholars, to comprehend each other. Second, Fish's description of literary criticism as the unreflective application of communal interpretive assumptions seemed belied by his own project. As already noted, Fish did not seem to be describing the reading practice of an existing interpretive community. But if he was prescribing a novel way of reading to members of alien interpretive

---

[124] Jonathan Culler, *On Deconstruction: Theory and Criticism after Structuralism* (Ithaca: Cornell Univ. Press, 1982), 65–66; see Dennis Patterson, "You Made Me Do It: My Reply to Stanley Fish," *Texas Law Review* 72 (1993): 67, 70 (citing and commenting on this passage).

[125] Fish, *Text*, 13–15.

[126] Culler, *On Deconstruction*, 68; Patterson, 67, 73–77; Ellen Schauber and Ellen Spolsky, *The Bounds of Interpretation: Linguistic Theory and Literary Text* (Stanford: Stanford Univ. Press, 1986), 146.

communities, how could he hope to persuade others to understand it, let alone adopt it?

About a decade after introducing the concept of discrete and unanimous interpretive communities, Fish solved the problem of explaining debate and persuasion by abandoning the claims of discreteness and unanimity. In an essay aptly entitled "Change," Fish dramatically revised his description of interpretive communities by restoring the account of language he had hinted at in "Literature in the Reader." First, he acknowledged that specialized discourses were often fractured forums for debate among competing views. Second, the "criteria of relevance" that Fish had always included within the defining assumptions of different interpretive communities now included criteria for the relevance of other discourses. Thus, interpretive assumptions were dynamic not only because they were pluralistic, but also because they were, after all, *interpretive* assumptions, that is, frameworks for organizing new information: "[It is] misleading . . . to think of change as a process by which something from the outside penetrates and alters the inside of a community or of a consciousness informed by community assumptions. It is misleading because it assumes that the distinction between outside and inside is empirical and absolute, whereas it is an interpretive distinction between realms that are interdependent rather than discrete."[127] Fish now described discourses as linked together in a larger network of relevance and organized as Quinean "webs," any part of which could be revised in light of the rest.[128]

For the second problem, Fish found no similarly satisfying solution. The need to account for his own creativity as a reader forced Fish to recharacterize literary criticism as a power struggle among competing subjectivities. He frequently described his own project as a kind of Nietzschean exercise of power, a performative act that created a new interpretive community: "What I had been doing . . . was not revealing what readers had always done but trying to persuade them to a set of community assumptions so that when they read they would do as I did."[129] It followed that literary criticism was not a Babel of incommensurable communal discourses, but a battle of competing subjectivities: "The business of criticism was . . . to determine from which of a number of possible perspectives reading will proceed. . . . In the end . . . I claimed the right, along with everyone else, to argue for a way of reading which, if it became accepted, would be, for a time at least, the true one."[130] Putting the claim more provocatively, Fish is reported (by an unsympathetic journalist) to have told an audience that he wanted readers "to do what I tell them to" and that he wanted "to be able to walk into any first-rate faculty anywhere and dominate it, shape it to my will."[131]

---

[127] Fish, *Doing What Comes Naturally*, 148.

[128] Willard V. O. Quine and J. S. Ullian, *The Web of Belief* (New York: Random House, 1978); Willard V. O. Quine, "Two Dogmas of Empiricism," in Willard V. O. Quine, *From a Logical Point of View* (Cambidge: Harvard Univ. Press, 1953); Fish, *Doing What Comes Naturally*, 153.

[129] Fish, *Text*, 15.

[130] Ibid., 16.

[131] Fred Siegel, "The Cult of Multiculturalism," *The New Republic* (Feb. 18, 1991): 34, 40.

The difficulty was how this lone gunfighter view of the literary critic squared with his account of interpretation as a necessarily social practice in which we do not choose our interpretive assumptions. Once Fish concedes, as he now has, that specialized discourses like literary criticism are not autonomous, the lone gunfighter view of the literary critic takes on an aspect of frivolity and decadence. For now the conventions of literary reading are affected by and affect other linguistic conventions and are not likely to be easily changed. Linguistic conventions, in turn, are part of practices that integrate people not only through discourse, but also through coordinated action. Thus, language use is determined not just by interpretive assumptions, but by shared purposes and institutions—our communities are not interpretive only. Fish treats persuasion as a matter of rhetoric. But before we are asked to change the way we not only *read*, but *live*, we deserve not just rhetoric, but reasons.

If anyone embraces the view of the interpreter as lone gunfighter it is Harold Bloom, who has developed a theory of poetic influence inspired by Nietzsche and Freud. Like Jauss, Bloom views literature as a tradition constituted by interpretation but paradoxically organized by a modernist aesthetic of innovation and discomfiture. Where Jauss focuses on the creative activity of readers, however, Bloom focuses on the interpretive activity of authors.

For Bloom, the literary status of a work consists not in its reception as such by readers, but in its provocation of subsequent rival works by writers. Authors are, for Bloom, Nietzschean figures, driven by a will to interpretive power and haunted by the fear of interpretive domination. The irony is that their drive for aesthetic autonomy is inspired by the exemplary originality of precursors, whose perspectival dominion they are driven to displace. The psychological agon between the aspiration to autonomous originality and embarrassment over that aspiration's origins in tradition makes authorship an Oedipal struggle against precursors:

> Every poem is a misinterpretation of a parent poem. A poem is not an overcoming of anxiety but is that anxiety. Poets' misinterpretations or poems are more drastic than critics' misinterpretations or criticisms, but this is only a difference in degree and not at all in kind. There are no interpretations but only misinterpretations, and so all criticism is prose poetry. Critics are more or less valuable than other critics only (precisely) as poets are more or less valuable than other poets. For just as a poet must be found by the opening in a precursor poet, so must the critic. The difference is that a critic has more parents. His precursors are poets and critics. But—in truth—so are a poet's precursors, often and more often as history lengthens.[132]

Bloom's claim that all reading is willful misreading may align him with Nietzsche, but it distances him from many in the hermeneutic tradition who see reading as enabled by shared linguistic competence or experiential horizons or traditions. For Bloom, traditions are linked by histories of repression, not mem-

[132] Harold Bloom, *The Anxiety of Influence: A Theory of Poetry* (New York: Oxford Univ. Press, 1973), 94–95.

ory; traditions consist in influence resisted and repressed, rather than embraced and revered.

Not surprisingly, Bloom's invocation of Nietzsche is itself a misreading. For Nietzsche, a powerful interpretation is one that frees the individual by achieving reality for him. The individual should aspire to fashion a sensibility worthy of enduring, but the societal response is of secondary importance. Worrying about whether one's virtues are appreciated by others is a symptom of weakness and resentment. For Bloom, by contrast, a powerful interpretation is one that sticks, that has enduring influence. Where Nietzsche's power is largely a matter of psychological self-dominion, Bloom's is unambiguously social.

In evaluating Bloom's argument it is important to realize that he is not making a conceptual claim that poetry and criticism are identical, but a time-bound claim that poetry and criticism have converged at the critical moment at which he writes. Bloom portrays poetry as an historically specific practice with a life cycle that has run its course.

According to Bloom, poetry is "about" its own originality. With Romanticism, poetic practice becomes self-conscious of its quest for originality and so comes to be the expression of anxiety about influence. The Renaissance poets could appropriate confidently, conscious of their superiority to their sources. That opportunity was lost to the Romantic poets who dwelt in Shakespeare's shadow. Exemplars of the Freudian moment in the development of the cultural sensibility of the European bourgeoisie, the modern poets stood in Oedipal relation to their poetic precursors, nostalgic for the narcissistic innocence of infancy.[133] Unable to sustain the fiction of originality, post-Romantic poets have defined their creative vocation by contrast to the hermeneutic vocation of the new profession of academic critics. Yet poetic self-consciousness inevitably becomes critical self-consciousness as poets read and misread poets through the eyes of critics and write to a critical as much as a creative audience. Finally, with the full acknowledgment of the inevitably hermeneutic, convention-bound nature of linguistic innovation implied by Wittgenstein, and the inevitably creative, antithetical nature of interpretation asserted by Nietzsche, the fiction of a distinctive poetic vocation becomes unsustainable and with it the delicate balance of originality and anxiety that enables modern poetry. Poetry surrenders to criticism, the new battlefield of the Nietzschean will to power.

The Intentionalist Revival

While the primary impact of hermeneutic thought in American literary scholarship has been to supply theoretical justifications for reader-response criticism, hermeneutics has also contributed to a revival of intentionalism. Two projects are discussed here, E. D. Hirsch's *Validity in Interpretation* and the polemic "Against Theory" developed by the historically oriented critics Walter Benn Michaels and

---

[133] See Carl Schorske, *Fin-de-Siècle Vienna: Politics and Culture* (New York: Vintage), 3–23, 181–207.

Stephen Knapp. Their arguments appear to support consulting authorial intent in legal interpretation. Yet to adequately account for the importance of conventions of reading in legal interpretation they have to strain their conceptions of authorial intent to the breaking point. Moreover, the difficulties they have in accounting for legal interpretation raise questions about the adequacy of an intentionalist account of literary interpretation.

In his pathbreaking *Validity in Interpretation*,[134] the American literary scholar E. D. Hirsch engaged the German hermeneutic tradition, acknowledging a debt to Schleiermacher and Husserl, as well as a less admiring familiarity with the work of Dilthey and Heidegger. Hirsch explicitly and extensively attacked the work of Gadamer.

Hirsch set out to provide a justificatory rather than an explanatory account of understanding, and to develop criteria for validating interpretation. By a "valid" interpretation Hirsch meant an identification of a text's meaning that, like an experimental result, could be reproduced by any investigator. Although chiefly interested in literary interpretation, Hirsch offered what he believed were criteria of validity for any interpretation, including the interpretation of legal texts.

For interpretive results to be reproducible, Hirsch reasoned, the object of interpretation must, like the laws of physics, remain the same over time. The only conception of meaning that could meet this criterion of "determinacy," according to Hirsch, was the meaning of a text to its author. The meaning of the text to anyone else was its "significance," not its meaning. Yet because Hirsch acknowledged that language is a social medium and that meanings cannot be private, he included within the author's meaning the author's beliefs about the meaning of the text to possible readers. Yet the meaning of the text was whatever the author, possibly mistakenly, believed it would mean to its readers, not what its readers believed it meant to the author.

If textual meaning depended on the actual or probable beliefs of readers, Hirsch reasoned, than it would cease to be self-identical over time or, in Hirsch's terms, "determinate." If textual meanings were capable of alteration, Hirsch reasoned, claims about textual meaning could not be valid or invalid. By this he apparently meant that if the validity of readings depended upon the beliefs of readers, there could be no fact of the matter and any reading would be self-validating.

Hirsch conceded that nothing prevents interpreters from identifying textual meaning with the actual or possible significance of a text to someone other than its author. Yet doing so, Hirsch claimed, would have two undesirable implications. First, by identifying the meaning of a text with the reaction of its readers, the interpreter would blind herself to the edifying impact of the text, narcissistically finding in the text only herself. Second, if readings are self-validating, Hirsch claimed, they cannot be judged better or worse, and the claims of literary critics to expert knowledge must be abandoned. Hirsch stressed the second claim, which, however, depended upon three false dichotomies.

---

[134] Edward D. Hirsch Jr., *Validity in Interpretation* (New Haven: Yale Univ. Press, 1967).

First, in equating validity with reproducibility by any investigator regardless of time and place, Hirsch demanded that the claims of critics be objectively, rather than intersubjectively, justifiable. But literary judgment can coherently claim status as expert judgment so long as it is reproducible among those who recognize each other as experts. Hirsch incorrectly treated private impressions as the only alternative to universally reproducible judgments.

Second, a factual claim about a temporary circumstance is no less determinate for being confined to a particular time and place. Scholars can marshall evidence about the actual or likely meaning of a text to readers of a particular milieu without giving up on the notion that they are debating a determinate matter of fact. Thus, Hirsch wrongly treated indeterminate meanings as the only alternative to permanent meanings.

Third, in condemning reader-centered interpretation as narcissistic and non-falsifiable, Hirsch confused inquiry into the likely responses of readers in a certain milieu with inspection of one's own responses. Thus, Hirsch incorrectly assumed that self-centered interpretation was the only alternative to author-centered interpretation.

Having conditioned interpretive validity on the identification of "determinate" meanings, Hirsch set out to prove that intentionalist interpretation could supply it. Textual meaning, according to Hirsch, is composed of two types of authorial intent, "verbal meaning" and "intrinsic genre." Hirsch acknowledged that neither intention is determinate by itself. He claimed that their combination determines meaning.

Hirsch defined verbal meaning as "whatever someone has willed to convey by a particular sequence of linguistic signs and which can be conveyed . . . by means of those linguistic signs."[135] He invoked Husserl's notion of intentional objects to explain how what might seem to be the private intentions of an author could be shared with readers: "An unlimited number of intentional acts can intend . . . the same intentional objects."[136] The puzzle was why, if meanings can be shared with readers, groups of readers cannot share the same meaning, irrespective of the author's intentions. Hirsch's answer was that because of the diversity of possible meanings any unit of language may bear, readers are unlikely to succeed in coordinating their own intentional acts unless they all attempt to reproduce the objects intended by the author.

But can they do so? When we read *Moby-Dick* or the *Metamorphosis*, the monster we imagine is not the same one Melville or Kafka envisioned (if indeed they visualized their creatures at all). To accommodate the text's underdetermination of the world it describes, Hirsch added that verbal meaning is a "type" or class of mental objects. Because all examples of the type share some characteristic,[137] it is not necessary for all examples or even the same examples to be intended by

---

[135] Ibid., 31.
[136] Ibid., 38.
[137] Ibid., 66.

author and reader for understanding to occur. It is sufficient for the reader to identify the shared characteristic to reproduce the verbal meaning.

Here Hirsch ran into difficulties, however. Wittgenstein famously and persuasively argued that linguistically expressed concepts cannot be defined by reference to a single essential characteristic—usage gives words unsystematic congeries of associations characterized by "family resemblance." Nor, on Wittgenstein's reasoning, can author and reader stabilize verbal meaning by holding a nonverbal "characteristic" in mind. Because there can be no private language of the mind, all concepts are linguistic.[138] We cannot intend what we could not say, and anything we say, as Hirsch admits, "can under the conventions of language, legitimately represent more than one complex of meaning."[139] If language is insufficiently determinate for Hirsch's purposes, so are intentions. Citing Wittgenstein, Hirsch obliquely acknowledged the difficulty. Verbal meanings turned out after all to be the family resemblances evolved by accretions of usage, and hence not to be "determinate."[140]

Hirsch's next attempt to delimit authorial intent, "intrinsic genre," was more sophisticated. Roughly speaking, "intrinsic genre" was Hirsch's term for the implied or idealized reader discovered by the New Critics. To this ideal reader, Hirsch added Husserl's idea that authorial "intention" is not limited to the intended "sense" but includes the intentions to associate that sense with certain signs, to address a particular audience and to convey the intended sense to it. Thus, Hirsch reasoned that an ideal reader could be the object of authorial intent.

How could this intended reader determine meaning? Hirsch argued that an indeterminate text acquires definition from reader expectations. These expectations proceed from an assumption about the overall purpose of the text. (Is it a love letter or devotional poetry? A prayer to God or a solicitation of funds?) This assumption is continuously revised during the experience of reading the text, in light of prior assumptions about the possible purposes of texts, and the textual characteristics associated with these purposes. The purposes that discerning readers ascribe to texts are not limited to stock generic forms.[141] Each text is sui generis, an example of its own "intrinsic genre."

The "intrinsic genre" is not, however, the actual purpose for which a text is written by its writer, for three reasons. First, the author's purpose does not sufficiently constrain the reader, if different readers can derive different expectations from it. Second, the author's purpose is constrained by the characteristics of available readers. If one writes with an overall purpose so unfamiliar as to be unintelligible to any user of the language, one's purpose is not, in fact, communication. Thus, *authorial* purpose turns out to be limited to purposes that are "conventional."[142] Third, since reading involves continuously revising one's conception

---

[138] See generally Wittgenstein, *Philosophical Investigations*.

[139] Hirsch, *Validity in Interpretation*, 4.

[140] Ibid., 72.

[141] Ibid., 108.

[142] Ibid., 92–94.

of the work's overall purpose, the reader's conception of the work's overall purpose is not self-identical over time. Accordingly, it cannot be the meaning intended by the author, which is determinate by stipulation. The "intrinsic genre" intended by the author must be capacious enough to include all of the overall purposes successively ascribed to the text by a properly constituted reader. The only intention that can be both determinate and authorial on Hirsch's terms is an intention to address a certain text to a reader familiar with certain linguistic conventions or "language games."

The difficulty with this solution is that language games are no more bounded or determinate than the "verbal meanings" that they are supposed to determine. Any specification of the game's rules will be in language and will have the same unbounded structure of "family resemblance" that Hirsch already found inadequately determinate for verbal meaning. Thus, language games cannot provide an account of intended meaning sufficiently determinate for Hirsch's purpose, which is to discipline groups of readers. This difficulty becomes apparent the moment we reflect on Hirsch's intended or idealized reader. Novelists address their works to an audience of uncertain identity and longevity. Is it likely they imagine their ideal readers any more precisely than they imagine the characters and other narrative furnishings that the characteristics of the ideal reader are supposed to render determinate?

The texts of greatest interest to hermeneutic theorists—literary, scriptural, and legal texts—are all addressed to groups of readers of uncertain scope. In discussing legal texts such as legislation, Hirsch admits that their authors may intend to delegate discretion to unknown later interpreters to apply these texts in light of their own experience. Thus, "for some genres, the author submits to the convention that willed implications must go far beyond what he explicitly knows. . . . The will to extend implications into the unknowable future . . . usually belongs to the convention system of a law whether it is mentioned or not."[143]

This admission yields two difficulties, however. First, the "convention" that "willed implications" exceed what the author knows may be said to "belong to the convention system" not just of a few specialized discourses, but of language itself. If so, Hirsch's conception of meaning ceases to be of much use in "determining" or "validating" interpretation. Second, Hirsch lets himself off the hook by specifying legislative "submission" to the convention system of the law. Is the legal interpreter not obliged to apply the conventions of the law whenever she recognizes a text as legislative, whether or not the legislative author has intended to "submit" to those conventions? Counterconventional intentions are arguably no worthier of credit than intentions too unconventional to be intelligible. Hirsch quite properly excludes the latter from interpretive relevance. By the same token, legal interpreters arguably may ignore intentions to be understood according to conventions other than those of legal interpretation. This suggests that it is the

---

[143] Ibid., 123–25.

conventions of the interpreter, not the purposes of the author, that properly govern textual interpretation.[144]

Just as the texts of interest to hermeneutic theory are generally those addressed to groups of uncertain scope, they are often authored by groups of uncertain scope as well. The American Constitution was framed and ratified by different groups of persons representing still other persons and at different times. The Pentateuch were collectively written over time by many authors, purporting to represent God. Homer's epics record oral tradition and Shakespeare's plays borrowed from many sources. The fiction of individual authorship may be conventional in appreciating Romantic and modernist literature but inappropriate for other interpretive enterprises. If authors, like intended readers, are often groups, Hirsch's author-centered criticism can be no more determinate than reader-centered criticism.

Pragmatic arguments suggest that intentionalism cannot provide an objective foundation for interpretation. Can intentionalism instead be defended on pragmatic grounds? In a series of articles Walter Benn Michaels and Steven Knapp have attempted to do so. But instead of merely defending intentionalist interpretation as a contingently useful practice, they have argued that interpretation is necessarily intentionalist.[145] The interpretation of linguistic utterances, they insist, is like the interpretation of any other sort of human action: it is an effort to explain why an actor chose to act as she did. There is nothing mysterious or special about language that requires a theory. Thus, Knapp and Michaels's pragmatic intentionalism rests on two claims: the meaning of any human act is the intention with which it is produced, not the reaction it provokes, and speech acts are like other acts. They devote the bulk of their argument to this second proposition, but they do not consider the possibility that speech acts are like other acts because all human actions have social meanings that transcend the intentions of the actor.

Their argument runs as follows: words become meaningful only when some agent ascribes meaning to them. Hence, to identify a set of marks with a meaning is not to read a text, but to write it. Only when we identify a set of marks as a text already written by someone else do we read it. Since it is the posited intention to mean something by an ordered set of words that makes it a text, to read is to ascribe such an intention to a textual author. From this Michaels and Knapp infer that to read a text is to look for a meaning intended by the author of the text read. Accordingly, they reason, all interpretation is intentionalist, and all evidence that illuminates a text's meaning is evidence of authorial intent. When we ascribe

---

[144] A point Hirsch denies, asserting that "there is no such thing as the philosophical interpretation of philosophy or the literary interpretation of literature, but there emphatically is such a thing as the intrinsic interpretation of a text." Ibid., 115.

[145] Walter Benn Michaels and Steven Knapp, "Against Theory," in *Against Theory: Literary Studies and the New Pragmatism*, ed. W. J. T. Mitchell (Chicago: Univ. of Chicago Press, 1985), 11–30; Walter Benn Michaels and Steven Knapp, "A Reply to Our Critics," in Mitchell, *Against Theory*, 95–105; Walter Benn Michaels and Steven Knapp, "A Reply to Richard Rorty: What Is Pragmatism?" in Mitchell, *Against Theory*, 139–46. (Additional works in this collection hereinafter cited to Mitchell, *Against Theory*.)

some other meaning to a text than that we believe intended by its author, we do not read the text, we write it.

Knapp and Michaels deny that meaning can inhere in words, sentences, or texts apart from the intentions of a speaker. They admit that there is a fact of the matter about what these signs commonly mean, but they deny that this forms any part of the actual meaning of signs. Granted that identifying meaning involves ascribing to someone an intention to mean something by language, does it follow that the meaning is *entirely* a function of the intention and not the language? Is an intention to convey some meaning the same thing as a particular intended meaning?

Knapp and Michaels argue that to read a text is not only to recognize it as authored, but to recognize it as authored in a particular language. Hence, the reader ascribes to the author an intent more specific than simply an intent to mean something by the words. To read a text as English is to ascribe to its author an intent that it be read as English. This argument can be extended to codes more specific than languages. In recognizing a text as an example of some genre, we recognize an authorial intent that the text be so read. Thus, even if a text is legible by virtue of shared conventions, it is the intentions of an author that make such conventions appropriate keys to decode the text.

But Knapp and Michaels's concept of intended conventions has the same problem as Hirsch's concept of "intrinsic genre." It still leaves plenty of room for ascribing conventional meanings to the text that were not contemplated by any author. Speakers and authors are motivated to use the words that they do because of what those words will probably mean to an expected audience. Recognizing signs as language means recognizing an intention that they be read as having the meanings commonly ascribed to them in contexts recognized as similar by likely readers or hearers. Presuming that actors intend the natural and probable consequences of their actions, courts often equate the intentions implicit in an act with the consequences an actor should have anticipated. In most practical contexts we interpret speech acts similarly, holding the speaker responsible for meanings conventionally assigned such words in such a situation. The pragmatic interpreter is not concerned about whether her own interpretive belief corresponds to an intention in the speaker's head. She is concerned about whether her own response to the speech act is justified under the circumstances.

If literary authors commonly aspire to lasting fame and literary influence, they cannot rationally expect the temporally dispersed and inventive audience they crave to read their work exactly as they do. Suppose an author associates her work with idiosyncratic ideas, uncommunicated because of ineptitude or intention. Are these relevant to interpretation?

The "pragmatic" answer is that the relevance of authorial idiosyncrasy depends on the purpose of interpretation, not on the author's intention. If the object of inquiry is the author's ideas, then the discovery of a diary reading a work as a political allegory or a roman à clef is highly probative. If the object of inquiry is the presuppositions of readers of popular fiction in nineteenth-century England, the private diary is not probative at all. Thus, the meaning of a work depends on the question of to whom it is meaningful.

"Pragmatic intentionalism" seems an oxymoron to the extent that a core idea of pragmatism is the acceptance of language as a social practice rather than the imperfect mirror of a private language of the mind. A pragmatist account of language is a conventionalist account of language, and it can only be intentionalist if "intention" is an idiosyncratic word for "convention." If Knapp and Michaels's "intentionalism" is a genuinely pragmatist position, then it must view the conventions invoked by a single or multiple author not as means for expressing some private meaning lying behind them, but as the "intended meaning." But this implies that the author "intends" her work to be read in light of that convention as it comes to be socially practiced, not as the author understands it. A truly pragmatic intentionalism can only identify meaning with "intentions" that are unstable, socially contingent, and incompletely known by those who hold them. This is an odd use of "intention." Given Knapp and Michaels's polemic against theoretical debate about meaning, it is a significant drawback that their terminology for defining meaning is idiosyncratic, even "theoretical." One follower of Knapp and Michaels has argued that "canonical" texts like the Bible, the Constitution, and Shakespeare's oeuvre that yield conflicting readings are not interpreted at all, but reauthored by a succession of putative interpreters.[146] Yet this is surely at odds with ordinary use.

"Pragmatic" intentionalism seems particularly inapt for legal texts, which are often authored by multiple persons. A constitutional or legislative text may be framed by one group and enacted by several other groups, whose members are agents of other groups still. It may be applied by additional bodies, and perpetuated by successors to the enacting authorities with the power to repeal, amend, or revise it, and by those subject to it, who may have the ability or the right to forcibly resist its authority. Within these groups there may be divided preferences papered over by vague language, and individual group members may have divergent preferences and expectations for the text's future application. They may have no preferences or expectations about many matters that future decision makers must decide.

"Pragmatic" intentionalists may finesse these difficulties by saying that legal interpretation is "really" rewriting and that theories of legal interpretation are "really" proposals for how best to write new law. In this way, pragmatic intentionalists may fence legal application of texts outside of their data set by definition. The problem with this strategy is it will fence out too much reading of literature. When we turn back to literature, we also find difficulties of multiple and indeterminate authorship, because literary texts appropriate precursor narratives. When an author records a saga handed down in oral tradition, we have multiple and unknown authors, over a range of different historical contexts, much like the

---

[146] Paul Campos, "Against Constitutional Theory," *Yale Journal of Law and the Humanities* 4 (1992): 279; Paul Campos, "That Obscure Object of Desire: Hermeneutics and the Autonomous Legal Text," *Minnesota Law Review* 77 (1993): 1065.

situation in which a statute purports to codify custom and is in turn passively "reenacted" by subsequent legislatures. In both settings, a reader seems "authorized" to choose or assemble an author.

Knapp and Michaels's need to account for multiplicity of meaning as multiple texts renders their terminology cumbersome, risking a scholastic proliferation of "texts." W. J. T. Mitchell has remarked on the sensation caused by Knapp and Michaels's elegantly spare and lucid style.[147] This style is an argument in itself, urging, by contrast to the density of theoretical language, the utility of the language of authorial intent. If so, the awkwardness of their language for describing all the genuinely interesting problems of interpretation is a decisive refutation.

Lessons from (and for) Literary Theory

We draw five lessons from our review of literary hermeneutics. First, for our purposes, meaning is simply whatever interpreters seek. Thus, while we find a reader-centered conception of meaning least cumbersome, this does not imply any special solicitude for Reader-Response criticism. Interpreters may seek to identify an author's intent, a text's verbal meaning, or the response of some group of readers. Any of these becomes the meaning of the text insofar as an interpreter seeks it. That meaning is reducible to the practice of interpreters is a "theory" of meaning with no implications for that practice. Hence, neither lawyers nor literary critics can learn how to interpret by achieving a correct philosophical account of meaning. From this it follows that legal and literary interpretation are not necessarily alike. If there are reasons for lawyers and literary critics to interpret in similar ways, they do not arise from the nature of meaning or the nature of language.

Second, interpretation is a convention-bound activity. Interpretation generally involves putting a text to use in some institutional context in a way that will be accepted by other participants as legitimate. Interpreters are disciplined by community norms. If lawyers and literary critics do read or should read in similar ways, the reasons are to be found in descriptive or prescriptive accounts of the institutions within which they read.

Third, writing is generally convention-bound as well. Authors produce texts for use in some institutional context. Accordingly, authors generally intend that their works will be interpreted in conventional ways. Because writing and reading are often governed by the same conventions and institutional purposes, author-centered and reader-centered methods of interpretation are often indistinguishable in practice. And to the extent that it becomes unnecessary or cumbersome to distinguish the conventions governing the writing and reading of a given work, it becomes possible to talk about the formal characteristics or linguistic meaning of the work. Formalism is the language interpreters use to describe conventional meanings when they do not wish to specify who is bound by those conventions. Interpreters may choose formalist rhetoric as a convenient shorthand when de-

---

[147] W. J. T. Mitchell, "Introduction: Pragmatic Theory," in Mitchell, *Against Theory*, 1, 3.

ploying uncontroversially applicable conventions, or they may choose formalist rhetoric strategically, to assert the exclusive applicability of certain conventions in the face of controversion. Formalism, intentionalism, and Reader-Response are all ways of talking about the same thing, linguistic conventions. It is possible to describe conventional meanings in any of these rhetorics, so that the reasons for adopting one or another rhetoric of criticism are practical.

Fourth, linguistic conventions have soft edges. Linguistic categories are defined by family resemblances rather than shared characteristics. These "resemblances" are historically contingent and so change with use. In addition, the communities or institutions subject to linguistic conventions have uncertain boundaries. Authors prepare texts for use in institutional contexts of unknown longevity and changing purposes. It is possible for authorial and reader conventions to diverge. Moreover, the conventions of writing or reading may recognize this and obligate writers to expect and accept the conventions of later readers, or obligate readers to seek and defer to the expectations of authors.

Finally, while most of the scholarship surveyed in the rest of this chapter assimilates legal to literary interpretation, our view of interpretation as the conventional use of texts in institutional contexts inclines us to see literary as more like legal interpretation. The analogy between legal and literary interpretation we propose does not so much ennoble law as it reveals literature, like law, to be a political arena subject to political critique.

2.2 LAW AS LITERARY INTERPRETATION

Constitutional Interpretation as Literary Criticism

The literary theory legal scholars found available in the 1970s and 1980s combined an increasingly freewheeling New Critical practice with an amalgam of hermeneutic and pragmatic philosophies of language. The dominant note was a celebration of the reader as the primary source not only of meaning but of creativity and aesthetic value. Even structuralism, which questioned the agency of all language users, could be understood primarily as an attack on the agency of authors, enhancing the authority of critics. Pragmatism seemed to stand for the contingency of textual meaning on the uses to which texts were put, rather than any practical constraints on interpretation. Critics displaced authors as sources of aesthetic value, but aesthetic value continued to be defined in Romantic terms as the subversion or "defamiliarization" of bourgeois culture.

Constitutional theorists were fascinated by this image of the literary critic as a creator of meaning and value unconstrained by the text and obliged to subvert prevailing cultural values. The Reader-Response critic seemed a role model for the activist, countermajoritarian judge. Constitutional theorists increasingly articulated this analogy but disagreed on whether the analogy legitimated or discredited legal interpretation. The debate over the legitimacy of countermajoritarian judicial review was reinterpreted as a debate over the objectivity of legal interpretation.

In "Law as Literature," an influential essay originally published in 1982,[148] Sanford Levinson announced that "the disputes currently raging through literary criticism precisely mirror some of the central problems facing anyone who would take law seriously. . . . If we consider law as literature, then we might better understand the malaise that afflicts all contemporary legal analysis, nowhere more severely than in constitutional theory."[149] Levinson explained that practitioners of each discipline suffer from " 'the loss of the sense of doing and speaking in the name of someone or something recognizable and unquestionably valid.' This loss undercuts the confidence in one's ability to ground description or analysis in a purported reality beyond the descriptions or analyses themselves."[150]

If "law" for Levinson meant "constitutional theory," "literature" meant reader-response theory. Levinson summarized the state of the art as follows:

> Against . . . the decoders [of texts] . . . Rorty posits "strong" [readers], who reject the whole notion of questing for the essential meanings of a text. "Strong," it should be emphasized, refers to the power of the critic, not the power of the text (or of its author). According to Stanley Fish, one of the leading proponents of this approach, "Interpretation is not the art of construing but the art of constructing. Interpreters do not decode poems; they make them." . . . The view endorsed by Fish regards "human beings as at every moment creating the experiential spaces into which a personal knowledge flows." Meaning is created rather than discovered, though the source of creative energy is the particular community within which one finds him- or herself. Critics more Emersonian in their inspiration, like Harold Bloom, are willing to credit individual acts of creativity, though Bloom's emphasis on the ubiquity of "misreading," rather than "truthful" renderings of what is inside texts, links him to Rorty's "strong" [readers]. . . . The patron saint of all strong [readers] is Nietzsche:
>
>> All events in the organic world are a subduing, a *becoming master*, and all subduing and becoming master involves a fresh interpretation, an adaptation through which any previous "meaning" and "purpose" are necessarily obscured or even obliterated.
>
> And the argument of Fish, Bloom, and other strong [readers], whether American or Continental, is *not* that they prefer to do their thing as an alternative to the more banal work of "truth-seekers" like . . . Hirsch, but rather that the project of ultimate truth-seeking is based on philosophical error. At the very least it presumes a privileged foundation for measuring the attainment of truth, and it is precisely this foundation that Nietzsche and most of the more radical literary theorists deny. Like Rorty, they do not substitute a new candidate for a winning method of how to recognize literary truth when one sees it; rather, they reject the very search for finality of interpretation.[151]

---

[148] Sanford Levinson, "Law as Literature," in Levinson and Mailloux, *Interpreting Law and Literature*, 155–75.

[149] Ibid., 157.

[150] Ibid., 158.

[151] Ibid., 160–61 (we have substituted the term "strong reader" for Levinson's more confusing "strong textualist").

Once conceding that there is no truth of the matter about interpretation, Levinson found it difficult to imagine any constraint on interpretation at all.[152] Thus, the implication of the law-literature analogy for Levinson was that legal interpretation was nothing more than the imposition of the interpreter's personal subjectivity— her idiosyncratic desires or values or prejudices—over the text interpreted:

> It would obviously be nice to believe that *my* Constitution is the true one, and, there-
> fore, that my opponents' versions are fraudulent, but that is precisely the belief that
> becomes steadily harder to maintain. They are simply *different* Constitutions. There are
> as many plausible readings of the United States Constitution as there are versions of
> *Hamlet.*[153]

Levinson concluded that unless the Constitution itself has determinate meaning there could be nothing separating the individual interpreter's interpretation from her personal whim. Thus, in assigning to each interpreter her own Constitution, Levinson assumed an interpreter constituted by individual preferences rather than any social identity or role. Indeed, Levinson elided the claim that meaning is socially constructed with the claim that meaning does not exist, equating relativism with nihilism:

> The notions of "truth according to the conventions of my community" and "objective
> knowledge as determined by my reference group" differ substantially from notions of
> unmodified "truth" or "objective knowledge." The former exist within the language
> of skepticism, including that most virulent form castigated as nihilism. It was
> Nietzsche, after all, who emphasized the reduction of "truth" to the views of one's own
> perspective.[154]

Levinson reasoned that if legal interpretations are reduceable to personal preferences, judicial power to coercively enforce interpretations amounts to despotism, since "the principal social reality of law is its coercive force vis-à-vis those who prefer to behave other than as the law 'requires.' "[155] If judicial power to interpret the Constitution entailed the ability to coercively enforce the judge's private preferences, Levinson concluded, the Constitution was an excuse for dictatorship rather than a defense against it:

> The role of our Constitution is not only to enable us to pretend that past linguistic acts
> can control future action. It is also presumably to prevent the rise of Nietzschean "mas-
> ters." Nietzsche seems to suggest, however, that a massive exercise in social deception
> is necessary if we are not to recognize the way that "interpretation" inevitably implies
> a struggle for mastery in the formation of political consciousness. . . . There is something
> disconcerting about accepting the Nietzschean interpreter into the house of constitu-
> tional analysts, but I increasingly find it impossible to imagine any other way of making
> sense of our own constitutional universe.[156]

---

[152] Ibid., 164.
[153] Ibid., 166.
[154] Ibid., 168.
[155] Ibid., 163.
[156] Ibid., 162.

The puzzle is whence Levinson derived the idea that the social construction of meaning is equivalent to the assertion of personal preferences. Certainly not from the philosophers and literary theorists he invoked. Pragmatists like Rorty and Fish present interpretation as a conventional practice, caught up in institutional settings, professional discourses, and "cultural conversations." Nietzsche presented interpretation as a projection of purposes, but not necessarily personal preferences. That "everything is interpretation" does not mean everyone's interpretations are idiosyncratic, or that interpreters can choose their interpretations. Indeed, Nietzsche saw the ability to place the stamp of one's personality on one's vision as a great and rare art, involving the subordination of desire to aesthetic discipline. The "mastery" he advocated was chiefly self-mastery. Similarly Bloom, though clearly an enthusiast of individual creativity, testifies to its rarity and enormous difficulty, to the unbearable weight of tradition and influence, to the Quixotic futility of the Romantic ideal of individual authorship. The pragmatist philosophies of knowledge and language undergirding Reader-Response criticism simply do not authorize skepticism in the face of the contingency of meaning on social practices and purposes.

For Mark Tushnet, the leading constitutional theorist of the Critical Legal Studies movement, Levinson's crisis of faith is symptomatic of a malaise afflicting all liberal thought. In *Red, White and Blue: A Critical Analysis of Constitutional Law*[157] Tushnet critiques a range of theories of constitutional interpretation, but his target transcends any particular approach to constitutional interpretation. Western society, claims Tushnet, is undergoing a profound crisis of legitimacy,[158] occasioned by the failures of liberal thought. According to Tushnet, the assumption that all meaning and value are reduceable to individual preferences is the fundamental axiom of such liberalism. Liberalism's reduction of meaning and value to individual preferences follows from a picture of human behavior as governed by acquisitive appetites. The restraint of these appetites requires government power, but the threat that government officials will deploy public power in pursuit of private appetite requires their restraint as well.[159] Liberal thought seeks to restrain officials by subjecting them to mechanical rules, and the device of a written constitution is one expression of this idea of a rule of law. But rules are texts requiring interpretation, interpretation implies discretion, and *discretion is private appetite.* The liberal ideal of a rule of law

> requires that we develop an account of the consistency of meaning—the meaning of rules and principles—within the liberal tradition. Yet the premises of that tradition tend to treat each of us as an autonomous individual whose choices and values are independent of those made and held by others. These premises make it exceedingly difficult to develop such an account of consistent meaning. The autonomous producer of choice and value is also an autonomous producer of meaning.[160]

---

[157] Mark Tushnet, *Red, White and Blue: A Critical Analysis of Constitutional Law* (Cambridge: Harvard Univ. Press, 1988).

[158] Ibid., 3.

[159] Ibid., 8–9.

[160] Ibid., 46.

Accordingly, Tushnet concludes "the liberal tradition makes constitutional theory both necessary and impossible:"[161] necessary, because of the threat to individual liberty posed by the "possessive individualism" of elected officals; impossible
"because . . . liberals had no reason to think that judges would be any less attached
to possessive individualism than were the representatives whom the judges were
to restrain."[162] According to Tushnet it is the function of "modern constitutional
theory . . . to provide the necessary limits on judges,"[163] and thereby "to specify
how judicial review can exist without becoming judicial tyranny."[164] Yet because
judicial interpretation is inevitably discretionary it can never be anything more
than an imposition of private desire. Accordingly, Tushnet concludes, constitutional theory is doomed to failure. The bulk of Tushnet's book is devoted to the
demonstration that no constitutional theory succeeds in the goal Tushnet ascribes
to it—eliminating any role for judicial discretion.

Yet Tushnet himself appears to reject as naive the "liberal" theory of meaning
that would equate judicial discretion with the pursuit of private appetites. He
bases his own arguments for the inevitable instability of constitutional meaning
on the hermeneutic view that meanings change over time, because author and
reader alike are caught up in ongoing social projects and processes. He thereby
rejects the "liberal" view of the author—*and interpreter*—as an "autonomous
producer of meaning."

Tushnet argues that while the search for original intent requires "unambiguous
historical facts," a determinate framers' intent can be produced only by means of
"fundamentally flawed historiographic methods" premised on the misconception
that "an individual's beliefs, intentions, and desires have their character independent of, or prior to, the larger social and conceptual context in which they
occur."[165] Tushnet finds more plausible "the view—sometimes called hermeneutics—that historical understanding requires an imaginative transposition of former
worldviews into the categories of our own."[166] But such hermeneutic interpretation defeats the rule of law because "such a transposition can take many forms,
none of which is more correct than the others. This indeterminacy means that
originalism cannot constrain judges."[167]

Tushnet demonstrates originalism's indeterminacy by generating three different
originalist resolutions of *Brown*. The first inquires into the attitude of Congress
towards segregated schools in 1868 and concludes Congress would have permitted it. The second reasons that public education is as important today as freedom
of contract was thought to be in 1868 and concludes that educational equality
should be considered the contemporary equivalent of the jural equality the Fourteenth Amendment's framers sought to provide. The third would argue that "edu-

[161] Ibid., 313.
[162] Ibid., 10.
[163] Ibid.
[164] Ibid., 16.
[165] Ibid., 38.
[166] Ibid., 32.
[167] Ibid.

cation today is an important part of American civil religion and that . . . the framers would certainly have regarded forced association in churches as improper" so that school segregation should remain permissible.[168]

The difficulty with this example is that given the constitutive contradiction between racist customs and egalitarian ideals in American political culture we would not expect a hermeneutic approach to be very helpful on this issue. The example hardly proves that tradition is always indeterminate. But more important, if we adopt the hermeneutic view of meaning Tushnet recommends, the need for determinacy disappears. Individuals are no longer the autonomous producers of meaning, choice, or value that must be restrained by a determinate rule of law. The interpreter's sense of who she is, and what sort of preferences are appropriate to such a person, is an interpretation of her situation. As with Levinson, the very theoretical sources to which Tushnet turns in arguing for the "subjectivity" of interpretation also bespeak the situated, interpreted character of that subjectivity.

Tushnet's critique of textualism argues that no text has any meaning apart from the potentially disparate purposes of its readers. Even the constitutional requirement that the president be at least thirty-five years of age may become ambiguous, Tushnet argues, if a religious group supports the candidacy of a child-guru whom they believe to be the reincarnation of an ancient sage. That Tushnet must strain this hard to blur the age qualification, however, suggests it exerts real interpretive constraint.

A better argument would be that a precise clause does not make for a determinate rule. Any such precise clause is surrounded by a larger document, by other legal sources, and by an institutional context; this broader body of law cannot be applied without an imprecise and perhaps unarticulated conception of its purposes. Suppose a faculty bylaw states that "no faculty member under the age of thirty-five shall serve in a leadership position." The precision of the age term fails to render this age qualification determinate because of the imprecision of the powers for which that age qualifies. Arguably, the age qualification for the presidency is indeterminate in the same way. The paragraph following the qualifications for office defines procedures for determining who shall "discharge the powers and duties of said office" in the case of the president's death, resignation, or inability to serve. It implies a distinction between a president and an acting president, between the office and the powers. Nothing in the original Constitution precluded Congress from appointing an acting president below the age of thirty-five. As it happens, Congress has never seized the occasion to select an acting president and has never had to decide if the qualifications for the *office* of president apply to all persons who discharge its *duties*. But this demonstrates that the apparently linguistic determinacy of the age qualification is parasitic upon extratextual assumptions about the duties and qualifications of the president, the proper role of Congress, the importance of stability, and so on.

Yet determinacy is determinacy whether it comes from language or social consensus. Tushnet concedes that much of the constitutional text has a meaning sup-

[168] Ibid., 41–43.

plied by practice rather than interpretation. But he counters weakly that the durability of settled practice "rests on contingent social facts."[169] His point is that textual language can never resolve social controversy. But this confirms that the roots of hermeneutic crisis are to be found in particular social controversies, like that over racial inclusion, not in the inherent indeterminacy of language.

How seriously should we take Tushnet's interpretive skepticism, given that it rests on a "liberal" account of language he condemns as naive? It is tempting to read him as arguing that the individualist premises of liberal thought should be rejected: that the socially constructed character of meaning implies that value is also embedded in social practices, not individual utility functions. If the motives of human action are social values rather than private preferences, perhaps collective action will not inevitably be hijacked by the officials elected to carry it out. Tushnet sometimes argues in this vein, invoking a communitarian and civic-minded "republican tradition" that rivals liberalism in American political thought. But in the end he shies away from endorsing a republican alternative to liberal political thought, on the ground that the civic community it exalts could be oppressive or exclusive. Could constitutional theory be aimed not at solving the philosophical contradictions that Tushnet ascribes to an atomistic liberalism, but at solving the problems of minority rights that trouble Tushnet himself? Rather than developing and defending a political theory better than the atomistic liberalism he critiques, Tushnet asserts—without argument—the futility of this aspiration, ending the book with the epigram "Neither the liberal tradition nor the republican one can accommodate the aspects of experience that the other takes as central. Critique is all there is."[170] This concluding non sequitur suggests that the skepticism that Tushnet ascribes to a philosophically naive "liberalism" is really his own.

Law and Literature as Crisis Management

Like the critics of legal interpretation, many of its defenders drew upon an amalgam of hermeneutic and reader-oriented literary theory. One of the most controversial of these hermeneutic defenses was Owen Fiss's 1982 essay "Objectivity and Interpretation,"[171] in which he joined issue with Levinson.

Fiss began by conceding that legal interpretation is not determined by text or authorial intent. He characterized legal interpretation as a dialogue between text and reader, citing hermeneutic theorists Charles Taylor and Clifford Geertz. Yet Fiss also agreed with Levinson that if legal interpretation is not "objective," it is illegitimate. Fiss sought to legitimize interpretation by developing an indulgent standard of objectivity. Interpretation is objective, Fiss posited, as long as individual interpreters do not interpret as they wish. Fiss drew upon the authority of such pragmatists as Wittgenstein, Thomas Kuhn, and even Fish to argue that, though

[169] Ibid., 64.
[170] Ibid., 318.
[171] Owen Fiss, "Objectivity and Interpretation," *Stanford Law Review* 34 (1982): 739.

unconstrained by text or authorial intent, individual legal interpreters are constrained by the norms of their communities of interpretation. In particular, Fiss added that legal interpreters are constrained by the "disciplining rules" of the legal profession. These rules required, among other things, that judicial interpreters strive to be impartial and to set their own desires aside.

Fiss emphasized that "objectivity" in his sense characterizes an attitude, not a result. Objectivity does not require that interpreters succeed in following rules, only that they strive to do so. It does not demand that interpretations be constrained by something outside of the interpreter; it demands only that interpreters *feel* constrained—that they do not feel free to do as they wish. He added that judicial and other authoritative interpreters feel constrained by the weight of responsibility implicit in knowing their decisions will be enforced, will make a difference for the parties to a dispute, and will reflect on the legitimacy of the institution the interpreter represents. The judge "quickly learns how to read in a way that avoids crises."[172]

Finally, Fiss argued that those who, like Levinson, assert that interpretation is not objective are "nihilists" in the sense that they deny that there is any external object of interpretation for the interpreter to defer to. Thus, he continued, Levinson's claim that constitutional interpretation is not objective implies that American society has no constitutive or public values. He warned that if Americans conclude that American society has no constitutive or shared values, social solidarity and cooperation will be seriously eroded and American culture will be impoverished. We are morally obliged to reaffirm "the truth of that which is being denied—. . . that the Constitution embodies a public morality and that a public life founded on that morality can be rich and inspiring."[173]

This defense of interpretation suffered from a surfeit of arguments for the objectivity of interpretation, inadequately distinguished. Fiss offered three quite different versions of the claim that legal interpretation, though unconstrained by text and authorial intent, is conditioned by social norms: (1) legal interpretation is constrained by the expectations of other lawyers, (2) legal interpretation is constrained by interpretive canons or "rules," and (3) constitutional interpretation is constrained by widely shared public values. This third argument is familiar to us as a variant of the evolutionary constitutionalism that played a prominent role in progressive jurisprudence. A fourth argument, drawn from Wechsler, claimed that legal interpretation is characterized by an attitude of self-effacing deference to norms that the interpreter experiences as independent of her own preferences. This claim replaced actual obedience to lawyerly expectations, interpretive canons, or public values with the subjective feeling of trying to obey them. It turned objectivity into a subjective attitude—a way of exercising discretion, not an absence of discretion. Thus, Fiss never clarified whether his three types of social norms actually determine results or merely inspire the authoritative interpreter with the requisite humility.

[172] Ibid., 754.
[173] Ibid., 763.

Fiss's failure to distinguish his four arguments for the objectivity of interpretation created an impression of confusion and meant that the weakness of any one claim could discredit the whole. His concluding warning of the dangers of conceding the subjectivity of constitutional interpretation sounded like an excuse for repressing an inconvenient truth. His assertion that authoritative interpreters are constrained by the awareness of the enforceability of their decisions dangerously approached a claim that authority is self-justifying, that power deserves deference merely because its exercise is such a chore. The result was that Fiss's encomium to objectivity seemed, in its partiality to the powers that be, to betray the very virtue it preached.

In "Fish v. Fiss" Fish strove to show that his own and Fiss's similarly sounding accounts of interpretation were not the same. Fish zeroed in on Fiss's phrase "disciplining rules":

> The claim is that, given a particular situation, the rules tell you what to do and prevent you from simply doing whatever you like. The trouble is that they don't. If the rules are to function as Fiss would have them function—to "constrain the interpreter"—they themselves must be available or "readable" independently of the interpretation; that is, they must directly declare their own significance to any observer, no matter what his perspective. . . . Unfortunately, rules are texts. They are in need of interpretation and cannot themselves serve as constraints on interpretation.[174]

Yet despite this rebuke, Fish in essence agreed with Fiss that meaning is determined by the exigencies of a shared social practice. Fish substituted for the idea of constraint by rules, a claim that readers are "constrained by the assumptions and categories of understanding embodied in" a practice.[175] He rejected the idea that these assumptions stand apart from the subjectivity or discretion of the interpreter, in favor of a view that they constitute that subjectivity. According to this view, while there is no (stable) object of interpretation, neither is there an interpreting subject. Instead, there is a practice, the point of which supplies an impersonal perspective on the problems it at once encounters and constitutes. Yet how different is this view from Fiss's equation of objectivity with fidelity to role? Fish concluded that Fiss's defense against the threat of nihilism was superfluous because the threat was impossible. Thus, Fish ascribed Levinson's anxiety about the legitimacy of legal interpretation to Fiss and ridiculed Fiss for offering Levinson substantially the same answer that Fish offered Fiss.

For other critics, including Levinson, the chink in Fiss's armor was his Bickelian notion of public values. Fiss all but admitted he was determined to believe that some values were genuinely public or shared, regardless of the evidence. Yet "the public" is not as homogeneous a community as the legal profession. Hence, the kind of agreement that, according to Fish, arises from participation in a common practice is less likely to inform the general public's notions of equality and freedom. Levinson confessed, "I share both Fiss's basic social and political values

---

[174] Fish, *Doing What Comes Naturally*, 121 (emphasis added).
[175] Ibid., 127.

... and his unhappiness about the implications of 'nihilism.' But a desire, however understandable, to combat it does not equal the ability to do so.... The united interpretive community that is necessary to Fiss's own argument simply does not exist."[176] A related objection was offered in "Objectivity and Interest,"[177] by Paul Brest. For Brest, the predictability of interpretive outcomes and the self-discipline of legal interpreters are not enough to legitimize legal interpretation, given legal interpreters' homogeneity and privileged status:

> Hopes for scientific objectivity in legal interpretation are on a par with the fantasy of a single, objective reading of *Hamlet* or Balinese culture. Therefore, one must confront the question of the relationship . . . between the composition of the dominant legal community and the outcomes of its interpretations. . . . It isn't a matter of good or bad faith. Try as we will, we cannot escape the perspectives that come with our particular backgrounds and experiences. . . . Professor Fiss regards both the exclusivity of the legal community and its tendency to impose its views on others as regrettable costs . . . that must be paid to ensure the rule of law. . . . I wonder whether our commitment to the rule of law, as to other "public values," is not related to our fortunate status within this society. Much of our commitment to *the* rule of law really seems a commitment to the rule of *our* law.[178]

Brest's "good-faith" questioning of the legitimacy of his own power and privilege contends with his admission that "good faith" cannot restrain power or erase privilege. He cannot quite give up the legal process scholar's "faith" that the savoring of deliberative ambivalence, the candid admission of doubt, can legitimize an admittedly dubious result. The constitutional theorist's honest confession that there are no constitutive values to interpret is not nihilism, but an expression of faith in the ultimate public value, the *process* value of honesty: "I do not think this is nihilism. Rather, I believe that examining the 'rule of law'—even at the risk of discovering that it is entirely illusory—is a necessary step toward a society that can satisfy the aspirations that make us hold to the concept so tenaciously."[179] The sincerity of the Legal Process scholars' commitment to the rule of law can only be proven by the very process of doubt that Fiss fears.

Levinson, who, like Brest, humbly confesses his own inability to self-deceive, closes with an identical profession of faith: "we who take the constitutional firmament seriously continue . . . to write our articles and dispute with one another. . . . All such writing (and reading) is a supreme act of faith. We can hope that some future conjunction of author and reader will provide a common language of constitutional discourse . . . but for now we can only await its coming."[180] While these responses reject the claim that shared public values can guide constitutional interpretation, they do not reject Fiss's argument that a self-

---

[176] Levinson, "Law as Literature," 172.

[177] Paul Brest, "Objectivity and Interest," *Stanford Law Review* 34 (1982): 765.

[178] Ibid., 771–72.

[179] Ibid., 773.

[180] Levinson, "Law as Literature," 173.

effacing attitude can legitimize interpretation. Instead, they aim to self-efface more successfully.

That the failure of "Objectivity and Interpretation" was more rhetorical than theoretical becomes apparent when its withering reception is compared to the warmth greeting an essay making a similar argument more elliptically: Robert Cover's "Violence and the Word."[181] In an earlier essay,[182] Cover had challenged Bickel's vision of the courts as society's harmless interlocutors. Society, according to Cover, houses a plurality of normative visions in a plurality of normative worlds. The courts, however, are "jurispathic": in resolving disputes they endorse one normative vision at the expense of others and may thereby destroy the social conditions in which the disfavored visions flourish. In "Violence and the Word," Cover appeared to extend his indictment of courts as more destructive than discursive:

> Legal interpretation takes place in a field of pain and death. . . . Legal interpretive acts signal and occasion the imposition of violence upon others: A judge articulates her understanding of a text, and as a result, somebody loses his freedom, his property, his children, even his life. Interpretations in law also constitute justifications for violence which has already occurred or which is about to occur. When interpreters have finished their work, they frequently leave behind victims whose lives have been torn apart by these organized, social practices of violence. Neither legal interpretation nor the violence it occasions may be properly understood apart from one another. This much is obvious, though the growing literature that argues for the centrality of interpretive practices in law blithely ignores it.[183]

This forceful opening acknowledges that "violence" and "the word" are both part of law. But in flaunting its own irreverence, this passage stresses the "violence" it calls unmentionable and slips "the word" by in its shadow. As a result, the paragraph appears to herald a rejection of the view, shared by Levinson and Fiss, that law is interpretation. Law, it seems to be saying, is violence rather than discourse.

Or is it? Immediately before the concluding indictment of the "blithe" legal humanities "literature" Cover quietly admits that law's violence may not be understood apart from legal interpretation. Though he attacks the law-literature analogy, he partially defends legal interpretation. In his account it is neither so harmless as its celebrants imply, nor so freewheeling as its critics fear—indeed, it is constrained by its very dangerousness. Law's violence is a cooperative achievement, requiring all the judicial diplomacy and tact that Bickel saw as an index of law's harmlessness.

On Cover's account, legal interpretation is constrained, not by language, not by disciplining rules, not by fundamental values. Legal interpretation is con-

---

[181] Robert M. Cover, "Violence and the Word," *Yale Law Journal* 95 (1986): 1601.

[182] Robert Cover, "The Supreme Court, 1982 Term—Foreword: *Nomos* and Narrative," *Harvard Law Review* 97 (1983): 4.

[183] Cover, "Violence and the Word," 1601.

strained in a legal system like our own by the dispersion of coercive power among many actors. The need to engage the cooperation of all these actors in making the judicial "word" effective as "violence" is what disciplines judges:

> Legal interpretation . . . can never be "free"; it can never be the function of an understanding of the text or word alone. . . . Legal interpretation must be capable of transforming itself into action; it must be capable of overcoming inhibitions against violence in order to generate its requisite deeds; it must be capable of massing a sufficient degree of violence to deter reprisal and revenge. In order to maintain these critical links to effective violent behavior, legal interpretation must reflexively consider its own social organization. In so reflecting, the interpreter thereby surrenders something of his independence of mind and autonomy of judgment. . . . Coherent legal meaning . . . is an element potentially in tension with the need to generate effective action in a violent context. And neither effective action nor coherent meaning can be maintained, separately or together, without an entire structure of social cooperation. Thus, legal interpretation is a form of bonded interpretation, bound at once to practical application (to the deeds it implies) and to the ecology of jurisdictional roles (the conditions of effective domination). The bonds are reciprocal. For the deeds of social violence as we know them also require that they be rendered intelligible—that they be both subject to interpretation and to the specialized and constrained forms of behavior that are "roles."[184]

The judge is unfree because she must motivate others to overcome their scruples and their fear of reprisal to commit violence. Though the judge must accommodate the will of other actors in the legal system, this in no way requires that the will of these other actors be transparently legible. To the contrary, pressure on all parties to conform arises from the diffusion of power in modern society among anonymous masses known only by function or social position. This situation entails that the legitimacy of any public act is frighteningly contingent on the barely predictable responses of countless pitiless strangers. The judge must convince those who execute judgments that their task is uncontroversial, unnoticeable, routine. Cover reveals judicial discipline as something more prosaic than the Nietzschean artistry feared by Levinson or the Ciceronian self-restraint celebrated by Fiss—it is the impulse of the petty bureaucrat in a world of petty bureaucrats to keep head down and butt covered. The predictability of judicial decision making is not a matter of conformity to rule, but of leaving undisturbed roles, routines, patterns of power, unspoken assumptions, and all the other sleeping dogs of authority—it is a matter of, in Fiss's phrase, reading in a way that "avoids crises." It is as far removed as possible from the modernist aesthetic imperative to defamiliarize and provoke. The mood of detachment experienced by legal functionaries is a symptom not of aesthetic contemplation but of moral inurement and self-alienation.

Cover's Kafkaesque account of a legal system as a hive of paranoid, craven functionaries, briskly moving death warrants off their desks and consciences, is not a pretty picture. It is no "vital national seminar"; its discourse is not poetry

---

[184] Ibid., 1617–18.

or prayer; its participants are neither "virtuous" nor "principled." Yet they are engaged in something like Bickel's "colloquy" with other institutions and power centers: they are discreet and deferential, they do avoid crises. They are fortunately less dangerous than they might be:

> As long as death and pain are part of our political world, it is essential that they be at the center of law. The alternative is truly unacceptable—that they be within our polity but outside the discipline of the collective decision rules and the individual efforts to achieve outcomes through those rules. The fact that we require many voices is not, then, an accident or peculiarity of our jurisdictional rules. It is intrinsic to whatever achievement is possible in the domesticating of violence.[185]

This, like "Objectivity and Interpretation," is a legal process *defense* of the rule of law. It owes a debt to Bickel—but a Bickel inverted, pickled in irony.

Unlike Bickel or Fiss, Cover makes no pretense that obedience to legal judgments is secured by the invocation of public values.[186] Judgments are justified, not to the public, certainly not to the victims, but to the perpetrators: "The function of ideology is much more significant in justifying an order to those who principally benefit from it and who must defend it than it is in hiding the nature of the order from those who are its victims."[187] Thus, Cover's defense of the rule of law declines to dignify the perpetrators and beneficiaries of official violence as genteel "elites," encaged by privilege, ennobled by good intentions. Far from Nietzschean supermen, they are stunted souls whose very self-delusions lack grace and scope. They are constrained, not by virtue, but by cowardice. The rule of law is a dirty job that—luckily—requires neither Bickelian virtue nor Nietzschean virtuosity. A rhetorical marvel, "Violence and the Word" offers us all the benefits of a rule of law free of any obligation to admire—or identify with—its administrators.

Like Fiss and Cover, Philip Bobbitt has also offered a defense of legal and especially constitutional interpretation that emphasizes the conventions of professional practice. In *Constitutional Interpretation* (1991), he criticizes Levinson and Tushnet for assessing constitutional interpretation from a position of skepticism external to the enterprise. Yet his claim is not that these conventions render the results of constitutional interpretation predictable. To the contrary, he argues that because the conventions of constitutional argument are diverse and incommensurable, constitutional interpretation is as indeterminate as its critics claim. What Bobbitt takes issue with is the assumption that the indeterminacy of constitutional argument renders judicial interpretation of the constitution illegitimate. He argues that the very flexibility of constitutional interpretation makes it an inclusive, adaptive, and ultimately co-optive process of dialogue.

Bobbitt rejects the assumption that a practice is presumptively illegitimate unless shown to be objective: that assumption, he endeavors to show, is the product of either a skepticism external to the practice of constitutional argument, or a

---

[185] Ibid., 1628.
[186] Ibid., 1608.
[187] Ibid.

single-minded empiricism that disrespects the pluralism of constitutional argument. For Bobbitt, legal argument is a culture or language game, not a science. Its validity consists in its continued use rather than its correspondence to any empirical state of affairs, whether authorial intentions, majority preferences, or economic welfare. It is a practice, rather than a product, warranted by its persistence rather than its pedigree: "Law is something we do, not something we have as a consequence of something we do."[188]

Bobbitt endeavors to implicate the reader in the practice of constitutional argument by placing her inside its culture. Of his 1982 work *Constitutional Fate*, he wrote "My aim . . . is to plunge the reader into a world, the experience of which will cultivate a particular sensibility toward the Constitution."[189] He proceeded to argue that having entered the culture of constitutional argument the reader had already collaborated in perpetuating its legitimacy. For readers of *Constitutional Fate*, acceptance of the legitimacy of constitutional interpretation was "fated" because it was the constitutive condition of the book's legibility.

Bobbitt identifies six different "modalities" of constitutional argument or ways of supporting a claim about constitutional law. These include such familiar practices as "textual" argument, the parsing of the Constitution's text; "historical" argument, the determination of original intent; and "doctrinal" argument, the application of precedent. But they also include some less familiar styles of argument: the "structural" argument that Charles Black explicated and defended; adversion to Bickel's "prudential" concerns about decisions provoking popular disaffection from the Court or constitutional principle; and finally, what Bobbitt calls "ethical" argument. This last type of argument invokes values central to the American constitutional "ethos"—something like Bickel's "principles." The American ethos does not, according to Bobbitt, include just any value popular with the American public, but values expressed in the Constitution itself, for the Constitution is "our Mona Lisa, our Eiffel Tower, our Marseillaise."[190] Constitutional "ethics" have a cultural authenticity that mere popular opinion does not. Bobbitt has in mind chiefly the "ethic" of limited government, so important in Charles Black's defense of judicial review.[191] Much of the argument of *Constitutional Fate* is devoted to showing that these styles of constitutional argument are authoritatively embedded in constitutional law, by virtue of their use by the Supreme Court in leading cases.[192] Yet the modalities do not fare equally in his hands: historical and prudential argument are disfavored relative to those modalities anchored in the constitutional text.

That the "grammar" of constitutional argument embraces a variety of incommensurable modalities of argument, premised on competing conceptions of the function of a constitution, "allows different groups in America to claim the Con-

---

[188] Philip Bobbitt, *Constitutional Interpretation* (Oxford: Basil Blackwell, 1991), 24.

[189] Philip Bobbitt, *Constitutional Fate: Theory of the Constitution* (New York: Oxford Univ. Press, 1982), ix.

[190] Ibid., 185.

[191] Bobbitt, *Constitutional Interpretation*, 120.

[192] Bobbitt, *Constitutional Fate*, 124.

stitution as their own in the face of reasoned but adverse interpretations."[193] Bobbitt describes the process of constitutional interpretation as a game of Twenty Questions in which the participants "agreed not to agree on any word at all. Each one around the circle could respond 'yes' or 'no' as he pleased to whatever question [was] put to him. But however he replied he had to have a word in mind compatible with his own reply—and with all the replies that went before."[194] Bobbitt comments that, in contrast to a conventional game of Twenty Questions, if the questioner "had chosen to ask a different question, he would have ended up with a different word."[195] In this sense, constitutional interpretation is not a search for a preexisting meaning. Bobbitt argues that the unpredictable, uncontrollable, and collaborative character of constitutional interpretation is the source of its legitimacy: "We do not have a fundamental set of axioms that legitimize judicial review. We have . . . a participatory Constitution, that accomplishes this legitimation."[196]

By enabling a pluralistic process of deliberation about the requisites of justice and democracy, the practice of constitutional argument respects and perhaps advances both ideals, without defining them. Bobbitt associates the realization of these values with artistic creativity. The indeterminacy of law is an aesthetic virtue because it permits the experience of "defamiliarization" so valued in modernist literature and criticism:

> Meta-rules [dictating just results] would make the art of decision into a kind of placid pornography, and for much the same reason, i.e., to assure a completely anticipated outcome. As Nabokov once observed: "Old rigid rules must be followed by the pornographer in order to have his patient feel the same security of satisfaction as, for example, fans of detective stories feel—stories where, if you do not watch out, the real murderer turns out to be, to the fan's disgust, artistic originality."[197]

To understand in what sense the open-ended process of constitutional argument described by Bobbitt "legitimates" judicial review, we must recur to Bobbitt's Wittgensteinian conception of legitimacy. On Bobbitt's account, legal language is made up not of empirical propositions, but arguments—"moves"[198] in a forensic game. The arguments are valid insofar as moves of the same type or "modality" remain a part of the game. To participate in the game at all is to accept and reproduce the legitimacy not only of the particular modality of argument used, but of the game itself. Hence, to use any modality is perforce to endorse them all.

Bobbitt uses this conception of legitimacy to catch up the critics of judicial review and constitutional interpretation in a performative contradiction. According to Bobbitt, the modalities of constitutional argument are traditions of judicial, not merely academic, argument. Hence, their use presupposes the long-

---

[193] Bobbitt, *Constitutional Interpretation*, 158.
[194] Bobbitt, *Constitutional Fate*, 238 (quoting physicist John Wheeler).
[195] Ibid.
[196] Ibid., 238.
[197] Bobbitt, *Constitutional Interpretation*, 162.
[198] Bobbitt, *Constitutional Fate*, 244.

standing practice of judicial application of the Constitution as law. Yet the critics of judicial review and constitutional interpretation couch their criticisms in these modalities. For example, many consider it necessary to argue that neither the constitutional text nor the records of the convention explicitly mandate judicial review, implying that these conventional modes of argument could establish its authority, were only the sources clearer. Moreover, many constitutional theorists question the legitimacy of judicial review only as a preface to arguing that one or another modality of argument uniquely solves the legitimacy problem. All such arguments, Bobbitt claims, are internal to the judicially developed practice of constitutional argument and so presuppose the legitimacy of judicial review.[199]

For Bobbitt, the "countermajoritarian" critique of judicial review poses a pseudo-problem: "notions of 'majoritarianism' are carefully boundaried in the constitution; not every group can declare itself a constituency and hold an election. . . . Insofar as judicial review preserves the legitimacy of the constitution, it preserves, not threatens, the operation of democratic representation."[200] Yet the claim of marginalized minorities to full participation in society does pose a different kind of "countermajoritarian difficulty," *internal to the conventions of constitutional argument*, that Bobbitt does not fully acknowledge. According to Bobbitt's account, the conventions of constitutional argument favor textually based argument and de-emphasize appeals to social fact. Yet our review of the Progressive tradition in constitutional interpretation suggests that, to the contrary, appeals to cultural tradition and social need have dominated constitutional thought. Bobbitt's textualist bias therefore suppresses the "modal conflict" that arises when a racially exclusive culture and an egalitarian constitutional text are at odds.

The epistemological objections to constitutional interpretation Bobbitt refutes were never the true sources of constitutional crisis. Constitutional interpretation has its skeptical critics like Levinson and Tushnet, its "strict constructionist" reformers like Robert Bork, and its pragmatic defenders like Philip Bobbitt. Taking the long view, all are engaged in the complicitous ritual of contriving and refuting foundationalist objections to a practice that fails its own internal standards.

Interpretation's Empire

The most elaborate defense of legal interpretation has been Dworkin's. Dworkin set out to meet skeptical objections to interpretation, while retaining its critical independence of majoritarian custom. To solve the first problem, Dworkin developed the argument, first in a 1982 article and then in *Law's Empire* (1986), that adjudication is an art not a science. Hence, in assessing the performance of judges, one should compare them to literary authors and critics. If legal interpretation is an art, it does not merely permit, but positively requires, subjectivity. To solve the second problem, Dworkin developed the idea of "integrity." Dworkin offered

---

[199] Bobbitt, *Constitutional Interpretation*, 25.
[200] Ibid., 9–10.

"integrity" as a criterion for internal criticism of culturally specific value systems and argued that the fact that laws cohere with each other and with culturally received norms offers a more realistic warrant for their legitimacy than consent. To put Dworkin's argument in a nutshell, because majority will is incoherent it cannot be applied without the construction of principles to render it coherent. Coherence or "integrity" is an evaluative criterion independent of both collective and individual will, constraining both. Integrity can therefore justify courts in protecting minorities against majority will, without recourse to putatively "objective" or "universal" principles.

Let us examine in turn Dworkin's conception of law as an art, his ideas of integrity and community, his views on minority rights, and finally his views on objectivity in law.

Dworkin characterized law as a practice of arguing that conduct is required or permitted by authoritative sources. Since disagreement about what counts as a source of law is a recurrent experience in legal practice, he reasoned, different theories of what law is are themselves sources of law. Dworkin added that law is an "interpretive practice," which combines the application of customary norms in light of their purposes, and the construction of purposes to explain customary norms. Participation in such a practice requires a common discourse rooted in what Wittgenstein called a common "form of life."[201] As a practice or "language game" law has no essence—it is an historically contingent assemblage of actions. Its content and purpose can only be identified by an act of "constructive" interpretation.[202] Thus, to offer a theory of law is to construct a purpose intended to explain, justify, and improve the law of some particular community.

What is "constructive interpretation"? Constructive interpretation is peculiar to two analogous enterprises: the interpretation of a social practice like law, and the interpretation of artistic works, such as works of literature:

> Both aim to interpret something created by people as an entity distinct from them, rather than what people say, as in conversational interpretation, or events not created by people, as in scientific interpretation. . . . Interpretation of works of art and social practices is . . . essentially concerned with purpose, not cause. But the purposes in play are not . . . those of some author but of the interpreter. Roughly, constructive interpretation is a matter of imposing purpose on an object or practice in an effort to make of it the best possible example of the form or genre to which it is taken to belong.[203]

The paradigm of constructive interpretation is literary criticism. Dworkin called his claim that legal interpretation makes its object the best that it can be, "the aesthetic hypothesis." Aesthetic value combined criteria of coherence (the purpose imposed on a practice must "fit" the data) and excellence (it must make the practice the best it can be). Coherence could be measured by comparing an

---

[201] Ronald Dworkin, *Law's Empire* (Cambridge: Harvard Univ. Press, 1986), 63–64.
[202] Ibid., 69.
[203] Ibid., 50–52.

interpretation to the data it was trying to explain. But excellence could only be measured by comparing the interpretation to some extrinsic standard.

Because law and literature both involve constructive interpretation, Dworkin assigned theoretical argument the same status in each. Thus, he claimed that theoretical disagreement among literary critics is not really about the source of meaning but about the nature of aesthetic or literary value.[204] Critical theory is part of the activity of criticism, which is involved in any aesthetic experience of literature. Similarly, jurisprudence—theoretical argument about the pupose of law—is part of legal argument and is implicit in experiencing a sense of entitlement or obligation.

While Dworkin held that lawyers and literary critics alike are "constructive" interpreters, he suggested, by means of a now-famous metaphor, that legal interpreters are even more creative than literary critics:

> We can usefully compare the judge deciding what the law is . . . with the literary critic teasing out the various dimensions of value in a complex play or poem. Judges, however, are authors as well as critics. A judge . . . adds to the tradition he interprets. . . . We can find an even more fruitful comparison between literature and law . . . by constructing an artificial genre of literature that we might call the chain novel. In this enterprise a group of novelists writes a novel seriatim; each novelist in the chain interprets the chapters he has been given in order to write a new chapter, which is then added to what the next novelist receives, and so on. Each has the job of writing his chapter so as to make the novel being constructed the best it can be, and the complexity of this task models the complexity of deciding a hard case under law as integrity.[205]

This "chain novel" metaphor was strikingly similar to Bobbitt's less-known metaphor of Twenty Questions. Dworkin used his law-literature analogy to address several problems.

First, literature offers interpreters a place to stand in critiquing law that is nevertheless culturally particular. If one is interpreting a literary or legal text, one chooses among interpretations that make it the best possible example of literature or law, by adverting to criteria of literary or legal excellence. We develop such criteria by interpreting the entire practice of law or literature so as to make it the best example of an interpretive practice it can be. But how can we develop criteria to determine what makes an interpretive practice the best interpretive practice it can be? We must deploy criteria of excellence extrinsic to the particular interpretive practice. Yet these criteria of value must still be drawn from some other social practice if they are to qualify as intepretive. Thus, Dworkin would derive criteria of value for each practice *interpretively* from other analogous practices of constructive interpretation. The availability of other interpretive social practices— literature paradigmatically—was what enabled Dworkin to regard extrinsic criticism of law as still *interpretive*.

---

[204] Ibid., 59–60.
[205] Ibid., 228–29.

A second point of the law-literature analogy was to enable the legal interpreter to sidestep the objectivity problem. Dworkin replaced objectivity with fidelity as the interpreter's aspiration. If interpreting law is like interpreting art, it involves appreciating rather than simply observing the object of interpretation.[206] Thus, the analogy of legal to literary interpretation supported Dworkin's Gadamerian methodological demand that the legal theorist suspend skepticism and engage law as a participant. Dworkin assumed that a literary critic similarly commits herself to participation in a literary culture when she interprets a work, asserting how the work *should* be read rather than observing how others *do* read it.

A third point of the law-literary analogy was to defeat originalism. Invoking Gadamer, Dworkin argued that construction is involved in applying artistic intent. Conveying the themes of the *Merchant of Venice* to a modern audience may require portraying the characters differently from what would occur in Shakespeare's time, translating the work from his society to ours.[207] Because a similarly wholesale translation is needed in applying framers' intent to modern constitutional controversies, Dworkin argued that this is a problem of constructive rather than conversational interpretation.

But Dworkin's most important use of the law-literature analogy was in arguing that law derives its legitimacy culturally rather than morally or politically. Law fulfills its "purpose" by realizing the aesthetic value of integrity within some particular culture:

> The adjudicative principle of integrity instructs judges to identify legal rights and duties, ... on the assumption that they were all created by a single author—the community personified—expressing a coherent conception of justice and fairness. ... According to law as integrity, propositions of law are true if they figure in or follow from the principles of justice, fairness, and procedural due process that provide the best constructive interpretation of the community's legal practice.[208]

Integrity entails making decisions that are consistent with past decisions; or correcting past decisions now acknowledged to be wrong.[209] Law as integrity "argues that rights and responsibilities flow from past decisions . . . , not just when they are explicit in these decisions but also when they follow from the principles of personal and political morality the explicit decisions presuppose by way of justification."[210] So the principles that characterize the communal persona are imaginative compositions.

The state's moral personality identifies its citizens with one another over time in a figurative relation. The ideal of legal integrity makes it possible for citizens to identify with and take responsibility for the actions of previous generations so that "white Americans who inherited nothing from slaveholders feel an indetermi-

---

[206] Ibid., 55.
[207] Ibid., 56.
[208] Ibid., 225.
[209] Ibid., 95–96.
[210] Ibid., 96.

nate responsibility to blacks who never wore chains."[211] Because the pursuit of integrity identifies people across time and space and makes them responsible for one another's actions, it forms the basis of community. Reconceived as cultural constructs rather than hypothetical rational bargains, principles become a legitimate basis for the countermajoritarian exercise of government power.

Dworkin reasoned that we have associative obligations to others insofar as we find ourselves in associative relations with others who meet their associative obligations to us, and the functioning of the association does not entail serious injustice to nonmembers. When associations meet these conditions, members are obliged to treat each other fraternally. For Dworkin, viewing citizenship as this sort of association explained the obligation to obey law without reference to the actual or hypothetical consent of the governed.[212] Such associations are "communities of principle." Their members

> accept that their political rights and duties are not exhausted by the particular decisions their political institutions have reached, but depend, more generally, on the scheme of principles those decisions presuppose and endorse.... Each member accepts that ... these obligations arise from the historical fact that his community has adopted that scheme, which is then special to it, not the assumption that he would have chosen it were the choice entirely his.[213]

Minority rights must be grounded in neighborliness rather than majority consent—the neighborliness without which, Dworkin implied, law cannot be accepted as legitimate no matter how appealing its moral content or desirable its policy benefits.

Dworkin's actual defense of the desegregation decisions derived largely from the arguments of Charles Black. Like Black, he argued that segregation expresses the unworthiness of blacks: segregation may, he conceded, treat blacks and whites equally, but it does not treat them *as equals*. But what, he asked, if majorities were to discriminate on the basis of mere antipathy, or even selfishness, unaccompanied by contempt? Dworkin pointed out that such discrimination could be defended as the outcome of a utilitarian calculus that, by weighing the utility of all individuals equally, showed the disfavored minority group equal respect. Hence, he conceded, invidious discrimination against minorities could be defended by a plausible interpretation of equality. Yet, he argued, the best interpretation of the principle of equal respect, the one most conducive to a fraternal *community* of principle, would require a greater measure of respect than is entailed in the weighing of utilities.[214] Ultimately, then, only the aesthetic discretion of the legal interpreter could shape the principle of equality into a sufficiently fraternal ideal of mutuality to ensure protection of minority rights.

[211] Ibid., 172.
[212] Ibid., 206–7.
[213] Ibid., 211.
[214] Ibid., 382–83, 387.

Dworkin commited himself to show this account of minority rights to be the "best" and therefore the "right" interpretation of constitutional equal protection. But he eschewed any additional obligation to show it to be "objectively" best or right. Thus, he urged that readers otherwise persuaded by his arguments not allow skeptical doubts about the subjectivity of interpretive argument generally to shake their agreement.[215] Dworkin argued that to answer an interpretive argument with the retort that interpretive judgments are matters of mere opinion is to leave the practice of interpretive argument. He took the pragmatic position that such skeptical argument gives participants in a practice no reason to change their views. If an interpreter feels constrained from reaching an otherwise appealing judgment by the lack of what she regards as sufficent evidence, the constraint is real even if *"merely* subjective."[216] For Dworkin, as for Wechsler and Fiss, a legal decision can be legitimated by the judge's subjective sense of constraint, manifesting itself as ambivalence, as suspense, as the *feeling* of suspending judgment. The very tensions or contradictions in legal doctrine that have induced critics to call adjudication indeterminate and therefore subjective seemed to be, for Dworkin, the sources of its legitimacy.[217]

Dworkin based an additional defense of judicial subjectivity on his idea that legal integrity implies a personification of the state. In interpreting the law as the unified expression of a coherent personality, the judge ascribes subjectivity to the law itself. A community of principle depends on the sharing of subjective opinion, the willingness of many to cooperate in keeping the community's actions "in character." Legal interpreters must strive to inculcate a communal moral character by reproducing in the reader their own feelings of ambivalence, deliberative suspense, and finally reconciliation and resolution. Dworkin showed legal interpreters how, placing a number of interpretive dilemmas before the character of Hercules, "an imaginary judge of superhuman intellectual power and patience who accepts law as integrity."[218] For Dworkin, the proof of an interpretive method, an interpretive subjectivity, and an intepretation all ultimately lay in the performance.

While Dworkin did not claim objectivity for legal interpretation, he did claim that legal interpretive dilemmas have one right answer. Yet the Reader-Response criticism that informed Dworkin's work rejects the view that literary works admit of one true meaning. How could Dworkin square his "right answer thesis" with his characterization of legal interpretation as a genre of literary art?

One plausible strategy would have been to present the "right answer" as nothing more than a convention peculiar to certain genres of legal reading and writing. But Dworkin regarded the "right answer" convention as not only appropriate for judges, but also morally obligatory for all legal interpreters. For Dworkin, the judge's obligation to decide between competing claims is never to be regretted as a necessary evil. There is no moment of mourning for the normative visions

---

[215] Ibid., 235–38.
[216] Ibid., 235–36.
[217] Ibid., 235–38.
[218] Ibid., 239.

necessarily suppressed in the act of judgment. Instead, decision is the recognition of both litigants' full membership in a community of principle. Thus, when citizens come into conflict, they have a right not just to a definite answer, but to a *right* answer—to the enforcement of a distribution of rights seen as *preexisting* the dispute, because entailed by the best principles that can be constructed to explain past practice.

Because this right answer must explain the entire corpus of legal practice and discourse, the demand for a right answer is not simply an artifact of pressure to decide an otherwise irresolvable dispute. Instead, all legal discourse is constrained to advance the end of enabling a right answer not just to an immediate dispute, but to every conceivable dispute. On this view, the deliberative search for the right answer is not merely a generic convention, but the organizing myth of all legal experience.

One difficulty is that, because legal interpretation is a social enterprise, "rightness" is arguably contingent on the future judgments and choices of others. Understanding this, individuals may offer interpretations with much more humility than Dworkin allows. They may be offered as suggestions for other contemporary or future participants in an interpretive institution to consider. Is a legal answer "right" if future decision makers will not maintain integrity with it? The contingency of normative judgments on future events—including the freely willed choices of others—makes it odd to say that there must be a " 'right answer' to the question which is best even when it is controversial what the right answer is."[219] When we engage in normative choice there are many attractive possible futures, each achievable by different paths, populated by different people. It would be as odd to say that one was uniquely right as to say that only one interpretation of *Hamlet* was right.

Yet Dworkin insisted that even debates in literary criticism proceed from the premise that one answer is right. While acknowledging that different interpretations of a complex literary work emphasizing different aspects can be right, he insisted that inconsistent interpretations must be better or worse, or at least must be thought so by one advancing such an interpretation.[220] Dworkin pointed out that every interpreter believes some interpretations wrong and adduces reasons in support of her own interpretation. But this commits the interpreter only to the view that interpretations can be more and less competent, not that one interpretation is uniquely best. Thus, Dworkin demanded that the literary interpreters' convictions outrun her reasons. If works can be polyvalent, why must the interpretations they give rise to be consistent? And if coherence is a contestable aesthetic value, we should also question the appeal of integrity as a political value.

The ideal of integrity lies at the heart of Dworkin's enigmatic figure of law as an "empire." We usually think of an empire as an extensive realm, internally articulated, built by conquest, subject to a single, centralized, autocratic power. Dworkin's conception of law has all of these features. That all public action im-

---

[219] Ibid., 80.
[220] Ibid., 76–77.

plies principles to which other public action should conform gives every public action a dimension of normative meaning accessed by means of interpretation. This dimension of normative meaning is an ideal realm, connecting, ordering, and controlling all public decisions. Yet this realm is, like an empire, internally articulated: while every legal issue is to be decided ultimately in light of the entire corpus of law, the data to be reconciled include the fact that law is "compartmentalized" into discrete doctrinal fields.[221] Dworkin's law is not pluralistic: it is governed despotically by a single personality or normative vision that expands its domain by conquest of rivals. The imperative that legal interpretations claim exclusive correctness means that the values that lose a legal dispute are adjudged wrong and thereby lose their status as values. The ideal of integrity turns that defeat into permanent conquest—having lost once, rejected norms must lose again and again if the legal system is to avoid the charge of hypocrisy. Moreover, citizens of a community of principle are bound by civic obligation to repudiate defeated norms. Just as the values vindicated in any legal dispute vanquish their rivals, so too law vanquishes rival normative systems like morality:

> Integrity insists that each citizen must accept demands on him, and may make demands on others, that share and extend the moral dimension of any explicit political decisions. Integrity therefore fuses citizens' moral and political lives: it asks the good citizen, deciding how to treat his neighbor when their interests conflict, to interpret the common scheme of justice to which they are both committed just in virtue of citzenship.[222]

For Dworkin, the seamless unity of the law implied it was self-legitimating—all the sources or "grounds" of law were already included within the law. Dworkin accorded law-as-integrity not just a monopoly on legitimate force, but a monopoly on legitimacy itself: "The courts are the capitals of law's empire, and judges are its princes."[223] Law-as-integrity is no mere aspect or dimension of governance: it is an inherently expansionist empire, reaching its natural boundaries only when it has subjugated the state and political society. Law's empire, ruled by judges, is the polity itself. Yet as Cover noted, in any but the most totalitarian polity, the power to enforce—and thereby to recognize—law is distributed among myriad social actors without whose cooperation the edicts of courts are not law at all. The courts do not and should not have a monopoly on legitimacy. A democratic polity is no one's "empire."

Pragmatic Deflations: Does Interpretation Come Naturally?

Dworkin's antiskepticism emerged in the course of an extended debate with Fish. Dworkin accused Fish of skepticism, while Fish accused Dworkin of metaphysical foundationalism. In fact, there was little separating the two antagonists. Fish admitted his fundamental agreement with Dworkin's characterization of

---

[221] Ibid., 251.
[222] Ibid., 189–90.
[223] Ibid., 407.

legal and critical practice as "chain enterprises," enterprises in which interpretation is an extension of an institutional history made up of "innumerable decisions, structures, conventions and practices." . . . I find this account of interpretation and its constraints . . . similar in important ways to the account I have offered under the rubric of "interpretive communities" in *Is There a Text in This Class?*[224]

Despite their agreement that interpreters are chained together in an institutional context, Fish objected to Dworkin's "chain novel" metaphor on the ground that Dworkin described later authors as constrained by what earlier authors had done. Fish objected that the view that later authors were constrained by what earlier authors had *written* implied that texts had meanings independent of the constructive activity of any interpreter. Fish added that Dworkin confirmed this implicit formalism by arguing that a reading of an Agatha Christie novel as a philosophical meditation on death would fit the data less well than a reading of it as a light mystery. According to Fish, Dworkin

> thinks that interpretation is itself an activity in need of constraints, but . . . interpretation is a structure of constraints, a structure which, because it is always and already in place, renders unavailable the independent or uninterpreted text and renders unimaginable the independent and freely determining reader. In searching for a way to protect against arbitrary readings . . . Dworkin is searching for something he already has and could not be without.[225]

Dworkin replied that it was he rather than the "skeptical" Fish who saw interpretation as a structure of constraints. Fish had misread the chain novel metaphor: Dworkin never meant that later authors were constrained in their interpretations by the uninterpreted meanings of what earlier authors had *written*. They were constrained in what they added to the chain novel *by their own interpretations* of what their predecessors had written. Dworkin protested similarly that any judgment of fit was the product of interpretive judgment. Thus, the judgment that a Christie novel would not work well as a meditation on death might involve imagining editorial improvements that might make it work better as such a meditation. The text and the genre to which it is being compared only take on discernible formal properties through such an effort of critical imagination. The judgment of generic fit was not a textual constraint on interpretation, but an interpretive constraint. In reading Christie as entertainment rather than philosophy, Dworkin's interpretive judgment that philosophy is the more valuable genre would be checked by his also interpretive judgment that her work makes bad philosophy. Interpretation, in short, was a "structure of constraints."

Both Dworkin and Fish saw interpretation as constrained by its own structure of concerns. Neither believed that interpretive practices could or should seek any warrant outside their own criteria of justification. Compare Fish:

---

[224] Fish, *Doing What Comes Naturally*, 87–88.
[225] Ibid., 98.

If an interpretation is grounded . . . in the interpreter's beliefs, then it goes . . . without saying that the interpreter believes in his interpretation. If he believes in his interpretation, then he necessarily believes it to be better. . . . And if he believes it to be better, then one need seek no explanation of how it is possible for him to think this, for it is flatly impossible for him to think anything else[226]

and Dworkin:

If some argument should persuade me that my views about slavery are not really true, then it should also persuade me to abandon my views about slavery. And if no argument could persuade me that slavery is not unjust, no argument could persuade me that it is not "really" unjust.[227]

The real disagreement between these two antagonists was not metaphysical but *aesthetic*. While agreeing that interpretation was a "structure of constraints," they disagreed about how interpretation was structured, particularly temporally.

For Dworkin, the complexity of interpretation's "structure of constraints" enabled interpreters to experience interpretive problems as "hard cases" that compelled them to suspend judgment and deliberate. In other words, for Dworkin, legal interpretation had to have an aesthetic quality of complexity, tension, or "difficulty" to produce its proper mood of deliberative ambivalence. This aesthetic quality, inhering in a dialogic rhythm, detaches the interpreter's persona from the result by phenomenologically separating the first, which is established early in narrative time, from the last, which is held in suspense until the end. By adopting the interpreter's persona, the reader can experience the feeling of being ruled by law. Thus, persuaded by her own experience that the interpreter's persona has been subordinated to law, the reader can accept the interpretive result as an expression of law rather than the personality of the interpreter. In this aesthetic tradition, the legal authority of interpretation depends upon its having the phenomenological structure of the *hard case*.

It is this aesthetic mood of deliberative difficulty, so prevalent in jurisprudence, that provokes Fish. The author of *Surprised by Sin* is a connoisseur of suspense, surprise, and other such readerly thrills. He prides himself on adroitly handling abstruse theoretical problems in a literary voice that is always brisk and irreverent. The handwringing earnestness that characterizes so much legal scholarship must strike him as hollow, the supposed suspension of judgment predictable, as far as possible from any true suspense.

Nothing piques Fish's irreverence more than the legal scholars' pious invocation of the angst-ridden Hamlet as the paradigmatic literary figure. Fish gave his initial response to Dworkin's vision of legal interpretation as collective literary creation the deflating title "Working on the Chain Gang." It argued that serious literature cannnot be distinguished from popular entertainment,[228] and that hard

[226] Ibid., 114.
[227] Ronald Dworkin, *A Matter of Principle* (Cambridge: Harvard Univ. Press, 1985), 172.
[228] Fish, *Doing What Comes Naturally*, 95–97.

cases cannot be distinguished from easy ones.[229] Fish reasoned that both distinctions depend upon textual formalism, but his real objection is a distaste for the aesthetic piety that motivates the construction of a canon of appropriately serious and difficult objects of reflection. Fish's attitude towards the characterization of professional judgment as an impossibly difficult labor of Hercules is summed up by the title of his collection of Law and Literature essays: professional judgment is merely *Doing What Comes Naturally*. For Fish, the professional at the top of his game is at ease, exercising powers of intuition that are not superhuman, but expressions of the situated human "nature" enabled by any densely textured social practice.

With the appearance of *Law's Empire*, Fish abandoned his philosophical critique of Dworkin. Despite the title of his review—"Still Wrong after All These Years"[230]—Fish conceded that Dworkin's account of legal interpretation was descriptively accurate.[231] What he objected to were the "hard cases" that Dworkin contrived for Hercules. He justly charged that these performative demonstrations of constructive interpretation, "although they are supposed to be the centerpiece of the book, are flat and uninteresting."[232] In fact, Hercules' opinions achieve such a disinterested voice that they detach the reader from any interest in the reasoning process or its result. They are suspenseless.

As far as Fish is concerned, the problem lies in Dworkin's aspiration to make legal argument sound like academic philosophy. Fish pretends his objection is conceptual, portraying Dworkin's claim that philosophical argument plays a role in law as a category mistake:

> "External skepticism" and "law as integrity" are [both] . . . philosophical practices . . . of speculation that emerge from the special context of academic philosophy where the constructing of a "perspective of no institution in particular" is the first order of business—and the mistake is to assume that as philosophical practices they have anything to say about practices internal to disciplines other than philosophy.[233]

But this "category mistake" objection is phony. The claim that since epistemological skepticism has nothing to say about law neither can moral philosophy is sophistry. Fish is obviously conflating two different kinds of philosophy: epistemology on the one hand, and theories of value on the other. Fish and Dworkin both agree that the first type of philosophy is categorically irrelevant to the practice of legal argument. Whether legal argument should be informed by theories of legal or ethical or aesthetic *value*, however, is obviously a normative question *within* law. Fish can offer no argument that theories of value are categorically irrelevant to law. Moreover, as an outsider to the "interpretive community" of lawyers, Fish is at a disadvantage in an argument about how the interpretive community should

---

[229] Ibid., 101.
[230] Ibid., 370.
[231] Ibid., 367–68.
[232] Ibid., 370.
[233] Ibid., 371.

conduct its practice. His rhetorical leverage arises from Dworkin's claim that the values served by normative theory are largely aesthetic. Here Fish can, from a position of authority, dismiss Dworkin's literary product as sanctimonious, grandiloquent, and dull. If the principal appeal of Dworkin's normative theorizing to lawyers is its literary preciosity, Fish is eager to expose "law's ambitions for itself,"[234] as parvenu pretension and *Law's Empire* as the Kingdom of Kitsch. Fish cannot argue with Dworkin's epistemological conclusions; but faced with an aesthetic choice between experiencing law as philosophy or as mystery, Fish will take Agatha Christie every time.

Taste aside, both Fish and Dworkin agree that the practice of interpretation needs no foundation in a meaning independent of interpretation. Meaning is determined within the practice of interpretation. Thus, while their literary taste differs dramatically, Fish and Dworkin share an assumption that law is rendered intelligible by acts of *literary imagination*. This common denominator has provoked the deflating rejoinder that it "turns the ordinary into the mysterious,"[235] offering an idealized picture of what is actually unreflective, bureaucratic routine.

For the pragmatist legal philosopher Dennis Patterson, the "law as interpretation" thesis is a form of metaphysical idealism needlessly "accounting for" the intelligibility of legal work. To Patterson, identifying linguistic meaning with a reader's interpretation is no less idealist than identifying meaning with authorial intention. Both involve inventing private languages to account for publicly observable facts. Rather than the practice of interpretation, it is the practice of law that determines legal meaning: "Meanings do not spring from interpretation but from action—ways of *using* signs. . . . Meaning arises not from interpretation but from regular use."[236] Not all ways of understanding a practical situation are aptly described as interpretive:

> It is not by virtue of interpretation that we have a common world. Rather we have a common world with others because we understand the manifold activities that constitute that world. Catching on to and participating in these activities—knowing *how* to act—is the essence of understanding. If understanding is primordial, then interpretation is of necessity a secondary endeavor; the very existence of practices of interpretation is dependent upon understanding already being in place.[237]

What organizes meaning in a social practice, Patterson insists, is not an interpretive assumption but familiarity with how other participants respond to and use signs. Most of the time, argues Patterson, the lawyer's work consists in using legal rules that are unreflectively understood, and not in constructing interpretations to account for their enigmas. For the most part, then, the lawyer is *neither* Hercules *nor* Hercule Poirot.

[234] Dworkin, *Law's Empire*, 407.
[235] Dennis Patterson, *Law and Truth* (New York: Oxford Univ. Press, 1996), 75.
[236] Ibid., 113.
[237] Ibid., 126–27.

Patterson largely agrees with Dworkin's characterization of interpretation,[238] but he sees the occasions for interpretation as arising rarely in law, and mostly in the rarefied context of appellate litigation. Thus, he agrees with Fish's description of legal practice as "doing what comes naturally"—but denies that what comes naturally includes interpretation. For Patterson, "interpretation" refers only to reflective, theoretical activity. By contrast, for Fish, the poetry teacher, interpretation is a prosaic workaday practice. Interpreting poetry does not ordinarily entail developing "theories" of what a poem means but simply experiencing the poem as meaningful. Only in the forensic activity of defending one reading against another—the literary equivalent of appellate litigation—does reflective distance from one's reading become necessary. The only real disagreement here is whether interpretation fits in the category of theoretical reflection (as Patterson claims it does for the experienced lawyer) or in the category of routine practice (as Fish claims it does for the cultivated literary reader). Patterson's claim is that interpretation is less routine for lawyers than for literary critics, that Fish has wrongly swallowed Dworkin's line that the lawyer's bread and butter is the interpretation that "comes naturally" to Fish.

Can Legal Hermeneutics Be Critical?

Feminist legal theorist Robin West, like Patterson, sees interpretation as freer and more creative than the routine judgment of legal professionals. For Patterson, this is part of a defense of legal reasoning against the charge of interpretive license. For West, by contrast, the claim that "Adjudication is not Interpretation"[239] is an indictment of adjudication. Like Cover, West sees effective coercion as adjudication's raison d'être and bondage to power as the price of effectiveness. But West is unconsoled by the hope that bureaucratic cowardice will at least curb the worst excesses of official power. Prudence is not justice. Justice may only be pursued by those who are independent not only of legal authority but also of prevailing customs and prejudices. If law has the legitimating and educative effects Bickel emphasized, "our moral beliefs and intuitions . . . cannot . . . serve as the standards against which we judge extant law, for they are themselves a product of it."[240] Law's "dialogic" power to influence social norms undermines the capacity of those norms to legitimate law.

In denying that law is interpretation, West rejects Dworkin's claim that legal judgment stands at a sufficient aesthetic remove from popular opinion to protect minority rights. Indeed, she argues that Dworkin's identification of adjudication with Reader-Response criticism misleadingly ascribed critical independence to

---

[238] Dennis Patterson, "Law's Pragmatism: Law as Practice and Narrative," *Virginia Law Review* 76 (1990): 937.

[239] Robin West, *Narrative, Authority and Law* (Ann Arbor: Univ. of Michigan Press, 1993), 89–178.

[240] Ibid., 95.

the judge and thereby legitimated judicially enforced law as having passed a test of conscience.[241]

The legitimating power of the law-literature analogy arises from what West takes to be literature's freedom. Literature provides an independent vantage point from which to criticize established authority. Yet literature's freedom from coercive power does not consist in creative license so much as in its determination by the invariant truths of human nature:

> We can and should rely on universal descriptions of human nature as a grounds for criticism of law, as well as for social and cultural criticism. The ... methods of the humanities, including the reading and interpretation of literature, the telling and hearing of stories, and the development of a capacity for empathizing with the experiences of others, might constitute one means of pursuing a rich understanding of human nature. ... Thus, the human capacities to which study of the humanities gives rise might constitute a set of moral capacities, and hence a sphere of consciousness, sufficiently removed from the influence of law to serve as a vehicle for moral criticism of it.[242]

This provokes the question why literature, any more than law, should be credited with insight into human nature. To be sure, authentic first-person accounts may expose natural human need, but why should the credibility of such accounts be extended to the designedly *inauthentic* accounts of imaginative literature? To put the problem the other way around, why does West characterize the contribution of autobiographical testimony to legal criticism as *literary*?

To value autobiographical testimony as literature is to value it for something other than its significance as social scientific data. West has elsewhere argued that the behaviorist assumption of legal economics that market choice always reveals preference is an imaginative construct comparable to the motivational structures authors give fictional characters.[243] Since behavioristic social science is committed to epistemological skepticism about hedonic experience it can say nothing about what behavior *means* and *feels like* to the actor. West rejects the skepticism implicit in behaviorism and argues that the meaning and hedonic quality of others' experience are knowable by the fundamentally literary methods of hermeneutics and phenomenology. That we can recognize a work of fiction as phenomenologically credible implies that we can also assess autobiographical testimony in the same way. Thus, for West, the function of literature is to produce a virtual experience in the reader; and the truth of that experience lies in the reader's empathic response rather than in correspondence to any actual event. The literary qualities of first-person testimony are primarily probative not of what occurred, but of what such an occurrence would feel like.

---

[241] Ibid., 94–95.

[242] Ibid., 7.

[243] Robin West, "Authority, Autonomy and Choice: The Role of Consent in the Jurisprudence of Franz Kafka and Richard Posner," *Harvard Law Review* 99 (1985): 384.

On West's view, reformist criticism inherently involves the literary imagination: to argue for reform is not only to claim that it would result in a different state of affairs than would the preservation of the status quo, but also to evoke what each state of affairs would feel like. West argues that law's bondage to power pressures the legal decison maker to repress this humane literary imagination. Thus, she implies, the dullness that Fish notices in Dworkin's narratives of legal decision making is symptomatic of the aesthetic poverty of legal thought generally. To assess law from within its own conventions, as both Fish and Dworkin endeavor to do, is to cut oneself off from the very source of critical insight. West therefore tests both theorists' accounts of legal decision making against narratives of legal thought drawn from imaginative literature and attempts to show that the experience of legal thought involves a self-alienation painful to anyone of moral sensibility.

West compares the communitarian hermeneutics of Dworkin's Hercules to the stratagems of Mark Twain's *Pudd'nhead Wilson*. Wilson, a Yankee lawyer, is transplanted to a small Missouri town where the social leaders hold slaves and strive to emulate Virginia cavaliers. Wilson craves social acceptance and professional success, but his hopes are frustrated for decades as a result of an ill-advised joke, which convinces the locals he is a fool. Wilson eventually wins acceptance by dramatically resolving a murder mystery in open court. The town's leading citizen, a judge of genteel Virginian ancestry, has been murdered. Two other outsiders, twin Italian "counts," have been accused. Acting as their attorney, Wilson demonstrates the counts' innocence by means of the newfangled technology of fingerprints. He uses the same method to identify the judge's craven nephew Tom as the culprit. Finally, he exposes this supposed nephew as an impostor—actually a slave, switched with the true nephew in the cradle. The "true" gentleman is freed from slavery, and the impostor, instead of being hung for murder, is sold down the river as a slave to satisfy the murdered man's debts. Ironically, the impostor not only looks white but is of mostly white parentage and descended from Virginia gentility. The "true" identities Wilson exposes are arbitrary conventions, but he flatters the community by representing them as scientific fact. West comments:

> Pudd'nhead does not achieve his legal triumph by convincing the community to abandon its noxious noble and racial codes in favor of the morally preferable legalistic code of individual responsibility. . . . Rather, what Pudd'nhead achieves is a Dworkinian, or Herculean, interpretive triumph: he convinces the town of Tom's guilt by interpreting the legal text prohibiting murder through the prism of the community's disciplining rules of race and family.[244]

As West emphasizes, Wilson's acquiescence in community norms represents a voluntary moral choice. Having exposed Tom as a murderer he did not have to also prove him a slave: "He chooses to. . . . By enforcing the community's code,

---

[244] West, *Narrative, Authority and Law*, 117–18.

Wilson perpetuated it; by incorporating the racial code into the legal code, he authored it."[245] West reasons that Wilson's "Dworkinian" success is a moral failure. He has realized communal integrity at the price of personal hypocrisy, integrating himself into the community but alienating himself from his own humanity.

Fish's "subjective interpretivism" recognizes that legal and social norms are mere conventions sustained by power. West complains that it accords the same relative status to natural justice: "There are no real human needs . . . by which to criticize law any more than there are real contracts or real neutral principles by which to adjudicate."[246]

West argues that the self-defeating psychological implications of this point of view are illustrated by John Barth's *The Floating Opera*. Todd Andrews, Barth's protagonist, is a morally skeptical lawyer who, believing "nothing has intrinsic value," concludes that "there's no final reason for living."[247] The "Floating Opera" is a tidewater showboat but also Andrews's metaphor for a world without foundation. Andrews vividly *experiences* life as an arbitrary social construct, an interpretation. Life is nothing more than a "floating opera," a foundationless and frivolous performance. West reasons that

> if the floating opera, our social history, provides the only text of moral value, then there is no way to criticize the opera itself as untrue to the real text of value. . . . Andrews . . . carries this argument one step further than Fish. . . . The lack of a real basis for criticism of the opera directly implies the lack of a real basis for its justification. . . . There is no ultimate reason why the floating opera should not be destroyed. And if that's so, Andrews asks, why not blow it up?[248]

Andrews, in fact, attempts to commit suicide by blowing up the showboat, with hundreds aboard. When the explosion mysteriously fails to ignite, however, he is too indifferent to try again. He considers drowning himself, but, unable to think of a reason, he gives it up.

Why is Andrews so devoid of scruples and motives? West traces his difficulties to a misinterpretation of "the real text of value," revealed in a wartime trauma Andrews experienced as a young man. Alone in a foxhole in the midst of battle, Andrews had been racked with terror. When an equally terrified enemy soldier dropped into his foxhole, the two at first struggled and then collapsed into an amazed and tender embrace. They spent the battle together, enjoying their own private truce and fell asleep. In the morning, Andrews's fear of his guest returned, however. Before Andrews could steal off, the enemy soldier awoke, and Andrews, torn between fear and guilt, killed him. He concluded from this experience that human beings are fundamentally selfish brutes, and their social bonds Hobbesian bargains serving no higher value than survival. But according to West,

---

[245] Ibid., 135–36. Note, however, that Wilson thereby freed one man from slavery and saved another's life.

[246] Ibid., 140.

[247] Ibid., 162.

[248] Ibid., 163.

Andrews has misinterpreted his own war story. It was not animalism, but professionalism, that prompted him to kill the German sergeant. . . . When stripped of their professional identities and roles, these two animals fed each other, embraced each other, protected each other, healed each other, and loved each other. It was only as their culturally created, socially constructed professionally defined roles returned, that the two men came, once again, to see themselves as in opposition to each other. . . . It was Andrews's participation in the floating opera, not his participation in nature, that dictated his final act of power.[249]

West argues, as Cover does, that violence is a collective project enabled by social norms. But that hardly implies that human nature is uniformly loving when unchanneled by social authority. The humanitarian catastrophes we have witnessed when state and society break down in the developing world discourage any such faith. Decency, no less than violence, is a collective achievement.

Most critics of adjudication sharing West's egalitarian and feminist political views will be reluctant to adopt her ethical naturalism: they are committed to some version of social constructivism. The challenge West poses for social constructivism is how socially constructed values can be used to criticize law, given the mutual complicity of legal and social convention asserted by interpretation's defenders. Once it is conceded that interpretation poses little threat to the descriptive legitimacy of law because it predictably conforms to social convention, convention-bound interpretation becomes a threat to law's normative legitimacy. If West is right, hermeneutic "defenses" of legal interpretation amount to little more than admissions that adjudication is governed by prejudice.

One social constructivist who has attempted to meet this challenge is the Canadian legal anthropologist Rosemary Coombe. In " 'Same as It Ever Was': Rethinking the Politics of Legal Interpretation,"[250] Coombe concedes that legal interpretation, though unconstrained by text and authorial intent, is disciplined by the expectations of interpretive communities. Coombe nevertheless denies that the routine predictability of most legal interpretation establishes its normative legitimacy. Like West, she criticizes both Fish and Dworkin as complacent and conservative. Yet Coombe's critique takes a different form, since she eschews the language of natural human need.

Coombe agrees with Dworkin and Fish both that legal interpretation is inevitably from a particular point of view and that this partiality is no criticism. Yet she objects to what she sees as Fish's assumptions that any point of view is as good as any other and that there is no point in criticizing a prevailing interpretation since its prevalence is inevitable.

Given her value relativism, how can Coombe distinguish among competing points of views? Coombe appears to define normative legitimacy in process terms. Invoking social theorist Pierre Bourdieu, Coombe treats the ability to influence the social determination of meaning as "symbolic power." As a form of political

---

[249] Ibid., 172.
[250] Rosemary Coombe, "Same as It Ever Was: Rethinking the Politics of Legal Interpretation," *McGill Law Journal* 34 (1989): 616.

power, interpretive authority should be shared. Hence, she reasons, the more inclusive and participatory the interpretive process, the more legitimate the interpretation. Her criteria of inclusiveness are pluralistic rather than majoritarian: broadening participation means including the perspectives of socially marginal or subordinate groups, and not limiting the interpretive process to legal and policy professionals: "To resign yourself, in the manner that Fish and Dworkin do, to the fact that the whole system is political is to concede the right of those with the licence and privilege to participate in legal interpretative decisions to determine the outcome of the struggle."[251]

Thus, one form of legal critique available to the social constructivist is that while law reflects social convention, it reflects the conventions of only some groups in society. A second form of critique might acknowledge that law reflects widely shared social norms, but object that the process by which these norms are formed and disseminated is coercive or unfair, imposing elite values on those who do not benefit from them. The difficulty with Coombe's aspiration to universal participation in authoritative discourse is that on Bourdieu's view exclusiveness is the very condition of authority, as it is of any form of "distinction." Will the powerless speak for themselves in Coombe's hermeneutic democracy, or will they inevitably be represented by experts in multicultural advocacy?

A third form of social constructivist critique might acknowledge that while the conventional values applied in legal interpretation are received, those values are also reproduced and reshaped in the legal process. As West argued, following Bickel, legal interpretation can influence social norms even where its coercive force is minimal. As critical legal historians have argued, legal norms cannot be seen simply as a function of social power or social norms, since they distribute social power and help shape the roles within which behavioral norms are developed and passed on:[252] "Accounts of legal interpretation which point to contexts, however defined, as stable referents which constrain practice, misunderstand the dynamic *process* whereby context or culture is both reproduced and transformed by the practices it enables."[253]

Consider the emergence of servitude in twelfth-century England, when royal courts began declining jurisdiction over tenurial disputes on the ground that peasants who had performed customary service to their landlords were subject to exclusive manorial jurisdiction. Peasants responded to this new initiative not by collectively resisting the legal construction of this new status, but by struggling to establish that it did not apply to them. Thus, by suing individually to establish their freedom they accepted the courts' characterization of the bulk of the peasantry as unfree.[254] The new status distinctions began as lines faintly drawn in the sand of custom by courts. The practical choices made by peasants negotiating this altered interpretive and strategic terrain wore them into deep ruts.

---

[251] Ibid., 631.

[252] Robert Gordon, "Critical Legal Histories," *Stanford Law Review* 36 (1984): 57.

[253] Coombe, "Same as It Ever Was," 634.

[254] Rodney H. Hilton, "Freedom and Villeinage in England," in *Peasants, Knights and Heretics*, ed. Rodney Howard Hilton (Cambridge: Cambridge Univ. Press, 1976), 174–91.

Legal interpretation did not merely reflect interests already present in society—it also helped to fashion them, and legal interpretation exerted its power not so much through the threat of official coercion but through a coordination effect. A legal norm, even backed by very modest coercion, may channel collective action by raising the visibility of a strategy that can succeed only if widely adopted. In deciding whether to accept or resist or escape the rule of a local grandee a peasant needs to know how other social actors ranging from government soldiers, to clerics, to other peasants will respond. One cannot adopt a group identity that others will not share, and one cannot adopt an individual identity that others will not recognize. Whether peasants find it most practical to identify themselves as clients of a patron, members of an agrarian movement, or upwardly mobile individuals may therefore depend upon what options law facilitates. Their interests may in turn flow from these identity-choices. Because judicial interpretation can have this kind of far-reaching effect on the shape of law's social environment, Coombe characterizes it as "political" even where judges unreflectively follow professional convention without any thought of their own individual or group interests.

Coombe characterizes legal interpretation not only as inherently "political," but also—drawing here upon Bourdieu—as inherently "violent." Coombe distinguishes this claim from Cover's claims that legal interpretation can trigger or threaten violence and that it is constrained by the conditions for mobilizing this violence.[255] Thus, where Cover and West point to law's violence in denying that law is primarily interpretative, Coombe insists that violence is characteristic of interpretation. Yet most of the difference between Cover and Coombe reflects different uses of the term "violence" rather than different accounts of interpretation. For Cover, "violence" is an ordinary language term referring to "pain and death." By contrast, Coombe borrows Bourdieu's theoretical term—"symbolic violence"—which refers to the act of "impos[ing] meanings and impos[ing] them as legitimate by concealing the power relations which are the basis of [the actor's] force."[256] Thus, "symbolic violence" refers to representing a situation one way when other representations are possible, denying the truth that other representations are possible, and coercing others by any threat (including the mere loss of esteem) to acquiesce in both the representation and the denial of its mere conventionality or "arbitrariness."[257]

Consider the example of a mental patient confined in a hospital and potentially subject to staff condescension, indifference to creature comfort, the administration of disorienting drugs, physical restraint, hydrotherapy, electroshock therapy, permanent confinement, and surgery. Which of these is violence? The diagnosis of the patient as mentally ill is the condition for the patient's vulnerability to all of these forms of "treatment"; but the patient's best chance of escaping the worst of these ordeals may lie in accepting the diagnosis and the staff's construction of

---

[255] Coombe, "Same as It Ever Was," 649.

[256] *Pierre Bourdieu and Jean-Claude Passeron, Reproduction in Education, Society and Culture* (London: Sage Publications, 1977), 4.

[257] Ibid., 5.

the treatment as therapeutic rather than violent. Hence, our patient is under enormous coercive pressure to collaborate in the denial that the coercion that surrounds her is violent. Insofar as an authoritative interpretation "straitjackets" its object in this way it may be likened to physical force.

Yet it seems hyperbolic to equate *all* authoritative interpretation with violence. To claim authority for any judgment is to claim the right to back it with some measure of coercion—the threat of a bad grade, for example. But if the coercion is not physical and is accepted as justified—if it does not *violate* anyone's person or rights—it seems odd to call it "violent." Social order is impossible without power, and if all exercises of power are equally "violent," the concept ceases to have much critical bite. Bourdieu's frankly figurative use of "violence" is an "arbitrary" coinage and as such an example of itself.

2.3 LEGAL HERMENEUTICS IN PRACTICE

If hermeneutics need not supply a theoretical foundation for legal argument, can it nevertheless inform legal argument? Dworkin urged us to read jurisprudential theories as interpretations of particular legal traditions, but his hypothetical interpretations in *Law's Empire* do not provide enough context to illustrate his claim. To illustrate the practice of hermeneutic argument, we turn instead to works on statutory interpretation by legal scholar William Eskridge and on justice by political philosopher Michael Walzer. In doing so, let us attend to the question raised by West and Coombe: can a *hermeneutics* of positive law or social norms also be *critical*?

Statutory Hermeneutics

Easily the foremost contemporary scholar of statutory interpretation, William Eskridge has drawn upon diverse intellectual traditions in arguing that statutory meaning must evolve over time, rather than being confined by original understanding or intent.[258] Lieber, Cardozo, Radin, Llewellyn, Bickel, Hart and Sacks, and Dworkin all figure in Eskridge's work. But perhaps the most important influence is Gadamer. In "Gadamer/Statutory Interpretation" Eskridge explicates Gadamer's hermeneutics, articulates a Gadamerian approach to statutory interpretation, and applies it to a 1960s Supreme Court decision construing a McCarthy Era immigration statute to exclude homosexuals.[259]

Eskridge identifies Gadamer with four ideas: first, that interpretation of a text can be neither simply "originalist" nor "present-oriented," second, that it must be traditional, third, that it should be tolerant of heteronomy, and fourth, that it is practical rather than theoretical, a craft rather than a science.

[258] William N. Eskridge, *Dynamic Statutory Interpretation* (Cambridge: Harvard Univ. Press, 1994).

[259] William Eskridge, "Gadamer/Statutory Interpretation," *Columbia Law Review* 90 (1990): 609.

As Eskridge understands it, Gadamerian interpretation is neither originalist nor present-minded. Instead, it treats the context in which the text was written as partly constitutive of the interpreter's purposes. To begin with, Gadamer rejects the positivist identification of meaning with preference or will, whether of author or reader. Instead, meaning consists in the world of purposes, projects, and possibilities discernible to participants in a given context—the "horizon" disclosed by a particular vantage point. The Gadamerian interpreter first seeks to reconstruct the horizon within which the text was written, and then asks how and how much her own horizon coincides with that of the text. Yet the interpreter's horizon is not simply given: it has already been broadened by its encounter with the text, just as the interpreter's reconstruction of the text's horizon is already limited by her own horizon. This mutual conditioning of the interpreters' purposes and her reconstruction of the author's world is what is meant by saying that text and interpreter participate in a dialogue or hermeneutic circle.

Eskridge notes that Gadamer views the past as available to the interpreter because practical action is inevitably traditional. To Gadamer, the interpretation of the past is not, as for "originalists," an alternative to consequentialist policy analysis. Instead, we experience our purposes as received, as the completion of a story already in progress when we joined in. If interpretation of the past is inherent in purposive action, it is not something we can decide to do, much less something we ought to do in order to restrain ourselves from enforcing our wills. Our wills are just interpretations and invocations of the past. When we apply a text authored in the past as a source of normative authority, we decide which past to identify with, not whether to identify with the past. The interpretation will be a narrative linking the text, and its context, to our present and future. Interpretation of a text, in other words, is the construction of a tradition, within which we can identify what it means to remain faithful to the text.

Eskridge sees Gadamer's deference to the past as motivated by tolerance and open-mindedness, rather than authoritarianism. To reconstruct the past as interlocutor in a dialogue is to make the past a foreign country, a distinct perspective that we can learn from and that can change us. Hermeneutics does approach its objects of interpretation with the Panglossian faith that they will prove intelligible and valuable. Yet Eskridge argues that this generosity towards objects of interpretation also enables a modest, self-critical attitude not conducive to dogmatism. Moreover, an open-minded and respectful attitude towards the past need not preclude subjecting it to searching questioning: "Interpretation is not merely an exercise in discovery, but involves a critical approach to the text. The interpreter questions the text, the presuppositions of which may be attenuated or undermined over time."[260] Finally, Eskridge argues that even conceding the conservatism of Gadamerian hermeneutics, such deference to the author's horizon may be appropriate for statutory interpretation "in a representative democracy . . . if we accept the premise of legislative supremacy."[261]

[260] Ibid.
[261] Ibid., 634–35.

Eskridge characterizes Gadamerian hermeneutics as a form of "practical reason," a craft of making judgments and applying standards in concrete contexts. Hermeneutics is not, in other words, a theory of meaning and is therefore indifferent to debates over where meaning is to be found. If the textual interpretations constructed by Gadamerian hermeneutics are not textual "meaning" according to someone's theory, so be it. The Gadamerian interpreter seeks the "truth of the text," that is, a reconciliation of the horizons of text and reader—yet hermeneutics offers no method that guarantees her success. To the contrary, the desire for a sure-fire "method" for producing true answers reflects a fear of the very openness to experience that a hermeneutic encounter with the text requires. Gadamer disdains instrumental rationality. The practice of interpretation is a matter of seeking harmony between means and ends, past commitments and future projects. It is an art involving aesthetic judgment, rather than a science grounding validity in technique.

Eskridge illustrates Gadamerian hermeneutics through a searching critique of the case of *Boutilier v. Immigration and Naturalization Service*. The case concerned the *Immigration and Nationality Act* of 1952, the relevant section of which excluded entrants "afflicted with psychopathic personality, epilepsy, or a mental defect." Clive Boutilier entered the United States from Canada in 1956, lived there continuously after 1959, and in 1964 applied for citizenship. At that point Boutilier admitted in an affidavit that he had engaged in sexual relations with men three or four times a year for thirteen years. The Public Health Service (PHS) ruled, for that reason, that Boutilier was excludable at the time of his entry into the United States. The INS decided, on that basis, not only to deny Boutilier's citizenship application, but to deport him as well. In 1967 the Supreme Court upheld their interpretation of the statute. Eskridge asks, "Was the Court's holding—that Congress used the term 'psychopathic personality' as a term of art to exclude homosexuals—a correct interpretation of the act in 1967? If the issue were one of first impression would it be a correct interpretation today? Having been decided, does *Boutilier* remain a correct interpretation of the statute?"[262]

Eskridge considers these questions from the standpoint of each of three conventional "methods" of statutory interpretation—textualism, originalism, and an approach advocated by some progressive jurists that Eskridge calls "presentism." Eskridge concludes that each approach is blindered by a dogmatically narrow temporal perspective. He argues that an honest and open-minded consideration of Boutilier's case requires acknowledging the relevance of a number of different temporal perspectives or "horizons." The statutory interpreter's task requires a narrative or tradition, linking the context of enactment to the possibly very different context of application. Only by adopting such an historicist conception of statutory meaning can the interpreter avoid an intellectually dishonest suppression of relevant data.

The problem with "textualism" is not so much that it imposes a narrow temporal perspective, but that it presumes that no temporal perspective is necessary

---

[262] Ibid., 610.

because linguistic meaning is timeless and self-sufficient. Eskridge notes that the key statutory term "psychopathic personality" is an esoteric term with no "plain" meaning beyond its apparent adoption of medical usage. But which medical usage? Eskridge argues that the term "psychopathic personality" was deemed meaningless by medical writers at the time of the statute's adoption. Nevertheless, many doctors saw homosexuality as pathological then, and the standard psychiatric diagnostic manual identified it as a "sociopathy." The current view, reflected in the diagnostic manual and the practice of the PHS in immigration cases, is that homosexuality is not pathological.[263] What meaning might have been ascribed to such language in 1964 when Boutilier applied for citizenship? Eskridge notes that in 1962 the United States Court of Appeals for the Ninth Circuit ruled that the phrase "psychopathic personality" was too vague to be applied against homosexuals. But in 1965 Congress, apparently reacting to this decision, included "sexual deviation" among the excludable traits. Eskridge argues that even this language can only be read against homosexuals because of what we know about its legislative history or what we suspect about the dominant social values at the time of its enactment. By itself, "sexual deviation" could be read to exclude anyone engaging in sexual conduct other than penile-vaginal intercourse (which would exclude many heterosexuals) or anyone engaged in sexual conduct harmful to others (which would not exclude homosexuals per se).

"Originalism" apparently supplies the temporal horizon that textualism lacks. But because a statute is always applied in a context somewhat different from the context in which it was enacted, a single horizon is never enough to generate a determinate interpretation. To use the past, originalist interpreters must select some features to emphasize and ignore others. The criteria of selection are imported from the present. In making this argument, Eskridge points to different legislative historical data supporting each side in the Boutilier case.

In support of Boutilier's exclusion, Eskridge recounts that some members of Congress called for statutory language explicitly referring to homosexuals, and that the PHS suggested the phrase "psychopathic personality," saying it would include homosexuals. Both the House and Senate reports agreed that this language was broad enough to refer to homosexuals. When the Ninth Circuit deemed this language unconstitutionally vague, Congress responded by making its intent to exclude homosexuals even more explicit.[264]

On the other hand, examination of the statute as a whole suggests that Congress's general aim in drafting the statute was to "exclude aliens who have socially destructive medical problems," rather than those deemed immoral. Congress considered and then rejected explicit reference to homosexuals, at the behest of the PHS. This suggests that the PHS successfully sought to define excludability in medical terms. Even if the PHS considered some homosexuals to be psychopathic, that does not mean it considered all homosexual activity psychopathic or promised Congress that anyone who had ever engaged in homosexual activity would

[263] Ibid., 639–40.
[264] Ibid., 642.

be excluded. At that time, the PHS defined psychopathy as a "personality structure manifest by lifelong patterns of action . . . a disturbance of intrinsic personality patterns." Eskridge argues that this definition may not have referred to someone like Boutilier, who engaged infrequently in the relevant behavior, and who had been found not psychopathic by doctors examining him.[265]

Suppose then, that in 1952 some congressmen thought aliens ought to be excluded if they had engaged in enough immoral conduct, and some thought aliens ought to be excluded if they were sufficiently crazy. That still does not tell us whether a majority of Congress would have thought Boutilier in particular excludable. Perhaps they would have approved excluding Boutilier out of deference to the judgment of the PHS. This would imply that *Boutilier* was rightly decided in its day, but that as soon as the medical profession stopped seeing homosexuality as a mental distrubance, *Boutilier* lost its authority. Thus, "originalism" may develop either a pro-exclusion, or an anti-exclusion interpretation, or even one in which the "originally intended" meaning of the statute shifts over time. We must choose among these different "original intents" on the basis of values drawn from some other source.

Because contemporary homophobia is primarily expressed in moral rather than medical discourse, hindsight suggests that a knowing exclusion of homosexuals "could not" have been motivated by health concerns. But to reason in this way is to forget the medical profession's role in presenting "homosexuality" as a chronic condition or character type; it is also to forget the cultural authority of science in general and psychiatry in particular in the 1950s. As bigotry moved from the mainstream to a reactionary fringe it may have become more irrational and invidious in content. Thus, the concerns we ascribe to yesterday's centrists may depend on whether we see them as the precursors of today's centrists or of today's reactionaries.

Presentists insist that deference to the past is an impossible fiction. Drawing on Justice Brennan's suggestion that we read the Constitution as if ratified today,[266] Alexander Aleinikoff has proposed that we read statutes as if currently enacted. In an important sense, statutes in force are currently enacted since they can be repealed by a simple majority of the current legislators (absent an executive veto). But when legislators "enact" an old statute by leaving it in force, just what do they enact? The text alone, or also that text's known history?

Aleinikoff argues that if enacted today, the exclusion of "psychopaths" and even "sexual deviants" would not be applied to homosexuals. According to Eskridge, however, Aleinikoff underestimates the conservatism of his contemporaries.[267] Thus, the problem with Aleinikoff's determination to apply only current values is that fidelity to tradition is central to most people's current value commit-

---

[265] Ibid., 643–44.

[266] William Brennan, "The Constitution of the United States: Contemporary Ratification," in Levinson and Mailloux, *Interpreting Law and Literature*, 13.

[267] Eskridge, "Gadamer," 645–46.

ments. In excising tradition from statutory interpretation, Aleinikoff risks a distorted portrait of the present.

Eskridge contrasts his own "Gadamerian" reflections on Boutilier with the interpretive "methods" he criticizes as dogmatically narrow-minded. Eskridge sets out to develop a narrative of the evolution of the statute's meaning that can resolve not only the original dispute but a hypothetical dispute involving the contemporary application for citizenship of "Jean Deau," a French national. Deau entered the United States in 1968 and today admits to the INS that he is gay. Pursuant to a 1979 policy change, the PHS refuses to certify him as a psychopath. Yet the INS concludes he was not "lawfully admitted" in 1968 and so cannot be naturalized. Eskridge is committed to resolving each case on the basis of readings of the applicable statute that reconcile text, legislative expectations, legislative reasons, subsequent administrative practice under the statute, subsequent changes in social and cultural conditions, and contemporary constitutional values.

Eskridge emphasizes that while the legislative history suggests Congress's desire to exclude homosexuals in both 1952 and 1965, it is not clear whether this desire was motivated by the now outmoded belief that all homosexuals posed a health threat, or by the still prevalent antipathy to homosexuals. As between these two possible legislative motives, Eskridge argues that the medical motive accords with the constitutional value of equal protection, which disfavors legislative classifications that are purely invidious. Moreover, the medical motive better accords with the health focus of the statutory text as a whole, which arguably confers sole jurisdiction on the PHS rather than the INS to investigate the health of aliens and exclude for medical reasons. The subsequent practice of the INS conformed to this expectation, and Eskridge argues that Congress has acquiesced in this practice.[268] Eskridge concludes:

> My ultimate fusion of horizons with the text is the following: . . . The story of this statute is that in 1952 both Congress and the PHS were committed to excluding at least some gay men and lesbians on medical grounds. The PHS persuaded Congress to define the exclusion broadly and leave virtually all the enforcement to the PHS. The PHS has changed its mind, in response to new medical developments. Interpretation of the statute should now follow the PHS's direction.[269]

Hence, the statute was rightly read in *Boutilier*, although Eskridge suggests that a conscientious judge could have admitted Boutilier on a sympathetic reading of the narrow facts of the case (he was never actually examined by the PHS).[270] By the time *Deau* is decided the meaning of the statute has changed. Deau is admitted among us, while *Boutilier* is deported to the past.

Eskridge renders *Boutilier* as a *hard case*. Like many other appropriations of literary theory in legal scholarship, Eskridge's "opinion" is a performative argu-

[268] Ibid., 657–59.
[269] Ibid., 659.
[270] Ibid., 676.

ment, aimed less at establishing the particular legal interpretation advanced than at establishing something about the persona of the interpreter. Eskridge's voice is personal (*"my* . . . fusion of horizons with the text")[271] and ruminative ("the more I consider the application [of the statute] . . . to exclude Jean Deau, the less sense it makes to me").[272] His interpretation is warranted less by the evidence that supports it than by the openness of the interpreter to countervailing evidence. Invoking Gadamer's critique of method, Eskridge insists that his analysis of the immigration statute not be read as the illustration of an interpretive *technique* for disposing of hard cases. Eskridge's reading does not so much resolve the case as conserve and savor its difficulty.

We are accustomed to reading such "opinions" allegorically as vindications of judicial discretion. Certainly "Gadamer/Statutory Interpretation" displays the requisite virtues of judiciousness and discretion. But it has an additional significance. By designing a narrative voice that discretely hints at but restrains itself from pressing a partisan interest, Eskridge engages in a performative legitimation not only of hermeneutics but also of the partisan interest he does not disclaim:

> My approach to the Boutilier issue is influenced at every turn by broader socioeconomic and political factors which may themselves be distorting. For example, my choosing to write a lengthy law review article about a twenty-three-year-old case, and the *Columbia Law Review*'s interest in publishing it, is incomprehensible without understanding the importance of gay rights among America's elites, some of whom are openly homosexual."[273]

The authorial voice stops short of identifying the author or the editors as gay, instead suggesting simply that the presence of open homosexuals among the producers and readers of law review articles makes it more possible for a gay person to write law review articles, for a person wishing to write articles to identify as gay, perhaps to do so publicly, for anyone to risk inviting speculation that they are gay by writing law review articles about gay rights issues. Thus, without identifying himself as gay, Eskridge points to his article as evidence of a gay presence in the legal academy and a gay voice in establishment culture. The point is that if he is gay, that fact does not discredit or distort his views; instead, the rationality, traditionality, moderation, and self-discipline of his argument for admitting gay immigrants shows that gayness is already "within our horizon," already admitted, whether or not any individual admits to it. By creating a possibly gay forensic voice with moderate views, deferential to tradition and majority views, even majority prejudice, by invoking and then eschewing a more "interested" tone of argument, Eskridge argues by performance that gays are at least as capable of cabining their desires as heterosexuals.

[271] Ibid., 659.
[272] Ibid., 658.
[273] Ibid., 677–78.

That the cases considered are about the admission of francophone homosexuals suggests that the article is also about admissibility into public discourse of European thought and literary theory: "Surely it is absurd to attribute to Congress a desire to exclude W. H. Auden, André Gide, Ludwig Wittgenstein, Marcel Proust, John Maynard Keynes, and millions of others based upon their sexual preference. No other country in the world excludes people because of their sexual preference."[274] The authorial voice of "Gadamer/Statutory Interpretation" embodies a gay advocacy and literary theory not—in the language of the PHS—"ill [adapted to] society and the prevailing culture."[275] In his stoic determination to tolerate even bigotry, to give it its due, Eskridge at once teaches a lesson of, and exacts a tuition of, tolerance.

The Hermeneutics of Justice

Eskridge's work offers a hermeneutic engagement with the paradigmatic form of positive law, the statute. We expect such an encounter to compromise the critic's independence, and Eskridge to some extent gratifies this expectation. But if we expect the interpreter of positive law to accommodate prevailing arrangements, we expect the apostle of justice to challenge them. Yet in *Spheres of Justice*[276] and *Interpretation and Social Criticism*[277] Michael Walzer argues for an internal, hermeneutic account of justice that begins with a "thick description" of prevailing arrangements. "Moral argument," he claims, "is interpretive in character, closely resembling the work of a lawyer or judge who struggles to find meaning in a morass of conflicting laws and precedents."[278]

Spheres of Justice defends a particular interpretation of egalitarianism that Walzer calls "complex equality." The aim of complex equality is an equality of social status that cannot be defined by reference to the equality of any particular good or basket of goods. According to this conception, "equality is a complex relation of persons, mediated by goods we make, share, and divide among ourselves; it is not an identity of possessions. It requires then a diversity of distributive criteria that mirrors the diversity of social goods."[279] Goods are tokens of social recognition and vehicles of self-expression. If all people are constrained to have the same "goods," they will have not equal status but the same social identity—which both restricts liberty and impoverishes social life.

The divergent aims of status equality and identity pluralism can be reconciled by maintaining boundaries among distributive criteria for different goods so that monopoly over one good does not lead to monopoly over others. Walzer's model of justice as complex equality is especially concerned with cabining the cor-

---

[274] Ibid., 652.

[275] Ibid., 643.

[276] Michael Walzer, *Spheres of Justice* (New York: Basic Books, 1983).

[277] Michael Walzer, *Interpretation and Social Criticism* (Cambridge: Harvard Univ. Press, 1987).

[278] Ibid., 20.

[279] Walzer, *Spheres of Justice*, 18.

rupting influence of wealth by means of alienation and accumulation restrictions for certain kinds of goods, and by means of the public provision of certain goods.

But if certain goods should not be bought and sold, how can we tell what they are? And if not bought and sold, how should they be distributed? Here hermeneutics is given its scope. In Walzer's view, the distribution of goods is a question of justice insofar as goods have social *meaning* and so shape the role, the place, the worth (including the self-worth) of individuals in a particular society. Justice has to do with goods—currencies of social meaning—rather than preferences—patterns of individual desire. Because goods are currencies of social interaction they are caught up in networks of distribution and circulation as soon as they are recognized. They have in-built criteria of distribution as part of their social meanings:

> The conception and creation [of goods] precede and control the distribution. Goods don't just appear in the hands of distributive agents who do with them as they like or give them out in accordance with some general principle. Rather, goods with their meanings—because of their meanings—are the crucial medium of social relations; they come into people's minds before they come into their hands; distributions are patterned in accordance with shared conceptions of what the goods are and what they are for.[280]

Thus, Walzer argues, we ordinarily assume that office should be distributed with some regard to competence, welfare with at least some regard for need, punishment and esteem with some regard for desert, political power with regard for who will be effected by its exercise, or who will exercise it competently. Each of these goods and each of the criteria governing their distribution is indefinite and subject to controversy. But to identify a distributive decision as involving one of these goods is to invoke a certain discourse for debating its justice. Argument about justice is therefore modal: it is organized by the particular goods recognized in a particular society.[281]

What counts as a good varies from culture to culture. Walzer regards even somatic needs like nutrition as culturally contingent since human beings are sometimes willing to sacrifice themselves for the vindication of a cultural value, and not necessarily irrationally.[282] Moreover, the institutions and values that sustain "community" also sustain the mutual concern that secures the fulfillment of our creature needs:

> The Athenian drama and the Jewish academies were both financed with money that could have been spent on housing, say, or on medicine. But drama and education were taken by the Greeks and Jews to be not merely enhancements of the common life but vital aspects of communal welfare. . . . These are not judgments that can easily be called incorrect.[283]

[280] Ibid., 6–7.
[281] Ibid., 8.
[282] Ibid.
[283] Ibid., 83.

Because different cultures create different "goods" the criteria of distributive justice vary across different cultural and historical settings.[284] We can never resolve the meaning of justice once and for all, in abstraction from a particular society or social institution. This means that *whenever questions of justice arise—* which is to say whenever social choices are made—*the methods of the humanities are implicated.* We have to "read" the society and its institutions anew, each time, and decide what reforms will best maintain or foster self-respect for these people, with these traditions, these institutions, these deep disagreements. Underlying this view of justice is a social scientific claim about the deepest well-springs of human motivation that challenges the behaviorist assumptions of economics: human beings are motivated not by the satisfaction of physical desires, but by the artistic quest to render a self in what we might call the "medium" of social norms.

Nevertheless, because justice is culturally specific, Walzer does not offer complex equality as a universal concept of justice. Complex equality is a conception of justice that he hopes to render appropriate and attractive to a society like ours, already devoted—or so he claims—to a plurality of goods. We are asked to assess the justice of Walzer's pluralism not by looking at the fairness of any particular distributive decision, but by determining whether the whole achieves his aim of equality of status.

And here is where Walzer's strategy of proliferating autonomous institutions appears vulnerable—there is no particular "sphere of justice" that must be governed by the aim of equal status. There is no particular institution whose responsibility it is to secure such equality. The result may be a collection of private spheres, each shirking the public responsibilities of justice.

The most visible inequality of status in American society is surely that of race. How does Walzer propose to cure it? Not by conventional means: he rejects affirmative action in employment as an intrusion of politics upon the calculus of qualifications intrinsic to the sphere of "office."[285] He similarly rejects "going beyond the remedies required to end willful segregation," in order to preserve the neighborhood school as a focus for political participation and community identity.[286] He suggests that these in any case are Band-Aids in place of the more radical social surgery he deems necessary to prevent the status degradation of any group: national health care, more and better public education, public subsidization of full employment with decent wages and conditions, workplace democracy, restrictions on employer mobility, union-friendly labor law reform, and campaign finance reform.

This is an appealing and progressive agenda that if systematically implemented would doubtless enhance the welfare and influence of the least well-off in our society. But it is unclear that a discourse of institutional pluralism and autonomy supports this agenda. One sphere that Walzer is anxious to protect is that of democratic politics. Yet political majorities show no contemporary inclination to sup-

[284] Ibid., 9.
[285] Ibid., 151–54.
[286] Ibid., 226.

port such a sweeping social democratic agenda. The rhetoric of autonomous institutional spheres seems better for protesting policies as corrupting intrusions than for defending policies as needed to sustain the independence of institutions. How will his social democratic proposals fare in the face of protests that they infringe the autonomy of property owners, political associations, the Federal Reserve Bank, and so on? The rhetoric of autonomy may yield a distribution of goods that is authentically American in its accommodation of racial hierarchy.

These objections may point to a deeper problem with Walzer's interpretive aesthetic. Walzer is committed to understanding social life as an array of discrete meanings: bounded nation-states, bounded communities, bounded institutions, each with its own defining ethos and purpose. But *are* meanings ever this discrete? Both structuralist and pragmatist approaches to anthropology regard cultural meaning as systematic. For Bourdieu, part of the meaning of any good—including such cultural goods as prestige, cultivation, distinction, chic—is its convertibility, its character as capital. On this view cultural action is *typically* an effort to convert one form of advantage into another—to buy esteem through the display of expensive taste in consumption, or to win lucrative employment through the display of cultivated speech. How realistic then is the aspiration to prevent inequality in one sphere from contaminating other spheres? Does the division of inequality into "distinct" spheres prevent its spread or simply insulate it from critique?

Is this apologetic tendency an artifact of Walzer's particular interpretation of American society, or is it endemic to interpretation? In *Interpretation and Social Criticism*, Walzer takes up this broader question: "Given that every interpretation is parasitic on its 'text,' " he asks, "how can it ever constitute an adequate criticism of the text?" He answers that "the critique of existence begins . . . from principles internal to existence itself."[287] The reason is that cultures always embody competing conceptions of abstract principles, contradictions between principle and practice, and tensions among different practices. Drawing on the young Marx and Gramsci, Walzer explains:

> What makes criticism a permanent possibility . . . is the fact that every ruling class is compelled to present itself as a universal class. . . . This self-presentation of the rulers is elaborated by the intellectuals. Their work is apologetic, but the apology is of a sort that gives hostages to future social critics. It sets standards that the rulers will not live up to, cannot live up to given their particularist ambitions.[288]

Thus, conceptions of justice are relatively autonomous, "texts" independent of any author. Standards of justification are "artifacts: subject to interpretation, and . . . interpreted in both apologetic and critical ways."[289]

Walzer offers the Biblical prophets as examples of hermeneutic social critics. Their message was neither universal nor esoteric but directed at all Israelites. They condemned the practices prevailing in their own societies, but not from the

[287] Walzer, *Interpretation and Social Criticism*, 21.
[288] Ibid., 40–41.
[289] Ibid., 48.

standpoint of universal justice. Instead they condemned their society for failing its own professed values. The prophets harped on the hypocrisy of elites, who hid their bad consciences behind the false piety of empty ritual, thereby compounding injustice with blasphemy. Walzer acknowledges that the critical impact of prophecy depended upon its address to a company of worshippers with a collective responsibility to interpret the law. Walzer twice quotes the biblical injunction that the law "is not in heaven. . . . The word is very nigh unto thee, in thy mouth and in thy heart, that thou mayest do it."[290] In this way he makes the point that the proliferation of a hermeneutic attitude towards justice fosters the social conditions for effective social criticism. Thus, the advantage Walzer claims for hermeneutic criticism is that it inculcates this attitude by addressing the critic's fellow citizens where they live. It may not be very radical in content, but it is democratic in process. And absent democratic debate, radical criticism will fall on deaf ears and can only be implemented by authoritarian means.

CONCLUSION

By contrast to the work of Eskridge and Walzer, much of what we have called Hermeneutic Criticism of Law is not genuinely interpretive in method. It is philosophical in method and questions—or reconfirms—the possibility of legal interpretation. But since legal interpretation is an unavoidable and practical activity, theoretical demonstrations of its impossibility—or its possibility—seem somewhat beside the point. Indeed, we have tried to show that epistemological critiques of legal interpretation derive their superficial plausibility from interpretive impasses rooted in the flaws not of language, but of American political culture. To seek epistemological explanations for the incoherence of American constitutional law is therefore to deflect attention from its political cultural meaning. This kind of epistemological criticism of legal interpretation implies that the incoherence of our peculiar Constitution is inevitable, rooted in the intractable duality of mind and body, rather than in a tragic but potentially correctable history of injustice. And this means, ironically, that the Hermeneutic Criticism of Law has somehow managed to avoid both interpretation and criticism.

However, we have sought to illustrate a more genuinely interpretive, or "hermeneutic," style of criticism in our own account of this genre. Thus, we have located the recent sense of interpretive crisis in law within a much longer tradition of reflection on legal interpretation, and in relation to an American political culture riven between egalitarianism and racial exclusion. We have thereby read—and criticized—abstract arguments about the possibility of interpretation, as interpretations of particular traditions.

The Hermeneutic Criticism of Law that has emerged among American legal scholars in the last two decades assumes that legal decisions depend on the interpretation of authoritative texts. But the hermeneutic tradition conceives interpreta-

---

[290] Deuteronomy 30:11–14, quoted in ibid., 22, 74.

tion as a necessarily broader enterprise entailing the interpretation of self and situation. If law is interpretive in this broad sense, it depends on the meanings not just of authoritative texts, but also of roles, social practices, institutional histories, and cultural identities, and it constantly reshapes these cultural contexts. Hence, a genuinely hermeneutic criticism would have to interpret and evaluate law as part of a larger culture. In our final chapter we will propose such a Cultural Criticism of Law.

Narrative Criticism of Law

Introduction: The Law as Narrative Trope

In the late 1980s, a symposium on "Legal Storytelling" appeared in the *Michigan Law Review*. Kim Scheppele's foreword announced that "narrative [has] become an important and recurring theme in legal scholarship."[1] Richard Delgado, the symposium's organizer, noted that numerous legal scholars had begun to write "dialogues, stories, and metastories," or had "dared" to "inject narrative, perspective, and feeling . . . into their otherwise scholarly, footnoted articles." He added that many of these scholars are members of "outgroups . . . whose voice and perspective—whose consciousness—has been suppressed, devalued, abnormalized."[2] Since the publication of this joint manifesto, narrative legal scholarship has continued to proliferate. While its proponents do not agree on all issues, a number of claims recur:

1. That human perception and thought inevitably rely on narrative.

2. That competing narratives may be told about the same events, reflecting the divergent interests and experiences of the tellers.

3. That legal argument and decision rely on the selective rendition of events in narrative form.

4. But that in this very selectivity, legal argument represses competing stories.

5. That the stories most often repressed may be those reflecting the perspectives of subordinated groups.

6. That legal discourse denies that it "privileges" some stories over others.

7. That legal decision making purports to achieve impartiality by applying rules that abstract away the very particularities of human experience that narrative emphasizes.

8. That by suppressing the concrete human consequences and meanings of legal decisions, rules make law morally obtuse.

9. That the authority of rules depends upon implicit narratives linking them to the will of authoritative decision makers, and explaining how those decision makers came to be authoritative.

10. That the inclusion of narratives, whether fictional or factual, in legal scholarship can morally improve the law, subvert its claims to impartiality, and advance the interests of subordinated groups.

[1] Kim Lane Scheppele, "Foreword: Telling Stories,"*Michigan Law Review* 87 (1989): 2073.
[2] Richard Delgado, "Storytelling for Oppositionists and Others: A Plea for Narrative," *Michigan Law Review* 87 (1989): 2411–12.

The "call"[3] to see law as narrative tends to be offered as something of a paradox, suggesting that law and narrative are ordinarily opposed. The Law as Narrative trope asserts that contrary to pretense, law is merely a story, one subjective rendering among many; or that it would be better for us all if law were more like narrative literature and less like itself; or that buried within the routines of legal practice lies an element of creativity that can redeem the practice of law or sustain the spirit of its practitioners. Typically, the trope is at once subjunctive in mood, imperative in voice, and wistful in tone: *imagine* law as narrative!

Thus, when lawyers and legal scholars liken law to narrative, they are offering what a linguist might call a performative remark—they are not so much describing law as they are dramatically presenting themselves as having a particular moral character with respect to law. In *The Word and the Law*,[4] Milner Ball tells the stories of several public interest lawyers working in close contact with the poor. Interweaving their stories with allusions to literary and biblical texts, Ball announces that he will not make linear arguments or advance propositions, but rather will make an "argument" in the sense of a ballet or poem—a performance. By narrating lives caught up in vocations, he witnesses to a theology of Christian service; but rather than arguing theology's relevance to law, he seeks to "*do* theology and either perform its relevance or fail to do so."[5] Ball will court faith the way a novelist courts the suspension of disbelief. As Steven Winter argues, all narrative persuades in this way, by enlisting the reader's collaboration: "Our very success in understanding [a] story is simultaneously the narrator's success in persuading us . . . to imagine the world in a particular way."[6]

The Law as Narrative trope makes this same performative appeal. Rather than denoting similarities between law and narrative, the Law as Narrative trope calls upon the reader to assimilate them *despite their presumed differences*, to make an imaginative leap, to participate in a *fiction*. Thus, scholars and lawyers who use the trope do not mean it literally—indeed, they offer it to oppose what they condemn as the literalism of the law. To understand the trope is already to heed its call, to perform it by imagining immanent within law a hidden character and potential awaiting dramatic realization.

The presumed antinomy of law and narrative is explicit in recent writing about legal themes in narrative literature. Much of this work assumes that law is mechanistic, abstract, rule-bound, and alienating, and that the experience of lawyers and legal actors and the justice of legal decisions would be improved if the abstracted, professional, rationalist voice of law were replaced or complemented by a more human voice. Typical are the many invocations in legal scholarship of *Billy Budd*, Melville's tragic tale of a simple, good-hearted sailor hanged for the unintended killing of his false accuser, whom he strikes in an inarticulate fit of righteous

---

[3] Kathryn Abrams, "Hearing the Call of Stories," *California Law Review* 79 (1991): 971.

[4] Milner Ball, *The Word and the Law* (Chicago: Univ. of Chicago Press, 1993).

[5] Ibid., 2.

[6] Steven L. Winter, "The Cognitive Dimension of the Agon between Legal Power and Narrative Meaning," *Michigan Law Review* 87 (1989): 2225, 2272.

indignation. The tale's true protagonist is Captain Vere, an intellectual, who uses all his powers of language and reason to convince the ship's officers—and himself—that Billy's execution, though undeserved, is required by law and good order. To Robert Cover, Billy's execution is a metaphor for the law of slavery whose enforcers, Vere-like, stilled the voice of conscience and played their roles.[7] To Richard Weisberg, the novella prefigures the verbal evasions that facilitated collaboration with the Nazi genocide.[8] To Brook Thomas, it bespeaks the seductive reasonableness in which law clothes oppression and injustice.[9] To all these authors, *Billy Budd* speaks the human truth of its namesake's mute innocence that the crabbed discourse of legal authority will not hear.

The use of narrative literature implied in these works is summed up by Paul Gewirtz in an essay commending Aeschylus to law students: "Literature makes its special claims upon us precisely because it nourishes the kind of human understanding not achievable through reason alone but often involving intuition and feeling as well."[10] Scholarly writing that implores us to see the human drama obscured by the rules and categories of the law tends to incorporate this sentimental view of literature as antithetical to reason.

In an essay entitled "Voices," Julius Getman laments that "the focus on general rules, which is one of the contributions of professional voice, ensures the use of language that removes some of the feeling and empathy that are part of ordinary human discourse."[11] The abstraction of "the professional voice" threatens the lawyers' psyche and emotional sensibility.[12] It drains much of the interest and drama from the "human situations" to which it is applied.[13] And it narrows the vision of lawyers, accommodating them to the powers that be and blinding them to possibilities of reform.[14]

To Getman, law is more than this professional voice. Counseling clients, negotiating deals, addressing juries, the successful lawyer is the one whose ear is attuned to the human voice. But, unfortunately, courts seem to speak in the professional voice. Getman discusses *Brown v. Board of Education*,[15] as well as the controversial rape case of *State v. Rusk*,[16] which implies that a victim must take the mortal risk of defending herself to sustain her accusation, and the well-known case of *State v. Williams*,[17] convicting a Native American couple of manslaughter for failing to bring a sick child to a doctor, out of fear that prejudiced social

---

[7] Robert M. Cover, *Justice Accused: Antislavery and the Judicial Process* (New Haven: Yale Univ. Press, 1975), 1–6.

[8] Richard H. Weisberg, *The Failure of the Word* (New Haven: Yale Univ. Press, 1984), xi–xiii.

[9] Brook Thomas, *Cross-examinations of Law and Literature* (Cambridge: Harvard Univ. Press, 1987).

[10] Paul Gewirtz, "Aeschylus' Law," *Harvard Law Review* 101 (1988): 1043, 1050.

[11] Julius G. Getman, "Voices," *Texas Law Review* 66 (1988): 577–78.

[12] Ibid.

[13] Ibid.

[14] Ibid.

[15] *Brown v. Board of Educ.*, 347 U.S. 483 (1954).

[16] *Rusk v. State*, 406 A.2d 624 (Md. 1979), rev'd, 424 A.2d 720 (Md. 1981).

[17] *State v. Williams*, 484 P.2d 1167 (Wash. 1971).

welfare authorities would take the child away. To each of these cases, Getman opposes a personal narrative—Charles Black's moving account of growing up in the segregated South,[18] Susan Estrich's frightening account of her own rape,[19] and the recollections of a Black law student from the Deep South of her family's demeaning treatment by White doctors.[20] In a concluding peroration, Getman invokes Huckleberry Finn's deliberation over whether to turn in the runaway slave, Jim: "When Huck thinks of Jim's situation in terms of legal concepts such as 'obedience to authority' or the judicially enforceable claims of property owners, he knows that he must turn Jim in. Only when he responds to his own more human expressions of empathy, friendship, and loyalty does he refuse."[21]

Narrative literature here stands for human feeling and is figured as alien to law but inherent in the persons who populate legal settings. Hence, narrative represents an insurgent potentiality within law, forever threatening to throw off the robes of reason that confine our passionate natures. This is how the Law-as-Narrative trope holds in suspense its two seemingly antithetical claims: that narrative is inherent in law, yet that narrative can also redeem or subvert it.

If the Law as Narrative trope trades on the currency of a sentimental opposition between law and literature in legal scholarship, it also capitalizes on wider currents in academic and professional culture. The sudden prevalence of literary terminology throughout academe bespeaks the declining stock of the ideal of objectivity. But where such other terms as "hermeneutics," "deconstruction," and "textuality" bristle with an intimidating theoretical erudition, "narrative" ingratiates itself as accessible and self-explanatory. The Law as Narrative trope is a particularly antiprofessional or antitheoretical version of the Law as Literature trope. After all, narrative is the aspect of literature most easily appreciated by those who are not technically trained, theoretically informed, or even literate. As Peter Brooks notes, "the desire and the competence to tell stories . . . reach back to an early stage in the individual's development, to about the age of three, when a child begins to show . . . the capacity to recognize narratives, to judge their well-formedness."[22]

Narrative denotes the simple activity of storytelling. To represent a phenomenon in narrative terms is to emphasize change and development. In a story events are related to one another over time, acquiring meaning from the order in which they happen, or the order in which they are revealed. To experience events as a narrative is therefore to grow or learn. According to the Aristotelian formula, a narrative has a beginning in which a problem or conflict is posed, linked by a

---

[18] Charles L. Black Jr., "The Lawfulness of the Segregation Decisions," *Yale Law Journal* 69 (1960): 421.

[19] Susan Estrich, "Rape," *Yale Law Journal* 95 (1986): 1087.

[20] Getman, "Voices," 583–84.

[21] Ibid., 58.

[22] Peter Brooks, "Reading for the Plot," in *Essentials of the Theory of Fiction*, 2d ed., ed. Michael J. Hoffman and Patrick D. Murphy (Durham: Duke Univ. Press, 1996), 327.

plausible sequence of events, to some climactic change or resolution.[23] Narratives promise suspense, curiosity, entertainment. They are pleasurable and even addictive, making a sensuous rather than "rational" appeal for attention and credibility. For all the creativity that reading is said to entail, the pleasure of reading narrative is partly the pleasure of giving up control, of regressing into childlike credulity and wonder.[24]

Of course, while fiction is always narrative, narrative is not always fictional. Nevertheless, the association of narrative with fiction identifies it with imaginative literature. To call a story a narrative is to emphasize the imaginative activity of a narrator. Hence, to narrate events is not simply to recount them as they occurred, but to impose an order, perhaps to embellish or invent. A narrative is a construction, an artifact. The early novels of the eighteenth century tended to overtly display the shaping sensibility of the author. Later "realist" writers instead told their stories through the experiences of their characters and established that fiction involves a choice of "point of view." Modern novelists have experimented with nonfictional memoirs or contemporary history in novel form, implying that the literary inventiveness of narrative could inhere entirely in the narrative point of view rather than in the events narrated.

Today, we expect a "narrative," even if factual, to reflect a particular, and often highly imaginative, point of view. The "New Journalists" of the 1970s sought to write in a way that was at once more narrative and more personal.[25] Their aim was not only to enhance the vividness and appeal of journalistic writing, but also to candidly confront the reader with the inevitably selective filtering function of the journalist. Such reportage presupposes that many narratives of an "event" are possible. The verity of a "New Journalistic"account lay not so much in its factuality as in its sincerity in reflecting the inner reality of subjective experience. Narration became self-revelation.

The "narratives" of interest to nonliterary academics are often "oral histories" or folktales that are told and retold. These narratives are artifacts without necessarily having been self-consciously produced as art and so may be viewed as data, revealing a worldview. The academic collector of folk narrative may seek to record and canonize a perspective otherwise unrecognized and suppressed. In so doing, she may reduce official discourse to the status of narrative, just one perspective among many.

If narration is an act of self-definition, and an implicit challenge to some official point of view, than narration seems to promise psychological and political liberation. A patient in psychoanalytic therapy presents her experience or her

---

[23] Aristotle, *Poetics*, trans. Ingram Bywater, in *The Works of Aristotle* (Oxford: Clarendon Press, 1908), 1447.

[24] See Roland Barthes, *The Pleasure of the Text* (New York: Hill and Wang, 1974).

[25] E.g., Tom Wolfe, *The New Journalism* (New York: Harper and Row, 1973); Norman Mailer, *Miami and the Siege of Chicago: An Informal History of the Republican and Democratic Conventions of 1968* (New York: World Publishing, 1968); Hunter S. Thompson, *Fear and Loathing: On the Campaign Trail '72* (New York: Warner Books, 1983).

dreams for analysis in narrative form. For the psychoanalyst Roy Schafer, "the self is a telling,"[26] to be compared to a generic narrative of the ego's mastery and sublimation of infantile desire in response to frustration: "In making interpretations, the analyst retells [the story of the self] along psychoanalytic lines. . . . The analyst's retellings progressively influence . . . the stories told by analysands. . . . The end product . . . is a radically new, jointly authored work."[27] The therapeutic subject gains access to a past or an inner reality previously suppressed. But the aim of the therapeutic dialogue is not the recovery of truth so much as the fashioning of a personal history that better enables the subject to cope. She emerges with a new, more aesthetically complete narrative of the self with a beginning (repressed trauma), a middle (neurotic conflict), and an end (self-knowledge, recovery, release).

The political therapy of consciousness raising has a similar dramatic structure, in which narration triumphs over not only a psychological process of repression but also a social process of "silencing." Testifying to an experience of victimization, receiving "validation" from similarly experienced victims, the victim resists intimidation, renounces self-blame, and, by helping others to do the same, recovers a sense of efficacy.[28] Indeed, to the influential feminist psychiatrist Judith Herman, psychoanalysis and consciousness raising are just two examples of a more general phenomenon of recovery from trauma, a phenomenon that is always narrative in method and political in significance. In Herman's vision, power consists largely of the capacity to inflict atrocity while silencing protest. At the same time, recovery from the traumatic effects of atrocity depends upon the capacity to integrate the memory of trauma into a coherent narrative of the self. Since power entails the suppression of the memory of trauma on which recovery depends, recovery from trauma entails a challenge to power. Thus, Herman argues, the accurate diagnosis and effective treatment of the psychological effects of trauma are political acts of resistance that require the social context of a political movement. At the same time, if power entails the silencing of victims and the erasure of its own effects, narrating trauma becomes essential to political resistance.[29]

As Herman describes it, the treatment of trauma-induced disorders involves considerable literary skill. The trauma victim often suffers dissociation, lacking

[26] Roy Schafer, "Narration in the Psychoanalytic Dialogue," in *On Narrative*, ed. W. J. T. Mitchell (Chicago: Univ. of Chicago Press, 1981), 25, 31.

[27] Ibid., 31–32.

[28] Catharine A. MacKinnon, *Toward a Feminist Theory of the State* (Cambridge: Harvard Univ. Press, 1989), 83–105; Katharine T. Bartlett, "Feminist Legal Methods," *Harvard Law Review* 103 (1990): 829, 863–67; Nancy McWilliams, "Contemporary Feminism, Consciousness-Raising, and Changing Views of the Political," in *Women in Politics*, ed. Jane S. Jaquette (New York: John Wiley and Sons, 1974), 157–70; Pamela Allen, "Free Space," in *Radical Feminism*, ed. Anne Koedt, Ellen Levine, and Anita Rapone (New York: Quadrangle Books, 1973), 271–79; Carol Williams Payne, "Consciousness Raising: A Dead End?" in *Radical Feminism*, 280–84; for a historical account of the origins of the consciousness-raising method among women involved in the civil rights movement, see Sara M. Evans, *Personal Politics* (New York: Knopf, 1979).

[29] Judith Lewis Herman, *Trauma and Recovery* (New York: Basic Books, 1992).

any coherent personal history, and any conscious or articulate memory of the traumatic events. The therapist must "read" evidence of victimization in disjointed dream images, psychosomatic or "hysterical" symptoms, and compulsive behaviors—indeed, the absence of memory may itself bespeak trauma. The therapist must, through "careful questioning," recover the patient's repressed experience and help shape it into the coherent narrative that will exorcise self-blame and underwrite a newly "integrated" personality.

Like Schafer, Herman emphasizes that the ultimate aim of this narrative is therapy, not accuracy. The therapist is properly a sympathetic listener, a "witness" to the victim's suffering, rather than a "detective" trying to ferret out truth.[30] The collaborative construction of the trauma narrative culminates in an act of "testimony," but the principal purpose of this ritual is to "empower" the patient rather than to record history. The Recovery Movement that Herman has helped inspire frames both psychological health and political justice in terms of narrative coherence. Whether self-narration is conceived primarily in political or in psychological terms, narrating and revising personal history is increasingly prescribed as the route to an aesthetic transcendence of suffering.

While narrative is often cast in a therapeutic role in feminist thought, it can also play a moral role. "Cultural" feminists like Carol Gilligan see the nurturing roles to which women have traditionally been socialized as a source of moral insight.[31] From this viewpoint, moral obligations spring from relationships to particular people rather than the abstract principles. A focus on relationships gives moral deliberation a distinctively concrete and particularistic "voice." Relational obligations have contingent origins, vest in particular persons, and may grow and change along with those persons. Thus, for a person socialized to nurture, moral reasoning involves *narrating* the past and future of relationships. It is particularistic, concrete, dynamic, and creative and so stands in contrast to a model of moral reasoning as the mechanical application of abstract, universal rules. Narrative morality may be celebrated as a kind of folk wisdom that challenges bureaucratic rationality.

In sum, to liken law to narrative may be to link it to popular culture rather than high art. The Law as Narrative trope imagines law as literature, but literature that is immediately accessible, unencrypted. Unlike the "interpretive turn," a "narrative turn" offers literature without the interdisciplinary middleman of literary theory. It promises not so much interdisciplinarity as extradisciplinarity, an escape from one's own discipline into a literary playground, unpoliced by literary professionals. The turn to narrative is a *re*turn, a *recovery* of an undamaged inner child beneath the professional shell. The antiprofessionalism implicit in the Law as Narrative trope is, therefore, closely related to its sentimentality. The sense that

---

[30] Ibid., 180.

[31] Carol Gilligan, *In a Different Voice: Psychological Theory and Women's Development* (Cambridge: Harvard Univ. Press, 1982); Sara Ruddick, *Maternal Thinking: Toward a Politics of Peace* (Boston: Beacon Press, 1989); Nancy Chodorow, *The Reproduction of Mothering* (Berkeley: Univ. of California Press, 1978); Jessica Benjamin, *The Bonds of Love* (New York: Pantheon Books, 1988).

narrative is a natural human capacity, obscured beneath the affectations of professionalism, gives the Law as Narrative trope its contradictory implications that narrative is already a part of law, yet is also antithetical to it.

Despite the antiprofessional and antitheoretical connotations of "narrative" in contemporary academic discourse, "narrative" remains a literary term of art. Part 3.1 of this chapter surveys accounts of narrative in literary theory. Two points emerge.

First, to recognize narrative as a kind of literature is to see it as the product of imagination working within and upon the constraints of convention. Thus, a literary training should discourage opposing narrative to other social practices as intrinsically more authentic, spontaneous, or sincere. Narrative is artifice, and it is not intrinsically free of the pressures of self-interest and social norms that influence all cultural practices, including law. This conclusion does not mean that narratives can never expose inconvenient truths, give voice to indecorous feelings, or challenge prevailing arrangements. But it does mean that we cannot *prejudge* whether particular examples of narrative are more truthful or authentic or subversive than particular examples of legal discourse.[32]

Second, literary scholarship of narrative reveals that the conventions governing narrative are historically contingent—including the very convention that associates narrative with originality and individual self-expression. Thus, narrative has social functions that vary with the social orders in which it is found. The characteristics that we now associate with "narrative" are likely to be those of the narrative genres peculiar to modern society—the national history and the novel. These genres presuppose certain legal institutions, which in turn rely on the narrative description of legal subjects and legal institutions that the novel and the academic history, respectively, exalt as art and science. Law and narrative may thus be mutually complicit rather than antithetical.

Accordingly, we proceed in part 3.2 to critically examine the prevalent claims that narrative can correct, redeem, or subvert law. To be sure, we will find that narrative is certainly useful and relevant in legal argument and deliberation, sometimes in politically progressive ways. But the hope that narrative will work some utopian transformation of law and legal culture is quixotic, resting on sentimental oppositions between reason and passion, objectivity and subjectivity, society and individual, convention and nature. Narrative legal scholarship cannot be evaluated categorically, but must be considered case-by-case. In this spirit, we will explicate particular examples of narrative scholarship, showing how particular narratives serve reasoned argument.

Part 3.3 will develop a variety of claims for the inherent link between law and narrative. It will show how legal claims necessarily narrate transactions, moral

---

[32] For an attack on the use of anecdotal narrative as a basis for legislation, see David Hyman, "Lies, Damned Lies, and Narrative," *Indiana Law Journal* 73 (1998): 787 (arguing that stories told to Congress promoting a bill to prevent hospitals from engaging in "patient dumping" were often unfairly unrepresentative or downright false).

dramas of condemnation and rectification, and institutional histories. Indeed, it will argue that the closer legal argument comes to fundamental questions about the authority of law, the more narrative it must become. Thus, the oft-posed dichotomy between the abstraction of theory and the concreteness of narrative appears specious. While it is commonly assumed that narratives reveal an authentic subjectivity that law suppresses, this last part argues that law helps to compose a liberal subject capable of assenting to law's authority, a liberal subject celebrated and dramatized in modern narrative literature. In this way law and narrative may be seen as different aspects of a single discursive process. These different aspects are brought together in a conclusion that recounts the theatrical political trial of John Brown to show how national mythology and personal biography can interpenetrate.

In sum, this chapter is a critique not primarily of narrative legal scholarship but of some of the extravagant and sentimentalist claims made on its behalf. Legal scholarship can hardly avoid narrating, especially if it is going to confront fundamental questions about the legitimacy of particular legal institutions. Our aim is merely to resist the sentimentality of categorical claims that narrative subverts or redeems law by opposing cold rationality with authentic human feeling. The task of narrative criticism is not to introduce the narrative subject into the alien and alienated discourse of the law—but to read, critique, and revise the field of narrative discourse that law already is. Attention to the narratives implied and enabled by law is a necessary part of the "Cultural Studies" of law endorsed in this book's final chapter.

3.1 LITERARY THEORIES OF NARRATIVE

Literary critics generally define narrative discourse as the conjunction of a story and a teller. A story is a sequence of events happening to a human or anthropomorphized subject over time, a sequence in which some sort of equilibrium is first disrupted and then restored. The mediation of such a story by a teller distinguishes narrative from drama, while the reference to events and characters external to the teller distinguishes narrative from lyric discourse.[33]

Literary critics analyze narrative in terms of at least four formal properties. First, plot—the structure of events making up the story. Second, the phenomenon of reader interest—the motives and characteristics ascribable to a properly engaged reader. Third, point of view—the identity and characteristics of the narrator or narrators of a story and of the characters with whom the reader is encouraged to identify. Fourth, combining all the others, narrative genre—the social practice of narrative the story exemplifies and presupposes. After surveying these formal devices, we will consider what literary theory has had to say about their rhetorical

---

[33] Robert Scholes and Robert Kellogg, *The Nature of Narrative* (New York: Oxford Univ. Press, 1966).

uses. Finally, we will survey the views of literary theorists concerning the historical contribution of literary narrative to the oppression and liberation of subordinated groups, attending especially to the political significance attached to the ideas of literacy and literary canons.

Plot

Robert Scholes and Robert Kellogg define plot as "the dynamic, sequential element in narrative literature."[34] Plot has particularly interested structuralist and other formalist critics. In his study of narrative discourse,[35] Gérard Genette offers what he calls a "Narratology," a system of concepts for analyzing the formal elements of narrative. This system analyzes plot structure by reference to the order of events, their duration and frequency. Genette demonstrates that plot events must be ordered and measured along two dimensions: "story time," which is the imaginary time within which the events of the story take place, and "narrative time," which is the time within which events are read about. Years of story time may receive a quick summary, while brief events may be ruminated over for hours of narrative time. Story time and narrative time are most closely synchronized in unembellished dialogue and in cinematic descriptions of action. Where the two temporal scales coincide, the reader may best sustain the illusion that the story is happening "before her eyes." Henry James called this sort of "realistic" narration "scene."[36] Genette's distinction between story time and narrative time also implies that there are two dimensions of plot, the order in which events occur, and the order in which they are told.

Roland Barthes also analyzes plot structure along two dimensions, a "proairetic" dimension of action and event, and a "hermeneutic" dimension of meaning. Questions of the cause, motivation, or purpose of events, ambiguities as to what really occurred, anxiety and curiosity about what will occur—these comprise the hermeneutic elements of plot that play such an important role in propelling the reading experience forward. Without the hermeneutic activity of a reader, a sequence of events is not yet a plot.[37] Barthes's hermeneutic recalls Iser's "virtual dimension," discussed in chapter 2.

Structuralists have sought not only to define the parameters of narrative plots, but also to map their characteristic elements and sequences. In *Morphology of the Folktale*, Vladimir Propp analyzed one hundred Russian folktales and showed that all were composed from a limited palette of character types and plot elements. More surprisingly, he showed that while not all plot elements were present in every tale, those present seemed to appear always in the same order: the head of a family departs on a journey, warning that some transgression is to be avoided,

---

[34] Ibid., 207.

[35] Gérard Genette, *Narrative Discourse: An Essay in Method*, trans. Jane E. Lewin (Ithaca: Cornell Univ. Press, 1980).

[36] Henry James, *The Art of the Novel: Critical Prefaces* (New York: Charles Scribner's Sons, 1934).

[37] Roland Barthes, *S/Z*, trans. Richard Miller (New York: Hill and Wang, 1974).

but the warning is not heeded. A "villain" arrives, seeking information. By trick, the villain makes off with a "victim" or valued object. A "sender" dispatches a "hero" after the villain. The hero enters a magical landscape, where he is tested by a "donor," shows virtue, and is rewarded with help. The hero defeats the villain, recovers the object of his quest, and returns, possibly pursued. But his heroism is not recognized, his glory usurped by an "impostor." The hero performs a further feat to win recognition. Finally, he is rewarded, and the villain or impostor punished. While Propp found this model plot in one tradition, he argued that similar plots could be found in the folklore of most European and some non-European peoples.[38]

In his classic *Anatomy of Criticism*, Northrop Frye attempted an even more ambitious morphology of plots, a scheme that purported to encompass all of Western literature, from its classical and biblical sources forward. Frye linked particular plot forms with characteristic patterns of imagery and with cosmological attitudes that in turn imply ideas about law, order, and legitimacy.

The demonic imagery of hell and damnation became attached in Western literature to the plot form of tragedy, and associated with suffering. Tragedy typically focused on a single figure of pronounced character and ability, a hero with sufficient social power to be little regulated by the will of others. The tragic hero confronts, and succumbs to, a natural order. Tragedy, is an "epiphany of law, of that which is and must be."[39] The tragic structure balances determinism with a cautionary portrayal of transgression and punishment. Typically the hero makes a self-constraining choice to submit to a certain law or instrumental program, thus "narrowing a comparatively free life into a process of causation."[40] Tragedy dramatizes a sacrificial ritual and so resonates with the Fall of man and the Passion of Christ.[41]

Pastoral settings provide the dominant imagery of salvation, social harmony, and fulfillment that Frye associates with the plot form of comedy. Comedies are typically narratives of social transformation, of return to the simple values of a lost golden age from a state of corruption, usurpation, and pretension. The comic plot often begins with a romance blocked by an illegitimate authority. The usurper imposes his own rigid personality on others in the form of an irrational law, the absurd results of which evoke laughter. Since the narrative is driven forward by the exposure of usurpation, it has the forensic structure of a lawsuit: "The action of comedy . . . moves from law to liberty. In the law there is an element of ritual bondage which is abolished, and an element of habit or convention which is fulfilled."[42] In the end, the hero and heroine are rewarded, while the usurper is humili-

---

[38] Vladimir Iakovlevich Propp, *Morphology of the Folktale*, trans. Laurence Scott (Bloomington: Research Center, Indiana Univ., 1958).

[39] Northrop Frye, *Anatomy of Criticism: Four Essays* (Princeton: Princeton Univ. Press, 1971), 208.

[40] Ibid., 212.

[41] Ibid., 212–14.

[42] Ibid., 181.

ated but reincorporated into a new, more inclusive society evoked by a concluding celebration.

To the basic narrative choice between tragic suffering and comic fulfillment, Frye added two psychological attitudes of withdrawal—romantic fantasy and ironic detachment. He associated each attitude with a "displacement" of the cosmological axis of heaven and hell onto a moral axis of good and evil. The romance asserts the compatibility of desire and morality, while the satire cynically asserts their incompatibility. The romance essentially follows the plot form laid out by Propp in his analysis of the folktale; it begins with authority enfeebled and prosperity played out, allowing villainy an opportunity. There follows a heroic quest or journey, a struggle with a villain, and a final drama of recognition and reward for the hero. The satire has no single plot structure, since its purpose is to disrupt and parody the other modes. Romantic heroes are exposed as deluded fools, while tragic heroes are reduced to pretentious comic villains who are traduced not by comic heroes and redeeming communities, but merely by other comic villains out for themselves.

Frye presented the four narrative modes as the poles of two perpendicular axes. Works could combine characteristics from two neighboring narrative modes such as comedy and satire, or tragedy and satire, but they could not combine the opposing modes of satire and romance or tragedy and comedy. Thus, the two axes defined a dial on which Frye hoped to be able to locate any narrative work of Western literature.

Reader Interest

The connection Frye drew between plot structure and certain conventional emotional attitudes suggests that plots presuppose a reader with an appropriate psychological constitution. According to Scholes and Kellogg:

> All plots depend on tension and resolution. In narrative, the most common plots are the biographical (birth to death) and the romantic (desire to consummation) because these are the most obvious correlatives for the tension and resolution which plot demands. . . . The reader of a narrative can expect to finish his reading having achieved a state of equilibrium—something approaching calm of mind, all passion spent.[43]

For Peter Brooks, this desiderative structure of narrative gives it an urgency and forward movement, held in check by suspense, by the sheer time it takes to read. Narrative is not only temporal but "time-bound,"[44] its movement "irreversible,"[45] as all its characters struggle to achieve glory, domestic happiness, self-realization, or enlightenment before the end so that "plot is the internal logic of the discourse of mortality."[46] The experience of plot then depends not just on a reader's curiosity, but on the mortal anxiety that engenders a sense of temporal urgency.

---

[43] Scholes and Kellogg, *Nature of Narrative*, 212.
[44] Brooks, "Reading for the Plot," 343.
[45] Ibid., 341.
[46] Ibid., 343.

Building on the work of Propp and Frye, Tzvetan Todorov has sought to map the structural features of narrative in particular oeuvres.[47] The key to his analysis is an analogy between the motives guiding the action of the characters and those guiding the experience of the narrative's ideal reader. For Todorov, a narrative is a three-part movement from fulfillment or equilibrium through loss or disequilibrium, back to recuperation or equilibrium. The disequilibrium is manifest in a protagonist's desire, and the story restores equilibrium by narrating the protagonist's strategy for pursuing her desire, and the outcome of this strategy. A narrative, in short, traces the career of a desire. But as experienced by a reader, the narrative is itself a desire, the desire to learn how the story turns out.

Todorov emphasizes how often a variant of the curiosity that motivates reading also seems to motivate narrative characters. For example, the characters in the medieval romance of the *Holy Grail* search not just for the location of the treasured object, but, with the reader, for its meaning.[48] Similarly, the entire premise of the *Arabian Nights* is that the story and its protagonist persist only as long as her antagonist's curiosity. Within the stories, too, characters seem almost uniformly motivated by an insatiable desire for stories, as each new character is greeted by others with a demand to tell his or her story. The *Arabian Nights* illustrates what Todorov calls the inevitable incompleteness of narrative, in that every narrative implies both a narrator and an ideal reader, with stories of their own. Thus, each narrative is embedded in a larger narrative, just as each narrative embeds the implied histories of all its characters and places.[49] Todorov shows that while Jamesian narrative is the exposition of a point of view, what we perceive through the protagonist's point of view is always some maddeningly elusive off-stage object of mystery. Although the narrative point of view is the only reality such "realist" fiction allows the reader to see, the reader's experience of that point of view requires her to share in a protagonist's obsessive search for an unmediated reality she can never see.[50]

Point of View and Narrative Voice

Narrative "voice" and "point of view" came to be important critical terms as a result of the finely etched realism exemplified and promoted by James and Flaubert. Each of them aimed at what Genette calls an experience of "directness" in reading narrative—a feeling of being inside the story. Yet according to Genette, they achieved this "directness" by two quite different strategies.

James's approach was to limit the reader's information to that which could be available to a person "within the frame of the action" or in a position to observe it. James aimed at a "realistic" mode of perception, an experience of being

---

[47] Tzvetan Todorov, *The Poetics of Prose*, trans. Richard Howard (Ithaca: Cornell Univ. Press, 1971).

[48] Ibid., 120–42.

[49] Ibid., 66–79.

[50] Ibid., 143–77.

"shown" rather than "told" the action. Typically, James's narrators observed rather than participated in the action. Yet the narrator could be anyone as long as the narrative was "focused" through the perspective of a particular character. As long as the narrator neither supplied information unavailable to the focal character nor suppressed information available to the focal character, she could comment on events without altering the point of view of the story. By contrast, Flaubertian "realism" aimed to de-emphasize the narrative voice, to prevent the reader from experiencing the narrator as a character. This stratagem in turn aimed to hide the shaping subjectivity of the author so as to allow a full suspension of disbelief. The transparent narrator favored by Flaubert could be the omniscient or "nonfocalized" narrator shunned by James.[51]

By contrasting Jamesian and Flaubertian realism, Genette shows that realism's aesthetic aim—the feeling of immediacy—is a contingent effect that derives from a variety of techniques. Indeed, he argues, what will strike a particular readership as a "realistic" narration depends upon historically contingent conventions of storytelling. Scholes and Kellogg concur that the strongest argument for James's identification of narration with participant observation is a historicist one. By the late nineteenth century, they suggest, the reliable omniscient narrator had ceased to be epistemologically credible. Thus, a nonironic posture toward the narrator had come to seem distractingly authoritarian for modern readers.[52]

Soon after the omniscient narrator became outmoded, Flaubert's transparent narrator met the same fate: the narrative voice became an important character in its own right. In the face of the moral and spiritual void of the twentieth century, artistic creation became an heroic action itself worthy of narration. Once the narrative voice was recognized as a character, authors could call attention to its change and development over the narrative time of the story. And if narration comes to be seen as a kind of action, all stories seem to lie nested within larger stories narrating these narrative acts. Genette calls these stories within stories different narrative levels. The intervention of characters or actions from one level of narrative into another—as when a character argues with a narrator about how the story should proceed—Genette calls narrative "metalepsis." A frequent device in modernist fiction, narrative metalepsis calls attention to exactly what Flaubert sought to suppress: the constructed quality of narrative, of its characters and viewpoints. By analogy, narrative metalepsis suggests that even the "characters" of author and reader are narrative devices.[53]

To some extent, the distinction between viewpoint or "focus," and narrative voice, reflects the emergence of a split between two different modes of characterization. Traditionally, narrative treated thought as unspoken soliloquy, a form of rhetoric following the conventions of public speech. By the eighteenth century, however, narrative began to reflect a *psychological* model of thought as the association of sense impressions "preparing the way for the stream of consciousness,"

[51] Genette, *Narrative Discourse*, 161–68.
[52] Scholes and Kellogg, *Nature of Narrative*, 275–77.
[53] Genette, *Narrative Discourse*, 227–77.

which purports to be a faithful transcript of a mind in operation.[54] Perception and association are psychological functions, dramatized by point of view. By contrast, narrative voice increasingly presents a speaker conscious of performing in front of an audience. In ancient literature, soliloquy and interior monologue are occasional devices, used to mark ambivalence and chart alternative paths of plot development. In modernist literature, however, the foregrounding of narrative voice can saturate a text with ambivalence and alienation. Monologue becomes less a process of deliberation than a shtick, an alibi, or a con game.

For the recently fashionable Russian critic Mikhail Bakhtin, the proliferation of voices and viewpoints in modern narrative fiction gives it a refreshingly pluralistic quality. Narrative is a "dialogic" structure in which the authority of a narrative or authorial voice can be challenged by the charisma of the characters.[55] Bakhtin implies that this "dialogic" element in modern fiction tends to subvert the totalitarian state and broaden the mind, by presenting a discourse that seems to comprehend and conserve contrarieties.

Genre

By narrative genre, we mean a historically particular social practice of narrative. A genre encompasses several narratives typically linked not only by formal conventions but also by a common purpose or social function. Narratives of the same genre are put to use in roughly the same way, and the use of one example of a narrative genre presupposes familiarity with other such examples. Historians of genre emphasize the distinction between oral and written narrative. Oral narrative—a phenomenon common to both traditional and modern societies, but obviously more important in traditional societies—involves a distinctive method of composition. In oral narrative, a performer must create a tale out of a standard plot, formulaic phrases and motifs, and sometimes a metric form. The narrative voice is typically omniscient, reliable, and impersonal. In traditional societies, the storyteller serves not as an author but as a more or less skilled performer of a collectively authored work.

The first stage in a written literature is often the recording of oral narrative tradition in the form of an epic, "amalgamating mythic, mimetic and historical materials in a fictional form."[56] From this amalgam different genres may emerge: the mimetic genres of history and satire, didactic genres such as fable and allegory, romantic genres like the fairy tale. Such discrete genres may in turn recombine to form new syntheses. Much literary history is written as the narrative of the epic's dissolution into discrete genres and their triumphal reintegration in the great modern synthesis of the novel. Literary scholars have been especially interested in

---

[54] Scholes and Kellogg, *Nature of Narrative*, 181.

[55] Mikhail Mikhailovich Bakhtin, *The Dialogic Imagination: Four Essays*, ed. M. Holquist, trans. Caryl Emerson and Michael Holquist (Austin: Univ. of Texas Press, 1981); Mikhail Mikhailovich Bakhtin, *Problems of Dostoevsky's Poetics*, ed. and trans. C. Emerson (Minneapolis: Univ. of Minnesota Press, 1984).

[56] Scholes and Kellogg, *Nature of Narrative*, 70.

explaining the novel's emergence, often treating the new genre as a symptom of distinctively modern ideas about society and individual psychology. The novel has been a particular focus of Marxist criticism, aimed at elucidating the social conditions for its popularity. A common theme of such work is the link between the novel and the emergence of liberal individualism.

According to Ian Watt, novels emerged in eighteenth-century England as a result of a decline in literary patronage.[57] To garner a larger reading public, authors sought to make their works more accessible. The novel was an innovation in that it told a story from the viewpoint of a particular individual. The characters were fully fleshed individuals with ordinary names and life histories, and the action took place in real time and space, giving the story an unprecedented verisimilitude. Verisimilitude made for an easier, more passive reading experience, less dependent on education, that stimulated the interest of new readers. Many of these new readers were participants in an expanding commercial economy, their economic individualism conducing to a sympathetic interest in the activities and well-being of individual characters. By presenting experience through the eyes of a particular person, the novel presented the individual mind as a free space where imagination and innovation might subvert tradition. This view of the mind may partly derive from new empiricist epistemologies focusing on the mind as the synthesizer of sense impressions. Yet these epistemologies also grew out of an earlier genre, the Calvinist diary that so interested Weber as a testament to "the Protestant Ethic and the Spirit of Capitalism." Many of the new readers were women, who in bourgeois households were expected to embody leisured refinement. In an effort to appeal to a new audience of cautious tradesmen and their wives, novelists came to emphasize moral rather than heroic virtue in their tales.

For György Lukács, too, the novel was the apotheosis of bourgeois individualism.[58] Yet it embodied individuality less in the protagonist than in the Romantic author. The novel's celebration of individualism was less a function of its biographical form than of its author's success in integrating the chaos and conflict of modern capitalist society into an aesthetic unity. Thus, the individualism of the novel was most expressed by what appeared to be its least individualistic and most objective aspect—its panorama of society, from court to country, and countinghouse to almshouse.

Where the premodern epic could achieve organic completeness by narrating the fate of a culturally coherent society, the atomized society of the nineteenth century could not be the protagonist of a story. Yet, for Lukács, the inability of such a society to provide individuals with a sure and safe "life path" in the face of the unpredictable dislocations of modernization meant that individuals were on their own in imagining their own futures and composing meanings for their

---

[57] Ian Watt, *The Rise of the Novel: Studies in Defoe, Richardson, and Fielding* (London: Chatto and Windus, 1957).

[58] György Lukács, *The Theory of the Novel: A Historico-Philosophical Essay on the Forms of Great Epic Literature*, trans. Anna Bostock (Cambridge: MIT Press, 1920).

lives to fulfill. The nineteenth-century novel provided a repertoire of imagined futures for readers, but these were never the futures their protagonists imagined. These novels often opposed two narratives: a rise or return from obscure poverty to social status as a result of cultural refinement, and the humiliating puncturing of self-delusion by external reality. Sometimes the two combined, as the protagonist achieved success only after he or she exchanged the pursuit of social status for the more fundamental refinements of spirit and conscience. The theme of social mobility enabled the author to display a cross section of society in biographical microcosm. Even if transcendence proved tragically temporary or illusory for the protagonist, it was achievable by the author, whose Olympian vision transcended that of his or her characters.[59]

For Edward Said, as for Todorov, the novel assumes an analogy between character and reader motivation. The novel presupposes a social world in which all persons fear anonymity and strive to articulate a distinctive point of view. In pursuit of identity, the protagonist struggles to realize an idealized or fictional self, initally currying the favor of others, but ultimately seeing the inauthenticity of this approach. So too the reader feels incomplete and seeks to supplement herself by adopting the fictional viewpoint of the protagonist. With the protagonist, the reader presumably learns the lesson of authenticity, transcending fantasy and dependence on others, and thereby bringing the reading experience to its conclusion.[60]

Said extends this parallel between the rise of the novel and the rise of the bourgeois individual to the rise of imperialism. The rhythm of outward exploration and return to self that structures the narrative of *Bildung* tracks the cycles of trade and empire, as experience must be paid for in the bitter coin of disillusionment and incorporated into the self. The Romantic hero must absorb stormy passion in some tropical adventure and bring it all back home to be tamed in the English drawing room. For Said, the novel is an incorporative, encyclopedic cultural form, with a highly regulated plot mechanism and a system of social reference depending on the rules of bourgeois society. The prototypical characters in the early novel are permitted the degree of restless energy appropriate to the enterprising class, but in the end they always submit to regulation.[61]

Fredric Jameson shares the view of Lukács and Said that the novel is fundamentally a narrative of *Bildung*, or character development. For Jameson, the motive force in such a narrative is the conflict between desire and the limitations of reality. In the face of experience, youthful aspiration accommodates itself to the finitude of life. Realizing it cannot become everything and achieve universality, desire shapes itself into a particular self. For Jameson, this lesson of limits, so prominent in the realist novel of the late nineteenth century, is essentially a version of the economic principle of scarcity. Hence, the model of individuality promoted

---

[59] Ibid., 60.

[60] Edward W. Said, *Beginnings: Intentions and Method* (New York: Basic Books, 1975), 82–93.

[61] Ibid., 69–75.

by realist literature essentially identifies maturity with accommodation to the "realities" of the marketplace.[62]

By contrast to the traditional emphasis among historians of the novel on voice, characterization, and plot form, "New Historicist" critic Catherine Gallagher emphasizes the novel's character as *fiction*.[63] She argues that the nineteenth-century novel's cultural and commercial success depended on its fictional status, because its social milieu was a speculative market. She also stresses the role in this marketplace of female authors and readers, who were more the objects than the subjects of property.

According to Gallagher, the popular genre that emerged in eighteenth-century England and France was not truly the descendant of archaic fictional genres like the romances satirized by Cervantes. As private patronage of poetry and drama declined in the early eighteenth century, writers had to rely increasingly on political parties for support. Thus, the novel's more immediate predecessors were such predominantly nonfictional genres as the political satire and the scandalous broadside. Yet scandalmongering, for the novelist, carried with it the risks of libel prosecution and of becoming identified with the very vulgarity one exposed to public view.

By midcentury, political patronage of literature was on the wane and Watt's new reading public was on the increase. To win the interest and patronage of these new readers, Gallagher argues, writers had to supply characters they could identify with. This was the "sentimental" age, and readers were willing to pay for opportunities to sympathize. But it was also the age of "possessive individualism," and readers were reluctant to sympathize with anyone real:

> If we grant that Humean sympathy works by appropriating emotions, by transforming them from the emotions of another (mere ideas) to our emotions (lively sentiments), we can see how property . . . serves as the invisible link between sympathy and fiction. . . . Our conception of the sentiments as appropriate to *that* rather than *this* body must be overcome in the process of sympathy. This proprietary barrier of the other's body is what the fiction freely dispenses with; by representing feelings that belong to no other body, fiction actually facilitates the process of sympathy.[64]

Fictional characters performed a marvelous alchemy, promising to increase everyone's capacity for altruism without requiring anyone to give up anything. Like corporations, fictional characters could be widely invested in without liability. They are "utopian common property, objects of universal identification."[65] Gallagher argues that fiction was especially useful in preparing women for courtship and marriage because it drilled readers in the conditional and temporary extension of sympathy to characters. Women had to be prepared to love any suit-

---

[62] Fredric Jameson, *The Political Unconscious: Narrative as a Socially Symbolic Act* (Ithaca: Cornell Univ. Press, 1981), 151–84.

[63] Catherine Gallagher, *Nobody's Story: The Vanishing Acts of Women Writers in the Marketplace 1670–1820* (Berkeley: Univ. of California Press, 1994).

[64] Ibid., 171.

[65] Ibid., 172.

able man, and to be amiable to any potential suitor, but could not overtly declare love until chosen.[66] In this respect, the sentimental investor had to practice the same psychological operations required of the financial investor. Gallagher notes that in one of Samuel Johnson's *Rambler* essays,

> the man of business and the feminine or feminized sentimental reader of love stories are juxtaposed in a way that reveals their abstract similarity: both hearts "flutter" to a set of signs that, although not personally addressed to them, seize and agitate them, inviting . . . an investment for a defined term. Each has entered that suppositional mental space where beings who are nobody in particular . . . provisionally solicit identification. As readers, they both speculate.[67]

Gallagher proceeds to argue that the cultivation of this speculative capacity was particularly open to those without a fixed public identity and social status. Accordingly, fiction writing was a craft open to women surprisingly early on. Gallagher suggests that if authorship had entailed a continuing proprietary right in one's literary creations, it would have seemed inappropriate for women. But since, as a practical matter, publication generally involved the permanent alienation of copyright for a small lump sum, authorship was more an experience of dispossession than of proprietorship. Accordingly, enslavement, prostitution, and betrothal became metaphors for publication, and authorship became "feminized." Gallagher thus presents the writing of narrative fiction as more an act of self-commodification than of self-definition.

Narrative as Rhetoric

If there has been an overall trend in contemporary literary theory of narrative, it has been a steadily increasing awareness of the wide array of strategic and aesthetic choices available to authors. Emphasizing these options, a number of literary theorists have portrayed narration as a rhetorical practice, a performance aimed at influencing an audience rather than a representation of events.

Certainly the most influential of these studies has been Wayne Booth's *Rhetoric of Fiction*.[68] Writing in the early 1960s, Booth made what today seems the obvious point that novelists exercise aesthetic discretion in telling a story. But Booth sought to combat the continuing critical legacy of the realist aesthetic, which demanded that information be "shown" through action and dialogue, and "seen" through the eyes of characters, rather than "told" to the reader by the narrator. These rules of composition were not only cumbersome, Booth argued, but disingenuous. The verisimilitude aimed at by realist authors was in fact a range of rhetorical effects, achieved by authorial choices of point of view, voice, timing, sequence, and the like. No one strategy always produced verisimilitude, nor was this verisimilitude the only rhetorical effect worth pursuing.

---

[66] Ibid., 192.
[67] Ibid., 194–95, discussing Samuel Johnson, *Rambler* no. 60.
[68] Wayne C. Booth, *The Rhetoric of Fiction* (Chicago: Univ. of Chicago Press, 1961).

Booth also questioned the aesthetic ideal of eschewing emotional manipulation of the reader. Unless the author exploited the reader's curiosity, sympathy, desire for coherence, and conventional expectations, Booth argued, the novel would never get read in the first place. The author of fiction may manipulate and dissemble, Booth implied, so long as she does not bore. Fiction is inevitably, and desirably, rhetorical. But the "rhetoric of fiction" consists not in procrustean generic conventions, so much as in a range of choices giving rise to diverse expressive possibilities.

In *The Sense of an Ending*, Frank Kermode offers a critique of the representational aspirations of the existentialist novel akin to Booth's critique of the aspiration to narrative realism.[69] Literary existentialism extended the realist attack on all versions of literary formalism; it sought to identify and create a literature that did not need to rely on convention and artifice to "mediate" experience. The existentialist novel sought to expose the narrative framing of experience in everyday life as entailing a sort of self-hypnosis, an anti-aesthetic dulling down of the vividness of sensation, a constant effort of bad faith. One consequence of the narrative organization of experience was the tragic illusion of one's actions being dictated by purposes, projects, and character traits that in fact one was free to alter. By experiencing each sensation as vivid and discrete, rather than part of a narrative flow, the existentialist hero came to see his own activity also as an unconnected sequence of spontaneous and ethically free acts.

Of course, this state of perception entailed alienation not only from convention and habit, but also from self. It posed the problem of how one could organize a meaningful life in such a state of self-critical alienation. But even apart from the difficulty of living a life unmediated by narrative convention, the existentialist novelist confronted the problem of how to construct a plotless novel:

> Novels have beginnings, ends and potentiality, even if the world has not. In the same way it can be said that whereas there may be, in the world, no such thing as character, since a man is what he does and chooses freely what he does—and in so far as he claims that his acts are determined by psychological or other predisposition he is a fraud . . . —in the novel there can be no just representation of this. . . . Novels have characters even if the world has not.[70]

Regardless of the conditions of living, Kermode argues, the novelist is existentially unfree. Like Dworkin's judge, what the novelist writes at each point is controlled by what has come before. Perhaps, from an existentialist standpoint, narrative perniciously reifies a false sense of necessity. But, Kermode insists, from a literary standpoint, existentialist fiction disingenuously denies its dependence upon the narrative coherence of the reading experience. When the reader suspends disbelief, her faith may be bad, but without that faith the novel has no existence.

---

[69] Frank Kermode, *The Sense of an Ending: Studies in the Theory of Fiction* (New York: Oxford Univ. Press, 1967), 127–51.

[70] Ibid., 138.

If narrative is inherently fictive and deceptive, as the existentialists claimed, it would follow that this is true even of narrative nonfiction, such as history. Kermode concedes that historical narration requires literary imagination and artifice. To locate one's self in history is to represent human experience as a plot with a beginning, an ordered conflict, and a future resolution bringing the episode to an end. Yet Kermode turns the edge of this critical insight back against existentialism, which, he argues, is itself merely the application of a characteristically modern convention for emplotting history. The sense of alienation to which existentialist fiction gives expression is a response to the experience of modernity as an apocalyptic crisis in which the end is not located at a particular moment, but is a temporally omnipresent potentiality. This diffuse apocalyptic threat is the sense of finitude that commands such attention in existentialist philosophy. Modernist literature generally emplots existential crisis in what Frye would call the mode of tragic irony. Existentialist authenticity is a rhetorical choice.

That historical experience is narratively ordered may have implications for law. Kermode argues that law is an intrinsically historical concept, contemplating the regulation of events in a particular domain, over some interval of time, and he thus implies that legal concepts follow a narrative order. To promulgate and apply laws is to employ narrative as a link to a source of authority, and to invoke a hypothetical narrative about the future consequences of disobedience.

The link that Kermode observes between historical thinking and the narrative imagination finds more careful explication in the philosopher Arthur Danto's *Narration and Knowledge*. Danto claims that histories are expected to explain a change in a narrative way; that is, to count as historical, an explanation must relate what happened between an initial state of affairs and some later altered different state of affairs that caused the change. A narrative explanation of change may combine an elaborate sequence of causal events in a single narrative, invoking many different causal generalizations that might not otherwise be juxtaposed. Thus, while narrative explanations rely on general causal laws, each such explanation is sui generis.

Danto argues that narrative discourse implicitly makes claims about at least two moments of time. A narrative claim identifies one event as the beginning, cause, or anticipation of some later event. A narrative claim presents one event as standing in some relation of significance to a later event, such that one is made meaningful by the other. Moreover, Danto argues, because events have no natural boundaries, the correct description of any event depends upon its significance within a narrative. And because the significance of any particular event within a historical narrative may depend on later events, a historian's version of events may legitimately differ from that of an eyewitness. Each event may be causally related to infinitely many others, and each event may stand in other relations of significance to many different events. Accordingly, many accounts of the same event are equally legitimate. The set of accounts that may legitimately be written at one time, however, is not identical to the set of accounts that may legitimately be written at another. And because criteria of significance and relevance will depend on the values and experiences of authors and readers of history, the value and even the accuracy of historical accounts will legitimately vary for differently situated readers. Thus, concludes Danto, the narrativity of historical claims makes their truth relative. The logic of narration necessitates authorial discretion, so that the aspiration to a purely objective narration of actual events is no more attainable than the aspiration to a purely realist narration of fictional events.[71]

Danto's analysis of narrative discourse implies that one could extend to historical narrative Booth's claim that fictional narrative is inherently rhetorical. In *Metahistory*, Hayden White does exactly that, proposing a poetics of historiography. Examining major European historians from Gibbon to Burckhardt and philosophers of history from Herder to Croce, White argues that both traditions can be analyzed in terms of Frye's taxonomy of plot forms. Together with ideological orientations and the patterned use of rhetorical tropes, plot forms make up part of each historical thinker's characteristic "style."

White characterizes historiography on the eve of the nineteenth century as a debate between ironists, like Gibbon and Voltaire, on one hand, and early Romantics, like Herder and Rousseau, who saw historical events as metaphors for larger spiritual forces.[72] Hegel, suggests White, resolved this particular debate to the satisfaction of his contemporaries by developing a more complex, "organicist," poetics of history, in which events continued to stand for larger principles, but in which these abstract principles had meaning only through their concrete expression in particular events.

For Hegel, historical explanation entailed more than mere causal explanation. For history to be meaningful to human beings, it had to be in some sense justifiable or "rational." Sin and suffering had to be explicable not simply causally, but teleologically, as a sacrifice for some later good if only the good of wisdom and moral progress. To Hegel, the modern idea of the liberal state gave meaning to the carnage of European history, by subjecting the passions to rational governance grounded in consent. The reconciliation of individual passion and the collective good was only an ideal, never an attainable reality, yet passionate striving for this ideal of justice permitted the reconciliation of individual passion and collective reason in a life. The new freedom to pursue this reconciliation in liberal politics was an achievement of history that could render its struggles retrospectively meaningful for nineteenth-century Europeans.[73]

As White notes, the idealist historiography inspired by Hegel was confronted throughout the nineteenth century by more functionalist or "mechanistic" models. Because mechanistic historiography treated events as mere symptoms of a deeper reality of causal laws, White characterizes its rhetoric as reductive or "metonymic." The later nineteenth century witnessed a reaction against theoretical historiography of both organicist and mechanist varieties, and the pursuit of a "realist" historiography that paralleled the contemporaneous pursuit of "realism" in fiction. But historical realism was undone by its own fertility. Competing realist

---

[71] Arthur C. Danto, *Narration and Knowledge* (New York: Columbia Univ. Press, 1985), 233–56.

[72] Hayden White, *Metahistory: The Historical Imagination in Nineteenth-Century Europe* (Baltimore: Johns Hopkins Univ. Press, 1975), 45–80.

[73] Ibid., 81–131.

accounts of the same events, ordered by different plot forms, revealed the impossibility of a purely descriptive discourse of history and the inevitability of rhetoric. The crisis of realist historiography provoked a return to irony, exemplified by Marx and Nietzsche.[74]

At the heart of this crisis of historiography, White argues, lies a truth embarrassing to the realist project: that historiography, because it is a genre of narrative literature, is a fundamentally Hegelian search for meaning and fulfillment. In a later essay[75] White critically explores the common claim that genuine history differs from the more primitive genres of the annal and the chronicle by its narrative form. Examining a medieval annal—a diary correlating events with their years of occurrence—White traces its narrative incoherence to its seeming indifference to institutions. Battles, natural disasters, deaths of saints or kings are recorded, selectively, but not according to any discernible principle of selection. Thus, the annal does not seem to dramatize any social struggle to achieve any state of affairs: "All this suggests to me that Hegel was right when he opined that a genuinely historical account had to display not only a certain form, that is, the narrative, but also a certain content, namely a political-social order."[76] White approves Hegel's claim that

It is the state which first presents subject-matter that is not only adapted to the prose of History, but involves the production of such history in the very progress of its own being. . . . Only in a state cognizant of Laws, can distinct transactions take place, accompanied by such a clear consciousness of them as supplies the ability and suggests the necesssity of an enduring record.[77]

White explains that "the reality which lends itself to narrative representation is the conflict between desire, on the one hand, and law on the other."[78] He suggests that neither historicity nor narrative "is possible without some notion of the legal subject which can serve as the agent, agency and subject of historical narrative"[79] and that "narrative in general . . . has to do with the topics of law, legality, legitimacy, or, more generally, *authority*."[80] This Hegelian theme is what enables narrative to present experience as a moral drama yielding a conclusion, a result, a *judgment*: "In so far as historical stories can be completed, can be given narrative closure, can be shown to have had a *plot* all along, they give to reality the odor of the ideal."[81]

In *The Postmodern Condition*, Jean-François Lyotard extends the rhetorical critique of narrative beyond fiction and history to all academic inquiry, including

---

[74] Ibid., 281–373.

[75] Hayden White, "The Value of Narrativity in the Representation of Reality," in Mitchell, *On Narrative*, 1–23.

[76] Ibid., 11.

[77] George Wilhelm Friedrich Hegel, *The Philosophy of History*, trans. J. Sibree (New York: Dover Publications, 1956), 60–61.

[78] White, "Value of Narrativity," 12.

[79] Ibid.

[80] Ibid., 13.

[81] Ibid., 20.

science. Lyotard reasons that the strength of any claim depends upon the legitimacy of the institution validating it. Arguing that defenses of the legitimacy of any institution must always take a narrative form, he concludes that the justification of even scientific claims depends at least implicitly on a narrative of institutional legitimation.[82] The recognition that all narratives are rhetorical constructs, Lyotard proposes, has provoked a general epistemological crisis. In particular, he argues, the validity of science depends upon some form of "grand narrative" of enlightenment, modernization, or technological progress. The recognition of the relativity and rhetoricity of all such "grand narratives" places us in an anomic condition of postmodernity, in which neither knowledge claims nor ethical projects can be treated as unreflectively legitimate.[83]

That knowledge depends on narrative "constructs" does not, according to Lyotard, entail its "subjectivity," since the idea of the liberal subject, whether in its Lockean or Hegelian variant, itself depends on some grand narrative of modernity. The postmodern crisis of legitimacy is general, destabilizing individuals as much as institutions. Postmodern selves are not subjects, but merely nodal points in a grid through which power and energy circulate.[84] In postmodern culture, narratives do not originate from or affix themselves to particular subjectivities, but simply circulate through a culture, like fashions or consumer fads. The stories people tell about themselves have no more authenticity—and no more originality—than the product images developed by advertisers. From this perspective, personal narrative is significant not of anything about the person, but of the popular culture that has circulated it through its speaker.

Victim Narrative and the Literary Canon

In part 3.2 we explore some of the claims made by *legal* scholars that the introduction into legal discourse of first-person narrative by members of subordinated groups could serve social justice. Yet the prospects and problems of such a program of "desegregating" elite discourse have long been debated by *literary* scholars interested in diversifying the literary canon. As explained in this book's introduction, the literary canon is a political institution, part of the cultural infrastructure of the modern nation-state. The compilation of a national literature has often accompanied the claims of an ethnic or linguistic minority to status as a self-governing nation. Thus, to recover and canonize a subordinated literature may be at once to seek recognition for a subordinated group's inclusion within a national citizenry, and to provide a scriptural focus for identification with a liberation movement.

Literary scholars have explained the importance of diversifying the canon by emphasizing that literacy and literature have historically been exclusive institutional practices. In the nineteenth century, for example, both blacks and women

---

[82] Jean-François Lyotard, *The Postmodern Condition: A Report on Knowledge*, trans. Geoff Bennington and Brian Massumi (Minneapolis: Univ. of Minnesota Press, 1984), 27.

[83] Ibid., 37–41.

[84] Ibid., 15.

were castigated as incapable of rigorous or creative thought, and their literary efforts were greeted with incredulity or condescension. If the Romantic author was the nineteenth century's emblem of self-realized individuality, the publication of an aesthetically coherent narrative by a member of these groups was a daring claim to liberal citizenship, for herself and her group.[85] Yet in claiming admission to liberal society for herself and her subordinated social group, the author also accepted its critical standards and its ideal of a sovereign, acquisitive self. Seen in this light, narrative authorship might have been less an act of rebellion than of collaboration, and its voice might have simply parroted mainstream literature rather than expressing a previously suppressed sensibility.[86] Thus, early narrative literature by members of subordinated groups tends to resist integration into the scriptural canon of a liberation movement and may contribute little diversity to the actual content of the mainstream canon.

Here, then, is the central problem: on the one hand, efforts to reform the canon seem to require criteria for identifying the authentic voice of the oppressed; on the other hand, we have seen that the literary theorist is likely to regard the narratives of the oppressed not as "authentic" self-presentation but as rhetoric, shaped by convention and strategy. Politically engaged literary scholars have assayed a number of responses to this problem.

VICTIM NARRATIVE AS THE RETURN TO ROOTS

If we are skeptical about the inherent authenticity of narrative literature by members of oppressed groups, perhaps we can find the authentic voice of the oppressed in the historical past, before oppression. In *The Journey Back*,[87] Houston Baker defines the task of Black criticism as a recovery of the African roots of African-American culture. In Baker's title trope, Africa stands for a realm of hidden or esoteric meaning to be decoded by the properly initiated critic. Baker argues that though Black and White early Americans may have shared a language or "lexical field," they participated in very different cultural systems with different semantic or "conceptual fields." A familiarity with African cultures, Baker suggests, would reveal hidden and subversive meanings in apparently conventional literary texts.[88]

Yet if Baker expects to find an authentic Black voice in eighteenth- and nineteenth-century Black autobiography, he is disappointed. Baker notes that the autobiographical form derives from the Puritan diary. It is highly individualistic, and so it attracted nineteenth-century Blacks because of their profound social alienation. Yet he finds that Blacks had no way of "transmuting an authentic, unwritten self . . . into a literary representation."[89] Rather, he writes, "the voice of the unwritten self, once it is subjected to the linguistic codes, literary conventions, and

---

[85] Henry Louis Gates Jr., *The Signifying Monkey: A Theory of Afro-American Literary Criticism* (New York: Oxford Univ. Press, 1988), 129–31.

[86] Sandra M. Gilbert and Susan Gubar, *The Madwoman in the Attic: The Woman Writer and the Nineteenth-Century Literary Imagination* (New Haven: Yale Univ. Press, 1979), 70.

[87] Houston A. Baker Jr., *The Journey Back: Issues in Black Literature and Criticism* (Chicago: Univ. of Chicago Press, 1980).

[88] Ibid., 20–21.

[89] Ibid., 39.

audience expectations of a literate population, is perhaps never again the authentic voice of American slavery."[90] Instead, Baker only finds a literature satisfying his criteria of authenticity in contemporary writing, writing inspired by Black liberation politics. Thus, it is not until the Black Power movement that Baker finally finds the "Africa" he is looking for in Black literature, in the form of an explicit theme of Black nationhood. The advent of authenticity tends to be the effect more than the cause of organized politics. *The Journey Back* never really leaves the here and now.

VICTIM NARRATIVE AS THE DEBUNKING OF STEREOTYPES

One approach to the problem of distinguishing subversive from collaborationist narrative emphasizes negative stereotypes of the oppressed group found in mainstream literature. Literature by members of the group that debunks these stereotypes is subversive, while literature that reproduces or reenforces such stereotypes is collaborationist. Yet this approach merely reformulates the problem rather than solving it: the critic must still strive to distinguish subversion of the stereotype from its mere repetition.

Consider Sandra Gilbert's and Susan Gubar's pathbreaking study of the tradition of female novelists, *The Madwoman in the Attic*. The book opens with a catalog of confining images of women prevalent in nineteenth-century England and America, such as the chaste "Angel in the House" and an "unnaturally" deceptive, aggressive, and whorish "Monster" figure who violates traditional gender norms. Yet Gilbert and Gubar find that early novels by women do not simply reject these stereotypes. Instead, the novels *appropriate* these stereotypes as metaphors for the confinement and frustration imposed on women by gender roles. Women's novels show how women were taught to view their natural aggressiveness, physicality, and creativity as monstrous desires to be kept "locked up." Women were taught to misinterpret their resulting unhappiness as attributable to the presence of these illicit desires rather than the repression of these desires. Hence, they were encouraged to view their own artistic impulses as a form of madness or hysteria. Images of madness and confinement in women's novels are therefore legible as both cries of protest and self-indictments.[91] These images involve the subversive use of stereotypes in a way that may nevertheless reenforce their cultural authority.

VICTIM NARRATIVE AS THE SYMPTOMATOLOGY OF OPPRESSION

Conceding that narrative literature by members of oppressed groups sometimes actually expresses self-hatred and reenforces demeaning stereotypes, critics may neverthless put narrative to a somewhat different political use. Such literature may be read diagnostically as part of the symptomatology of oppression. Thus, Gilbert and Gubar present women's literary discourse as "infected" with "anxiety" about violating gender roles, and as "colonized" by patriarchal ideology.[92] The

---

[90] Ibid., 43.
[91] Gilbert and Gubar, *Madwoman in the Attic*, 45–104.
[92] Ibid., 74.

recurrent imagery of madness, confinement, and disease in women's writing is therefore a symptom of a kind of trauma-induced psychic illness, to be read clinically. The "Madwoman in the Attic" is a "projection" of the author's "rebellious impulses" that are "liberated" by "the very process of writing."[93] The author is not the mistress of her own narration, but rather a plaything of rebellious impulses and repressive forces.

In another classic critical exploration of women's literature, *A Literature of Their Own*, Elaine Showalter measures all women's fiction from the standpoint of the self-realization of author and heroine and finds most of it disappointing. Showalter critiques what she calls the "feminine" novelists from Austen through Eliot for accepting the confining Victorian role of "Angel in the House." Showalter objects that, even where feminine heroines insist on equality, "men and women become equals by submitting to mutual limitation, not by allowing each other mutual growth."[94] Apparently as committed to a modern ethic of "self-actualization" as she is to feminism, Showalter objects to the Victorian morality of impulse restraint as pathological, regardless of its implications for sexual equality.

Showalter critiques the feminist novelists of the turn of the century for promoting an ideal of women as asexual symbols of a morality of self-denial.[95] She even seems annoyed that many feminists, while equating femininity with maternal love, avoided motherhood.[96] Finally, she critiques "the female aesthetic" of the diffident Virginia Woolf, who rejected political commitment as an expression of the masculine zeal to win, and dismissed protest and advocacy as bad art. Showalter characterizes this posture as a self-annihilating withdrawal to "a secret room."[97]

If Showalter reads literature clinically, she reads clinical symptoms as literature. Thus, hysterical symptoms are legible as composed symbols that appropriate culturally available systems of signification. Similarly, she argues, the narratives of trauma "recovered" in therapy or support groups are literary inventions that express suffering but do not accurately depict its form. Showalter suspects that many people are driven to invent traumatic episodes because society has failed to recognize or acknowledge less vivid forms of suffering. For Showalter, "recovered" memories of satanic ritual abuse or alien abduction are forms of hysteria that testify to routinized oppression, oppression that is silent not because someone has covered it up, but merely because it is nonnarrative, undramatic. Thus, a trauma narrative may be psychologically empowering even if it is not strictly true, because it gives a name to oppression that would otherwise seem diffuse and ineffable.[98]

---

[93] Ibid., 77–78.

[94] Elaine A. Showalter, *A Literature of Their Own: British Women Novelists from Brontë to Lessing* (Princeton: Princeton Univ. Press, 1977), 124.

[95] Ibid., 29.

[96] Ibid., 189–90.

[97] Ibid., 297.

[98] Elaine Showalter, *Hystories: Hysterical Epidemics and Modern Culture* (New York: Columbia Univ. Press, 1997).

THE LIBERATION MOVEMENT AS CRITIC

If the literary traditions of subordinated groups are records of pathology, then perhaps critical insight must be found elsewhere. The works we have discussed so far emplot these traditions as struggles towards rather than lapses from an authentic voice; and all imply that a truly authentic and subversive victim literature is possible only in the reenforcing social context of a liberation movement. Accordingly, contemporary movements of the oppressed tend to plot the cultural history of their groups according to a narrative of therapeutic progress— a movement from enforced silence through pathological false consciousness to true self-knowledge. The movement makes available for the first time an uncorrupted collective identity and so reveals to members of the subordinated group their authentic identities as group members. Thus liberated, group members are in a position to critically read their own literary tradition. And literature can now be assessed in terms of its contribution to this project of liberation. The contemporary liberation movement becomes the critic of its own literary antecedents.

In moving authority from the authors of narrative literature to a contemporary liberation movement, politically engaged critics of the 1970s simply followed out the implications of the Reader-Response theory then in vogue. According to Baker and other exponents of "the Black aesthetic," meaning and aesthetic value are produced by communities of readers in the act of reading. Literary value had traditionally been defined by reference to the putatively inclusive "communities" of "humanity" or "America." Yet the liberal values of humanity, pluralism, and tolerance associated with these abstractions were simply the values of the White intelligentsia. Blacks could not hope to create their own meanings unless they created their own community of readers.[99]

The stratagem of reading the literature of the oppressed through the eyes of a liberation movement poses difficulties, however, recognized even by some of its proponents. Larry Neal, for example, laments that "the Black aesthetic" may be afflicted with a vanguardism and censorious Puritanism borrowed from Marxism. Thus, it may be an elite discourse that is neither "Black" nor "aesthetic."[100] Similarly, Baker points out the obscurantism in claims that Black writing exhibits an aesthetic quality of "Blackness" perceptible and intelligible only to Black readers, and definable only by reference to their experience.[101]

---

[99] LeRoi Jones, *Home: Social Essays* (New York: William Morrow, 1966); Larry Neal, "The Black Arts Movement," in *The Black Aesthetic*, ed. Addison Gayle (Garden City, N.Y.: Doubleday, 1971), 272; Stephen Evangelist Henderson, *Understanding the New Black Poetry: Black Speech and Black Music as Poetic References* (New York: Morrow, 1973), 272.

[100] Larry Neal, "The Black Contribution to American Letters: The Writer as Activist—1960 and After," in *The Black American Reference Book*, ed. Mabel M. Smythe (Englewood Cliffs, N.J.: Prentice-Hall, 1976) 781–84.

[101] Houston A. Baker Jr., *Blues, Ideology, and Afro-American Literature: A Vernacular Theory* (Chicago: Univ. of Chicago Press, 1984), 82–83.

VICTIM NARRATOR AS CRITIC

Another strategy for identifying the voice of an oppressed people is showcased in two important works on the African-American literary tradition: *Blues, Ideology and Afro-American Literature* (1984) by Baker and *The Signifying Monkey* (1988) by Henry Louis Gates. These works share two distinctive features. First, they identify an authoritative Black voice neither in the Black literature of the past nor in contemporary Black politics. Instead, they turn to the folk traditions of oral discourse and song that Baker calls "the Black vernacular." Here they find an authentic Black speech and aesthetic creativity neither tailored for White audiences, nor obscured beneath Marxist cant. Second, Baker and Gates see the Black vernacular less as a record of experience than as a lively process of invention. To Gates, the key to Black culture is the practice of "signifying," a playful ritual of rhetorical appropriation, mockery, and innuendo. "Signifying" covers the range of rhetorical double-talk from the calumny contest called "the dozens," through the sly encoding of slave-quarter schemes in the pious language of Scripture. For Baker, the African-American tradition of blues improvisation provides the proper metaphor for Black literary inventiveness.

Both "signifying" and "the blues"—like all traditional forms of oral composition—involve appropriating and modifying available cultural materials. Accordingly, they are apt metaphors for the creativity of a captive people constrained to make their mark within an alien culture. They identify authentic self-expression in the ways that black authors worked with and upon prevailing literary conventions, rather than equating authenticity with isolation and retreat. For Gates in particular the premodern practice of oral composition provides both a metaphor and a precursor for the postmodern notion of the author as interpreter and critic of her literary precursors. The homeboy signifying on the street corner and the trope-turning semiotician are just two ends of the same simile, linking folk authenticity with the avant-garde effete.

Implicit in this simile is an antinomy between the antic folk rhetoric of the African diaspora and the staid literary depictions of bourgeois society and subjectivity associated with the novel. It is as if captive Africans, by virtue of having been denied recognition as liberal subjects, anticipated the postmodern critique of the liberal subject. As emblems of displacement, alienation, and commodification, African slaves may "serve" to represent the anonymity and impotence menacing all participants in market society. Female slaves could symbolize the vulnerability of all nineteenth-century women to brutality, objectification, sexual exploitation, and other forms of heteronomy. By virtue of their status as objects of property, slaves were particularly well positioned to see the material underpinnings of the selfhood idealized in romantic literature. Thus, slaves could subvert or "signify upon" literary convention merely by participating in it.

This view of the slave narrator is evident in the ways that Baker and Gates reread the texts Baker found so disappointing in his earlier book. Rereading the autobiographies of Gustavus Vassa and Frederick Douglass, as well as that of

Harriet Jacobs, Baker now sees them less as the encounters of alienated souls with an isolating Christian literacy. Instead he sees them as the records of crushing and transformative encounters with commercial capitalism, in which the protagonists give voice to the lesson that they can become their own masters only by commodifying themselves. Thus, the slave narratives are stories of self-possession achieved through a harrowing ordeal of self-alienation, in which the narrator emerges as a trickster or sharp dealer, joining the alienation of humanity she cannot beat, "negotiating slavery's tight spaces,"[102] improvising a strategy rather than conserving an authentic self.

Gates concentrates on some of the earliest slave narratives, mostly from the eighteenth century. He calls these "sacred" narratives because they link salvation to the acquisition of literacy, but he reads them as expressions of a subtle ambivalence about the written letter and about assimilation. Gates's texts all "signify" upon a common image, "the trope of the talking book." This trope involves an illiterate African or Indian witnessing a literate Westerner reading Holy Writ. The non-Westerner assumes that the book is somehow speaking to its reader, but is disappointed to find that the book will not speak to him. The problem posed by this recurrent trope is not simply that of learning to read, but that of "making the white written text speak with a black voice."[103] White people are often portrayed in these narratives as deficient in spirituality, or as twisting and misusing Scripture, but the dead letter of Scripture can be brought to life by the narrator's spirituality voiced in prayer. The Word speaks *to* the Black narrator when it *answers* to his prayer, and writing speaks in a Black voice when it is experienced not as the letter of authority but as divine inspiration.

VICTIM NARRATIVE AS PERFORMANCE

A final stratagem portrays the early literary product of members of subordinated groups neither as authentic nor as failed self-expression but as artful role-play, as the creation of an author character no less fictive than that author's creations. Gallagher informs us that the Restoration Era practice of paying the playwright with the third night's receipts made authors directly dependent on their audience's patronage. In one play Aphra Behn apologizes to any ladies in the audience who might be offended by its bawdiness. In essence she pleads poverty as an excuse for pandering to the prurience of her public:

> By selling bawdiness and then complaining of the necessity to do so, she assures her female readers that there is an innocent self above the exchange. Authorship for the marketplace and selfhood are here dissevered, for the author that can be inferred from the work is merely a "way of writing" dictated by the age, an alienable thing outside and beneath the true self. But it is precisely this severing, this inauthenticity, that is supposed to oblige the audience, to make them feel an obligation to the compromised author.[104]

[102] Ibid., 63.
[103] Gates, *Signifying Monkey*, 131.
[104] Gallagher, *Nobody's Story*, 16.

Another of Gallagher's authors, the early-nineteenth-century novelist Maria Edgeworth, rejects the aspiration to a true self in favor of one artistically composed. For Edgeworth, says Gallagher, "there is no unproblematically given personality against which false and fictional identities might be simply contrasted." Instead, fictional models or stock characters are necessary to guide self-definition. The literate woman must "provide her own stock of characters and match each against a 'self' that is not given but rather consciously made."[105] Rather than expressing or winning recognition for an authentic self, Edgeworth offered model identities for sale.

Gallagher's argument challenges the conventional picture of literature as a discursive arena from which subordinated groups were excluded. After all, the modern conception of literature as an art produced for mass aesthetic consumption involved the separation of aesthetic value from the elite preserves of civic, scientific, and religious authority. The emergence of this conception of literature coincided with the rapid expansion of the reading public, the rise of the novel and other popular narrative genres including the slave narrative,[106] and the emergence of a new ethos of civility and sentiment that opened moral discourse to the participation of women. Seen in this light, the emergent institution of literature may have been shaped by the struggles of subordinated groups to participate in culture.

Thus, Gallagher suggests that women were in some ways the paradigmatic authors of eighteenth-century fiction. She "trie[s] to convince the reader that the apparent negativity in [early female novelists]—their emphasis on disembodiment, dispossession and debt—points not to disabling self-doubts but to an important source of their creativity."[107] Thus, she presents alienation as the social condition for authorship and its inspiration. Since propertyless, dispossessed women were emblems of alienation in the eighteenth century, they could make themselves metaphors for authorship. This was particularly true insofar as they served the new market for fiction. Readers did not want real people to sympathize with or worry about; they wanted fictional characters to consume for their own ends. Fiction was a substitute identity most easily proffered by one without identity; the new narrative genres therefore provided an opportunity for marginal social groups to influence a public discourse as yet unprepared to acknowledge them.

We have examined literary theories of plot, reader experience, narrative voice, and point of view, narrative genres, narrative rhetoric, and the political significance of narrative. At a minimum, we can draw two lessons from this discussion: that narratives are literary artifacts, conditioned by imagination and convention, and that legal institutions must be counted among the cultural conditions shaping narratives.

---

[105] Ibid., 281.

[106] Sara Faherty, "Slave Narratives and the Novel" (unpub. ms., 1997); Joseph Bodziock, "The Weight of Sambo's Woes," *Journal of American Culture* 12 (1989): 89–97.

[107] Gallagher, *Nobody's Story*, 327.

3.2 Instrumental Claims: Narrative as Law's Antagonist and Salvation

Literary theories of narrative emphasize that narrative is artifice and that narrative literature is the expression of a culture shaped by legal institutions. Nevertheless, many legal scholars offer narrative as a reproach and antidote to legal discourse. No sound argument for the instrumental value of narrative can be maintained that simplistically treats narrative as the voice of authentic humanity or that caricatures legal thought as necessarily abstract, inflexible, and epistemologically naive. Yet more modest claims can be made for the contribution of narrative to critical argument within law. Thus, while "Narrative" cannot be shown to redeem or oppose "Law," particular narratives can improve or destabilize particular legal regimes. In this part we will explicate a number of instrumental claims for narrative and consider responses offered by critics of narrative legal scholarship. Our own conclusions are that (1) narrative is useful *in* legal and policy argument, not as a corrective to it, and (2) whether narrative argument is morally improving or disabling, subversive or conservative depends on its particular content and context.

Advocates of the integration of narrative into law and legal scholarship make five intertwined claims: that it can be a source of (1) practical wisdom, (2) epistemological insight, (3) moral improvement, (4) political subversion, and (5) psychological integration. The first two of these claims require only brief treatment. The latter three require more detailed treatment, each of them implicating distinctive types of narrative legal scholarship. Thus, the claim of moral improvement requires us to consider "phenomenological" arguments articulating the experience of victims of injustice. In assessing the political subversion claim we examine scholarly efforts to marshal popular memory in order to challenge official history, define the aims of subordinated communities, or illuminate the popular contribution to the lawmaking process. Finally, the claim that narrative advances psychological integration envisions narratives of a certain sort: postmodern authorial performances aimed at reconstructing subjectivity in the face of alienation. Ultimately, we conclude that the value of narrative legal scholarship cannot be determined categorically. There is much valuable scholarship that uses the propositional or performative aspects of narrative in making reasoned arguments that address legal and related policy issues. But the value of this scholarship does not depend upon the sentimental assumption that narrative is the concrete and "human" alternative to law's cold abstraction, nor does it consist in any other categorically redemptive or subversive implications of the narrative form.

Practical Wisdom

The first instrumental claim for narrative is fairly uncontroversial: narrative is sometimes praised as an important aspect of practical reasoning.[108] Cognitive psy-

---

[108] See generally Winter, "Cognitive Dimension of the Agon."

chology suggests that expertise requires not just knowledge but also skill at picking relevancies, learned largely through experience. We develop patterns of response to recognizable situations and anticipate familiar consequences, and so we situate our actions in a narrative. When faced with a new situation or problem, we use narrative to integrate the unfamiliar into our experience, and so to determine how to "go on" with a practice—to continue its story.[109]

Scholars of law and narrative typically cite a consensus of psychologists, philosophers, linguists, and aestheticians that we make sense of actions and events by placing them within narrative frames.[110] From the first moment that children can form sentences, narrative structure is the means by which they take in the world.[111] Only through story can a person learn the norms of the culture and recognize deviations from them,[112] and anthropologists tell us that social relations are organized around narratable social dramas, whether stock scripts or imaginative revisions of those scripts.[113] According to sociologists like Goffman, however "authentic" people believe their behavior, thoughts, feelings, and perceptions to be, human activity is always assembled out of available bits of narrative:

> In many cases, what the individual does in . . . life, he does in relationship to cultural standards established for the doing and for the social role that is built out of such doings. . . . The associated folklore itself draws from the moral traditions of the community as found in folk tales, characters in novels, advertisements, myth, movie stars and their famous roles, the Bible, and other sources of exemplary representation.[114]

Often citing these authorities, contemporary legal scholars have relied on terms like "stock stories"[115] or "pre-understandings"[116] for the notion that people apprehending narratable facts that bear on legal questions cannot help but construe those facts according to certain received frames. Pragmatist philosophers point to the utility of such unreflective stereotypes in enabling action. Without them, one would have to devote all of one's energy to inventing and maintaining concep-

---

[109] Dennis Patterson, "Law, Practice, Interpretation and Argument: Toward a Narrative Conception of Legal Discourse," in International Association for Legal Methodology, *Le Recours aux Objectifs de la Loi dans son Application* (Brussels: E. Story-Scientia, 1990), 324–37.

[110] Louis Mink, "Narrative Form as a Cognitive Instrument," in *The Writing of History: Literary Form and Historical Understanding*, ed. Robert H. Canary and Henry Kozicki (Madison: Univ. of Wisconsin Press, 1978), 129–31.

[111] Jerome S. Bruner, *Acts of Meaning* (Cambridge: Harvard Univ. Press, 1990).

[112] Ibid., 49–50.

[113] Victor Turner, "Social Dramas and Stories about Them," in Mitchell, *On Narrative*, 137–41.

[114] Erving Goffman, *Frame Analysis: An Essay on the Organization of Experience* (Cambridge: Harvard Univ. Press, 1974), 561.

[115] Gerald P. Lopez, "Lay Lawyering," *U.C.L.A. Law Review* 32 (1984): 91.

[116] Anthony V. Alfieri, "Reconstructive Poverty Law Practice: Learning Lessons of Client Narrative," *Yale Law Journal* 100 (1991): 2107–47; Marc A. Fajer, "Authority, Credibility, and Pre-understanding: A Defense of Outsider Narratives in Legal Scholarship," *Georgetown Law Journal* 82 (1994): 1845.

tual schemes. When the practical actor encounters an obstacle, it is rational for her to make the smallest adjustment to her beliefs and attitudes possible for her to go on with the practice. According to William James, "in this matter of belief we are all extreme conservatives."[117]

Narrative thinking is useful, then, because of its *conservativeness.* It maintains continuity in the midst of change. But in so doing, it enables moderate change, by obviating any need to rethink first principles before choosing a course of action. Its efficiency consists in its *unreflectiveness.* Described as conservative and unreflective, narrative thinking does not sound very subversive or liberating. Yet it has a certain populist appeal—it preserves customary practices and meanings against the systematic reforms of technocratic elites like legal scientists or economists. Accordingly, legal realists contrasted the narrative "situation sense" of practicing lawyers to the "formalism" of academic and judicial proponents of laissez-faire.

Epistemological Insight

The second instrumental claim is indeed controversial, but, given the background of literary theory we have laid out, it needs only relatively brief treatment here as well: the claim that narrative can shape the preconceptions that enable practical action is closely connected to the claim that narrative scholarship or argument can yield epistemological insight. The perceptions available to those deeply engaged in a practice are *necessarily* highly selective. By confronting practitioners with familiar events as perceived from an unfamiliar perspective, scholars or advocates can arguably awaken practitioners to the selectivity of their own perceptions, and perhaps to the relationship between those perceptions and the interests and purposes presumed by the practice. Kathryn Abrams points out that "the narratives of those who occupy a comparatively powerless position are not only evidence of what has been excluded, but testimony to the law's relentless perspectivity."[118] According to Richard Delgado,

> Stories, parables, chronicles and narratives are powerful means for destroying mindset—the bundle of presuppositions, received wisdom, and shared understandings against a background of which legal and political discourse takes place. . . . Ideology—the received wisdom—makes current social arrangements seem fair and natural. Those in power sleep well at night—their conduct does not seem to them like oppression.[119]

The audience for narrative argument that Delgado envisions here consists of mainstream or elite lawyers, who contribute to oppression through their unreflective adherence to prejudicial stereotypes about the oppressed and complacency about unfair social arrangements:

[117] William James, *Pragmatism: A New Name for Some Old Ways of Thinking: Popular Lectures on Philosophy* (New York: Longmans, Green, 1907).

[118] Abrams, "Hearing the Call of Stories," 976.

[119] Delgado, "Storytelling for Oppositionists," 2413.

> The stories or narratives told by the ingroup . . . provide it with a form of shared reality in which its own superior position is seen as natural. The stories of outgroups aim to subvert that ingroup reality. . . . For many minority persons, the principal instrument of their subordination . . . is the prevailing *mindset* by means of which members of the dominant group justify the world as it is.[120]

Narrative will subvert these prevailing "mindsets" by exposing their selectivity and partiality.

There are two difficulties with this claim, however. First, that legal judgment is based on selective preconception is not, by itself, a criticism. All practical judgment is necessarily based on selective preconception.[121] Delgado complains that "traditional legal writing purports to be neutral and dispassionately analytical, but *too often* it is not."[122] By his own premises, however, legal writing cannot be neutral and dispassionate. Hence, critics of the preconceptions and purposes of legal judgment must be prepared to show why some other set of preconceptions and purposes is better. Second, if the claim is that practical judgment narrows vision and discourages reflection, storytelling seems an odd way of correcting the problem. After all, part of the usefulness of narrative thinking is that it enables us to bypass reflection, to identify and respond to "problems" without questioning our assumptions. We generally associate reflective critique of practices with theory, which often articulates unspoken premises and compares them to alternative premises. If the true aim of narrative scholarship is to induce reflection, it would be most useful in conjunction with some more systematic theory. Otherwise storytelling seems better suited to the project of modifying existing practices without challenging their premises.

In a controversial critique of narrative legal scholarship, Daniel Farber and Suzanna Sherry argue that "storytelling . . . can and should be judged by standards that include the requirement of an analytic component."[123] This is probably an unfair standard in judging individual works of scholarship, since an illuminating narrative may be put into a theoretical context by another scholarly work. But it seems plausible that theory or analysis must play *some* role if storytelling scholarship is meant to induce reflection on the part of those caught up in a practice. For cognitive psychology suggests that if readers of a "counterstory" can avoid reflection on fundamental purposes and premises, they will. Delgado argues that the "dialogic" address of stories makes them ingratiating rather than challenging: "They invite the reader to suspend judgment, listen for their point or message, and then decide what measure of truth they contain."[124] But if a story deviates too much from the preconceptions of practical actors, it may be dismissed as anomalous.

---

[120] Ibid., 2413.

[121] This point is nicely stated in Jane B. Baron and Julia Epstein, "Is Law Narrative?" *Buffalo Law Review* 45 (1997): 141, 171–72.

[122] Delgado, "Storytelling for Oppositionists," 2440.

[123] Daniel A. Farber and Suzanna Sherry, "Telling Stories Out of School: An Essay on Legal Narratives," *Stanford Law Review* 45 (1993): 807, 846.

[124] Delgado, "Storytelling for Oppositionists," 2415.

Moral Improvement

The claim that narrative morally improves the law generally associates narrative with empathy for others and views law as deficient in just that dimension. In her important article "Legality and Empathy," Lynne Henderson argues that empathic responses to suffering are discouraged by some features of legal thought. Henderson identifies legality with rule following and role morality, arguing that fidelity to rules and role will sometimes induce legal decision makers to cause suffering. These decision makers in turn will suffer "empathic distress," unless they learn to inure themselves to the suffering of others. Hence, legality discourages empathy, treating it as a temptation or indulgence to be resisted in favor of fidelity to role.[125] According to Henderson, rule formalism depends on predictability and stability, values that are subverted if rules are selectively modified when they cause suffering.[126] The application of rules requires the lumping of diverse situations into general categories, categories that may reenforce empathy-blocking stereotypes about socially marginal groups.[127]

On the other hand, while legality discourages empathic responses to suffering, legal decision makers can be influenced by "empathic narratives, [which include] descriptions of concrete human situations and their meanings to the persons affected in the contexts of their lives." Empathic narrative counteracts rule formalism and role morality with "phenomenological argument."[128] Empathic narrative improves the law, Henderson concludes, because empathy should always play a role in legal reasoning. She points to *Brown v. Board of Education* as a case in which empathic arguments were well made and reflected in the ultimate opinion. She points to *Roe v. Wade*[129] as a case in which such arguments were not made effectively by abortion rights advocates and are absent from the court's opinion, and she suggests that their absence undermined the decision's popular legitimacy.

Arguing in a similar vein, Richard Weisberg asserts that judges are more likely to achieve justice if they eschew the cold abstractions of conventional legal doctrine and instead render the concrete human story underlying a legal dispute. For Weisberg, good narrative exposes concrete facts that belie procrustean legal categories. Moreover, good narrative has more than ornamental value in appellate decision: its aesthetic integrity reflects the moral integrity of the decision. Thus, Weisberg offers the arresting claim that "No bad judicial opinion can be 'well written.' "[130] He asserts that the holding in a case cannot without some alteration be abstracted from its words, that no opinion with a misguided outcome has ever

---

[125] Lynne N. Henderson, "Legality and Empathy," *Michigan Law Review* 85 (1987): 1574, 1590.

[126] Ibid., 1588.

[127] Ibid., 1591.

[128] Ibid., 1592.

[129] *Roe v. Wade*, 410 U.S. 113 (1973).

[130] Richard H. Weisberg, *Poethics, and Other Stratagies of Law and Literature* (New York: Columbia Univ. Press, 1992), 251.

been well crafted, and that even opinions with salutary effects will lose power if "they fail to harmonize sound and sense in working their outcome."[131]

For Weisberg, both *Brown* and *Roe* are *morally* bad decisions because they are badly written—they reach salutary results but fail to morally insulate these results against political backlash because they rely on science: *Brown* on social science experiments about the effect of segregation on self-esteem, *Roe* on the increased safety of abortion and on the limits of medicine's ability to maintain the life of fetuses outside the womb. By deploying the bland voice of scientific rationality, each fails to capture "in its writing the essence of the human situations they so courageously attempted to alleviate."[132]

For his affirmative example of the fusion of sound and sense in a judicial opinion, Weisberg relies on Cardozo, particularly the opinion in *Hynes v. New York Central Railroad Co.*[133] Weisberg believes that something useful can be learned about justice from the sheer fact of Cardozo's reference to the plaintiff as a "lad" rather than as a "plaintiff." More generally, he insists that Cardozo's prose captures reality in some ineffable way. Yet contrary to Weisberg's claims, the *Hynes* opinion illustrates just how stilted Cardozo's prose can get (almost down to the level of Hallmark card cliché), particularly in its blending of somewhat concrete physical images with legal abstractions. Thus, in the key sentence in which a "lad of 16 . . . swam with two companions," we see that they swim in a "navigable stream"; later, "Bathers in the Harlem River on the day of the disaster were in the enjoyment of a public highway."

It may seem intuitively right to align linguistic precision with sensitivity to moral value, and abstraction to the opposite. But this is not a very necessary matrix, in part because such a view is itself so abstract. It ignores the possibility that poetic language can distort or distract. Moving victim-impact statements may exploit the social distance between sentencers and defendants to block empathy, or they may lead to defendants being differentially punished based on the moral qualities of their victims rather than their own.[134]

On the other hand, abstract deduction or statistical analysis can be the rhetoric of powerful moral enlightenment. Consider *McCleskey v. Kemp*, in which the petitioner offered a powerful statistical argument that death sentences are handed down in hugely disproportionate numbers to killers of Whites, rather than killers of Blacks.[135] The moral power of McCleskey's argument came precisely from its use of McCleskey as a mere statistic—that, and not anything in his subjective life, was his moral significance. By abstracting away other variables, statistics showed that the death penalty expresses a view of the relative worth of White and Black lives. And though the argument finally failed, it won a moral victory in Justice Powell's deeply conflicted assertion that the argument truly proved

---

[131] Ibid., 8.

[132] Ibid., 9.

[133] Ibid., discussing *Hynes v. New York Central Railroad Co.*, 131 N.E.2d 898 (N.Y. 1921).

[134] *Payne v. Tennessee*, 501 U.S. 808 (1991).

[135] *McCleskey v. Kemp*, 481 U.S. 279 (1987).

too much—it not only logically called for the end of all capital punishment, but threatened the legitimacy of all criminal justice.

The philosopher and classicist Martha Nussbaum offers a more successful argument for the moral—but not necessarily legal—value of narrative. Nussbaum argues that our most salient moral obligations arise from love relationships and other sorts of personal commitments.[136] This relational view of moral obligation means that moral obligations are always highly contingent, premised on their context in a particular human life, rather than an integrated theory. Moral deliberation is therefore a species of practical rather than theoretical reason, responsive to peculiarities of context rather than principle. And since our most salient obligations are not organized by any coherent theory, they may turn out to be both inconsistent and incommensurable. The resolution of such dilemmas must in turn proceed by reflection, imagination, and passionate commitment because calculation is simply inapposite. Moral deliberation is like writing a novel and living in it at the same time: "The well-lived life is a work of literary art."[137] Thus, even to understand morality philosophically requires narrative: we must "study the loves and attentions of a finely responsive mind . . . through all the contingent complexities of a tangled human life."[138]

Nussbaum's relational conception of moral obligation also has implications for the nature of moral virtue. Since to live well is to love well, the virtuous person must cultivate the ability to love. This ability involves an altrustic orientation, of course, but it also necessitates certain capacities for perception of the kind we associate with aesthetic experiences. The person well prepared for love is capable of giving in to the unpredictability and contingency of a life ruled by passionate attachments to others and so must be alive to his or her own feelings, rather than attuned to propriety. Such a person also must be capable of perceptively appreciating others: seeing not only what they need or want, but also what they are capable of becoming. This sort of perception requires narrative imagination. Nussbaum points to the character of Adam in Henry James's *The Golden Bowl*, who moves abroad so as to free his too-devoted daughter to marry without guilt or distraction. His ability to take his leave gracefully and without regret turns on his ability to imagine his daughter's future flourishing, in figurative terms. He suddenly sees her as a gleaming sea creature confidently afloat and fearlessly at play in a swelling ocean of feeling: "Adam sees his daughter's sexuality in a way that can be captured linguistically only in language of lyrical splendor. . . . To this moral assessment the full specificity of the image is relevant. . . . It could not be captured in any paraphrase that was not itself a work of art."[139] In choosing her example from the perspectivist fiction of Henry James, Nussbaum makes clear that the perception required by love is not cognitive but imaginative, because for

[136] Martha C. Nussbaum, *Love's Knowledge: Essays on Philosophy and Literature* (New York: Oxford Univ. Press, 1990).
[137] Ibid., 148.
[138] Ibid., 140.
[139] Ibid., 152.

James, the inner life of another cannot be known in any directly perceptual or referential way. Thus, moral perception requires aesthetic precision, not scientific accuracy.

Nussbaum makes a powerful argument for the moral salience of love, and for the role of the literary imagination in a passionate life. But it is disconcerting how much this argument uncritically accepts the ethical imperatives and social presuppositions of nineteenth-century drawing-room fiction. Here morality is confined to the sphere of private relationships; virtue presupposes the opportunity for leisurely self-reflection and consists in a grace of manner refined to the point of preciosity; the self is cultivated as an objet d'art to ornament the domestic tableau.[140] Moreover, Nussbaum's ethic of love is not easily transported to law. Nussbaum's is nothing so dilute as an ethic of empathy. It is an ethic of passionate attachment, of fierce partiality, of blinding, intensely selective attention, and such love cannot be universal. Yet we expect legal decision makers to be impartial, or at least broadly attentive, and we expect participants in legal decision making to stake their claims on *public* reasons. This is not to say that Nussbaum's arguments are irrelevant to law, since public reasons may embrace historically particular loyalties, traditions, and institutions. Political deliberation, like moral deliberation, may require practical wisdom rather than theoretical consistency and may engage the narrative imagination. But not because justice demands love, if love is as Nussbaum depicts it.

If empathic or "phenomenological" argument, allied to the narrative imagination, is not always superior to more abstract forms of moral reasoning, it is nevertheless clearly relevant to a host of legal issues, including disputes about harm, consent, and culpability.

Assessments of harm are relevant to criminal liability, civil damages, and the policy judgments that inform legislative, judicial, and administrative lawmaking. Yet aside from death and maiming, the harmful nature of consequences is not self-evident. Many legal disputes and legislative issues involve conflicting or incompatible activities, each of which can be deemed harmful to the other. When courts or legislatures must draw lines between conflicting claims, a phenomenological narrative can give meaning to the stakes on both sides, enabling the very interpersonal comparison of utilities that economists eschew but that the law cannot avoid.[141] For example, in a conflict involving a home or a job, phenomenological narrative can explicate the special role these goods might play in the identity of its holder, showing the presence of what economists call an "endowment" effect. Phenomenological narrative can show how sexual harassment or any other form of intimidation affects the options and enjoyment available to its victims.

Many legal issues turn on the consensual transfer or waiver of entitlements. Phenomenological narrative can show how the pressures implicit in a situation,

---

[140] To their credit, both Nussbaum and James himself anticipate this objection. Nussbaum, *Love's Knowledge*, 164–65; Henry James, *Art of the Novel*, 221–24.

[141] Margaret Jane Radin, "Property and Personhood," *Stanford Law Review* 34 (1982): 957.

or the outright intimidation of another person, coerced a choice or an expression of consent.

Both criminal and civil liability assume that we can attribute to an actor intention, recklessness, or negligence with respect to a harmful result. Phenomenological narrative can reveal the purposes, reasons, and social norms that motivate the person's action, or the fears and pressures that may monopolize attention and cause him to take inadvertent risks. Narrative can also show how environmental factors like trauma might have diminished responsibility for wrongdoing.

To acknowledge the relevance of phenomenological narrative to legal issues, however, is to question the assumption that legality and empathy are necessarily opposed. In a critique of Henderson's article, Toni Massaro notes that law often involves fidelity not to rules but to standards, standards that define "spheres of relevant conversation, not mathematical formulas."[142]

On the other hand, while phenomenological narrative is undoubtedly relevant to legal issues, it has struck some legal authors as unreliable. Thus, Farber and Sherry distinguish between reports of how an event would have looked to a third-party observer, how it actually felt to a participant, and how it seems to a participant on subsequent reflection. Revealingly, they assert that the first is the conventional understanding of a true description of an event and that therefore the second or third are misleading and so must come with warnings.[143] Yet it seems odd to say that speculation as to what a *hypothetical observer* would have seen is a core case of true description, whereas a report of the *actual* feelings of a *participant* is a metaphoric extension of the concept of true description. In thus elevating observable behavior over feelings, Farber and Sherry adopt a behavioristic skepticism about the reality of intangible mental states that is simply inapt in law, since many legally significant events are *defined* by reference to the mental states of a participant. It is one thing to favor "you would not have seen any violence" over "I felt as if he had slapped me." But it is quite another to favor "you would not have seen any manifestation of nonconsent" over "I did not consent."

Perhaps swayed by the claims of its proponents that empathic narrative opposes legality and even rationality, mainstream critics of phenomenological narrative scholarship appear to have underestimated its pertinence as legal argument. An examination of some of the most controversial examples of phenomenological narrative will confirm that they offer reasoned arguments that, persuasive or not, are clearly pertinent to law.

A good place to start is "The Difference in Women's Hedonic Lives,"[144] in which Robin West offers a performative argument for the centrality of phenomenological method to feminist legal theory. She criticizes prevailing models of feminist legal theory for relying on formal proxies for women's well-being, in-

---

[142] Toni M. Massaro, "Empathy, Legal Storytelling and the Rule of Law: New Words, Old Wounds?" *Michigan Law Review* 87 (1989): 2099, 2111.

[143] Farber and Sherry, "Telling Stories," 833.

[144] Robin West, "The Difference in Women's Hedonic Lives: A Phenomenological Critique of Feminist Legal Theory," *Wisconsin Women's Law Journal* 3 (1987): 81, 96–97.

stead of listening to women's experience. Thus, "liberal" feminist legal theory seeks to expand the range of women's choices, while "radical" feminist legal theory seeks to enhance women's power. West interprets both her own experience and published accounts of other women's experiences in arguing that neither of these aims correlates sufficiently with the aim of increasing women's subjective happiness. Women, she avers, do not always choose what they want, and do not always want more power.

Her critique of the liberal ethic of choice relies on (1) a detailed picture of the violent, coercive threats confronting women in the form of domestic abuse, rape, sexually predatory courtship, and harassment in public spaces; and (2) a phenomenological analysis of the effect of this menacing environment on the self-images, preferences, and pleasures of women. Her claim is that the harm of abuse far exceeds the pain it inflicts, and that the harm of coercion far exceeds the options it forecloses. These forms of terror instill a pervasive fear that kills desire and ambition—a fear that *constitutes* women as "giving selves" who are neither self-regarding nor self-defining:

> a woman will define herself as a "giving self" so that she will not be violated. She defines herself as a being who "gives" sex, so that she will not become a being *from whom sex is taken*. In a deep sense . . . , this transformation is consensual: she "consents" to be being a "giving self"—the dependent party in a comparatively protective relationship—for self-regarding liberal reasons; she consents in order to control the danger both inside and outside of the relationship, and in order to suppress the fear that danger engenders. Once redefined, however, . . . she becomes a person who gives her consent *so as to ensure the other's happiness* (not her own).[145]

West's critique of radical feminist legal theory argues that its ideal of equal power is at odds with many women's reported experience of erotic pleasure in submissiveness. She explains "the erotic appeal of submission" as rooted in the desire "to safely depend on another to look after one's own well-being."[146] West suggests that this need is particularly strong for women and explains why this should be the case in cultural feminist terms: "a mother is not *autonomous*; she is both depended upon and thereby dependent on others. . . . To the considerable degree that our potentiality for motherhood defines ourselves, women's lives are relational, not autonomous."[147] West cites appreciative responses to sadomasochistic pornography by some feminist writers and argues against the efforts of other feminists to suppress such pornography.

In a provocative critique of West's essay, Anne Coughlin links West's phenomenological method and the pornographic writing West defends. For Coughlin, "The Difference in Women's Hedonic Lives" is an example of the venerable genre of confessional erotica by women. It urges women to "articulate the truth about their sexual experiences if they would redeem themselves from the bonds of patri-

---

[145] Ibid., 96–97.
[146] Ibid., 132.
[147] Ibid., 140–41.

archy," and thereby achieves "a secular version of the Christian confessional."[148] Drawing on Foucault's *History of Sexuality*, Coughlin argues that there are traditionally thematic connections among confession, domination, and eroticism. Confession implies the participation of "a partner who is not simply the interlocutor but the authority who requires the confession,"[149] and this "enhances or perhaps, even, creates in the first instance the erotic pleasure that the participants attribute to the sexual experiences confessed by the speaking subject."[150] Thus, Coughlin implicitly confesses to arousal by what she takes to be West's confession of pleasure in submission—and by this erotic response she "proves" West's performative argument for the erotic appeal of submission. Coughlin cannot resist repeating this seduction as she confesses her own scandalized reading of West to her readers and invites them to share her titillation.

An oft-cited example of feminist phenomenological argument is Marie Ashe's "Zig-Zag Stitching and the Seamless Web."[151] Ashe's essay is often viewed as an illustration of the challenge that the uniqueness of personal experience poses to categorical thought and indeed to coherence itself.[152] Yet it is a perfectly cogent meditation on the moral implications of two narratives. One is an account of the harrowing Angie Carder case, in which a court compelled a dying woman to undergo a Caesarean birth of a child who died anyway. The other is an account of Ashe's own pregnancies—five births, two miscarriages, and one abortion.

One clear implication of this dual narrative is that doctors, no matter how well intentioned, underestimate pain, discount patients' desires and knowledge, and pretend to more knowledge than they have. Ashe describes one doctor who interferes with her ability to push during labor by placing her on a labor bed where she cannot brace her elbows and by forbidding her to groan. He then complains that she is not pushing hard enough and uses forceps. He forbids her to ease the passage of the baby by massaging her own perineum because that would interfere with his performance of an episiotomy—a procedure that she believes massage would render unnecessary. Later Ashe describes visiting her gynecologist after a home birth, when her placenta fails to pass. He treats the situation as an emergency requiring immediate, on-the-spot treatment without the anaesthesia that would be available in a hospital. The ensuing scraping out of her still raw womb is excruciating and, she implies, punitive—a brutal "rape." Both doctors take advantage of a pregnant woman's physical distress and concern for the health of herself and her child to establish psychic dominance and painful physical invasion.[153]

---

[148] Anne M. Coughlin, "Regulating the Self: Autobiographical Performances in Outsider Scholarship," *Virginia Law Review* 81 (1995): 1229, 1334.

[149] Ibid., 1335, quoting Michel Foucault, *The History of Sexuality*, trans. Robert Hurley (New York: Pantheon Books, 1978), 61–62.

[150] Coughlin, "Regulating the Self," 1337.

[151] Marie Ashe, "Zig-Zag Stitching and the Seamless Web: Thoughts on 'Reproduction' and the Law," *Nova Law Review* 13 (1989): 355.

[152] Abrams, "Hearing the Call of Stories," 1009–12; Farber and Sherry, "Telling Stories," 847.

[153] Ashe, "Zig-Zag Stitching ," 366–70.

Surprisingly, "Zig-Zag Stitching" is presented by both critics of narrative, like Farber and Sherry, and enthusiasts of narrative, like Abrams, as cryptic. But Ashe offers a very clear thesis: medicalization of the abortion decision deprives women not only of autonomy but also of responsibility, inuring them to the consequences of their decisions. Ashe thereby implies that more complete reproductive freedom for women might actually result in fewer abortions, because women would be less alienated from their own bodies and the fetuses they carry and would thereby be forced to confront the violence of abortion. Ashe illustrates this violence with an account of drowning puppies, and she implies that she regrets her own abortion in part because a privately experienced miscarriage made her aware of the physicality and humanity of the fetus.[154]

Ashe acknowledges that other women do not regret and are not troubled by abortion, concluding that "each singular body is the site of a singular subjectivity, a unique personhood. . . . For some women, abortion is nothing other than a relief, while for others it becomes nothing other than a kind of dying—suicidal if not murderous. Different constructions of bodily experience."[155] Because we have special access to our own bodily experience, the body serves as her metaphor for an individual moral sense. But it is only a metaphor—bodily experience must still be "constructed" by conscience. Truth to conscience and self-awareness, Ashe insists, are the only universal ethics, and compliance with them cannot be monitored.

Ashe then offers what is to her a more admirable perspective on fetal life— that of Angie Carder's disabled mother Nettie Stoner, who anticipated that if her daughter's baby survived the C-section it would be severely impaired, and that the surviving family members would be incapable of caring for it: "Who wants it? . . . I would do the best I could, but we don't want it. Angela wanted that baby. It was her baby. Let the baby die with her."[156] This is a view that urges allowing fetal life to die without denying the violence of it, and that views the developing life as an extension of its mother. Ashe ends with an image of the deregulation of reproduction as "cut-work," a type of embroidery that frames a hole in the fabric, and that destroys at the same time it constructs. This is an arresting and effective metaphor for her claim that reproductive autonomy is both a space of freedom and a power of life and death.

While Ashe does not provide a "model statute," it is clear enough what values she is arguing for. Ashe is no relativist: she insists that morally responsible women *must* attend to their body-based moral intuitions. She clearly thinks that the medicalization and legalization of abortion have prevented most women from doing so, with the result that the position of the organized feminist movement on abortion and other issues is morally superficial. She preaches to other women from what she clearly regards as the rare and morally privileged position of one who has successfully struggled against authority to mobilize her own embodied moral

---

[154] Ibid., 371–72, 377.
[155] Ibid., 379.
[156] Ibid., 381–82.

sensibility. The morality she preaches will not endear the pro-choice movement to the wider public: it implies on the one hand that women should have an absolute power of life and death over their offspring that might extend to infanticide, and on the other, that most current abortion decisions by women are cavalier and morally obtuse. Feminist readers have taken Ashe's rather formulaic bow to the uniqueness of each woman's bodily experience as an excuse to evade this dangerous and discomforting moral message. They take this one isolated passage as a license to pretend that Ashe's bodily experience could hold no moral message for them, or for the feminist movement more generally. By emphasizing the uniqueness of bodily experience, these readers deny the clear message of *Ashe's* experience that abortion is infanticide *and* its regulation is rape.[157] Instead, they misleadingly praise the piece as an example of the resistance of concrete experience to reason and categorical thought. They read Ashe as exquisitely cryptic because they find her meaning unacceptably dangerous, and thereby collaborate with critics of narrative in the pretense that feeling is incompatible with reason and that a literary style precludes a cogent argument.

One way that feminist phenomenology can serve a cogent argument is in supporting a counterstory that challenges the more familiar stories underwriting influential policy arguments. A useful example is Martha Mahoney's "Legal Images of Battered Women."[158] Mahoney deploys the personal stories of numerous battered women—including her own—in challenging the image of the passive, dysfunctional battered woman underlying the legal recognition of a battered woman's defense. According to this now conventional account, women subjected to repeated severe abuse within domestic relationships "learn helplessness" because their actions seem to have no influence on the violence that terrorizes them. As a result they are incapable of extricating themselves from the abusive relationship and leaving the home. Hence, they may come to see self-defense as their only chance for survival. The psychological damage wrought by abuse explains and excuses their unnecessary resort to self-defense. An important element in this generic narrative is the abuser who is portrayed as little more than a pressure valve repeatedly cycling through stages of tension, explosive violence, and relaxed, contrite amiability.

Mahoney opposes to this generic narrative of dysfunction a counternarrative in which domestic violence punctuates a continuous power struggle between strategic actors. In this scenario the batterer is often an emotionally needy person, trying to hold his own vulnerability at bay by asserting a suffocating control over his partner. Battering is just one tactic in this overall program of control, typically triggered by the victim's assertions of autonomy. Mahoney reports the following exchange between two battered women: "R: They say we have this thing called 'learned helplessness'. . . . Y: Really? I always thought it was when I was getting too *much* power."[159] Another domestic violence victim recounts:

---

[157] E.g., Abrams, "Hearing the Call of Stories," 1009–112.

[158] Martha R. Mahoney, "Legal Images of Battered Women: Redefining the Issue of Separation," *Michigan Law Review* 90 (1991): 1.

[159] Ibid., 39.

The way it came out for me was not a battered woman's thing. I wanted to go out with my girlfriends, and that triggered possessive jealousy . . . he wouldn't let me do the things I wanted to do, therefore the marriage wouldn't work. The problem didn't start with his beating me up. After I made my stand on that ground, then the violence started.[160]

According to Mahoney, acute incidents of battering are often "separation assaults"—efforts to prevent or punish attempts to leave the relationship. Thus, battering is not controlled by some endogenous rhythm of tension and release, but is a response to the self-assertive agency of the victim. Victims of domestic abuse are not passive and helpless, but insubordinate and indomitable.

An important feature of Mahoney's counterstory is that she locates separation on a continuum with other expressions of autonomy and highlights coercive pressures and other obstacles to separation. In these ways she resists the inference that women who "stay" in abusive relationships acquiesce in the abuse. Mahoney's counterstory also stresses the burdens and coercive pressures that battered women share with other women who are not battered—for example, the burdens of responsibility for children, or the threat of spiteful custody claims by separated husbands.

Mahoney acknowledges that the "learned helplessness" narrative has helped some victims of domestic violence win acquittals, and that it is sometimes accurate. Nevertheless, she argues, it has several objectionable consequences. Most obviously, battered women who kill are seen as excusably acting out of fear rather than justifiably defending their autonomy. In addition, women who admit to suffering battery may be viewed as incompetent to look after their own children.[161] Mahoney asserts that the prevailing image of battered women as pathologically damaged zombies prevents more self-possessed victims from recognizing themselves as abused. But perhaps Mahoney's most subtle argument is that the typing of both battered women and their abusers as deviant disguises the dynamic of power and control in all relationships. In an ironic reversal, Mahoney implies that some women may avoid the most atrocious forms of abuse only by passively remaining in relationships in which they are subordinated and controlled. Thus, the "learned helplessness" narrative legitimates all nonviolent relationships as noncoercive and freely chosen, while Mahoney's insubordination narrative critiques these relationships as "a site of domination."

Phenomenological argument typically tells stories unrecognized by law. But that is not to say that phenomenological argument replaces abstract reason with authentic experience. The stories told by phenomenological argument are framed by convention and imagination and appeal to reason. West's confessional intimacy, Ashe's shocking naturalism, Mahoney's ironic reversal—all of these are rhetorical achievements. These texts achieve their subversive effect not by opposing reason with experience, but by offering reasons to replace one narrative "construction" of experience with another.

[160] Ibid., 32.
[161] Ibid., 49.

Political Subversion

Richard Delgado recommends that "outgroups" tell stories in order to "subvert" the "mind-set" or "reality" by virtue of which "ingroups" justify to themselves their own oppressive conduct. Steven Winter similarly claims that the "highest use and greatest facility of narrative is as an iconoclastic tool of persuasion to legal and social change."[162] Such assertions of the subversiveness of narrative combine a number of distinct claims of varying plausibility.

Two claims we have already dealt with. One is the idea that personal narratives debunk prevailing preconceptions by showing that other perspectives are possible. This sort of epistemological critique is politically pointless since, by its own terms, preconceptions and perspectives are unavoidable. While it is useful to identify the preconceptions on which laws and legal judgments rest and to evaluate them in comparison with other views, such ideological diagnosis and critique goes beyond the platitude that different perspectives are possible. A second such claim is that narrative is a useful rhetorical weapon because it mimics actual experience and so is easily integrated into practical reason. But we have seen that whether a particular narrative "feels" realistic to a particular reader is culturally contingent, and that the more a narrative subverts the reader's preconceptions, the less persuasive it is likely to be. Personal narratives, unframed by theory, seem ill-suited for "iconoclastic" attacks on the self-justifying "mind-sets" of elites.

A more substantial claim is that decision makers *should* attend especially to the personal narratives of those without power. Mari Matsuda, for example, urges that both society at large and critical legal scholars in particular should "look to the bottom"[163] and "consider the victim's story."[164] This popular position combines two distinct claims. One is that a society or institution that purports to be egalitarian or democratic should attend especially to the concerns of the least powerful. This is an appealing position, but one with no necessary connection to narrative. Presumably, the powerless should be listened to regardless of what "voice" they speak in. The other claim is that attention to narrative *ipso facto* entails attention to the powerless, because they characteristically speak in the "voice" of personal narrative. The notion here may be that storytelling is a folk method of political thought available to all, whereas technical methods of policy or legal analysis are the preserve of those trained to serve in bureaucratic roles. As a corollary, cultural feminist thought identifies a more organic relationship between the subordination of women and a narrative sensibility: not only are women less often trained for service to institutions, they are more often trained for nurturing roles that encourage a narrative pattern of moral deliberation.

---

[162] Winter, "Cognitive Dimension of the Agon," 2228.

[163] Mari J. Matsuda, "Looking to the Bottom: Critical Legal Studies and Reparations," *Harvard Civil Rights–Civil Liberties Law Review* 22 (1987): 323.

[164] Mari J. Matsuda, "Public Response to Racist Speech: Considering the Victim's Story," *Michigan Law Review* 87 (1989): 2320.

Assuming that narrative is the characteristic voice of the oppressed, some scholars imply that integrating narrative into law or legal scholarship automatically advances the interests of the powerless. But others counter that this effort depends on the form and content of the narrative. Patricia Ewick and Susan Silbey evoke the example of consciousness raising in arguing that "subversive stories are narratives that employ the connection between the particular and the general by *locating the individual within social organization*."[165] Yet they emphasize that not all narratives are subversive in this sense. Narrative can acclimate us to prevailing social norms or ideological beliefs about the causes of social problems. Moreover, narratives can "depict understandings about persons and events while simultaneously effacing the connections between the particular persons and the social organization of their experience, . . . and thus help to reproduce the taken-for-granted hegemony."[166]

In a recent article Anne Coughlin agrees, arguing that the autobiographical form generally reenforces the individualist premises of liberal market society that many feminist and minority scholars profess to reject. One of the few legal scholars to actually engage literary theories of narrative, Coughlin rightly rejects the opposition implicit in much narrative legal scholarship between an ideologically distorted legal representation and an unvarnished narrative representation of human experience. Quoting the Marxist literary critic Terry Eagleton, she scorns efforts to subvert ideology by invoking " 'experience'—as though that, precisely, were not ideology's homeland."[167] Autobiography, no less than law, is ideological and indeed is "shaped by the same cultural values reflected in law."[168] Coughlin argues that "American cultural ideals, including specifically the mythic connection between the 'heroic individual . . . [and] the values of free enterprise,' are 'epitomized in autobiography.' "[169] Accordingly, "By affirming the myths of individual success in our culture, autobiography reproduces the political, economic, social and psychological structures that attend such success."[170]

These arguments suggest that narrative is politically subversive only if it illuminates the links between individual experience and larger patterns of social life. Assuming that scholars lend theoretical depth to personal narrative by placing personal experience in a social context, they may use such "subversive" narrative in several ways. One use is to address lawyers, showing them how to use the experiences of underprivileged clients in fashioning arguments under prevailing legal standards. Another use is to address judges and other lawmakers and to make moral and policy arguments for law reform. Both of these uses of narrative,

---

[165] Patricia Ewick and Susan S. Silbey, "Subversive Stories and Hegemonic Tales: Toward a Sociology of Narrative," *Law and Society Review* 29 (1995): 197, 220.

[166] Ibid., 222.

[167] Coughlin, "Regulating the Self," 1332, quoting Terry Eagleton, *Criticism and Ideology: A Study in Marxist Literary Theory* (London: Atlantic Highlands Humanities Press, 1976), 15.

[168] Coughlin, "Regulating the Self," 1232.

[169] Ibid., 1284, quoting Sacvan Bercovitch, "The Ritual of American Autobiography: Edwards, Franklin, Thoreau," *Revue Française d'Etudes Americains* 14 (1982): 139, 149.

[170] Ibid., 1286.

aimed at other legal professionals, fulfill traditional functions of legal scholar-ship. A third use is to address popular opinion generally, perhaps by winning the attention of the newsmedia. A fourth use is to address, and attempt to mobi-lize or "raise the consciousness" of, oppressed populations, directly or through activist intermediaries. These last two uses of narrative break from tradition by addressing popular, nonelite audiences. Yet they otherwise serve a traditional function of legal scholarship: influencing the development of law by informing legal advocacy.

Nevertheless, Farber and Sherry have questioned the scholarly worth of both advocacy and consciousness raising. Responding to Mary Coombs's suggestion that "outsider" narrative be judged by its contribution to the interests of "outsider" communities,[171] they object that a focus on influencing lawmakers "detracts from the basic question of whether the work is good scholarship as opposed to good advocacy."[172] As for the use of narrative in consciousness raising, Farber and Sherry dismiss it as a kind of psychotherapy without relevance to the scholarly enterprise of "increasing understanding of the law."[173]

These objections to politically motivated legal scholarship come a little late in the day. Legal scholarship has always been prescriptive and has always addressed legal decision makers. A purely *de*scriptive legal science is a chimera, at least in a pluralist democracy where the ultimate source of legal authority is always contestable. If legal scholarship must illuminate legal issues, therefore, it must illuminate normative issues. Coombs's proposal is simply that scholars who iden-tify themselves as advocates for oppressed groups should consider these norma-tive questions from the standpoint of those groups. Surely one legitimate function of legal scholarship is to try to identify the interests of subordinated groups. This effort would usefully inform the professional work of their advocates and of legal decision makers concerned with the social welfare as a whole. Consciousness raising addresses the members of oppressed groups in two capacities—as advo-cates for their own interests, and as lawmakers. In a democracy, ordinary citizens must be deemed lawmakers, as worthy of scholarly address as judges and legisla-tors. As Robert Cover argued, the force of law depends on the sufferance and support of ordinary citizens,[174] and the substance of the law is supplied by social life. "The creation of legal meaning . . . takes place always through an essentially cultural medium" and does not depend primarily on state officials.[175] Seen in this light, consciousness raising is not just therapy, but an extension of the traditional function of legal scholarship: informing lawmaking.

One way that narrative can inform lawmaking is by helping to mobilize disaf-fected populations to contend within institutional arenas. A substantial body of

[171] Mary J. Coombs, "Outsider Scholarship: The Law Review Stories," *University of Colorado Law Review* 63 (1992): 683, 717, 722–23.

[172] Farber and Sherry, "Telling Stories," 843.

[173] Ibid., 824.

[174] Robert M. Cover, "Violence and the Word," *Yale Law Journal* 95 (1986): 1601.

[175] Robert Cover, "The Supreme Court 1982 Term, Foreword: *Nomos* and Narrative," *Harvard Law Review* 97 (1983): 4, 10.

research in the sociology of law suggests that the portals of the law are guarded by narrative. The classic Felstiner-Abel-Sarat article "Naming, Blaming, Claiming"[176] conceives legal claims as a three-stage process of narrative framing. Only after an injury has been identified and attributed can it become the basis of a claim. Yet the burdens and risks of pursuing a claim can dissuade a relatively powerless or disaffected claimant, unless her commitment can be sustained by some sense of solidaristic commitment to others. In order to pursue a claim in an institutional process, an actor must (1) characterize herself as a grievant, (2) identify an antagonist, and (3) compose a quest romance in which she is *called* to go forth and right injustice. The dispute forum becomes the magical space, the haunted forest, which the actor must brave to win her way. This sense of being called by a commitment or group identification that transcends the self may require the creation and conservation of group memory or myth.

In "Origin Myths: Narratives of Authority, Resistance, Disability, and the Law," David Engel evokes the scripted nature of confrontation between families and bureaucratic or medical authority.[177] In Engel's cases, the script begins at a very distinct moment, when parents learn that their child is disabled. Parents of disabled children tell strikingly similar stories about the first day of diagnosis, when an authoritative announcement of deviance initiates them into a newly divided and alienating world. These mythic encounters clarify earlier relations with doctors and later relations with legal authorities and provoke dreams of transcendence and reunification. Engel presents these recountings as a pragmatic form of family myth making that helps parents sustain the energy required to negotiate their way through legal and educational systems. Thus, Engel shows how participation in a social myth helps build communal strength among parents who have shared suffering and reinforces their ability to hold lawmakers morally accountable to do justice. Engel conceives these parents as insurgents who help create law by making demands on bureaucratic lawmakers, emboldened to do so because they now conceive themselves as mythic figures liberated from conventional concerns about proper deference to legal authority.

Culturally available narratives play a role in determining who will assert themselves in institutional arenas and to what ends. Thus, one role for narrative scholarship is to make available narratives that can help mobilize participation by recovering and emphasizing aspects of historical experience that prevailing institutional narratives ignore.

Kendall Thomas pursues this task in his "popular constitutional history of the Angelo Herndon case,"[178] an essay that "refuses to view constitutionalism in American culture as the exclusive preserve of elites and institutions."[179] In 1932

[176] William L. F. Felstiner, Richard L. Abel, and Austin Sarat, "The Emergence and Transformation of Disputes: Naming, Blaming, Claiming . . . ," *Law and Society Review* 15 (1981): 631.

[177] David M. Engel, "Origin Myths: Narratives of Authority, Resistance, Disability, and the Law," *Law and Society Review* 27 (1993): 785.

[178] Kendall Thomas, "*Rouge et Noir* Reread: A Popular Constitutional History of the Angelo Herndon Case," *Southern California Law Review* 65 (1992): 2599.

[179] Ibid., 2610.

Herndon, a young African-American Communist, was arrested in Atlanta for attempting to incite insurrection against the state government.[180] He was convicted and sentenced for life. Five years of litigation later, in *Herndon v. Lowry*,[181] Herndon won a Supreme Court decision declaring that the Georgia anti-insurrection law violated the First Amendment by suppressing political speech and violated due process by failing to furnish a reasonably ascertainable standard of guilt. This was a "landmark" case that revived the "clear and present danger" test. Two years earlier, however, the Supreme Court had handed down a very different decision in the same case. In *Herndon v. Georgia*,[182] the Court originally denied appellate jurisdiction because of appellant Herndon's failure to properly present the question; this case was quietly approved by legal process scholars as a prudent exercise of restraint, an example of what Alexander Bickel would later call the "passive virtue" of deciding not to decide.

Thomas subverts received Whiggish history by suppressing the landmark *Herndon v. Lowry*, concentrating instead on the crabbed jurisdictional discussion in *Herndon v. Georgia*. Part of his critical effort is directed at showing how hard the Court strained to achieve its virtuous restraint. The jury had convicted despite the judge's instructions that conviction required a showing of clear and present danger of violence—the test later applied in *Herndon v. Lowry*. Consequently, Herndon's initial appeal was premised on the insufficiency of the evidence, not on any error of law. The state appellate court affirmed the conviction, however, on the grounds that the jury instructions were wrong and that the state had a much lower burden to bear, for which the evidence at trial sufficed. The Supreme Court, however, refused to review this apparent violation of its First Amendment jurisprudence because the defense had not anticipated and objected *at trial* to the *appellate* court's *subsequent* speech-inhibiting interpretation of the statute.

Thomas explains this contorted evasion of jurisdiction by juxtaposing it to two features of the historical context. First, he argues that the Herndon case is properly read as a case about the frightening prospect of Black militance in the crisis-ridden atmosphere of the Depression. The trial was highly publicized and conducted in a hysterical atmosphere. Harping constantly on the defendant's race, the prosecution identified his Communist views with miscegenation and armed revolution. An unapologetic Herndon, supplied with a Communist Party defense team, hectored the jury on the cause of the working class. Thomas is at pains to show that—in the context of the time—the cause of Black liberation was closely and genuinely identified with Communism. He locates Herndon's political autobiography *Let Me Live!* in the tradition of African-American autobiography, substituting Communism for evangelical Christianity as the redemptive force in his life, and the *Communist Manifesto* for the gospel as the site of literary instruction. Thus, to say that the Herndon case was about Communism is not to deny that it was about Black liberation.

---

[180] Ibid., 2630–32.
[181] 301 U.S. 242 (1937).
[182] 295 U.S. 441 (1935).

This insight brings Thomas to another feature of the case's context—the Supreme Court's treatment of race cases during the Depression. The absence of any mention of race in the *Herndon v. Georgia* opinion finds stark contrast in numerous other cases in which the Court premised review on the vulnerability of Southern Black criminal defendants to prejudicial treatment. The point of the story, then, insists Thomas, is the Court's sharply differential treatment of unsophisticated Black victims like the "Scottsboro boys," and an articulate, militant Black leader—the former rescued, the latter abandoned, while legal scholars looked on and approved this prudent disengagement from "political controversies."[183] The result is a coldly ironic destruction of legal process mythology, and a reinscription of racial struggle into the long chapters of our constitutional history that are supposed to have been merely about "federalism" or "institutional competence."

In "Claiming our Foremothers: The Legend of Sally Hemings and the Tasks of Black Feminist Theory,"[184] Stephanie Phillips identifies a rich example of popular historical memory: the narration and interpretation among African-Americans of interracial sexual relations under slavery. Phillips suggests that such stories retain provocative significance in American culture generally and for African-Americans in particular in part because of American society's categorization of race by the "rule of hypodescent"—the rule that a single African ancestor "marks" an individual as "Black." This scheme implicates all Americans in a kind of cognitive dissonance in which they deny the reality that most Americans of African descent also have "White" ancestors. And it places African-Americans in a position of ambivalence or antagonism towards some of their own ancestors. In this way White ancestry serves as a potent metaphor for African-American feelings of dispossession at the hands of a society that is nevertheless their own.

As Phillips shows, the topic of miscegenation implicates not only racial but also gender hierarchy. For most of America's history, sexual relations between Black men and White women have been attended by enormous social sanctions for both. Thus, most interracial sexual relations, especially during slavery, involved White men and Black women. This pattern meant that Black women were both valued and degraded by Whites in ways that Black men were not, so that the oppressions faced by Black men and women were in some respects different and incommensurable.

Because this complex legacy is evoked whenever African-Americans acknowledge White ancestry, to recount or interpret master-slave sexual encounters today is to take a position on what it means to be a Black woman or a Black man in America. By examining and classifying these tales Phillips identifies a rich debate on racial and gender identity within Black popular culture, that she hopes can inform Black feminism. She regrets that an attitude of political piety has often reduced Black feminist commentary on miscegenation to a single, predictable

---

[183] Thomas, *"Rouge et Noir* Reread," 2677, quoting Felix Frankfurter and Henry Hart, "The Business of the Supreme Court at October Term, 1934," *Harvard Law Review* 49 (1935): 68, 107.

[184] Stephanie L. Phillips, "Claiming our Foremothers: The Legend of Sally Hemings and the Tasks of Black Feminist Theory," *Hastings Women's Law Journal* 8 (1997): 401.

emplotment. In an effort to promote the status of Black women as paradigmatic victims of oppression, Phillips charges, Black feminists have denied even the possibility that slave women sometimes sought sexual relations with Whites out of such diverse motives as romantic love, protection from the worst rigors and dangers of slave status, or the thrill of exercising a form of power denied them in other spheres. Phillips urges that Black feminists acknowledge the continuing significance in Black culture of these alternative interpretive frames, and incorporate their psychological insight into the diversity and complexity of human experience under conditions of oppression. The result, she argues, will be a movement more hospitable to women of African descent with White parents or partners, or light skin, and more open to dialogue and coalition with progressive Black men and Whites.

Psychological Therapy

Closely related to the political claims for narrative considered above are some claims for narrative's therapeutic value. Narrative, of course, plays a role in consciousness raising, which is a process of therapy as well as political mobilization. In consciousness raising, the victim of oppression may come to see that she is not alone in her suffering, that others share it and care about it, that the suffering has roots in systematic injustice, that it is not her fault. Thus, consciousness raising can be thought of as a process of recovery from the trauma of oppression. Yet consciousness raising is not always such a cosy, "supportive" process. It does not always emphasize the participants' commonality and solidarity, but often instead is the occasion for coerced public "self-criticism," for exposing other participants' complicity in oppression or insensitivity to difference. When participants in consciousness raising draw general conclusions or lessons from the experiences of others, they may be chastened for misappropriating others' suffering, or presuming to define them. The participant may be told that the self she brings to the consciousness-raising group—or the contemporary classroom—is unworthy, while the collective identity she seeks is an "essentialist" myth.[185]

This, according to Anne Dailey, is the problem that narrative legal scholarship addresses. Such narrative concedes that there is no authentic self, untainted by oppression, waiting to be liberated from false consciousness. Instead, it creates an exemplary self, an authorial voice alive to the gendered, raced, scripted, mass-mediated, culturally determined nature of the postmodern self, yet somehow transcending ideological determination through irony and imagination:

> In contrast to the spontaneous, open-ended dialogue of consciousness-raising, narrative as practiced by feminist legal scholars is a supremely self-conscious art form. The stories feminists tell are sometimes autobiographical and sometimes true, but they

---

[185] Anne C. Dailey, "Feminism's Return to Liberalism," *Yale Law Journal* 102 (1993): 1265, 1274–75 (review of Katharine T. Bartlett and Roseanne Kennedy, eds., *Feminist Legal Theory: Readings in Law and Gender* [Boulder: Westview Press, 1991]; Wendy Kaminer, *I'm Dysfunctional, You're Dysfunctional: The Recovery Movement and Other Self-help Fashions* (Reading, Mass.: Addison-Wesley, 1992).

are as often fictions or even fantasies. Feminist narrative in law is literature with a political point.

The reconstructive power of narrative lies in its potential for arresting the infinite regress of anti-essentialist critique. At its most profound, anti-essentialism leaves us weakened and dazed, paralyzed by self-doubt and schizophrenic impulses. We can reconcile these internal conflicts and achieve a comprehensive sense of identity by a process akin to storytelling. When we imagine our lives, integrating our experiences and emotions into a coherent story, we create ourselves whole. . . .

Narrative thus tempers the view that self or identity is created entirely by social discourse: it injects an element of individual will into the socially constructed postmodern subject. Like the process of psychoanalysis, the practice of narrative recognizes that there is enough of a storyteller in us to create a coherent, if unstable self.[186]

This account of the psychological benefits of narrative scholarship has a certain air of paradox. Where consciousness raising was once prescribed as the cure for the trauma of oppression, narrative is here prescribed as the cure for the trauma of consciousness raising. At first blush, Dailey's account of narrative as postmodern therapy appears to avoid Anne Coughlin's charge that narrative's celebration of the individual protagonist reenforces the individualism of liberal society. The exemplary self offered by postmodern narrative is, after all, presented as a fragile construct, a therapeutic fiction. Yet if we recall Lukács's critique of the novel we may be less sanguine. For Lukács, the true center of bourgeois individualism in the novel is the authorial sensibility, not the character of the protagonist. The contradictions of modern society may render the romantic project of *Bildung* quixotic, Lukács argues, but the all-embracing vision of the novelist teaches the alienated reader that coherence may still be found in art. The bourgeois individual may have little hope of realizing herself in social life, but she may seek solace for civilization's discontents in the aesthetic detachment enabled by the consumption of cultural commodities. So, too, Dailey reassures us that we can sustain identities as radical intellectuals amid the routines and compromises of professional life by fantasizing that at least we are the authors of our own fantasies.[187]

In pursuit of such a program, many works of feminist legal narrative direct the reader past the normative implications of the experience narrated to consciously reflect on the rhetorical process by which experience is framed as narrative. This reflective project goes beyond the assertion that different narrative constructions of experience are possible and that one story should be preferred to another on moral or political grounds. Instead, it celebrates the constructive or narrative element of experience as inherently liberating—as a source of the author's power to create a coherent self and thereby resist heteronomy. Yet this integration of the self is a hard-won and often tenuous achievement, the outcome of a suspenseful

---

[186] Dailey, "Feminism's Return to Liberalism," 1274–75.

[187] See Pierre Bourdieu, "Men and Machines," in Karin-Knorr Cetina and Aaron Victor Cicourel, eds., *Advances in Social Theory and Methodology: Toward an Integration of Micro- and Macro-Sociologies* (Boston: Routledge and Kegan Paul, 1981), 304–17 (the pretense of Sartrian self-consciousness and freedom to change roles is the role to which intellectuals are unself-consciously habituated).

struggle against the forces of fragmentation. When feminist legal narrative focuses attention on the constructive activity of the author, that author's struggle for autonomy and integrity often provides the motor of narrative suspense. Often the author dramatizes the struggle for self-integration by composing an authorial voice acutely sensitive to the aesthetic and ethical choices it confronts in narrating either its own experience or another's. While purporting to worry about how it should constitute itself, this voice is of course already constituted as that of a self-conscious intellectual, struggling to achieve a recognizable individuality while remaining independent of all identifying commitments.

A common occasion for this sort of authorial performance is the ethnographic encounter between an activist lawyer and a subordinated client who faces the awesome bureaucratic power of the state. The lawyer is typically caught between obligations to advocate effectively for the client's interests and to recognize and give way to the client's authentic voice. The client is typically presented as a kind of noble "natural," possessed of an enigmatic moral wisdom or strategic cunning that her technically trained lawyer cannot quite grasp. The attorney narrates how she came to realize that while purporting to represent her client she has collaborated with the state in suppressing the client's authentic story. This sort of ethnographic parable has become so prevalent in the writing of clinical professors as to constitute a discrete genre in its own right.[188]

The most celebrated example of the genre is Lucie White's "Subordination, Rhetorical Survival Skills, and Sunday Shoes, the Hearing of Mrs. G."[189] Mrs. G., a Black single mother of four children who lived on AFDC money, received a $600 insurance settlement for an auto accident. She told her caseworker about it, and the caseworker wrongly reassured Mrs. G. that this settlement did not have to be set off against her monthly welfare payments. Later, the supervisor discovered the error and ordered Mrs. G. to pay back $600, which she had already spent on personal articles and shoes for her children. Mrs. G. sought the advice of White, then a legal aid lawyer, who told her she had done nothing wrong and that she should not sign a contract agreeing to repay the money. Nevertheless, Mrs. G. signed such a contract and then returned to White, apologized for ignoring her advice, and agreed, somewhat grudgingly, to challenge both the reimbursement order and the contract at a hearing.

White told Mrs. G. she could tell one of two stories at the hearing to support her legal claim: first, an estoppel story, whereby the caseworker clearly told Mrs. G. that no set-off was necessary; second, a necessities story, whereby the payment was used to buy, for example, new shoes because the children's older shoes were beyond repair.[190] White was confident the estoppel story was true, and that it expressed Mrs. G.'s indignation at being unfairly accused of fraud after she had

---

[188] Christopher P. Gilkerson, "Poverty Law Narratives: The Critical Practice and Theory of Receiving and Translating Client Stories," *Hastings Law Journal* 42 (1992): 861.

[189] Lucie White, "Subordination, Rhetorical Survival Skills, and Sunday Shoes: Notes on the Hearing of Mrs. G.," *Buffalo Law Review* 38 (1990): 1.

[190] Ibid., 27.

been candid. Yet she feared that its accusation of unfairness and ineptitude would provoke the welfare department's retaliation against Mrs. G. As for the necessities story, White sensed that Mrs. G. resented having to present herself as a supplicant flaunting her poverty and seeking approval for her purchases. Yet White had been told that state officials were sympathetic to "necessities" claims in cases like this. Mrs. G. offered to tell both stories at the hearing, and White prepared her accordingly.

To White's shock, at the hearing Mrs. G. broke from the script. She hedged and stammered. She refused to blame the caseworker for estoppel, now saying that she was unsure whether she ever even told the caseworker of the payment. As for necessities, Mrs. G. now said that the children's older shoes were quite adequate, but that she wanted the children to have finer ones for church. At this point "her voice sounded different—stronger more composed—than I had heard her before."[191] Mrs. G. lost the hearing before the state examiner, but the County Welfare Authorities withdrew their claim against her in the interest of "fairness."

White views Mrs. G.'s improvisation as an act of heroic self-assertion. On the estoppel story, White surmises that Mrs. G. simply refused to grovel, or perhaps was protecting the welfare worker, who was also a Black woman. As for the shoes, Mrs. G. did not want to equate material objects with life's true necessities. Rather, she wanted to affirm the "necessity" of religion as central to the spirit of Southern Black life. In so doing, she affirmed her respectability before the Black welfare worker but "condemned the welfare system" and its "systemic disregard for her point of view."[192] She "claimed a position of equality in the speech community."[193] She refused to be "respectful,"[194] or to "legitimate" the "patterns and priorities that had kept her down."[195] She also revealed her mistrust of White, the White lawyer who was part of a system devoted to "assisting, but also controlling the poor."[196] White implies that the humiliation she herself suffered as the hearing spun out of her control was a well-deserved rebuke for her efforts to channel Mrs. G. into the role of a compliant supplicant. By betraying White in front of the welfare officials, Mrs. G. taught White that she had betrayed Mrs. G. from the outset.

White concludes that Mrs. G. proved herself a "better strategist then the lawyer—more daring, more subtle"[197] and that her "unruly participation" was a form of "political action."[198] Mrs. G. triumphed over the efforts of the legal system—including those of her own lawyer—to objectify her. She forced the assembled professionals to confront her subjectivity, thereby breaking them out of their own confining bureaucratic roles and enabling them to respond to "their own human

[191] Ibid., 31.
[192] Ibid., 49–50.
[193] Ibid., 50.
[194] Ibid., 49.
[195] Ibid.
[196] Ibid., 46–47.
[197] Ibid., 47.
[198] Ibid., 52.

judgment."[199] Yet the larger conclusions she draws somewhat belie this romantic characterization of Mrs. G.'s narrative act as a political, rhetorical, and aesthetic triumph.

White presents Mrs. G. as a speaker subordinated because of race, sex, and class and argues that such speakers typically adopt a deferential posture, eager to accommodate and please authority. When officials show that they view welfare recipients as conniving frauds, they coerce welfare recipients to confess to wrongdoing so as to make a sacrificial display of their candor. The legal system's objectification of the welfare recipient further silences her by allowing her to speak only to the legal issues in dispute—yet White admits that informal, discretionary decision making is likely to disadvantage the subordinated even more. The only way to provide Mrs. G. with a *process* that duly hears her and recognizes her as equal before the law is to make her *substantively* equal, White concludes. Thus, White arrives at the whimsical position that wealth and power must be equalized, not to achieve social justice or democracy, but to perfect judicial process.

White's account of the pressures arrayed against Mrs. G. is convincing—so convincing that it is hard to read Mrs. G.'s conduct at the hearing as an act of insubordination. At every stage she deferred to the welfare officials. It is possible to read her submission as a dramatic performance—she equips herself with the prop of a lawyer and the stage of a hearing in order to remind the officials that she could be troublesome, and then ostentatiously spurns her lawyer and abandons her legal claims. That her submission may have been strategically staged for maximum effect does not make it rebellious, however. She may have won the indulgence of officials on this occasion, but she nevertheless reenforced their power to withhold such indulgence on another occasion, or against a less compliant welfare recipient.

Mrs. G.'s political triumph is primarily over her own lawyer. The humble but streetwise client teaches the intellectual lawyer a lesson in humility that she in turn passes on to us. This edifying lesson—that genuine beneficence must recognize its objects as subjects in their own right—becomes the main point of the story, as Mrs. G. not only bears witness to the centrality of Christianity in her own life, but teaches its ethical meaning to her pharisaical attorney. Mrs. G. will go on in her dogged project of survival, while it is the young lawyer who comes away transformed by her encounter with grace. Mrs. G. is the familiar "donor" character of the quest romance, the shrewd forest-dwelling troll who tests and teaches a callow protagonist. Thus read, the clinical narrative embodies a paradox: its ethical message inveighs against the lawyer's narcissistic appropriation of the client as a means to her own ends, while its narrative form reduces the client to an instrument of the author's ethical redemption.

The clinical narrative, then, is a somewhat covert authorial performance. Just as the legal process opinion performatively demonstrates the virtue of deliberative restraint in its Quixotic effort to ground judicial decision in objective principle, the clinical narrative performatively demonstrates the virtue of self-effacing sen-

---

[199] Ibid., 51.

sitivity in its Quixotic effort to represent the client's authentic subjectivity. Both performances display the authorial persona by purporting to efface it.

By contrast, Patricia Williams's much-admired "diary of a law professor," *The Alchemy of Race and Rights*, involves no such coyness.[200] From the outset it is not only a presentation of self, but also a meditation on the presentation of self in a public space framed by commerce, mass media, and racial hierarchy. The book interweaves Williams's self-reflections with a number of different elements: commentaries on language, property, objectification, race, and reproduction; narratives of quotidian encounters with demeaning store clerks, smug neighbors, and alienated homeless people; commentaries on news stories and other media images; narratives of professional experiences in which Williams presents her views to sometimes unsympathetic, defensive, or dim-witted audiences; family history involving discussions of her slave (and slavemaster) ancestry; and dreams. The narrative connections among these elements are diverse. Sometimes a theoretical discussion is "quoted" at length within a narrative of a professional encounter; a conference might be interrupted by a shopping trip; a colleague's comment might prompt remembrances or musings on recent media stories; channel hopping might create juxtapositions that resemble the associative connections that structure stream of consciousness. Indeed, if there is a dominant narrative form here at all, it is the stream of a consciousness buffeted by the steady pulse of demeaning images and stories circulating through mass culture.

The self Williams presents is "fashionably" fragmented: "Some part of me knows that it is intelligent for me to be schizophrenic . . . to hear a lot of voices in my head: in fact, it is not just intelligent but fashionable, feminist, and even postmodern."[201] Williams mourns this incoherence as a state of alienation.[202] Yet to try to "compose" one's self neatly (and fashionably?) is to oblige the inconsistent demands of an oppressive culture:

> When I get up in the morning I stare at the mirror and stick on my roles: I brush my teeth, as a responsibility to my community. I buff my nails, paving the way for my race. I comb my hair in the spirit of pulling myself up by my own bootstraps. I dab astringent on my pores that I might be a role model upon whom all may gaze with pride. I mascara my lashes that I may be "different" from all the rest. . . . When I am fully dressed, my face is hung with contradictions.[203]

The composed, public self is one of the many meanings of Williams's polyvalent metaphor of "the Obliging Shell," the title of one of the book's essays. This shell is, first, the set of abstract categories in which the rules of antidiscrimination law collect the complexity of human experience, yielding a "seductive . . . stone cool algebra of rich life stories."[204] The reduction of discrimination to color-con-

---

[200] Patricia J. Williams, *The Alchemy of Race and Rights: Diary of a Law Professor* (Cambridge: Harvard Univ. Press, 1991).

[201] Ibid., 207.

[202] Ibid., 228–29.

[203] Ibid., 196.

[204] Ibid., 98.

scious rules is a "shell-game" substituting "reverse discrimination" for real racism.[205] The *Richmond v. Croson* affirmative action decision, which belittled evidence of past discrimination in the construction industry, makes a similarly formal shell of experience.[206]

Williams next asserts the obliging plasticity of these word-shells—and shows the plasticity of her own metaphor—by likening words to sausage skins. She recalls her summation to the jury in a consumer fraud case about impure sausages: "You have this thing called a sausage-making machine. You put pork and spices in at the top and crank it up, and because it is a sausage-making machine, what comes out the other end is a sausage. . . . One day, we throw in a few small rodents of questionable pedigree and a teddy bear and a chicken."[207] In posing the question whether to call the result sausage, Williams challenges the jury to "acknowledge" their own "participation in the creation of reality" by recognizing that they have the choice of "enlarging the authority of sausage makers" to decide what sausage is, or "expanding the definition of sausage" to include all usage, or of confining the meaning of sausage to its useful social function as healthful food.[208]

Next, the metaphor stretches from sausage skin to human skin and so to racial identity. The repudiation of formal segregation has not eliminated the privilege associated with Whiteness, Williams argues, but has stretched its "protective shell" to encompass those Blacks willing and able to assimilate.[209] The shell then becomes the privileged spaces to which assimilation might admit one—middle-class neighborhoods, professions, trendy stores, and the obliging civility with which one hopes to be treated. Yet this protective shell of civility depends in turn on one's own docility. The price of fitting in is not only the implicit condemnation of those who do not, but obliging complicity in the brutal incivility with which they are treated. In a Greenwich Village boutique, Williams finds herself flattered by the pleasant young salesclerks into silent acquiescence in their sly anti-Semitic jokes. She is chagrined that the fear of humiliation by these preening adolescents had seduced her into debasing herself. This kind of betrayal of others, Williams concludes, is a self-betrayal that divides the self. We may hope the obliging shell of civility will hold together our fragmented selves, but true integrity requires that we "transgress" the "encompassing circle" of social acceptance and bear witness to conscience.[210] We may not then appear composed, but we will be "well, . . . strong," whole: our schizophrenia will be merely skin deep, a postmodern presentation of a romantic self.

Most of the recurrent elements, themes, and narrative devices of the book are introduced in its subtly compressed opening scene. Her first address to the reader is a caveat emptor: "Since subject position is everything in my analysis of the

[205] Ibid., 103.
[206] Ibid., 106.
[207] Ibid., 107.
[208] Ibid., 107–8.
[209] Ibid., 116.
[210] Ibid., 129–30.

law, you deserve to know that it's a bad morning. I'm very depressed."[211] She has positioned the prospective reader as a skeptical consumer and questioned her own psychological fitness to serve as the author/subject/product. Why is she depressed? She hates her chosen profession of law, because of its objectification of human suffering and its smug racism, as in the commercial law case she is reading that morning, in which

> The plaintiff alleged that he purchased of the defendant a slave named Kate, for which he paid $500, and in two or three days after it was discovered the slave was crazy, and run away, and that the vices were known to the defendant. . . . It was contended [by the seller] that Kate was not crazy but only stupid, and stupidity is not madness; but on the contrary, an apparent defect, against which the defendant did not warrant.[212]

Suddenly, the prospective reader is engaged in a like purchase of human property, and Williams is revealed to be confessing craziness so the buyer will infer no warrant of reliability. In this way Williams connects the self-promotion and self-commodification required by modern mass culture with the expropriation of the slave's humanity and draws connections between legal categorization and racist stereotyping. Williams offers herself for sale, but with no promise of docility: "I let my hair stream wildly and my eyes roll back in my head. . . . You should know this is one of those mornings when I refuse to compose myself properly."[213]

Uncomposed, she cannot compose: she feels like a "monkey" at the keyboard,[214] a projection of racist stereotypes, a nonsubject—but capable, according to the old joke, of writing *Hamlet* by some quirk of chance. In search of such a quirk, she spins the dial of the TV set and becomes a receptor of fragmented postmodern culture. The news blandly reports, amid other catastrophes, several stories revealing societal animosity towards Black people, expressed in exploding incarceration rates and thinly disguised eugenic proposals. All of these stories leave her disabled by depression, until she sees a story announcing that "Harvard Law School cannot find one Black woman on the entire planet who is good enough to teach there, because we're all too stupid." Harvard does not want to purchase anyone with such an "apparent defect." "So now you know," Williams continues. "It is this news item . . . that finally pushes me over the edge and into the deep rabbit-hole of this book."[215] *Over the edge*—crazy, not stupid as charged.

Anne Coughlin, reviewing *The Alchemy of Race and Rights*, reads this opening as locating Williams's narrative in the venerable genre of the "apology, a conventional autobiographical form in which the author undertakes to defend her intellec-

---

[211] Ibid., 3.
[212] Ibid., 3, quoting *Icar v. Suares*, 7 La. Rep. 517 (1835).
[213] Williams, *Alchemy*, 4.
[214] Ibid.
[215] Ibid., 5.

tual career."[216] As far as Coughlin is concerned, there is nothing particularly avant-garde or rebellious about this apologetic project. Williams postures as "the scourge of the academy" who will "lay bare the errors and biases that permeate its craft" but is impeded by her apologetic project of "aggrandizing"[217] her academic status and achievements so as to win recognition in conventional terms. Moreover, argues Coughlin, the apologetic project undermines what would otherwise be the considerable literary merit of the book. Avant-garde literature, she reasons, is supposed to be richly dialogic, pregnant with polyvalent meanings the reader is left to ponder. But, she charges, Williams tends to present her ideas framed within narratives in which she jets to one or another prestigious venue where she lectures skeptical, sullen listeners who are portrayed as "flat, unreflective, ill-educated and bigoted." Their objections are always "impatient, insensitive and dull." Rather than savoring multiple meanings, readers must "endorse Williams's meaning" on pain of being associated with these yahoos.[218]

Coughlin adroitly exposes the performative contradiction in this work, its join-what-you-can't-beat emulation of the objects of its critique. But Coughlin overstates the parochialism, and hence the pettiness of this ambivalence. Williams is unabashed about her identification as a comfortably situated intellectual. It is not primarily in relation to the academy that Williams's narrator is divided against herself. In *every* public interaction, she fears that embodying a stereotype is the price of recognition. It is the stereotypes of black women circulating through the circuitry of mass culture that depress her more than the muted resonance of those images in academe. Every story on the news insults her; the story that *inspires* her is the one in which legal academics *like her* get on MacNeil-Lehrer to deliver the insult on national TV. The Harvard soundbite is not just a provocation to apologetic narrative, it is the postmodern equivalent of the slave narrative's *scene of literary instruction*, the trope of the Talking Book refigured as the trope of the Talking Head. Williams's inspired response is to write a popular book that not only will win her an appointment at an Ivy League law school, but will get her in front of the national media as a pundit. It is this aim of plugging into the media power-grid that accounts for the features of the text Coughlin remarks upon. Williams's narrator glamorizes herself because that is necessary to the rhetorical project of composing herself as a celebrity, and she reduces her antagonists to stereotypes because stereotypes are the currency of mass culture. As Williams herself stresses, it is nothing *personal*.[219] Like Baker's slave narrators and Gallagher's fiction-mongers, Williams is joining what she cannot beat, substituting a strategy for a self.

---

[216] Coughlin, "Regulating the Self," 1303.

[217] Ibid., 1305–6.

[218] Ibid., 1311–12.

[219] As Williams explains, "I have fictionalized the identities of people and collapsed several conversations . . . into the mouths of only a few characters. . . . I generalized because the power of these events is precisely their generality. . . . The lesson lies in the principles, not in the personalities." Williams, *Alchemy*, 91.

3.3 LAW AND NARRATIVE AS MUTUALLY INHERENT

While much narrative criticism of law is premised on an antinomy between law and narrative, some of the most interesting work on law and narrative reverses this hackneyed trope and explores the ways in which narrative inheres in law, or law inheres in narrative. The claim that narrative inheres in law can be made at a number of levels: first, and most obviously, that in requiring that legal authorities "find facts," legal disputes require them to fashion or choose a narrative. Second, that basic patterns of legal thought link causation to disapprobation, obligation to rectification, and means to ends in narrative structures. Third, and most fundamentally, that some narrative of legitimation is implied in the very ideas of legal authority, legal system, and the state. We will consider each of these claims for the inherency of narrative in law. Next, we will draw upon literary as well as legal scholarship in discussing the constitutive role of law in narrative. Finally, we will recur to the question of narrative legal scholarship. If narrative is inherent in law and legal thought, there is little point in urging legal scholars to write narrative, for they are already doing so. The point of narrative criticism is to read the narratives that are already immanent in law and legal thought; to propose and defend criteria for evaluating legal narrative rather than to embrace all narrative uncritically; and to urge not more, but better, narratives.

Narrating Facts

The intense moral and political conflicts in criminal cases make the criminal courtroom the most visible of all narrative arenas. Kim Scheppele interprets the rape trial as a contest of narratives.[220] Truth in law, Scheppele argues, is not the property of an event; rather, it is a property of an account of an event. Women's stories continue to be disbelieved in court, but whereas law used to be sexist in its abstract doctrine, now it is sexist in its framing of the facts: Where the victim no longer has to prove the rapist used aggressive force or knew she had not consented, she now has trouble convincing courts she did not consent. Scheppele argues that a subtly sexist premise of legal narrative is that truth is singular, apparent, and narratively coherent. When women are attacked, among the many harms they suffer is the loss of their grasp of the conventional coherence of an event, because the attack disrupts their normal expectations of reality. Their stories therefore do not comfortably jibe with the culturally available narratives. Before a new story becomes acceptable to courts and juries, we must see larger numbers of tellers, and corroboration, and even expert testimony that the story makes sense.

Alan Dershowitz offers a different objection to narrative coherence.[221] Countering talk of competing narratives in criminal cases, Dershowitz argues that the

---

[220] Scheppele, "Foreword: Telling Stories," 2085–94.

[221] Alan Dershowitz, "Life Is Not a Dramatic Narrative," in *Law's Stories: Narrative and Rhetoric in Law*, ed. Peter Brooks and Paul Gewirtz (New Haven: Yale Univ. Press, 1996), 99.

role of the defense lawyer is to *disrupt* narrative form, which he regards as an uninformed fantasy wholly exploitable by the prosecution. Thus, if the jury hears that O. J. Simpson has once assaulted Nicole Brown Simpson, and if it sees physical evidence at least consistent with Simpson's guilt, the prosecution urges it to use this information to form a well-wrought story with a resolute climax. But, Dershowitz argues, the overwhelming majority of men who assault their wives do not kill them, and most encounters between jealous ex-husbands and ex-wives end in boring anticlimax. For Dershowitz, law as narrative means law as the imposition of a procrustean form on a protean reality. Dershowitz, of course, faces the counterargument that while most wife abusers do not kill, most previously abused murder victims may have been murdered by their abusers. Yet the larger point, that the criminal trial is often a battle between a prosecutorial narrative and a defense strategy of disrupting the coherence of that narrative, is one heard with increasing frequency. An obvious case in point is the first "Rodney King" trial, in which the defense seemed to perform the miracle of persuading the jury to disbelieve their own eyes by deconstructing the videotape of King's beating into discrete frames.

The risks and paradoxes of this deconstructive strategy are explored in a recent article by Richard Sherwin.[222] Sherwin examines the case of Randall Adams, the death-row inmate who won retrial and acquittal because of Errol Morris's film *The Thin Blue Line*. Sherwin notes that in this controversial litigation the state of Texas had the advantage of a linear, logical narrative. In the state's story, Randall Adams picked up a sixteen-year-old runaway named David Harris, shared an evening of drinking and thieving with Harris, and was driving Harris around when they were stopped by a police officer. Fearing arrest, Adams killed the officer. Harris testified against Adams, and Adams was convicted and sentenced to death.[223]

Adams was ultimately saved by the public persuasive power of Morris's film, so Sherwin treats the film as if it were a legal presentation of the defense case. He posits the defense's narrative dilemma: technical burdens of proof aside, you might try to win an acquittal through a counternarrative whereby you show incontrovertibly that someone else did the crime. Conversely, since your job as defense counsel is only to provoke reasonable doubt, you may be tempted to exploit postmodernist skepticism about the possibility of linear narrative or meaningful order in human events. Morris, says Sherwin, tried both these strategies—a linear counternarrative and an antilinear antinarrative.

The counternarrative was a story whereby Harris had indeed briefly become Adams's companion, but was the sole killer and was alone at the time of the killing, and that Harris was helped in framing Adams by corrupt state authorities who wanted to pin the blame on Adams because he, unlike Harris, was old enough to get the death penalty. As for the antinarrative, says Sherwin, Morris reveals

---

[222] Richard K. Sherwin, "Law Frames: Historical Truth and Narrative Necessity in a Criminal Case," *Stanford Law Review* 47 (1994): 39.

[223] *Adams v. State*, 577 S.W.2d 717 (Tex. Crim., App. 1979), rev'd in part by *Adams v. Texas*, 448 U.S. 38 (1980).

plenty of factual ambiguities about the counternarrative. Disorienting the viewer through nonlinear arrangements of images and accounts of the crime and even interpolated clips from clichéd crime movies, Morris raises doubts as to whether Adams might after all have at least been with Harris when the officer was killed, and whether Adams lied about some of the other events of that evening.

Sherwin admires the film because it goes beyond a simple (and questionable) counternarrative and thus, to the more discerning viewer, induces a deeper skepticism about how well-made actual human stories are. But Sherwin thinks that if we view the film essentially as a lawyer's argument, Morris took a huge risk in making the film so "postmodern" that he was overtaxing the audience's tolerance for skepticism and underestimating its fear of moral nihilism. While lawyers are "inescapably part of postmodern culture," he warns them not to repeat Morris's questionable strategy of offering a "lay" audience a skeptical postmodernist view of human events. Such an audience cannot quite let go of its need for the principles of intentionality and causation that make possible moral accountability. Sherwin concludes that the movie's "aesthetic and psychological failures offer a cautionary lesson about the art of persuasive legal storytelling: The law has little use for the kind of skeptical, radically subversive postmodernism that has been featured of late in some legal and much nonlegal scholarship."[224] Instead, lawyers should adopt an "affirmative postmodernism" that emphasizes "particularity, contextuality, multiplicity," but that still somehow affirms the possibility of "truth and justice." On the question of how the defense could have satisfied the jury's craving for literary order while still inducing agnosticism about the knowability of the key facts in the case, Sherwin is not altogether helpful.

One answer to this dilemma is to create a counternarrative with the jury as protagonist. Using a homicide trial focusing on the issue of intent to kill, Anthony Amsterdam and Randy Hertz identify narratives built into the competing arguments.[225] They show that the prosecutor's posture is that the facts of the case are largely undisputed and that the inference of intent to kill follows fairly directly from these undisputed facts. As Amsterdam and Hertz note, the prosecutor places this undisputed narrative at the heart of her argument, and her various rhetorical and linguistic stratagems serve that goal; for example, the language of the argument is largely physical ("iconic") and the verbs are almost all in the past tense. Often the prosecutor will underscore the firmness of the narrative by reminding the jury of what is *not* at issue: "You don't have to decide whether the defendant was the one who pulled the trigger of that gun and who caused the bullet to penetrate Mary's heart and liver and eventually lodge in her back and eventually cause her to bleed to death."[226] The prosecutor thereby rhetorically separates the facts of the defendant's actions from any matter of jury interpretation or construction—or moral responsibility in deciding what happened.

[224] Sherwin, "Law Frames," 71.

[225] Anthony G. Amsterdam and Randy Hertz, "An Analysis of Closing Arguments to a Jury," *New York Law School Law Review* 37 (1992): 55.

[226] Ibid., 61.

The defense lawyer, as Dershowitz suggests, needs to destroy this narrative, but he is caught in Sherwin's dilemma: he may not risk underestimating the jury's need to see the facts through a narrrative, so he has to construct one for them. But he may not have an alternative story to tell—unless perhaps his defense is alibi and he is willing to take on the burden of "prosecuting" an alternative defendant. One solution, Amsterdam and Hertz argue, is to produce a "present-tense" narrative drama, figuring the jury itself as the protagonist of a heroic quest. In this narrative, the jury is tempted by the prosecutor to follow the easy path to conviction, but the defense lawyer calls the jury to enlist in a high-minded moral crusade: to accept their civic duty to follow the law, gird themselves with the presumption of innocence, resist temptation, and find the holy grail of reasonable doubt.

Narrative Legal Concepts

Some of the most basic patterns of thought in law appear to be narratively structured. We will briefly discuss causation and blame, obligation and rectification, and the relation of means to ends in both instrumentalist and formalist legal reasoning.

To assign legal responsibility for harmful or wrongful consequences often involves judging cause. A causal relationship implies a sequence of events in time, but this by itself is not enough to render causal explanation narrative in nature. According to Danto, a narrative explanation must involve a sequence of causal explanations. What is a cause? Philosophers tell us that the entire set of conditions necessary to a result is its cause.[227] When the law assigns causal responsibility to an individual, however, it apparently selects only one among many necessary conditions, a single act or omission, and calls that a cause. Yet that single necessary condition is deemed causally responsible because of the culpable mental state of the perpetrator. The perpetrator's intention to cause a harmful result, or reckless or negligent disregard of the risk that such a result would occur, was a necessary condition to the action or omission that caused harm. Thus, an assignment of causal responsibility involves a short *chain* of causal explanation, a simple narrative linking a harmful result to a blameworthy character.

Of course, lengthening the narrative chain may negate the inculpatory inference of bad character. Perhaps the defendant knowingly risked harm in response to the command of a desperate gunman. Thus, the point is not that narrative necessarily establishes blame, but rather that narrative is inherent in the general legal problem of assigning or denying cause and blame. As Mark Kelman has shown, many simple criminal scenarios can be narratively conceived as inculpatory or exculpatory, depending on alternative "time frames."[228] An addict causes harm under the

---

[227] Richard Taylor, "Causation," *The Encyclopedia of Philosophy*, ed. Paul Edwards (New York: Macmillan and Free Press, 1967), 2:56, 63.

[228] Mark Kelman, "Interpretive Construction in the Substantive Criminal Law," *Stanford Law Review* 33 (1981): 591.

influence of an intoxicating drug. At the time of his harmful act he is incapable of entertaining a culpable mental state. Yet his earlier decision to ingest the drug may be considered reckless. Even this earlier decision may be exculpated, however, as part of a larger pattern of compulsive, addiction-driven behavior. Yet his state of addiction itself may perhaps be blamed on earlier voluntary acts of experimenting with drugs or forswearing regular habits. These choices may in turn be exculpated by reference to peer pressure, limited opportunity, a deprived or abusive upbringing.

Rectification is a recurrent theme in legal thought that seems to involve narrative. Drawing on structuralist analysts of narrative like Propp, Steven Winter has isolated some of the basic structural features of a text that identify it as a story: movement from an origin to a goal, balance between beginning and ending scenario, and some conflict or transformation in the middle.[229] This structure obviously closely parallels the sequence of events we associate with rectification: after an initial equilibrium an event occurs to trigger an obligation—a benefit is conferred, a promise is made, a right is violated, harm is done. There follows a struggle—a claim is made, contested, and then vindicated. Finally, the benefit is repaid, the promise is performed, compensation or penance is paid, and equilibrium is thus restored. Philosophers tend to explain retributive punishment in narrative terms that reflect this structure. For Herbert Morris, just punishment presupposes something like a social contract, conferring the "benefit" of security in return for the "burden" of self-restraint. By renouncing these burdens, the offender "has acquired an unfair advantage." Punishment "restores the equilibrium of benefits and burdens by taking from the individual what he owes, that is, exacting the debt."[230] Jean Hampton asserts that "by victimizing me, the wrongdoer has declared himself . . . a superior who is permitted to use me for his moral purposes." Proportionate punishment "corrects" this "false" claim: "If I cause the wrongdoer to suffer in proportion to my suffering . . . I master the purported master, showing that he is my peer."[231] According to R. A. Duff, wrongdoing alienates the offender from society, just as sin alienates from God. Punishment is meant "to bring the criminal to understand the nature and implications of her crime; to repent that crime and thus, by willing her own punishment as a penance that can expiate her crime, to reconcile herself with the Right and her community."[232] For all of these authors, retributive punishment is the completion of an expressive drama.

Laws are sometimes applied as flexible means to policy ends like consumer confidence or optimal deterrence. Such purposive interpretation obviously deploys narratives linking legislation, through discretionary application, to a telos. But laws are sometimes applied inflexibly, without regard to future consequences,

[229] Winter, "Cognitive Dimension of the Agon," 2225, 2240.

[230] Herbert Morris, *On Guilt and Innocence: Essays in Legal Philosophy and Moral Psychology* (Berkeley: Univ. of California Press, 1976), 34.

[231] Jean Hampton, "The Retributive Idea," in *Forgiveness and Mercy*, ed. Jeffrie G. Murphy and Jean Hampton (Cambridge: Cambridge Univ. Press, 1988).

[232] R. A. Duff, *Trials and Punishments* (Cambridge: Cambridge Univ. Press, 1986), 261.

and most Law and Narrative scholarship treats such rule formalism as antithetical to narrative. But Leo Katz has recently suggested that rule formalism actually contributes to the narrative structure of moral and legal reasoning. Rule formalism excludes certain *means* regardless of the desirability of the *ends* to be achieved. It sets up these proscriptions as obstacles encountered along a desiderative journey towards an otherwise legitimate goal. As a result, it renders moral choice *path-dependent*. Among Katz's many examples is the situation facing a hospital administrator who finds he is frequently unable to connect life-support equipment to the patients who could most benefit from it because it has previously been hooked up to relatively less promising patients. The hospital can choose among patients who have not yet been put on life support, but it cannot detach a patient for the purpose of saving another. The initial allocation of life-support equipment is a fork in the road from which there is no going back: "What occurs to the hospital administrator is that if he buys equipment that has to be disconnected regularly and replaced and serviced, he obtains a flexibility he didn't have before."[233] The administrator redesigns the topography of moral choice, turning prohibited actions into permissible omissions that achieve the same ends. In such cases, certain paths to utility maximizing are open at certain times and others are foreclosed. The open paths are sequences of permissible choice, channeled by formal rules.

Narratives of Legitimation

Narrative is implicit not only in the facts law judges, and in the moral judgments it makes, but also in legal authority itself. To invoke the authority of law as an official, judge, lawyer, litigant, or protestor is to tell a story. In "*Nomos* and Narrative," Robert Cover writes:

> No set of legal institutions or prescriptions exists apart from the narratives that locate it and give it meaning. For every constitution there is an epic, for each decalogue a scripture. Once understood in the context of the narratives that give it meaning, law becomes not merely a system of rules to be observed, but a world in which we live.
>
> In this normative world, law and narrative are inseparably related. Every prescription is insistent in its demand to be located in discourse—to be supplied with history and destiny, beginning and end, explanation and purpose.[234]

At the simplest level, Cover reminds us that the authority of any legal rule rests on a "pedigree,"[235] a narrative linking it to an authoritative decision maker. Even when a rule is defended in consequentialist terms, its authority rests on the consequences having been identified by a competent decison maker and process of decision. Narratives of legitimation are implicit in the application of any legal source, including constitutions, decisional precedents, and statutes.

---

[233] Leo Katz, *Ill-Gotten Gains: Evasion, Blackmail, Fraud and Kindred Puzzles of the Law* (Chicago: Univ. of Chicago Press, 1996), 58.

[234] Cover, "*Nomos* and Narrative," 4–5.

[235] H. L. A. Hart, *The Concept of Law*, 2d ed. (Oxford: Clarendon Press, 1994), 1–17, 51–65.

Constitutions are framed at discrete moments in history that seem to necessitate a fresh start, a hiatus in legality. Their preambular language often refers to these conditions in stating the principles that justify a new constitution and the purposes it serves. We can think of the American Declaration of Independence as an extended preamble that not only states principles justifying a conditional right of revolution, but recounts the "long train of abuses" that trigger the right.

Common law decision making narrates and continues the evolution of legal principles through analogy. Common law decisions must be warranted by past decisions read together, against the background of historical experience. Thus, past rules of decision can be confined to their narrow facts or to the broad historical conditions of their emergence. A "trend" of the progressive narrowing of a rule or the carving out of exceptions can be marshaled as evidence that it is ripe for overruling. Thus, even though common law judges can innovate, their innovation must be defensible as the continuation of the story of a legal doctrine, a legal system, or a society.[236]

Statutory codes may be read as a timeless collection of legal rules equally binding regardless of the sequence of their passage, but their authority obviously depends upon a previous act of legislative enactment. And it has often been assumed that coherent and stable codes could be developed only following a lengthy process of customary legal development and scholarly study.

Communitarian philosophers insist that the very notion of a moral obligation assumes a narrative past. According to Alasdair MacIntyre, "I can only answer the question 'What am I to do?' if I can answer the prior question 'Of what story or stories do I find myself a part?'"[237] David Luban adds that even when we argue consequentially, "the consequences we seek are in large measure to be sought in the past" in the sense that we strive to "resurrect the memory of our dead ancestors," or "rescue their history from the defamations of their enemies," and achieve "a past that makes us comprehensible."[238] Even utility, Luban suggests, is a matter of fidelity to the interests our traditions confer upon us.

Against such assertions of the necessary traditionality of values, the literary theorist Steven Knapp voices the suspicion that the authority of the past depends upon our current values, so that "the lines of authority run from present to past and not the other way around."[239] Knapp wonders, "why should it ever matter . . . that an authoritative narrative correspond to, or have anything much to do with, historical *actuality*?"[240] Why care about the actual circumstances under which

[236] This is of course the main point of Ronald Dworkin's chain-novel metaphor in "Law as Interpretation," *Texas Law Review* 60 (1982): 527.

[237] Alasdair MacIntyre, *After Virtue: A Study in Moral Theory* (Notre Dame, Ind.: University of Notre Dame Press, 1985), 201.

[238] David Luban, "Difference Made Legal: The Court and Dr. King," *Michigan Law Review* 87 (1989): 2152, 2221–22.

[239] Steven Knapp, "Collective Memory and the Actual Past," *in Literary Interest: The Limits of Anti-Formalism* (Cambridge: Harvard Univ. Press, 1993), 116.

[240] Ibid., 107.

"canonical texts" like the Bible and the Constitution were authored?[241] If past deeds seem noble and inspiring, Knapp argues, that is because of values we hold independent of those past deeds: "But in that case our sense of what is symbolically useful in the past will depend on our present sense of what matters, and the values represented by what we borrow from our past will only be the ones we already have."[242] We might just as well turn to fiction or to the history of some other society or social group for inspiration.

What difference should it make that a particular history is in some sense "ours"? In other words, why should the fact that a practice preceded and caused our current circumstances recommend it? Knapp offers as an example Edmund Morgan's revisionist history of colonial Virginia, *American Slavery, American Freedom*:

> [Morgan] argues convincingly that . . . American ideals of freedom and equality can be traced in part to an ideology that arose in colonial Virginia, where the possession of even a few slaves gave a modicum of independence and social prestige to small landholders; "equality" thus meant solidarity among slaveholders. . . . It is hard to see how such causal "roots and beginnings" of egalitarian values collectively affirmed in the present can function usefully as a means of symbolically promoting or reinforcing those values. Certainly the explanatory significance of the social reality Morgan reconstructs does not confer any present authority on that past reality; it's not as if one feels inclined, after reading Morgan's account, to advocate slaveholding as a way of living up to one's egalitarian commitments.[243]

Knapp implies that the opposition between slavery and our egalitarianism should discredit the ideology of the American revolution wholesale, so that it has nothing further to teach us.

But surely that does not follow. A hermeneutic encounter with the Virginia yeomen would identify common ground between our world and theirs and would require us to sympathetically understand as much of their value framework as we could, condemning only those elements, like slavery, that appall us. Having composed a tolerable Virginia yeoman, we might critically assess our society from his "horizon," identifying weaknesses previously invisible to us. From his perspective we might see our own society as largely composed of economically dependent wage-servants without productive property and dominated by plutocrats and demagogues. Morgan teaches us that the Virginia yeomen saw the broad dispersal of slaves as contributing to freedom and equality, for two reasons. First, they saw freedom in material terms, as economic independence guaranteed by ownership of productive property. Second, they saw freedom in political terms, such that the freedom of all would be threatened by the dominion of rich men or demagogues over large concentrations of the unfree.

---

[241] Ibid. 109.
[242] Ibid, 116.
[243] Ibid., 116–17.

Today we can appreciate this "civic republican" vision of freedom as material independence and political equality, even as we abhor the price at which it was realized. Morgan provokes us to wonder whether the abolition of slavery really required giving up on this substantive vision of freedom and equality. Indeed, we might wonder whether White Americans abandoned their substantive conception of freedom in order to avoid sharing material wealth and political power with the African-Americans they nevertheless claimed to free. Neither colonial nor contemporary America is faultless, and each moment has moral standing to criticize the other.

Knapp acknowledges that the past is at least ethically relevant: we hold people "accountable for their pasts" and expect them to "experience guilt, pride, regret, or a sense of obligation" as a result of them.[244] But why, he wonders? Why blame and punish people for committing bad acts in the past rather than for approving those acts now (whether committed by themselves or someone else)?

Knapp offers a two-part answer. First, he concedes as a matter of psychological fact that "no one could have what we mean by a self unless she were disposed to identify . . . with at least some features of her own actual past."[245] As the psychoanalysts say, the self is a telling, a narrative. Second, punishment is an effort to police the narratives that constitute the self, to determine which features of the past will be foregrounded and which suppressed. Punishment compels people to treat their transgressions as a permanent part of their identity, a painful prospect likely to deter crime. Because enforcing obedience to law assumes that we contemplate what our individual or collective lives would be like if we did not obey, law induces us to conceive the future—that is, to create imaginary narratives. Thus, Knapp concludes,

> the ethical relevance of the actual past . . . derives, paradoxically, from an agent's imaginative relation to the future consequences of some contemplated action. It is what we want her to imagine about the future, and not a debt owed to the past as such, that justifies, if anything does, our sense that an agent's present ethical status may properly be affected by discoveries about the actual content of her . . . past.[246]

Knapp next asks whether this same rationale applies to groups. Should current group members feel guilt and suffer punishment for the transgressions of past generations? Does it make sense to encourage citizens to think of their policy choices as a permanent part of a national identity they bequeath to future generations? Certainly orators routinely call upon their compatriots to keep faith with their ancestors by handing down traditions to posterity. Prophetic discourse berates a decadent society for failing to keep its covenant;[247] every Sunday sermon

---

[244] Ibid., 120.

[245] Ibid., 124.

[246] Ibid., 128.

[247] Michael Walzer, *Interpretation and Social Criticism* (Cambridge: Harvard Univ. Press, 1987), 67.

exhorts Christians to redeem the sacrifice of their savior; and funeral orators from Pericles to Lincoln have called on the mourners to rededicate themselves to the principles served by their fallen comrades.[248]

No rhetorician has been more influential in articulating an American national identity than Lincoln, whose characteristic trope was an intergenerational teleology. Thus, he called on his compatriots to keep faith with the founding fathers by fulfilling the promise of the Declaration of Independence and the Northwest Ordinance. By resisting slavery's spread, Americans could at once complete the framers' supposed intention to set it "upon the path of ultimate extinction," and redeem the framers' sin of personally holding slaves. Lincoln also invoked future generations in warning that the extension of slavery would choke off free labor, and that compromise on the question could corrupt the public mind. He seemed to accept punishment for the sins of the past when he speculated that God might justly allow the Civil War to continue "until all the wealth piled by the bondman's two hundred and fifty years of unrequited toil shall be sunk, and until every drop of blood drawn with the lash shall be paid by another drawn with the sword."[249] If the prosperity and social peace sought by the Virginia yeomen were purchased at such a terrible moral price, Lincoln implied, they were undeserved. Slavery clouded America's title to both the republic of free labor and the union for which the Civil War had been fought.

But Lincoln was speaking to a generation of Americans of whom many could be said to have both benefited from and acquiesced in slavery. What about generations more remote from the actual practice of slavery, like our own? Obviously some modern Americans benefit directly from slavery by inheriting wealth it produced. Yet Alasdair MacIntyre has argued forcefully that all Americans bear continuing responsibility for slavery, regardless of whether they have personally benefited from it: "I inherit from the past of my family, my city, my tribe, my nation, a variety of debts, inheritances, rightful expectations and obligations."[250] In the recent debate over a national apology for slavery, some Whites argued that slavery was the responsibility of the "Confederacy" or "the South," while the "United States" had spent its blood and money in the fight against slavery. Others argued that the South's debt was paid in the last century when it was laid waste, conquered, and driven into economic decline. For MacIntyre, all such "nice calculations" are evasions. Responsibility for slavery is entailed in the identity of "being an American," an identity that cannot be shed when it becomes burdensome.[251]

Knapp responds that this kind of collective responsibility makes no sense unless individuals identify not only with their own past acts, but the past acts of collectivities.[252] And Knapp is skeptical that people identify with traditions in

---

[248] See generally Garry Wills, *Lincoln at Gettysburg: The Words That Remade America* (New York: Simon and Schuster, 1992).

[249] Abraham Lincoln, "Second Inaugural Address, March 4, 1865," in *Speeches and Writings, 1859–1865* (New York: Literary Classics of the United States, 1989), 686–87.

[250] MacIntyre, *After Virtue*, 220–21.

[251] Ibid., 205.

[252] Ibid., 138–41.

modern liberal societies.[253] But this sort of skepticism seems to misapprehend what an identity is. Identities are tales told to others to win *social recognition*. They are constrained by the narrative conventions prevailing in the teller's social milieus and restricted to the stock of socially recognized roles. MacIntyre may exaggerate when he insists we cannot act without knowing what stories we find ourselves to be already implicated in.[254] But without this knowledge we cannot act in a way that is *meaningful to others*. Even the rationally self-interested egoist will develop the human capital needed to fulfill socially valued and recognized roles. This in turn will give her a stake in the continuity of cultural values and social roles which she will work to conserve and reproduce.

Even were one to conclude that the modern self is wholly unencumbered by tradition, it would be a mistake to assume that the past can matter ethically only as part of the narrative of individual identity. Institutions like the modern state have narrative identities as well. Perhaps citizens of a liberal state identify less intimately with their governing institutions than do members of a traditional society—although we do not see why this should be so. But whether we identify personally with the liberal state is immaterial if we identify the liberal state with its own past. A liberal state's past may influence our evaluation of it, even if it does not influence our self-evaluation.

In arguing that collective identities retain little hold in modern society, Knapp offers an arresting, but in the end self-defeating, example. He argues that MacIntyre's notion that collective responsibility for slavery inheres in American identity has the untenable implication that contemporary Black Americans are responsible for slavery, and its continuing effects: "If present benefits and ongoing injuries are beside the point; if collective guilt for the past is taken seriously in its own right and is not just a figurative way of referring to present inequities; then it is hard to see why current black Americans are any less responsible for the effects of slavery than Americans generally."[255] Knapp implies that if an African-American can opt out of American responsibility for slavery, so can a recent European immigrant or the White descendant of a Civil War veteran.

Knapp's example raises questions about the coherence and universal appeal of a generic American identity but does not thereby diminish the ethical significance of the past. Quite the contrary. African-Americans are unlikely to identify enthusiastically with America's slave-holding past, because of the depth of their identification with a different past—that of the slaves. Contrary to Knapp's implication, many Black Americans probably *do* feel morally implicated in slavery. Though himself a victim of slavery, Frederick Douglass felt a continuing obligation to struggle for the freedom of others after his own escape. Though formally free he felt "bound in chains" with those still enslaved.[256] Indeed, he broke with the

---

[253] Knapp, "Collective Memory," 143.
[254] MacIntyre, *After Virtue*, 201.
[255] Knapp, "Collective Memory," 143.
[256] Frederick Douglass, *My Bondage and My Freedom* (New York: Dover Publications, 1969), 441–45 (appendix).

Garrisonian abolitionists over their impulse to evade responsibility for slavery by seceding from the South.[257] Contemporary African-Americans may not feel responsible *for* slavery, but many Black Americans feel responsible *to* their enslaved ancestors, to struggle to eradicate slavery's effects not only for themselves, but for others. Slavery is the common heritage of African-Americans that makes the oppression of any one an affront to all. Only the responsibility of Black Americans to the past can fully account for the depth of their current solidarity, their sense that to deny or de-emphasize Black identity is not only a surrender to prejudice but a betrayal.

Second, while MacIntyre insists that identifying as an American obliges one to accept responsibility for slavery, is it not clear that this legacy makes it more difficult for Blacks to identify as Americans? If African-Americans are alienated from America, that is because they are not indifferent to its sinful past. And if other Americans are tempted to opt out of American identity to avoid the moral burden of its past sins, then an atrocious past makes a difference. It imposes a cost in terms of the legitimacy and effectiveness of government. We can explain the disadvantage of an atrocious past to a liberal state like the United States by reference to two familiar problems of liberal political theory, the problem of collective action and the problem of political obligation.

The problem of collective action is said to arise among individuals who are rationally self-interested, uncoerced, and well informed. Such people have no incentive to cooperate in producing or conserving public goods like air, water, renewable resources, and common defense, or in enforcing private entitlements. By defecting, they can receive the benefits of the public good without bearing the costs of its provision. Hence, all will defect, and none will enjoy the public good, and so, the argument concludes, government is needed to coerce free riders into cooperating to produce public goods. Convinced by the security of government enforcement that one's fellow citizens will cooperate in the provision of public goods, each citizen will ungrudgingly cooperate in turn.

But this compliant attitude depends upon each citizen's faith in the stability, effectiveness, and civic responsibility of the institutions charged with enforcing cooperation. If government has already demonstrated these qualities over a period of time—if it has a creditable past—such faith may be warranted. But rational self-interest maximizers will be very skeptical of any government that lacks such a pedigree. For government is itself a public good requiring cooperation to establish. Such cooperation includes (1) the effort of politics to plan and establish, (2) restraint on the part of these political participants from designing in advantages to themselves that will impede the provision of public goods, (3) the effort of widespread obedience before it is clear that enforcement will be effective, (4) the effort of enforcement before it is clear that it will be supported by others, (5) the effort of supporting the enforcement apparatus if it is resisted, and (6) nondefection by those with the most access to enforcement power, who may be tempted

---

[257] Frederick Douglass, *The Life and Writings of Frederick Douglass*, ed. Philip Foner (New York: International Publishers, 1950), 467–80.

to use it to enrich themselves rather than to enforce cooperation in the provision of public goods.

So government arguably cannot come into existence among people who are uncoerced, rationally self-interested, and well informed, even if they desire it. Launching a government requires either prior coercion, altruism (which here means simply a disposition to forego defection and so suffer the risk of being exploited), or myth. By myth we mean faith that others will participate politically, enforce the law, obey the law, and defend the state when these have not been proven by experience. Typically, myth takes the form of an invented past characterized by heroic altruism or solidaristic cooperation. As Carol Rose points out,

> there is a gap between the kind of self-interested individual who needs exclusive property to induce him to labor, and the kind of individual who has to be there to create, maintain, and protect a property regime. The existence of a property regime is not predictable from a starting point of rational self-interest; and consequently, from that perspective, property needs a tale, a story, a post-hoc explanation.[258]

Liberal states do not arise as a result of uncoerced contracting among rationally self-interested individuals. Instead, they emerge out of traditional societies ordered by myth, tribal loyalty, and authoritarian governance. Rationally self-interested individuals devoid of solidaristic commitments and authoritarian belief systems are only likely to arise in an up-and-running modern state that securely protects private property and permits its free alienation. Only in such a state can people identify themselves with their property holdings and their manifestations of consent rather than their social claims within a group.

Thus rationally self-interested individualists are unlikely to ever face the problem of establishing a political society. They can establish a new state only by seizing or being given control of an existing state, or one of its administrative units. Rationally self-interested persons pose no threat to an up-and-running state as individual free riders. They only threaten the existing state if they organize to resist it—in other words, if they are already engaged in collective action and already mobilized by a mythology of solidarity or altruistic virtue.

The story of a social contract among freely consenting persons may provide part of the justificatory mythology for such a revolution, but it can never provide the whole. Some element of solidarity or heroic virtue is needed for two reasons: first, to explain why rational people would stake their lives and fortunes on an unproven state; second, to explain why they had a right to revolt, *but their successors do not*. Thus, the point of legal narrative, argued Robert Cover, is that every legal order must conceive of itself in one way or another as emerging out of that which is itself unlawful, and this sacred transgression always provides the typology for a dangerous return. Authoritative narrative is an effort to hold this risk at bay, even as it invites the symbolic insurgency of counternarrative.[259]

---

[258] Carol Rose, "Property as Storytelling: Perspectives from Game Theory, Narrative Theory, and Feminist Theory," *Yale Journal of Law and the Humanities* 2 (1989): 37, 53.

[259] Cover, "*Nomos* and Narrative," 23.

The liberal state cannot induce cooperation and provide public goods unless it is stable. But it cannot promise stability if it holds that citizens are only bound to obey law as long as they consent to do so. Thus, the authority of the liberal state can never be explained by reference to consent alone. The narrative mythology of the liberal state must offer a reason why the consent of the founders binds their successors. It must distinguish the virtuous will that justifies revolution from the licentious will that merits suppression. To distinguish the founding exercise of will from future defections, the liberal revolution must be remembered as virtuous, motivated by altruism rather than selfishness. Hence, the exposure of the founding as less than virtuous, or of subsequent governance as inconsistent with the virtues ascribed to the founding, is potentially destabilizing in a liberal state, like the United States.

It may well be that the liberal state can survive without the intense personal identification of most of its citizens. But its functioning depends upon the widespread expectation that its authority and coercive power will be effective. In a liberal society this effectiveness requires a broad, if thin, acceptance of the state's normative legitimacy, a manageable level of passive disaffection, and very little intense opposition mobilized by a competing political identity. And even in a liberal society, the credibility of the state's coercive power may be enhanced if the state has a hard core of intensely motivated supporters. In short, a liberal state does not require an equal level of commitment from all its citizens, but its credibility depends upon an aggregate amount and intensity of commitment. The moral worth of the state's past may not make a decisive difference to all of its citizens, but an atrocious past may marginally reduce the intensity of commitment at every level. As the aggregate level of civic commitment falls, the credibility of the state's enforcement power erodes and its ability to coordinate collective action is reduced, provoking disaffection even from those who do not care about the state's history or moral legitimacy.

In posing the question why the past matters in politics, Knapp has implicitly proposed a model of modern society as a natural or spontaneous market composed of calculating consequentialists, unencumbered by culture or tradition, free to choose and pursue any ends they fancy. But such a model misconceives both modernity and the liberal individual. Markets are not spontaneous or natural but depend upon demonstrably stable and effective institutions and the liberal individual depends for his freedom upon the stability provided by the authoritarian or solidaristic commitments of others.[260]

If the disenchanted liberal individual parasitically depends on the solidaristic commitment of others, then most citizens of the functioning liberal state will have a stake in a national identity legitimized by a virtuous past. They will also have a strong motive to fashion a national identity that can be accepted as legitimate

---

[260] Carol Rose borrows a page from Engels in suggesting that a market society of acquisitive males would have to be held together by the sacrifices of altruistic women. Rose, "Property as Storytelling," 46, 50; Friedrich Engels, *The Origin of the Family, Private Property and the State* (London: Lawrence and Wishart, 1943).

by any substantial group of disaffected citizens. This accounts for MacIntyre's idea that all Americans are responsible for the wrong of slavery and responsible for correcting it. This is true of everyone who benefits from the American national identity and the state it sustains, whether or not they benefited from slavery.

Stephen Holmes offers a somewhat different account of the function of narratives of constitutional foundation within liberal political theory.[261] Holmes examines the paradox that democracy flourishes best when citizens supposedly exercising untrammeled majority rule in fact operate within the bounds of pre-set limits on the power of that majority. For Holmes, this is the essence of liberalism, not a contradiction of it. Though there are many old explanations for the anti-majoritarian nature of constitutionalism—based on natural law, paternalism, intergenerational justice, contract theory—Holmes favors the notion that we choose constitutional restraints over ourselves for the purpose of collective self-realization, in order to become what we want to be.

Early versions or liberal political theory would hold that ancestors cannot rightfully bind their descendants—that the people can always alter or abolish their form of government. Paine was most extreme on this point, arguing that it is immoral and also in a sense conceptually impossible for a generation to bind future generations. Jefferson passionately attacked rules of perpetuity and held that constitutions should not outlive the generation that ratified them, while Adam Smith attacked the notion of testators binding heirs to the testators' debts. Locke tried to solve the problem by saying that the property one inherits necessarily includes the debts entailed by that property and by implicitly extending that principle to the inheritance of political regimes. Madison deployed this Lockean argument against Jefferson's rigid opposition to precommitment. A frequent disestablishment of fundamental law was bad for the security of property and commerce, he asserted, while descending public obligations are simply a form of intertemporal division of labor often necessary to achieve important national goals like financing a war for independence, the benefits of which are presumably enduring.

Jon Elster has restated the problem as a paradox: each generation wants both to be unbound, but to have the power to bind. Holmes responds that one escape from this paradox lies in our ability to freely choose limits that will sustain our optimal freedom over time. Thus, one generation may bind another precisely by constraining it from overly constraining a third. Holmes argues that liberal constitutions consist largely of "metaconstraints: rules that *compel* each decision-making authority to expose its decisions to criticism and possible revision, rules that *limit* each generation's power to rob its own successors' power of significant choices."[262] Just as Ulysses, by binding himself to the mast, was able to safely enjoy the Sirens' song, our constitutional framers bound us in order that we might have a country in which to enjoy freedom. Past constitutional choices do not just

[261] Stephen Holmes, *Passions and Constraint: On the Theory of Liberal Democracy* (Chicago: Univ. of Chicago Press, 1995).

[262] Ibid., 162.

constrain: they also enable, like the rules of grammar or chess. They constitute the very power that they hedge.

Writing in the institutional positivist tradition of Lieber and Lincoln, Holmes reasons that far from displacing popular will, constitutional rules render it effective. Unless concretized in stable institutions, he implies, popular will is a pernicious fiction:

> The power of the street (in the capital city) is never the power of the numerical majority. So how can the majority make its voice heard? Through competitive elections and public discussions. Neither of these historically rare mechanisms are available in a state of nature or condition of sovereignless anarchy. . . . Both are highly artificial constructs, requiring patient acceptance of elaborate procedures, institutions, rules. Without regular elections and open debates in civic forums such as the press, and without the political culture that makes both seem legitimate in the eyes of the public, majoritarianism is purely fictitious. . . . For a society with millions of citizens . . . there is no such thing as a collective choice outside of all prechosen procedures and institutions.[263]

Holmes argues that both the desire to be unbound by the past and the desire to bind the future can never be more than partially achieved. No framer of law could conceivably be unbound at the moment of framing. To influence a situation, Holmes asserts, a wielder of power must adapt himself to preexisting patterns of force. On the other hand, the conventional image of constitutions as permanent radically overstates the power of founders over future generations. Basic changes in the American Constitution— the expansion of federal Executive powers during World War II for example—arose outside the formal amendment process. In this sense, constitutional politics is a perpetual task. All politics is constrained by the past; all politics is about the farther future as well as the near term. In a continuous polity, politics simply cannot have the kind of temporal discreteness that Paine's idea of the absolute sovereignty of the living implies.[264] To the extent that politics is institutionally situated it is also narratively embedded.

That ordinary politics is narratively embedded is the basis for a recent response to Social Choice theory's charge that democracy cannot meaningfully reflect individual preferences. Kenneth Arrow's impossibility theorem demonstrates that no social choice mechanism can assure a coherent social preference ordering of more than two alternatives that bears any fair relation to the preference ordering of individuals arrived at in advance of the social choice process.[265] Arrow's claim expresses the following intuitions: first, the number of alternative possible futures polities must choose among is infinitely large. Second, choosing among these alternatives by vote means one of two things: a sequence of pairwise comparisons of alternatives decided by majority rule, or a ranking of alternatives based on some system of weighting the preference rankings given by individual voters.

---

[263] Ibid., 9.

[264] Ibid., 161.

[265] Kenneth Arrow, *Social Choice and Justice* (Cambridge: Harvard Univ. Press, Belknap Press, 1983).

Third, as the number of alternatives and voters increases, it is increasingly likely that the winner of a pairwise comparison will depend on the order in which they are compared, and that different ways of weighting the preference rankings of individuals will yield different results. Social Choice theorists add that voters aware of the preferences of other voters, and the procedure for aggregating them, may strategically misreport their preferences. The upshot is that if we understand democratic politics to include agenda setting as well as voting, its results seem to depend on luck or strategic manipulation, not voter preferences.

In sum, Arrow's theorem suggests that even under the fairest of conditions, voting is a game of chance and skill. Yet Arrow's entire line of argument that social choice does not reflect individual preferences assumes the existence of individual preferences independent of processes of social choice.[266] Proponents of deliberative democracy argue that far from delegitimizing democracy, Arrow's theorem invalidated this assumption of individual autonomy and showed that individual preferences must be discovered or refined in the social choice process. For them social choice is neither a math problem nor a game, but a drama of collective self-discovery.

Richard Pildes and Elizabeth Anderson have recently argued that Social Choice theory's skepticism about democracy results from its assumption that

> individuals are . . . capable of rationally ordering their preferences on their own, apart from social practices or institutions in which they participate. Individualism is implicit in the assumption of social choice theory that citizens arrive at the process of democratic decision-making with their preferences already well-ordered. . . . The assumption of individualism . . . denies . . . that the rationality of . . . preference-rankings is dependent on participation in social practices.[267]

This individualist picture of rationality is wrong if people's preferences are themselves democratically determined. This might be the case if people base their preferences on the interests or moral commitments of the social groups with which they identify, or the social roles they have assumed. Political conflict is not always conflict between the coherent preferences of competing individuals or groups; sometimes political conflict occurs within individuals, and political debate helps resolve it through a process of "collective self-determination."[268]

Not all individual preferences are relevant to that process of collective self-determination, argue Pildes and Anderson: "norms of democratic political interaction constrain the expression of preferences in political processes to those that can be justified by publicly acceptable reasons."[269] Political debate appropriately filters individual preferences because "rational choice should not be understood

---

[266] Ibid., 10.

[267] Richard H. Pildes and Elizabeth S. Anderson, "Slinging Arrows at Democracy: Social Choice Theory, Value Pluralism, and Democratic Politics," *Columbia Law Review* 90 (1990): 2121, 2143–44.

[268] S. L. Hurley, *Natural Reasons: Personality and Polity* (New York: Oxford Univ. Press, 1989), 326.

[269] Pildes and Anderson, "Slinging Arrows at Democracy," 2201.

as a matter of satisfying undefended preferences, but of articulating good and convincing reasons for choices."[270] If individual preferences are tied to the preferences and norms of groups and institutions with which individuals identify, then individuals need information about the values and intentions of others to determine their own preferences. And when group or institutional values and interests change as a result of changing conditions, changing membership, new information, or collective deliberation, individual preferences will be affected.

Pildes and Anderson criticize Social Choice theory for its failure to appreciate the "path dependence" of social choice—the legitimate and inevitable dependence of certain social choices on earlier choices: "Past choices change our evaluations of future possibilities, not just instrumentally, but constitutively: past choices often alter a political community's self-understanding."[271] Pildes's and Anderson's embrace of path dependence rests ultimately on the institutional positivism defended by Stephen Holmes. In their view, politics is never about the private preferences of individuals. People can only act politically if they act through an institution with a temporally continuous and historically particular identity:

> Because different decision procedures lead to different outcomes . . . social choice theorists argue that political outcomes are meaningless or cannot reflect a coherent collective will. But this view imagines a collective will already in existence, lying in wait for democratic institutions to discover. Before institutions are formed, however, no such collective will exists. Political institutions and decision procedures must create the conditions out of which, for the first time, a political community can forge for itself a collective will. . . . No uniquely "rational" institutional architecture exists for constructing that will. *Each* bundle of institutions and practices represents a *distinct* social constitution of the collective will.[272]

The connection drawn here between institutional positivism and path dependency was the very essence of Lincoln's political philosophy, and his response to the problem discussed by Knapp, MacIntyre, and Morgan: the entrenchment of slavery in the American constitutional tradition. For Lincoln, the continued presence of slavery was at odds with the national aspiration and destiny ordained in the Declaration of Independence. In the long run, that national destiny had to be regarded as prior to or constitutive of the will of the American people on the slavery question.

Two paths beckoned opponents of slavery, argued Lincoln. The abolitionist path would involve the arrogation to the federal government of an unconstitutional power to abolish slavery, or the unconstitutional secession of the free states. This Lincoln condemned as the path of extremist intolerance, breaking faith not only with the Southern states but with the Founders. In threatening the Union and the Constitution, abolitionism threatened the institutional embodiment of the Declaration's principles. No national telos could be realized without the preservation of the nation. The other path was the anti-extensionist path upon which the

[270] Ibid., 2193.
[271] Ibid., 2195.
[272] Ibid., 2197–98.

Founders had placed the nation by cutting off the slave trade and banning slavery from the Northwest Territories. Along this path, free labor society would spread westward, surrounding and choking off slavery, which could not survive economically and culturally without spreading to new victims. The anti-extensionist strategy was the longer path to abolishing slavery in the South, but the surer one, and the only one faithful to the Founders' vision of a *nation* dedicated to freedom.

Two paths likewise beckoned to slavery's supporters. The faithful, constitutional path was to acquiesce in slavery's ultimate demise, while the extremist alternative was to oppose the Constitution. Should slavery's supporters choose this forbidden path, the Constitution, in providing for its own defense, would authorize the emancipation of the slaves by martial law.

To ask whether Lincoln's ultimate aim was to preserve the Union or to abolish slavery misunderstands his peculiarly narrative conception of American national identity. That identity connected a particular origin to a moral principle through the medium of a teleological history. For Lincoln, the convergence in history of the causes of Union and Abolition was the providential fulfillment of the founder's dedication of the nation to a proposition. Rather than seeing the revolutionary founding as a discrete event, Lincoln saw it as coterminous with the republic, which existed to complete its own founding in the fullness of time. Like a character in a Romantic novel, the American Constitution needed the medium of narrative to discover its true nature.[273]

Teleological narrative operates to give Lincoln's Constitution another dimension of meaning beyond its immediate applications and so to negotiate what Bickel called the Lincolnian tension between expedience and principle that lives to fight another day. This narrative dimension of legal meaning is reminiscent of the Iser's "virtual" dimension of narrative or Barthes's "hermeneutic" dimension. The relationship between the Constitution's present applications and its narrative meanings gives Lincoln's constitutional vision what Cover called "depth of field." It was this depth of field to which Cover referred when he said that narrative makes of law, as law makes of narrative, a *nomos*, a "world in which we live":

> A nomos is a present world constituted by a system of tension between reality and vision.
>
> Our visions hold up reality to us as unredeemed. By themselves the alternative worlds of our visions—the lion lying down with the lamb, the creditor forgiving debts each seventh year, the state all shriveled and withered away—dictate no particular set of transformations or effort at transformation. But law gives a vision depth of field, by placing one part of it in the highlight of insistent and immediate demand while casting another part in the shadow of the millennium. . . .
>
> The codes that relate our normative system to our social constructions of reality and to our visions of what the world might be are narrative.[274]

---

[273] Guyora Binder, "Revolution as a Constitutional Concept," in International Association for Legal Methodology, *Le Recours aux Objectifs de la Loi dans son Application* (Brussels: E. Story-Scientia, 1992); 341, 350–52.

[274] Cover, *"Nomos* and Narrative," 9–10.

The Constitution of Narrative

As Cover's last sentence suggests, he regarded law and narrative as "inseparably related." Not only is "every prescription insistent in its demand to be located in [narrative] discourse," but "every narrative is insistent in its demand for its prescriptive point, its moral. History and literature cannot escape their location in a normative universe."[275] To tell a story, Cover implied, is to evoke a normative order.

Certainly a normative order enables storytelling. Legal or moral prescriptions create a narrative context for action, infusing it with expressive meaning:

> There is a difference between sleeping late on Sunday and refusing the sacraments, between having a snack and desecrating Yom Kippur, between banking a check and refusing to pay your income tax. . . . Law is a resource in signification that enables us to submit, rejoice, struggle, pervert, mock, disgrace, humiliate, or dignify.[276]

Stories are about human and or anthropomorphized protagonists, confronting disorder or order as an obstacle to their goals. For the story to hold a reader's interest, these goals must engage sympathy or antipathy. Hence, the reader is called upon to normatively judge human purposes, and principles of order that are human, or if natural or divine, anthropomorphized.

In the Western narrative tradition modeled by Frye, legal and moral orders play a paradigmatic if not an indispensable role. Comedy typically narrates the subversion of an arbitrarily rigid legal regime, and the humbling and forgiveness of its proud administrators. Tragedy typically portrays a conflict of normative orders—its protagonists are often brought low by their own virtues. In romance, the stage is cleared for heroic adventure by the decline or departure of authority, which is restored or replaced only at the adventure's end. Finally, satire generally exposes the hypocrisy and contradiction of a normative order, without the "comic relief" of its replacement by a more lenient and humane order.

When we consider the modern narrative genres of the history and the novel, the centrality of law is even more apparent. Following Hegel, Hayden White directly links historical narrative with law. For Hegel, there is no possibility of history without law, since only in law-bound societies do definable and hence recordable social transactions take place. In that sense, the proper, if implicit, subject of all history is the legal state itself, and the endless conflict between law (or authority) and desire. Only where there is law can there be a legal subject to serve as the individual or collective agent of historical narrative. Only thus do we get the tensions and conflicts that make history. The legal system is the form in which the subject encounters most immediately the social system in which he must seek his humanity.

In embracing Hegel's position, White is not ignoring trendy historical genres like social, economic, and cultural history, which deflect attention from the martial

[275] Ibid., 5.
[276] Ibid., 8.

dramas of traditional political history. He is arguing that, fundamentally, these newer histories are still about the dialectic of state and subject, but with a sharper focus on the meaning of history in the everyday lives of its subjects. Braudel's classic social history of the sixteenth-century Mediterranean, with its quotidian focus on peasant diets, is still ultimately aimed at explaining the shift in political power from the Mediterranean to the Atlantic sea powers.[277] Economic history is increasingly the study of the economic role of *institutions*, that is, of law. And cultural history in the wake of Foucault is about the role of bureaucratic social control in shaping the inner sensibility of the cultural subject, or the role of nationalism and imperialism in shaping conceptions of culture.

The modern nation that enacts and enforces a modern legal system is a work of imagination. The building of a geographically dispersed system of distribution, administration, and defense requires replacing local dialects and attachments with a common language and a mobilizing ideology. According to Ernest Gellner, the modern state requires that all individuals be educated into a common high culture that combines literacy with civic mythology.[278] This effort to make culture coincident with political order requires a strategic form of amnesia, by which the diverse local folk cultures of the common people are replaced with an invented tradition that vulgarizes the culture of a clerical elite and produces the illusion of nationhood created upward from the folk. The mass production of high culture permits the mass production of the fungibly educated and "socialized" workers whose mobility is crucial to a capitalist economy.

In Benedict Anderson's much-admired study of nationalism *Imagined Communities*, we see the self-conscious creation of the regulatory state as a phenomenon parallel to the development of the self-regulating individual, and equally dependent on a narrative of development.[279] Unlike the traditional village community, the community of the nation cannot consist in the intimacy of face-to-face encounter—it must be an imaginative artifice, sustained by print media and other forms of publicly accessible culture. It is this imagined community in which the subject of the modern state must seek recognition and esteem. Hence, the modern state requires that the social order be internalized, that each individual develop within herself a disciplining cultural sensibility.

That historical consciousness attends to the dialectical encounter between social authority and the desiderative subject implies that it expresses itself not only in historical narrative but also in the novel. The modern nation under capitalism requires a type of individual citizen who can be a subject and object of regulation within liberal principles. The rise of the novel depicts the social development of that individual and coincides with the emergence of the modern self-regulating market actor. The novel depicts both the adjustment of the individual to social norms and the creation of the self according to self-regulating norms.

[277] Fernand Braudel, *The Mediterranean and the Mediterranean World in the Age of Philip II*, vols. 1 and 2, trans. Sian Reynolds (New York: Harper and Row, 1972).

[278] Ernest Gellner, *Nations and Nationalism* (Ithaca: Cornell Univ. Press, 1983).

[279] Benedict Anderson, *Imagined Communities: Reflections on the Origins and Spread of Nationalism* (London: Verso, 1983).

The link between the narrated nation and the narrated individual lies in the disciplinary society described by Foucault.[280] The modern prison is Foucault's metaphor for the modern social institution more generally—an ordered space where the subject is constantly on display, to be measured against norms of docility, productivity, and conformity. For Foucault, the new penitentiaries of the early nineteenth century were just the visible face of a larger system of social control that enabled modern industrialized society to function smoothly, despite the erosion of traditional sources of authority and networks of community. This new social order relied on organization, regimentation, surveillance, examination, record keeping, rational incentives, paradigms of normality, and diagnostic profiles of deviance. Its consequence was the inculcation of self-awareness. The soul, Foucault quips, became the prison of the body. And it was this self-regulating soul that the novel at once addressed and modeled.

Regenia Gagnier describes this modern "literary subject" as

> A mixture of introspective self-consciousness, middle-class familialism and genderization, and liberal autonomy. The modern literary subject assumed individual creativity, autonomy, and freedom to create value by satiating its subjective desires as a right; it considered self-reflection as problem-solving, and thus valued reading and writing; and it developed in a progressive narrative of self in gendered familial relations and increasing material well-being. This was the self of Victorian literature as it was studied in the academy. Subjects who did not assume creativity, autonomy, and freedom; who expressed no self-consciousness; who did not express themselves in individuated voices with subjective desires; who were regardless of family relations; and who narrated no development or progress or plot never appeared in literature courses. In short, what appeared was private individuals and families in pursuit of private gain for whom society was generally an obstacle to be surmounted.[281]

This is the novelistic protagonist as portrayed by Watt, Lukács, Jameson, Said, and Gallagher—the rational utility maximizer who disciplines desire to the reality of economic scarcity and social authority by becoming self-aware. The modern narrative subject may be a dispossessed woman or a slave. Nevertheless, she has the inner sensibility of the legal person. Her story narrates her profitable investment of self in a civil society constituted by law.

Narrative is hardly antithetical to law. Law must become narrative when we question its authority, when we ask the most fundamental questions about its legitimacy. It is tempting to try to close the question of legitimacy by invoking the consent of individuals. For this answer to work, however, the subjects of law must be autonomous sources of value, self-authored narratives. Thus, it is also tempting to see the stories that individuals tell about themselves as the expression of an authentic human voice independent of social authority. Yet this view of

---

[280] Michel Foucault, *Discipline and Punish: The Birth of the Prison*, trans. Alan Sheridan (New York: Vintage Press, 1977).

[281] Regenia Gagnier, "Social Atoms: Working Class Autobiography, Subjectivity and Gender," *Victorian Studies* 30 (1987): 335.

personal narrative does not subvert legal authority, it collaborates with it by senti-mentalizing the self. The narrative subject is a cultural artifact, and in modern society culture is inextricably bound up with the liberal state. For better or worse, law does not suppress subjectivity, it confers it. To question the legitimacy of law is therefore to question our own subjectivity, not to defend it against alienation.

Legal Scholarship as Narrative

If legal authority must be established by narrative, it follows that law's narrative nature is most apparent from the perspective of the legal theorist. Ronald Dworkin developed his account of legal judgment as the continuation of a chain novel in order to explain why legal theory had to be part of law. His argument was that applying the law to unforeseen situations requires a narrative linking judgment to the ultimate bases of legitimacy of the legal system. If narrative is inherent in legal theory there is something deeply confused both in the call to make legal scholarship more narrative and in fears that narrative is a perversion of legal scholarship. Certainly legal scholarship should identify and *criticize* the particular narratives implicit in or enabled by law. But it need not *become* narrative—it *is* narrative.

In *Narrative, Authority, and Law*, Robin West argues that narrative is inherent in all legal reasoning because almost any vision of society or justificatory ideology can find its place in Northrop Frye's typology of narrative myth. Legal theory tracks the recognizable plot forms of myth because law is not only an historical and political actuality, but "also an ever-present possibility, potentially bringing good or evil into our future. The nature of law is also revealed, then, by our aspirations for and our fear of law: fantasies and nightmares revolving around power, reason and authority."[282]

In "Jurisprudence as Narrative," West draws her correlation between jurispru-dential traditions and Frye's narrative genres. Recall that Frye's generic spectrum is organized by two polar oppositions. One opposition is that between the redemp-tive or "apocalyptic" imagery of comedy and the predestinarian, "demonic" imag-ery of tragedy. Comedy presumes a freedom on the part of characters to learn and improve, whereas tragedy presupposes that its characters are governed by necessity. A second dichotomy opposes the Romantic "method of innocence" to the ironic "method of experience." The method of innocence idealistically pre-sumes the unity of morality and desire, whereas the method of experience cyni-cally presumes their opposition. For West, the dichotomy between comedy and tragedy in literature corresponds to the dichotomy between liberalism and authori-tarianism in political theory, and the dichotomy between romance and irony cor-responds to the dichotomy between natural law and positivism in jurisprudence.

According to West, "Natural law scholarship, like romantic narrative, is domi-nated by moral quest. 'Law' is the natural lawyer's romantic hero: it is morally

[282] Robin West, "Jurisprudence as Narrative: An Aesthetic Analysis of Modern Legal Theory," *New York University Law Review* 60 (1985): 145–46.

virtuous and historically triumphant."[283] Like the romantic hero, natural law sometimes must travel incognito through a corrupted world governed by usurpative
authority, awaiting the moment when it can break the spell, reveal its true identity,
and assume its rightful place. West associates irony with a reductive empiricism
that insists that the world is nothing more than it appears to be. Similarly, "The
positivist's story of law is rigorously experiential: Law is the consequence of
legislation and adjudication. . . . Human beings, not 'neutral principles,' decide
cases and enact statutes. . . . Jail sentences and damage remedies, not 'general
rules of law' . . . are law's essence."[284] At the tragic end of irony, West locates
Hobbes, the legal economist Richard Posner, and Kafka as authors envisioning
individuals trapped in isolation and conflict. West notes that Frye associates comedy with the mockery and overthrow of arbitrary conventions and laws and argues
that "The political traditions loosely called 'liberalism' share comedy's optimistic
assessment that democratic societies progress through history from a stage of
'ritual bondage' to a state of 'pragmatic freedom.' "[285]

West's reinterpretation of the major schools of jurisprudence as literary genres
presents them as unified by aesthetic attitude rather than philosophical principle:
"There does not appear to be a single core of philosophical beliefs unifying liberalism. This does not mean that liberalism is incoherent. . . . It only suggests that
what ties the strands of liberalism together is not a shared philosophy [but a]
common *aesthetic* thread."[286] Similarly, it is not the philosophical differences between competing schools that account for their passionate debates. Natural lawyers and positivists appear to argue over the meaning of the word "law," but "the
natural law tradition in jurisprudence is not just a particular way of defining
words—it is a manifestation of a romantic literary impulse. Similarly, the legal
positivist tradition is a manifestation of the ironic impulse. . . . They are engaging
in contrasting aesthetic projects."[287]

If all legal reasoning is narratively emplotted, it would follow that calls to
introduce narrative into legal scholarship are pointless, except as performative
demonstrations of the speaker's commitment to humane values. On West's view,
legal scholarship is inherently narrative, but this in no way implies that legal
scholarship is inherently humane or uplifting. As Frye's typology suggests, literature has different narrative conventions, striking different attitudes toward human
nature, ranging from indulgent sentimentality to bitter irony. None of these is
uniquely literary and none is alien to law.

West's most wickedly dialectical reading of legal theory as narrative is her
extended comparison of Kafka and Posner.[288] For West, Kafka and Posner are both
tragic ironists in that they portray the subjects of modern society in a seemingly

[283] Ibid., 160.
[284] Ibid., 171.
[285] Ibid., 186.
[286] Ibid., 206–7.
[287] Ibid., 204–5.
[288] Robin West, "Authority, Autonomy, and Choice: The Role of Consent in the Moral and Political
Visions of Franz Kafka and Richard Posner," *Harvard Law Review* 99 (1985): 384.

inalterable state of social isolation. Kafka's protagonists tend to be fussy para-
noids, mystified and vaguely threatened by every social situation. Posner's "characters" are isolated by the assumptions of microeconomics, each rationally pursuing self-interests knowable only to themselves. Both character types are socially
alienated, but Kafka's characters are also alienated from themselves. That we
cannot trust one another, Kafka implies, does not entail that we can trust ourselves.

On West's reading, Kafka's characters typically consent to market transactions,
employers' imperatives, and legal and familial authority and thereby get exactly
what they think they want. Kafka thus poses ironically what legal economists
pose seriously—consent as a moral trump to claims of injustice. Where law-and-
economics presents a Panglossian world of characters satisfied by all they have
consented to, Kafka presents a world of hapless schlemiels anxious to salvage
their bourgeois dignity by consenting to their own discontents. Consumed with
self-doubt, they are eager to delegate choice to others as the only guarantee that
their choices will meet with approval, even as they know their deference will
inspire contempt and their yearning for approval will be requited with indifference. Joseph K., the Hunger Artist, the failed entrepreneur of "The Judgment,"
and all the others "consent" to humiliating sexual, commercial, and employment
situations and "voluntarily" assume the risk of loss. The Hunger Artist is obsessed
by—and then destroyed by—his need to be autonomous. West argues that Kafka's
characters always hypothesize a welfare-maximizing excuse for giving in.

As a critique of Posner's legal economics, West's essay operates at two levels.
First, it debunks economists's scientific pretensions by representing some of their
key assumptions as literary constructs. Economics may be able to predict and
model market behavior, but to evaluate it as welfare maximizing or explain it as
rationally motivated is to exercise the narrative imagination. Thus, West's essay
critiques law and economics for *being* literature. Yet it also critiques legal economics *as* literature. By contrast to Kafka's fully integrated realization of tragic
irony, Posner's narrative is presented an aesthetic pastiche, which first envisions
tragic alienation and conflict and then purports to resolve it all with glib happy-
talk about rational consent and allocative efficiency.

West's critique provoked a series of denials by Posner that literature had anything to do with law, politics, or economics, culminating in his well-known book
Law and Literature: A Misunderstood Relation.[289] Posner's book entertainingly
reviews a wide array of imaginative literature on legal themes, but its ultimate
point is to defend market-oriented legal thought against West's literary reading.
Posner's argument is that legal thought cannot be criticized as literature because
literature can never be about anything as specific as law. Posner argues that the
specific legal content of significant works of literature is adventitious.[290] Literature
is only about timeless, universal themes: maturation, desire and its frustration,

[289] Richard Posner. "The Ethical Significance of Free Choice: A Reply to Professor West," *Harvard
Law Review* 99 (1986): 1431; *Law and Literature: A Misunderstood Relation* (Cambridge: Harvard
Univ. Press, 1988).

[290] Posner, *Law and Literature,* 71–79.

loss, loneliness. In making this argument, he is compelled to deny any connection between the modern experience of individuality and the institutions of modern society. Whereas West presents "economic man" as a contingent social construct, Posner simply equates the experience of the liberal individual with the human condition.

Because great literature is timeless, its themes of freedom and necessity cannot be about social freedom and compulsion, its themes of alienation cannot be about markets or urbanization, its themes of subjectivity cannot be about responsibility. Law is just a metaphor:

> Law's apparently arbitrary and undeniably coercive character, combined with the inevitable . . . miscarriages of justice and with law's "otherness"(law, like . . . the state, and the market economy, is a human institution frequently . . . perceived as external to man . . .) makes law a superb metaphor for the random, coercive and "unfair" light in which the human condition—"life" appears to us in some moods.[291]

But if law has this figurative significance for us in literature, why not in life? Indeed, the life that sometimes "appears" random, coercive, and " 'unfair' " is always lived in a particular society composed of particular institutions constituted by law.

Predictably, Posner tames the bleakness of Kafka's world by denying that it has anything to do with the intermediating force of society. Here are some of the themes of Kafka's fiction that Posner considers to have nothing to do with law, politics, economics,[292] or the organization of society:[293] "people's indifference to the interior lives of strangers,"[294] "the disquieting acceptance of suffering, cruelty, and death,"[295] the futility of trying "to find a meaning in a universe that . . . is arbitrary, impersonal, cruel, deceiving, and elusive,"[296] "the sense of guilt, . . . life's unfairness," people's tendency "to accept the valuation placed on them by other people, . . . the dislocated 'feel' of modern life to highly sensitive souls, . . . the indifference of others to our personal turmoil,"[297] and that "we can never make our aspirations fully understood" and "we can never really . . . enter the interior life of another person."[298] So convinced is Posner of the interpersonal incomparability of utilities that he simply sees it as a feature of human nature rather than a political claim. It may be the subject of tragic literature, but it cannot be a subject of legal or political debate.

Maturity is Posner's recurrent example of a literary theme of sufficient generality and universality to transcend the merely topical. In work after work he finds the story of a romantic or violent personality purged of illusion, excess, and pas-

[291] Ibid., 77.
[292] Posner, "Free Choice," 1433.
[293] Ibid., 1435.
[294] Ibid., 1434.
[295] Ibid., 1433.
[296] Posner, *Law and Literature*, 125.
[297] Posner, "Free Choice," 1436.
[298] Ibid., 1438.

sion, so as to achieve pragmatic maturity.[299] What he fails to see is how political, how historically particular this maturity theme is. Recall that for Fredric Jameson, maturity in Posner's sense—accommodating one's self to reality—is specifically the theme of the nineteenth-century novel, particularly of post-Romantic realism. It reflects the market-oriented ethic of accommodation to the reality of scarcity and rejects as illusory the Romantic interpretation of the newly dynamic social world of the nineteenth century as a horizon of unlimited possibility. For Edward Said, the nineteenth-century novel and its overt theme of maturity are just as much about the governance of "primitive" by "developed" societies as about the governance of savage impulses in the parlors of the European bourgeoisie.

Posner's effort to drain literature of all legal and political meaning deprives it of aesthetic interest as well. Thus, Kafka's fiction is not only about interior despair but also about the social world that helps create it. While Kafka's work is spare and given to parable, it is full of the realistic detail necessary to one of his characteristic aesthetic effects: the seating of the absurd in the compulsive routines of a social world ordered by the pursuit of an inconspicuous normality. Posner must strain to deny that this ironic effect has anything to do with the mechanization of production, the commodification of labor, and the bureacratization of social choice, or with careerism and role morality and bourgeois respectability, just as he must strain to miss the manifest link between inurement to absurdity and inurement to atrocity. Kafka's work is, like all art, a unity of form and concrete medium, and the concrete medium of literature is meaning, including political meaning. An interpretive strategy that renders the social world evoked by narrative literature "adventitious" effaces much of the aesthetic experience of the work. But this anti-aestheticism is intended: Posner urges us to resist experiencing even the imaginary social and legal worlds of literature aesthetically. This insulates us against what he regards as the immature, Romantic impulse to assess our actual institutions aesthetically rather than economically.

By contrast to Posner's opposition between the legal and the literary, West, Cover, and Dworkin make a persuasive case that legal authority depends upon the narrative imagination, so that legal theory is a kind of narrative literature, while modern narrative literature is centrally conditioned by and concerned with the dialectic of state and subject, or, in short, law. We will conclude with a vignette that shows this dialectic at work in an extraordinary act of myth making that was at once legal practice and bombastic autobiographical invention.

CONCLUSION: PERFORMING THE LAW AND NARRATING THE NATION

According to Louis Mink, our intellectual heritage assumes a commonsense distinction between fiction and history, and the premise of that distinction is the assumption that history is a unity while an infinity of fictions can coexist in imagination.[300] With White and Lyotard, Mink concludes that the idea of universal

---

[299] Posner, *Law and Literature*, 81.
[300] Mink, "Narrative Form as Cognitive Instrument," 129.

history has given way before the experience of relativity and particularity. Mass culture displays decreasing faith in the idea of progress, but it seems to have absorbed the Hegelian notion that no person can fully understand the history he goes through, that all of us are stuck in the haplessly peripheral roles of Rosencrantz and Guildenstern. The problem, Mink argues, is that any effort to perceive history requires the subject to partake of the aesthetics of narrative form, and that this obligation blurs our commonsense distinction between fiction and history. We have no way of perceiving history without making artistic decisions.

As Homi Bhabha puts it, political narrative is torn between the role of the *pedagogic* and the *performative*.[301] "The nation" is at once the popular sovereign that creates the law and legitimates the state and the creature of state policies of national integration and mobilization. It both invents and learns its own culture. The state has this same dual aspect: it instructs the populace in an invented cultural tradition, yet it purports to derive its political and cultural authority from that populace. Nationality, on Bhabha's view, is a continuous process of narration, linking a constantly shifting cast of persons, places, events, artifacts, and practices. In any act of lawmaking, we are both reading and writing a national narrative. The "people" are not simply historical events or parts of a patriotic body politic. They are imaginative conceptions and self-conceptions. They follow the lesson of their received historical narrative, yet they also continually perform new narrative acts of self-definition.

This double process is aptly illustrated by Robert Feguson's remarkable essay "Story and Transcription in the Trial of John Brown." Here Ferguson demonstrates how a bungling bankrupt managed to exploit the narrative and dramatic materials of the American criminal trial and draw on the conventions of the literary romance, to embed himself forever in historical memory as a sacrificial hero, turning dross into gold.[302] Brown enacted a myth of sacred inevitability, making it up as he went along. As Ferguson says, the

> underlying homologies between courtroom performance and the genre of the American Romance helped to turn Brown into Emerson's "hero of romance." The result was a story of mythopoeic proportions. . . . On trial for his life, John Brown achieved a special imaginative power by mixing legal artifice with religious understanding.[303]

Ferguson shows that Brown was perhaps the first "celebrity" in American history in that he was the first to control the public perception of a major event through self-dramatizing manipulation of the press. He transformed himself from a man of questionable character, a feckless loser in both business and the military, into a mythic hero by artfully blending legal rhetoric, courtroom dramaturgics, and shards of junk culture from popular American romance.

---

[301] Homi K. Bhabha, "Introduction: Narrating the Nation," and "DissemiNation: Time, Narrative, and the Margins of the Modern Nation," in *Nation and Narration*, ed. Homi K. Bhabha (London: Routledge, 1990), 1–8, 291–321.

[302] Robert A. Ferguson, "Story and Transcription in the Trial of John Brown," *Yale Journal of Law and the Humanities* 6 (1994): 37.

[303] Ibid.

What deeper nation-story was Brown reenacting? In *The Slave Power Conspiracy and the Paranoid Style*, David Brion Davis examines the deep structure of the paranoid style in our politics, a peculiarly American discourse of conspiracy, corruption, and recrimination,[304] reflecting the deep cultural demand that America be morally pure. The fundamental source of the American Revolution, by this measure, was not so much concrete concerns about central control and taxes, but an almost primal sense that the British represented a corruptly European defilement of Edenic virtue. Our true origin is not the Revolution, but the Reformation, a ritual to be reenacted throughout American history. This ritual had to involve a ripping off of veils and cloaks, an abolition of secrecy and monopoly. The slavery crisis occasioned two opposed and closely related manifestations of this paranoid style. To the abolitionists, the Slave Power was a dangerous atavism of European corruption. To the South, abolitionism threatened the defilement of civilized American society by slave rebellion.

Each side accused the other not just of malevolent intentions but, as in most conspiracy theories, of subtle deceptions that made their malevolence even more insidious. To the abolitionists, the evil of the Slave Power was obscured by a thin veneer of Southern etiquette and civility. To the Southerners, the evil subversive force of the abolitionists was obscured by their pretense to zealous humanitarianism. Only in the 1850s, in response to the 1850 Missouri Compromise and the Kansas-Nebraska bill, did the defensive rhetoric get transmuted into hardened conviction, which required a reassessment of American history and a mobilization of sectional power. The Fugitive Slave Law, the repeal of the Missouri Compromise, and the *Dred Scott* decision suggested a degree of Southern unity, premeditation, and control that would have been incredible years earlier. At the same time, the emergence of Black Republicans and the appearance in Kansas of immigrant aid societies confirmed Southern fears that abolitionist conspirators had nearly gained control of the North. These two opposed menacing forces mirrored each other in their lurid imagery.

A sociologist might say this paranoid style had a stabilizing function in a period of unprecedented fluidity and growth. This was a mobile society of rootless strangers where success depended on the effective presentation of self, a society of hucksters lampooned in Twain's novels and Melville's *Confidence Man*.[305] Goffman would probably say that to depict oneself as open and sincere and one's enemy as deceptive was a strategy, but also a way of affirming democratic values. Garrisonian crusades struck at the heart of the national morally expedient accommodations that had long defined slavery as a necessary evil. So pro-slavery forces found a receptive audience for their portrayal of abolitionists as fanatics, not humanitarians. The notion of a Slave Power conspiracy had a similarly conserva-

---

[304] David Brion Davis, *The Slave Power Conspiracy and the Paranoid Style* (Baton Rouge: Louisiana State Univ. Press, 1970); see Richard Hofstadter, *The Paranoid Style in American Politics* (New York: Knopf, 1965).

[305] Herman Melville, *The Confidence Man, His Masquerade* (London: Longman, Brown, Green, Longmans, and Roberts, 1857).

tive function, distracting the guilty consciences of Northerners from the manifest atrocity of slavery to the hidden evil of devious purposes. Thus, the national paranoid style helped both factions endure the growing dissonance between slavery and liberal ideology. Both conspiracy theories worked to relabel the slavery conflict as the vice of incivility, and so to confine its divisiveness to the margins of the political spectrum.

Brown's performance disrupted this delicate ballet of denial by embodying and confirming the Southerners' only half-believed fantasies of a demonic abolitionist plot. At the same time it broadened abolitionism's appeal in the North, drawing on the powerful currency of evangelical Christianity, to evoke millenarian yearnings for purgation and redemption.

The great event was not the raid itself. Not only was that a failure, but it was a lucky failure. Had Brown died in the raid, he would have missed the chance for iconography; had it succeeded at all, Brown would have aroused too much wrath and fear, even in the North. He lived long enough to make his death the most ritually important nonpresidential death of the century, and to cause a sea change in the national debate over slavery. The anomaly of slavery in a republic ceased after Brown's death to be a matter of negotiation. Once he raised the issue in the fiercely adversarial context of a criminal trial, slavery debates became, in Ferguson's view, truly adversarial.

Brown exploited all the narrative resources (and apparent constraints) of the trial process. The rules of evidentiary relevancy enabled him to erase his unsavory past, and a series of procedural concessions from the judge and prosecutor—designed to calm him down and lend an image of generous legitimacy to the trial—enabled him to embellish his life with heroic speeches and fabrications. His insensitivity became a quality of fierce principle, while his financial failure became a matter of transcendence over the material life. (Oddly, his sordid experience with the bankruptcy courts is what gave him experience in the courtroom.) A past full of grimy compromising was transformed into a life of unyielding principle.

Ferguson compares Brown's trial performance back to his brief epistolary autobiography, which was itself a shameless act of romance fabrication where, Gatsby-like, Brown made himself into a rising young businessman, a swashbuckling western adventurer, a descendant of revolutionary warriors, a Quaker pacifist, a humble shepherd, a great leader, and a martyr. The remarkable thing is not any originality or sophistication, but the shameless conventionality of his writing—and later of his trial performance. All his passionate expressions of idealism and belief were tropes out of popular romance literature, full of melodrama and sanctimony.

As Ferguson shows, a trial by or in a community is also a trial *of* that community. Virginia authorities felt that an image of rigorous legal decorum would quell any fear of abolitionist violence. Thus, in a ritual battle over forms and tropes, Brown would decry the denial of his various trial rights, and the court would in turn make remarkable legal concessions to him, which he would then use as further opportunities to denounce the trial as a mockery. In this regard, the state appears partly as the magnanimous, self-legitimating hander-down of favors, and partly as a narrator itself, telling a story about the proper constraints on emotion in the courtroom. ("One more outburst, and I'll . . .") Decorum was not really the absence of emotion so much as a particular structure of boundaries of emotion designed to vindicate the communal majesty of the law. When Brown threatened disruption, he won more concessions, and soon he became an independent agent, free to engage in colloquies with witnesses and prosecutors.

Brown crossed all the boundaries of legal formality and thus became the legal version of the frontier romance hero. The trial was his medium for assembling multiple frames of reference. He rhetorically declaimed the unfairness of the trial, even as he was granted every concession. He challenged the trial as mere form, and yet it was the form of the trial that he so brilliantly exploited. Exhausted and exasperated, a prosecutor permitted him irrelevant speeches, and Brown then fended off later attacks on relevancy grounds by resort to a sort of estoppel or waiver. His own lawyers Brown constantly dismissed and rehired and dismissed on various grounds of conflict. He lamented that he was denied counsel, all the while preferring no counsel because he wanted to be able to speak his "own" voice. He exploited his wounded condition so that though he was able to stand, he managed to appear lying on a hospital cot. Emerson recognized that Brown's ideal character, formed in the trial, would remain forever in the American imagination. Brown had used the tools of the confidence man to instill the courage of conviction.

Ferguson's reading serves as a corrective to the familiar constructions of narrative as the authentic story suppressed by law or as the scandalous subjectivity of the law exposed. Narrative is here the performance enabled by law and cultural convention. Narrative is also the authority we give the law by telling our stories. Narrative is the self we would become and the allegiance that invented self demands. Narrative is likewise the nation we would dwell among and the obedience that imagined community commands. Narrative is the promises we make and the excuses and amends we make when we break those promises. Narrative is the aspiration that guides us, the tradition that commits us, the hollow-seeming hope that accommodates us to the limits we live within. It is the order we submit to, the law by which we govern ourselves.

Rhetorical Criticism of Law

INTRODUCTION: LAW, RHETORIC, AND THE PROBLEM OF AUTHORITARIANISM

One important strand of the Law and Literature movement urges that law re-connect to its roots in rhetoric.[1] While the claim that law is really a kind of litera-ture has an air of paradox, identifying law with rhetoric—the art of persuasion—seems almost obvious. Yet the venerable history of "rhetoric" gives the Law as Rhetoric trope connotations that are more esoteric than self-evident.

Rhetoric's origins associate it with classical literature and philosophy. For con-temporary legal scholars, it is often linked to the ideal of a civic republic in which politics engages all citizens, but in a disinterested way. According to this ideal, the virtuous citizen experiences politics as an intellectual debate or dialogue rather than a contest of opposing interest groups. To refer to legal argument by this classical term is therefore to locate the lawyer in the ancient forum, within a society that valued oratory as a civic responsibility. In Classical Greece or Rome, rhetoric was the art of persuasion by which public actors sought to channel the natural sentiments of an audience towards proper social behavior and political practice. The *rhetor* persuaded an audience towards a political goal, often "model-ing" the desired public behavior by proffering the figure of the speaker as an heuristic example of ethical character. Rhetoric in this sense was not merely a tool of law but was itself a kind of legal order, a personal and public discipline, fusing social authority with personal virtue.[2] The Law as Rhetoric trope therefore suggests that the contemporary lawyer is both a noble statesman and a quaint anachronism, the vestige of a more virtuous age.

Yet the connotations of "rhetoric" are not uniformly positive. Plato initiated a tradition of portraying rhetoric as a superficial technique of verbal and emotional manipulation, at odds with the sincere pursuit of wisdom. Thus, to call law rheto-ric is at once to acknowledge the popular stereotype of lawyers as sly dissemblers and to parry it with a learned euphemism suggesting that lawyers are practitioners of an esoteric virtue intelligible only to the classically educated. It is to suggest that the gulf of suspicion separating lawyers from the lay public is to the discredit

---

[1] E.g., James B. White, "Law as Rhetoric, Rhetoric as Law: The Arts of Cultural and Communal Life," *University of Chicago Law Review* 52 (1985): 984; Gerald Wetlaufer, "Rhetoric and Its Denial in Discourse," *Virginia Law Review* 76 (1990): 1545; Francis J. Mootz III, "Rhetorical Knowledge in Legal Practice and Theory," *Southern California Interdisciplinary Law Journal* 6 (1998): 491.

[2] Ian Worthington, ed., *Persuasion: Greek Rhetoric in Action* (London: Routledge, 1994); Renato Barilli, *Rhetoric*, trans. Giuliana Menozzi (Minneapolis: Univ. of Minnesota Press, 1989).

of the public and reflects the decline of classical literacy and its associated virtues. Thus, the Law as Rhetoric trope offers a tantalizingly concealed defense of law that persuades by praising as cultivated and wise those capable of unraveling its mystery. In this way the Law as Rhetoric trope is an example of the very art it praises, a performative demonstration of its claim that the art of persuasion depends not on superficial technique, but on cultivation, virtue, and penetrating insight into fundamental truths.

The Law as Rhetoric trope bears a complex relationship to the larger enterprise of reading law as literature that is the subject of this book. In one important sense, rhetoric is not literature at all. As we noted in this book's introduction, the "literature" to which most law-literature scholarship turns is the idea of literature as an art originating in the Romantic Era. This idea of literature involves a characteristically modern conception of writing as the expression of emotion presented for aesthetic contemplation by a professional literary artist. It presumes a psychological conception of the mind as an imaginative synthesizer of sensations; a conception of value as rooted in human desire rather than a transcendent order; a distinction between instrumental and aesthetic value; widespread literacy in a national language of governmental administration; a mass market for objects of aesthetic consumption; and a division of learning into discrete professions and disciplines. In sum, the modern conception of imaginative writing as literary art makes sense in a social world made up of discrete subjectivities who represent distinct perspectives and sources of value. Literature is an aesthetic discourse of subjectivity defined by contrast to such instrumental discourses of administration as law, economics, and politics. It presupposes the separation of personality and institutional structure and asserts the priority of the former over the latter.

Rhetoric, by contrast, does not assume that legal discourse can help give voice to the personhood that society otherwise suppresses; rather, it assumes that personhood is precisely a status of political participation expressed in the rhetorical activity of reaffirming and revivifying the social order. Rhetoric is civic and instrumental rather than expressive or aesthetic. It is classic rather than Romantic, and it preceded the modern division of letters into discrete disciplines including its division into instrumental and aesthetic discourse. Rhetoric presumes that the point of language is not to express subjectivity but to communicate knowledge of the nature of things. It presumes that speech reveals something about the self only in the way that any other action does—by displaying character. The significance of this character to an audience does not lie in its idiosyncrasy or uniqueness. Character can be virtuous or corrupt, well-formed or deformed. Thus, even the performative dimension of rhetoric is ultimately significant not for what it reveals about the self, but for what it teaches about the nature of virtue. Accordingly if we understand "literature" in Romantic terms, rhetoric is not literature at all.

Yet part of the point of praising law as rhetoric is to deny the division of letters into discrete disciplines and the subjectivist assumptions of modern thought on which this division seems to be premised. A world in which rhetoric is still an important category of human enterprise is a world in which rhetoric includes not only law, but imaginative literature as well.[3]

Regardless of whether rhetoric is properly seen as literature, the Law and Literature movement includes the Law as Rhetoric trope within its pedigree by virtue of the prominence of the Ciceronian ideal of republican virtue in antebellum American legal—and literary—culture. While this ideal may be said to have died with Lincoln, it remains available as a resource for nostalgic appeals to a noble past, with Lincoln perhaps replacing Cicero as its heroic exemplar. Such appeals have been part of the Law and Literature movement from its inception. That movement may be said to have begun with Alexander Bickel's argument that judicial artistry could overcome the presumptive illegitimacy of countermajoritarian judicial review. In developing his model of the judicial artist as the prudent conservator and inspiring professor of principle, Bickel turned not to any contemporary judge, but to Lincoln, the last great rhetorician.

Moreover, despite the divergent premises of classical rhetoric and Romantic literature, they share convergent themes that permitted them both to be invoked on the same side of certain quarrels among legal academics. Both enterprises may be said to involve the sublimation of passion. Romantic literature of course invites us to recollect and savor emotion in tranquility. But neither are the admirers of classical rhetoric indifferent to passion. Contemporary admirers of classical rhetoric emphasize its aims to make the contradictions of error not just known, but *felt*, and to instill a passion for wisdom or virtue that drives out baser desires. Classical rhetoric and Romantic literature have the common aim of refining the passions; this shared aim enables both to be invoked against materialist and hedonist currents in modern thought. But because both seek to evoke passion, they seem opposed to a calculating rationality, or an abstract conceptualism. In the polemical context of legal academe in the 1970s and 1980s classical rhetoric, like Romantic literature, seemed useful to opponents of law and economics and utilitarianism. And so both came to stand for a humane liberalism that defended the dignity of the individual against the crass materialism and cynical instrumentalism of cost-benefit analysis.

The key exponent of this liberal vision of law as rhetoric has been James Boyd White. For White, law, literature, and rhetoric are all parts of the same activity of "constituting" a culture of discourse. On White's view, rhetoric is a literary form that exploits an array of aesthetic tools to achieve moral ends. It follows that aesthetic form has moral salience and that the ethical responsibilities of the lawyer or judge include an attention to aesthetic form. The lawyer, acting in this combined capacity of artist and exponent of legal standards, acts to create "community." The lawyer must so express legal norms as to induce social harmony and

[3] Taken in a different sense, rhetoric remains an important term of art in contemporary literary studies. Here it refers less often to oratorical performance or ethical significance, than simply to figuration—to the tropes of metaphor, simile, and the like that, to the modern reader at least, seem ornamental and therefore intrinsically literary.

solidarity by reaffirming and revivifying common values. In so doing, the lawyer makes an ethical appeal, modeling a virtuous character.

Now, there is an obvious difficulty with this project of rhetorical revival, one that accounts for White's elision of rhetoric and literature. Rhetoric represents a remembered ideal, evoking a lost time when all public action and discourse was a search for right action and governance; when law, custom, religion, and ethics were unified; and, indeed when all uses of language were harmonious in purpose.[4] The result—but the premise as well—was an organically unified society where no notion of individual will or desire conflicted with civic duty—where indeed civic duty was the apotheosis of selfhood. If the rhetorical enterprise depends on shared values and virtues, and on faith in the prevalence and perspicuousness of civic motives, it does not seem very credible in the modern liberal society we have and that—White implies—we are lucky to have. The rhetorician can hardly reaffirm value consensus where none exists, or model public virtues where self-presentation is seen as a mask for private interest.

While White rarely addresses this problem directly, he implies a two-part answer for it. First, he would argue that the distance between traditional and modern society is smaller than our formulation assumes. That there is no consensus in our society, he would say, is a demeaning self-caricature. There is a great deal on which we agree, at least at an abstract level—elected leaders, freedom of opinion and worship, equality before the law, some system of permitting and rewarding initiative—and at this abstract level, our principles are superior to those of the ancients. We need only to give life to these values, to live them as virtues by integrating them into our habits of discourse. On the other hand, classical societies were less stable and harmonious than we might think. Such unity as they had was the product of a constant rhetorical effort to *re*constitute and revitalize consensus in the face of challenges.

Thus, the second step in White's implied argument for the contemporary relevance of rhetoric is to argue that a similar effort today can create community on the basis of shared values and virtues. The requisite rhetoric would not simply reflect or reproduce a community of value already present; it would also bring such a community into being through an effort of the literary imagination. Modern rhetoricians cannot simply reveal their characters in the rhetorical act; they must also create them. They are obliged to create themselves, by an effort of the Romantic literary imagination, as characters that are nevertheless, in the classical sense, well-formed.

For White, the "literary" stands for the possibility of individual and collective self-creation. In yoking the Romantic project of self-creation to the classical ideals of civic virtue and public discourse, White resembles those legal theorists who have sought to root a contemporary politics of deliberative democracy in America's early history of civic republicanism. Some, like White, have proffered the

---

[4] E.,g., Christopher Carey, "Rhetorical Means of Persuasion," in Worthingthon, *Persuasion*, 26–45.

Bickelian judicial artist as a model of deliberative discourse. What these authors either forget or suppress is Bickel's urgent sense that the rhetorician was necessarily a marginal and politically weak element in a democracy, who must speak neither too boldly nor too candidly. Behind this diffidence lay a prudential conservatism, even a discreet authoritarianism, that has been typical of twentieth-century proponents of the revival of classical rhetoric.

Whether conservatism and authoritarianism are necessary or merely accidental elements of the rhetorical ideal, whether something like a liberal practice of rhetoric is possible—these are the chief questions of this chapter. The problem is sharply posed by Peter Goodrich's searing essay "Antirrhesis: Polemical Structures of Common Law Thought."[5] As Goodrich notes, the modern liberal proponent of rhetoric believes that this classical art can return language to nature, and comity to law; that it can establish civic character and save law from nihilism, drawing it away from the evils of theory and back to literature. But in fact, as Goodrich warns, a powerful, underrecognized alternative strand in the rhetorical tradition dating back to the Middle Ages is a theological model of calumny against heresy and iconoclasm. He calls this "antirrhesis"—a form of speech by which the orator rejects error and perversion.[6] Indeed, Goodrich traces many of the principles of specifically legal rhetoric to this discourse of defense and denunciation. Rhetoric in law has always been sophistical, notes Goodrich, and though figures from Cicero to Vico tried to associate it with civic virtue, the practice of legal oratory, as adopted from the classical models by the medieval rhetoricians, was always part of casuistry, apologetic, proof, and polemic. At its roots, Goodrich implies, the venerable alliance of law and rhetoric may be not so much harmonizing as denunciatory, and dogmatic. Goodrich's essay is of course an example of the very polemics it warns against. But it usefully raises the question of the compatibility of liberal politics with the orthodoxy presupposed by much of the rhetorical tradition.[7]

We will approach this question with a brief review of the history of rhetoric in part 4.1. We will then move in part 4.2 to explore the conservative politics of the twentieth-century rhetorical revival. We will proceed from Bickel's invocation of Lincoln, to his source in the profound rhetorical analysis of Harry Jaffa, and from thence to Harry Jaffa's philosophical mentor, the conservative political theorist Leo Strauss. We will consider the efforts of the "Chicago Critics" to develop a classically inspired rhetorical criticism, including the call of Richard Weaver to restore rhetoric to a central place in the college curriculum.

These figures tended to view classical learning as a fragile flame to be kept alight, but sheltered, in the dark age of modernity. They feared that modern culture is constitutively opposed to the essential teaching of the classics, that there are

[5] Peter Goodrich, "Antirrhesis: Polemical Structures of Common Law Thought," in *The Rhetoric of Law*, ed. Austin Sarat and Thomas Kearns (Ann Arbor: Univ. of Michigan Press, 1996), 57–102.

[6] Ibid., 57–59.

[7] For models of constrained public dialogue, see Bruce Ackerman, *Social Justice in the Liberal State* (New Haven: Yale Univ. Press, 1980); John Rawls, *Political Liberalism* (New York: Columbia Univ. Press, 1993).

objective, rationally discernible values, transcending human will and opinion. Some of these conservative rhetoricians allowed that modern culture had good reason to fear this teaching, which is easily corrupted into a violently purgative orthodoxy or a corrosive skepticism in the hands of the discontented. Thus, a certain discretion in the dissemination of classical learning seemed prudent, to preserve it against persecution by established authority or perversion by zealots, and to preserve the social order against the disruptive effects of such zealotry. Those privy to the wisdom of the classics had a special responsibility to conserve both social authority and the higher, but inevitably weaker, authority of reason. This was a delicate task requiring considerable rhetorical skill. It involved recognizing that not everyone was capable of wisdom, and instilling piety and deference to authority among the uninstructed. Those capable of instruction needed to learn prudence and respect for social order, before being admitted to the secrets of wisdom. Hence, instruction had to involve a long probation. To sustain the patience and commitment of the pupil the teacher had to both mobilize and control a passion for learning, tantalizing without gratifying a yearning for wisdom, teaching an erotics of impulse control. The conservative rhetorician did not assume that classical rhetoric could or should again become the everyday currency of public discourse for all. Instead he saw rhetoric as an occult knowledge, a powerful and subtle instrument of persuasion, instruction, and concealment to be deployed by an embattled intellectual and moral elite in addressing different messages to different audiences.

On this conservative rhetorical model, rhetoric serves to check rather than enable popular democracy and personal liberty. Nevertheless, it may be prudent for rhetoric to present itself as a friend to these modern institutions. And so it may speak in the ambiguous language of "self-governance," encoding a sermon on self-discipline within an apparent endorsement of popular power. Or it may praise tolerance and dialogue without conceding that different opinions are of equal authority. Tolerance and civility are valued by the conservative rhetorician in four ways. First, as a rhetorical tactic that engages ignorance and invites it into an unequal dialogue with wisdom. Second, as a prudential stratagem that avoids provoking ignorance to persecute wisdom. Third, as a check against the zealous pursuit of virtue at the cost of social stability. And finally, as a discipline of restraint and discretion that reenforces the virtues of the wise. But however much it may value tolerance, conservative rhetoric is pedagogy, not democratic dialogue.

Can rhetoric nevertheless serve liberal democracy? Is a liberal rhetoric possible? In part 4.3 we will examine the efforts of White and other legal scholars to develop a progressive rhetorical vision. What would qualify as such a liberal rhetoric? It would refigure dialogue as an egalitarian democratic process, rather than an intrinsically hierarchical process of pedagogy. It might abandon the classical teaching that there is an ultimate truth of the matter about questions of value, or it might presume that true values could only be discovered through an open-ended and universally inclusive process of rational discussion. In such a process the transformation of preferences inherent in deliberation would be mutual rather than one-sided.

What might be the role of rhetoric in such an egalitarian process? It might be a filter, screening out the expression of views that are intolerant, or that cannot be defended by reference to public reasons.[8] Or it might be a set of conventions specific to a particular community, assisting collective action by channeling opinion towards a limited number of agenda choices. Or it might reaffirm certain process values important to democratic deliberation, such as tolerance, willingness to compromise, or trust in the good faith of antagonists in debate. Finally, it might be a process of invention, defining new identities and interests that enable the participants to move past intractable conflict. Participants in democratic dialogue might be moved to adopt new self-definitions by the aesthetic qualities of these self-definitions, or by compelling narratives linking these new self-definitions to older ones. It is this last, inventive role for rhetoric in democratic dialogue that would make it most resemble "literature."

Thus, liberal democratic dialogue might plausibly be enhanced by a culture of argument involving a set of disciplining conventions and motivating myths continually renewed by a practice of literary invention. And we might choose to call such an enabling culture of argument "rhetoric." Rhetoric's liberal proponents insist that rhetoric is a component of all cultures and of all normative traditions competing within cultures. Thus, these proponents insist that rhetoric is a form of cultural expression as well as cultural regulation and can be the instrument of pluralist competition within a single culture. But in choosing this venerable term to describe an enabling culture of argument for liberal democracy, we invoke a specifically classical cultural heritage at odds with the egalitarian, pluralist, and relativist values of modern liberalism. Conservative rhetoricians would insist that this idea of a pluralist rhetoric is inherently confused. They would note that liberal rhetoricians treat tolerance and the equal standing of all participants as intrinsically important process values; they would argue that if any values, including process values, are intrinsic, not all opinions can be equally valuable. They would insist that conversation about value is pointless if there is no truth of the matter and if every opinion is as good as any other.

To rhetoric's liberal proponents, the subjectivity of value is an intractable reality that political discourse must accommodate. What we might call "liberal rhetoric" promises to charm the public into assent to institutions rooted in values that are ultimately arbitrary and subjective. By contrast, for the conservative rhetoricians the liberals' faith in the subjectivity of value is an irrational prejudice that rhetoric ultimately refutes. This disagreement is fundamental, but not always perspicuous. Because conservative rhetoricians regard the objectivity of value as a dangerous doctrine, corrosive to existing institutions and offensive to the Luddite masses, they teach it with discretion. The result is that we can never be entirely sure whether ostensibly liberal rhetoric is what it professes to be.

---

[8] For concise histories, see Barilli, *Rhetoric*, 2–23; Samuel Ijsseling, *Rhetoric and Philosophy in Conflict* (The Hague: Martinus Nijhoff, 1976), 7–33.

This difficulty is particularly apparent where scholars offer *law* as their model of liberal rhetoric. There is something disconcerting about the notion that litigation should be the setting for democratic deliberation, and that we should take judges as our models of democratic citizenship. The implication is that the deliberative discourse enabled by rhetoric is the preserve of a professional elite ("Have your attorney call my attorney and we'll dialogue"). If rhetoric is the special competence of experts, we get a rather chilling picture of liberal society as a charade of pluralist conflict disguising an inner reality of elite consensus and professional courtesy.

Any effort to bring rhetoric to the service of modern liberalism and cultural pluralism must contend with the centrality of political authority and moral virtue in the rhetorical tradition. To set the liberal and conservative models of rhetoric in the context of that tradition, we begin with a brief history.

4.1 A VERY BRIEF HISTORY OF RHETORIC

Classical Origins

From our first historical sources we discover that rhetoric has always been controversial, both as to what it really is and what values it serves. Plato and others denounced rhetoric with as much vitriol as a stereotypical modern American lawyer-basher denounces corrupt lawyers; yet while Aristotle offered a complex and nuanced defense of rhetoric, the Platonic dialogue is an enduringly influential model of rhetorical form.[9]

At one pole, the Platonic end of the continuum, rhetoric enables the speaker to retrieve the ideal forms he learned in pre-life. Rhetoric strives to achieve ethos, the inner harmony of language, character, and truth made incarnate in the person. Under this model, the speaker must actually *have* good character to impress his audience; the quality of one's discourse is an index and instrument of one's moral health, so that as one lives so one speaks. The other pole lies on the far side of Aristotle, leaning towards the world of the Sophists. Here, rhetoric aims only at *seeming* to be good, at constructing an image of good character. The speaker is not an exogenous force of virtue creating the text, but is, in effect, simply the key signifier within the text. This notion of rhetoric is always susceptible to degeneration into the manipulation of an audience to achieve some ignoble end.[10]

[9] James S. Baumlin, "Introduction: Positing Ethos in Historical and Contemporary Theory," in *Ethos: New Essays in Rhetorical and Critical Theory*, ed. James S. Baumlin and Tita French Baumlin (Dallas: Southern Methodist Univ. Press, 1994).

[10] Goodrich's recent work develops this critique of the "historically ill-informed revivals of rhetoric as felicitous communication, eloquence, community, or ethics of speech." See *Oedipus Lex; Psychoanalysis, History, and Law* (Berkeley: Univ. of California Press, 1995), 71. Goodrich views traditional or conventional Anglo-American jurisprudence as a mixture of common law interpretive and customary principles and legal liberalism, mixing positivism, instrumentalism, and various species of natural law principles. To Goodrich this jurisprudence is ahistorical, because it fails to acknowledge that the emergence of common law and liberalism was not a comfortable transition, but rather a highly con-

The conventional history of rhetoric tells us that Aristotle's slightly begrudging acceptance of rhetoric is the ultimately winning position. As conceived by Aristotle, persuasion through rhetoric is more contingent and topical than proof through logic. In the case of rhetoric, the audience is supposed to identify with the terms, character, motives, and values of the speaker. The Aristotelian version of the art of rhetoric is functional and pragmatic, a study of the argumentative role of public speech, focusing not just on style, but on the invention and classification of arguments.

Plato is too often viewed simply as a condemnor of rhetoric along with poetry, who warns us that all verbal construction built on contingent opinion is a dangerous illusion. As Martha Nussbaum shows, however, Plato can also be seen as the keeper of the flame of the true rhetoric, the source of the nobler model of rhetoric as a tool of philosophical enlightenment that motivates the more idealistic promoters of rhetoric in later eras.[11]

Nussbaum shows how Plato's criticism of tragedy expresses his concern about the link between literary style and philosophical content. Plato's ambivalence about rhetoric is reflected in our uncertainty about the status of the Platonic dialogue as literature. Although not written for the stage, the dialogues closely resemble drama and lend themselves to performance. Yet the question is not why they are more dramatic than treatise-like, because ethical treatises like Aristotle's *Nichomachean Ethics* did not yet exist. Rather, since the poets were then the key ethical teachers, the question is why the dialogues were not poetic dramas. Before Plato, the Greeks did not distinguish between philosophical and literary discussions of human practical problems.[12] For Plato, the choice of style or form was also a moral choice, and it was therefore significant that he rejected the available model of the tragic poem in favor of the discursive and relatively dispassionate dialogue.

As Nussbaum shows, the theatrical dialogue form bespoke the value of spoken conversation in a way that a written treatise could not. For Socrates, written philosophy, especially in the form of a didactic treatise, would have been a virtual oxymoron. Philosophy was a way of living in a social world, not of representing it.[13] It required responsive interaction between teacher and pupil. Books were

---

flicted and often politically violent suppression of what he calls the "iconographic"—a deeply religious and even mystical basis of justice, in favor of what he calls the "textual" or the "scriptural," most obviously in the early Renaissance and Reformation. Thus, Renaissance European writers resurrected the art of rhetoric as a revival of Classical learning, but in the hands of liberal jurisprudes like James B. White, the rhetoric is drained of the violent content and transformed into a Panglossian civic humanism. See also "*Ars Bablativa*: Ramism, Rhetoric, and the Geneaology of English Jurisprudence," in *Legal Hermeneutics: History, Theory, and Practice*, ed. Gregory Leyh (Berkeley: Univ. of California Press, 1992); "Rhetoric as Jurisprudence: An Introduction to the Politics of Legal Language," *Oxford Journal of Legal Studies* 4 (1984): 122; "The Continuance of the Antirrhetic," *Cardozo Studies in Law and Literature* 4 (1992): 207.

[11] Martha Nussbaum, *The Fragility of Goodness* (Cambridge: Cambridge Univ. Press, 1986), 122–35.

[12] Ibid., 122–25.

[13] Ibid., 125.

inert. In Nussbaum's words, they "lull the soul into forgetfulness, both of the content and the manner of real philosophizing,"[14] teaching passive reliance. Books, moreover, induce the false conceit of wisdom, offering mere information in place of true understanding. But after the death of Socrates, Plato had to accommodate the philistines of the written word. Though Plato obviously opposed the crass trickery of the sophistic rhetoricians, and though he opposed tragic theater because it distracted the mind with emotion, the dialogue nevertheless engages in a form of seduction. Whereas a treatise by, say, Parmenides announces its purpose and asserts its authority, the Platonic dialogue draws the perhaps resistant reader into philosophizing by exploiting the context of ordinary conversation between ordinary people. Indeed, it relies on the sense of honor of any person capable of articulating a self-image, and experiencing humiliation on being forced to admit he cannot live up to it. The dialogue also "models" ethical behavior by demonstrating the moral development of the characters in process. This ethical "role-modeling" is the heart of rhetoric.

Good rhetoric, for Plato, was not very "rhetorical." It dramatized the movement of the soul from emotion to intellect, and from contingent opinion, through contradiction, and the acknowledgment of ignorance, towards enduring truth. Socrates governs rather than displays his emotions, and so we would be embarrassed to respond emotionally.[15] Yet after he has made his point clear Socrates often clinches the point with an extended analogy or allegory. "It is so regularly the method of Plato to follow a subtle analysis with a striking myth," concludes Richard Weaver, "that it is not unreasonable to call him the master rhetorician."[16] Thus, though widely viewed as condemning rhetoric, Plato was only condemning one genre practiced in Greece. That genre, the kind associated with Aristotle, Isocrates, and ultimately Cicero, erred, in Plato's view, in the most fundamental way—by taking the social unit rather than the soul as the ideal starting point. This rhetoric was hence too corrupt to achieve the ideal of statesmanship. In his attack on sophistical rhetoric, Plato establishes the dilemma that will persist through two millennia: Do we rely on some capacity to apprehend absolute truth as the epistemological starting point for rhetoric; or is rhetoric nothing grander than a toolkit of tropes and evidentiary devices to help us do our best in assessing the relatively probable, plausible, or useful?

The latter view is compatible with Aristotle's approach. His *Rhetoric* is unabashedly a manual of techniques of audience manipulation. There is *Docere*—the subject matter exposited—the instructive or informative aspect; *Placere*: pleasing or entertaining the audience, through eloquence; *Movere*—moving the audience to pass ethical judgment.[17] Aristotle conceives two types of arguments: extrinsic and intrinsic. The extrinsic are technically the nonrhetorical ones that

---

[14] Ibid.

[15] Otis M. Walter, "On Views of Rhetoric, Whether Conservative or Progressive," in *Contemporary Theories of Rhetoric: Selected Readings*, ed. Richard L. Johannesen (New York: Harper & Row, 1971), 18–38.

[16] Richard Weaver, *The Ethics of Rhetoric* (Chicago: Regnery, 1963).

[17] Ijsseling, *Rhetoric and Philosophy in Conflict*, 26–33.

rely on some source of authority, such as laws, contracts, and confessions. But the intrinsic arguments rely on the ethos of speaker, the pathos of public, and the logos, or logic. Logic in turn can be in the strict form of a syllogism or the loose form of the *enthymeme*. The latter is the crucial, defining form of Aristotelian argument, representing neither pure logic nor pure manipulation, but uniting intellect, will, and emotion.[18] The enthymeme is Aristotle's effort to solve two problems: how to reason logically with an audience indisposed to careful analysis, and how to reason logically when one lacks indisputable major premises.[19]

Aristotle himself offers an example: that Darius invaded Greece after he conquered Egypt, and that Xerxes invaded Greece after his conquest of Egypt—these facts suggest that the Greeks should not now allow Egypt to be conquered by Persia.[20] This is the inductive wisdom of experience, where practical judgment does not require certainty that all Persian conquerors of Egypt invade Greece, and where the causal hypotheses that might link current to past circumstances do not need to be spelled out for a credulous and impatient audience. Indeed, the likely audience for this argument will be more moved by these particular examples than by some such general proposition as "Allowing a powerful empire to conquer a neighbor strengthens it and feeds its ambition." The enthymeme relies on brevity and omission of steps to surprise and entertain its audience, and the steps omitted communicate something about the audience—"You are an insider who does not need this spelled out"—as well as about the speaker—"I am an insider who knows I need not spell this out for you." But it thereby runs the risk that a skeptical or offended audience will reject either the unstated major premise or the implied relationship between speaker and audience.[21] So what strikes the modern reader as a mundane shift from analytic logic to the tactics of rational persuasion was for Aristotle a dramatic and risky redefinition of the very nature of reason.[22]

In the stock story about the rise and fall of Aristotelian rhetoric, we begin with the civic ideal in which eloquence was an expression of the individual's virtue

---

[18] Andrea Lunsford and Lisa Ede, "On Distinctions between Classical and Modern Rhetoric," in *Essays on Classical Rhetoric and Modern Discourse*, ed. Robert J. Connors, Lisa Ede, and Andrea Lunsford (Cambridge: Cambridge Univ. Press, 1984), 37–49.

[19] James C. Raymond, "Enthymemes, Examples, and Rhetorical Method," in Connors, Ede, and Lunsford, *Essays on Classical Rhetoric*, 140, 144.

[20] Aristotle, *Rhetoric*, II.20.1393a.

[21] Renato Barilli gives a deceptively simple example: a humorous advertisement proclaims that a new sportscar would "juvenate" its owner. The major premise is that youth is desirable, the conclusion that the juvenating car is therefore desirable. To offer to "juvenate" rather than "rejuvenate" is to flatter a presumably mature and wealthy audience by implying that youth is an acquirable property rather than a temporal state. Barilli, *Rhetoric*, 14.

[22] A modern exponent of the Aristotelian conception of rhetoric as a form of practical reason is the Belgian philosopher Chaim Perelman. See Chaim Perelman, *Justice, Law, and Argument: Essays on Moral and Legal Reasoning*, trans. John Petrie (Boston: Reidel, 1980); Chaim Perelman and L. Olbrechts-Tyteca, *The New Rhetoric: A Treatise on Argumentation*, trans. John Wilkinson and Purcell Weaver (Notre Dame: Univ. of Notre Dame Press, 1969). For a treatment of Perelman's work on legal rhetoric, see Mootz, "Rhetorical Knowledge."

and of the spirit of the *polis* as a whole. The material precondition of an engaged rhetoric was the intimate and participatory politics of the democratic city-state, in which speech was conventionally expected to express a judgment about the public good, rather than partisan advocacy. In a sense, rhetoric may be defined as the craft of changing self-organization, by overcoming self-conflict.[23] In its "original" domain, however, the divided self was a collective self, not an individual self.

Rhetoric was not simply the communication of ideas: it was a form of public *performance*. To properly appreciate the oratorical performance it was necessary not only to grasp its meaning but also to recognize it as virtuous social action, to read in it, for example, the forebearance or modesty of the great, or the restraint of the aggrieved, or the courage implicit in a grave commitment undertaken. Appreciating oratorical performance therefore required highly local cultural knowledge. It entailed the ability to recognize the status and situation of the speaker, and to recognize and value the virtues he sought to display. In this sense, rhetoric required "virtue"—a culturally specific ethical sensibility—not only of the speaker but also of the audience.[24]

The "virtue" of eloquence was associated with ownership of property. On the one hand, despite the fiction that rhetoric was always public-spirited, much public legal rhetoric took the form of a citizen arguing for his right to a disputed property. The result was that eloquence earned ownership. On the other hand, ownership established eloquence, because a citizen's grounding in the propertied class was the true badge of character that won him the right to credibility in the local marketplace of persuasive performances.[25] In the political history of Greece itself, historians trace a movement from the local multiformity of oratorical conventions to Panhellenic uniformity, ultimately elevating formal composition over oral improvisation and intellectual over ethical authority. The *rhetor* ceased to personally recompose and instead relied on the authority of well-developed and recorded tradition, and so the performative dimension of rhetoric fell into decline. Rhetoric is supposed to have then lost its focus on argument and audience in favor of pure, self-conscious style; rhetorical study became formulaic and didactic, focused on figures of speech. As Athenian democracy ended and public speech contracted, rhetoric moved from argument to ornament, from dialectics to aesthetics, from semantics to grammar, and from persuasion to poetics.[26]

By the time the rhetorical baton is passed on to the Romans, we find little left of the Platonic end of the continuum. Instead, skill in producing belief is seen as the key to civilization, and hence Quintilian's and Cicero's view of man as a barely

[23] Marshall W. Alcorn Jr., "Self-Structure as Rhetorical Device: Modern Ethos and the Divisiveness of Self," in Baumlin, *Ethos*, 3, 24–25.

[24] Indeed, the precondition for the prolixity of "literature" is a kind of nostalgia for the lost occasion of the performative. Gregory Nagy, "The Crisis of Performance," in John Bender and David Wellbery, eds., *The Ends of Rhetoric: History, Theory, Practice* (Stanford: Stanford Univ. Press, 1990), 43–59.

[25] Ijsseling, *Rhetoric and Philosophy in Conflict*, 11.

[26] Stanley Fish, *Is There a Text in This Class: The Authority of Interpretive Communities* (Cambridge: Harvard Univ. Press, 1980), 471–502.

governable animal for whom Platonic quest for truth is an irrelevant fantasy.[27] In this tradition, rhetoric rightly deals only with the probable and contingent and aims not at truth but at social peace. The city begins when savages submit to reasoned eloquence.

The Decline of Rhetoric

Though we hardly purport here to recount the history of rhetoric over the next two millennia, it is worth briefly tracing how these complex and often contradictory premises of rhetoric play themselves out after the Fall of Rome.[28] The classical rhetorical art forms certainly persist in the early Christian Era. Early Christian apologists offered legalistic arguments to defend Christianity against charges of bestiality and incest and child killing. And though their cautious prudentialism hardly seems compatible with revelational notions of truth, Cicero and Seneca served, for early Christians, as models of stoic argument for those exhorting the faithful to endure persecution and martyrdom.[29] Augustine himself was a lifelong admirer of Cicero, yet after his conversion he had to struggle to incorporate eloquence into an honored place in the hierarchy of the Two Cities. But Augustine found Cicero's probabilistic notion of practical reason useful in combating the epistemological claims of the Skeptics, and Cicero's stoicism served as an antidote to their reductive materialism. Augustine read Cicero as actually disdaining the formal rules of eloquence in favor of the true source of eloquence lying in an intuitive grasp of nature; in this way Augustine managed to reconcile Cicero with the Platonism that served as the most important classical legacy for the early Church.

On the whole, however, classical rhetoric fit poorly with the rise of Scripture as the true eloquence. Rhetoric might aspire to marry form to content, but for believers Scripture fully integrated letter and spirit and therefore left no place for rhetoric in Christian life. Christian scholars were able to sustain some of the study of the classical tropes, largely in their writing about the forms of analogy between the earthly and the spiritual phenomena. But even when contact with Arab philosophers in the later Middle Ages began to revive for Europeans the study of Aristotle, it was more Aristotelian logic and metaphysics that aided Christian scholasticism, not Aristotelian rhetoric. We see the repudiation of the inherently particularist civic ideal in the universalistic vision of Dante, with all society and history subsumed in a theological unity; here, rhetoric, the tool of the topical and the local, could play only a minor role.[30]

It is a cliché, of course, to say that the Renaissance meant the revival of classical learning, and certainly rhetoric became an important part of the Italian model of

[27] Ibid., 481, n. 18.

[28] John Bender and David Wellbery, "Rhetoricality: On the Modernist Return of Rhetoric," in Bender and Wellbery, *The Ends of Rhetoric*, 3–39.

[29] Ijsseling, *Rhetoric and Philosophy in Conflict*, 41–45.

[30] Ibid.; Barilli, *Rhetoric*, 38–45.

education and learning in its honored place in the classical *trivium*. But at least two factors complicated the strength of the classical rhetorical tradition in Renaissance Europe. First, the development of printing and the rise of literacy put the written above the spoken and thus diminished the special role of oratorical eloquence. Second, though Renaissance poets certainly drew on the rhetorical arts, the conscious rise of a "poetic" aesthetic and the exploration of the lyric mode moved the arts of language out of the public square and into a world of private contemplation. Hence, we see what Vasile Florescu calls the "literaturization of rhetoric."[31] Absorbed into poetry, rhetoric lost its distinctness as it gained prestige.

The stock stories of the postclassical era of rhetoric include both Whiggish and decline-and-fall versions, but both undermine the Classical ideal. One Enlightenment story shows rhetoric abetting the cause of serious reason in dispelling the mists of superstition. In another, we trace a line from Vico to Foucault and find rhetoric abetting a carnivalesque world of exuberance and possibility struggling against soulless reason. But our own contemporary "loss of faith" in Enlightenment reason has returned us to an ironic, even perverted version of classical rhetoric. While science supposedly destroyed rhetoric, Kuhnian relativism now seems to reduce science to rhetoric.[32]

Here is the conventional story of the decline and fall of classical rhetoric: classical rhetoric once covered all aspects of public discourse, from performative speech acts, to grammar and stylistics, to cultural and political forms—all that logic did not cover. Rhetoric had originally been a codification of oratory, matching conventions of speech to the status of the speaker and the nature of the occasion. This meant that rhetoric delineated the anatomy of social power and provided, in an age before revelational religion and depth psychology, an etiquette of thought itself. As John Bender and David Wellbery show in their recounting of the fall of rhetoric, though rhetoric once subsumed all other language-based disciplines, the Enlightenment disconnected rhetoric from science, and the Romantic Era disconnected it from literature. The supposed reunification of discourse in the postmodern age means a revival of rhetoric, but really a revival of the phenomenon of "rhetoricality."[33] Certain cultural changes meant the demise of rhetoric, and some of those changes have now partly reversed. Rhetoric has become literary criticism, linguistics, communications, and the sociology of knowledge.

The newly authoritative discourse of the Enlightenment was the language of science—neutral, transparent, nonpositional.[34] Evocative, passionate language was increasingly suspect in public discourse as "subjective." It had to be rejustified as a lyrical, "literary" language of the inner self, largely irrelevant to public debate. In legal proceedings in particular, the stylized ballet of rhetorical disputa-

---

[31] Barilli, *Rhetoric*, 52–69; Ijsseling, *Rhetoric and Philosophy in Conflict*, 46–59.

[32] Vasile Florescu, "Rhetoric and Its Rehabilitation in Contemporary Philosophy," *Philosophy and Rhetoric* 3 (1970): 193, 210.

[33] Bender and Wellbery, "Rhetoricality," 1315.

[34] Ibid. 13–15, 22–39.

tion gives way to a quasi-scientific model of empirical inquiry.[35] Though in Italy Vico tried to sustain the notion of history and language at the center of civic life, the premise that language was a repository of wisdom could hardly survive the combined assault of rationalism and empiricism, both asserting that truth is independent of speech and social activity.

With the increasing influence of these new epistemologies, Neoclassical aesthetics became the theory not of discourse but of sensate cognitions and of the signs that convey them. Its frame of reference was not social interaction within a hierarchical culture, but the soul as a faculty of representation. In neoclassical literature, the novel represented the most "written" of genres. Such novelistic techniques as free indirect discourse have no oral counterpart, and the novel was more psychological and visual than oratorical in its expository method. More generally, the proliferation of literacy and the mass production of written works threatened rhetoric, as writing for publication is neither so social nor so intimate an act as speech.

Poetry remained a more oral genre than the novel, yet it too grew less oratorical. The Romantic lyric offered a creative, self-forming subject, independent of audience function and public responsibility, and it shared the novel's unadorned natural language.[36] Though the early history of the lyric shows a poetry that is formal and rhetorical in issuing praise and blame on ceremonial occasions or subjects, the Romantic lyric was built upon a unique epiphanic moment in the life of a single speaker and reflected the Romantic notion of speech that could not be paraphrased, and so could not be rhetorically enhanced. A final step in this conventional history of the demise of rhetoric was the early-nineteenth-century rise of nationalism in Europe, which undid the supposed internationalism of classical rhetorical forms—and focused on the romance of a national vernacular tradition. Political representation was mediated by the administrative machinery of the nation-state, while the citizenry "participated" in the fictive community of an institutionally disseminated national culture. Romantic literature may be said to have replaced classical oratory not only as a mode of discourse, but as a source of social solidarity and political legitimacy.

The Rise and Fall of the Ciceronian Ideal in America

In America, the career of rhetoric lasted longer and was part of the elaboration of an American nationalism. Historians tell us that the American revolutionaries inherited from English Whigs a civic republican ideology that conditioned political authority on the participation in governance of a broad class of virtuous and materially independent citizens. The young political societies of America fancied themselves latter-day versions of republican Rome and derived their most exalted visions of virtuous political participation from the recorded speeches of Roman orators. Thus, virtue came to be associated in America not only with property but with literacy, a bit of classical education, eloquence, and experience in public debate. Early republican America had, or fancied it had, a kind of organic

---

[35] Ibid., 8.
[36] Ibid., 21.

culture in which law and literature were so united that we could regard leading statesmen as special figures we might call political artists. As described by Robert Ferguson, the early American republic provides an example of a sort of original unity that answers the law-literature question by integrating both into rhetoric.[37]

As Ferguson notes, in the early republic it would have been foolish even to ask what the relation of law and literature was: lawyers were ministers and maestros of culture as well as of politics. Recognizing that no republic would survive without the backing of a culture, America's leaders saw the building of a republic and the building of republican culture as a single task. The unity of law and culture was not so hard to conceive, because the legal rules and principles the republic had to lay down were so broad and fundamental that they bore a connection to wider cultural values. This was a world where, because of political urgency, even imaginative and academic talent had to be directed toward practical ends, where Neoclassical poetic genres were wholly susceptible to patriotic and political themes.[38]

Hence, a kind of legal aesthetic could unify early republican political writing. Lawyers were the cultural elite, partly because the ideological rhetoric of revolution had been so legalistic. The rights that the revolution protected derived from right reason and natural law, but operated through the positive laws of statutes and royal charters. At the century's end, law replaced the potentially divisive discourse of theology as the most authoritative language, so the poet and lawmaker combined in the role of the new secular priest. Chief Justice Marshall's courtroom became the studio for creating the symbolic forms of the republic, the theater of public values.[39]

Law, literature, and rhetoric were linked because the professional man's broad cultural responsibilities and literary impulses were the same. Joel Barlow's goal in *The Columbiad* was "to inculcate the love of rational liberty . . . to show that on the basis of the republican principle all good morals, as well as good government and hopes of permanent peace, must be founded."[40] Literature was to help carry out the "great experiment of republican influences upon the security, the domestic happiness of man, his elevation of character, his love of country." In a new country trying to define itself, law provided the necessary imagery of control. Law dealt in a prudence of means that reached toward ideal totalities. What was meant by "literary" language in this milieu was the rhetorical language of advocacy, exhortation, methodological caution, abstract argument. Justice Story sought to apply "the universal empire of juridical reason" to realize "the splendid visions of Cicero, dreaming over the majestic fragments of his perfect republic."[41] The goal was a fusion of beauty and utility, not mere ornamentation to add classical quotation to oral argument. Kent and Story saw their treatises as literature,[42]

---

[37] Robert Ferguson, *Law and Letters in American Culture* (Cambridge: Harvard Univ. Press, 1984).

[38] Ibid., 11–33.

[39] Ibid., 23.

[40] Joel Barlow, "The Columbiad," quoted in Ferguson, *Law and Letters*, 25–26.

[41] Ibid., 32.

[42] Ibid., 33.

and lawyers were natural authors in an era when literature aimed to establish America's collective identity, and when "republic," "constitution," and "rights" were handy tropes.

As Stephen Botein demonstrates, the dominant figure for American lawyers was Cicero—and not so much Cicero the philosopher as Cicero the fiery orator and prosecutor of the traitor Cataline (represented in the American demonology by Governor Hutchinson).[43] We find an absolute infatutation with Cicero as a model of political behavior. In New England, a newly self-assertive bourgeois elite, eager to act out untraditional roles without the benefit of legitimization from immense landed wealth or securely aristocratic family station, found Cicero an inspiration to "clarify their self-estimates and thereby sustain their aspirations in public life." The Ciceronian speeches were usually read in English translations; Adams read the speeches aloud and praised them for virtues independent of their content. He had to "look out for a cause to speak to, and . . . cut a flash, strike amazement, to catch the vulgar." A key example is James Otis's 1761 speech before the Supreme Court of Judicature to attack the Writs of Assistance:

> I have taken more pains in this cause than I ever will take again, although my engaging in this and another popular cause has raised much resentment. But . . . let the consequences be what they will, I am determined to proceed. The only principles of public conduct that are worthy of a gentleman or a man are to sacrifice estate, ease, health, applause, and even life, to the sacred calls of his country. These manly sentiments, in private life make the good citizen; in public life, the patriot and hero. I do not say, that when brought to the test, I shall be invincible. I pray God I may never be brought to the melancholy trial; but if ever I should, it will be then known how far I can reduce to practice principles, which I know to be founded in truth.[44]

Adams and other lawyers in the post-Revolutionary period faced circumstances far less conducive to Ciceronian behavior: the self-imagery of the bar changed when politics moved from elitism to representativeness. The new anti-Roman attitude was expressed by Rantoul: "The grinding despotism of the privileged orders of Rome . . . never permitted any real liberty, save to the patricians liberty to oppress." Story admired Cicero but looked more generally to classical culture as a means of "refining the taste" and "warming the heart" to "elevate sentiment," seemingly reducing rhetoric to an aesthetic function. Adams's letters then show the Ciceronian decadence—the orator as melodramatic figure: "My morning always ends with a hearty execration of Caesar, and with what is perhaps not so right, a sensation of relief at the 23 stabs of the Ides of March, and the fall at the feet of Pompey's statute." This decadent version resulted from the irrelevance of the true Cicero to the needs of elite professionals servicing the business community, and it troubled men who now feared the emotions of the political public.

---

[43] Stephen Botein, "Cicero as Role Model for Early American Lawyers: A Case Study in Classical Influence," *Classical Journal* 73 (1978): 313–21.

[44] Ibid., 316, citing Charles Francis Adams, *The Works of John Adams* (Boston: Little, Brown, 1850), 247–48.

Choate said reading Cicero would "form the sentiments and . . . enlarge the mind" of an aspiring lawyer. This was no longer the role of "actions daring . . . the new things of a new world . . . large, elementary, gorgeous ideas of right, of equality, of independence, of liberty, of progress through convulsion."[45] Classicism instead became associated with the Federalist-Whig project of conserving the achievements of the Founders. It implied the continuing authority of established institutions and the prudent stewardship of elites.

By midcentury, politics had become more Jacksonian, Classical knowledge became peripheral to legal practice, and the educational and cultural standards of the bar declined. The principal political mouthpiece of the elite bar, the Whig Party, failed. But more significantly, the failure of the great lawyer-orators to craft a rhetorical solution to the slavery conflict signaled, and perhaps caused, the decline in their cultural prestige. The grand style of the generalist ended with the Civil War. To be sure, the old model of the lawyer as cultural statesman may have survived in a rather mugwumpish way. But if the lawyer represented cultural values, it was no longer as the creator of an organic society, but rather as the elite museum keeper of cultural values no longer embodied by the democratic mass.[46] At the same time, according to standard literary history, we observe a shift in literature from the public values of neoclassicism to the private values of Romanticism. As had happened in Europe, the broad neoclassical domain of letters split into discrete discourses, separating the political and the cultural. As enterprise became larger in scale and more complex, American law became more technical and specialized. Where lawyering formerly required only a classical education topped off with a reading of Blackstone, after the Civil War it came to entail a technical education.[47]

In modern democracies, as compared to the early republic, statesmen have lost their inherent moral authority, and it now seems comically anachronistic to conceive serious artists as possessing political authority. Were such a union of cultural and political authority reproducible in this century we would probably find it dangerous to democracy. Thus, to the extent that the Law as Rhetoric trope points us towards a Ciceronian unity of ethics, politics, and aesthetics, it points us towards a world that we cannot have and perhaps should not want.

4.2 THE CONSERVATIVE MODEL OF RHETORIC

Bickel, Lincoln, and Burke

To understand the place of rhetoric in the Law and Literature movement, it is necessary to recur to the role of Alexander Bickel in American jurisprudence. As we argued in chapter 1, the Law and Literature movement had a crucial precursor in Bickel, who provided the most influential formulation of the recent hermeneutic

[45] Botein, "Cicero as Role Model," 320–21.
[46] Ibid., 287–88, 297–304.
[47] Ibid., 34–35.

crisis in American constitutionalism. For Bickel, the political and social crisis of
race relations precipitated by the Civil Rights movement was above all a problem
of judicial discretion to interpret the Constitution. The proper way to confront
this crisis was to treat it as a problem of judicial craft, and the best way to meet
this challenge to judicial craft was through ever greater artifice and ever more
subtle aesthetic vision. Drawing on such progressive precursors as Thayer, Cardozo, and Hand, as well as such contemporaries as Wechsler and Black, Bickel
offered the most fully developed example of the character of the judicial artist in
legal process writing, and he gave this character the leading role in his thought.
In this way he set the stage for the legal interpretation debate and the emergence
of a Law and Literature movement.

Bickel's jurisprudence was thoroughly classical in aesthetic sensibility and rhetorical in method. Bickel's aesthetic vision was *classical* in the sense that it sought
a balance of "principle" and "expedience," a reasonable course moderating the
opposing and equally dangerous passions of moral indolence and moral zeal; it
aimed at a controlled, deliberate, motion towards the good. Bickel's was an aesthetics of stoic self-restraint rather than Romantic self-expression. The Bickelian
judicial artist would not invent or impose new values, but would become a monu-
ment to enduring virtues, saying less than he thought and doing less than he might.
He would unite form and substance, cordially restricting himself to moderate
means in pursuing the ends of cordiality and moderation. Bickel's method was
rhetorical in the sense that it combined prudential reason with eloquence, in that
it aimed at reaffirming the normative basis of social solidarity, and in that it aimed
at modeling the political virtues of restraint, forbearance, and commitment to
deliberative dialogue.

Not only did Bickel *evoke* the classical rhetorical ideal in his sensibility and
method, he *invoked* the classical rhetorical ideal in offering Lincoln's leadership
as a model of the proper balance between prudence and principle. For Bickel, the
segregation cases exposed the "countermajoritarian difficulty"—the presumptive
democratic illegitimacy—of judicial review. It was no solution to argue, as Hamil-
ton and Marshall had, that judicial review simply imposed on the government the
constitutional constraints earlier enacted by the people, since the problem only
arose when a majority of the people did not wish to be so bound. The Hamilton-
Marshall argument was self-defeating because it conceded the crucial premise
that the only measure of legitimacy was popular will, thereby acquiescing in a
debased language of politics. A better response could be built on Lincoln's argument in his debates with Douglas: that democratic self-government had to be
constituted by principles independent of the will of the citizenry, else it was not
government at all, but merely license. In arguing that popular sovereignty meant
that a majority could "vote slavery up or down," Douglas was thereby perverting
political language and "corrupting" the "public mind."

Properly understood, democracy was not a license but a principle, imposing
constraints on majority will. Otherwise, by permitting the sequential disfran-
chisement or destruction of a succession of minorities, democracy could eventually destroy itself. Yet neither could self-government permit principle to stand

completely apart from the people and rule over it in the guise of a Platonic philosopher-king. That might be wise government, but not *self*-government. Nor would it necessarily be prudent even from the standpoint of principle, since taking the power to discern and apply principle from the people would encourage them to become irresponsible and hostile to principle. Because a dictatorship of principle cannot increase the authority of principle in the public mind, it is as corrupting to the public mind as licentious majoritarianism. Lincoln apparently associated abolitionism with such dictatorial principle. Principle had to prevail by persuasion rather than lawless violence to contribute to self-government.

Following Charles Black, Bickel argued that legitimacy is a feature of systems of government, not particular institutions such as judicial review. Judicial review, he reasoned, is justified insofar as it contributes to the legitimacy of the system as a whole, by judging majority will as principled or unprincipled. Were principle to simply overrule the majority and govern, it would destroy the system's majoritarian character and leave principle with nothing outside itself to legitimate. Legitimacy, Bickel implied, arises from the dialogue between institutions that forces majoritarian institutions to articulate the principles by which they govern. The purpose of principled review by the relatively powerless judiciary—Bickel's "Least Dangerous Branch"—is simply to force that dialogue. So the function of judicial review is to conserve a legitimating language of principle, by which the people may judge the products of their majoritarian politics. The "system" needed to produce legitimacy included not only institutions, but a popular culture of principled democratic deliberation—a virtuous "public mind." Thus, the role of the judiciary is to lead by persuasion, not coercion, and by example rather than regulation. Its function is rhetorical rather than dictatorial. Yet if the Court could not coerce at all, neither its message nor its model would compel attention. This is what Bickel calls "the Lincolnian tension."[48] Leadership of the public mind is a prudential art of the possible lying somewhere between command and persuasion.

The Lincolnian tension required a Lincolnian genius for moral leadership. This in turn required the rhetorical judgment to instruct without hectoring, and the ability to inspire tolerance and self-restraint by example more than by exhortation. Applying these lessons to the Court, Bickel reasoned that prudence and respect for self-governance dictate that in some cases, the justices, even if they know great truths, must refrain from saying or applying them. To avoid great tragic choices, the Court must sometimes decide not to decide because even though "no good society can be unprincipled," neither can any "viable society . . . be principle-ridden."[49] It is necessary to be, in Gerald Gunther's biting phrase, "a hundred percent principled twenty percent of the time."[50]

Yet there is no contradiction in an "occasional principle" if principles are themselves culturally contingent values rather than universal absolutes, received tru-

---

[48] Alexander Bickel, *The Least Dangerous Branch: The Supreme Court at the Bar of Politics* (Indianapolis: Bobbs-Merrill, 1962), 65–69.

[49] Bickel, *Least Dangerous Branch*, 64.

[50] Gerald Gunther, "The Subtle Vices of the Passive Virtues: A Comment on Principle and Expediency in Judical Review," *Columbia Law Review* 64 (1964): 1.

isms rather than revealed truths. Bickel implied this particularist view of principle in proclaiming himself a Burkean Whig.[51] He contrasted liberal contractarianism, rooted in Locke, and resting on pre-political rights and absolutist theories, with the Whigs' reliance on culture-bound social reality. For Bickel, the Whig disdains theory and absolutes, preferring a pragmatic, flexible, slow approach to legal change. He recognizes that the possibilities of social life are constrained by historical circumstance and human fallibility. The mature statesman learns that no principle can be an absolute, and that the call to moral zealotry is more likely the voice of sanctimony than of conscience, of self-doubt rather than self-confidence. Bickel suspected the liberal contractarian of moral puerility, of fearing the responsibilities of exercising judgment in a morally uncertain world. The liberal contractarian model assumes that ontologically independent rights and preferences can determine a scale of values and a set of rules by which all members of a society can be bound. The contractarian world, therefore, is moralistic, hyper-principled, authoritarian, and prone to catastrophic moral error. For Bickel, the very epitome of the contractarian is Chief Justice Taney, who, in his *Dred Scott* opinion, confidently read the Constitution as an arm's length contract among independent sovereign states who could not possibly have intended to alienate any of their power over property and personal status to the federal government.[52]

Bickel's Burkean model implies narrow jurisdiction for courts, limited to unavoidable incremental decisions when action allegedly violates a legal norm. By contrast, the liberal model relaxes jurisdiction to enable litigants to force the courts to prematurely decide matters of general and abstract principle. In Bickel's view, Burke opposed a politics of theory and theology in favor of the political arts of prudential compromise. For Burke, the rights of man were not pre-political values, but creatures of civil society best preserved by preserving the social order and the culture of civility that made them possible. Judging, then, must be narrow and incremental. The judge must model self-restraint and resist the egotistical temptation to destabilize constitutional liberty by uprooting it from the solid soil of social habit and setting it upon the fragile foundation of a contestable theory.

Jaffa's Lincoln

The choice of Lincoln as a model for the rhetorical function of the modern judge is an odd one. Certainly Lincoln was a great rhetorician and an important constitutional thinker, and his role in precipitating the Civil War Amendments gives him a particular authority in questions concerning their application. Yet Lincoln was the powerful elected leader of the *most* dangerous branch: his influence on events did not depend on rhetoric alone. Moreover, Lincoln could draw upon a wealth of intellectual and cultural resources for his grand rhetorical performances that are unavailable to contemporaries. Among these was the model of the American

---

[51] Alexander Bickel, *The Morality of Consent* (New Haven: Yale University Press, 1975), 3–4.
[52] Ibid., 36–37.

lawyer as Ciceronian statesman of culture. This conception of statesmanship was tied to a Whig constitutional vision of evolutionary change and social peace achieved through a capacious public rhetoric of legal principle and institutional conservation. But with the outbreak of civil war it appeared to have failed and become discredited. Bickel must reach back to Lincoln because there is no more recent exemplar of the Ciceronian ideal.

This gives Bickel's idealization of Lincoln a strange quality of multilayered anachronism: he appears to implausibly hold out as a model of the judicial role an inherently nostalgic cultural form that itself died a century ago. But rightly read, Bickel does not honor Lincoln as the last representative of an organic Ciceronian culture. Instead, Bickel honors him as the founder of a tradition of tragically displaced and alienated rhetoricians, Ciceronian statesmen in exile. And it is in this belated, alienated, exiled capacity that the Ciceronian statesman can serve as a model of the "passive virtues" of the "least dangerous branch." Bickel's revival of Lincoln is not so much an effort to restore a lost rhetorical culture as an effort to define a nobly tragic role for the rhetorical enchanter in the disenchanted and debased culture of modern mass society.

Bickel's invocation of Lincoln should therefore be seen as part of a mid-twentieth-century movement of rhetorical revival that acknowledged and lamented the disappearance of rhetoric's constitutive cultural conditions. The Lincoln on which Bickel relied was Lincoln as interpreted by this movement.

Bickel's acknowledged source for his interpretation of Lincoln was Harry Jaffa's *Crisis of the House Divided*.[53] Perhaps the single greatest modern work on rhetoric, Jaffa's masterpiece provides an essential link between the literary character of rhetoric and the rhetorical character of law. Its key theme is that Lincoln's greatness derived from his capacity for self-governance, and his rhetorical capacity to educate others in the spirit of self-governance.

"Self-governance" takes on three complexly related meanings throughout the speeches Jaffa recounts. It obviously refers to democracy, and on first hearing suggests simply freedom from the constraints of government by some superior authority. Yet inevitably it becomes, over the course of Lincoln's orations, the governance of passion through reason, whether by a self-disciplining individual or a moderate political movement. In that sense, Lincoln is drawing on the venerable traditions of classical rhetoric in which the orator would demonstrate his exposure to and his conquest of conflict in the very act of his oration, therefore "modeling" self-governance for his audience. But the concern with self-governance as an aspect of character is connected to the deeper constitutional theme of Lincoln's major speeches—the need to sustain the possibility of fulfilling high moral aspirations precisely through concessions to a parallel morality of prudence and expedience—through a self-governing constraint on the passion of the ideal aspired to, that accommodates the settled expectations of the majority.

[53] Harry Jaffa, *Crisis of the House Divided: An Interpretation of the Issues in the Lincoln-Douglas Debates* (Chicago: Univ. of Chicago Press, 1982).

Though Jaffa ultimately focuses on the great Lincoln-Douglas debates, he first treats two great earlier Lincoln speeches. The "Lyceum speech,"[54] Lincoln's first major address, is a defense of law as an instrument of social peace. Lincoln begins with a ritual invocation of the Founding Fathers, declaring that American liberties had not been earned by his contemporaries, but had been bequeathed by departed ancestors. Yet, he argues, these Founders were lucky to live in a time that gave scope for heroic creativity rather than imposing an obligation to conserve a legacy. Thus, in an ironic reversal, Lincoln implies that the Founders may have revolted out of a Caesarist desire for glory, rather than true republican virtue. And so now, he warns, Americans face a greater test than those Fathers faced—the threat of mob rule, and of a Caesar created by the mob. Recounting the murder of an abolitionist and other instances of lynching, Lincoln admonishes his audience that mob rule not only threatens direct violence, but also encourages those lawless in spirit to become lawless in practice, and finally discourages the virtuous from respecting government. The mob and Caesar, Lincoln warns, complement each other. The Lyceum speech is then a defense of the rule of law against all forms of arbitrary rule.

Lincoln frankly laments the infeasibility of discretionary justice, which, though superior to legal rules as an ideal, is inferior as a practical matter. Law, says Lincoln, is a means to justice because it is informed by the discretionary judgments of wise men. Indeed, men will accept abuses of law if they are tolerated rather than required or abetted by law. Hence, that all men are created equal is an abstract truth, whose implications had only been partly realized. Then, in explaining why the United States cannot abolish slavery outright, Lincoln argues that it would have been disastrous to try to achieve all that might and ought ultimately to be demanded in the name of justice, at least too soon. This is because, as with mob rule, so with abolition—its direct consequences are not the only consequences. It is equally wrong to believe that all that is sanctioned by law is right and that law should only sanction that which is right.

As Jaffa argues, the task of a leader is to find the point of coincidence between the moral demands that are dear to the men he would lead and their self-interests, and to turn this coincidence, not only against the unjust self-interests of others, but against the unjust self-interests of his own followers. The popular leader must be prepared to gratify the less-than-noble but not immoral demands of his would-be supporters if he is to have their support for the higher purposes of statemanship. To hold these meaner services in contempt is to abandon popular government to those who have only mean ends, and to make of popular government a mean thing. Men may be led toward higher purposes of which they are scarcely conscious, if those who hold these purposes first show concern for and ability to gratify their less noble demands. The moral zealot—including the abolitionist—despairs of this possibility of leading the public toward virtue, and so envisions a despotism of principle rather than self-governance according to principle.

[54] Ibid., 191–232, 236–45.

The truly virtuous do not claim to be so. Thus, while it is not literally true that all men are created equal, it is *rhetorically true* "because those who might with justice deny it have no motive to deny it, while those who do deny it can only do so because of an unjust motive."[55] The true leader, with the highest of ambitions and abilities, sees in the idea of equality the principle that requires of all the highest degree of moral self-government.

The next major oration, the Temperance address,[56] is a wryly ironic and even condescending speech in which Lincoln purports to feel grave moral concern about temperance with respect to mundane sumptuary pleasures. But in this tour de force the temperance theme gives Lincoln a chance to develop the theme of self-government further, and to exhibit more clearly the elements of his rhetoric. As Jaffa notes, the speech ultimately is not about liquor at all but about the right and wrong way to effect moral reform. Lincoln presents himself to a convention of the temperance movement as a fellow moral reformer—but, appropriately enough, a temperate one. He aims for control not of the body but of thought. And he only adopts the cause of temperance here for the sake of reaching this larger lesson. Lincoln suspected these moral zealots of a perverted sensualism, a morbid irreconcilability to earthly reality; and he was afraid of a movement that exploited misery for legislative ends rather than relieving it. Indeed, Lincoln hated theological denunciation of sinners, because his goal was friendship in civil society. So the irony is that much of the speech is an attack on the temperance movement as itself intemperate.

Jaffa uses these two early speeches to set up his main theme, which is how Lincoln, in his debates with Douglas, fulfilled his vision of self-government and prudential political morality.[57] Lincoln hated the Nebraska Bill because it encouraged the view that men should have slavery if they wanted it and because slavery engendered despotic manners. For Lincoln, freedom was conditional upon self-denial of the impulse to despotism. Douglas's doctrine of "popular sovereignty"—that Whites in the Western territories should decide by majority rule whether to have slavery—was less an opposing moral position than the abdication of any moral position and hence a dangerously exemplary failure of self-government. It not only denied that slavery was wrong, but also denied that men had an obligation to act on what they thought was right. It was a calculated indoctrination in moral incontinence.

Lincoln rejected abolitionism because he saw it, like the temperance movement, as a politics of moral purity, a zealotry fed by the same impulse to despotism it so piously opposed. While working towards higher principles moral reformers risked reducing principle to partisanship, righteously aiming to exclude all the "impure" from political participation. But for Lincoln the primary task of political leadership was to maintain and strengthen the opinion that alone secured the place

---

[55] Ibid., 222.
[56] Ibid., 245–72.
[57] Ibid., 305.

of principle. Lincoln believed that in a free society, in which opinions formed by speech are the basis of all government, it is idle to forbid changes in the government while permitting changes in the opinion upon which government rests.[58] It is one thing to tolerate slavery as an evil beyond the powers of a limited government to eradicate. It is quite another to permit its extension; worse to do so upon the ground that it is a matter of moral indifference; worst of all to treat this moral indifference as a principle, a "right" to choose. Lincoln articulated the danger of fascism that arises when the passion surrounding perceived principle attaches itself to private interest.

Thus, despite the tragic concessions to prudence the political idealist must make, Jaffa's Lincoln resists modern liberalism in two related senses. First, he is no utilitarian—he does not see politics as an efficacious balancing of private interests. Private motive always threatens public order; and it can be counteracted solely by the moral leadership of superior men who sacrifice private interest. Second, Lincoln resists the notion that the irreducible material of the constitutional order is a set of rights, for he fears the danger that the people will confuse their rights with their passions and mistake liberty for licentiousness. That was what was wrong with popular sovereignty. It was not true that desire created right; rather, people who wanted rights first had to respect those rights themselves. For, as Jaffa says, the whole struggle with Douglas revolved precisely around the question of the moral demands that must be obeyed by a people if the people themselves are to possess the title deeds to respect and obedience.[59] Jaffa reads Lincoln as teaching his audience that popular virtue must precede popular sovereignty.

Douglas, by contrast, fails in the role of public leader because of his disbelief in—and indeed his lack of—true self-governance. The doctrine of popular sovereignty, with its professed indifference to whether slavery survives or not, demonstrates what Jaffa calls Douglas's "incontinence"—not so much his lack of an *awareness* of the virtuous path but his failure to *adhere* to it. Jaffa's Lincoln catches Douglas in a gross inconsistency. Simply put, the doctrine of popular sovereignty is based on the norm of self-government, and slavery is the despotic government of others, and the licentious indulgence of the self. Put in constitutional terms, Douglas's attempts to protect the legal basis for a new territory rejecting slavery are inconsistent with his belief that the Constitution protects the rights of slaveowners against expropriation. Douglas, in other words, cannot resolve the tension between majoritarianism and constitutional limits on majority will. His Constitution is a house divided against itself, not just between slavery and freedom, but between popular will and private rights.

To Jaffa, both of these alternatives are corrupt because both root political authority in human will. The only consistent position is to root political authority in moral principle. On Jaffa's tendentious reading, Lincoln does exactly that. Lincoln shows that to have any stable meaning, popular sovereignty must presuppose

[58] Ibid., 306.
[59] Ibid., 321.

and be limited by the particular moral principle that all are created equal. This principle, enunciated in the Declaration of Independence, is Lincoln's "Apple of Gold" around which the "Silver Picture" of popular government is framed. But the larger point that Jaffa imputes to Lincoln is that political will is categorically subordinate to moral principle. Jaffa reads Lincoln as flattering his audience— these are after all election campaign speeches—by appearing to endorse popular sovereignty and liberty, but he endorses them only after redefining them as moral principles independent of human will. While appearing to court and defer to the will of his audience, Lincoln really defers only to his principles. Rightly understood, argues Jaffa, the Lincoln-Douglas debates are Socratic dialogues between reason and will, with reason, in the figure of Lincoln, utterly traducing will, in the figure of Douglas. Yet this understanding is available only if we read between the lines: had Lincoln made his true message explicit, it would have defeated itself by insulting the very audience he sought to persuade. By intemperately revealing the full depth of his commitment to principle, Lincoln would have weakened rather than strengthened the influence of principle on the public mind.[60]

Jaffa's argument is paradoxical. In the most obvious sense it is egalitarian. But on other levels it is elitist and even authoritarian. First, he asserts that value questions have right answers, and that those who correctly perceive and act on those answers merit political authority, while others do not. Second, he admonishes that the wise should not reason candidly with those who are in error, because this will diminish the influence of the wise. The proper attitude of the morally wise to the general public is benevolently manipulative. Yet third, just as the wise need not take Lincoln's argument entirely at face value, we would be wise not to take Jaffa's argument entirely at face value either. Jaffa presents equality as an absolute principle when comparing it with democratic will, because he argues that democracy *presupposes* equality. Thus, democracy, by presupposing a principle independent of popular will, refutes itself. But does democracy thereby establish the validity of the principle it presupposes? Does Jaffa really regard equality as an absolute? His reading of the Lyceum speech instead presents equality as a necessary governing principle in a modern age that disrespects authority. It provides an alternate basis for the inculcation of an edifying self-restraint. Thus, what is attractive about the "principle" of equality to Jaffa is primarily the fact that it is a principle and that as such, it restrains the will. "Equality" happens to be a principle demonstrably implicit in the irreverent culture of modernity, but its appeal to Jaffa is that taken as a principle, equality demands reverence and self-restraint. Principles appear to be intrinsic values, but Jaffa paradoxically values them as means to the intrinsic value of self-discipline. In this sense, the principle of equality is only the silver picture framed around the golden apple of obedience to reason. And thus equality's presentation to a modern public as a categorical principle is a benign deception, hiding the dangerous truths that equality is itself a contingent value and that people are unequal in the qualities of virtue and wisdom that most count.

[60] Ibid., 328–29.

318 *CHAPTER FOUR*

Like Jaffa's normative argument, his interpretive method also yields more than meets the eye. Jaffa reads between the lines of Lincoln's argument to discern a hidden message. He extends Lincoln's argument by defining the deep problem of the nature of self-government addressed by Lincoln and then engaging in his own Socratic dialectic to determine its right solution. He concludes that in defining the problem in this way Lincoln was implicitly inviting his listeners onto the path of Socratic self-examination that would lead towards its right understanding. And that right understanding is therefore the ultimate, hidden meaning of Lincoln's argument, available only to those virtuous enough to take this hard road and wise enough to understand where it has taken them. But in reading Lincoln in this way, Jaffa has ascribed a meaning to Lincoln's discourse defined neither by extrinsic evidence of his intentions, nor by the likely reactions of Lincoln's audience (most of whom are, one hopes, deceived). This may appear to be simply the standard new critical procedure of eschewing intentional and affective in favor of formal interpretation that hews to the "data" of the text. But Jaffa's method is instead classical. To Jaffa, the meaning of Lincoln's text is given by the nature of the subject on which Lincoln discourses. Lincoln's speeches, like all great texts, gesture beyond themselves and disclose the nature of things. And so too with Jaffa's book. What appears to be a historical investigation into the subjective opinions of Lincoln is a secret treatise on the objective truths of reason.

Socratic Teaching and Esoteric Writing: The Straussian Model

Jaffa's purposes are clearer if they are interpreted in light of the teachings of his mentor, the conservative political philosopher Leo Strauss.[61] A German Jewish refugee who had studied with Husserl and Heidegger, Strauss came to the University of Chicago in 1949 and soon collected around himself a circle of historians of political philosophy devoted to his methods. More than any contemporary philosopher, Strauss reached back to classical models of dialectic and rhetoric as expressions of natural values but also as desirable methods for instilling those values in those able to receive them. Strauss advocated the close textual study of the classics as a prerequisite to authentic philosophical thinking. He argued that to help free our minds from modern prejudices, we must encounter alien modes of writing, especially the classics. For Strauss, self-critical reading of classical texts was the proper path to spiritual liberation.

Strauss conceived of political philosophy as a civic responsibility imposed by the dangerous incoherence of modern liberalism, which he believed provided no

---

[61] Strauss's views are best revealed in Leo Strauss, *The Rebirth of Classical Political Rationalism* (Chicago: Univ. of Chicago Press, 1989); *Persecution and the Art of Writing* (Glencoe, Ill.: Free Press, 1952); *Natural Right and History* (Chicago: Univ. of Chicago Press, 1953); *Liberalism, Ancient and Modern* (New York: Basic Books, 1968); *On Tyranny* (New York: Free Press, 1963), *What Is Political Philosophy?* (Westport, Conn: Greenwood, 1973); and *The City and Man* (Chicago: Univ. of Chicago Press, 1978).

adequate defense against the dual menaces of fascism and communism.[62] Strauss taught that modern liberalism is premised on the fact-value distinction. Thus, liberalism assumes that there can be no truth of the matter about values, and that scientific truth is value-free. Yet, Strauss argued, this assumption is merely a dogma. Thus, while modern liberalism purports to value open inquiry it is in fact closed-minded on value questions. Furthermore, since value relativism has not been established as true by open-minded inquiry, it follows that its sources lie elsewhere—in an excessive egalitarianism that presumes that all opinions are equally wise, and in a licentiousness that presumes that we have only the responsibilities we choose. Thus, Strauss concluded, value relativism is actually an expression of the self-indulgent values associated with pure democracy and the cult of popular opinion. Since value relativism is merely a value rather than a scientific truth, it contradicts itself. Moreover, Strauss argued, the value neutrality to which science aspires is a chimera, as the classically inspired Nietzsche and Heidegger conclusively demonstrated. Indeed, Strauss thought the profundity of these relativist critiques of modern scientific rationality had left political liberalism with neither the will nor the wherewithal to defend itself against totalitarian populism. This, concluded Strauss, was unfortunate because although modern liberalism lacked virtue and conviction, it had genuine achievements—prosperity, tolerance, and order—worthy of defense.

Strauss challenged liberals who professed to be committed to open inquiry to test their faith in value relativism and value neutrality against the ancient view that value questions have true answers, and to accept the latter view if, after open debate, it proved superior. But, reasoned Strauss, sincere and intellectually serious expressions of the view that values are subject to rational debate were unlikely to be found in modern liberal society, whose members were products of their debased political institutions. Strauss therefore invited modern liberals to engage the great minds of the ancient world—Plato paradigmatically—in dialogue. But to learn what the ancients have to teach, moderns must try to understand the ancients on their own terms, free of modern prejudices and preconceptions. They must be especially careful to abandon their faith in the progress of knowledge, a faith that would tempt them to condescend to these ancient texts. They must humble themselves and accept the guidance of those already initiated into the mysteries of ancient wisdom.

Strauss taught that understanding ancient philosophers on their own terms requires careful attention to their terminology and premises, the rival views they debated, and the characteristics and concerns of the audience they addressed. Yet this rhetorical context was to be gleaned primarily from the language and rhetoric of the texts themselves. Moreover, to understand a classical text in light of its

---

[62] Thomas Pangle and Nathan Tarcov, "Epilogue: Leo Strauss and the History of Political Philosophy," in *History of Political Philosophy*, ed. Leo Strauss and Joseph Cropsey (Chicago: Univ. of Chicago Press, 1987), 907–9; see generally Leo Strauss, *On Tyranny* (Ithaca: Cornell Univ. Press, 1968).

own premises is to remember that its author and original readers equated the understanding of a text with the true understanding of its subject, rather than with understanding of the subjective will of its author. An ancient text cannot be understood without being taken seriously as a challenge to one's own views. To understand the text is to consider the subject itself and to decide if the proposed view of it is true.[63]

Close attention to the rhetoric of ancient texts reveals that they operate at different levels of meaning, addressing different audiences in different ways. In their apparent, or "exoteric," meanings they defer to traditional authority and historically received values or to popular opinion. In their "esoteric meanings" they exalt untrammeled reason and universal truth. This dualistic rhetorical structure at once embodies and teaches wisdom. Esoteric writing covertly implies the following unstated argument:

1. Truth, reason, and the good are distinct from mere opinion.
2. Reason is dangerous to constituted authority, and hence to social order.
3. Social order is inherently valuable.
4. The good is difficult to discern, even for the wise.
5. Therefore social order cannot await discovery of, or consensus about, the good.
6. Therefore prudence requires the sustenance of social orders not founded upon reason, until reason can prevail.
7. Not everyone is capable of wisdom and not every capable person has attained wisdom.
8. Hence, prudence alone will not suffice to motivate everyone to sustain social orders not founded in reason.
9. Nor will reason alone persuade everyone to build social orders founded in reason.
10. Hence, among those who have not attained wisdom, support for imperfect social orders must be sustained by faith in tradition, or opinion, or some other such arbitrary value.

For these reasons, the esoteric expression of the eternal truths of reason must masquerade as the exoteric flattery of prevailing opinion. In this way, truth will be revealed only to those initiates capable of using it prudently rather than destructively.[64]

To understand ancient texts in Straussian terms is to grasp and take seriously not only their esoteric claims about what is universally true, but their prudential assumptions about why it is necessary to express these truths esoterically. Thus, to understand the texts is to reflect on one's own responsibilities as a person of discernment who has been intitated into privileged knowledge. It is to take seriously not only the notion that there are moral truths, but also that there is a pruden-

---

[63] Pangle and Tarcov, "Epilogue: Leo Strauss," 912–14.
[64] Strauss, *Persecution and the Art of Writing*; Pangle and Tarcov, "Epilogue: Leo Strauss," 914–15.

tial morality of truth telling. It follows that the polyvalence and deceptiveness of rhetoric need not imply its amorality. The very deceptiveness of rhetoric may indicate its profound moral insight.[65]

It was Strauss's view that by hiding their truths, ancient texts engage the open-minded reader in a dialogic and pedagogic process of initiation into rational knowledge and moral wisdom, a process that moves from condescending flattery to candid debate, and so from contingent opinion to knowledge of what is universally and permanently true. This process of initiation into esoteric mysteries is designed to have a pleasurable quality of suspense that cultivates an erotic passion for knowledge.[66] The cultivation of this noble passion restrains baser passions by sublimation rather than mere abstinence. Once the pupil experiences the pleasure of pursuing knowledge, he will value the admission of his own ignorance and error as the condition of the pleasure of instruction. This acknowledgment of ignorance is the beginning of wisdom. The open-minded pupil will move from sophomoric arrogance to humble respect, or from deference to the authority of tradition to deference to the authority of reason; he or she will also move from narcissistic prolixity to self-disciplined discretion. She will be not just intellectually, but passionately, attached to the good.

On the Straussian model, the rhetorical form of ancient philosophy reveals that philosophy is itself a political regime in which wisdom guides and governs ignorance, and which—like all political regimes—produces a distinctive character. An additional function of rhetoric is conservation: conserving authority by keeping the powerful weapon of skeptical inquiry in the hands of the prudent, and conserving the philosophical truth by making it harmless to authority. The Straussian conception of rhetoric as pedagogy presumes that there is a truth of the matter in politics, and that the ultimate ground of political authority is not democratic will but natural right. From this perspective, democratic participation in politics is valuable only instrumentally, as a check against tyranny. The proposition that citizens have an inherent right to govern themselves is an error, since legitimate governance depends upon wisdom. While some interpreters of the classical tradition assert that political participation builds civic character, Straussians counter that this depends on the character of the polity. In modern society, at least, good character is best inculcated by pedagogy, rather than egalitarian deliberation.

It should be apparent that Jaffa's interpretation of Lincoln, on which Bickel relied, is an exemplary "esoteric" reading in the Straussian tradition. Strauss's influence of course extended well beyond Jaffa and has shaped the teaching of the political philosophy and the classics at many North American universities. Strauss's most visible disciple was Allan Bloom, whose controversial attack on the moral relativism of American higher education, *Closing of the American Mind*,[67] unabashedly asserted the elitism of the search for truth. This popular

---

[65] Strauss, *What Is Political Philosophy*, 221–32; Pangle and Tarcov, "Epilogue: Leo Strauss," 926.

[66] Pangle and Tarcov, "Epilogue: Leo Strauss," 920–26, and passages from Strauss's works cited therein.

[67] Allan Bloom, *Closing of the American Mind* (New York: Simon and Schuster, 1987).

polemic called upon American education to recapture the spirit, and indeed the actual methods, of the Platonic dialogue. Though truth seekers could come from any group, race, or class, their common goal should be to transcend circumstance and accident, to overcome dependence on history and culture, to live immune to the noise of history in the quest for natural justice: "They become the models for the use of the noblest human faculties and hence are benefactors to all of us, more for what they are than for what they do. Without their presence . . . no society . . . can be called civilized."[68] Admission to this exclusive circle requires acknowledgement that there are certain things audiences and readers simply must accept to understand truth-seeking writers and speakers. Yet in a typical Straussian rhetorical formulation, this acceptance on faith of the pedagogic authority of an elite and its Platonic metaphysics is presented as unbiased open-mindedness.

Bloom particularly attacks what he sees as the twisted relativism and skepticism of modern higher education. Students reduce all disagreements in the search for truth to unresolvable differences of perspective, opinion, and culture. By contrast, their teachers purport to destroy their prejudices with searing analytic skepticism, and yet have nothing to offer in return. But students, argues Bloom, may have to be *induced* to have prejudices that they deeply believe in before they learn how to overcome prejudices, because the absence of professed prejudices is the sign of value-nihilism, a false openness.[69] Bloom wants us to acknowledge that every educational system has a moral goal that it tries to attain and that informs its curriculum. It wants to produce a certain kind of human being. For example, the original model individual in American culture was a rights bearer, one whose rights gave scope to a spirit of righteousness. But the rights model has now decayed into a permissive tolerance that indulges others without respecting them because it neither disciplines nor respects the self.

A less visible but, for law, more important adherent was George Anastaplo.[70] Anastaplo presents the intriguing example of a Straussian resister of McCarthyism. Anastaplo was for several decades denied admission to the Illinois bar because he refused to answer the then-obligatory question about any Communist affiliations. Though he had nothing to hide, he did have something to demonstrate: a Socratic refusal to acquiesce in the intolerance of the state where he believed that intolerance ill-served the civic-humanist project of modeling good character. Instructively, then, Anastaplo fell into a debate with Jaffa, who denounced Communism in the very same terms that he denounced Nazism. As Anastaplo discerned, the debate between him and Jaffa was about the relative importance of two strands of the natural rights theme immanent in their revered Declaration of Independence. For Jaffa, the key value was equality. For Anastaplo, it was liberty.[71]

---

[68] Ibid., 21.

[69] Ibid., 41–43.

[70] George Anastaplo, *Human Being and Citizen: Essays on Virtue, Freedom, and the Common Good* (Chicago: Swallow Press, 1975), 43.

[71] Ibid., 64–71.

How did this abstract distinction play itself out in contemporary politics? For Jaffa, the great sin of Nazism was its hierarchy of humanity—treating the Aryans as superior and others as inferior and therefore less deserving of fair treatment. And, says Anastaplo, Jaffa then illogically found an analogy in Communism's elevation of the proletariat as "the sole subject of moral right" over other classes of society. According to Anastaplo, Jaffa's one-dimensional interpretation of the Declaration blinded him to the patent inadequacy of this analogy. More important, Anastaplo complained that Jaffa's refusal to see Communism's "equal" denial of human liberty also blinded him to the inconsistency between virulent (and intemperate!) anti-Communism and the very rhetorical civic model that both he and Jaffa embraced. Anastaplo argued that we must open ourselves to the intellectually legitimate—even if incorrect—political views of the Communists.[72] This was true not just because their position might prove instructive, but also because intolerance of it reflects—and induces—a loss of self-confidence in us and a fraying of our public life. Anastaplo argues that the *rhetor* can invoke the liberty principles of free speech not as a form of promiscuous intellectual permissiveness, but rather as a method of stern instruction in the civic virtue of tolerance.

One of Anastaplo's key themes in reviewing the work of Jaffa and Strauss is that both men sought to unite the teachings of our two great sources for the Western tradition—Jersualem and Athens. For Anastaplo, Jaffa's Old Testament–like authoritarianism in the face of subversive ideas caused him to undervalue the confidence the Athenian model offers us in sweet reason leading us to the truth.[73] Yet Anastaplo may underestimate the authoritarianism inherent even in his own tolerant version of Straussian pedagogy. For Anastaplo, the United States "is alone of modern states in being the product of human deliberation applied to political problems." Thus, in Anastaplo's republic, reason rather than will is the ultimate authority. Debate is open—to all who are faithful to this conception of a deliberative polity, constituted by debate not about will or interest or policy, but about the true meaning of liberty, equality, and justice. These questions constitute a polity belonging "to the people who think about them—to the people, that is, who understand, refine, and, if need be, revive the heritage which has been handed down even to this generation."[74] American democracy, then, does *not* belong to the many adherents of the common view that political questions are ultimately subjective matters of will, opinion, and interest.

The Academic Revival of Rhetoric in This Century

As we have noted, the late nineteenth century was a time of declining prestige for the academic study of rhetoric. Where present at all in American universities, rhetoric was most often taught in English departments. In 1914 teachers of rhetoric formed a national association under the leadership of James Winans of Cornell

---

[72] Ibid., 68–69.
[73] Ibid., 72–73.
[74] Ibid., 45.

and James O'Neill of Dartmouth and began to lobby for the creation of speech departments. Not until the 1920s was there any serious revival of rhetorical scholarship, when Charles Sears Baldwin of Columbia began to publish on ancient and medieval rhetoric. In the 1940s "communication" courses and departments began to proliferate, and speech teachers began to exert an influence over the teaching of composition in English departments. Kenneth Burke began to draw on Aristotelian rhetoric, and finally an aggressive "school" of rhetorical criticism developed in the literature and classics departments at the University of Chicago, under the leadership of R. S. Crane, Richard McKeon, Richard Weaver, and Wayne Booth.[75]

THE CHICAGO CRITICS

Upon Strauss's arrival, the University of Chicago already had an active community of scholars devoted to the study of classical rhetoric. According to the history offered by its key member R. S. Crane,[76] there arose between the world wars a school of rhetorical critics who sought to revive the academic study of rhetoric at a time when the study of literature was becoming the anchor of institutional study of the humanities. These "Chicago Critics" lamented that the growing field of literary studies was increasingly ignoring the traditionally edifying function of the humanities, in favor of various forms of subjectivism and scientism: psychology, topical historical research, and value-free formal analysis. The literary critic had become more of an academic technician and was no longer the key figure in the maintenance of culture and value envisioned by Matthew Arnold.[77]

The Chicago Critics sought to revive the humanities and to insulate them from the sciences. Though rigorously concerned with methods of argument, they opposed science in the sense that they opposed reconsidering foundational assumptions. The impulse to tear down and rebuild on objective foundations impaired not only the ability to believe in received values but even the ability to comprehend and appreciate them as aspects of an integral cultural whole. Thus, they shared the Straussian view that scientific rationality was a kind of blinding prejudice. Like the Straussians they saw themselves from the outset as an isolated minority, battling against the current. But where the Straussians saw themselves primarily as Socratic dialecticians in pursuit of the absolute, the Chicago Critics saw themselves as Aristotelians chiefly concerned with understanding texts as practical action rendered meaningful or authoritative by the contingent purposes of particular communities. They particularly drew inspiration from Aristotle's focus on discrete forms of discourse serving distinctive purposes, and within the poetic form, his focus on discrete genres, practices of writing imposing constraints of conventional form and social function that confronted authors with distinctive aesthetic challenges.[78] They used an Aristotelian vision of a discourse

---

[75] Connors, Ede, and Lunsford, "The Revival of Rhetoric."

[76] R. S. Crane, Introduction to *Critics and Criticism: Ancient and Modern*, ed. R. S. Crane et al. (Chicago: Univ. of Chicago Press, 1952), 1–26.

[77] They include such figures as W. R. Keast, Richard McKeon, Elder Olson, Norman Maclean, and Bernard Weinberg.

[78] Crane, Introduction to *Critics and Criticism*, 12–13.

divided into discrete rhetorics to account for their own Aristotelian enterprise within modern criticism.

The Chicago rhetoricians delicately confronted a pluralism of critical theories in the modern academic world. Though they recognized that no one critical theory could dominate, they would in any event have been wary of promoting a single "theory" precisely because any such theory would likely rely on the key premise of most of the then-current theories—the notion of criticism as the play of the critic's mind upon constant objects or aesthetic data. This premise united two enemies of the rhetoricians—science and Romanticism.[79] Indeed, the Chicago Critics were determined to avoid the scientistic terminology of theory and data. Instead, they talked of multiple "languages" of criticism. A "language" is the specialized discourse of a community engaged in a common practice, organized around shared purposes and problems, with its own traditions and articles of faith. It is, in short, a *rhetoric*. As classical rhetoric presupposed the polis, so a "language" of discourse presupposes a social context, although in the postclassical world it might be a church, a profession, or an intellectual movement.

From this perspective, criticism, as opposed to mere aesthetic perception or appreciation, had to be reasoned *discourse*, a "rhetoric of terms and propositions—depending as much on factors operative in the construction of the discourse itself as upon the object or the mind and circumstances of the author."[80] Rather than responding to literary "data," a critic chooses a frame of discourse, which then constructively delimits what he can say about any literary work. So in evaluating a critic, we try to describe her "rhetorical grammar," the characteristic form of her argument's movement. Does the critic move from general principles to applications by dialectical division and then resolution? Or from observed effects via causal inference? For Crane, our goal must be to determine the sense and assess the validity of the critic's arguments, but to do so we must recognize "the necessary relativity of all critical utterances" and observe the critic's choice of basic terms and operational devices.

To understand a text on its own terms, it was necessary to reconstruct the tradition to which it contributed, the audience it addressed, and the shared purposes and problems that united that audience. This might involve historical research, but the critic should resist the temptation to focus through the text on social conditions because she will almost certainly fail to understand those social conditions as the author did. If the critic began with historical research she would either force into the text her own view of the author's historical circumstances, or reduce the text to nonsense.

For the Chicago Critics, understanding the text on its own *terms* meant exactly that: it meant identifying pivotal terms of value in the text itself, and then reading the text as a performative argument about how these terms should properly be used. Thus, the Chicago Critics read rhetorically, treating each text as a contribution to a dialogue within a particular community not only about how its members

---

[79] Ibid., 13–15, 22.
[80] Ibid., 6–7.

should act but also about how they should speak and deliberate. To read in this way enabled one to map the parameters of the discourse to which the author sought to contribute. To grasp what an author *did* say it was first necessary to know what an author writing in that "language" *could* say.

Criticism of a poetic work involves an inquiry into its constitutive elements, a taxonomy of its working parts and organizing purpose:

> The undeniable fact [is] that what a poet does *distinctly as a poet* is not to express himself or his age or to resolve psychological or moral difficulties or to communicate a vision of the world or to provide entertainment or to use words in such-and-such ways . . . but rather, by means of his art, to build materials of language and experience into wholes of various kinds to which, as we experience them, we tend to attribute final rather than merely instrumental value.[81]

The key phrases in this passage are "wholes of various *kinds*," "language *and experience*," and "final rather than *merely* instrumental significance." Rhetorical critics agreed with their contemporaries the New Critics that poems were aesthetic wholes with intrinsic value. But the wholes were not isolated artifacts, and their aesthetic integrity depended upon a fit between form and social purpose, or desired effect. These social purposes were always more specific than the writing of "poetry," and the forms were always generic forms integrating the entire work rather than assemblages of formal elements. These forms made works "more than the sums of their parts,"[82] and indeed these parts were "necessary constituent elements"[83] of different "species,"[84] of works or "possible kinds of poetic wholes."[84] Both literary works and literary genres then were ideal objects, each possessed of an essence. This means that for the Aristotelian critics, the different schools of criticism were not simply different perspectives on poetry. Aristotelian criticism purported to disclose a metaphysical reality that other critical rhetorics lacked the conceptual vocabulary to discern. This was the different set of assumptions and purposes that distinguished the rhetoric of Aristotelian criticism from the rhetorics of science and Romantic subjectivism.

THE SERMONIC SPEECH OF RICHARD WEAVER

For one of the Chicago School's key spokesman, Richard Weaver, rhetoric was more than just one critical approach to literature alongside others. It was and should remain a distinctive discipline. It should have its own department, and courses in rhetoric should be the heart of the undergraduate curriculum. Weaver's ideas have served defenders of "speech" departments as well as those seeking to raise the professional status of teachers of composition.

[81] Ibid., 13.
[82] Ibid., 14.
[83] Ibid., 20.
[84] Ibid., 13.

For Weaver, the Chicago Critics provided a response to a crisis of values in Western civilization signaled by the declining prestige of rhetoric,[85] the ascendance of science, the rise of totalitarianism and bureacratic social planning, and the totemistic authority of liberal abstractions like "democracy."[86] Rhetoric had once meant the art of persuading people to adopt and act on right attitudes, and it had thereby required more skill and wisdom than "subject courses." By contrast, "Literature" was once viewed as merely an informational subject anyone could teach. But the academic roles had become reversed, the literary critic now enjoying the mystery of cult and craft, all, says Weaver, because of a change in the image of man toward the scientistic. "Rhetorical Humanism" had fallen into disparagement.

For Weaver, the task of language is to be *sermonic*. While rationality is an indispensable part of humanism, humanism "includes emotionality, or the capacity to feel and suffer, to know pleasure, and . . . the capacity for aesthetic satisfaction, and, what can only be suggested, a yearning to be in relation to something infinite."[87] Rhetoric, Weaver argues, is the "most humanistic of the humanities" since it speaks to the "whole man," and always to a particular audience in a particular context. For Weaver, all language use is rhetoric, an attempt to influence others motivated by purposes. Even the pure scientist is moved by some motive about the role of science. All people are naturally rhetoricians

> because they are born into history, with an endowment and a passion and a sense of the *ought*. There is ever some discrepancy, however slight, between the situation man is in and the situation he would like to realize. His life is therefore characterized by movement toward goals. It is largely the power of rhetoric which influences and governs that movement.[88]

Properly understood, rhetoric is the art of motivating to the good. It may be combined with understanding where knowledge is likely to be used wisely. But Weaver agreed with Strauss that rhetoric may be combined with obfuscation, where knowledge is dangerous. Two lectures from *The Ethics of Rhetoric* make the point.

In "The Phaedrus and the Nature of Rhetoric,"[89] Weaver derives a Platonic defense of rhetoric from a dialogue that does not appear to be about rhetoric at all, but about love. But the view of love that Socrates is here challenging is a defense of dispassion as conducing to rationality, objectivity, and impartiality. Weaver likens this to the dispassionate speech of modern scientific writing and so likens rhetoric to passion, because it is partial, "inclined." Socrates encounters Phaedrus fresh from hearing the eloquent, seductive defense by Lysias of dispas-

---

[85] Richard M. Weaver, "Language Is Sermonic," in Johannesen, *Contemporary Theories of Rhetoric*, 163–79.

[86] Weaver, *Ethics of Rhetoric*, 211–32.

[87] Weaver, "Language Is Sermonic," 165.

[88] Ibid., 176.

[89] Weaver, *Ethics of Rhetoric*, 3–26.

sion. To be moved by eloquence to such a view is already, for Weaver, to be caught in contradiction. Socrates responds with an alternative attack on love, not as a loss of reason by the lover, but as an exploitative consumption of the beloved that in seeking to trap the beloved in dependence weakens and demeans rather than strengthens and ennobles him. Love on these terms is false friendship, akin to manipulative and deceptive rhetoric that seeks to win the hearer's assent to what is not best for him. But, Socrates proceeds, it is also false love. True love loves not the tangibility of the body, but its qualities of beauty and strength and health; not the agreeableness of the mind, but its reason; not the licentiousness of the character, but its virtue. Hence, true love puts itself in the service of improving and ennobling the beloved, of moving it to realize its ideal potential. This is the proper function of rhetoric as well: passionate friendship aimed at improving the mind and character of the hearer. And indeed Socrates illustrates his redefinition of love with an elaborate rhetorical figure, likening the properly moved soul to a charioteer. Weaver continues that true rhetoric contains two elements: a dialectic effort that establishes what is just or good, and a further effort to motivate the pursuit of the just or the good. To do this it must exert the imagination to "prophesy" the ideal potential to be realized by the pursuit of the good. This should not be seen as exaggeration or fiction because within classical metaphysics the potential and the ideal were as real as the actual.

That persuasion to the good does not always entail enlightenment is evident from Weaver's defense of William Jennings Bryan's rhetorical performance during his prosecution of Scopes for teaching evolution in the famous "Monkey Trial." The gist of Bryan's position, and Weaver's, was that regardless of its truth, evolution could plausibly be regarded as a morally dangerous doctrine. The linchpin of Bryan's argument, according to Weaver, was a Socratic effort to catch his opponent Clarence Darrow in a contradiction. In the Leopold-Loeb trial, Darrow had famously used determinist arguments to mitigate the guilt of the two murderers. Darrow had suggested that these wealthy young intellectuals should be seen as impressionable young men who had tried to act out the Nietzschean ideal of the superman they had been taught in college. Bryan attempted to link Nietzschean and Darwinian thought in making an argument that evolutionism was a dangerous doctrine. Weaver quotes Bryan on evolution:

> It is this doctrine that gives us Nietzsche, the only great author who tried to carry this to its logical conclusion, and we have the testimony of my distinguished friend from Chicago in his speech in the Leopold and Loeb case that 50,000 volumes have been written about Nietzsche, and he is the greatest philosopher in the last hundred years, and have him pleading that because Leopold read Nietzsche and adopted Nietzsche's philosophy of the superman, that he is not responsible for the taking of human life. We have the doctrine . . . that the universities that had it taught, and the professors who taught it, are much more responsible for the crime that Leopold committed than Leopold himself.[90]

[90] Ibid., 37.

Having conceded that a profound philosophy could be morally dangerous, Darrow could not deny that the same might be true of a scientific truth; nor could he deny that a legislature could rationally proscribe the teaching of such a dangerous truth. Natural science should therefore be esoteric knowledge, available only to those morally educated to resist its misuse. Weaver finds implicit in Bryan's argument an Aristotelian view of truth as polydimensional. From such an Aristotelian perspective, the natural history of humanity could never be more than a partial truth, describing humanity's material and efficient causes, but not its formal or final causes, its equally real ideal and potential. Thus, to allow natural scientists to teach what they regarded as the exclusive truth about the human species to impressionable children might preclude the children from learning the morally more important truths taught by religion.

The Conservative Model Summarized

1. Conservative rhetoricians oppose classical thought to modern thought, and so oppose rhetoric to both the subjectivism of Romantic literature and the objectivism of science. In the eyes of conservative rhetoricians, both of these concern themselves with mere facts, whether psychological or physical. Rhetoric directs our attention not to what is, but what should be.

2. Conservative rhetoricians apparently adhere to a classical metaphysics made up of natural wholes, classes, and values. Yet it is not always clear whether they believe that this metaphysics is true or merely that it is useful to the maintenance of desirable forms of social authority.

3. Conservative rhetoricians regard the question of how to speak as a practical, political question, primarily. While they add that speech is also an ethical reflection on the speaker's character, it is not always clear whether virtuous character is an end in itself or merely a resource of persuasion.

4. Conservative rhetoricians present themselves as open-minded pluralists, seeking to make room for classical ideas in modern debate rather than to replace modern ideas. Yet this position may simply reflect an effort to exploit the vulnerabilities of liberal ideas like value relativism, value neutrality, and tolerance. And it may reflect the awareness of these rhetoricians that classical ideas are unlikely to prevail with the general public in a modern liberal state. In any case, their teachings are not primarily directed at the public but at intellectual and political elites.

5. Conservative rhetoricians place relatively little value on candor, which they associate with incontinent self-revelation and an irresponsible disregard for how information may be misused.

6. Conservative rhetoricians place rhetoric within a narrative of cultural decay and corruption. They tend to associate together as corrupting forces Romantic individualism, hedonism, populism, empirical science and social science, and social planning. Although they value property as tying self-interest to social order and authority, they seem hostile to market bases of valuation. Rhetoric properly

functions to conserve excellence—the authority of natural values or intellectual elites—against these reductionist and leveling tendencies.

7. Conservative rhetoricians see themselves as a relatively powerless intellectual elite—a "least dangerous" elite—that must ally with and civilize other sources of political power in order to conserve itself and its values.

8. Conservative rhetoricians see the structure of rhetorical discourse as hierarchical. For those interlocutors unfit for initiation into wisdom, rhetoric serves to deceive and mollify. For those fit for instruction, rhetoric is pedagogic. Yet it does not deliver its lesson directly or expeditiously. A lengthy, suspenseful, and eroticized process of initiation serves to confirm the charismatic authority of the teachers and to socialize the pupils to deference and patience. Thus, conservative rhetoric is a performative pedagogy that teaches the lesson of authority first and foremost.

4.3 Is a Liberal Rhetoric Possible?

Constituting Liberal Values

If the conservative model of legal rhetoric rejects the elision of classical rhetoric and Romantic literature, the liberal model is quite willing to indulge the overlap of the literary and the rhetorical. Where the conservative model opposes classical to modern thought, the liberal model opposes the humanities to the sciences within modern thought. Thus, for the conservative model, the Romantic self-expression so prevalent in modern literature is just another form of hedonism, no more noble than utilitarianism or welfare economics. All of these indulge appetite and reduce the transcendent potential of human nature to brute facts. But for liberal rhetoricians, literature is the core of the humanities and opposes the brute facticity of natural and social science. Thus, when liberal rhetoricians refer to the subjects of politics and law as "rhetoric," they claim them for the humanities as opposed to the social sciences.

The general claim of liberal rhetoricians of law is that law and literature are parallel cultural phenomena; both are efforts to shape reality through language, and both are concerned with ambiguity, interpretation, and necessarily imprecise judgment. Rather than stressing the difference between rhetoric and literature, scholars of this model hold that rhetoric is the aspect or element of law that operates "in the place where law and literature meet."[91] The major practitioner of this liberal version of the rhetorical criticism of law, James B. White, argues that law

> is most usefully seen not, as it usually is by academics and philosophers, as a system of rules, but as a branch of rhetoric, and that the kind of rhetoric of which law is a species is most usefully seen not, as rhetoric usually is, either as a failed science or as the ignoble art of persuasion, but as the central art by which community and culture are established, maintained and transformed. So regarded, rhetoric is continuous with law, and like it, has justice as its ultimate object.[92]

[91] Weaver, "Language Is Sermonic," 178.
[92] White, "Law as Rhetoric," 684.

White complains that with the death of religious authority in law, the influence of social science has left law in the grip of value neutrality. In the bureaucratic conception of law now dominant in the West, law runs societies according to "policy science," designed and implemented by supposedly neutral cost-benefit calculators. Citizens are reduced to the roles of either expressing or serving preferences. Rhetoric, if acknowledged at all, is reduced to deception or manipulation in a corrupt political market.[93]

If conservative rhetoric responds to this predicament by seeking to conserve authority, rather than accept its death, a liberal rhetoric instead seeks to create authority anew, in a a discursive process that is open rather than dogmatic, and egalitarian rather than hierarchical. It is this aim of creating new values that suggests the analogy to literary creation. Just as the Romantic artist creates herself anew in disciplining herself to create art, the political community can aspire to re-create itself through the discipline of deliberation. It can re-create its lost sense of common identity and common purpose as something collectively willed rather than received or imposed.

In associating rhetoric with literature, liberal rhetoricians assert rhetoric's openness to the new. They present it as compatible with modernity. To speak of rhetoric in this way is to de-emphasize rhetoric's history as a limited and limiting repertoire of oratorical conventions, but instead to associate rhetoric with the creative choices a speaker inevitably makes in constructing a discourse. Thus conceived, "rhetoric" refers to style, figuration, narrative suspense, emotional appeal, all the ways in which the medium may modify the message. Rhetoric then comes to stand for the contingency of what is said on how it is said. Hence, it becomes associated with the subjectivity of meaning and value, and with creative possibility. Gerald Wetlaufer invokes this literary conception of rhetoric in associating rhetoric with complexity, contingency, and uncertainty:[94]

> If the purpose of a judicial decision is to close what has been open, the motive behind literature is to likely to be the desire to open what has been closed. Thus, literature is likely to celebrate and explore the problematic, the uncertain, the ambiguous, the subjective, the irrational, the insoluble. It will, at least usually, acknowledge and examine the multiplicity of perspectives and the personal contingency of reality. . . . Indeed, it will confront the limits of knowledge and reason, often casting the rational and logical man not as the hero but as the fool.[95]

But if rhetoric is reconceived as a force for openness and contingency, how can it underwrite the authority of law? Can a liberal rhetoric of law eschew reliance on ethical and metaphysical orthodoxy, while also avoiding the audience-manipulating maneuvers that the conservative rhetoricians deem necessary?

In responding to this problem White and other liberal rhetoricians tend to emphasize what we might call "process virtues." These might include the following: (1) careful and precise speech, which entails rigorous self-examination before

---

[93] Ibid., 686.
[94] Wetlaufer, "Rhetoric and Its Denial," 1594.
[95] Ibid., 1564.

one speaks; (2) careful listening—avoiding stereotypic assumptions about what someone else must be saying, and the arrogant assumption that one has already considered all that might be said; (3) tolerance, civility, and mutual respect; (4) candor; (5) deliberation—the offering of public reasons for public action, rather than the mere assertion of preferences, even if they are majority preferences.

It is this last virtue that is most troublesome, since to assume that there are discernibly *public* reasons is arguably to assume away the problem of authority. A possible response is to assert that in any society there is a wealth of cultural values that transcend self-interest. These values need not be shared by all participants for debate to be deliberative. As long as all participants cite their own values and principles rather than their preferences, debate will have a deliberative character. The experience of careful, cordial deliberative debate may provide the setting for the emergence of new values and principles that achieve consensus, and for the emergence of feelings of solidarity and mutual sacrifice as well.

But to argue in this way is to blame the erosion of traditional authority on self-interest rather than on profound disagreements of value and principle. It presumes that as long as opponents defend principle rather than interest they will see that they are all engaged in the common enterprise of finding or inventing a common constitution of principle for society. On this view, the specific content of the principles that encounter each other in deliberative debate is unimportant. What matters is the attitude of moral earnestness that unites all interlocutors once talk of principle begins. This association of principle with an almost aesthetic mood of contemplative detachment perhaps grows out of certain high church Protestant traditions of spirituality. Certainly it comports with a view of religion as a vague attitude of benign religiosity chiefly expressed in private efforts to compose the spirit and calm the conscience. By analogy, to be "principled" would mean to have warm feelings about principle, but not about any particular principle. In any case, such a view of principle ignores the association of principle with dogma, group identity, institutional authority, martyrdom, and purgative violence prevalent in many religious traditions. And so it purports to value principle, while presuming that no specific principle can be worth fighting for; and its enthusiasm for deliberative dialogue seems heedless that differences of principle may be mediated by machete rather than metaphor.

The liberal rhetoricians seem to forget that what discredited religious authority in European history was not the loss of faith attending an excess of self-interest, but the catastrophic consequences of competing religious zealotries. It was, in short, the recognition that conflicts of principle were inevitably more violent and less amenable to compromise than conflicts of interest. That is why liberal political theorists sought to *cultivate* self-interest as a relatively pacifying and stabilizing force.[96] Thus, the claim that a repression of self-interest is *all* that is needed to restore value consensus and social authority is either naively sentimental, or deceptive.

---

[96] Albert O. Hirschmann, *The Passions and the Interests: Political Arguments for Capitalism before Its Triumph* (Princeton: Princeton Univ. Press, 1977).

If a purely procedural conception of liberal rhetoric cannot achieve the stated aim of restoring the cultural authority of law, then literature might serve liberal rhetoric as a source of—or more accurately an alternative to—substantive values. Richard Sherwin charges that liberal rhetoricians express nostalgia for a time

> when the power of the word seemed to shine forth with greater radiance than it does today; for a time when high culture seemed to blossom for everyone (or at least the citizenry, if not their servant class); for a time when great stories (of gods or heroes) were broadly shared as part of the politics as well as the popular and artistic culture of the day.[97]

If the shared beliefs that once integrated culture and politics now seem both unavailable and undesirable, perhaps it is still possible to build a political culture around shared artifacts. Literature seems to offer a secular substitute for religion, evoking some of the same feelings of attachment and reverence but without the clear normative implications that can yield bitter, intractable conflict. A literary sensibility—sensitive, humane, self-doubting, ironically bemused—can give the citizens of the modern liberal state a shared sense of *being principled*, but without bearing the full burden of *having principles*.

Rhetoric as Literary Ethics

The most important contemporary figure in exploring the link between rhetoric and literature has surely been the Chicago Critic Wayne Booth, who has argued forcefully for recognizing the ethical significance of literary form, especially by viewing literary narrative as one version of the broader art of moral rhetoric.[98] Although an important figure in the Aristotelian school we have associated with cultural conservatism, Booth offers an imaginative rhetoric more compatible with nineteenth-century Romanticism. He provides a key literary model for rhetorical affirmers of the law like White.

For Booth, the very act of creating a fictional or historical narrative has ethical significance because it creates an alternative world for our moral imagination; it changes the quality of life by determining how at least one moment—the moment of reading—is to be lived. Building on Iser's notion of the implied reader, Booth poses the question of who a literary text asks us to become during its reading, and who it changes us into by virtue of the reading experience we have had. The ethical critic does not merely, like the New Critic, praise poems for exhibiting the aesthetic quality of vitality. She praises poems for giving this life, this fullness of experience, to the reader, and praises the reader for opening herself to the poem's vitality and incorporating it into her everyday experience.[99]

---

[97] Richard Sherwin, "A Matter of Voice and Plot," *Mich. L. Rev.* 87 (1988) 543, 556.

[98] Wayne C. Booth, *The Company We Keep: An Ethics of Fiction* (Berkeley: Univ. of California Press, 1988); *The Rhetoric of Fiction*, 2d ed. (Chicago: Univ. of Chicago Press, 1983).

[99] Booth, *Company*, 53.

Perhaps the prime virtue cited by ethical critics of literature and rhetoric is a moral and imaginative openness, a proclivity to questions, rather than answers, a resilience in the face of the morally unexpected, a willingness to shatter and subvert preconceptions. Booth notes, of course, the necessary limits on the professed value of openness. Truly universal openness is impossible, since all language determines as well as opens, and the very notion of a story demands closure of some sort. Moreover, to value art as the means to openness may close the question of art's value. With such limits in mind, Booth stresses that the praise of literary craft always entails some sort of ethical approval. For one thing, the exercise of artistic skill usually requires a vast, and morally laudatory, investment of one's life's energy. For another, when we proceed to particular analyses of texts, we recognize the moral virtue in aesthetic choices.

For example, Booth offers an exemplary pedagogic exercise, by taking a brilliant and famous Yeats poem—"After Long Silence"—and deliberately rewriting it into dogmatic or "unliterary" language.[100] To do so, shows Booth, is to undo and denigrate the moral sensibility invested in the original poetic language, and thereby to expose the moral significance of the linguistic choices the poet made. Here is the original language:

> Speech after long silence, it is right,
> All other lovers being estranged or dead,
> Unfriendly lamplight hid under its shade,
> The curtains drawn upon unfriendly night,
> That we descant and yet again descant
> Upon the supreme theme of Art and Song:
> Bodily decrepitude is wisdom; young
> We loved each other and were ignorant.

And some possible "improvements":

> Speech after long silence; it is appropriate,
> All other lovers being estranged or passed to the other side.[101]

Merely to turn careful into careless language suggests a *moral* defect in the author. Character and craft are related; a writer who shows indifference to the perfection of her words is ethically flawed for her lack of devotion to fulfilling the inherent order and promise of the work, and in particular is unethically indifferent to the needs and expectations of her audience.

Thus, Booth marries his ethical aesthetics to reader-response theory: the author and reader, and implied and idealized versions of each, are mutual friends engaged in aesthetic and then ethical acts of exchange. Booth begins with an engaging but obscure passage from Joyce's *Ulysses*:[102]

---

[100] Ibid., 101–9.

[101] Ibid., 102.

[102] Ibid., 273, quoting James Joyce, *Ulysses*, ed. Hans Walter Gabler (New York: Random House, 1986), 31.

Ineluctable modality of the visible: at least that if no more, though through my eyes. Signatures of all things I am here to read, seaspawn and seawrack, the nearing tide, that rusty boot. Snotgreen, bluesilver, rust: coloured signs. Limits of the diaphane. But he adds: in bodies. Then he was aware of them bodies before of them coloured. . . . Stephen closed his eyes to hear his boots crush crackling wrack and shells. You are walking through it whomsoever, I am, a stride at a time. A very short space of time through very short times of space. . . . Am I walking into eternity along Sandymount strand?

The passage inspires the reader to ask, "What kind of life do I live as I decipher this immensely compact bundle of actions, thought, and allusions?" But the reader is also expected to ask, "What sort of character, what sort of habits, am I likely to take on or reinforce as I live that life? What 'better desires' does it lead me to desire?" Booth recalls his own youthful jealousy in first reading the novel—jealousy not of Joyce but of Stephen, and specifically of Stephen's highly enlightened consciousness. But ultimately he learns to read the passage as moving him towards imagining, and imagining having, the character of a philosophical person grappling with metaphysics. The reader imagined, implied, and hoped for by the writer then not only aspires to be like Stephen, but in fact, at least for the duration of the reading, does become like Stephen.[103]

Thus, Booth develops the terms of ideal author-reader friendship. The fullest friendship means sharing not only pleasures and utilities but also aspirations. Such a friend is one who "has the same relations with me that he has with himself." That literary friendship will vary along several dimensions such as intimacy, intensity, and candor. The rhetorical critic cannot devise a formula but can lay out the criteria by which a book establishes the terms of proffered friendship, and by which it creates and shapes the moral world in which the reader will be embraced. As Booth says to a hypothetical literary friend:

> You are an idealized version of the writer who created you, the disorganized, flawed creature who in a sense discovered you by expunging his or her duller times and weaker moments. To dwell with you is to share the improvements you have managed to make in your "self" by perfecting your narrative world. You lead me first to practice ways of living that are more profound, more sensible, more intense, and in a curious way more fully generous than I am likely to meet anywhere else in the world. You correct my faults, rebuke my insensitivities. You mold me into patterns of longing and fulfillment that make my ordinary dreams seem petty and absurd. You finally show what life can be, not just to a coterie, a saved and saving remnant looking down on the fools, slobs, and knaves, but to *anyone* who is willing to earn the title of equal and true friend.[104]

But how does this correction and inspiration of character work? Booth acknowledges that the process is subtler than the general statement of it. For Booth, moral edification through literature requires a considered and deliberated experience of conversion—not a charismatic bolt of lightning or a passionate rebirth. To make

---

[103] Ibid., 274–77.
[104] Ibid., 223.

the process more concrete, we can examine Booth's important example of Jane Austen's *Emma*, and then later link Booth's treatment of the book to the remarkably parallel treatment by James B. White.[105]

Young Emma Woodhouse, a woman of means and station, is unmarried but shows a proclivity to arrange marriages for others. She gives herself credit for the marriage of her longtime governess and friend, Miss Taylor, to Mr. Weston, but as a result is now left alone with her aging, dotty father. To prove her success at matchmaking to the doubting brother of her sister's husband, Mr. Knightley, she tries to marry off the young rector, Mr. Elton, to the young and illegitimate Harriet Smith. Emma discourages Harriet's interest in a devoted suitor, Robert Martin, on the ground that Harriet should aspire to a higher social station. Her intrusion proves near-disastrous: Mr. Elton assumes Emma is flirting with him on her own behalf. He is insulted when he learns the truth and insults Harriet in vengeful spite. Emma begins to doubt her own judgment in matchmaking. (Mr. Elton proves himself a snob and marries the well-born but obnoxious Miss Hawkins.)

Mr. Weston's son Frank Churchill, a dashing stranger, comes for the holidays. Emma recognizes Frank as a potential beau for herself. Emma must then spend time with the dotty old Miss Bates and her orphan niece, Jane Fairfax. Emma becomes briefly entranced by Frank Churchill, who feigns interest in her to cover his secret relationship with Jane Fairfax. Meanwhile, Mr. Knightley tries to tutor Emma in learning better and more selfless judgment, especially after Emma shows gracelessness in insulting the annoying but helpless old Miss Bates. Ultimately, Emma realizes both her love and respect for Mr. Knightley over the likes of Frank Churchill. Her spirit and his judgment harmonize into a perfect marriage, while, appropriately, Harriet finally joins with Robert Martin.

Emma and Knightley are of course themselves "readers" of their social surroundings, and from Knightley Emma receives an education in reading generously and carefully, without prejudice or self-superior narcissism. Presumably the reader receives a like education from Austen and learns that her initial impressions both of Emma, and of Austen, must be revised.

Thus, Booth acknowledges that, on the surface, the "ideal" reader implied by *Emma* is one suspiciously amenable to accepting a world in which women are relegated to a subordinate role. But Booth demonstrates that on a deeper reading, the novel contains "antidotes" to its own apparent position on the role of women. It both exploits and undermines the conventional form. Booth examines how the underlying texture of the novel is all disappointment and chastening. The novel participates in the conventional genre by imputing to Emma conventional aspirations and all-too-neatly fulfilling those aspirations at the end. But along the way, Austen reminds the perspicacious reader of both the need and the difficulty of making one's way in the world with moral clarity, of the hard ethical work of "keeping one's wits about one." Indeed, at a key moment, Austen warns the reader, "Seldom, very seldom, does complete truth belong to any human disclo-

---

[105] Ibid., 426–35.

sure; seldom can it happen that something is not a little disguised, or a little mistaken; but where, as in this case, though the conduct is mistaken, the feelings are not, it may not be very material."[106] We are reminded that all is not well even in the small and placid world of this book, and we return to our world with a more vigilant moral alertness. If we do not condescend to Austen, she will repay our friendship with edification. It is this model of ethical friendship that lies at the heart of James B. White's effort to analogize legal argument to imaginative literature.

White and the Rhetorical Lawyer

For White, law is an imagined social world. Although the lawyer starts with available cultural resources, she imagines a new cultural world as she argues not only how a case should be *decided* but about how such cases should be *discussed*. She frames not just a "policy question" about what we will get, but a conversation about what we should want. And her work, finally, is ethically constitutive. The lawyer is always establishing an ethical identity in making an ethical argument, a performative answer to the question of what sort of society we want and what sort of lives should we lead. White suggests that if we see law this way, as a rhetorical practice, we will be less disturbed by textual ambiguity and discretion in the application of law. We will understand legal texts as settings for conversation rather than commands. Through legal conversation we try to determine not what we want, but what we should want, and even more importantly, who we should be as we discuss what we should want:

> Law is in a full sense a language, for it is a way of reading and writing and speaking and, in doing these things, it is a way of maintaining a culture, largely a culture of argument, which has a character of its own. . . . . Reading literature (like reading law) is not merely a process of observing and receiving, but an activity of the mind and imagination, a process that requires constant judgment and creation. Like law, literature is inherently communal: one learns to read a particular text in part from other readers, and one helps others to read it. . . . This is an interpretative culture rather like the culture of argument established by lawyers.[107]

White's approach to rhetoric epitomizes the gentle, communal comparison between law and literature as cultural constructions of value. And for him, the joint study of law, literature, and rhetoric promises a reintegration of the segmented modern mind. White assumes that the essence of social life is the creation of a world of meaning to share, that this world of meaning is a kind of public good constantly threatened by self-interest, and that it is also an imaginative construct threatened by positivism, literalism, and dry conceptualism. He also assumes that

---

[106] Ibid., 434, quoting Jane Austen, *Emma*, in *The Novels of Jane Austen*, ed. R. W. Chapman (London: Oxford Univ. Press, 1960), 4:431.

[107] James B. White, *Heracles' Bow* (Madison: Univ. of Wisconsin Press, 1985), 78.

the authority of law depends upon this shared world of meaning, so that the effort to build law on a foundation of economic rationality, majority self-interest, or science is self-defeating. Each of these ideas implies a reductive discourse of justification that destroys the shared world of meaning on which the authority of law depends.

Thus, while law depends upon a shared world of meaning, that shared world may depend upon law. Law not only aims at just consequences, but also creates a conversational community within which justice can be defined. It also makes explicit the contingency of conversation on institutional ground rules and substantive standards, and in this way candidly confronts the rhetoricality of all cultural activity:

> Law is thus not only an interpretive but a compositional process, for the judge as well as the lawyer. . . . It is a composition in which the speaker must choose a language for telling a story and justifying a result, and must do so against the reasonable claims of the losing side that he or she speak differently. In this sense, it offers a perpetual training in the artificiality of culture and the responsibility for what we say and do.[108]

White's rhetorical criticism is in a sense one long elaboration of a pun on the term "constitution." Legal language is "constitutive of" culture, and the formal act of establishing a legal constitution is a metaphor for all actions by legal actors. All law is "constitutional" in that it constitutes a culture of argument, and all culture is likewise constitutional in that it asserts how we should speak, according to what terms of value, and in what roles. All cultural expression is rhetoric, and all legal discourse is also rhetoric. In this formulation, rhetoric is simply the performative dimension of meaning—the way in which what is said affects what can be said, by redefining or reaffirming or reevaluating terms, speakers, discursive rules, sentiments, forms, and so on. Every cultural expression reshapes the landscape of authority—and authority, at once a form of power and a form of meaning, is the point where law and culture meet in rhetoric.

But this is also the point at which White begins to evade important questions. Does every cultural expression influence authority in the same way? Is there a fixed and finite amount of cultural authority, such that to reduce the authority of one value is to increase the authority of another, or is it possible to influence the amount and role of authority within a culture? Is it possible, as liberals fear, to have an excess of authority? Or, as conservatives fear, to have a deficiency? Does it matter what values are authoritative? Does a plurality of authoritative values enable liberty or threaten social peace? Are there important differences between state authority and private authority, or between the formal authority conferred by law and the informal authority conferred by high or popular culture? White seems content merely to point out that there is a performative dimension to advocacy, so that it is possible for lawyers to improve the culture of conversation in

---

[108] Ibid., 240–41.

some way in arguing for a bad or futile cause.[109] This is consoling news for the young idealists whom law schools send off to serve corporate clients, or to "service" the indigent, but it does little to vindicate their decision to burnish the particular corner of the conversational culture that is law. And it gives little guidance as to how to recognize an improvement in—or a corruption of—that culture.

Rhetoric as Ethical Friendship

In his most systematic book, *When Words Lose Their Meaning*, White develops Booth's idea of the relationship between reader and writer as an ethical friendship, arguing that there is or can be a redemptive ethical dimension to legal argument:

> The basic idea is this: in each text the writer establishes a relation with his or her reader, a community of two that can be understood and judged in terms that are not bound by the language and culture in which the text is composed; this community can become a basis for judging the writer's culture and his own relation to it.[110]

The relationship between reader and writer White admires is friendship, especially as it is defined in two of the texts he reads, Plato's *Gorgias* and Austen's *Emma*. In each, friendship is associated with candid criticism, in the form of Socrates's dialectical questioning or "refutation," and Mr. Knightley's similar tutelage of Emma. This tutelage is mirrored in Austen's correction of the reader, who, like Emma herself, is too quick to judge.

For White, ethical friendship presumes a background set of values against which it is possible to judge a friend's conduct and language. The ethical friend persuades the backslider to return to or live up to the values on which his or her self-respect depends. The ethical friend shows respect for her interlocutor by equating her aims and interests with principles of justice rather than appetites. The ethical friend is not indifferent to her interlocutor's behavior and so bestows concerned attention. Thus, ethical friendship is, in a sense, flattering: it is a conditional offer of social esteem that promises self-esteem. This is part of its persuasive appeal.

While ethical friendship presupposes principles of justice, it is not important that these principles be absolute, founded in natural or divine law. They can be the contingent principles particular to a culture or tradition. Thus, White presents ethical friendship as a technique by which normative authority can be created within a culture, when absent, and restored, when decayed. If citizens can be shown the appeal of ethical friendship, they will be willing to adopt a language of principle and justice in order to have the enriching experience of edifying conversation it enables. By engaging in a discourse of principle, they will be committing themselves to the authority of law—or at least the possibility of

---

[109] Ibid., 215–37.

[110] James B. White, *When Words Lose Their Meaning* (Chicago: Univ. of Chicago Press, 1984), 13–14.

authoritative law. And so rhetoric, in the sense of ethical friendship, is crucial to the authority of law. It constitutes law's authority, and reconstitutes it, when that authority has been eroded by the language of self-interest and materialism.

White begins his argument with readings of two classical texts, Homer's *Iliad* and Thucydides' *History*. These chapters each display a "language" of justification in crisis, a shared world of social meaning dissolving under the pressures of unrestrained egoism.

White reads the *Iliad* as the story of the dissolution of a heroic culture organized around honor and martial virtue. Such a culture proves instable: its dual values of social power, embodied by Agamemnon, and martial virtue, embodied by Achilles, vie for preeminence. Its ethic of unrestrained pride precludes reconciliation and so leads to violent conflict rather than social peace. But the culture also proves incoherent: while it values self-mastery in the form of conquering fear, it places the self in bondage to the passions of anger, jealousy, and pride. The heroic culture creates a character in Achilles that its values cannot regulate, that is immune to its persuasive appeal. The language of honor proves to be flawed and must give way to the discourse of justice that founds the polis.

The next chapter reads Thucydides' history of the Peloponnesian War as an account of the breakdown of the language of justice on which the polis is founded. Athens has developed into an empire. Its relations with its neighbors are no longer equitable, and it succumbs to the temptation to justify this situation in the "realist" language of self-interest. But to do so is to abandon the language of justice, and the dialogic relations of reciprocal respect such a language implies. The result is that Athens can no longer form alliances on the basis of equality and good faith. Diplomatically outmaneuvered by its rivals, Athens's position becomes progressively weaker: "The ultimate sanction of outlawry . . . has been brought by Athens upon herself."[111] Together these two chapters teach the Socratic lesson that only a language of principle is consistent and stable, whereas languages of self-aggrandizement are incontinent and incoherent and so destroy meaning. The choice of classical examples of the dissolution of meaning also undercuts the assumption that classical culture was a seamless unity, and that only modern cultures face the challenge of subjectivism and materialism. White wants to present his dialogic version of rhetoric as a response to these challenges, and to deny that rhetoric presupposes an organic society.

White's version of rhetoric restores and conserves a shared world of meaning in the face of these challenges by offering ethical friendship on the model of Socratic dialogue. Thus, White paradoxically offers as models of *good* rhetoric, two of history's great critics of rhetoric, Socrates and Plato. In the *Gorgias*, according to White's reading, Plato offers Socratic "dialectic" as a desirable form of friendship to be contrasted with mere rhetoric, which Plato presents as a form of manipulative flattery. While White associates good rhetoric with dialectic, White shows us that Plato treated dialectic and rhetoric as antithetical. White tells us that for Plato,

---

[111] Ibid., 79.

The goal of rhetoric . . . is the power to persuade others, to reduce them to one's will. The goal of dialectic is the opposite of persuasion: it is to be refuted, humiliated, corrected. . . . Rhetoric persuades another not by refuting but by flattering him, by appealing to what pleases rather than what is best for him; if successful, it therefore injures him.[112]

The dialogue begins with Socrates telling the rhetorician Gorgias that he is not interested in hearing eloquent speeches, but that he welcomes being corrected when he is in error, and that if Gorgias shares that feeling, he is happy to converse with him.[113] Socrates' conversations consist of question and answer. He begins by asking interlocutors who they are and what they do:

In the ensuing conversation the interlocutor's account of himself is shown to make no sense even in its own terms; it is seen to be internally incoherent. The one who claims to know knows nothing at all. This is the . . . refutation of which Socrates repeatedly speaks, and it is the heart of dialectic. It results in a mortification or humiliation.[114]

Socrates asks Gorgias what a rhetorician is: "He defines rhetoric as the art of persuading others, especially those with power in the state, primarily about questions of justice."[115] Socrates then poses the question whether the rhetorician must know justice and other values about which he talks. While Gorgias concedes that he must, other rhetoricians do not. Polus presents the rhetorician as one who rules through the power of rhetoric. Socrates forces him to concede, however, that the rhetorician can be said to rule only if he achieves what is best for him, that it is worse to do than to suffer injustice, so that unless he has knowledge of justice he cannot know what is best for him and cannot rule. Self-rule or continence is the prerequisite to rule. Callicles rejects this association of power with morality, offering a hedonistic conception of the good. Socrates forces Callicles to concede that power can be associated only with the gratification of heroic rather than cowardly desires. Thus, desire is once again subordinated to transcendent value, and power over others subordinated to self-discipline and knowledge of the good.[116] White concludes that "dialectic proceeds . . . by exposing contradictions in one's thought, which are for Socrates, contradictions in one's very self" and that "an aim of the dialogue . . . is to offer the reader an experience . . . that changes his sense of things, including his sense of his language and himself."[117]

Dialectic is a form of friendship, one that influences the whole person, not just the mind. It is intimate and paternalistic: the dialectician is more concerned with making his interlocutor worthy of respect than with treating him respectfully. Thus, a dialectical text "might evoke [aggressive or racist feelings] against the will of the reader in order to help him understand and correct them, and this would

---

[112] Ibid., 109.
[113] Ibid., 102.
[114] Ibid., 95.
[115] Ibid., 98.
[116] Ibid., 98–101.
[117] Ibid., 102–3.

be an act of the deepest friendship."[118] Dialectical "friendship" is also erotic, as implied by both Strauss and Weaver: "One accepts refutation gladly, for it reduces the divisions and disharmonies within the self. . . . One can see why the language of sexuality seems natural to describe these two relations: dialectic is a recognition of self and other, rhetoric a reification and seduction."[119] While Socrates evokes and praises this erotic friendship in the *Gorgias*, he does not achieve it within the dialogue. The rhetoricians respond to his teachings with sullen acquiescence rather than conviction and gratitude. The true audience, White argues, is the reader: "In this text Plato makes himself his reader's dialectical friend."[120] Thus, in keeping with its paternalistic structure, dialectical friendship need not be reciprocal or genuinely dialogic. While dialectic supposedly teaches "recognition of the equal value of other people,"[121] its structure belies this message.

White identifies a difficulty with Platonic dialectic that bedevils conservative rhetoricians: the destabilizing critical potential of Platonic natural law. Talk of absolute principles that transcend human will can undermine the authority of human institutions, if those institutions are not clearly identified with absolute principle. Thus, White reasons, "The Platonic premise . . . is that, beyond language, the absolutes themselves exist, and it is towards these that we struggle. . . . But until [the absolutes] are discovered, this kind of absolutism produces a radical relativism in method." This is threatening to "the larger world and . . . our fidelities to the language that constitutes it." Like the conservative rhetoricians, White proposes rhetoric as a solution to this problem. Thus, "something can be said on behalf of rhetoric by . . . the modern lawyer" who

> can claim to be one of those who maintains the culture . . . by which the world is constituted and made real; in which materials for the definition of self and motive can be found; and without which nothing human can occur. An inherited language, as the repository of our collective experience, can have much to teach its users.[122]

The lawyer offers the inculcation of tradition as a model of friendship. Regardless of content, all traditions impose values that transcend the self and channel desire. Thus, the learning of any tradition provides an edifying training in continence, and the dialectical friendship that the lawyer offers society is an edifying lesson in submission to authority.

There follow two chapters that, together, pose the problem of the authority of tradition. These chapters—a reading of Jonathan Swift's *Tale of a Tub*, followed by a reading of Samuel Johnson's *Rambler* essays—constitute a kind of dialogue on the worth of received wisdom. Swift mocks cliché and blind faith, but White argues that Swift shows irreverence and skeptical reason to be equally superficial. Johnson provides White with a model of the revivification of received wisdom.

---

[118] Ibid., 15.
[119] Ibid., 110.
[120] Ibid., 111.
[121] Ibid., 18.
[122] Ibid., 112.

White shows that the method of the *Rambler* essays is to pose a tired homily, usually in praise of moderation, to consider the consequences of ignoring it, and to close with a firmer sense of the homily's meaning and point. Moderation is not a matter of stasis or regular habits, or following the path of least resistance—it is a precarious equipoise among deeply compelling claims on the soul. To White, these essays show that received wisdom can be rescued from cliché if the rhetorician reproduces in the reader something like the experience that initially gave rise to it. What was formerly assented to without understanding, merely because it was the common opinion, can then be embraced with conviction. Johnson is White's answer, not only to Swift, but also to Plato; he shows that dialectical questioning can conserve rather than subvert traditional values, by restoring their basis in reason and experience.

In his reading of *Emma*, White brings together the figures of Socrates and Johnson in the figure of Mr. Knightley: "For Mr. Knightley, as for Socrates . . . , true friendship is corrective and refutational, and to please by flattery is an act not of friendship but of its opposite."[123] Yet the mature Knightley "formed partly on the model of Johnson"[124] represents Johnson's wisdom of social experience rather than Socrates' passion for truth.

Emma and Knightley encounter each other in an almost purely rhetorical world: "For Jane Austen [language and character] are one. . . . It is in speech and behavior that character is at once expressed and determined."[125] Emma's problem is a problem of rhetoric. Her character is defective because her speech is defective: "Her speech is a definition of what she is, and she cannot change it without changing herself."[126] What is wrong with Emma's speech is its lack of dialectical tension and its resulting self-indulgence: "The language that defines 'the attachment of friend and friend' as 'Emma doing just what she liked' and that links 'affectionate' and 'indulgent' as practical synonyms is . . . a highly defective language . . . for we know that the the term 'friendship' . . . also includes discipline, correction and the speaking of unwelcome truths."[127] In contrast to Johnson's neoclassical language of contrast, symmetry and balance, Emma's "has no internal opposition, no tension to give it life and to make meaning possible: the terms run into one another, without contrast or definition."[128]

Knightley is the one source of resistance in Emma's indulgent world, and she gradually comes to realize that she most feels alive and most respects herself when embroiled with him in debate, whether in actuality or in her imagination. Thus, what Knightley offers Emma is not only the benefit of dialectical correction, but also the pleasure of experiencing herself as a dialectician in his company. He teaches, not just by disproving her errors intellectually, but by giving her the experience of speaking critically and precisely: "The kind of education she needs

[123] Ibid., 173.
[124] Ibid., 163.
[125] Ibid., 184.
[126] Ibid.
[127] Ibid., 165.
[128] Ibid., 166.

is not merely a matter of cognition—of receiving the right lessons—or of adapting her behavior to prescriptions. It is not enough to repeat truisms learned from others or copy their conduct."[129] Emma must make what she receives alive to herself to truly receive it.

The lessons the Johnsonian Knightley teaches Emma are traditional lessons: "Emma ends as one who remakes her world and her language in constant conversation with another, but the terms in which she does so are the standard terms of her moral culture, clarified by experience and context. Her new world is an old world remade."[130] She reaffirms convention by finding fulfillment in marriage to a superior man, but redefines marriage as an ethical friendship and redefines superiority as virtue and wisdom rather than social class. In this way she transcends the immaturity of her father fixation, avoids the danger of becoming a socially isolated and sexually unfulfilled "old maid," and makes the best of her world.[131]

Nevertheless, a key point for White is the relevance of Emma's drawing room world to the modern reader: "What Emma [finally] perceives . . . is the essential subjectivity and relativity of this world—what we might call its modernity. Contrary to the surface impression, it turns out that . . . even in this world . . . there is no stable culture external to the self, on which one can simply rely."[132] One cannot simply rely on culture because one must constantly remake it in order to conserve it. In order to learn the lessons of her culture, Emma must "reconstitute" not only her own language, but tradition as well. Happily, then, cultural traditions are never truly alien or oppressive; they are merely resources for realizing our better selves.

Certainly a major aim of White's is to make "the classics" available to readers as a resource for self-improvement. Almost all of the texts read in this book are classical or neoclassical, none dating from later than the early nineteenth century. Austen's is the only novel, and White presents it as part of

> an ethical literature that includes among its central concerns the character of the reader. It is one lesson of the novel that there is an important connection between friendship and what I have called reading, for it is only through speech and interpretation, through the manifestation and recognition of character in relation with others, that friendships can exist. One can be a good friend only if one utters what will not mislead and reads correctly what one is told.[133]

Thus, Knightley's relation to Emma is a model for the pedagogic relation of author to reader. So arrogant and narcissistic is Emma in her early efforts to manipulate her world that the reader is tricked into judging Emma as Emma judges others,

[129] Ibid., 184.
[130] Ibid., 189.
[131] Ibid., 187–89.
[132] Ibid., 188.
[133] Ibid., 163–91.

not as Mr. Knightley, who sees Emma's potential for good, judges her. We come to see that we have condescended to Emma in much the same way that she has condescended to Harriet and Miss Bates:

> *Emma* thus trains its reader not only in conversation but in a certain sort of kindness. It does so partly in the way it teaches us to understand who Emma is, for the extra error it corrects is not our failure to see the secret evil behind the plausible surface . . . but our failure to see the unobtrusive and easily missed good beneath an unappealing surface. This is a training in sympathy and generosity as well as in accuracy of observation.[134]

For White, the reading experience is like taking a series of tests in which we progress in our moral acuity. Like Emma, we find what is best in ourselves by seeing the best in what we read. By becoming an ethical friend to what we read, we learn to become an ethical friend to our cultural traditions, making the best of ourselves by making the best of our world.

Thus, while White acknowledges that *Emma* is not a political novel in the conventional sense, he finds it implying a politics by inviting us to assume a certain character in our dealings with others: "If I become the ideal reader the text defines, the version of myself it calls into being, what will I do, what will I be, when I turn to my own larger world and act within it?"[135] The reader learns, with Emma, that the capacity for dialectic is a privilege not vouchsafed to all, and that with it comes the responsibility of kindness towards those less capable, like the foolish Miss Bates.[136] White suggests that this combination of dialectical conversation among the clever and kindness towards the simple is an appropriate model for politics. But beyond this, White implies that the good citizen will be similarly generous towards her society's culture and institutions. She will attribute her own dialectical capacities to her cultural inheritance and see herself as its steward, obliged by privilege not to criticize it destructively, but to make of it the best it can be. It is a politics of patrician statesmanship and benevolence, to be reproduced by inculcating an ethical appreciation of the works of high culture that mark the boundaries of privilege.

Civic Friendship

White makes this model of the citizen as ethical friend to her culture explicit in his generally admiring treatment of Edmund Burke's conservative tract *Reflections on the Revolution in France*. Burke presents this work as a series of letters to a young French friend, explaining his disapproval of the French Revolution and his contrasting admiration for the venerable, evolving, unwritten constitution of England. White reads *Reflections* as a performance, an act of fashioning a consti-

---

[134] Ibid., 190.
[135] Ibid., 191.
[136] Ibid., 190.

tution out of metaphor, for a polity that lacks a constitutional text.[137] An important element in this performance is a strategy of rhetorical inversion, in which hereditary monarchy turns into democracy, prejudice becomes reason, and paternalistic governance is refigured as "virtual" representation. Thus, he produces a political language that is unabashedly esoteric, a political language meant to be as quaintly English as thatched roofs and high tea. Burke, says White, invites the English reader to learn and use this reconstituted language, so that the ideal Burkean reader will identify himself differently as a result of the reading. As constitutional rhetorician, Burke avoids merely intellectual persuasion. He seeks to evoke veneration by making the reader feel as though he had lived the entire accumulated experience of the English people. Though he does not narrate the events of English history, his metaphors offer a virtual experience of English history, a kind of emotional correlative.[138] Burke's chosen genre for this performance is epistolary, because it speaks in the intimate language of friendship, and it mirrors his view that the British constitution fuses the public and private. Burke's rhetoric

> unites fact, value, and reason; thought and emotion; the family and the crown; the social and the natural worlds; ethical motives and material results. It has an integrative force not only in the political and social world but in the reader himself, for Burke addresses him not merely as a fellow subject or as a political philosopher but as a parent, child, farmer, landlord, church member, tenant, voter, and so on.[139]

For Burke, the British constitution is a personal relationship, not an abstract set of principles or procedures. It is a social relationship among particular persons, across generations, and a proprietary relationship between those persons and their land and institutions. In Burke's view only such a relational constitution can command the personal loyalty necessary to secure the authority of law. Governing institutions must be maintained by affection, which requires that they have developed organically. Citizens should "own" their institutions in the way that they own their property—as indeed they do, since it is on those institutions that their property depends. Thus, Burke justifies even hereditary monarchy as an expression of the rights of the people, since the principle of inheritance secures the people's property rights.[140] In Burke's language, property ownership is not just a qualification for political participation, it is political participation itself. Because the English identify their constitution with their estates, they come to see themselves collectively as trustees of a national family estate they must improve and pass down.[141] Thus, the British constitution is bound up with the English citizen's sense of who he or she is in relation to family, place, and community.

The English constitution is a personal attribute of the English citizen, a constitution of the self, not in the classical sense that the constitution of the polity shapes

---

137 Ibid., 192–97.
138 Ibid., 218.
139 Ibid., 208.
140 Ibid., 203–4.
141 Ibid., 206–8.

the character of the citizen, but in the modern sense that makes participation in the nation part of the citizen's identity. The Burkean citizen belongs to England in exactly the way that Austen's provincial gentry belong to the county.

According to Burke, the British attachment to venerable institutions is a kind of "prejudice" in favor of tradition. To Burke, prejudice enhances reason: first, because prejudice is the accumulated wisdom of a nation that is bound to outweigh the reason of an individual; second, "because prejudice, with its reason, has a motive to give action to that reason, and an affection which will give it permanence."[142] One important source of the motives of affection required for stable government is religion, which must be established in order to be independent of government and so capable of legitimating it. White explains that for Burke, religion "civilizes and ennobles power by teaching those in positions of authority to 'have high and worthy notions of their function and destination.' . . . In a democracy, in particular, religion will help impress it on the people that no more than the will of kings can the 'will' of the people be the 'standard of right and wrong.' "[143] Religion also reconciles the majority to the "disproportion" between "endeavor" and "success" and reenforces "principles of natural subordination."[144] With Straussian irony, White complains that Burke's approval of the establishment of religion is "difficult for the modern American to comprehend since our prejudices run so strongly the other way."[145] He mocks our "self-congatulatory" condescension towards Burke as one that grows out of our "prejudice" in favor of the equal right to vote.[146]

White argues that Burke's conception of representation merits a closer look, in that it exposes the poverty and hypocrisy of our own. Our insistence on equal voting is premised on our mutual mistrust and our assumption that, ultimately, the interests of all voters conflict. Yet an equal right to vote is obviously an inadequate response to this problem, since it does not guarantee equal power or equal outcomes. It is merely a formal, a sham equality. On Burke's account, however, the English constitution made no pretense of equal political participation. Yet it reconceived political participation as representation of the interest of the whole rather than self-interest, and it relied on culture and fraternity to discipline officials and overcome mutual mistrust.

Burke's "virtual" representative is not a flattering, manipulative servant of the people, but a *true* ethical friend. The virtual representative represents the people's moral interests, their *virtues* rather than their desires. He exercises judgment rather than indulging preference. For Burke, "representation . . . has, like Burke's own text, an essentially rhetorical and ethical character." Accordingly, the representative "is not subject to direction by the constituency," for that would be indulgence and license. Instead, "each member of parliament is understood to represent

---

[142] Ibid., 212, quoting Edmund Burke, *Reflections on the Revolution in France* (1790, London: Penguin, 1969), 183.

[143] Ibid., 214.

[144] Ibid., 223, quoting Burke, *Reflections on the Revolution in France*, 372.

[145] Ibid., 213.

[146] Ibid., 225–26.

the nation as a whole and to represent not its temporary will but its largest interests."[147] All political decision makers, including citizens, should be seen as operating within the limits of a " 'moral competence . . . subjecting, even in powers more indisputably sovereign, occasional will to permanent reason.' "[148] Here, in Burke's defense of elite rule, and in White's defense of Burke's elitism, we find the familiar pattern of argument. Reason is permanent and implies the superiority of the wise; while equality is an ephemeral fashion, not taken seriously even by its defenders, who thereby show their self-indulgence and superficiality.

In developing his critique of the French Revolution, Burke repudiates his own reputation as an enthusiast of liberty. "The effect of liberty to individuals is to do what they please: We ought to see what it will please them to do, before we risque congratulations," quotes White with approval.[149] To do otherwise would be to serve the people as a flatterer, not a true ethical friend. According to White, Burke "loves not 'liberty' itself, but 'manly, moral, regulated liberty.' " White sees this conditional approval of liberty as the manifestation of a Johnsonian appreciation that "the essence of moral thought is the simultaneous comprehension of contrary tendencies in the mind." White sees this Johnsonian aesthetic of complexity and balanced tension in turn reflected in Burke's vision of the English constitution organized not on a single principle but as a "composition" of "various anomalies and contending principles."[150] The sensibility praised here—moderate, pluralistic, prudent, is Aristotelian in spirit.

Yet here White finds himself in difficulty, for Burke's *Reflections* are anything but moderate. His critique of the French Revolution—though written before the Terror—is self-consciously hyperbolic, its vitriolic excess testifying to the passionate loyalty England's organically evolved constitution inspires. White argues that this display of violent hatred simply shows the need for the restraints of authority and tradition, as if authority and tradition could not be as hateful and violent as reform. "In an important sense," argues White, " 'the French Revolution' Burke so violently opposes is in fact most clearly located not in his description of it but in the very violence of his opposition to it."[151] Here White seems to deceive himself as to the source of Burke's virulent hatred, which is his passionate patriotism. The toleration and moderation that Burke praises in the English constitution rest upon the mutual friendship and organic attachment of the English people, a friendship that does not extend beyond the domain of their shared kinship and estate. Burke argues that a political community can function only when its citizens accept *as their own* a good deal that cannot be rationally justified. The logic of Burke's argument is that social happiness requires stable institutions; stability depends on authority; authority depends on passionate attachment; and passionate attachments are necessarily particular and partisan. White's liberalism

---

[147] Ibid., 199.
[148] Ibid., 203, quoting Burke, *Reflections on the Revolution in France*, 104.
[149] Ibid., 200–201.
[150] Ibid., 201.
[151] Ibid., 228.

makes him hesitate, one foot in the air, before the final step. But this step is necessary to the argument: unless England's lower orders could be assured that they were the special object of paternalistic solicitude, they could have no motive to accept the authority of England's elites. When Austenian "kindness" becomes universal it ceases to be paternalistic and it can no longer evoke gratitude and paternalistic authority. The metaphor of civic "friendship" would seem to have its limits.

The Lawyer as Cultural Conserver

White's political sensibility is flexible and evolutionary, equating conservation with reconstitution. It is roughly compatible with a tradition of evolutionary constitutionalism and prudential conservatism in American legal thought, extending from Kent and Story through Hand, Levi, and Bickel. But from the perspective of a true conservative, like Strauss, it is ultimately confused in its deference to the liberal values of liberty, equality, and above all progress. Consider the contradiction confessed in the following passage:

> Of course . . . there has been no progress since the *Iliad* and never will be. But I do think Swift and Johnson and Austen are right to see more merit in their inherited language of morality and community than Plato could see in his, and I think, too, that the self-conscious constitution-making of the eighteenth century, especially in America, represented a new stage in the possibilities for collective life.[152]

In his last chapter, "The Possibilities of American Law," White suggests a broadly egalitarian vision of dialectical conversation, an Austenian politics, which, he implies, is realized in American law. Law is a dialectical friend, not merely doing the will of the people but instructing them in their responsibilities:

> The judicial process not only recognizes the individual but compels him to recognize the other. For the litigant, the lawyer, and the observer alike, the central ethical and social meaning of the practice of the adversary hearing is its perpetual lesson that there is always another side to the story. . . . The law can thus be seen as a discipline in the acknowledgment of limits, in the recognition of others, and in the necessity of cooperation. It is a method of individual and collective self-education, a way in which we teach ourselves, over and over again, how little we can foresee, how much we depend on others, and how important to us are the practices we have inherited from the past.[153]

The language of the law is Burkean and rhetorical—White tells us that it is always concrete and situated rather than conceptual and abstract.[154] He adds, "In the law, as in Johnson and Austen, we find that 'principles' are not mere generalities applied to particular cases, but complex and disciplined attitudes of the mind and

---

[152] Ibid., 282.
[153] Ibid., 266.
[154] Ibid., 266.

self, educated positions from which difficulty (in Burke's sense) can be acknowledged and addressed."[155]

Thus, White offers law as a contemporary arena of dialectical conversation, the presence of the jury ensuring that it proceeds in the inclusive language of the people, rather than that of elites.[156] But this is doubly misleading. First, law is an elite language in which the jury must be instructed, and the vast bulk of disputes never arrive in front of a jury. Second, law is not simply a language; it is a set of precepts that neither jurors nor litigants are permitted to question. White presents this preceptual order as a merit, building legitimacy and solidarity: "One of the functions of a culture of argument, the law among others, is to provide a rhetorical coherence to public life by compelling those who disagree about one thing to express their actual or pretended agreement about everything else."[157] But it means that law is not a rhetorical world made by the litigants and jurors it instructs.

The far more important arena for popular participation in governance is in the making of laws, which proceeds at best in the utilitarian language of policy analysis and more often in the idiom of partisan interest. Not only is White exaggerating and sentimentalizing the democratic element of legal decision making; he is attempting to substitute legal judgment for legislative will as the arena for democratic "conversation." In White's vision of democratic conversation, the people are constrained to talk only about what is just, not what is useful or desirable. Thus, as with Strauss, the chief function of democratic participation is educative, and self-government is government and improvement of the self, rather than the definition and implementation of collective will. The key figure in this educative model of democracy is the judicial artist who models the sober judgment and reconstitutive passion that all citizens should bring to democratic conversation:

> The best judge, like Socrates, exposes himself to refutation. The most important achievement of judicial writing, indeed, is ethical and intellectual: The manifestation in performance of a serious, responsible and open mind, faithful to the sources of authority external to the self even while contributing to their transformation. . . . His most significant legacy by far is his definition of his own role and the institution of which he is a part.[158]

Subject to the judge's authority and example, the lawyer-rhetorician fulfills the same ethical function:

> The lawyer is not committed simply to power through persuasion but to persuasion of a special kind that perpetually recreates an ideal version of his inheritance. . . . The lawyer's audience is always ideal as well as real: he speaks to the judge or jury not as they are defined by their indvidual interests, passions, and biases but as they are defined

[155] Ibid., 269.
[156] Ibid., 265.
[157] Ibid., 268.
[158] Ibid., 270.

by their role, which is to do justice. He thus speaks to, and becomes like, his own view of the best judge or juror he can imagine, and this is one form of the best version of himself.[159]

Of course, not everyone holds as sanguine a view of the ethical effects of litigation. As White tells us, Burke thought the prominence of lawyers in the leadership of the French Revolution chiefly responsible for its excesses, because their livelihood depended upon the insecurity of property rights. Such men, "habitually meddling, daring, subtle, active, of litigious dispositions and unquiet minds," were "not taught habitually to respect themselves."[160] Perhaps in imagining and addressing idealized lawyers, White intends the same performative lesson that he calls on lawyers to teach: by addressing idealized lawyers the law professor will summon such lawyers into being, teaching them self-respect and quieting their minds. In essence, White argues that a democratic discourse of desire and self-interest is doomed to incoherence and periodic dissolution, whereupon it must be reconstituted as a rhetoric of justice and principle. The calling of lawyers, then, is to forge and maintain such a rhetoric in the crucible of litigation, holding it in readiness for the crisis of meaning that inevitably will come.

This is an elite calling of cultural conservation that in some ways resembles the vocation of the Straussian philosopher. Yet it is less self-assured, less orthodox, and that has everything to do with White's substitution of literature for philosophy as his model for a language of principle. We may explain White's literary conception of rhetoric by contrasting it with two other models. One is the model of rhetoric as dogmatic instruction in orthodoxy. Fundamentally, this is the aim of Straussian dialectic, even though the political weakness of philosophy forces it to proceed by indirection and persuasive seduction. Conceived as dogmatic instruction, rhetoric confronts popular opinion with authoritative knowledge and subjective desire with objective principle. An alternative model would conceive rhetoric as a form of radical criticism. Without purporting to speak with authority, the radical rhetorician might challenge the authority of prevailing arrangements by speaking in the language of principle. By what principle, the radical critic might demand to know, do the rulers rule? If the rulers respond that they are answerable to no principle of legitimacy, they give up any claim to authority and admit that they rule by force alone. Such an answer concedes that the ruled have no obligation to obey their rulers and may justifiably revolt. On the other hand, if the rulers admit that they are subordinate to a principle, they thereby provide a criterion by which their power can be criticized and found illegitimate. In this way the rulers may also provide their opponents with a justification for revolt. Both the model of dogmatic instruction and the model of radical criticism treat principles as absolute, and for that reason White rejects them both.

[159] Ibid.
[160] Ibid., 210, quoting Burke, *Reflections on the Revolution in France*, 130–31.

In contrast to these two models, White conceives rhetoric as restorative, not denunciatory. This requires a modest, tentative language of principle, one that eschews absolute principles, a language of literature rather than philosophy. For White, as for the New Critics, a literary work is that which resists paraphrase, a complex ineffable unity in which opposed values and qualities can be held in delicate equipoise, without contention or compromise. He suggests that literary discourse is more humane than conceptual discourse because it remains aware of how dependent it is on the contingencies of language. White says that by using language we all participate in the

> remaking of our shared resources of meaning, and thus of our public or communal lives. This is obviously the case with great artists and thinkers—their work changes the terms in which we think and talk, the ways in which we imagine and constitute ourselves. . . . The ineradicable flux of language, and of the world, so recently "discovered" and lamented by the modernist who learns at last that the language and methods of science are after all not good for all forms of thought and life, is actually structural to human experience. . . . What is required to face this circumstance is not a science in the usual sense but an art—the art of reconstituting language, self, and community under conditions of ontological relativism, an art that is literary and rhetorical in character and of which we ourselves are the most important subject.[161]

For White, all conduct is a form of linguistic expression because it is an effort of individuals to establish their sense of the significant. What distinguishes literary discourse from the rest of expressive human action is its self-consciousness about the contingency of meaning on fragile cultural contexts. The literary model of rhetoric encourages a self-consciousness about the contingency of language that educates us to be skeptical about our assumptions, whereas the pretenses of social science only reinforce those assumptions. Thus, "there is . . . no privileged subject by explaining which we can explain . . . everything else. . . . Our work cannot claim to be the kind of science that assumes a validity beyond culture, beyond language, but should hope to be a literary or rhetorical art, a way of working with and within our language." For White, the art of rhetoric lies in learning to qualify a language while we use it "in finding ways to recognize its omissions, its distortions, its false claims and pretensions, ways to acknowledge other modes of speaking that qualify or undercut it."[162] The aesthetic vision animating this view of literary art is the New Critical "tolerance of ambivalence" which

> has long been thought to be an essential ingredient of intellectual, emotional, and political maturity: the capacity to see, with Virgil for example, at once the greatness of Rome and its terrible cost or with Wallace Stevens at once the fictional character of the poetic world and its reality . . . the comprising of contrary tendencies, the facing of unresolved tensions.[163]

---

[161] James B. White, "Thinking about Our Language," *Yale Law Journal* 96 (1986): 1960, 1962–63.

[162] Ibid., 1964.

[163] Ibid., 1972.

White argues for the relevance of this aesthetic to law, saying that "at its central moment, the legal hearing, [law] works by testing one version of its language against another, one way of telling a story and thinking about it against another, and by then making a self-conscious choice between them." Law "remakes its own language" and permits that

> simultaneous affirmation of self and recognition of other [that] is the essential ethical task of a discoursing and differing humanity. These ethical possibilities arise from the fact that the premises of the legal hearing commit it to a momentary equality among its speakers and to the recognition that all ways of talking, including its own, may be subject to criticism and change.[164]

Thus, the language of justice and principle that lawyers are charged with conserving is not, as in Straussian dialectic, a set of substantive values. It is the familiar legal process language of justice as procedure and of principle as an attitude of deliberative detachment and open-mindedness. White's literary version of rhetoric opposes utilitarianism, because the utilitarian proceeds on the basis of values defined in advance of the discourse; but it also opposes deontological moral theories on the same basis. It opposes all such theorizing as too aggressive, too given to staking out conversational terrain. White regards literary language as more modest, more aware that no one can be compelled to submit to an idea, that all categories are evanescent. For White, rhetorical authority cannot precede the performance but lies in the relationship established between speaker and audience. Rhetoric must win its way by virtue not of prudence but of "principle." Yet the "principle" is a process value of civility, of leaving room for disagreement, rather than any substantive principle of justice.

White's literary rhetoric aims to evoke in the hearer an *attitude* of devotion to principle, an attitude that might be jeopardized by confrontation with any *particular* principle. The hope is that carefully composed language will inspire the hearer to give a carefully composed response. Passions will be sublimated in art, and opponents will be soothed by the complex symmetry of the discursive world they make together. Aesthetic self-discipline will replace moral self-discipline, and righteous indignation will give way before gracious gestures. A literary rhetoric invites the citizens of liberal society to recollect their opposing interests and values in tranquility, to reinterpret their own political conflicts as elevated cultural experiences.

White v. Jaffa

A sharp test of the capacity of White's liberal rhetoric to resolve crises of value, and an inviting comparison to Jaffa's conservative model, lies in his treatment of the antebellum slavery cases *Dred Scott v. Sanford* and *Prigg v. Pennsylvania*, both of which diminished the legal protections of blacks outside the slave South

---

[164] Ibid., 1963–64.

and extended the legal protections of slaveholders.[165] White attacks both decisions as illustrations of the moral bankruptcy of intentionalist interpretation, and he suggests that we condemn each decision not for its oppressive result, but for its character as "an ethical and political act, as a way of defining the judge himself, the court of which he is a part."[166]

In *Prigg v. Pennsylvania*, Margaret Morgan, a slave held by Margaret Ashmore under the laws of Maryland, escaped to Pennsylvania in 1832.[167] Prigg, a slave catcher from Maryland, went to Pennsylvania, seized Morgan, and brought her back to Maryland. Pennsylvania prosecuted Prigg under a state law making it a crime to take "any negro or mulatto by force, fraud or seduction with the intent" to take the captured person into slavery. The case therefore posed three federal questions: Was the Pennsylvania anticapture statute unconstitutional by virtue of conflicting with the Fugitive Slave Clause of the Constitution? Was it in any event preempted by the Fugitive Slave Act of 1793? Or was it an impermissible exercise of state power?

The Fugitive Slave Clause states:

> No person held to service or labor in one state, under the laws thereof, escaping into another, shall, in consequence of any law or regulation therein, be discharged from such service or labor, but shall be delivered up on claim of the party to whom such service or labor may be due.

The 1793 congressional law essentially provided that when a slave escaped to another state, the owner or owner's agent could seize the slave, wherever found, and take him or her before a state or federal court.[168] Once the court ruled that the petitioner was the rightful owner, it had to issue the petitioner a judicial certificate that would serve as a warrant authorizing return of the slave to the home state. As White points out, the state statute is arguably compatible with both the Fugitive Slave Clause and the Fugitive Slave Act, because it does not bar the slaveowner from ultimately recapturing his slave and preventing discharge. Rather, it bars pure self-help, implicitly requiring the slaveowner to prove his right of ownerhip in some sort of judicial proceeding, and in that sense, is quite consistent with the clause and the statute.[169] Thus, White argues, Story could easily have upheld the state law on strictly textualist grounds.

White then attacks the Story opinion. For Story, the intention behind the clause, not its strict language, was the source of its meaning. Story in turn found the intent underlying the clause in the attitudes of the Southern states; had they not been guaranteed full slaveowning rights, they would not have consented to enter the Union in the first place.[170] In this spirit, Story read the term "discharge" in the Fugitive Slave Clause improbably to include any state process that delays or

[165] James B. White, *Justice as Translation* (Chicago: Univ. of Chicago Press, 1990), 113–40.
[166] Ibid., 112.
[167] *Prigg v. Pennsylvania*, 41 U.S. (16 Pet.) 539 (1842).
[168] Fugitive Slave Act, ch. 7, sec. 3, 1 Stat. 302, 302–5 (1793) (repealed 1850).
[169] White, *Justice as Translation*, 115–17.
[170] Ibid., 117–23.

regulates the recapture of slaves. Thus, to plumb legislative intent is to look into the motives, desires, and expectations of the dead, not the language they uttered. White describes this sort of inquiry as "factual"—that is, empirical, and not literary, and hence he finds it ethically suspicious.

In White's view, Story's construction is a terrible distortion of language. Understood in this way, laments White, the Constitution fails to achieve a true rhetorical vision of law as "a testamentary trust of words," thereby treating "an instrument meaning to constitute a national community"[171] as a mere act of will. But White's fundamental objection is not exactly to the search for original intent but rather to the manner in which Story defines it—essentially as a mere matter of political preference, power, and will, modified only by the pragmatic need to compromise with others' wills. Interpretation, laments White, then becomes a mundane empirical matter of discerning where the predominant power lay. The scientific determinacy of this approach is also illusory since it simply presumes that all actors are more concerned with protecting private interests than with realizing a common good. Thus, White accuses Story of inventing a story of how the South wanted to extort the North. But if we must inevitably imagine the motives and hopes of the framers, if we must construct an interpretive fiction, should we not employ the Austenian art of ethical fiction? White invites constitutional interpreters to become the framers' ethical friends, reading the text as a noble effort to harmonize opposing voices. He complains that Story's approach eliminates this aspirational element in law. The law becomes simply a matter of what someone wanted, and hence, for White a destruction of law itself.

White develops a similar criticism of the *Dred Scott* case,[172] in which Chief Justice Taney ruled that free Blacks could not be citizens of the United States with the right to sue in federal court, because the Constitution's framers could not have so intended. As White reads the case, Taney found an original intent to treat Blacks as citizens inconceivable because it would have conflicted with the motive of the Southern states to ratify the Constitution.[173] By contrast, White suggests that the absence of explicit reference to race in the Constitution proves that the Framers, though aware of the racism of the South, hoped to write a document that might eventually escape it, and so mentioned servitude but not race. White seems uncertain whether to attack Taney for an unimaginative reduction of constitutional aspiration to historical fact, or for fabricating a constitutional mythology of racial community with insufficient basis in historical evidence. He declares his primary target to be the reductive positivism of "the economist who wishes to reduce us to utility-maximizers, of the political radical who sees law simply as an expression of class interest, or the psychological realist who sees it as the expression of subconscious needs."[174] Yet his objection to these styles of reading is ultimately less epistemological than aesthetic. On the one hand, he

[171] Ibid., 119–20.
[172] *Dred Scott v. Sandford*, 60 U.S. (19 How.) 393 (1857).
[173] Ibid., 123–32.
[174] Ibid., 136–37.

concedes that these styles of reading involve as much interpretive discretion and imaginative myth making as his own. On the other hand, his aspirational reading of the Constitution as a document left vague to permit a process of deliberative dialogue to generate moral progress is itself an historical claim about Framers' intent. Both Taney's and White's readings of the Constitution constitute a future by inventing a past.

As White reads him, Taney, like Story, invents a past that irrationally constrains us to serve the most selfish desires of a generation past and gone. By contrast, White invents a past that constrains us to seek the good by our own lights. But there are other alternatives to the backward-looking hedonism that White attributes to Story and Taney: a forward-looking hedonism that seeks to maximize the welfare of current and future generations, or a backward-looking moralism that seeks to realize a preordained vision of the good. For White, however, both of these are deficient in that they do not edify and improve us; whereas White's forward-looking moralism invites constitutional interpreters to deliberate on the good and thereby to become "an idealized version of themselves."[175]

The heart of White's argument appears in the following key passage:

> [Story's] way of reading legal texts is inconsistent with the fundamental idea of law on at least two counts: first, as we think of it, law is a way of creating a world that accommodates opposing interests and claims, a world in which distinct voices can be heard. The fugitive slave clause seems in fact framed upon exactly that principle, offering neither the South nor the North everything they might want, but creating a text tolerable to both, with the open questions to be resolved by future interpretration. . . . Second, Story's method eliminates the aspirational or idealizing element that is essential to what we think of as law. . . . This is to destroy the ground of authority upon which the law rests: the authority that derives not from the power of the person who makes the law but from the character of the law that is made, from the kind of conversation by which it is to become real in the world. Instead of participating in an argumentative or discoursing community that struggles with the questions, what kind of world we ought to have, what the authoritative language ought to mean, we are offered a world in which the only question is what someone wanted. The vice of this opinion is worse than authoritarianism; it is to destoy authority.[176]

This is a remarkable piece of rhetoric, one that wonderfully obfuscates its own meaning. If anything, it is White who cannot accept any serious notion of authority, at least any authority "authored" by any political instrument of power. Were he a committed postmodernist, he might assert the incoherence of any notion of authority. But White cannot: he is committed to the humane values that postmodernists critique, and he believes that conversations among competing positions resolve themselves not into the triumph of one will over another, nor anything so crass as compromise, but rather some new moral principle that exerts its own authority. By contrast, were he willing to assert some deeper notion of Framers'

[175] Ibid., 137.
[176] Ibid., 120.

intent, or some transcendent notion of natural rights, he might argue that Story's view of intention is simply incorrect as a matter of law. But either of these two premises would involve the kind of preconversational authority that White is unwilling to allow. "Authority" functions in White's rhetoric as an empty place-holder: while purporting to defend the idea of authority, he empties it of any possible content.

White's critique of Taney's originalism is therefore usefully contrasted with that of Jaffa, a conservative rhetorician who takes the idea of authority seriously. In 1987 Jaffa attacked the campaign of Reagan conservatives to restore their notion of textual originalism to constitututional interpretation.[177] But in doing so, Jaffa did not seek so much to refute originalism as to correct it—to replace an originalism of past preferences with an originalism of first principles.

Jaffa's hapless target was then Attorney General Edwin Meese, who in his campaign for an originalism of text and Framers' intent invoked Taney's *Dred Scott* opinion as a misbegotten exercise in judicial activism.[178] For Meese, the case before the Court was a technical one about federal jurisdiction and the power of Congress, and Taney committed the anti-originalist sin of using the case as an occasion for opining on slavery. But Jaffa points out that Taney was the ultimate originalist and argues that if one "simply" reads the Constitution, Taney had the better of any originalist argument.

Jaffa implicitly disdains as pharisaical White's careful semantic distinctions, his reliance on the apparent significance of the Constitution's failure to use the words of slavery or race. For Jaffa, that would be a lawyerly evasion of the Consti-tution's obvious compromise with slavery, as evident in its text as in its historical context. Slavery, based on race, is obviously contemplated, accommodated and enforced. And it is not unreasonable to wonder how the Framers could have ac-cepted slavery if they considered their Black compatriots part of the civic commu-nity and clothed with civil rights. Moreover, this is not really a question about the Framers' intent, but a matter of what Charles Black has called the "structures" and "relationships" implied by the text itself. If even segregation implies a subor-dinate status inconsistent with full citizenship, what sort of relationship between the republic and persons of African descent is implied by the Constitution's en-forcement of the race-based institutions of slavery and the slave trade? Once it is conceded that slavery based on race was a *constitutive* feature of the republic, it becomes reasonable to conclude, as Taney did, that the original Constitution de-fined a racially exclusive civic community. On such grounds, Jaffa thought Taney perfectly faithful to the constitutional text—*provided that the constitutional text was nothing more than the text of the Constitution.*

The difficulty with originalism, Jaffa maintained, is the question of *what* is to be originally construed. Jaffa's Lincolnian argument was that the Constitution depended upon the earlier authority of the Declaration of Independence, and so

---

[177] Harry V. Jaffa, "What Were the 'Original Intentions' of the Framers of the Constitution of the United States," *Puget Sound Law Review* 10 (1987): 351.

[178] Ibid., 351–62.

perforce incorporated the Declaration's natural law principles. The Declaration states unequivocally the equality of all people. The original Constitution never mentions equality and in fact contains several clauses that obstruct, though not permanently, the passage towards equality. But for Jaffa, the self-evident natural law principles of the Declaration must be read as part of the Constitution, part of the broader act of "constituting" the nation. And so once, and only once, we invoke the Declaration, we can attack Taney for wrongly treating the Constitution as denying the equality of the races. Taney's originalist interpretation is wrong not at the superficial, exoteric level at which Meese attacks it, but at the deeper, less visible level of the ideal. And for Jaffa, the Constitution's ideal meaning does not depend on our aspiration or imagination any more than it depends on the Framers' will. For Jaffa, substantive moral ideals are not, as they seem to be for White, acts of imagination: they are *truths*.

Thus, for Jaffa, the Declaration tells us why the political authority of the United States is also a moral authority, not just the expression of collective self-interest. Unlike the Constitution, it is not "ordained and established" by fiat, by the will of "We, the People." It is an argument of principle, directed to the conscience of "mankind," and it is only after justifying its sovereignty on the basis of and in subordination to such principles that the people of the United States earned the right to ordain and establish governing institutions. To Jaffa, what modern conservatives like Meese expound is not true conservatism, but the vicious positivism of Calhoun, a mean-spirited sense of sovereignty in which state's "rights" depend on positive state law and not on residual social consent or natural law. Calhoun's was a narrow positivist notion of sovereignty as untrammeled power—not the real sovereignty of a continent, self-governed people announced by the Declaration. The mighty "will of the people" of the modern positivist is "factum brutum."[179] But Madison thought the constitutional compact was formed under the laws of nature and God, for the purpose of rational, civil government. The necessary accommodation of slavery in the frame of government did not imply otherwise since, as Lincoln recognized, only a foolish purist would have formed a smaller union without slavery, leaving slavery unrestrained and a weaker republic imperiled by external threats. For Jaffa, the Constitution is a prudential compromise of natural law with historical circumstance, subject to the superior authority of the Declaration—it is not a delegation to the whimsy of future readers. The founders

> meant to set up a standard maxim for a free society, which could be familar to all, and revered by all, constantly looked to, constantly labored for, and even though never perfectly attained, constantly approximated, and thereby constantly spreading and deepening its influence and augmenting the happiness and value of life to all people of all colors everywhere.[180]

[179] Ibid., 364–68.
[180] Ibid., 415–22.

Madison, says Jaffa, believed that the will of the people was that of a body incorporated under "the laws of nature and of nature's God."[181] Ours was to be a civil society deliberately and rationally formed, its underlying purposes given by nature and flowing from that nature as rationally apprehended. Such a society would be ruled not by will or imagination, but reason, and dedicated to natural human equality. Thus, Jaffa invokes Strauss's pronouncement that "the United States was the first country in the world to be founded in explicit opposition to Machiavellian principles."[182] These "Machiavellian principles" consist in accepting that politics is cast adrift from ultimate values and that social order therefore depends upon inherently fragile, ephemeral, corruptible cultures of value. This "Machiavellian" predicament is, of course, precisely the premise of White's notion of rhetoric as the art of temporarily reconstituting authority in the face of the inevitable corruptions of time.

"Machiavellian Principles": The Civic Republicanism School

The most prominent interpreter of this "Machiavellian" predicament is J. G. A. Pocock, the intellectual historian renowned for his exposition of the "Republican" tradition in political thought in Renaissance Italy, seventeenth-century England, and Revolutionary America. Like Strauss, Pocock is an historian of political theory who has been concerned with modern treatment of classical ideas and motifs, and whose primary focus has been on the language or rhetoric of political thought. However, Pocock's approach is closer to the Aristotelian method of the Chicago Critics than the Socratic dialectic of the Straussians. His aim is to reconstruct the rhetorical contexts of archaic political debates—the conventions and key terms of value organizing their traditions and genres—so as to render them intelligible on their own terms. The rhetorical historian is less concerned with the particular aims and interests of a political actor or movement than with terms and paradigms by which the content will take shape. He is concerned not so much with what the speaker intended but what means he had to say what he intended. Thus, the English of the eighteenth century cast all debates in terms of the common law and real property. Machiavelli's Italy cast debate in terms of the Florentine *pratiche*.[183] The Puritans cast all issues in the rhetoric of the eschatological and the apocalyptic. And Strauss notwithstanding, the American Founding Fathers drew from Machiavelli himself a language directed at exposing the risks and incidents of corruption.

In recent years, many left-of-center legal scholars have sought inspiration from the intellectual model of civic republicanism expounded by Pocock in *The*

---

[181] Ibid., 363.

[182] Jaffa, "What Were the 'Original Intentions," 351, 363–64, quoting Leo Strauss, *Thoughts on Machiavelli* (Chicago: Univ. of Chicago Press, 1984), 13.

[183] J. G. A. Pocock, *The Machiavellian Moment: Florentine Political Thought and the Atlantic Republican Tradition* (Princeton: Princeton Univ. Press, 1975), 116–21.

Machiavellian Moment.[184] This prototypical "moment" is an era's discovery of the contingency of its legal and political order, which is now seen as an ephemeral human creation rather than something divinely ordained. There ensues a search for the human qualities of virtue that render a polity stable or at least resilient and for the institutional design that reproduces these virtues in those with the greatest influence over events. In Renaissance Italy this search turned to reflection on the fate of the Roman republic. The Puritan revolt in England produced a similar sense of crisis and also inspired a turn to civic humanist models of republican virtue, in the thought of James Harrington, and the polemics of the "Country" party against what they saw as the nefarious party of the "Court."

The Country Englishman conceived his life according to Aristotelian and civic humanist notions of virtue, which for Machiavelli had rested on private ownership of arms and for Harrington freeholds in land, since the Courtly enemies were standing professional armies and the rentier class. Virtue was associated with independence, corruption with economic and social dependence. The common law was the security of virtuous freeholders, while corruption came from the paid army, parliamentary patronage, the rentier class, and the phantasmagorical economy of credit. The Country gentleman lived free of interest and passion because he had all he required in his own back yard and so could devote himself unselfishly to his country, while those dependent on government presumably regarded public affairs from the standpoint of private interest.

The opening of the American continent was an opportunity to build a republic of yeoman farmers in an uncorrupted Edenic landscape, and the American revolutionaries perceived the annoyances of Parliamentary rule through categories received from the Country ideology. Historians have portrayed the revolutionary state constitutions as republican in inspiration, and while the federal constitution compromised republican principles, the debates over its framing and ratification were conducted in reference to those principles.[185] The Ciceronian classicism that informed the interpretation and veneration of the Constitution between the Revolution and the Civil War testified to the continuing vitality of the republican motif in American political culture.

Many contemporary legal scholars understand American constitutional law to be experiencing a kind of "Machiavellian Moment," in which the lack of objective foundations for adjudication has prompted a search for political virtues that judges can model or otherwise encourage. Certainly Bickel's vision of the Supreme Court as a deliberative forum of principle, to be protected by its prudence and rhetorical artistry, is such a model of virtue; so is Dworkin's conception of adjudication as a personification of the moral traditions of the polity, as is White's vision of the judge and lawyer as ethical friends to the culture.

---

[184] Ibid.

[185] Gordon Wood, *The Creation of the American Republic* (Chapel Hill: Univ. of North Carolina Press, 1969).

Another such project is the proposal of some constitutional theorists to develop a modern rhetoric of civic republicanism as a guide to constitutional interpretation. According to Cass Sunstein, a leading proponent of this approach, neo-republican constitutional theorists draw four principles from the republican tradition: (1) political decisions should result from a deliberative process that alters the preferences of participants by subjecting them to rational dialogue; (2) participants in this deliberative politics should be equal in participation and influence; (3) deliberation should aim to reach agreement on the common good; (4) participation in deliberative politics should be broad.[186] In essence, these theorists equate civic virtue with the activity of deliberative debate over the common good, debate that is disinterested in the sense of articulating public reasons rather than private preferences. Thus, they identify civic virtue with a certain kind of rhetorical pursuit.

There is a difficulty with this deliberative model of politics, one that its proponents usually acknowledge but do not always resolve. Republicanism has traditionally sought to restrict participation to the virtuous. While republicans have sometimes sought to distribute virtue broadly, they have sometimes been pessimistic about the capacity of most citizens for virtue. If virtue consists in deliberative reason and few citizens have both the capacity and the opportunity to exercise this faculty in making political choices, then deliberative reason becomes a restrictive qualification for political participation—or a reason to reduce mass politics to a merely cathartic or expressive function while restricting decision making to a deliberatively rational elite.

This is no idle concern. Sunstein understands Madison's conception of the original Constitution to have been premised on pessimism about the prospects of popular virtue.[187] Madison argued that, contrary to prevailing ideas, virtuous government was more attainable in a large than in a small republic precisely because of the distance between the people and their governing representatives. A carefully designed constitution, it was hoped, could disable partisan and parochial pressures on government by setting them against each other and allow a cosmopolitan elite to govern above the fray. And the most obvious and common use of republicanism in contemporary constitutional theory is to justify countermajoritarian judicial review as a means of requiring majoritarian decision making to be deliberative or of supplying the deliberation that majoritarian decision making would otherwise lack.[188]

Of course a neorepublican constitutional theory need not be elitist and antidemocratic if it emphasizes broadening and deepening political participation. Several critical legal scholars have proposed taking more seriously the Harringtonian con-

---

[186] Cass Sunstein, "Beyond the Republican Revival," *Yale Law Journal* 97 (1988): 1539.

[187] Cass Sunstein, "Interest Groups in American Public Law," *Stanford Law Review* 38 (1985): 29, 38–48; see also *Federalist Papers Nos.* 10, 51 (James Madison); Garry Wills, *Explaining America: The Federalist* (New York: Doubleday, 1981), 197–264; David Epstein, *The Political Theory of the Federalist* (Chicago: Univ. of Chicago Press, 1984) 88–110, 154–55.

[188] E.g., Sunstein, "Interest Groups," 47.

nection between material independence and the capacity to participate meaningfully in politics. Richard Parker has proposed on this basis that democratic citizenship should be thought to entail a right of income security for all,[189] while William
Simon and William Forbath have suggested that collective ownership or management of productive property might be a necessary condition to meaningful democratic citizenship.[190] Gerald Frug has instead proposed that government power be
devolved to the local level to enhance opportunities for direct political participation.[191] These proposals are more concerned with the social requisites for political
participation than with its deliberative character, and so they do not emphasize
the identification of virtue with rhetoric.

Our concern is with the variants of neorepublicanism that emphasize deliberation over participation. These are the most rhetorical and potentially the most
elitist. And that elitism may manifest itself in the form of a particularly decadent
version of the Law as Literature trope, in which lawmakers envision themselves
not as representatives but as artistic representations of the people that *portray*
deliberation for popular edification and entertainment. In this scenario, popular
participation in politics is illusory, and official deliberation is largely ornamental
rhetoric, so that most of what passes for "politics" is nothing more than a pacifying
aesthetic spectacle.

These risks are apparent in Frank Michelman's "Traces of Self-Government."[192]
Here Michelman strives to expound a republicanism compatible with his liberal
commitment to the subjectivity of value, and with the character of the American
Constitution as a continental scheme of representative government. He pursues
this aim by emphasizing the deliberative strand of republican thought. The essay's
generative trope identifies deliberation with "self-governance," not primarily self-
governance in the sense of democracy, but self-governance in the esoteric sense
of individual autonomy or self-control. Michelman's wistfully pessimistic and
aestheticized attitude towards democracy is aptly expressed by his title. "Traces"
of self-government suggests that self-government is not something we have, but
something we have lost, a sign of redemption to be sought in an object of interpretation that is at once our Constitution, our past, our institutions, and ourselves.

Michelman prepares his audience by beginning with a brief discussion of a
freedom of religion case that seems aimed at distinguishing desirably "self-governing" or "republican" judgment from regrettably "authoritarian" or "imperial"
judgment. The "authoritarian" opinions uphold the decision of the Air Force to
preclude an Orthodox Jewish airman from wearing a yarmulkah while in uniform.
They rest on deference to military judgment concerning discipline and concerns
about the implications for military discipline of requiring accommodation for a
wide range of religious practices. The "self-governing" dissent would overturn

---

[189] Richard Parker, "The Past of Constitutional Theory—and Its Future," *Ohio State Law Journal*
42 (1981): 223; Richard Parker, *"Here, the People Rule"* (Cambridge: Harvard Univ. Press, 1994).

[190] William Simon, "Social-Republican Property," *U.C.L.A. Law Review* 38 (1991): 1335; William
Forbath, "The Ambiguities of Free Labor," *Wisconsin Law Review* (1985): 767.

[191] Gerald Frug, "The City as a Legal Concept," *Harvard Law Review* 93 (1980): 1059.

[192] Frank Michelman, "Traces of Self-Government," *Harvard Law Review* 100 (1986): 3.

the Air Force decision on grounds that no compelling reason was shown to infringe the free exercise of religion in this particular case. Michelman lauds the dissent's apparent call for ad hoc, case-by-case interest balancing as an act of "commitment" to "the country's project of resolving normative disputes by conversation, a communicative practice of open and intelligible reason-giving, as opposed to self-justifying impulse and ipse dixit. She speaks in a voice of colloquy, not authority, persuasion, not self-justification."[193]

Thus, a thoroughly conventional Supreme Court opinion becomes Michelman's illustration of deliberative virtue. Judges "govern" or control themselves, not by deferring to other decision makers, but by making up their own minds: "Every norm, every time, requires explanation and justification in context."[194] Deference to other authorities is "authoritarian." In this case the other authority is that quintessentially arbitrary, undemocratic authority of the military, but of course in most cases courts will defer to elected political authorities. Nevertheless, judges do not support democracy by deferring to elected officials. Such "authoritarian" jurisprudence "debases the community by slighting its self-transformative capacity,"[195] while deliberative jurisprudence vindicates the "aspirational content of American constitutional discourse, expressed in its organizing tension of self-rule and law-rule."[196] So, "if the Justices have any way to further the cause of our self-government it is through the exercise of their own."[197] In deciding for themselves what law should govern us, the Justices give expression and inspiration to our aspirations to govern ourselves according to a self-chosen law.[198]

Having prepared his readers with this inspiring example of deliberative virtue, Michelman then proceeds to his argument. He begins by asserting that the republican tradition has understood deliberation to serve two values. One is the "anthropological" value of "public happiness," the Aristotelian idea that human beings fulfill their nature and realize themselves by participating in politics. The other is the "epistemological" value of practical reason in revealing the public good. The difficulty is that both of these values seem to offend the liberal premise of the subjectivity of values by implying an objective human nature or public good.[199] Liberals, concludes Michelman, can only endorse deliberation as a *process* leading to the realization of individual preferences or values. Thus, he rejects the Aristotelian idea that "citizenship . . . is the essence of the human subject" and treats practical reason as a means to individual freedom as self-governance.

He explains his notion of self-governance in terms of a "Kantian" ideal of autonomy, requiring that the self be chosen rather than determined by desire. Self-governance then consists in making a considered and well-informed choice of a

---

[193] Ibid., 34–36.
[194] Ibid., 76.
[195] Frank Michelman, "Law's Republic," *Yale Law Journal* 97 (1988): 1493, 1496.
[196] Ibid., 1596.
[197] Michelman, "Traces," 17.
[198] Ibid.
[199] Ibid., 23.

"law" or moral principle to guide one's conduct:[200] "We are free only in so far as we are self-governing, directing our actions in accordance with law-like reasons that we adopt for ourselves, as proper to ourselves, upon conscious critical reflection on our identities (or natures) and social situations."[201] Michelman argues that our reflections must begin with our received identities and social situations because deliberation is a form of practical reason that cannot yield specific results unless the deliberator situates herself in the narrative of a life, a community, or an institution. He rejects the assumption that individual preferences are given in advance of social choice and associates republicanism with the contrary view that there are no prepolitical preferences.[202] It follows that "Kantianism implies republicanism—self-government implies citizenship—to all who conceive of the human individual as in some degree socially situated or constituted. . . . Normative reason, it then seems, cannot be a solitary activity."[203]

Thus, Michelman concludes that Kantian deliberation must take the form of political dialogue—but *only* as a means to achieve individual autonomy, *not* as a means to realize the common good or the individual good of a politically engaged life. Individual normative deliberation cannot get off the ground unless it is fueled by a "nomos"—a collective normative tradition—but it cannot achieve autonomy if it is governed by any "telos"—including the telos of deliberative politics.[204] Yet Michelman's fastidious efforts to evade teleology are futile: he treats individual freedom as an intrinsic good, a telos, and he *equates* individual freedom with collective deliberation. He cannot argue, for example, that individual freedom is realized as long as individuals have the option of such collective deliberation but choose not to avail themselves of it, because on his terms, any such choice is free only if it follows *from* such deliberation. It follows that individual autonomy is not merely facilitated, but *constituted* by "public happiness"; if the first is an intrinsic good, so is the second.

Possibly to Michelman's chagrin, his discussion of self-governance has far-reaching critical implications. It implies that without meaningful, deliberative participation, neither voter nor consumer preferences express autonomous individual choice, and that no government decision can be democratically legitimate. It seems to point in the direction of the kind of fundamental reforms suggested by Parker, Simon, Forbath, and Frug. But by framing his argument as yet another vindication of judicial review, Michelman drains it of any of these radical implications. Before we even encounter this implicit democratic critique of all government we have already been taught to respect a particular process of government—Supreme Court adjudication—as not only compatible with self-governance, but as its very paradigm. Government decisions are therefore legitimate *not* insofar as they are made with the participation of all affected persons; government decisions are legitimate insofar as the officials who made them *deliberated*.

[200] Ibid., 24.
[201] Ibid., 26.
[202] Ibid., 27.
[203] Ibid.
[204] Ibid., 28–29.

Michelman concludes that the republican "ideal of freedom as self-govern-ment" is "obviously impractical" in the "national constitutional setting," and even "ominously" illiberal. Yet

> as a result, the courts . . . seem to take on as one of their ascribed functions the modeling of active self-government that citizens find practically beyond reach. Unable as a nation to practice our own self-government . . . we—or at any rate we of "the reasoning class"—can at least identify with the judiciary's as we idealistically construct it.[205]

Michelman is more or less resigned to the unattainability of the ideal of a self-governing democracy in the United States. He acknowledges that the ideal of self-governance cannot be realized vicariously through the deliberation of Burkean virtual representatives.[206] Yet he concludes that the American Constitu-tion presumes that the American people are incapable of deliberation. It seeks to moderate the clash of their private and partisan interests, by balancing the actual but nondeliberative representation of those interests against deliberation by virtual representatives. Judges, he concludes, exemplify the latter category of representation.[207]

But rather than regretting this situation, Michelman renders it as an aesthetic object. Thus, "the judge . . . represents by his own self-government our missing self-government, by his own practical reason our missing dialogue";[208] and simi-larly, "the Court . . . appears not as *representative* of the People's declared will but as *representation* and trace of the People's absent self-government."[209] We may not govern ourselves, and our government may not represent us—but by governing us deliberatively it provides us with an idealized portrayal of ourselves. Our rulers imagine what we might decide to do if we were a self-governing people, or, if necessary, we imagine that they do; and so we flatter ourselves that our rulers imagine us as self-governing. Thus inspired, we of the "reasoning class" perhaps deliberate in the manner of the Supreme Court over the issues of the day—not to affect public life, but the better to appreciate our rulers' rhetorical performance. Michelman's liberalism reduces his republicanism to ornament and restricts it to a small class of officials. Like White, Michelman invites us to experi-ence politics aesthetically. But White at least assumes we are party to that politics, authors of our own aesthetic experiences, players on the set of a grand political theater. Michelman appears to relegate us to the role of sophisticated spectators.

The Liberal Character

It may seem an odd anti-authoritarianism that fawns over judges as inspiring models of ethical character, but this paradox may be inherent in the liberal variant of the Law as Rhetoric trope.

---

[205] Ibid., 73–74.
[206] Ibid., 51.
[207] Ibid., 73.
[208] Ibid.
[209] Ibid., 65.

The anti-authoritarianism is, of course, a defining commitment of liberalism. And in some ways, the Law as Rhetoric trope serves this anti-authoritarianism by implying that law is persuasion rather than fiat or truth. The Law as Rhetoric trope thereby makes the authority of law seem contingent on the assent of an audience, one that can perhaps answer back and participate in a lawmaking dialogue. Yet these subversive implications tend to be undercut by a focus on the judge as rhetorician, and by an implicit identification of the rhetorician with noble character.

The focus on judicial rhetoric is hard to avoid, since the culture of the American legal profession treats the judicial opinion as the model forensic performance, which appellate advocates and doctrinal legal scholars imitate. And despite the attachment of liberal rhetoricians to the conceit that the law is a dialogic process, it is hard to ignore the fact that in the courtroom at least, lawyers speak *to* the law, while judges speak *for* it. The judge's dignity, civility, and dispassionate deliberation may provide an appealing model of personal demeanor, but they are luxuries of power that do not win but rather presuppose a deference secured by force.[210] We "talk back" to judges at their sufferance and our own risk.

Ideally, the rhetorician wins persuasive authority by force of character and argument rather than by force of arms. Part of the appeal of rhetoric to liberal legal theorists lies in this identification of authority with ethos or character. The liberal legal theorist strives to restore the possibility of an authoritative law in the face of the subjectivity of values. Yet the liberal legal theorist cannot simply ascribe authority to every subjective preference without confronting the paradoxes of social choice that seem to preclude the legitimacy of any law: a world in which all subjective preferences are equally authoritative is arguably a Hobbesian state of nature, not law at all. Hence the appeal of rhetoric: rhetoric promises to restore the authority of law in the face of the subjectivity of values, by at least provisionally establishing the authority of a certain kind of subject, one capable or worthy of persuading others.

We have already explored one approach to establishing an authoritative subject, which is to condition ethical authority on criteria of virtue that are *impersonal* in the sense that they derive from nature, or from the traditions and institutions of a particular civic community. Insofar as this approach is true to rhetoric's classical roots, it is somewhat alien to the sensibility of the modern liberal. A more modern, more Romantic conception of ethical character might view it as a unique quality, different in each individual. The ethical evaluation of personality would be similar to the aesthetic appreciation of works of art in that both would be essentially noncomparative. Thus conceived, rhetoric is a form of literary self-expression, and ethical authority is an aesthetic effect that is different in every case.

Such an overtly aesthetic model of character implies a conception of self-governance as self-creation rather than self-control. The "character" on which rhetorical authority rests is then an artistic creation, like a character in a novel. The virtuous discipline involved in achieving this Romantic conception of rhetorical authority

---

[210] See Robert Cover, "Violence and the Word," *Yale Law Journal* 96 (1986): 1601.

is the discipline of the artist, sublimating passion into creative expression. In order to create her own character, the rhetorical artist will have to be imaginative and will have to be flexible enough to change herself, even at the cost of flouting tradition. Thus, a Romantic model of rhetoric also suggests a reinterpretation of the liberal values of open-mindedness and irreverence as attributes of artistic creativity rather than scientific rationality.

One example of this effort to ground the authority of law in Romantic authorship is Joseph Vining's *The Authoritative and the Authoritarian*. The book addresses what the author takes to be a crisis of meaning and value both in modern society generally and in the American legal profession in particular. The crisis of modern society is the inability "to order our wants" resulting from the rejection of meaning and value as merely subjective.[211] This results in efforts to invest authority in various emblems of "objectivity": science, markets, bureaucracy. All such efforts are misguided, in Vining's view, because neither individuals nor societies can "order their wants" without professing values, and without meaning what they profess. The ability to formulate a goal or a judgment depends upon accepting some value as authoritative.

Vining adds that the modern crisis of value and meaning expresses itself in two ways within the legal profession. One expression of this crisis is a contradiction between the hermeneutic method of lawyers and their cynical view that meaning is a fiction. Another is a loss of respect for the Supreme Court and its opinions, which Vining insists should be, and once were, texts interpreted with the care and veneration literary critics lavish on Milton.[212] The judgments of the Supreme Court may retain coercive force, Vining concedes, but they are losing authority. Vining links this loss of respect to what he calls the "bureaucratization" of opinion writing as a result of the increasing reliance on staffs of law clerks. The inauthenticity of Supreme Court opinions reflects a creeping cynicism about values that assumes that the reasons for the exercise of power do not matter. To the extent the Justices do not take seriously the obligation to win authority for their judgments, their decisions of power have become authoritarian rather than authoritative.

But this "authoritarian" or positivist understanding of law is mistaken, Vining proclaims. Law is not a cause of behavior, but a reason for behavior: to apply or obey law as law requires belief in its authority. This in turn requires belief that the law is promulgated by an intending mind that has deliberated in good faith on the public interest, and decided as she sincerely believes anyone in the same role should have done. True authority, Vining insists, requires not objectivity, but authenticity combined with devotion to role. Authority can inhere only in an identifiable author, not a bureaucratic process.

Vining insists that to interpret the law is to personify it, to construct a character who could coherently think the thoughts attributed to the text. For Vining, law

---

[211] Joseph Vining, *The Authoritative and the Authoritarian* (Chicago: Univ. of Chicago Press, 1988), 4.

[212] Ibid., 10, 12, 150–53.

must reflect the authentic deliberative judgment of an author, even if that author is taken to be a sovereign people. Why cannot the people simply do their will? Why must they deliberate? Why isn't majority preference self-authorizing? Because, says Vining, without law, without procedural ground rules for social choice, there is no popular will: "An election begins with a world of alternatives, and it is a party structure or some other system of rules that finally brings the decision down to a bipolar one."[213] These procedural rules must be authoritative law for an aggregation of votes to be recognized as the sovereign popular will. Moreover, most elections are won with a small minority of the eligible electorate. The authority of such elections as a measure of popular will may depend on an assumption that the participants have acted as virtual representatives of the nonparticipants, that they have considered everything that the nonparticipants would have considered relevant.[214] To be fully authoritative as law, Vining concludes, law must be seen as the coherent, deliberative, sincere judgment of a single mind, even if it was promulgated by numerous people. Like Dworkin, Vining believes that to interpret and apply law is to personify the polity.

Vining fears that unless the polity is personified in this way, we are incapable of personifying ourselves. He argues that because individuals are shaped by the larger forces of culture and language, we cannot govern ourselves individually, even by deliberating about our values and preferences. Language and culture can only be shaped collectively, through law. But because the meaning and authority of law are also contingent on language and culture, law's influence on language and culture may influence its own development in unanticipated ways. Hence, in order to shape the cultural conditions for the development of individual personality, law must imagine its own biography, composing itself as a character. Only by personifying law and deliberating over its character development, Vining concludes, can individuals have any role in shaping the future conditions of their own development.

Vining argues that it is much easier for law to deliberatively shape its own development if it is declared by a single authoritative institution, like the Supreme Court. But to achieve this kind of collective self-determination Vining considers it necessary that such an institution seek authority for its decisions in a deliberative and personal voice, and that the individuals writing for the institution convincingly express a sense of responsibility to the institution's past and for its future. This is why Vining considers it so important to the authority of law that the Supreme Court's opinions be ascribable to the venerable figures of the Justices themselves. The Supreme Court seems to him ideally designed to personify the Constitution to the public. The Justices' authorial personalities are, to Vining, a fund of ethos upon which the Constitution draws for meaning and authority, a fund that they squander if they allow hacks to churn out bureaucratic boilerplate in their name. Thus, Vining endeavors to bring together, in the figure of the judicial author, the classical ideal of ethos and the Romantic ideal of self-expression.

---

[213] Ibid., 138.
[214] Ibid., 139–40.

Vining attempts to establish the proposed linkage between literary voice and rhetorical authority performatively, by modeling it. He identifies his own authorial voice as literary in a variety of ways. The work opens and closes with a poem and consists otherwise of a series of ruminative essays, drafted with much greater attention to cadence, symmetry, and elaborate metaphor than to argumentative rigor. While the work contains arguments, it affects an oracular tone, as if to create the impression that the reader is being persuaded even of small points by the personal authority of the author rather than by argument.

But in the end this strategy is undermined by the author's idiosyncratic concerns. It is simply narcissistic to hinge the fate of the republic on whether "serious analysts"[215]—presumably legal academics—feel betrayed by a Court that is not providing them with texts worthy of their hermeneutic prowess. If we really need to rely on the institutional authority of the Supreme Court to sustain our faith in values, nihilism must have more going for it than meets the eye.

A more successful effort to ground values in the ethical authority of the subject is Martha Nussbaum's lecture "Valuing Values: A Case for Reasoned Commitment."[216] Nussbaum challenges the assumption that we have unavoidably entered something called a "postmodern" world where we can never justify a value. As a corollary she pairs with a glib postmodernism, represented by Stanley Fish, the glib marginalism of Richard Posner and Robert Bork that skeptically opposes the "intersubjective comparison of utilities." Both treat the subjectivity of values as a reason to avoid value choices. Nussbaum claims that any argument against the rationality of value judgment will fail in the same way: on close inspection, it will turn out to equate rationality with some impossibly exacting standard like certainty or universal agreement. This is an impractical and hence irrational way to assess values, which should be judged according to the probabilistic standards of Aristotelian practical reason.

Yet Nussbaum's more distinctive and rhetorically effective argument is to catch her interlocutors up in a performative contradiction. To do so, she turns to the classical predecessors of modern skeptics and shows that their skepticism was not in fact an epistemological attitude of disbelief in values but a rhetorical and therapeutic art aimed at achieving a valued emotional state. Skepticism was a practice of argument aimed at maintaining detachment from commitments so as to avoid an emotional investment in events. The desired emotional state—"freedom from disturbance"—was roughly the same state sought by stoics, who sought to suppress desires rather than values in order to maintain what we still call a "philosophical attitude" towards events. Like Vining, Nussbaum believes that to value is to embrace a certain sort of character. But she also reverses the relationship, so that to adopt a character is to embrace a value. This in turn implies that the brisk, unruffled, cocksure characters projected by both Fish and Posner are aesthetic sensibilities—valuations that belie their expressed value skepticism.

---

[215] Ibid., 10.

[216] Martha Nussbaum, "Valuing Values: A Case for Reasoned Commitment," *Yale Journal of Law and the Humanities* 6 (1994): 197–217.

But Nussbaum extends her performative argument to implicate not only her opponents, but also her readers in valuing. After showing that skeptics, both ancient and modern, are valuing by creating characters who pursue an implicit conception of the good, it becomes possible to evaluate their skepticism by evaluating these characters.

Thus, Nussbaum recalls a story told by Diogenes Laertius concerning Pyrrho and the pig. On a ship facing shipwreck, Pyrrho notices that the pig is blissfully indifferent to the imminent disaster and concludes that he thereby exemplifies the wise person, who lives in a state free of disturbance. To Nussbaum, this piglike wise man is none other than the glib skeptic who relieves himself of the tension and challenge of moral choice by assuming the impossibility of justifiable choice; his failure, in a sense, is another example of a failure of self-governance. This is the "allure of freedom from normative commitment."[217] His is also an aesthetic failure: his life lacks the drama of striving and the narrative development that attends a project of self-realization. Such an existence, she implies, is unworthy of a human being.

What Nussbaum has done here is to take advantage of the fact that we are always readier to judge character than to commit ourselves to a value. We may be tempted with the skeptic to say that value is only a matter of opinion, but we cannot help holding such opinions with conviction when faced with the practical question of whom to befriend or trust. She has directed our attention past the arguments of skeptics to the smug self-assurance these arguments afford them. In so doing she already has us judging, evaluating, and by that very evaluation rejecting, skepticism.

To be morally alive, Nussbaum implies, is to be capable of being disturbed. This capacity for disturbance can serve liberalism in three ways: by enabling the feeling of empathic distress that can undergird humane and egalitarian impulses; by enabling the painful self-alteration implicit in deliberation, self-realization, or acceptance of progressive social change; or by enabling tolerance of alien views and practices. In these ways the capacity to tolerate disturbance may be an aspect of open-mindedness, of being willing and able to listen.

While a capacity for disturbance and inner conflict may conduce to a freer or fairer society, it may be valued intrinsically as a self-discipline that enlarges and deepens the soul. Hence, we might endorse liberal practices that challenge our complacency merely because of their beneficial effects on character. This is the gist of Lee Bollinger's surprising defense of freedom of speech in *The Tolerant Society*.[218]

For Bollinger, the practice of protecting speech through the courts is designed to model and induce good character in society; that is, we engage in tolerance beyond what is necessary to protect harmless or valuable speech, because we thereby train ourselves not to yield to the very intolerant impulses that often manifest themselves in extremist speech. Tolerance of such speech trains us to

[217] Ibid., 197–201.
[218] Lee Bollinger, *The Tolerant Society* (New York: Oxford Univ. Press, 1986).

deal more moderately and deliberatively with the provocative practices and social encounters we face in a pluralist society: "The operation of free speech may be seen as reflecting a determination to create a general intellectual character through the creation of a kind of tolerance ethic."[219]

Bollinger's argument proceeds from the premise that all speech, and indeed all behavior, is a kind of self-expressive rhetoric: a performative demonstration of one's character and values and an implicit model for others to follow. Every act implicitly asserts that such conduct is permissible and worthwhile, and implicitly attacks the character and status of those who disagree or are disadvantaged. Thus, all social behavior expresses a commitment to certain values, and hence both a measure of intolerance and a provocation to the intolerance of others.

Similarly, Bollinger views the social attitudes of both tolerance and intolerance as communicative performances. Intolerance, he notes, is designed to say that we do not believe what we will not tolerate, or that we have the courage to condemn the enemy. What we will not tolerate defines who we are.[220] It is a sign of conviction, but also of insecurity, even self-contempt. Like White writing on Burke's immoderate critique of the French Revolution, Bollinger thinks what we least tolerate in others is what we most hate in ourselves: "As painful as the acknowledgment is, each of us bears some aspect of the character of mind reflected by the Nazis. And it is the intolerance we feel toward our own intolerance that contributes to our wanting to censor the external, exaggerated reflection of that part of ourselves."[221] In this sense, intolerance is an admission of self-alienation.

By contrast, Bollinger views tolerance as a form of resistance to the controlling effects of the flux of social life, a technique for ensuring personal coherence and integrity. Tolerance therefore is a form of self-governance that invites others to exhibit similiar moderation. Intolerant "feelings must arise and must be controlled in the basic operation of a self-governing political society, where a willingness to compromise and a willingness even to accept total defeat are essential components of the democratic personality."[222] Tolerance of extremist speech serves to reinforce tolerance in civic life generally, by serving as a kind of civic self-mortification that "symbolizes" public commitment to tolerance.[223] By making a ritual of tolerance, the citizens of modern society can substitute an aesthetic for a moralistic response to the provocative self-expressions of their fellow citizens, without losing a sense of themselves as morally serious.

Bollinger argues that the rhetorical task of teaching and modeling tolerance is appropriately left to judges, because

> judges are members of a professional group whose central intellectual ethic is identical with the aspirations of the free speech principle. To a degree more than with any other group, judges are expected to have mastered the tolerant mind, to have the capacity to

---

[219] Ibid., 124.
[220] Ibid., 104–42.
[221] Ibid., 127.
[222] Ibid., 117.
[223] Ibid., 124, 131, 143.

set aside their personal beliefs and predilections, and to control the impulses that accompany them as they set about interpreting and administering the society's laws. . . . The ideal judge . . . is . . . a paradigmatic illustration of the qualities of mind pursued through the free speech principle.[224]

Like other liberal rhetoricians, Bollinger regards judges as icons of open-minded self-governance, paragons of the liberal character. He offers the Bickelian argument that judges may be particularly sensitive to the value of tolerance, since their weakness makes them dependent on public forbearance.[225] And like Bickel, Bollinger regards judicial instruction of the public as a delicate rhetorical task, requiring restraint and moderation.[226] Zeal and absolutism in the protection of speech undercut the rhetorical point of the practice. Thus, for Bollinger, judicial forebearance is not a prudential posture required to conserve judicial authority; forebearance is the very virtue judges seek to model. Forebearance—even in the pursuit of principle—is the liberal character.

For Gerald Frug, there is no single liberal character, but a field of possibilities. In "Argument as Character," Frug urges us to regard "legal argument as an example of rhetoric" in which the speaker " 'show[s] himself to be of a certain character' and seeks to have his listeners . . . identify with that kind of character."[227] Frug invokes Aristotle's association of persuasive authority with character, but according to Frug, "character" takes on new meanings in the modern era, associated less with notions of virtue and ethos, and more with individual personality, social and dramatic roles, and literary self-expression. Members of modern society conceive themselves as something like characters in a novel—having experiences, making choices, pursuing careers and love objects, undertaking and fulfilling obligations, developing and acting in accordance with self-understandings. Thus, for Frug, moderns are ultimately motivated neither by desires nor by principles, but by identities that fit them with both. Accordingly, the "subjectivity" of value does not disable choice, it enables it. An "ordering of wants" is implicit in each person's conception of who she is, and rhetoric can therefore persuade and motivate by mobilizing these identities.

That is not to say that identity is stable in modern society. A defining feature of the experience of modernity is the sense that character is capable of development, social position is subject to change, and belief is responsive to reason and experience. One's "character" is a work-in-progress, and its development is subject to influence and persuasion: "the subject . . . is not something from which our decisions are derived. The 'subject' itself has to be interpreted."[228] At the same time, the individual in modern society is not really free to be whoever she wishes. Identities always depend upon social recognition and support, and Frug

[224] Ibid., 134–35.

[225] Ibid., 135.

[226] Ibid., 214–15.

[227] Gerald Frug, "Argument as Character," *Stanford Law Review* 40 (1988): 869, 872, quoting Aristotle, *The Art of Rhetoric* 1377b (J. H. Freese trans., 1926).

[228] Ibid., 878.

believes that recognition in modern society is largely mediated by bureaucratic institutions. Thus, a "character" is primarily an interpretation of the relationship between one's institutional roles and one's subjective inner life, a strategy for accommodating one's dignity as a supposedly self-determining person to the reality of bureaucratic power. Modern or liberal rhetoric persuades by offering solutions to this problem in the form of model characters.

Frug identifies several such characters in his analyses of arguments. One argument he examines is that offered by Harvard University President Derek Bok, in opposing divestment of the university's stock in companies doing business in South Africa. Bok offered several rationales.[229] First, the university must maintain some distance from the outside world—in part to protect itself from harmful economic pressure; second, divestment would be costly and less effective than Harvard acting in its role as stockholder to influence South African employers; and third, the argument for divestment rests on no coherent moral principle that its proponents are willing to implement in their own lives. Bok also invokes, in bolstering the sincerity of his position, his own vocal opposition to apartheid in, for example, congressional testimony. Frug reconstructs Bok's argument as one resting its ethical appeal on two stock characters, the academic and the establishment liberal. The academic is a unique combination of strength and weakness. The academic has persuasive power secured by material autonomy and the appearance of disinterestedness, and this power would be squandered if the academic tried to use power politics and economic leverage to influence events. The establishment liberal is liberal in his personal political views while remaining a loyal servant of conservative institutions.[230]

The character of the "new conservative"—who some will recognize as a revival of the classical liberal—mediates the tension between individual autonomy and social role in a different way: by identifying market transactions as the sphere of individual self-expression, in which people consent to confining social roles, or seize the rewards and assume the risks of entrepreneurial innovation. Frug sees this character as the rhetorical motor of Justice Rehnquist's opinion in *FEC c. NCPAC*,[231] striking down a statutory limit on PAC spending. The contrary image from Justice White's dissent sees the world as overwhelmed by corporate power and seeks accommodation and balancing to constrain this power—to make the best of a bad thing. This is the character of the "pragmatic postwar liberal."[232]

Finally, Frug considers the jurisprudential debate over the implications of the subjectivity of value as a contest of characters, a debate about how to interpret social roles. One contending character is the skeptic—or "tragic modernist" in Frug's terminology—who equates the subjectivity of values with their arbitrariness and so presents herself as disabled from making choices.[233] Such a character

---

[229] Ibid., 882–96.
[230] Ibid., 893.
[231] Ibid., 896–909.
[232] Ibid., 910–7.
[233] Ibid., 877.

is not actually disabled from choosing, Frug implies, because choice is inevitable—but her tragic posture absolves her from responsibility from her choices and allows her to acquiesce in institutional roles without disturbance. In this sense, Frug agrees with Vining that there is a link between skepticism and authoritarianism. Frug presents his own rhetorical voice as that of an "active modernist"— roughly speaking, an existentialist—who sees the inevitability of choice as a source of responsibility to compose, out of some interpretation of the available social roles, an admirable self.[234]

Yet in preaching an ethical responsibility to choose an admirable self, Frug may in the end slight the social constraints on character he earlier seemed to emphasize. Frug's "active modernist" character exemplifies a tendency in liberal rhetoric to conceive ethics as an individual project—the Romantic authorship of an ethical character—rather than a collective project of reshaping the cultural constraints on selfhood. In presenting the liberal ethos as the product of such a heroic act of literary invention, liberal rhetoricians imply that in modern society ethics is an aesthetic project *rather than* a political project. This dichotomy between the aesthetic and the political is implicit in the Romantic conception of literature as individual self-expression often presupposed by Law and Literature scholarship. This is not the first time we have encountered legal scholars responding to the subjectivity of value by trying to construct an exemplary authorial subject. The disappointing feature of these "literary" stratagems is how mutually unaffected they leave the literary and the legal. They reduce the "literary" to a prepolitical practice of fashioning a valuing individual who can then introduce fully formed subjective values into the "political" arena of the law. Literary invention can never become a collective political practice on these terms, while law can never be more than a bargain among liberal subjects.

Yet Frug points to the richer possibilities of a modern rhetoric in his repeated invocation of Nietzsche,[235] whose philosophical project could be described as the effort to imagine a modern analogue to classical virtue. For Nietzsche, the harmonious classical culture that fused personal virtue, political authority, and eloquence was unrecoverable. While Nietzsche did see the modern pursuit of virtue as a Romantic project of self-authorship, he drew from the classical world a sense that the development of virtue depended upon cultural conditions, and he saw the creation of an enabling culture as a chief aim of artistic self-expression. Thus, Nietzsche saw self-authorship as a kind of public, rhetorical, activity aimed in part at enriching the cultural resources of self-composition available to others; and he saw the values and characters individuals fashioned for themselves as vital matters of public concern. The more rhetorical criticism of law concerns itself with the cultural conditions of character formation—and the role of law in shaping those conditions—the more it resembles the "Cultural Criticism of Law" recommended in chapter 6.

---

[234] Ibid., 878–79, 923.
[235] E.g., ibid., 869 n. 1, 878 nn. 35, 36.

Yet for such criticism to yield insight it must investigate the actual functioning of law in shaping institutional conditions for the development of identity and character throughout society. By contrast, the liberal rhetoricians tend to reduce all of law to the figure of the appellate judge, and so to see law's chief cultural function as providing in that figure a model of the disinterested deliberative character. In equating law with appellate courts, liberal rhetoricians drastically restrict the significance and redemptive potential of the Law as Rhetoric trope by focusing narrowly on the self-presentations of a judicial elite. We could instead regard every social act as a rhetorical performance that models character and contributes for good or ill to the cultural repertoire of values. This would be a more democratic notion of rhetoric—but also a more demanding, less tolerant one. Insofar as it would expose our self-definitions to caustic cultural criticism, and treat our personal values as matters of public concern, such a "Nietzschean" model of rhetoric might no longer qualify as liberal.

The Liberal Model Summarized

In the view of its modern liberal proponents, rhetoric solves the problem of encouraging civic mindedness in a world dominated by the subjectivity of value by granting the self the power to create its own values while encouraging the self to conceive those values as some version of the general good. The liberal conception of rhetoric borrows heavily from the Romantic literary sensibility: instead of reason, an aesthetic posture provides the detachment from selfish desire required for a deliberative, public-regarding attitude. Like conservative rhetoric, liberal rhetoric requires that the rhetor establish ethical authority through a display of virtue. But liberal virtue is procedural rather than substantive, emphasizing civility, tolerance, open-mindedness, and flexibility, yet paradoxically also requiring concern, commitment, a capacity to be disturbed. It is the earnest desire to be principled, while deliberating interminably, deferring the embrace of any particular principle. Liberal rhetoric is deeply committed to dialogue and open-ended inquiry, yet for all its talk of self-governance and self-determination, it is ambivalent about democracy and it tends to find its models among judges rather than political leaders.

Is the rhetorical ideal incurably authoritarian? Not if by "authoritarian" we mean "dogmatic." Liberal rhetoricians seem sincere in their rejection of intellectual authoritarianism. On the other hand, they seem committed to a kind of intellectual authority—not perhaps the authority of particular ideas or principles or theories, but the authority of an intellectual of suitably refined aesthetic sensibility. Thus, liberal rhetoric rejects the dogmatism of conservative rhetoric, but not necessarily its elitism.

There may even be an ironic connection between liberal rhetoric's antidogmatism and its tendency towards elitism. It may be that the impulse to restrict the rhetorical function to a representative elite is aimed at protecting the ordinary citizen from moral scrutiny. In the rhetorical tradition, to address the public is to present one's whole self for judgment—an ordeal that not everyone would relish.

It may be that such an intensity of civic engagement is simply incompatible with the privacy and tolerance liberalism values. The liberal character may crave such "disturbance"—but liberal institutions generally promise freedom from disturbance of this kind. The price of privacy may be a vicarious politics in which our virtual representatives dramatize, for our aesthetic contemplation, a civic ideal most safely appreciated at a distance.

Conclusion

How much difference is there finally, between the two models of rhetoric we have explored? In some respects, the division is an artificial one: Bickel was a legal process liberal as well as a Burkean conservative, while the liberal White is an admirer of Burke; Booth and Nussbaum are both Aristotelians although also liberals; Anastaplo was a martyr in the struggle against McCarthyism as well as a Straussian. Even Strauss proclaimed himself a friend to liberal government although a critic of modernity and the idea of progress. All of these figures oppose racism; all believe in the worth of rational discourse and the superiority of persuasion over coercion. Clearly these are different strands of a single tradition.

One reason for the seeming convergence of the conservative and liberal models of rhetoric is the circumspection of the conservatives. They see themselves as untimely vestiges of a lost tradition, keepers of the flame in a dangerously hostile world. Figuratively speaking they are all, like Strauss, refugees. Hence, they are circumspect in criticizing the liberal institutions that provide them refuge, even if they regard those institutions as monuments to licentiousness. And so they typically make their arguments about authority, wisdom, self-discipline, and natural right indirectly, in the guise of praising some liberal article of faith, like liberty or equality or "self-government." Thus, this is a fairly benign version of conservative authoritarianism, one that does not even aspire to overt political authority. It seeks first and foremost to preserve itself, and only secondarily to help elites discreetly preserve their rule while bowing to the forms of liberal democracy. In their practical aims, the conservative and liberal models may differ very little.

It may be that where the two models differ most profoundly is in their attitude towards literature and the Romantic quest for individual and collective self-expression. For the liberal model, rhetoric conceived as a form of self-expressive literature is the basis for reconstituting the authority of law in the face of the subjectivity of value. As a rhetorical form of literature, law becomes a somewhat vicarious project of collective self-determination that promises to rescue the modern citizen from the anomie of mass society. For the conservative model, however, rhetoric is conceived as esoteric pedagogy in the service of classical philosophy. It views self-government as impulse control and submission to the authority of the wise rather than as expressive self-realization. And it views rhetoric as the basis for conserving the quest for what is truly good in the face of modern mass society's illegitimate demands for self-gratification. On the liberal rhetorical model, self-expression sublimates hedonistic impulses and so elevates the public mind. On the conservative rhetorical model, self-expression falsely asserts the worth of hedonistic impulses and so corrupts the public mind.

The dialogue between these two models may point to the possibility of a third model of modern rhetoric that is neither conservative nor liberal. Such a model would accept the subjectivity of value but not its privacy. It would view values as imaginative products but treat the resources of the normative imagination as matters of public and political concern. It would equate "rhetoric" with the performance and criticism of culture.

CHAPTER FIVE

Deconstructive Criticism of Law

INTRODUCTION

Poststructuralist literary theory, especially in the form of Jacques Derrida's "deconstruction," has been influential in legal scholarship since the early 1980s. This influence is most immediately traceable to the conjunction of four events. First, of course, the interpretation debate raised the salience of literary theory in the legal academy. Second, in the late 1970s, Duncan Kennedy incorporated the non-literary structuralism of psychologist Jean Piaget and anthropologist Claude Lévi-Strauss in law review articles that became the canonical texts of the Critical Legal Studies movement. Third, the American publication in the late 1970s of Derrida's two most important theoretical works, *Of Grammatology* and *Writing and Difference*, as well as other poststructuralist work, dramatically increased the influence of poststructuralist literary theory in American universities. Fourth, the economic decline of the humanities and the corresponding rise of the professional schools in the 1970s brought many aspiring academics into law who had recently been exposed to poststructuralist literary theory in college or graduate school. These scholars were familiar with structuralism primarily as a method of linguistics and literary theory. To them, structuralism was the tradition within which deconstruction had developed and against which it had rebelled. Many of these aspiring scholars became active in the Critical Legal Studies movement. The convergence of these influences has resulted in a genre of critical scholarship that treats law as language and views all language use as a figurative or literary practice of signification.

This deconstructive criticism of law is an inherently ambivalent enterprise. It is ambivalent, first, about sentimentality. While literature often stands for authentic human feeling in critiques of the law, no critical movement has more scorned the sentimentality implicit in this "humane" conception of literature's mission than deconstruction. And yet when they encounter law, even deconstructive literary critics cannot resist the temptation to give Nobel Prize acceptance speeches, celebrating human dignity by regretting the "reductive," "objectifying" tendencies of legal thought. The apparent contradiction is explained by the ambitions of deconstructive theorists in both the aesthetic and political realms. Within literature, the authority of critical theory depends upon challenging the Romantic equation of authority with authenticity of feeling. To the extent that literature is irreducibly artificial, arcane, and mediated, deconstructive critics can argue that a theoretically informed practice of reading is not marginal but central to the literary enterprise. But if critics are the pharisees of literature, lawyers have long ago preempted them as the pharisees of public life. In public life, the authority of literary critics depends upon the authority of literature, and so simply to be heard, even deconstructive literary critics must fulfill the public function of literature: to edify and inspire.

Deconstructive legal study is similarly ambivalent about left politics. In its home terrain of France and its home field of literature, deconstruction opposes as totalitarian a radical tradition associated with Marxism. But in the United States, deconstruction is merely the latest representative of the post-Kantian critical tradition in continental thought that for more than thirty years has offered a discreet cover for affiliation with a genteel and humane Marxism. Thus, in the United States to invoke deconstruction is to signal a vague identification with the New Left themes of community and participatory democracy, even if deconstruction's canonical texts explicitly repudiate these values. The reason is that the political identification of American intellectual work has long since ceased to depend upon its normative conclusions. The intellectual American left has so long had to hide its hunted, heretical politics beneath the enigmatic rhetoric and epistemological skepticism of continental philosophy that it has blurred politics with aesthetic form.

Among legal scholars, deconstruction has been most frequently invoked by participants in the overlapping movements of Critical Legal Studies and feminist jurisprudence. Critical legal scholars have primarily interested themselves in deconstruction as the latest model of imported epistemological critique. They have accordingly invoked the skeptical implications of deconstruction to buttress—or at least ornament—their critical accounts of "liberal" legal doctrine as indeterminate and fatally contradictory. Feminist scholars have tended to see a humane, ethical message in deconstruction's demonstrations that categorical thought is reductive and exclusive of "difference." In deconstructive thought, "difference" usually means the distinguishability and comparability of particulars that enables their variable categorization. In feminist deconstruction, however, "difference" also means the deviance ascribed to women and other underprivileged groups. Thus, feminist legal scholars have invoked deconstruction in support of an ethic of tolerance and inclusion, while critiquing legal categorization as determinably sexist.

In this chapter we will evaluate both the epistemological and ethical variants of the deconstructive criticism of law. We will proceed by first reviewing the epistemological claims most associated with deconstruction's leading exponent, Jacques Derrida, and their role in Derrida's ethical critiques of participatory democracy and group identity. Next we will assess the epistemological deconstruction of legal doctrine initiated by American critical legal scholars. Finally we will assess the efforts of American feminist legal and political theorists to develop a deconstructive ethics of "difference."

Because both Critical Legal Studies and feminist jurisprudence define themselves first by political rather than by methodological commitments, we will be seeking in each case to understand and evaluate claims that the deconstructive criticism of law is politically progressive. Despite their oft divergent interpretations of deconstruction and legal doctrine, Critical Legal Studies and feminist jurisprudence have seen themselves as more allied than opposed, and a number of individuals embody both movements. We present the necessarily artificial division between them only as a heuristic device for sorting out the epistemological and ethical interpretations of deconstruction.

5.1 DERRIDEAN DECONSTRUCTION

Deconstruction in Ten Easy Lessons

Before evaluating the application of deconstruction to law, we need to introduce its most influential themes; but even before we can introduce deconstruction we need to dispose of two related objections: first, that deconstruction resists description or definition because it refers not to a theory or technique but simply to an assortment of texts authored by Derrida and others; and, second, that deconstruction is a practice, a particular juncture of means and ends, not an instrument that can be abstracted from its context and "applied" to law.[1]

In hopes of preempting such objections, it has become de rigueur to preface every summary of deconstruction with a ritual disclaimer about the impropriety of identifying and thereby objectifying a body of work that critiques the concepts of identity and objectivity.[2] While exhibiting our acquaintance with this convention we decline to perform it for three reasons.

First, no amount of prior genuflection to the subtlety and complexity of deconstructive writing can absolve its subsequent criticism of the original sin of reductionism. Since no such ritualized incantation can forestall this equally ritualized accusation, we might as well admit straightaway: we are all for reducing deconstruction.

A second, and related, reason to dispense with the expected handwringing is that the charge and the disclaimer of reductionism contradict themselves: to claim for deconstruction any special privilege against definition is already to identify, to define, to reduce it.

Third, the efforts of proponents of deconstruction to protect it against misappropriation are at odds with deconstruction's most valuable insights: that authors cannot own their words; that the condition of any sign's meaning is its "iterability," or capacity for repetition in a variety of contexts; that any term is open to an infinite variety of meanings, each of which can be thought of as implicit in the term's every use. If, on its own terms, deconstructive writing has any import at all, it is iterable, identifiable, reducible, appropriable, or, in short, useful.

Implicit in the ritual accusation of reductionism, and explicit in Derrida's writings, is an assumption that combating reductionism is politically progressive, regardless of context. It seems to us that the ritual mortification of reduction is a variant of the sentimentality deconstruction purports to eschew. Deconstruction

---

[1] See generally Pierre Schlag, *"L'hors de Texte c'est moi," Cardozo Law Review* 11 (1990): 1631.

[2] For an example of this sort of disclaimer, see Jack Balkin, "Deconstructive Practice and Legal Theory," *Yale Law Journal* 96 (1987): 743, 745–46.

is said to counter the "totalizing" tendencies of theory in much the same way that literature is supposed to leaven law's reified abstraction with concrete experience, its harsh logic with tender feeling, its authority with justice and its justice with mercy. Yet it is just this kind of sentimentality that Derrida, in his better moments, incommodes by reminding us that there is no unmediated feeling, no unreified reality, no griefs or grievances that are not already interpretations of conventional rules.

Having thus banished reductionism guilt, we blithely reduce deconstruction as practiced by Derrida to the following ten basic themes.

1. *The Principle of Differentiation.* Derrida borrows from structuralism a conception of language as a synchronic or static structure, which is to say that the meaning of any unit of language depends not on its reference to an object, but on its relation to or difference from other linguistic units.

2. *The Principle of Iterability.* Derrida adds a temporal dimension to his description of meaning by stressing the capacity of any language unit to have a different meaning in a different context, and hence its incapacity to mean the same thing twice. Yet in order for signs to be defined by this difference from one another, they must be iterable, that is, recognizable as the same in different contexts in which their meanings differ. Language is a public medium that must remain meaningful at a considerable remove from its speaker and its original context.

3. *The Principle of Rhetoricity.* Since no two iterations mean the same thing, we cannot ever be sure which sign any language use iterates. Thus, even though meaning depends upon differentiation, to read at all—to recognize something as a text composed of signs—is to repress awareness of the differences between iterations. Paul de Man expressed this point by claiming that every language use is ambiguous between referential and figurative meaning.[3] Derrida urges us further down this road, arguing that reference depends upon the rhetorical figure of iteration. Where de Man might say any use of "night" might refer to the hours between dusk and dawn or the dark night of the soul, Derrida would argue that even to assign "night" the first, "referential" meaning is to marshal a simile, likening one use of "night" to another. "Night" can be recognized as a conventional sign only by virtue of this simile. On this view, every use of language is ultimately figurative or rhetorical.

4. *The Concept of the "Trace."* Combining the operations of differentiation and iteration, Derrida reasons that every sign refers to all the signs from which it is differentiable, and to the meaning of the same sign in all past and all possible future iterations. These implicit references or connotations—Derrida calls them "traces"—are infinite.

5. *The Principle of Unbounded Textuality.* For Derrida the concept of the trace and the principle of rhetoricity combine to efface the distinctions among contexts in which a sign appears and between a semiotic text and its context. Since all

[3] Howard Felperin, *Beyond Deconstruction: The Use and Abuses of Literary Theory* (Oxford: Clarendon Press, 1985): 124–27.

textual elements are iterable, and therefore bear the traces of all their possible contexts, no juxtaposition of times or texts places an object of interpretation "out of context." At the same time delimiting the text—like identifying the signs of which it is composed—is an act of *reading*, which is to say of rhetorical figuration. If context is boundless and the text/context distinction arbitrary, "there is no beyond the text." There is nothing knowable that has not already been read in some text, and nothing conceivable that cannot be read into any text.[4]

6. *The Critique of Closure.* Frequently Derrida invokes the principle of unbounded textuality by figuring meaning as movement along an endless "chain" of "signifiers." Such chains are not merely endless in the way that a circle has no beginning or end, because Derrida aspires to transcend the structuralist image of meaning as constituted by a closed system of static relations. Instead, these chains of connotation extend out into a future of infinite—but already implicit—possible iterations. Against the background of this figure of the infinite chain, any attempt to close the circle—to reduce meaning down to even a very large set of present possibilities and constraints—is reductive and exclusive.

7. *The Critique of "Presence."* Reducing and excluding are traits or symptoms of a metaphysical belief that the traces of meaning excluded are not real because absent or remote. By the "metaphysics of presence," Derrida means the belief that only what is "objectively present" is real, and that the interpretability of experience, its traces of infinite meanings, are impurities introduced by the "subjectivity" of "representing" what is objectively present. Derrida ascribes the effort to distinguish present from absent meaning to a neurotic or "totalitarian" impulse to "control" difference or to close the text.

8. *The Critique of Dualism.* The critiques of closure and of the ideal of "presence" express themselves in a critique of dualism. Derrida sees dualistic analysis as a particularly prevalent technique of closing the circle of meaning. Thus, categories will be defined by the particulars that compose them, which will in turn be identified by the categories that collect them. For example, objective truth and subjective opinion will be mutually defining. Typically, argues Derrida, such oppositions will be hierarchically arranged, with one "privileged" or "essential" term producing, regulating, or controlling its inessential opposite. This control allows the two terms to remain fixed in place and hence avoids their reverberating into a dialectic of unending mutual transformation. Hierarchical and dualistic figures are, for Derrida, symptoms of the metaphysics of presence. Derrida's typical argumentative strategy is (1) to identify hierarchical distinctions in a text, and then (2) to blur the opposed terms, or reverse their priority, by finding the belated and subordinated term already implicit in the original and dominant one, as its constitutive condition.[5]

9. *The Critique of Narrative.* According to Derrida, the narrative conventions of Western literature are structurally congruent with metaphysical dualism. Dual-

---

[4] Jacques Derrida, *Of Grammatology*, trans. Gayatri Spivak (Baltimore: Johns Hopkins Univ. Press, 1976), 158, 163.

[5] See Patrick Martin, "Deconstruction and Duncan Kennedy's' The Structure of Blackstone's Commentaries" (unpub. ms., 1986).

ism has a narrative structure in that the subordinate term is secondary not only in importance but also in time. Thus, the second term is the corruption of, the fall from, the wilderness beyond, the first. Hence, the metaphysics of presence is implicit in Western literature's stock narratives of fall and resurrection, temptation and redemption, passage from innocence through experience to wisdom, and profit from prudent investment and sober delay of gratification. By the same token, these closed, circular narrative paths are implicit in any dualistic analysis. We differentiate only in order to reappropriate, so that difference is always regulated by an implied narrative.[6]

10. *The Critique of Figuration.* Derrida finds dualist metaphysics implicit not only in the narrative pattern of Western literature, but also in its stylistic exuberance. Embarrassed over its derivative status as a mere representation of presence, literary language struggles to outshine presence, to render descriptions more vivid than any sight, to invent figures more spectacular than the reality they represent, to tell stories more true to the human condition than the experience of any human being. In distracting attention from presence to the medium of representation, literary language paradoxically expresses envy of a presence that it wrongly supposes to require no representation. Hidden within every literary figure, therefore, is a narrative of longing to transcend fantasy, to put away childish things, to mature: every simile is a frog prince, a tin woodsman, a velveteen rabbit yearning to be real.

These ten themes—the concepts of differentiation, itertability, rhetoricity, trace, and textuality, and the critiques of closure, presence, dualism, narrative, and figuration—comprise deconstruction's most portable conceptual baggage.

In our view, the first five are quite useful but less original. They may be seen as adaptations of the anti-essentialist themes of pragmatist epistemology to the practice of reading. On the other hand, the second five themes of Derridean deconstruction together comprise a highly original reading strategy—but one that is of limited use, particularly for a "progressive" critique of law.

Derrida's reading strategy ascribes essentialist metaphysics to every text. Yet the mental operations criticized by Derrida may be motivated by practical goals rather than metaphysical commitments. The critique of closure seems to debar reaching the conclusions that guide action; the critiques of presence and dualism seem to condemn even the temporary division of knowledge into theory and data; the critique of narrative makes us suspicious of the practice of explanation, particularly in terms of equilibrium models, with their rhetoric of displacement and return; finally, the critique of figurative language seems to condemn comparison and analogical reasoning. *Yet a pragmatist could engage in all of these practices without evidencing any residual commitment to essentialist metaphysics.*

Of course, a pragmatist epistemology of reading suggests that there is nothing inherently wrong with Derrida's reading any and every instantiation of these practices as symptoms of "the metaphysics of presence." To a pragmatist, such readings may be no less "true" than any others. But from this pragmatic standpoint, the mere fact that a belief is not objectively false is not a good enough reason for

[6] Ibid.

holding it. Pragmatically speaking, we should not join Derrida in interpreting every text as essentialist unless this repetitive, reductionist reading strategy serves some purpose.

We can understand deconstruction as a technique for revealing or, more accurately, *producing* epistemological errors in texts. But the very perspective from which the texts are condemned as erroneous—pragmatism—also condemns epistemology as a pointless pursuit. Hence, the pragmatism of deconstruction invites its assessment not merely as a method of epistemological critique, but as a juncture of critical means and ethical ends in a practice. Thus, to understand, to evaluate, and to imitate what is most distinctive about Derridean deconstruction require attention not to Derrida's rather mechanical critical technique, but to his *targets*.

On this view, the central purpose of deconstruction is an attack on the Romantic radicalism associated with Rousseau, Fourier, the young Marx, Sartre, and Fanon. The values chiefly condemned are those of participatory democracy and group solidarity: Derrida sees both as expressions of a metaphysically essentialist ideal of authenticity, an ideal with totalitarian implications.

The perspective from which these potent political values are criticized is that of a supremely talented man of letters who has experienced multiple forms of marginality and exile. Derrida is an intellectual emigré of colonial origins (Algerian) who is a member of a minority (Jewish) now despised in his original homeland and only recently tolerated in his adopted land (France) after surviving threatened extermination. As an Algerian, he is a member of a nationality historically oppressed by and still discriminated against in France. But as a Jew rather than an Arab Muslim, and as an immigrant to France, he is no longer likely to be seen as authentically Algerian in Algeria.

The ultimate target of Derrida's deconstruction is not the metaphysics but the *politics* of "presence," the politics of popular sovereignty, which, he fears, tends to exclude all that can be seen as foreign, cosmopolitan, sophisticated, artificial, or intellectual. Hence, although claimed by the left, particularly in America, Derrida attacks many of the left's most cherished aspirations.[7] Let us now examine Derrida's critiques of popular sovereignty, of the concept of cultural identity that he believes underwrites it, and of the revolutionary quest for justice that he believes legitimizes it.

Deconstruction and Democracy

This section will explicate and evaluate Jacques Derrida's critique of the ideal of direct, or participatory, democracy.

Derrida's most important critical work, *Of Grammatology*, questions the priority of speech over writing that he finds implicit in the ideal of direct democracy,

---

[7] In his *Spectres of Marx*, trans. Peggy Knauf (New York: Routledge, 1994), Derrida somewhat sheepishly attempts to ingratiate himself with his leftist fans by struggling to find something in the Marxist tradition to endorse, and daringly concludes that Marxism's aspiration to improve humanity's lot makes it part of the intellectual heritage of liberal social democrats like himself.

as developed by Rousseau. Derrida argues that political communication is always mediated rather than direct, so that Rousseau's critique of representation undermines all political arguments, including Rousseau's own.

Distinguishing social from natural freedom, Rousseau associated social freedom with direct, deliberative participation in politics—the open assembly or town meeting.[8] Rousseau's critique of political representation was based on the educative, virtue-inculcating function of participatory democracy.[9] Believing that "everything was radically connected with politics, and that however one proceeded, no people would be other than the nature of its government,"[10] Rousseau favored participation for its effects on character.[11] He stressed political participation because he believed that both independence and cooperation required self-reliance:[12] "In a country that is really free, the citizens do everything with their hands and nothing with money."[13] Rousseau rejected political representation because he believed that human beings fulfill and develop their capacities only through action, and that only by trying to affect the world could they learn from it: "Man is born to act and to think, and not to reflect."[14] Rousseau therefore conceived political participation as active experience, not just as the use of language. Deprived of the opportunity to deliberate with others, Rousseau implied, citizens could develop no political will.[15] Unless citizens made their own decisions, they could develop no preferences or interests for their representatives to represent.

Derrida offers two related attacks on this position. First, he objects that a preference for direct rather than representative democracy reflects a sentimental belief that direct democracy enables the expression of authentic or unmediated desires. By Derrida's account, Rousseau favored speech over writing because writing is a dry, formulaic representation of speech. Rousseau actually admitted that even speech represents something else—passion—and that it contains conventional elements.[16] Yet Rousseau argued that speech also contains a nonformulaic, nonconventional element—the musical inflection of the particular living voice.[17] Derrida responds that even this "live" element of speech turns out to be conventional

---

[8] Jean-Jacques Rousseau, *The Social Contract*, trans. Lester Crocker (New York: Pocket Books, 1967): 98–101 (only direct democracy preserves freedom); ibid., 19–23 (social contract entails exchange of natural for civil liberty).

[9] See Guyora Binder, *Treaty Conflict and Political Contradiction* (New York: Praeger, 1988), 75–76 (discussing Rousseau's critique of representation).

[10] Benjamin Barber, *Strong Democracy: Participatory Politics for a New Age* (Berkeley: Univ. of California Press, 1984), 213, n. 1 (quoting Rousseau, *Confessions*, book 9).

[11] See Carole Pateman, *Participation and Democratic Theory* (Cambridge: Cambridge Univ. Press, 1970), 24–25; John Plamenatz, *Man and Society* (New York: Longmans, 1963), 440–42.

[12] James Miller, *Rousseau: Dreamer of Democracy* (New Haven: Yale Univ. Press, 1984), 31–32 (discussing the benefits of work—particularly farming—and commitment to family and community).

[13] Rousseau, *Social Contract*, 98.

[14] Janis Forman, trans., preface to Jean-Jacques Rousseau, *"Narcisse*: or the Lover of Himself," *Political Theory* 6 (1978), 543, 550.

[15] Rousseau, *Social Contract*, 28, 99 (the "general will" cannot be divided).

[16] Derrida, *Of Grammatology*, 195.

[17] Jean-Jacques Rousseau, *The First and Second Discourses and Essay on the Origin of Languages*, ed. and trans. Victor Gourevitch (New York: Perennial Library, 1986), 239, 255–58.

as well. The alterations of pitch that give expression to the spoken word also depend on regular, notable intervals—the intervals that allow music to be reproduced.[18] To deny the conventionality of music, Rousseau was driven to say that music grew out of song, which grew out of impassioned speech.[19] Thus, the non-linguistic aspect of speech turns out to be a representation of language. Hence, Derrida concludes, Rousseau has failed to find any origin at which the expression of feeling is any less conventional, or mediated than in writing.

Now, all this might be quite devastating if Rousseau did in fact object to writing's artificiality, as Derrida charges. To the contrary, however, Rousseau scorned writing as more private and hence as less socially coded than conversation. Writing facilitates the representation of what the sovereign people would say if they were assembled together, and Rousseau feared that such representation might fix individual preferences in advance of the political dialogue that alone can transform them into a sovereign will. The direct dialogue demanded by Rousseau would mediate individual preferences more than does representation. From a Rousseauian perspective, representative democracy rests on the fiction that individual preferences can be accurately depicted and reflected in social decision making, whereas direct democracy openly aims at changing them.

Derrida's second objection to Rousseau's critique of representation is that this critique was self-consuming. After all, Rousseau expressed his critique of writing in writing. And although his work inspired much political struggle in his native community of Geneva, Rousseau lived in exile and resisted engagement with that struggle, so that his own political views hardly derived from political participation.[20] Derrida demonstrates that Rousseau's view of writing as shameful, sterile, and solitary frequently found expression in an association of writing with what Rousseau regarded as his own particular vice of masturbation.[21] To write, according to Rousseau, is to fantasize in isolation and spill ink at an absent reader who is helpless to argue or respond.[22] Writing is sterile, unable to engender the fertile dialogue established by conversation.[23] Derrida, by contrast, argues that isolation, far from being the haven of unnatural acts, is natural and original: masturbation, he says, precedes sexual relations, writing precedes speech, self-reference precedes communication. Derrida sees all experience as requiring the active interpretation of its recipient. Thus, all experience is a form of self-stimulation: "Auto-affection is a universal structure of experience. All living things are capable of auto-affection. And only a being capable of symbolizing, that is to say of

---

[18] Derrida, *Of Grammatology*, 199–200; see also Rousseau, *The First and Second Discourses*, 288–90.

[19] Derrida, *Of Grammatology*, 195–97.

[20] See generally, Miller, *Rousseau: Dreamer of Democracy*, 52–54 (describing Rousseau's voluntary lifelong exile); ibid., 126–27 (describing how Rousseau provoked unrest in Geneva, then denied responsibility and refused involvement).

[21] Derrida, *Of Grammatology*, 150–54.

[22] Ibid., 151.

[23] Ibid., 168.

auto-affecting, may let itself be affected by the other in general. Auto-affection is the condition of an experience in general."[24]

This startlingly solipsistic position—that others affect us only if we "let" them—leads to a thoroughly subjectivist account of language, one in which meaning is not cultural but individual: "Conversation is, then, a communication between two absolute origins that, if one may venture the formula, auto-affect reciprocally, repeating as immediate echo the auto-affection produced by the other. Immediacy is here the myth of consciousness."[25] In conversation—or any other social experience—we are affected not by others, but by a fantasy that we conjure up and control. Thus, "speech and the consciousness of speech—that is to say consciousness simply as self-presence—are the phenomenon of an auto-affection lived as suppression of differance."[26]

Derrida's reinterpretation of social life as nothing more than a solitary communion between each individual and a fantasy of her own creation is individualism pure and simple. Few accounts of communication better illustrate Marx's claim that "in bourgeois ethics speaking and loving 'are interpreted as expressions and manifestations of a third artificially introduced Relation, the Relation of utility.' "[27] The Derridean self relates not to other people but only to her own desires. While ostensibly deconstructing the concepts of subjectivity, nature, and origin, Derrida in fact treats the autonomous subject, isolated in an experiential world of her own creation, as natural and original.[28]

And so, ironically, it is Derrida rather than Rousseau who gives voice to nostalgia for a presocial origin. Granted, Rousseau's "conjectural histories"[29] explored the *origins* of society, government, language, and music. But as deconstructive theorist Paul de Man observes, Rousseau's rhetoric favored

> diachronic structures . . . over pseudo-synchronic structures . . . because the latter mislead one into believing in a stability of meaning that does not exist. The elegiac tone that is occasionally sounded does not express a nostalgia for an original presence but is a purely dramatic device. . . . The origin here "precedes" the present for purely structural and not chronological reasons.[30]

[24] Ibid., 165.

[25] Ibid., 166.

[26] Ibid. *Différance* is Derrida's term for the distinction between contexts that prevents any unit of language from ever meaning—or even being—the same thing twice.

[27] Bertell Ollman, *Alienation: Marx's Conception of Man in Capitalist Society*, 2d ed. (Cambridge: Cambridge Univ. Press, 1976), 41, quoting Marx's *German Ideology*, trans. R. Pascal (London, 1942).

[28] See Anne Norton, *Reflections on Political Identity* (Baltimore: Johns Hopkins Univ. Press, 1988), 30.

[29] On this genre see "Dugald Stewart's Account of Adam Smith," ed. I. S. Ross, in Adam Smith, *Essays on Philosophical Subjects*, ed. W. P. D. Wightman and J. C. Bryce (Oxford: Clarendon Press, 1980), 292; Robert Nisbet, *Social Change and History* (New York: Oxford Univ. Press, 1969), 157; M. Royce Kallerud, "Conjectural History: Rousseau, Shelley, and Blake in the New World" (unpublished dissertation, S.U.N.Y. at Buffalo, 1998).

[30] Paul de Man, *Blindness and Insight: Essays in the Rhetoric of Contemporary Criticism*, ed. Wlad Godzich (New York: Oxford Univ. Press, 1971), 133–34.

Seen in this light, Rousseau's "nature" is not a presocial condition located in the historical past; it is instead the world conjured by the imagination.[31] But the exclusive pursuit of this "natural" freedom is contrary to a human nature that fulfills itself by transcending the natural. Human beings live in a social world and so can experience only social freedom. In Benjamin Barber's interpretation,

> If the human essence is social, then men and women have to choose not between independence or dependence but between citizenship or slavery. . . . To a strong democrat, Rousseau's assertion . . . that man is born free yet is everywhere in chains does not mean that man is free by nature but society enchains him. It means rather that natural freedom is an abstraction, whereas dependency is the concrete human reality, and that the aim of politics must therefore be not to rescue natural freedom from politics but to invent and pursue artificial freedom within and through politics.[32]

Rousseau therefore presented all of his key political values—freedom, community, and democracy—as achievements of human artifice.

Yet Derrida insists on associating these Rousseauian values with a metaphysics of "presence" that views artifice as inauthentic. Derrida mocks the "affective impulse" he detects in Rousseau and in Claude Lévi-Strauss towards the "islets of resistance" to commercial capitalism found in "the small communities that have provisionally protected themselves from . . . a corruption linked . . . to writing and to the dislocation of a unanimous people assembled in the self-presence of its speech."[33] Derrida then broadens his attack from Rousseau and Lévi-Strauss to the whole radical tradition:

> Self-presence, transparent proximity in the face-to-face of countenances and the immediate range of the voice, this determination of social authenticity . . . relates . . . to the Anarchistic and Libertarian protestations against Law, the Powers, and the State in general, and also with the dream of the nineteenth-century Utopian Socialists, most specifically with the dream of Fourierism.[34]

Derrida's charge that radicalism embodies a metaphysics of presence extends to all radicals his reading of a Rousseau wracked by self-hatred and self-delusion.

First, Derrida means to generalize his charge that a written critique of representation is self-contradictory. In exalting presence over representation, radicals reveal themselves to be self-hating intellectuals, romanticizing ignorance as innocence and inarticulateness as authenticity. Derrida, whose idiosyncratic coinages and daunting constructions resist interpretation, could not disagree more with Rousseau's axiom that "any tongue with which one cannot make oneself understood to the people assembled is a slavish tongue. It is impossible for a people to

---

[31] Miller, *Rousseau: Dreamer of Democracy*, 177.

[32] Barber, *Strong Democracy*, 216 (footnote omitted). In rhetoric deliberately evocative of Rousseau, Barber continues, "We are born insufficient, we need cooperation; we are born with potential natures, we require society to realize them." Ibid.

[33] Derrida, *Of Grammatology*, 134.

[34] Ibid., 138.

remain free and speak the tongue."[35] For Derrida this requirement of rhetorical humility debases political argument and ultimately requires the intellectual to present herself inauthentically. But this characterization of direct democracy as anti-intellectual ignores the educative function of political participation. Radical democratic theory presumes that all parties benefit from participating in debate. Thus, for intellectuals to address the public does not require them to *disguise* their views, but to *communicate* them. And while their views may change in the process of communication, that is what politics is all about: transforming its participants, not preserving an authentic, prepolitical self.

In associating radical democracy with the metaphysics of presence, Derrida depicts radical democrats as not only self-hating, but self-deluded. Accordingly, the radical ideals of direct democracy and community rest on the "delusion" that face-to-face politics can avoid the alienation and mediation that are the preconditions of communication.[36] But radical democrats need not so delude themselves. What they demand is not simply speech but transformative dialogue.[37] Derrida's mischaracterization of democratic deliberation as "speech" assumes that its purpose is to reveal rather than to change preferences.[38] The advantage claimed for face-to-face political debate is not that it "presents" citizens to one another without distortion, but that it enables citizens to change and be changed by one another.[39]

In sum, the democratic critique of representation does not assume that conversation is more "natural" than writing. To the contrary, the objection to political representation is that it leaves people in their original state, whereas political deliberation engages them and transforms them into citizens. This transformation is possible only to the extent that citizens are different from each other. Ideally, participation in a political community continually transforms the participants by exposing them to one another, not by making them all the same.[40] Derrida, by contrast, viewing discussion as a solipsistic exercise, assumes it cannot change people.

[35] Ibid.

[36] Ibid., 139.

[37] Barber, *Strong Democracy*, 173.

[38] Ibid., 174.

[39] After studying participation in a cooperative crisis intervention center and a New England town meeting, Jane Mansbridge concludes, "In an assembly of all the members, ideas, emotions, and points of view surface that rarely reach elected or appointed representatives. The rank-and-filers can themselves listen to points in a debate, mull the issues over, ask questions, draw their own conclusions, and make their decisions on how to act. By acting themselves, they make themselves responsible for the collective action. The government becomes us not them. Moreover, in an assembly, one sees the opposition. Ideas that one would normally reject out of hand come from people one knows, people who may have believable reasons for espousing them. Finally, when an assembly struggles through to a satisfactory conclusion on a difficult issue, the very act of congregating produces mutual pride and a feeling of communion." Jane Mansbridge, "Fears of Conflict in Face-to-Face Democracies," in *Workplace Democracy and Social Change*, ed. Frank Lindenfeld and Joyce Rothschild Whitt (Boston: Porter Sargent, 1982), 125–27. See also Jane Mansbridge, *Beyond Adversary Democracy* (New York: Basic Books, 1980).

[40] Barber, *Strong Democracy*, 185.

Deconstruction and Identity

This section develops and evaluates Derrida's critique of the concept of identity, particularly cultural identity. Derrida's attack on this concept should be seen as part of his polemic against the tradition of Rousseauian radicalism. Rousseauian radicalism depends upon the concept of identity in at least three ways.

First, the idea of popular sovereignty depends upon group identity. Judging action by reference to the will of the sovereign people requires criteria for identifying its membership and its preferences. The popular sovereign is not reducible to some collection of persons. Traditionally even the sovereignty of kings inhered not in themselves but in the corporate fiction of the "crown."[41] Popular sovereignty depends upon such similar corporate fictions as "political society," "the nation," "the proletariat," or "the electorate." Only through the mediation of these corporate fictions—group identities for our purposes—can popular will become articulate.

Second, the notion of radical social change depends upon group identity. To identify radical change, at the very least we must be able to distinguish one social order from another. But radicals since Rousseau have seen such social change as a means to transform human nature. From Robespierre through Sorel to Guevara, radicals have also seen the solidarity and sacrifice called forth by the experience of revolution as formative for its participants, conferring a new social identity upon them. In this longing for a "New Socialist Man" Derrida detects a totalitarian impulse to mold personality and extirpate nonconformity.

Third, the aspiration to community or solidarity that often motivates radical change seems to imply the sharing of an identity. Derrida assumes that this shared identity entails more than common membership and mutual concern. The pursuit of mutuality against the background of a revolutionary struggle against evil suggests a conformity enforced by the threat of expulsion and demonization. Hence, Derrida worries that fraternity, or its illusion, can only be purchased through the totalitarian suppression of heterogeneity.

Thus, Derrida's critique of group identity elaborates the themes of his critique of the ideal of the popular assembly. Identities are reductionist, insofar as they deny the difference between and within individuals. Identities are essentialist: they exalt "presence" over representation insofar as they ascribe to group members a culture that outsiders cannot authentically understand, represent, or participate in. Identities are therefore also exclusive and intolerant—intolerant not only of foreigners but of "foreign elements" within group members themselves.

Finally, because identities are reductionist, essentialist, and exclusive, they are deconstructible. In coining his slogan that "there is no beyond the text," Derrida deconstructs not only the distinction between formal and contextual criticism, but also the distinction between orthodoxy and heterodoxy. Hence, he challenges the integrity of all those cultural traditions that define themselves by their fidelity

---

[41] Ernst Kantorowicz, *The King's Two Bodies* (Princeton: Princeton Univ. Press, 1981).

to a canon or a sacred text. There is nothing but endless textuality, no place outside of one's culture from which to critique it, but also no boundary beyond which alien values may be expelled. Because authenticity is an impossible ideal, to claim it is immediately to contradict oneself, to catch oneself in a lie. And so Derrida detects in orthodoxy and radicalism alike the same futile purgative obsession. In orthodoxy this takes the form of ritual; in radical politics it takes the form of cycles of factional division and violent purgation. Every effort to eradicate sin or oppression somehow seems to reproduce it. Unable to purify ourselves of shameful traits we disown them, blaming their presence on foreign influences. And the more we dishonestly project our sins onto others, the greater burden of sin we have to displace. Thus, far from repositories of authentic memory, our cultural traditions are bequests of repression—lies violently erasing the evidence of earlier lies.

DECONSTRUCTING IDENTITY

The crucial site for Derrida's argument that identity is inherently inauthentic is his confrontation with the problem of Jewish identity in the wake of the Holocaust. But insofar as Derrida's critique of all group identity as totalitarian is itself the expression of a version of Jewish identity, it involves him in a series of paradoxes.[42] Seeing all identity as defined by exclusion, Derrida must view even his own Jewish identity as tainted by the totalitarian "logic" of Nazism. Yet in defining deconstruction as opposition to Nazism, Derrida employs the very logic of identity that he condemns as totalitarian. We suggest that since the concept of identity is unavoidable, Derrida's critique of identity is not pragmatic. Moreover, Derrida's critique of identity is undermined by its own hyperbole—any argument that implores us to implicate Jewish identity in responsibility for the Holocaust has run off the rails.

In an essay called "Edmond Jabès and the Question of the Book,"[43] Derrida rejects the idea that Jewishness makes Jews identical to one another or identifies them all with any one thing. Derrida explicitly questions whether one can speak of "the Jewish community."[44] Like much of Derrida's work, this essay attacks the idea that a group or culture can be identified—unified, made the same—by adherence to Scripture, because Scripture is always contradictory, disjointed. For Derrida, God has nothing meaningful to say to humanity. "God," writes Derrida, "separated himself from himself in order to let us speak. . . . He did so not by speaking but by keeping still, by letting silence interrupt his voice, . . . by letting the tables be broken."[45] God's silence, his mystery, makes possible "our writing, certainly, but already his, which starts with the stifling of his voice and

[42] Gayatri Spivak, Translator's Preface to Derrida, *Of Grammatology*, ix.

[43] Jacques Derrida, *Writing and Differences*, trans. Alan Bass (Chicago: Univ. of Chicago Press, 1978), 64–78.

[44] Ibid., 74.

[45] Ibid., 67.

the dissimulation of his face. This difference, this negativity in God, is our free-dom."[46] God dissembles and His Scripture hides his face which "no man may look upon."[47] God, concludes Derrida, "is not truthful, he is not sincere."[48] For Derrida, Scripture cannot unify, it cannot be a source of identity because its author, God, is not one.

This position is so heterodox that it places in question its author's identification with Judaism. Derrida attributes this apostasy to the poet Edmond Jabès, but with obvious sympathy. Jabès, he insists, is Jewish in the sense that he is following the footsteps of Kabbalists and other Jews into "exile" from the law, and hence from Jewishness: "traditionality is not orthodoxy." One can be Jewish by virtue of contributing to a tradition of speculation and commentary, without being orthodox, that is, without accepting the authority of Jewish law.[49] Derrida con-cludes that "the Jew's identification with himself does not exist," because ambiva-lence between particular identity and universal significance is essential to Juda-ism.[50] Derrida critiques Jewish identity as divided between insularity and universality; yet his own critique proves to be divided as well. Because Judaism is contradictory, he argues, it cannot identify Jews with one another, or even with themselves. This is a critique of Judaism as inadequate to the full particularity of Jews. Yet he also expresses anxiety that this internal critique of Judaism will be interpreted as "too universalistic"—in others words, as reflecting a desire to iden-tify with gentiles, to hand over one's own particularity in the face of anti-Semitic persecution.

More elaborately, in "Violence and Metaphysics: An Essay on the Thought of Emmanuel Levinas," Derrida defends himself against this potential accusation of betrayal by arguing that Jewish identity is not only contradictory, but also immoral and violent. "Violence and Metaphysics" is a critique of the existentialist philoso-pher Levinas's effort to reconcile Jewish identity with openness and tolerance towards strangers. In *Totality and Infinity*,[51] Levinas asks his readers to identify themselves without relying on a biblical Scripture that purports to account for all creation and to legislate all human behavior. Levinas rejects the image of God as totally omniscient and omnipotent because it eliminates the human freedom

---

[46] Ibid.

[47] Exodus 33:20–23.

[48] Derrida, *Writing and Difference*, 68.

[49] Ibid., 74. Derrida further complicates the question of his own identity and that of his "subject" Jabès by ending the essay with a "signed" quotation from Jabès's fictional character "Reb Rida." In so doing, Derrida claims a place in the rabbinic tradition and questions whether the "Jabès" Derrida interprets is his own invention, or whether Jabès creates Reb (der) Rida in the act of being read by him. Ibid., 78; see also ibid., 300 (additional essay on Jabès signed "Reb Derissa," another of Jabès's characters).

[50] Ibid. "The [Jew's] history would be but one empirical history among others if he . . . nationalized himself within difference. . . . He would have no history at all if he let himself be attenuated within . . . an abstract universalism."

[51] Emmanuel Levinas, *Totality and Infinity*, trans. Alphonso Lingis (Pittsburgh: Duquesne Univ. Press, 1969).

prized by the existentialist.[52] Rather than abandoning religion, however, he invites his readers to worship a God that is infinitely mysterious rather than infinitely knowledgeable and powerful. Thus, he redefines the wonder of God's creation as its infinite indeterminacy rather than its total determinacy and transforms the creator from exacting lawgiver to fecund artist. By worshiping a God that is infinitely remote, infinitely other, people can be drawn together, but they will also be encouraged to respect the otherness of their fellow humans.[53] Accordingly, by imagining God as infinitely other, Jews can affirm their own particularity, their own distinctness, while accepting gentiles as divine creations, reflecting the mystery of God.[54]

While Derrida shares Levinas's hostility to the harsh determinacy of Scripture, he rejects Levinas's effort to ground a specifically Jewish identity in infinite distance from an admired other. Although Derrida lobbies for the recognition of difference in every context, he argues that recognition of difference requires some similarity, some basis for communication. Thus, to identify oneself as radically different from others, to learn to be tolerant of the "infinite otherness" of strangers, is to isolate oneself behind a wall of silence. And this, argues Derrida, is the ultimate "violence."[55]

For Derrida, such silence is violent because tolerance without communication is nothing more than the cruel indifference of a self-sufficient God. Further, an abstract commitment to tolerate an infinitely distant other may be compatible with violent efforts to expel the stranger in one's midst. From the standpoint of a vulnerable minority, isolating oneself behind a facade of tolerance leaves a community conspicuous and vulnerable to sacrificial violence, as the Jews of Europe discovered. In this sense, the collective isolation implicit in the attitude of disengaged tolerance may be not only unethical but also imprudent. Recognizing another's difference may be admirable, but insisting on your own difference can get you killed. Thus, Derrida's critique of Jewish identity is both an ethical and a

---

[52] Ibid., 292–94 (totality opposed to infinity, which Levinas equates with freedom).

[53] "Infinity . . . cannot be as violent as is totality." Derrida, *Writing and Difference*, 107; see also Levinas, *Totality and Infinity*, 292 (infinity contrasted to totality). According to Derrida, Levinas sees God as infinitely other, and because Levinas sees all otherness as resembling God, he believes all relations with others are made possible by religious faith. Derrida, *Writing and Difference*, 95–96, 104, 107, 108; see Levinas, *Totality and Infinity*, 292–93 (otherness a miracle, facilitating divine creation); see also ibid., 291, 305 (pluralism is the good).

[54] Levinas never makes the Jewish focus of *Totality and Infinity* explicit, but as Derrida remarks, at its "heart" is "the face of Yahweh, who of course is never named." Derrida, *Writing and Difference*, 108. Levinas does, however, admit the thorough influence of Jewish theologian Franz Rosenzweig's "opposition to the idea of totality," in *Totality and Infinity*, 28. Rosenzweig devalued the modern state in favor of family and descent, which he saw as the source of Jewish identity and eternity. Rosenzweig identified Jews as strangers everywhere, even from God, giving them an unusual tolerance for strangers and estrangement and a detachment from history. Eliezer Berkovits, *Major Themes in Modern Philosophies of Judaism* (New York: Ktav Pub. House, 1974), 40–46. Without naming it as Jewish, Levinas advocates this conception of identity. Levinas, *Totality and Infinity*, 268–69, 282–85. Derrida, *Writing and Difference*, 94, 97.

[55] Derrida, *Writing and Difference*, 117, 130.

prudential assimilationism. In the wake of the Holocaust, he worries that to define himself at all is to incorporate and validate what he considers the Nazi logic of defining the other outside of oneself. Yet in defining his own deconstruction by contrast to this antinomian logic of exclusion, he cannot avoid incorporating it.

A CASE OF IDENTITY: THE DECONSTRUCTION OF PAUL DE MAN

Derrida presents deconstruction as a response to Nazism in a reading of apparently pro-Nazi newspaper columns written by the late Paul de Man, in the latter's early adulthood. An originator with Derrida of deconstructive criticism, de Man was later discovered to have authored a number of essays for a collaborationist newspaper in occupied Belgium during World War II. One of these articles, "The Jews in Present Day Literature,"[56] concludes that European culture would suffer no loss if Jews were eliminated from Europe. The discovery of this essay prompted accusations that deconstruction is tainted with Nazism.

There are at least three possible bases for this charge. First, because deconstruction shows every argument to contain its own opposite, it seems nihilistic and therefore unable to generate moral reasons to resist Nazism. Second, because deconstruction is said to "annihilate the subject"—to deny the individual identities of authors and of characters—it may seem to deny individual responsibility for evil. Third, because it exposes the futility of efforts to deny loss, contradiction, and violence, deconstruction seems to urge acceptance of their necessity.[57] Perhaps an "antihumanist" philosophy that attempts to annihilate the subject sees no great loss in the annihilation of subjects.[58] For all these reasons, many observers greeted the discovery of de Man's wartime journalism as a confirmation of their suspicions about deconstruction.[59] In an anguished essay entitled "Like the Sound of the Sea Deep within a Shell: Paul de Man's War,"[60] Derrida undertakes a difficult task: to justify deconstruction and to excuse de Man, without justifying the charge that deconstruction excuses anti-Semitism. Derrida meets this challenge with his deconstructive critique of identity.

Derrida attempts to detach de Man's mature deconstruction from de Man's youthful anti-Semitism *by denying that de Man can be identified with himself over time*. The problem with Derrida's effort to detach the deconstruction of identity from de Man's anti-Semitism is that Derrida's deconstructive arguments are

---

[56] Derrida, "Like the Sound of the Sea Deep within a Shell: Paul de Man's War," *Critical Inquiry* 14 (1988): 590.

[57] See Jonathan Culler, *On Deconstruction* (Ithaca: Cornell Univ. Press, 1982), 93 (deconstruction critiques rhetoric of recuperation; Kate Soper, *Humanism and Anti-Humanism* (London: Hutchinson, 1986), 122 (pessimistic implications of deconstruction).

[58] Soper, *Humanism and Anti-Humanism*, 10–12; Mark Poster, *Existential Marxism in Postwar France* (Princeton: Princeton Univ. Press, 1975), 319, 336–37 (antihumanist slogans of various structuralist and poststructuralist thinkers); see also Richard Bernstein, "Critics Attempt to Reinterpret a Colleague's Disturbing Past: The de Man Affair," *New York Times*, July 17, 1988, §4, p. 6, col. 1 (deconstruction accused of nihilism).

[59] See generally David Lehman, *Signs of the Times: Deconstruction and the Fall of Paul de Man* (New York: Poseidon Books, 1991).

[60] Derrida, "Like the Sound of the Sea."

anticipated by the anti-Semitic text he deconstructs. "The Jews in Present Day Literature" heaps contempt on Jews for having no distinctive identity and expresses annoyance that their claims to distinction force de Man to express anti-Semitic opinions that are foreign to him. Because the young de Man's anti-Semitic text deconstructs itself in this precocious way, it undermines Derrida's later claim that deconstruction is the opposite of anti-Semitism.

To make this claim plausible, Derrida is forced to redefine anti-Semitism in universalist terms, as "totalitarianism." Thus, his deconstruction responds to anti-Semitic persecution by denying that there is any such thing as a Jew. The following reading of "Paul de Man's War" reveals how deconstruction's flexibility enables Derrida to excuse anti-Semites by refusing to identify them with their anti-Semitism, and to implicate Jews in their own persecution by claiming that it is "totalitarian" to identify as a Jew.

Derrida argues that the young de Man lacked commitment to the collaborationist and the anti-Semitic sentiments in his own essays, that he did not identify with them. Derrida points out ways in which the young critic's complex prose seemed to undermine the authority of his conclusions. Thus, Derrida notes de Man's ironic failure to heed his own prescient warning that politics is " 'totally alien to [men of letters], so that when they venture onto this terrain in that offhand way that only the ignorant are capable of one may expect the worst.' "[61] Yet this may be read as the protest of a young aesthete at being forced by his editors to write about politics, one who perhaps is more upset at having to collaborate with politics than at the politics with which he is forced to collaborate.

Consider Derrida's argument that "The Jews in Present-Day Literature" is really an attack on "vulgar anti-Semitism." For the young de Man, anti-Semitism was vulgar if it rejected literary modernism as a Jewish invention.[62] According to de Man, to notice any Jewish influence on European literature was to insult it: "It would be a rather unflattering appreciation of Western writers to reduce them to being mere imitators of a Jewish culture that is foreign to them. The Jews themselves have contributed to spreading this myth. Often they have glorified themselves."[63] Derrida is quite right in saying that de Man condemned "anti-Semitism as regards literature."[64] The young de Man wanted to save modern literature from anti-Semitism by denying its Jewishness, just as he wanted to save literature from political repression by denying its politics.[65]

In de Man's defense, Derrida argues that de Man was pleading for the autonomy of literature from politics at a time when authors were being judged and persecuted for resisting Nazism rather than serving it.[66] Hence, de Man's hollow boast

---

[61] Ibid., 612 (quoting de Man).

[62] Ibid., 624.

[63] Ibid.; also see ibid., 625 (Derrida's unconvincing argument that de Man's ascription of this "unflattering myth" to Jewish vanity undermines the statement's anti-Semitism).

[64] Ibid.

[65] Derrida asserts that the "History of Art and Literature . . . does not merge with sociopolitical history." Ibid. (Derrida summarizing de Man's text).

[66] Ibid., 615, 628.

that European literature was free of foreign influence revealed an anxiety that the occupier's politics might invade his own literature: "If our civilization had let itself be invaded by a foreign force, then we would have to give up much hope for its future."[67]

But whom did de Man blame for this predicament? To whom did he attribute this invasion? What was the "foreign force" that threatened to corrupt the literary sensibility that Derrida calls de Man's "culture"?[68] Not German occupiers, but Jews: "By keeping, in spite of Semitic interference in all aspects of European life, an intact originality, that civilization has shown its basic nature is healthy."[69] De Man here argued that Jewish influence no longer threatened European culture because it had been resisted successfully.[70] But in offering this argument, de Man also congratulated himself that he had prevented "vulgar anti-Semitism"[71] from invading his own personal "culture." In short, the success of refined anti-Semitism in keeping European culture free of Semitic influence had obviated the need for the vulgar anti-Semitism of the Nazi invader. And if de Man had failed to resist anti-Semitism, he blamed not himself, but an invader, who was not even the real invader, but the invader's scapegoat, the Jew.

Thus, the young de Man argued that he had not been occupied by anti-Semitism, on the grounds that unlike the vulgar occupiers, he was not preoccupied with Judaism. Derrida suggests that the complex excuse already embedded in this youthful text explains why the mature de Man never felt called upon to apologize for it directly.[72] However, in "Excuses," an essay on Rousseau's *Confessions*, de Man would assert the futility of all attempts to excuse what one has said: "the text can never stop apologizing for the suppression of guilt that it performs." For this futility de Man blamed "a foreign element, that disrupts the meaning, the readability of the apologetic discourse, and reopens what the excuse seems to have closed off."[73] De Man's example is Rousseau's famous excuse for falsely accusing a friend, that he did so only to excuse himself of the same misdeed. This scapegoat—implicit in every excuse—is the foreign element that renders every excuse inexcusable. Where the youthful de Man wished to see such foreign elements as contingent and dispensable, as not really influencing his language, the mature de Man acknowledged the necessity and ineradicability of such foreign elements.

As Derrida suggests, de Man's mature deconstructive theory, which insists that language is always alien to its speaker, implies repentance. We can imagine the mature de Man congratulating what he calls the "foreign element" in his own youthful language: Thank God, my friend, that I could not eradicate you! Thank

[67] Ibid., 631.

[68] Ibid., 636.

[69] Ibid., 631.

[70] Ibid., 630.

[71] Ibid., 624.

[72] Ibid., 638

[73] Paul de Man, *Allegories of Reading* (New Haven: Yale Univ. Press, 1979), 289–90, 300.

God I could not mean what I said! But de Man's theory also implies an excuse: After all, I could not say what I meant. My language was invaded. My cruelty towards you, though unavoidable, was not my own.

And Derrida, de Man's embarrassed "friend," accepts this excuse: Derrida describes the nationalist and anti-Semitic rhetoric of de Man's collaborationist essays as already familiar to him as part of a preexisting "ideological configuration," appropriated by de Man. Here the deconstructive critic that was his friend is not the youthful de Man who wrote an anti-Semitic essay. Like the Jew, de Man is not identical with himself but is divided from his past by a "rupture."[74] Yet de Man's innocence is over-determined: bearing no responsibility for his past, de Man has nevertheless rectified it. Thus, Derrida insists that de Man's mature deconstruction always deconstructs de Man's own youthful writing. This conflict between de Man's deconstruction and de Man's anti-Semitism is what Derrida calls, in the subtitle of the essay, "Paul de Man's War."[75]

Thus, Derrida uses de Man to argue that deconstruction is essentially opposed to Nazism and is also essential to opposing Nazism.[76] He claims that attempts to identify this early anti-Semitic article with de Man's later work are "guided by [the] principle of the worst totalitarian police."[77] To identify de Man with himself is to seek a "historical totalization" that subordinates "discontinuities" to a "totalitarian logic":[78] "Since we are talking at this moment about discourse that is totalitarian, fascist, nazi, racist, anti-Semitic and so forth . . . I would like to do . . . whatever possible to avoid the logic of the discourse thus incriminated."[79]

Yet Derrida reveals that this resistance to "the logic of totalitarianism" is one of his "rules" for interpreting all discourse, not just de Man's: "[A] formalizing, saturating totalization seems to me to be precisely the essential character of this logic whose project, at least, and whose ethico-political consequence can be terrifying. One of my rules is never to accept this project and consequence."[80] Indeed, rejecting the totalitarian is the very purpose of deconstruction: "One must analyze as far as possible this process of formalization and its program. . . . It has occurred to me on occasion to call this deconstruction."[81] Deconstruction, in short, *is* this critical analysis of totalitarian logic,[82] this discovery of the contradiction in every text:

---

[74] Derrida, "Like the Sound of the Sea," 635, 641, 646, 648.

[75] Ibid., 594. This argument that de Man's deconstruction developed as a reaction to his youthful error suggests that Derrida is not only defending de Man as a man capable of learning from his mistake—he is defending de Man's anti-Semitic essay as a mistake capable of teaching de Man the value of deconstruction.

[76] Ibid., 600.

[77] Ibid., 641.

[78] Ibid.

[79] Ibid., 645 (emphasis in original).

[80] Ibid. (emphasis in original).

[81] Ibid., 646.

[82] Ibid., 647.

Do we have access to a complete formalization of this logic? . . . Is there a systematic set of themes . . . which, forming a closed and identifiable coherence of what we call totalitarianism, fascism, Nazism, racism, anti-Semitism, never appear outside these formations and especially never on the opposite side? . . . Is there some property so closed and so pure that one may not find any element of these systems in discourses that are commonly opposed to them? . . . I do not believe that there is.[83]

Yet in confidently ascribing the Holocaust to a "totalitarian logic," Derrida himself engages in an act of "totalization" that ascribes an illusory coherence to this atrocity. The Holocaust was made possible by the convergence of ideology, expedience, technology, bureaucracy, economic depression, and the immigration policies of many nations. The attribution of Nazi crimes to a "logic" or "ideology" attributes more consistency to Nazi thought than is warranted, and Derrida's cavalier assimilation of the quite disparate phenomena of racism, anti-Semitism, and totalitarianism exemplifies the "logic of identity" he criticizes as "totalizing."[84] Ironically, Derrida's own effort to identify Nazism with a "logic" whose "essential character" is a "formalizing, saturating totalization" is motivated by the hope of defining himself in opposition to that atrocity. Only if Derrida can perpetuate Judaism's Nazi antagonist in the more refined guise of a "totalitarian logic" legible in every text can he allow himself to perpetuate Judaism's tradition of critical alienation in the more refined form of deconstruction.

Deconstruction and Justice

Derrida's more recent lectures on jurisprudence combine his critiques of popular sovereignty and of the purgative impulse he detects in both political radicalism and religious orthodoxy. These lectures, published under the title "Force of Law: The Mystical Foundation of Authority,"[85] depict both Marxism and messianic Judaism as expressions of a dangerously apocalyptic yearning for justice that finds fulfillment in revolutionary violence. Seeing such purgative violence as disturbingly evocative of the Holocaust, Derrida rejects the utopian or "messianic" vision of justice that inspires it. Yet these lectures, delivered to American audiences, also manifest the tension between Derrida's politics and that of his American following, particularly in the legal academy. If the role of European literary theory in American intellectual life is to authorize—or at least ornament—radical criticism of existing institutions, to condemn utopian politics within the confines of this assigned role is no small chore. Derrida opens these lectures on a note of exasperation, as with a laborious sigh: "This is an obligation, I must address myself to you in English."[86]

[83] Ibid., 645.

[84] Guyora Binder, "Representing Nazism: Advocacy and Identity at the Trial of Klaus Barbie," 98 *Yale Law Journal* 98 (1989): 1321, 1344–47 (multiple causes of the Holocaust, incoherence of Nazi ideology, difficulty of identifying an ideological cause of the Holocaust).

[85] Jacques Derrida, "Force of Law: The Mystical Foundation of Authority," *Cardozo Law Review* 11 (1990): 919.

[86] Ibid.

The gathering Derrida thus addresses is a symposium on "Deconstruction and the Possibility of Justice," sponsored by the Cardozo Law School and the New School for Social Research. His annoyance results from the symposium's title. He feels called to account, forced to answer the oft-voiced suspicions that "deconstruction doesn't in itself permit any just action,"[87] and that it does not "have anything to say about justice." In response, Derrida at once complains and boasts that "if I were to say that I know nothing more just than . . . deconstruction . . . I wouldn't fail to shock"[88] critics and supporters alike. By thus acknowledging that the claim is implausible, he manages to suggest that it therefore exposes an unpleasant truth—that it is a surprising claim not because false, but because scandalous, irreverent, daring, unflinching, honest, true.

Derrida proposes to use two different rhetorical strategies to identify deconstruction with justice. The first employs the "demonstrative and apparently ahistorical allure of logico-formal paradoxes. The other, more historical . . . seems to proceed through reading of texts."[89]

Dividing his response into two lectures, Derrida offers two distinct and ultimately incompatible arguments. In the first lecture, Derrida distinguishes law and justice in order to identify deconstruction with the normative critique of legal institutions that motivates popular revolution. The second lecture, however, in reading Walter Benjamin's "Critique of Violence,"[90] deconstructs the distinction between law and revolution on which the argument of the first lecture depends. Critical concepts of justice are revealed to be always institutionalized somewhere within the social text, so that the longing for a pure, transcendent justice proves both disingenuous and dangerous. In the end, the justice with which Derrida would identify deconstruction must transcend both legal institutions and popular will, maintaining a critical distance from any possible political action.

Taken as a whole then, Derrida's text, like Benjamin's, "lends itself to an exercise in deconstructive reading" that "is in some way the operation . . . that this text does itself by itself, on itself."[91] Accordingly, its answer to the charge of ethical emptiness is self-consciously equivocal. When Derrida threatens to say that he "know[s] nothing more just than deconstruction," he immediately announces that he "will not say it, at least not directly." The claim is itself an equivocal response to the question implicit in the symposium's title: "Does deconstruction insure, permit authorize the possibility of justice?"[92] While proclaiming at one point that "deconstruction is justice,"[93] Derrida also raises "a question about the possibility of deconstruction," cautioning his audience that "the most rigorous deconstructions have never claimed to be possible" because "for a deconstructive

---

[87] Ibid., 923.

[88] Ibid., 957.

[89] Ibid., 959.

[90] Walter Benjamin, *Reflections*, ed. Peter Demetz, trans. Edmund Jephcott (New York: Schocken Books, 1979), 277–300.

[91] Derrida, "Force of Law," 979–81.

[92] Ibid., 921.

[93] Ibid., 945.

operation possibility would rather be the danger, the danger of becoming an available set of rule-governed procedures, methods, accessible approaches."[94]

So deconstruction identifies and empathizes with justice only, in a Judo-like maneuver, to demonstrate its impossibility, to show that institutionalizing justice would profane it. The first lecture, in which Derrida offers his equivocal identification of deconstruction and justice, was delivered to the audience of legal scholars who organized the symposium, thereby calling Derrida to account before the law. The second lecture, in which he subverts the premises of the first, was delivered off-site, on the other side of the continent, to a group of Holocaust historians.[95] We are tempted to read Derrida's edifying expression of noble sentiments in the first lecture as a joke on his earnest interrogators from Yeshiva University and the New School for Social Research. In his second lecture, on the Jewish Marxist critic Walter Benjamin, he is less flattering to the traditions of Jewish piety and Frankfurt School Critical Theory with which these two institutions are, respectively, affiliated.

Before proceeding to the second lecture's scathing critique of Benjamin's "neo-messianical Jewish mysticism"[96] as "too messianico-Marxist,"[97] let us outline the no less theological conception of justice with which Derrida sets out to beguile the audience of Lecture 1.

Derrida begins his apologia for deconstruction's silence on questions of justice with an expression of piety: "One cannot speak directly about justice, thematize or objectivize justice, say 'this is just' even less 'I am just,' without immediately betraying justice."[98] Hence, to name justice is blasphemy, like speaking the name of God, and so deconstruction's silence on questions of justice is to be taken as a kind of reverential mysticism.

Derrida extends this mystical status from God to persons. Justice, he reasons, is a discursive matter—one can only act justly or unjustly towards those to whom it is possible to address justifications.[99] And yet such justification is "impossible ... since I cannot speak the language of the other except to the extent that I appropriate and assimilate it."[100] Accordingly, the pursuit of justice is nothing more than the struggle against reductionism, a sort of Kantian imperative against taking the other's name in vain:

> Justice always addresses itself to singularity, to the singularity of the other, despite or even because it pretends to universality. Consequently, never to yield on this point, constantly to maintain an interrogation of the origins, grounds and limits of our conceptual, theoretical or normative apparatus surrounding justice is, on deconstruction's part anything but a neutralization of interest in justice, an insensitivity toward injustice. On

---

[94] Ibid., 981.
[95] It was, however, circulated in manuscript at the symposium.
[96] Ibid., 979.
[97] Ibid., 1045.
[98] Ibid., 935.
[99] Ibid., 949–53.
[100] Ibid., 949.

the contrary, it . . . strives to denounce not only theoretical limits but also concrete injustices . . . [perpetuated by] the good conscience that dogmatically stops before any inherited determination of justice.[101]

This discursive, relational, and mystical conception of justice is not, of course, original to Derrida. It is "the unwillingness to name or describe the 'other' " familiar not only in the Jewish existentialism of Martin Buber and Emmanuel Levinas, but that Martin Jay locates "at the heart of Critical Theory."[102] In short, it is a vision of justice certain to go down pretty easily with Derrida's audience on this occasion.

The balance of the lecture derives a predictable reconciliation of deconstruction with this conception of justice: epistemological deconstruction is really ethically motivated normative critique of the inevitably demeaning, reductive effects of legal institutions. "Law," reasons Derrida, "is essentially deconstructible" because it is constructed, instituted by human will.[103] By contrast, the ideal of justice is never instituted and so never defined. There is no "construction" to deconstruct: "Justice is not deconstructible, no more then deconstruction itself, if such a thing exists. Deconstruction is justice. . . . The deconstructibility of law makes deconstruction possible. . . . The undeconstructibility of justice also makes deconstruction possible."[104] In short, it is the vulnerability of legal institutions to deconstruction that makes justice possible. But note Derrida's equivocation: "possible" now means "conceivable," not realizable in institutions. The justice enabled by deconstruction is nothing more then nostalgia for an unrealizable ideal.

Nevertheless, Derrida associates the deconstructive critique of legal institutions with a revolutionary politics:

In the moment that an axiom's credibility . . . is suspended by deconstruction, in this structurally necessary moment one can always believe that there is no more room for justice . . . but . . . this anxiety-ridden moment of suspense—which is also the interval or space in which transformations, indeed juridico-political revolutions take place—cannot be motivated . . . except in the demand for an increase in or supplement to justice.[105]

Derrida supports this suggestion that deconstruction is politically motivated by reinterpreting its antireductionism as a challenge to institutions rather than concepts.

Derrida first explains his identification of deconstruction with justice by stressing the subversive quality of the ideal of justice: "To be just . . . the decision of a judge . . . must not only follow a rule of law . . . but must also . . . approve it, confirm its value, by a reinstituting act of interpretation . . . as if the judge himself invented the law in every case."[106] Just judgment is at once responsible to rules,

---

[101] Ibid., 955.
[102] Martin Jay, *The Dialectical Imagination* (Boston: Little, Brown, 1973), 200.
[103] Derrida, "Force of Law," 943.
[104] Ibid., 945.
[105] Ibid., 955–57.
[106] Ibid., 961.

but free to test their justice, to justify them. This decisional freedom is acknowledged whenever the outcome of justificatory discourse is held in suspense. Hence, indeterminacy, "a theme often associated with deconstruction,"[107] is not an embarrassment to judgment, but a prerequisite to its appearing just. Here Derrida reverts to mysticism, suggesting that the deconstructive ideal of justice, like the Levinasian God, is infinite, and that this infinity renders the invocation of justice in finite decision making contradictory. This elusive ideal of justice is a "ghost," the "ghost of the undecidable."

Against this figure of the ghost, Derrida opposes a very different figuration of the ideal, the messiah who represents a definite promise of justice:

> Deconstruction . . . operates on the basis of an infinite "idea of justice," infinite because it is irreducible, irreducible because it is owed to the other, owed to the other before any contract. . . . This "idea of justice" seems to me irreducible in its affirmative character, in its demand of gift without exchange without economic circularity, without calculation and without rules. And so we can recognize in it . . . a kind of madness . . . and . . . mystique. And deconstruction is mad about this . . . desire for justice. . . . I would hesitate to assimilate too quickly this "idea of justice" to a regulative idea . . . to a messianic promise.[108]

Because founded on a promise or a covenant itself without juridical foundation, any messianic ideal of justice can be deconstructed and found wanting, in debt. To this, Derrida contrasts a ghostly ideal that would come into currency owing to nothing, constructed by no one.

Having shown that the ideal of justice involves a contradiction that precludes justifying institutions, Derrida finally argues that deconstruction depends upon this unjustifiability of institutions. In other words, the epistemological skepticism manifest in deconstruction depends upon an implicit ethical critique. Derrida reasons that the descriptive statements of interest to epistemology all imply such performative statements as "I promise to faithfully report the truth." These performatives in turn presuppose institutions of promising, contracting, and the like that in turn are founded on "other anterior performatives." The truth claims challenged by deconstruction therefore depend ultimately upon social conventions that can only be defended as just rather than true. Yet because justice is indeterminate, and irreducible to existing institutions, these conventions are always vulnerable to overthrow in the name of idealized justice.[109] Thus, Derrida suggests, deconstruction's challenge to truth claims is ultimately ethical.

The difficulty with this guarantee of deconstruction's ethical earnestness is that we cannot take it in earnest, depending as it does upon the sentimentality and essentialism that Derrida condemns not only in earlier texts, but later in this same text. Derrida's first lecture is sentimental insofar as it evokes the ideal of justice as the unmediated understanding of the other. In figuring justice as the expression

---

[107] Ibid., 963.
[108] Ibid., 965.
[109] Ibid., 967–71.

of the full particularity of each person, which is inevitably distorted by the law's rigid categories, deconstruction plays the familiar role of literature as law's sentimental helpmeet, leavening its harsh judgment with tender feeling. This first lecture is essentialist in evoking not only an authentic individual personality, but also an unmediated, ahistorical concept of justice. If deconstruction offers any valuable lesson, it is the pragmatic point that every concept is instituted, situated, "constructed," if it has meaning at all. There are no sentiments that are not already conventional, no values that are not already the product of negotiation and exchange, no personalities that are not already legal personalities.

Yet the first lecture's uncharacteristically sentimental and metaphysical tendencies are inserted in the argument only for later deconstruction. We are asked to "hesitate" in identifying the ideal of justice with messianism only to permit Derrida time to pursue his suspicion that the "incalculable and giving idea of justice is always very close to the . . . worst"[110] and then to dramatically announce the arrest at the close of his next lecture when he indicts "messianico-Marxis[m] as "complicit . . . [with] the worst."[111] The tip-off that the detective-writer is scattering red herrings to lead his readers astray is the first lecture's heavy reliance on that favorite target of Derrida, the dualistic opposition. The oppositions transsecting the first lecture include those between law and justice, realized institutions and idealized values, rule and discretion, gift and exchange, and finally, most importantly, legal order and revolution. Justice, in Lecture 1, is that ideal which inspires revolutionary change, the refounding of a legal order, and deconstruction is "just" insofar as revolutionary.

The surprise here is that Derrida momentarily pretends to endorse a distinction between rule intepretation and rule invention. Revolution, after all, is a form of invention that claims a complete break with the past. It changes not only the content of the law, but its principle of legitimacy, its rule of recognition. Thus, revolution is distinguishable from reform only if we can distinguish between the application and the alteration of rules of recognition for legal rules. The idea of the revolutionary "refounding of law and politics"[112] is therefore parasitic on the distinction between interpretation and invention. *And it is this very distinction that Derrida's principle of iterability denies.*

Derrida had already drawn attention to the instability of the distinction between perpetuating and subverting legal order in an insightful commentary on the Declaration of Independence. Who, Derrida wonders, authorizes the independence of a heretofore dependent people? Who signs the Declaration of Independence?

> It is the "good people" who declare themselves free and independent by the relay of their representatives and of their representatives [Jefferson] of representatives. One cannot decide . . . whether independence is stated or produced by this utterance. . . . It is not a question here of an obscurity or of a difficulty of interpretation. . . . It is not a question of a difficult analysis which would fail in the face of . . . events. This obscurity,

[110] Ibid., 971.
[111] Ibid., 1045.
[112] Ibid., 971.

this undecidability between, let's say, a performative structure and a constative structure, is required in order to produce the sought-after effect. It is essential to the very positing or position of a right as such. . . . I would even go so far as to say that every signature finds itself thus affected. . . . This people does not exist . . . before this declaration, not as such. The signature invents the signer. And yet . . . They sign in the name of the laws of nature and in the name of God . . . creator of nature. He comes, in effect, to guarantee the rectitude of popular intentions, the unity and goodness of the people. He founds natural laws and thus the whole game which tends to present performative utterances as constative utterances.[113]

The assertion of a right to independence is at once a claim of untrammeled sovereignty and a respectful argument to and from preexisting legal authority. Itself dependent, the claimed independence must be warranted by reason, custom, natural law, the virtue of its claimants, the corruption of its opponents, and so forth. Natural rights and popular sovereignty authorize each other, while the "justice" demanded by revolutionaries must already in some fashion be instituted, if it is to justify anything at all.

In light of this earlier text, it can come as no surprise that Lecture 2 deconstructs the very distinctions on which the argument of Lecture 1 depends. Derrida attacks the revolutionary longing for justice voiced by Benjamin as a self-deluded and dangerously apocalyptic aspiration. Derrida's target is the "Critique of Violence,"[114] in which Benjamin offered a radical critique of representative democracy, while evoking the violence and mystery of divine judgment.

The unspoken starting point of Benjamin's analysis was an image of revolution as an untrammeled expression of popular sovereignty, a moment of pure democratic participation. Benjamin lamented modern parliamentary democracy because, if the police had a monopoly on legitimate force, popular soverignty would more likely develop into a police-state than a participatory democracy: "When the consciousness of the latent presence of violence in a legal institution disappears," Benjamin argued, "the institution falls into decay. In our time, parliaments . . . offer a . . . woeful spectacle, because they have forgotten the revolutionary violence from which they are born."[115] Unwilling to mobilize the sovereign people, parliamentary democracies were powerless to represent them and were easily coerced into craven compromises. Yet, Benjamin argued, this cycle of the decay of democracy is inevitable so long as popular power must exhaust itself in legal institutions.[116] In a cryptic peroration, Benjamin prophesied a moment when humanity will give up the mythic idols of the law and allow itself to be ruled only by an "expiatory" and "bloodless"[117] divine violence that Benjamin concluded by calling "sovereign."[118]

[113] Jacques Derrida, "Declarations of Independence," *New Political Science* 15 (1986), 9–11.
[114] Benjamin, *Reflections*, 277.
[115] Ibid., 288.
[116] Ibid., 300.
[117] Ibid., 297.
[118] Ibid., 300.

Derrida subjects this formulation to three criticisms. First, he finds it fatally dependent on a distinction between the law-founding violence of revolution and the law-enforcing violence of the police. Parliamentarism threatens to take the violent power of lawmaking away from its rightful owners, the people, and give it to officers appointed only to enforce the law. But all revolutions, Derrida responds, undermine the legal orders they found by implying the legality of future revolution; on the other hand, all revolutions are potentially limited by their own discourse of justification:

> I shall propose the interpretation according to which the very violence of the foundation of law must envelop the violence of conservation and cannot break with it. . . . It belongs to the structure of fundamental violence that it calls for the repetition of itself and founds what ought to be conserved. . . . A foundation is a promise. . . . And even if a promise is not kept in fact, iterability inscribes the promise as guard in the most irruptive moment of foundation. With this, there is no more a pure foundation . . . of law, and so a pure founding of violence, than there is a purely conservative violence.[119]

As Derrida correctly observes, "what threatens the rigor of the distinction between the two types of violence is at bottom the paradox of iterability."[120] Having come clean on this point, Derrida can no longer liken deconstruction to revolution: "these Benjaminian oppositions [e.g., between revolution and compromise] seem to me to . . . deconstruct themselves, even as paradigms for deconstruction."[121]

A second line of argument recapitulates the case against the Rousseauian ideal of participatory democracy: Benjamin had expressed a kind of metaphysical essentialism in his promotion of popular revolt over parliamentary deliberation. "The very passage from presence to representation . . . forms the trajectory of decline, of institutional 'degeneracy'."[122] Like Rousseau, Benjamin adopted a self-deluded pose of anti-intellectualism, approvingly quoting Sorel's statement that "the revolution appears as a clear, simple, revolt, and no place is reserved either for the sociologists or the elegant amateurs of social reform or for the intellectuals who have made it their place to think for the proletariat."[123] Finally, like Rousseau, Benjamin was dangerously sentimental: "Benjamin intends to prove that a nonviolent elimination of conflicts is possible in the private world when it is ruled by the culture of the heart, cordial courtesy, sympathy, love of peace, trust. . . . Yet this nonviolence is not without an affinity to pure violence."[124] By this Derrida probably means that Benjamin longs for a finality, a placidity beyond conflict which could only be achieved by violence.

This brings us to the third, and most troubling accusation. Derrida moves beyond the familiar characterization of Rousseauian radicalism as totalitarian to associate Benjamin with Nazism. There are really three distinct points here. First,

---

[119] Derrida, "Force of Law," 997.
[120] Ibid., 1007.
[121] Ibid., 995–97.
[122] Ibid., 1015.
[123] Ibid., 1019; Benjamin, *Reflections*, 286.
[124] Derrida, "Force of Law," 1019–21.

Benjamin's idea that parliamentary democracy represents "decay" or "degenera-tion" from an earlier state of health expressed in violence reminds Derrida of Nazism's Darwinist notions and eugenic methods.[125] Second, in a striking reversal, Derrida now detects an affinity with Nazism in the very rhetoric of revolution he embraced in his first lecture. Purporting to summarize Benjamin's conclusions, Derrida writes,

> 1. Democracy is a degeneracy of droit . . . ; 2. There is not yet any democracy worthy of the name. Democracy remains yet to come. . . . And so Benjamin's argument, which then develops into a critique of the parliamentarism of liberal democracy, is revolution-ary . . . , but in the two senses of the word . . . which include . . . the sense of a return to the past of a purer origin. This equivocation is typical enough to have fed many revolutionary discourses on the right and the left, particularly between the two wars.[126]

Finally, Benjamin's strange discussion of a bloodless divine judgment suggests to Derrida the compulsive neatness of the Nazis, endeavoring to exterminate with no trace. Benjamin's characterization of divine violence as expiatory leaves open

> a temptation . . . notably to the survivors or victims . . . to think the holocaust as an uninterpretable manifestation of divine violence. . . . When one thinks of the gas cham-bers and cremation ovens, this allusion to an extermination that would be expiatory because bloodless must cause one to shudder. One is terrified at the idea of an interpreta-tion that would make of the holocaust an expiation and an indecipherable signature of the just and violent anger of God.[127]

Against the background of these unsavory associations, Benjamin's concluding identification of divine violence as "sovereign" is all the proof Derrida needs that sovereignty—however popular, however participatory—is inherently extermina-tory. Concluding his address to the Holocaust historians, Derrida warns:

> This text . . . seems to me finally to resemble too closely . . . the very thing against which one must act and do and that with which one must break. . . . This text, like many others by Benjamin, is still too Heideggerian, too messianico-Marxist or archeoeschato-logical for me. . . . If there were a lesson to be drawn [from this nameless thing called the final solution] . . . the lesson that we . . . must [draw today]—is that we must think, know, represent for ourselves, formalize, judge the possible complicity between all these discourses and . . . the final solution.[128]

This identification of a Jewish Marxist Holocaust victim with Nazism in order to score a point off neo-Marxist critical theory seems disturbingly exploitative.[129] Derrida's effort to associate Benjamin's elusive figure of divine judgment with

---

[125] Ibid., 1013–15.

[126] Ibid.

[127] Ibid., 1044.

[128] Ibid., 1045.

[129] Benjamin committed suicide in 1940 under the apparently mistaken belief that he was about to be captured by the Gestapo. Peter Demetz, introduction to Benjamin, *Reflections*, xiv–xv.

gas chambers that Benjamin could hardly have imagined in 1921 is unconvincing and evokes familiar Christian critiques of Judaism as vengeful. Benjamin is quite explicit that human beings may not stand in judgment of one another, in God's place,[130] and that life is rendered sacred rather than superfluous by the messianic possibility of justice.[131] It is odd to blame the triumph of Nazism on the left's failure to support parliamentary democracy in the face of the more familiar account that the Weimar Republic's political center sold out to the Nazis for fear of the left. Nor did Benjamin endorse dictatorship or characterize "democracy [as] degenerate." Instead, and like Rousseau, he reserved his scorn for representative democracy, while endorsing participatory democracy. If Benjamin's revolutionary radicalism neither contributed to nor encouraged the Nazi Holocaust, the complicity Derrida seeks to establish is somewhat mysterious.

But regardless of the persuasiveness of Derrida's critique of Benjamin in the second lecture, it dramatically alters the meaning of the first lecture. While the first lecture denies that justice can be institutionalized in a state, the second lecture argues that efforts to institutionalize the messianic yearning for justice in a subversive social movement lead to atrocity. *Any* political effort to institutionalize justice is totalitarian, Derrida implies. Thus, the affiliation between deconstruction and radical politics suggested in the first lecture is firmly repudiated in the second. And if he affiliates deconstructive criticism with justice, that is because he views the idea of justice as too dangerous to play a role in any affirmative political program. Far from identifying deconstruction with radical politics, he advocates deconstruction as a safely ineffectual outlet for the messianic yearning for justice that inspires radical politics.[132]

Conclusion to Part 5.1

Derridean deconstructive practice may be thought of as a conjunction of three elements: first, a pragmatic epistemology of reading that figures every sign as suspended in a boundless web of meaning, any strand of which a reading may legitimately follow; second, a critical strategy of reading that finds essentialist claims implicit in any practice of signification; and third, an ethical target of critique consisting of the ideal of popular sovereignty and the various concepts by which democrats attempt to identify a sovereign people. Having explicated the relationship between Derrida's epistemological arguments and his ethical goals, we are now in a position to understand and assess the efforts of legal scholars to adapt various aspects of his practice. First, in part 5.2, we will examine the efforts of several critical legal scholars to adapt deconstruction to the project

---

[130] Benjamin, *Reflections*, 298.

[131] Ibid., 299.

[132] For a withering analysis of the political implications of Derrida's recent writings on justice, see Mark Lilla, "The Politics of Jacques Derrida," *The New York Review of Books* 44, no. 11 (June 25, 1998): 36–41.

of an epistemological critique of legal doctrine. Later, in part 5.3, we will examine the efforts of several feminist legal and political theorists to articulate a deconstructive ethics of "difference."

5.2. DECONSTRUCTION AS EPISTEMOLOGICAL CRITICISM OF LAW

In evaluating the use of deconstruction for an epistemological critique of law, we will first review the efforts of critical legal scholars Jack Balkin and Duncan Kennedy to develop a deconstructive "semiotics" of legal argument. Second, we will explore a debate between Balkin and Pierre Schlag over the political implications of such deconstructive epistemological critique. Third, we will consider at length the explanatory potential of such critique by giving searching examination to two epistemological histories of legal doctrine, "The Ideology of Bureaucracy in American Law" by Gerald Frug, and "The Metaphysics of American Law" by Gary Peller.

We will ultimately conclude that critical legal theorists have often understood deconstruction to authorize an epistemological skepticism, which, it turns out, equally undermines all political arguments and so says nothing distinctive about any. Where deconstructive readings root error in a dualistic "Western Metaphysical Tradition" spanning three millennia, they can say little of interest about the particular historical and political contexts of legal thought and action. Celebrating the particular as the manifestation of a difference inherently resistant to comprehension and critique, deconstruction paradoxically absolves its practitioners of the obligation to even explore the explanatory power of cultural and historical context in reading texts. Deconstructive legal study can usefully complicate and enrich situated accounts of the production and formation of cultural identities. But without such a conscious effort to put legal thought in context, deconstructive analysis simply spins on its axis, drilling holes in the air.

"Legal Semiotics": Deconstruction as Analytic Technique

Critical legal scholars have invoked deconstruction in mapping the structure of legal argumentation in many fields of law. Arguing that the meanings of rules are always indeterminate, these "semiotic" critics have urged that we redescribe legal doctrine, not as a code of rules, but as an inventory of opposing arguments for resolving ambiguities in rules. They have suggested that such a focus yields a parsimonious description of a doctrinal system, because the arguments used to fill in gaps in rules tend to repeat themselves. Because the rule choices motivated by these arguments merely open up new ambiguities, argue Duncan Kennedy and Jack Balkin, the opposing arguments marshaled in selecting a rule tend to recur in the process of applying or interpreting the rule selected.[133]

---

[133] Jack Balkin, "The Crystalline Structure of Legal Thought," *Rutgers Law Review* (1986): 1; Duncan Kennedy, "A Semiotics of Legal Argument," *Syracuse Law Review* 42 (1991): 75; see also

Typically, familiar arguments reappear at ascending levels of doctrinal specificity wherever legal doctrine conditions results in "mental" states such as intent, consent, culpability, and pain that cannot be directly observed. In tort and criminal law, for example, we hold liable those whom we deem responsible for results: in deciding whether liability will be based not only on causation but also on fault; whether fault will be based on available knowledge of risk or actual knowledge of risk; whether the knowledge ascribable to the defendant was that available to most people, or those in the defendant's circumstances, or those with the defendant's characteristics; whether fault turns on awareness of a larger or smaller risk; and whether the defendant should bear the burden of proof on any of these points—in all these contexts, the same arguments are likely to recur. Defendants are likely to argue on grounds of both fairness and deterrence that liability should be based only on proof of knowing wrongdoing. Prosecutors and plaintiffs will respond that more knowledge was available to the defendant at the price of effort, so that the defendant's ignorance was both culpable and deterrable; further, the defendant's psychological states and dispositions are unverifiable, so that the defendant must be judged by external circumstances.

If we think of the possible standards of responsibility for harmful results as a continuum, with strict liability for harm caused at the left end and liability for harm intended at the right, every standard in between must be defended against alternatives to the left by deploying the principle of no liability without knowing wrongdoing, and against alternatives to the right by arguing that ignorance is culpable and unverifiable. Thus, each of the innumerable positions in the middle is inherently instable, relying on incompatible arguments that, taken together, could equally well justify any position on the continuum.

To take one example, consider the defense of mistake of law. In the case of *People v. Marrero*,[134] a federal correctional officer mistakenly concluded that he was among the "state and other correctional officers" authorized by statute to carry an unlicensed weapon. In invoking New York's statutory defense of mistake of law based on an official statement of the law, Marrero argued that he had relied on a reasonable, although apparently mistaken, reading of the statute itself.

Rejecting this argument, the New York Court of Appeals ruled that interpreting the statute to permit a defense of reliance on a reasonably mistaken interpretation of a statute would encourage ignorance and lying, elevate the individual's interpretation of the law over the law itself, and violate the maxim "ignorance of the law is no excuse." Yet these arguments, as the saying goes, prove too much. Any defense of mistake discourages inquiry beyond a point and so rewards ignorance, and any defense of mistake rewards claiming one made a mistake. So much is true even of the mistakes based on inaccurate official statements of the law that the Court would excuse, not to mention the mistake of fact that acquits the unwitting recipient of the wrong garment at the coatcheck counter. Any defense based on

---

Jeremy Paul, "The Politics of Legal Semiotics," *Texas Law Review* 69 (1991): 1779; James Boyle, "The Anatomy of a Torts Class," 34 *American University Law Review* (1985): 1003.

[134] 507 N.E.2d 1068 (N.Y. 1987).

ignorance of one's legal duty elevates the individual view of the law over the law. This is true not only of the mistakes based upon inaccurate official statements of the law, but also of the inability to distinguish right from wrong produced by mental disease.

The dissent responded that the Court's position imposed liability without knowing wrongdoing and punished diligence. Yet these arguments also prove too much. Punishment of any offender believing his conduct lawful—however unreasonably—offends the principle of no liability without knowing wrongdoing. And if reasonable mistakes of law based on reasonably diligent inquiry are sufficient to excuse, why limit them to those based on an official statement of the law?

Both majority and dissent rely on arguments that, taken seriously, would undermine the very standard they are interpreting. We might therefore conclude that the arguments offered and the values urged by the majority and dissent have already been considered and rejected by the legislature. But that is not the way legal "discourse" is structured. Legislatures do not so much select among ends as they agree on means, or even on ineffectual language that expresses competing ends. Courts decide cases on narrow grounds, distinguishing cases on the facts to avoid articulating a standard; where a standard is unavoidable it will consist of a formula for balancing competing values. These forensic habits—legislative compromise, judicial restraint, interest balancing—may or may not embody a liberal ideal of value neutrality. But their effect is to preserve the authority of the competing arguments that enable doctrinal discourse. And so, comments Duncan Kennedy, "the play of [argument] bite and counter-bite settles nothing (except the case at hand). As between the bites themselves, every fight is a draw, and all combatants live to fight another day, neither discredited by association with the losing side nor established as correct by association with a winner."[135] To Kennedy and Balkin, the reappearance during norm interpretation of arguments rejected during norm promulgation suggests a model of doctrinal discourse as an endless sequence of similarly shaped disputes "nesting" inside one another.

What does this "nesting" model of doctrinal discourse share with deconstruction? What does it have to do with progressive politics? And how illuminating is it? While Kennedy has identified his "semiotic" analyses of legal argument primarily with deconstruction's parent movement, structuralism,[136] Jack Balkin has

---

[135] Kennedy, "A Semiotics of Legal Argument," 103.

[136] Ibid., 106, 107, 109. Kennedy recognizes as exponents of this semiotic approach authors who clearly are influenced by deconstruction—David Kennedy, Gerald Frug, Pierre Schlag, and Jack Balkin. The lines of influence here are quite complex. Kennedy's article explicating his semiotic approach appeared in 1991, whereas the works he cites by the above authors appeared between 1984 and 1988. Yet both Kennedy's own article and Balkin's 1986 article represent efforts to formalize and explicate Kennedy's teaching method in common law courses, and Kennedy claims to have used the method "tentatively"in his influential articles "Form and Substance in Private Law Adjudication," *Harvard Law Review* 89 (1976): 1685, and "The Structure of Blackstone's Commentaries," *Buffalo Law Review* 28 (1979): 205. Balkin, interestingly but not entirely convincingly, interprets both of these articles as examples of deconstruction. Jack Balkin, "Deconstructive Practice and Legal Theory," *Yale Law Journal* 96 (1987): 743 , 762–63. In his recent book *A Critique of Adjudication (Fin-de-Siècle)*

identified his almost identical analyses with deconstruction. The model of doctrinal discourse as nested conflict resembles deconstruction in three ways.

First, it illustrates the structuralist principle that meaning is produced by difference or contrast. In practice, arguments are not so much briefs for particular standards of liability—such as strict liability or intent—as they are briefs for relatively more inclusive or exclusive, relatively more objective or subjective, criteria of liability. They get their meaning, in short, from the arguments they oppose rather than the rules they endorse, or to which we might say, they normatively "refer."[137]

Second, the nested conflict model shares deconstruction's rejection of the structuralist distinction between a fixed and finite structure of rules (*langue* in de Saussure's phrase) and an infinitely repeatable practice of rule application (*parole*). Instead of viewing legal doctrine as a body of rules, Balkin and Kennedy view it as a discursive practice for generating rules by appeal to arguments.[138] At first blush the practice appears to proceed according to a kind of genetic code, consisting in a finite number of arguments—but the iterability of arguments in different contexts permits them no fixed meaning. Because the arguments come in neatly opposed pairs, they simply define axes, any point along which can be explained by reference to either argument. Within its domain of relevance, then, each argument can literally mean anything. In this way doctrinal discourse illustrates how iterability disrupts structural models of meaning: every argument is defined by what it excludes, but over an infinity of available iterations, every argument comes to exclude nothing.

Third, because it interprets doctrinal discourse as the repetition and reconciliation of opposed principles, the nested conflict model resembles Derridean critique of any doctrinal argument as a failed effort to sustain a dualist metaphysics.

And this last point raises our second question: is the nesting model politically corrosive? Kennedy proposed a partial answer in observing that

> legal argument has a certain mechanical quality, once one begins to identify its characteristic operations. Language seems to be "speaking the subject" rather than the reverse.

(Cambridge: Harvard Univ. Press, 1997) Kennedy rejects what he regards as the implication of some deconstructive criticism that deconstruction is always possible and that legal doctrine is always equally indeterminate, since practical contexts can contrain adjudication, as he illustrated in "Freedom and Constraint in Adjudication: A Critical Phenomenology," *Journal of Legal Education* 36 (1986): 518. In other respects, he endorses the position of the English critical legal scholar Matthew Kramer, that structuralism and deconstruction are compatible. Kennedy, *Critique of Adjudication*, 413 n., citing Matthew Kramer, *Legal Theory, Political Theory and Deconstruction: Against Rhadamanthus* (Bloomington: Indiana Univ. Press, 1991).

[137] Kennedy, "Semiotics of Legal Argument," 76.

[138] Kennedy, in keeping with his own understanding of his enterprise as structuralist, describes this conflation of "langue" and "parole" in the opposite way as "reducing the 'parole' of legal argument to a 'langue' composed of argument-bites." Ibid., 106. Yet he traces his conception of legal argument to Lévi-Strauss's notion of "bricolage," a practice of adapting received cultural materials to new uses and that seems closer to 'parole.' Ibid., 107. See Claude Lévi-Strauss, *The Savage Mind* (London: Weidenfeld and Nicholson, 1962), 16–22.

It is hard to imagine doing this kind of argument in utter good faith, that is, to imagine doing it without some cynical strategy in fitting shoe to foot.[139]

Kennedy may be read as suggesting that each iteration of an argument is informed by traces of other contexts in which the same argument could be deployed against the proposition for which it is cited. In defending any standard of liability, for example, judges must invoke arguments knowing that they must be prepared to oppose them not just in some other case, but in their next breath, in explaining why the argument does not push farther than the constraints of precedent or policy permit. This can give judicial discourse a kind of studied, cynical quality that aptly illustrates the deconstructive view of all language use as citation, the iteration of scripted discourse.

Thus, a court will implicitly admit that "social protection" can be invoked against virtually any defense in any context when it says "society would be almost completely unprotected against criminals if it permitted a blind or irresistable impulse or inability to control oneself to excuse or justify murder or to lower it from first to second degree."[140] Similarly a court will admit that the conflict between social protection and the conditioning of punishment on voluntary wrongdoing justifies any result when it reasons that

> our jurisprudence, while not oblivious to deterministic components, ultimately rests on a premise of free will. This is not to be viewed as an exercise in philosophic discourse, but as a governmental fusion of ethics and necessity, which takes into account that a system of rewards and punishments is itself part of the environment that influences and shapes human conduct.[141]

Beyond a comfortable posture of ironic detachment, what then follows from the recognition that lawyers and judges cannot take their own arguments seriously? The deconstructive critique of doctrinal discourse as inauthentic must contend with the deconstructive critique of the aspiration to authenticity. If, as Balkin acknowledges, all discourse is necessarily artificial and mediated, the charge of inauthenticity cannot be very corrosive.[142]

A Derridean response might contend that a claim to earnestness is internal to doctrinal discourse—that the discourse's dualistic structure implies a "metaphysics of presence," with its values of truth and authenticity. But imagining such a response merely illustrates the underdetermination of Derrida's deductions of metaphysical faith from rhetorical form. The question, after all, is how seriously lawyers take their own rhetoric, and this question cannot be answered by recourse to the rhetoric alone. When we factor in additional information about the cultural context of doctrinal discourse, however, we have reason to believe that lawyers

[139] Kennedy, "Semiotics of Legal Argument," 104.

[140] *Commonwealth v. Tyrrell*, 174 A.2d 852 (Pa. 1961); *Commonwealth v. Carrol*, 194 A.2d 911 (Pa. 1963).

[141] *United States v. Brawner*, 471 F.2d 969 (D.C. Cir., 1972) (Leventhal, J.).

[142] Jack Balkin, "The Promise of Legal Semiotics," *Texas Law Review* 69 (1991): 1831; see also Paul, "The Politics of Legal Semiotics."

and judges are already onto themselves. Lawyers, after all, are encouraged to view their own arguments with detachment. In role, their obligations are to client and case, not conscience. In judges, detachment is the virtue of impartiality. The "exposure" of advocacy as a role in no way alienates the performer or impedes the performance. Thus, Duncan Kennedy's claim that exposing legal argument's inauthenticity can break its spell seems unconvincing.

Although both avoid Kennedy's political claims for a deconstructive semiotics of legal argument, Jack Balkin and Pierre Schlag offer contradictory accounts of why such deconstruction can be, nevertheless, politically progressive. Their arguments against one another are each compelling, yielding a nicely rounded picture of the deconstruction's potential for epistemological critique—but also yielding the conclusion that deconstruction has no particular political implications.

Balkin argues that deconstruction shows the inevitability of contradiction, hence discretion, hence indeterminacy. And, he contends, it thereby liberates the audience from the objectifying grip of a necessarily partial or perspectival view. But, Balkin adds, by demonstrating that discretion is inevitable, deconstruction also reminds legal decision makers of their ethical responsibility for whatever decision they make. This amounts to an existentialist ethics of radical individual freedom, imposing a responsibility to acknowledge and courageously exercise discretion.

Now, the difficulty, pointed out by Schlag, is that this account of deconstruction's liberating or transformative potential presumes the autonomous individual subject of existentialist humanism—generally seen as a chief target of deconstruction's critique. Schlag fixes on the following revealing passage in Balkin's "Deconstructive Practice and Legal Theory," in which he compares deconstruction to psychoanalysis:

> In the same fashion, the deconstructionist must engage in a process of self-reflection to determine when the insights provided by deconstruction have produced sufficient enlightenment with respect to a view of law, legal doctrine, or human society previously accepted as privileged, natural or complete. This decision is, of course, a political or moral choice, but it is one informed by insights gained through the activity of deconstruction itself. At the moment the choice is made, the critical theorist is, strictly speaking, no longer a deconstructionist. However, the purposes of engaging in the deconstruction have been served.[143]

Schlag has two related objections to this form of argument. First, he objects to reducing deconstruction to the status of a technique, temporally bounded and held firmly in control by the critic's ends. This objection exemplifies the Derridean critiques of closure and dualism, in this case the dualism of ends and means. Schlag also objects that by positing a continuity of purpose throughout the decon-

---

[143] Balkin, "Deconstructive Practice and Legal Theory," 766, quoted by Schlag, *"L'hors de Texte,"* 1641; for a quite similar account of deconstruction's inherently limited utility as a practice see Thomas Heller, "Structuralism and Critique," *Stanford Law Review* 37 (1984): 127.

structive "process," Balkin implies a continuous subject, always in charge. While deconstruction critiques the identity of the self, Balkin seems to see this dissolution of the self as partial, temporary, like the temporary risks the personality must undergo in a therapeutic process of healing. Thus, deconstruction remains caught within narrative convention: it is a dangerous journey from which the subject returns intact and enriched.

For Schlag, however, criticism cannot be genuinely deconstructive if it leaves the subject in charge by addressing itself to a normative decision maker. Conversely, Schlag implies, there is some disruptive or transformative implication in getting people to acknowledge that, in fact, they have no discretion and can engage in no morally responsible choice. At the very least, Schlag asserts, they will have to stop reproducing normative thought and do something else. But there are two difficulties here.

First, we encounter a problem of self-contradiction: to presume, as Schlag seems to, that merely admitting our lack of moral discretion will get us to desist from the meaningless exercise of reasoned normative deliberation, or to change our practices in any other way, is to ascribe to us the discretionary agency, which by hypothesis we lack. To this, Schlag makes two responses: first, that rational consistency is our criterion, not his. Finding in deconstruction a warrant for the inevitability of contradiction, he can offer his own as more proof of his point. Second, he implies, he is not really ascribing agency to us by rationally appealing to us to desist from normative thought; rather, he is bullying, manipulating, tricking us into desisting by feeding parts of the machinery of rationality into itself so that it chews itself up in what he has called a "cannibal move."[144] Of course, he would acknowledge that the contradiction in his thinking reappears at one remove: in thus manipulating our rationality into immobility he may objectify us, but he thereby subjectifies himself, attributing free agency and normative discretion to himself. Schlag cheerfully acknowledges this difficulty as one of a species of "performative contradictions," that is, critiques of a practice that reproduce the practice. For Schlag this difficulty is endemic to internal critique, and situated within an infinite text as we are, internal critique is all there is.

This brings us to the second difficulty with Schlag's critique of normative subjectivity: so what if we do give up the meaningless exercise of normative deliberation and admit our impotence? Why should change in this practice change power relations or the distribution of wealth or anything else we might be tempted to call political? Of course, if we were capable of free agency, the revelation that we are less free than we supposed might impel us to action by undermining an otherwise settled social order. But this sort of subversion through critical enlightenment is precisely the exercise that Schlag rejects as meaningless. More information does not make us more free, and in any case the sources of the unfreedom revealed by deconstruction are metaphysical, not social. Why should desisting from rational inquiry into justice undermine an unjust social order? To be sure,

---

[144] Pierre Schlag, "Cannibal Moves: An Essay on the Metamorphosis of the Legal Distinction" *Stanford Law Review* 40 (1988): 929.

we might stop rationalizing the social order as just, but would we not be equally likely to stop criticizing the social order as unjust? Would we not give up the meaningless, naive, immature habit of worrying about whether or not it was just?

Moreover, even if we knew that deconstructive critique would change the social order in determinate ways, what would authorize us to judge the change an improvement? How, after giving up the bankrupt enterprise of normative deliberation, could we even compare possible social orders from the standpoint of justice? How can any claim that deconstruction is politically progressive survive our abandoning any normative criteria by which we would identify progress?

Balkin's response to the difficulties of Schlag's position is to reject the claim that the actual practice of deconstruction (as opposed to its epistemological premises) in any way subverts normative thought. Instead he argues that it is part of the normal operation of normative thought; that is, normative thought is enabled and constituted by the very contradictions that render the closure of deliberation impossible.[145] But if so, there is nothing distinctive or original about deconstruction as a practice, and, coextensive with normative thought, it cuts in no particular normative direction.

In sum, Schlag argues that Balkin's undetermined chooser is underdetermined, so that the very indeterminacy that appears to enable choice deprives it of motivation. Then Balkin reverses the paradox, arguing that normative indeterminacy creates the experiences of deliberation and choice. Schlag finds a metaphysical error in Balkin's text: the error of placing the reader outside of the deconstructed text, so that she can control the deconstructive operation. Yet Balkin finds a similar error in Schlag's text: the error of placing the deconstructive operation outside of a text that includes the reader, so that deconstruction can change the reader. But the act of deconstruction cannot be so neatly separated from the act of reading. Because textual indeterminacy is not only the condition for deconstruction, but also the condition for reading, deconstruction adds nothing to the text. As Derrida himself suggests,

> the very condition of a deconstruction may be at work, in the work, within the system to be deconstructed . . . , participating in the construction of what it at the same time threatens to deconstruct. One might then be inclined to reach this conclusion: deconstruction is not an operation that supervenes afterwards, one fine day.[146]

Already implicit in the text, deconstruction is also implicit in any reader of that text. Thus, at the end of their exchange of flanking maneuvers, Balkin and Schlag both find themselves circumscribed by Derrida's infinite textuality. We are left with a text that produces its own deconstructive reader. This deconstructive reader turns out to be none other than His Honor, the normative deliberator, who was speaking French literary theory all along and never knew it.

[145] See Drucilla Cornell, "The Violence of the Masquerade: Law Dressed Up as Justice" *Cardozo Law Review* 11 (1990): 1047.

[146] Jacques Derrida, "The Art of *Memoires*," in *Memoires for Paul de Man* (New York, Columbia Univ. Press, 1989), 73.

This is a much less subversive result than Kennedy, Balkin, or Schlag expect, but one that would be just fine with Derrida. Derrida, you may recall, tells us that "deconstruction is always to be found" in "the space between law and justice," that is, in the exercise of normative judgment. This is also the space between sign and meaning, expression and purpose, that the reader inhabits. For Derrida, then, reading is a refuge for the individual reminiscent of the space conservative political philosopher Leo Strauss finds "between the lines" in his essay "Persecution and the Art of Writing"—a refuge from the intimidating presence of the assembly, a place where the cloistered scholar can safely register his doubts.

Thus, we can think of Derrida as one who, impressed by the structuralist critique of existential humanism, attempts a belated, poststructuralist defense of individualism and subjectivism. The structuralist critique of "humanism," initiated by Derrida's targets Lévi-Strauss, Althusser, and Foucault, was a critique of the individual as a cultural construct. Derrida wants to argue—probably on the side of Balkin and against Schlag—that the individual subject can be reconceived as a reader of texts. Derrida sees this subjective reader as a potentiality within any culture. This subject is not a hard precultural reality, but instead a product of culture—of any culture, not just that of capitalism or modern society. Writing always implies—and produces—an autonomous reader: that is the political point of Derrida's principle of iterability. Derrida's project is to refound liberal individualism on culture rather than natural law. The linguistic crafting of human experience means that natural law liberalism must ultimately succumb to the Aristotelian-Rousseauian-Marxist argument that humanity is constitutively social. Resting on error, natural law liberalism is dangerously vulnerable to refutation and so invites the suppression of civil liberties. Thus, Derrida objects to the humanism of the existentialists, but *not* to their embrace of subjectivity.

Schlag seems to assume with the Marxian tradition that the critique of subjectivity is politically progressive; here he is consistent with the anti-individualist structuralism of Lévi-Strauss, Althusser, and Foucault. But this project, with which Derrida has been so often associated, is not his. Balkin, on the other hand, may associate Derrida's subjectivism with a Sartrean ethic of responsibility to the authentic voice of conscience. But the Derridean reader cannot be forced to respond to the imprecations of any voice. It prefers to receive inquiries in writing and preserves its freedom by interminably reserving decision.

If semiotic analysis is unlikely to affect doctrinal argument, can it at least illuminate doctrinal argument? Here we suspect that precisely what appears to give semiotic analysis explanatory power—its capacity to class together vast numbers of arguments, irrespective of context—blinds it to the politics at play in legal argument.

Typically, these analyses read bodies of legal doctrine as futile, Sisyphean efforts to purge legal decision making of its discretionary elements. Legal doctrine purports, in other words, to rest legal decision making on the determinate will or consent of legal persons rather than contestable moral principles. This positivist project founders, however, on epistemological difficulties. The subjective will of legal persons is unknowable, perhaps nonexistent. Any inference from action to intention seems to require assumptions about what a rational person would intend by such action. Any such notion of rationality, in turn, requires a theory of the objective interests of human beings.[147] Thus, positivists' attribution of subjective will to legal persons turns out to depend on an objectivist moral theory, rooted in an account of human nature. The exposure of these objectivist moral assumptions embarrasses legal positivism in much the same way that the pragmatist's exposure of hidden metaphysical assumptions embarrasses logical positivism. Intentions turn out to have the same mythic status in legal positivism that sense-data do in logical positivism. In line with this reading, semiotic analysis represents legal doctrine as a series of nested oppositions between subjective and objective standards—between the positivist ideal of a jurisprudence of consent and its inevitable adulteration by reliance on formal proxies for representing and measuring consent. Thus read, legal doctrine exhibits the dualistic and hierarchical structure Derrida finds symptomatic of Western metaphysics.

The difficulty with this deconstructive critique of legal doctrine is that it proceeds from the unexamined and unsupported assumption that all doctrinal reliance on mental concepts is motivated by a commitment to legal positivism. It reduces all doctrinal argument to the tired jurisprudential theme of natural law versus positivism, without any account of why this issue would be of such obsessive concern to lawyers and legal scholars in so many different contexts. In so doing, it obscures normative debates of far greater moment to the participants. If a purely formal, "semiotic" deconstruction of legal doctrine merely missed these value conflicts, it could be used selectively and combined with an account of when and why the positivism/natural law debate is likely to be politically and culturally significant. We might then conclude that Derridean deconstruction could contribute to an illuminating interpretation and critique of legal doctrine. Unfortunately, however, by focusing right through the normative issues at stake in legal argument to the *supposedly* deeper issues of metaphysics and epistemology, "semiotic" deconstruction tends to render the political and historical context of doctrinal debate invisible.

In explicating this difficulty, we offer critical readings of two of the most historically informed examples of the epistemological deconstruction of legal doctrine, "The Ideology of Bureaucracy in American Law" by Gerald Frug, and the "The Metaphysics of American Law" by Gary Peller. These are richly suggestive articles, well repaying the reader's attention. But in each case a methodological commitment to epistemological critique intervenes between a skilled interpreter and well-chosen material.

"The Ideology of Bureaucracy in American Law"

In "The Ideology of Bureaucracy in American Law," Gerald Frug presents bureaucracy as a controversial feature of modern life and traces four stages of efforts to justify it. According to Frug, claims that bureaucracy could routinize government decision making, confer policy-making discretion on experts, observe judicially defined due process, or aggregate social interests are all functionally equiva-

---

[147] Martin Hollis, *Models of Man* (Cambridge: Cambridge Univ. Press, 1977), 99–100.

lent. Each is an effort to reassure us that bureaucracies, by reducing decision making to a ministerial or technical matter, can reduce the conflict, domination, and unpredictability of "face-to-face interaction." Thus, for Frug, the claimed illegitimacy of bureaucracy is not a matter of controversy between organized sectors of society so much as a psychological fault line running through all members of modern society, bureaucracy's defenders included.

Frug does not present the different theories of bureaucracy as policy proposals designed to settle disputes between identifiable societal interest groups or to improve the functioning of bureaucracies. Nor does he present them as strategies by which bureaucratic elites attempt to check threats to their power, or platforms on which place-hungry intellectuals mounted campaigns for elite status. To Frug, this sort of instrumental analysis of the process of legitimation would replicate the bureaucratic mentality he critiques. Instead, he treats all proposed criteria of legitimacy as rhetorical formulations, defense mechanisms, tropes of self-delusion.

One might imagine a Nietzschean formulation of Frug's psychological critique of bureaucracy, in which the ultimate fright implicit in face-to-face interaction is not the threat of domination by the other, but the pressure to win the other's respect through the display of virtue, whether martial or of some other kind. Thus, William Miller has suggested that we read our own Uzi-streaked surroundings as much less violent than the pastoral world described in the Icelandic Sagas, because we have delegated our defense to the bureaucratic state. We may be helpless to avoid violence—but we are absolved of the responsibility to establish and defend our worth. Having traded personal honor for formal equality, we can be brutalized, but not dishonored.[148]

In light of Frug's attraction to classical democracy[149] and his belief in the persuasive power of personal virtue in deliberative politics,[150] we might have expected this sort of Nietzschean account of bureaucracy's appeal for "the last man" as a flight from republican responsibility. Such a formulation of Frug's critique would place bureaucracy in the familiar historical and moral drama of modernity, reiterating the Nietzschean irony that the effort to liberate the self has debased it. By placing the rise of bureaucracy in a moral narrative, Frug could offer the reader a perspective from which to critique bureaucracy, one that avoids the cynical instrumentalism of more familiar critiques of bureaucrats as rent seekers or as agents of the ruling class.

But Frug eschews this Nietzschean strategy in favor of a deconstructive critique according to which the dilemmas troubling the citizen of the bureaucratic state are epistemological rather than moral. Thus, the fear of others that Frug detects in the justificatory discourse of bureaucracy is not the Nietzschean fear of the exposure of one's own moral vacuity. For Derridean skepticism about the possibil-

---

[148] William Ian Miller, *Humiliation and Other Essays on Honor, Social Discomfort, and Violence* (Ithaca: Cornell Univ. Press, 1993).

[149] Gerald Frug, "The City as a Legal Concept," *Harvard Law Review* 93 (1980): 1057.

[150] Gerald Frug, "Argument as Character," *Stanford Law Review* 40 (1988): 869.

ity of interpersonal communication insulates us against any such fear of being known. What we fear instead is that others will *not* know us, that their view of us will be distorted by their own subjectivity. Read in this light, bureaucratic discourse is a Sisyphean effort to cabin subjectivity by maintaining its separation from objectivity. It feverishly searches for some locus of purely objective knowledge that can contain and define the subjective desires of the public, even as it portrays those desires as sovereign.

Borrowing a phrase from Derrida, Frug portrays objectivity and subjectivity as one another's "dangerous supplements." Thus, the subjective desires of the public can only be determined through a process of objectification that transforms them, but this necessary gap between representation and reality makes the process of objectification inherently subjective. Efforts to constrain the subjectivity of those bureaucrats charged with determining the public will depend on this same process of objectification, which will depend in turn on the subjectivity of those charged with checking the bureaucrats. And so on. Because objectively knowable subjectivities are constructs, they can be endlessly deconstructed, whereupon like Russian dolls, each subjectivity will reveal another, that of its objectifier, "nested" inside. Nesting characterizes the structure of each of the four models of legitimate bureaucracy Frug critiques, as well as the relations among them. As each model crumbles into contradiction, it gives way to the next.

Frug presents the original ideal of bureaucratic rationality championed by Weber as the goal of "effectuating 'subjective' constituent goals through an 'objective' bureaucracy."[151] This he calls the "Formalist Model" of bureaucracy. Yet the nondelegation doctrine, invoked by courts to prevent legislatures from delegating "legislative" powers to administrative agencies, shows that bureaucracies cannot be restrained from exercising subjective judgment without the subjective desires of their constituents being cabined as well.[152] In corporate law, similarly, the fear that corporate directors would manipulate their shareholder constituents has sometimes induced courts to require that directors act as "trustees" of shareholders' objective interests rather than "agents" of their subjective desires. And because such "objective interests" cannot be specified with any great precision, their pursuit by bureaucracies will involve subjective judgment.[153]

Conceding that subjective judgment inheres in administration, New Deal Era and postwar proponents of the "Expertise Model" hoped to constrain subjectivity by limiting it to a technical elite. Likewise accepting the inevitable objectification of constituents, the Expertise Model regarded them entirely as passive repositories of interests, rather than sovereign decision makers. The expertise model's "aporias" are the problem of qualifying bureaucratic judgment as expert and delineating the expert's sphere of competence. Courts defer to the judgment of corporate managers and public administrators, provided these judgments are "rational," "informed," and "impartial." Yet implementing these standards reintroduces an

---

[151] Frug, "Ideology of Bureaucracy."
[152] Ibid., 1300–4.
[153] Ibid., 1307.

element of objective restraint into the subjective discretion of the manager. Further, the requirements of information and impartiality seem to cut against each other, as experience is not easily distinguished from prejudice. Thus, the conflict between objectivity and subjectivity reappears, nested inside the doctrines that purport to resolve the conflict in favor of subjectivity.[154]

Acknowledging the inevitability of judicial policing of bureaucratic judgment, contemporaries of the Warren Court hoped to legitimate bureaucracy by subjecting it to judicial review. This "Judicial Review Model" divides into its Formalist and Expertise variants, depending on whether judicial review is supposed to prevent action unauthorized by the bureaucracy's constituents or action outside its sphere of competence. For the Judicial Review Model, the aporetic problem lies in distinguishing the spheres of competence of the bureaucracy and the courts.[155] Judicial supervision of bureaucracy is required because of the dangers inherent in allowing bureaucracies to set the limits of their own authority—but these same dangers reappear when the courts must set the limits of their own authority. Proponents of judicial supervision defend the judiciary as formally rational or as expert, thereby reproducing the contradictions of the Formalist and Expertise Models of bureaucracy.[156] The result is a thoroughly indeterminate system of "nested oppositions": courts, using a formalist or expertise model of institutional competence, can justify (subjective) discretion or (objective) restraint on the part of either themselves, or the bureaucracies they review.[157] Courts typically mediate these oppositions through a technique of "interest balancing" that strikes critics as fatally subjective.[158] Thus, the stratagem of supplementing bureaucratic judgment with judicial review simply displaces the subject/object problem onto the judiciary.

Conceding that courts can no more reliably determine societal interests than bureaucrats can, participants in bureaucratic society substitute the market and the arena of pluralist politics for the courts. In corporate law, proponents of the "Market Model" claim that the market for corporate management will ensure management responsiveness to the shareholder interest in profitability, while assuming that the interests of such other constituent groups as consumers and labor are recognized, summed, and protected through competitive markets as well. Proponents of the "Pluralist Model" of administrative law similarly claim that a competitive political marketplace can adequately aggregate and protect interests of all constituencies "relevant" to administrative decision making. Concerned about the permanent entrenchment of victorious interests in winner-take-all majoritarianism, however, and recognizing that administration is an arena for policy

---

[154] Ibid., 1324.

[155] Ibid., 1335.

[156] Ibid., 1338.

[157] Ibid., 1342.

[158] Ibid., 1349; see also Al Katz, "Studies in Boundary Theory: Three Essays in Adjudication and Politics," *Buffalo Law Review* 28 (1979): 383; Katz, "Balancing," *In the Public Interest* 7 (1987): 18; Alexander Aleinikoff, "Constitutional Law in the Age of Balancing," *Yale Law Journal* 96 (1987): 943.

making, pluralists conceive the administrative process as a series of micro-arenas for the struggle of contending interest groups. The two models can colonize one another's terrain, as Marketeers call for privatizing public functions and Pluralists call for public representation on corporate boards or more extensive regulation of corporations.

At first, it appears that markets and majorities, unlike courts, are substitutes for, rather than supplements to, bureaucratic discretion. For the "visible hand" of bureaucracy, the market and majoritarian processes appear to substitute "invisible" or nondiscretionary mechanisms for translating individual preferences into social choice. In this way they seem to achieve the formalist ideal of objective measurement of subjective preferences without bureaucracy: recognizing that "subjective" issues of policy making inevitably nest inside the task of implementing policy, the "Market-Pluralist" model simply redefines administration as policy making and turns it over to institutions of unquestioned legitimacy.

Frug's answer is that just as policy-making discretion can never be excised from administration, the administrative function of objectifying subjective preferences can never be excised from policy making. That the "mechanisms" of market and majority rule require designers and operators follows from the fact that each mechanism embodies conflicts that will reappear nested inside the policy choices that purport to resolve them. The decision to protect the interests of shareholders by strengthening the bargaining power of acquiring managers relative to that of incumbent managers can never be final. Shareholder interests cannot be equated with the interest of acquiring managers, and indeed no end is ever fully reducible to the means chosen to pursue it. In Derridean terms, the very distinction between ends and means implies that ends bear the semantic "traces" of all possible means to pursue them. What should be done when conflicts inevitably develop between the bargaining power of acquiring managers and shareholders, or between the bargaining weakness that motivates incumbent managers to pursue shareholder interests and the bargaining strength they need to do so effectively? To select any one means of pursuing an interest is to objectify that interest, building into any policy choice a tension that will reopen it again and again.

Ultimately, then, subjective interests have import only through the objectifying policies they justify, but policies inevitably betray the interests they serve, and interests cannot resist condemning the policies they once anointed. Bureaucrats are the objectifying policies in this story, and their discontented constituents are the subjective interests. They are each other's dangerous supplements.

Thus anthropomorphized, Frug's dialectic of dangerous supplements takes on political drama. That the anthropomorphosis of conflicting concepts is such a prevalent rhetorical figure in the Hegelian tradition within which Derrida writes[159] suggests an ambiguity: is the subject-object problem in continental philosophy,

---

[159] "Derrida always reminds us, we cannot easily—if ever—escape from the shadow of Hegel." Drucilla Cornell, "Post-structuralism, the Ethical Relation, and the Law," *Cardozo Law Review* 9 (1988): 1587–88 (portraying poststructuralism as a rebellion against the Hegelian effort to synthesize all oppositions into a single totality).

as in analytic philosophy, about the mind? Or is it about society?[160] Is it occasioned by the epistemological critique of the mind's subjective perception of real objects, or the political critique of society's alienating objectification of its constituent subjectivities?

Given Hegel's unreserved historicism, he is best read as trying to understand the distinctively modern society to emerge from the French Revolution. It was Hegel's distinctive achievement to realize that subjective desire had replaced objective reason as the fount of legitimacy in the era of capitalist and democratic revolution. Accordingly, philosophy's old ambition to rid the mind of the distractions of desire had to be discarded, and the traditional problems of epistemology with them.[161] The only remaining epistemological question was how desire could be known.

Derrida is best read as arguing that the insolubility of this problem undermines the entire effort, so that repressed epistemological doubt returns, now regnant. Without reembracing reason, Derrida rejects the politics of desire and the problem of alienation. And he rejects them because the critiques they generated of the ancien régime proved too powerful for modern representative democracy to withstand. Ultimately, then, Derrida is also more political than epistemological; but he is willing to use epistemological skepticism to disable the radical political movements that, he fears, might lead to the Gulag or the gas chamber.

Yet American legal academics find this strategy completely illegible, for two reasons. First, the Hegelian philosophical tradition to which Derrida is responding remains foreign. Anglo-American philosophy has remained much more committed to epistemological inquiry than to questions of value. Second, circumscribed by the ideal of judicial objectivity, legal scholarship remains obsessed with the eigtheenth-century problem of ridding reason of desire.

Radical American legal academics seem to find Derrida mesmerizing. It is as if they turn to the Hegelian tradition for authority, flip to the "pocket part" to find its most recent exponent, and there find what look like skeptical arguments against the ideal of judicial objectivity. In an eddy in the backwaters of intellectual history, we find radicals deploying a postmodern critique of radicalism to hasten the advent of modernity. Frug, who wants to advocate participatory democracy over bureaucracy, keeps getting distracted by the problem of indeterminacy. Since he cannot invoke Derrida's authority to claim that direct democracy can overcome the indeterminacy of representation, his critique of conceptions of bureaucracy exemplifies the very incoherence he ascribes to them. According to Frug, "this dangerous supplement analysis can help demonstrate that the legal system's effort to answer the political attack [on the formalist bureaucratic vision] through line-drawing is a meaningless endeavor."[162] Similarly, "the project of drawing a line

---

[160] Jonathan Bush, "Hegelian Slaves and the Antebellum South,"*Cardozo Law Review* 10 (1989): 1517, 1526 (on social versus speculative readings of Hegel's *Phenomenology*).

[161] Andrew Prior, *Revolution and Philosophy: The Significance of the French Revolution for Hegel and Marx* (Capetown: D. Philip, 1972).

[162] Frug, "Ideology of Bureaucracy," 1315.

between bureaucratic subjectivity and objectivity is meaningless: each of these concepts can only be understood in terms of its relationship to the other."[163] Surely, for anyone working in the Hegelian and structuralist traditions, the mutual consti-tution of opposing concepts renders them *meaningful*, not *meaningless*. Even if the arbitrariness of doctrinal distinctions between objectivity and subjectivity pre-vents them from legitimating bureaucracy, Frug does not—and within the con-fines of his ahistorical method cannot—show that legitimation, rather than mere dispute resolution, is the purpose of these distinctions.

It simply does not seem plausible that the possibility of objective knowledge has been the most pressing political issue of modern times. That bureaucracy fails to overcome the epistemological conundrums that have amused philosophers for two millennia does not seem a terribly severe indictment. Moreover, the epistemo-logical focus of Frug's deconstructive reading of administrative and corporate law blunts its explanatory as well as its critical bite. Given that Frug presents all four models as equally flawed from an epistemological standpoint, the historical movement among them seems unmotivated. Without a persuasive account of the legitimacy crises these models were designed to solve, Frug cannot explain why one or another model succeeded or failed in legitimating bureaucracy at a particu-lar time.

Thus, in accounting for the rise of the judicial review model, it helps to recall that the national security state that emerged from World War II derived its legiti-macy from the struggle against "totalitarianism" of the right and left. It was the problem of distinguishing bureaucracy from totalitarianism that engendered a re-newed commitment to the rule of law; and it was that commitment that inspired concern about bureaucratic subjectivity.[164] In understanding the earlier emergence of the Expertise Model, we might wonder why the Great Depression and World War II occasioned the proliferation of bureaucratic discretion not just in the United States, but around the world. Taking an even longer view, we will want an historically specific account of the underlying commitment to bureaucracy that motivates all four forms of legitimation. As a response to a two-thousand-year-old subject-object problem, bureaucracy seems wildly underdetermined. Why did this characteristically modern response to the subject-object problem develop when it did?

How did bureaucracy, that most prosaic of social contexts, get charged with solving the problems of philosophy? One answer, suggested by Foucault's ac-count of the development of "disciplinary" human sciences in the nineteenth cen-tury, is that bureaucracy provides the historical and semantic condition for the development of a particular philosophy, roughly, utilitarian political philosophy. Bureaucracy is at once the solution to the problem of utilitarian social choice, and

---

[163] Ibid., 1313.

[164] Gary Peller, "Neutral Principles in the 1950's," *Michigan Journal of Law Reform* 21 (1988): 561; Mary Dudziak, "Desegregation as a Cold War Imperative," *Stanford Law Review* 41 (1988): 61.

the laboratory in which problems of social choice and all of their operational concepts—utility, interests, abilities, incentives, and the like—are invented.[165]

It is well to remember that at the inception of utilitarianism, democracy was far more controversial than bureaucracy. Traditionally associated with mob rule, democracy was viewed by classically trained political theorists as a corruption of the mixed constitution that ensured republican virtue.[166] Nor did the advent of modernity, symbolized most vividly for Europeans by the French Revolution, extinguish this mistrust of democracy. And when Europeans looked to America, what impressed them was not the Constitution of which Americans were so proud, but the very penal institutions of which Foucault writes. In classical political theory, virtue was democracy's necessary supplement; to the modern mind, bureaucracy suggested itself as a substitute for virtue. Or, as Foucault puts it, "the 'Enlightenment' which discovered the liberties, also invented the disciplines."[167]

While "bureaucracy" signals an insidious force of social control, undermining the democracy in whose name it speaks, its utilitarian discourse has more ambiguous connotations. Utilitarian policy discourse is, after all, a language of the public good, a deliberative discourse that could guide democratic as well as bureaucratic decision making.[168] A democratic public that sought the greatest good of the greatest number would presumably be a virtuous public, fit to govern itself. In this sense, utilitarian policy analysis spoke not only *about* but also *to* the newly enfranchised public. Insofar as it was offered to educate and motivate an unwashed electorate to its civic responsibilities, utilitarianism's talk of the greatest good of the greatest number served at once to legitimate and contain democracy. In this sense, bureaucracy invented our modern conceptions of the public interest and public opinion. But once authored, "the public"—like any text—took on a life of its own. Provided it spoke *in* the utilitarian voice of the social policy expert, the public was not constrained to speak *through* him.

Seeing bureaucracy and its characteristically utilitarian language in this way as a set of historically located political practices, we can also see the limits of Frug's deconstructive critique of bureaucracy. Frug is right to see bureaucracy as a mentality that pervades modern society, uniting the constituents, the administrators, the objects, and the critics of social policy in a consciousness at once common and divided. And Frug is right to see the divisions in the bureaucratic mentality as the site of philosophical struggle: within these fissures Frug finds and displays a dizzying maze of bridges and buttresses worthy of Escher or Piranesi.

[165] Michel Foucault, *Discipline and Punish*, trans. Alan Sheridan (New York: Vintage Books, 1977).

[166] J. G. A. Pocock, *The Machiavellian Moment* (Princeton: Princeton Univ. Press, 1975), 69–77, 272–77, 297–98, 307–8, 382–83.

[167] Foucault, *Discipline and Punish*, 222.

[168] The interpretation of utilitarianism offered here relies in part on Jeremy Bentham, *The Collected Works of Jeremy Bentham: Securities against Misrule and Other Writings for Tripoli and Greece*, ed. Philip Schofield (Oxford: Clarendon Press, 1990), and Robert Goodin, *Utilitarianism as a Public Philosophy* (Cambridge: Cambridge Univ. Press, 1995).

But the philosophical problems that torment the bureaucratic mind are not the two-thousand-year-old dilemmas of epistemology: they are the roughly two-hundred-year-old difficulties of representing and aggregating the desires of individuals. Only at some point between the English and French Revolutions did desire become a source of political authority rather than profanity;[169] and only at this point did political theory—and literature—take up the problem of conceiving the individual, this mysterious being hopelessly divided between discretion and passion, contingency and necessity, sociability and venality, sovereign and subject. Only at this point did political theory embrace "the liberal creed" from which Kenneth Arrow derived all his paradoxes of preference aggregation: the faith that individual preferences exist independent of processes of social choice.[170]

In his repetitive variations on the theme of subject and object, knower and known, Frug always seems to just miss the most fertile contradictions in the modern mentality. The problem is one of misemphasis rather than mischaracterization: what Frug fails to convey is that the interesting contradictions are no longer between subjectivity and objectivity, because the authority of subjective will is no longer seriously controversial. The fertile contradictions in modern social thought tend to be among competing visions of subjectivity—for example, the freedom and contingency associated with discretion, versus the necessity associated with desire. Because representing individual subjectivity is a cognitive operation, it raises the epistemological problems that undermine the objectivity of all cognition—the dependence of data on theory, language, and perspective. But because the concept of individual subjectivity is uniquely contradictory and contestable, the knowledge of subjectivities produced by bureaucratic society raises additional problems. It is these problems, the problems of legitimating social choice by reference to individual desires, that give energy to the exfoliating tropes of bureaucratic discourse that Frug so patiently catalogs.

What renders bureaucratic discourse susceptible to deconstruction is that its authority rests in representing interests that can exist only through that process of representation. But the circularity of bureaucratic discourse counts as an argument for what is sometimes called direct democracy only if direct democracy can escape it. And direct democracy involves deliberative speech, requiring, Derrida would claim, the same process of objectification of social interests that proves bureaucracy illegitimate. If anything, deconstruction cuts *in favor* of bureaucracy, by arguing both that policy making is inherent in administration and that the public is a creature of bureaucratic discourse that can never participate directly in policy making. Frug complains that we unthinkingly assume that bureaucracy is an inevitable feature of modern life. But it is just that assumption that deconstruction supports by arguing that democracy is unthinkable without the mediation of bureaucracy. From a Derridean perspective, bureaucracy is democracy's necessary supplement.

---

[169] See generally Albert O. Hirschman, *The Passions and the Interests: Political Arguments for Capitalism before Its Triumph* (Princeton: Princeton Univ. Press, 1977).

[170] Kenneth Arrow, *Social Choice and Individual Values* (New York: Wiley, 1963).

"The Metaphysics of American Law"

In "The Metaphysics of American Law,"[171] Gary Peller invokes Derridean deconstruction in making three related claims, one epistemological, one historical, and one political.

The epistemological claim is that all knowledge is mediated, or dependent upon discretionary schemes of representation. All description depends upon purposive criteria of relevance—yet to identify any agent's purpose is itself a descriptive problem. Thus, knowledge is inherently evaluative, and since the practical implementation of value choices in turn involves descriptive knowledge, value choice is a Sisyphean task.

The historical claim is that the formalism supposedly dominant in American judicial decision making from the Gilded Age to the New Deal, and the legal realism supposedly influential on American jurisprudence since the New Deal, committed the same epistemological error. They both claimed to justify normative choice on the basis of an unmediated description of society. According to Peller, formalism built its picture of society up out of the contractual relations of individuals. It thereby "took individual subjects as the ultimate source of social relations, as prior to and constitutive of objective social structures." Realism, which applied private bargains in light of unequal bargaining power, trade custom, and the public welfare, "merely flipped the order of the terms so that objective social structures (or contexts), were viewed as prior to and constitutive of subjective practices."[172] Both formalism and realism relied on the distinction between subject and object. Each regarded one of these entities as real, or in Derridean terms "present," while regarding the other as nominal, as mere representation.

Peller's political claim is that because it is premised on this "metaphysics of presence," all legal thought "violently" excludes other descriptions of the social world. While all social decision making is necessarily discretionary, legal thought "suppress[es] the socially contingent metaphors upon which the legal representation of the social world depends," generating an "experience of alienation" in such quotidian contexts as fast food restaurants and factories.[173]

Peller's epistemological argument nicely summarizes the main points of pragmatism, which arguably anticipated much that deconstruction has to offer on this subject. The question raised by Peller's ambitious effort to deconstruct two generations of American jurisprudence is this: can an epistemological history of legal thought have any political bite?

Peller's subjects, "liberty of contract jurisprudence" and "legal realism," are particularly inviting targets for epistemological critique. Liberty of contract jurisprudence coincided with the advent of academic legal education in America, a development founded on the claim that law was a science. Legal realism was one expression of a later rise in the authority of social and policy science. Peller's

---

[171] *California Law Review*, 73 (1985): 1151.
[172] Ibid., 1154.
[173] Ibid., 1156.

objection to legal realism in particular dovetails with Frug's critique of the expertise model in administrative and corporate law. For Peller, legal realism makes social policy a matter of expert knowledge rather than politics, technocracy rather than democracy. Since both movements Peller reviews claimed political power on the basis of intellectual authority, it is tempting to think that a political critique of these movements must undermine their epistemological claims.

But the difficulty with such an epistemological strategy is that it leaps to the conclusion that the authority of lawyers, legal scholars, and policy analysts rested on their exaggerated claims to scientific expertise. If the social authority of a group rests on such historical accidents as its perceived independence from other discredited groups, its governing experience, its recruitment from the ranks of other elites, or its perceived association with ill-understood forces of modernity, the "subjectivity" or "arbitrariness" of its decisions may not undermine its legitimacy. An epistemological critique is a useful starting point, but only because the disjunction it reveals between the authority and the achievements of an intellectual elite invites further inquiry into how such authority was achieved and maintained. Thus, a sociology of knowledge is more likely to yield a politically informative history of formalist and technocratic legal thought than is a disembodied history of ideas, and the most direct route to a political critique of technocracy is to expose it as bad politics rather than bad epistemology.

Peller ascribes to Derrida a pragmatist epistemology that treats all metaphysical beliefs as nothing more than regulative fictions. Yet as others have pointed out,[174] the power of this kind of pragmatic epistemology to corrode political arguments tends to be overrated. Deconstruction creates its illusion of powerful critique only by turning the pragmatist insight on its head, and reading all regulative fictions— even in works presented as fiction—as implying surreptitious commitment to metaphysical realism. One difficulty with this repeated charge of secret idolatry is that it is often untrue, so that texts Derrida criticizes as covertly metaphysical often turn out to anticipate his own critique of metaphysics.[175] But to a pragmatist, the more serious problem with treating every use of a concept as evidence of metaphysical belief is that it makes a point of no practical importance. One impli-

---

[174] E.g., John Stick, "Can Nihilism Be Pragmatic?" *Harvard Law Review* 100 (1986): 332.

[175] John Ellis asserts that though identified with metaphysics in *Of Grammatology*, de Saussure is "decidedly anti-essentialist." *Against Deconstruction* (Princeton: Princeton Univ. Press, 1989), 45. Ellis also complains that Derrida claims originality for anti-essentialist insights that might have been credited to de Saussure, Wittgenstein, and others. Ibid., 37–43. Similarly, Paul de Man points out that Derrida's *Of Grammatology* "deconstruct[s] a pseudo-Rousseau by means of insights that could have been gained from the 'real' Rousseau." De Man, *Blindness and Insight*, 139–40. Consider Peller's claims that "the liberal notion of freedom is rooted in idealism's notion of an ontologically free subject which exists prior to the constraining world of experience," and that in idealist representational modes, "the other is never immediately 'present' to consciousness the way that the self in subject/object dichotomization is taken to be immediately present in self-consciousness." Peller, "Metaphysics," 1267, 1267–77. Each of these claims was explicitly critiqued by Hegel, who saw individual identity as an idea arising out of experience, and self-consciousness as necessarily mediated by others. Far from taking identity to be a presocial given, Hegel saw it as a socially constructed regulative fiction. Not every use of a concept is metaphysical.

cation of the pragmatist epistemology deconstruction endorses is that thought is mediated by simplifying concepts because they are useful. If "metaphysics" means nothing more than "the abstraction and generalization inherent in all thought," it ceases to be an epithet. Why should a pragmatist care whether political actors "reify" their concepts? The pragmatic question is how the use of these concepts affects experience and action.

Peller's answer to this pragmatic question is a claim that legal doctrine's "reification" of individual wills and societal needs leads to a pervasive experience of alienation. Yet this concern with alienation, reminiscent of such Marxist humanists as Marcuse and Sartre, sounds odd coming from a deconstructive critic, for two reasons.

First, the leading deconstructive critics, Derrida and de Man, have stressed the *inevitability* of alienation in order to critique humanism as sentimental. All self-expression is necessarily mediated and the intelligibility of mediated expression, even to the speaker, depends upon its iterability by others. Thus, for the deconstructive critic, self-expression can be nothing but the role playing that Peller describes as alienating.

Second, that legal doctrine causes alienation in everyday life is a much more ambitious empirical claim than deconstruction can tolerate. Supporting such a claim would require detailed description—and therefore "reification"—of the social world, showing the causal connections between the courtroom and the food court. In addition, causal accounts are narrative accounts, and deconstructive critics see narrative as one telltale symptom of the "metaphysics of presence." According to Derrida, narrative's cyclic figures of journey and return, fall and redemption, loss and recuperation all falsely imply that meaning can pass through the travail of mediation and return to its origin, enriched but unadulterated.[176]

Thus, Peller's deconstructive method precludes him from supporting his claim that legal thought imprisons the subjects of the liberal state in alienating social roles. Rather then growing organically out of his argument, the claim is supplementary, a politically correct afterthought apologizing for a politically inert argument. Scorning narratives of conflict and resolution as sentimental fairy tales, Peller portrays a monistic world in which all political conflict masks a much more fundamental metaphysical agreement.

For Peller, the relevant category for grouping and dividing historical experience is "metaphysical assumptions," by which he means "background" or "representational metaphors" such as the distinction between subject and object. According to Peller, a belief is metaphysical if it "goes without saying" and hence is not the site of controversy and political struggle.[177] Peller urges the usefulness of this category of analysis by arguing that the Supreme Court's early-twentieth-century decisions that progressive labor legislation violated "liberty of contract" were driven by metaphysical assumptions rather than interests or ideology. In a crucial passage, Peller concludes that

---

[176] Derrida, "Limited Inc. abc," *Glyph* 2 (1977): 162, 247–48.
[177] Peller, "Metaphysics," 1154.

There appears to be no source except the metaphysical assumptions themselves for the representation of social life created by the liberty of contract legal actors. It is not as if the spatial and temporal metaphors were established as valid or useful in one area and thereby assumed to be valid analogies for the interpretation and representation of other areas of social life. . . . The integration of the representational language did not flow from, say, a decision to achieve a particular result with respect to constitutional questions or with respect to the relationship between labor and capital. Rather, it appears that the metaphors were part of a metaphysical root system that had no particular origin. No part of the discourse demonstrated that it was positive and free standing without the rest of the representational practice to orient and confirm it. Each analogy pointed to another, which itself pointed to another.[178]

A closer look at this claim underscores the fundamental tensions between the enterprises of deconstruction and historical explanation. Peller's effort to read history as the reiteration of unspoken and uncontested metaphysical assumptions places him in a dilemma. Finding this sort of unanimity in history is likely to require one of two filtering strategies. One strategy filters out disagreement by describing beliefs at a very high level of generality—in this case, treating all distinctions between public and private or between subject and object as functionally similar. A second strategy filters out disagreement by looking at a very narrow range of evidence—in this case, selected appellate opinions of a particular era. The first strategy yields an account so reductive that it ceases to reveal the meaning of events for participants who believe they are engaged in struggle against one another, while the second strategy excludes the evidence that would enable the reader to compare a "metaphysical" explanation to competing hypotheses emphasizing ideology or interests. How can we assess the effect of ideology and interests on adjudication if we learn nothing about the social context of disputes? These filtering strategies, moreover, are themselves vulnerable to deconstructive critique as examples of, respectively, "objectification" and "exclusion."

The liberty of contract decisions that Peller sets out to explain are *Lochner v. New York*[179] decided in 1905, and *Coppage v. Kansas*[180] decided a decade later. The first decision struck down a New York law limiting bakers' working hours to no more than sixty per week. The second struck down a Kansas "yellow-dog" statute, precluding employers from conditioning employment on nonmembership in a labor union. Peller claims that "while these opinions rested on metaphysical assumptions, within the representational metaphors of the legal discourse the decisions were not subjective or political choices to favor, say, laissez-faire ideology over welfare, or owners over workers."[181] These assumptions were "part of 'what goes without saying' . . . [and were] not . . . subject to question in the cases. [They were] part of the background structure within which argument took place."[182]

---

[178] Ibid., 1218–19.
[179] 198 U.S. 45 (1905).
[180] 236 U.S. 1 (1915).
[181] Peller, "Metaphysics," 1194.
[182] Ibid., 1205.

To establish this claim, Peller needs to persuade us (1) that the two decisions shared "metaphysical assumptions," (2) that these metaphysical assumptions were uncontested in other opinions and other discourse within the experience of judges, (3) that metaphysical assumptions general enough to unify such a broad range of discourse are also specific and determinate enough to explain the results in these two cases, and (4) that the results cannot be better explained by reference to interests or ideology. Peller's argument is vulnerable at all four of these points.

For Peller, the decisive metaphysical assumptions were two: first, a division of the social world into "public" matters wholly subject to governmental regulation and "private" matters wholly immune to government regulation, and, second, a "privileging" of the category of private over public based on a view of social conditions as resulting from the choices of individuals.

Peller explains the *Lochner* decision as following unproblematically from the judgments that public power could regulate employment contracts only to redress coercion, incapacity, or the health effects of the contract, and that the presence and absence of each of these justifications for regulation was absolute rather than relative.[183] Faced with a choice of finding bakers completely coerced, incompetent, and sickly, or completely free, competent, and healthy, the *Lochner* Court chose the latter in order to favor the private over the public and the individual over the social.[184] Concerning *Coppage*, Peller tells the same story, minus the discussion of health risk, which was never alleged to justify the yellow-dog statute in this case.[185] In both cases, concludes Peller, "the conclusion that a laborer was 'entirely free' within the context of the market seemed 'rational' . . . within a conceptual space in which individual intent was seen as the source and origin of social context."[186] Thus, "economic context could not be coercive. Coercion, conceived as the subordination of one will to another, had to be rooted in another's will. But no one willed the economic context."[187]

This account obscures important inconsistencies within *Lochner*, between *Lochner* and *Coppage*, and between *Lochner* and its precedential and ideological context. We suggest that when read in context, the various articulations of the liberty of contract doctrine look more like evolving efforts at conceptual innovation than unthinking applications of uncontroversial assumptions.

It is unlikely the architects of liberty of contract believed that "economic context could not be coercive." They could not so believe without countenancing contractual slavery, by which inequalities of bargaining power could be translated into physical coercion. But contemporaneously with the liberty of contract decisions, the Supreme Court held that the private use of force and the public use of criminal punishment to enforce labor contracts would both violate the Thirteenth Amendment's proscription against involuntary servitude.[188]

---

[183] Ibid., 1198–200.
[184] Ibid., 1212.
[185] Ibid., 1201, 1208.
[186] Ibid., 1195.
[187] Ibid., 1209.
[188] *Clyatt v. United States*, 197 U.S. 207 (1905); *Bailey v. Alabama*, 219 U.S. 219 (1911).

Peller correctly notes that for Justice Peckham, author of the *Lochner* decision, such physical coercion was categorically distinguishable from economic coercion,[189] *but it would be naive for us to assume that the existence and location of the boundary between economic and physical coercion were self-evident.* In 1867, uncertain that debt-peonage constituted involuntary servitude, the Thirteenth Amendment's authors passed a statute prohibiting "voluntary servitude."[190] Just eight years before *Lochner* a Supreme Court already including all of the Justices voting with the majority in that case upheld a statute authorizing the forcible return to their vessels and criminal punishment of absconding merchant sailors, arguing that the "epithet 'involuntary' does [not] attach to the word servitude continuously . . . [but] only at the inception of the servitude," so that "a servitude which was willingly and knowingly entered into could not be termed involuntary."[191] A year after the *Lochner* decision, the Court indicated that the forcible interference with the efforts of employees or potential employees to seek other employment would not violate the Thirteenth Amendment.[192]

But if the *Lochner* Era Court could view physically compelled servitude as voluntary, it could also view economically compelled service as involuntary. Just seven years before *Lochner*, in *Holden v. Hardy*,[193] the Court upheld a statute limiting the working hours of miners. The Court's discussion of coercion is impossible to square with an unspoken assumption that "economic context could not be coercive." As the majority notes,

> the legislature . . . has recognized the fact, which the experience of many legislatures has corroborated, that the proprietors of these establishments and their operatives do not stand upon an equality, and that their interests are, to a certain extent, conflicting. The former naturally desire to obtain as much labor as possible from their employees while the latter are often induced by fear of discharge to conform to regulation which their judgment, fairly exercised, would pronounce to be detrimental to their health or strength. In other words, the proprietors lay down the rules and the laborers are practically constrained to obey them. In such cases self-interest is often an unsafe guide, and the legislature may properly interpose its authority. . . . The fact that both parties are of full age and competent to contract does not necessarily deprive the state of the power to interfere where the parties do not stand upon an equality, or where the public health demands that one party to the contract shall be protected against himself.[194]

True, the majority opinions in *Coppage* and *Lochner* both rejected this view that states could regulate the employment relationship in order to redress inequalities of bargaining power. But they rejected this view for very different reasons,

---

[189] *Lochner v. New York*, 52, quoted in Peller, "Metaphysics," 1198.

[190] Robert Steinfeld, *The Invention of Free Labor* (Chapel Hill: Univ. of North Carolina Press, 1991), 183–84.

[191] *Robertson v. Baldwin*, 165 U.S. 275, 280–81 (1897).

[192] *United States v. Hodges*, 203 U.S. 1 (1906) (striking down federal statute punishing the private interference with labor contracts because of race as unauthorized by the Thirteenth Amendment).

[193] 169 U.S. 366 (1898).

[194] Ibid., 397.

as they were forced to by a fundamental doctrinal change that occurred between the two cases. The *Lochner* court rejected the assumption that employees "do not stand upon an equality" with their employers, asserting that "there is no contention that bakers as a class are not equal in intelligence and capacity to men in other trades or manual occupations, or that they are not able to assert their rights and take care of themselves. . . . They are in no sense wards of the state."[195] The *Coppage* Court, however, made no such claim that workers and employers were equally autonomous, instead asserting that unequal constraint was the inevitable and therefore legitimate result of combining liberty of contract with protection of property:

> No doubt, wherever the right of private property exists, there must be inequalities of fortune; and thus it naturally happens that parties negotiating about a contract are not equally unhampered by circumstances. This applies to all contracts, and not merely that between employer and employee. Indeed, a little reflection will show that wherever the right of private property and the right of free contract coexist, each party when contracting is more or less influenced by the question whether he has much property, or little, or none; for the contract is made to the very end that each may gain something that he needs or desires more urgently than that which he proposes to give in exchange. And, since it is self-evident that, unless all things are held in common, some persons must have more property than others, it is from the nature of things impossible to uphold freedom of contract and the right of private property without at the same time recognizing as legitimate those inequalities of fortune that are the necessary result of the exercise of those rights.[196]

Far from justifying liberty of contract as an appropriate regime for relations between equals, the *Coppage* Court justified inequality as the inevitable consequence of liberty of contract. But such an argument was unavailable to the majority in *Lochner*, for the simple reason that before *Lochner* there was no constitutional protection of liberty of contract. Constrained to justify—not simply invoke—liberty of contract, the Lochner court had to present it as a guarantor of equality rather than inequality.

Peller treats the constitutional proscription of labor regulation as entailed by a foundational distinction in postbellum legal thought between public power and private relations. He borrows this theme from other critical legal scholars, especially Duncan Kennedy.[197] And yet Kennedy was prompted by such inconsisten-

---

[195] *Lochner v. New York*, 57.

[196] *Coppage v. Kansas*, 236 U.S. 1, 17 (1915).

[197] Duncan Kennedy, "Toward an Historical Understanding of Legal Consciousness: The Case of Classical Legal Thought in America 1850–1930," *Research in Law and Sociology* 3 (1980): 3; see also Elizabeth Mensch, "A History of Mainstream Legal Thought," in *The Politics of Law*, ed. David Kairys (New York: Pantheon Books, 1982); Robert Gordon, "Legal Thought and Legal Practice in the Age of American Enterprise, 1870–1920," in *Professions and Professional Ideologies in America, 1730–1940*, ed. Gerald Geison (Chapel Hill: Univ. of North Carolina Press, 1983); Frances Olsen, "The Family and the Market: A Study of Ideology and Legal Reform," *Harvard Law Review* 96 (1983): 1497.

cies as the view of the marketplace as private relative to government and public relative to the family to question whether "the public/private distinction" can be taken "seriously as a description [or] an explanation . . . of anything."[198] Thus, it seems unlikely that "the public/private distinction" had an unexamined metaphysical status for Gilded Age lawyers.

We will argue that a richer explanation for the emergence of a view that government could not legislate the terms of employment contracts lies in the convergence of a doctrinal distinction between public regulation and private property with a social vision of the unpropertied laborer as the proprietor of a small business.

In the Republican political thought that many historians consider the dominant intellectual impetus for the American Revolution,[199] independence and civic responsibility both depended upon ownership of productive property. While the ability to make contracts was of some use in acquiring property, inalienable liberty depended upon holding onto rather than alienating one's property, and credit was more often seen as encumbering than as enabling, a source of bondage rather than freedom.[200] Contracting therefore occupied no special place in the pantheon of liberty, and contractual employment in particular was likely to be seen as service, manifesting the dependence of the propertyless servant upon a propertied master.[201] *Blackstone's Commentaries*, the most influential lawbook in postrevolutionary America, listed only Locke's triad of personal security, personal liberty, and property as natural rights for the protection of which polities were established: contract and other methods for the transfer of property were mere "civil" rights, created and defined by the state.[202] Personal liberty, involving mobility and freedom from arbitrary detention, might imply a right to *leave* service,[203] but not to *enter* it. The Due Process Clause of the Fourteenth Amendment, applied in *Lochner*, adopted this same Lockean formula.

From the outset, the Republican dichotomy between material independence and propertylessness ill-fit the complexity of circumstance in a market society in which property could be acquired and lost. In theory, a skilled slave, seeing his value as a capital asset, might see simple self-ownership as involving an increase in material independence.[204] Similarly, a journeyman might see the power of organized artisans to set the price of their skills as evidence of their control over a

---

[198] Duncan Kennedy, "The Stages of Decline of the Public/Private Distinction," *University of Pennsylvania Law Review* 130 (1982): 1349, 1357.

[199] Bernard Bailyn, *The Ideological Origins of the American Revolution* (Cambridge: Harvard Univ. Press, Belknap Press, 1967); Gordon Wood, *The Creation of the American Republic* (Chapel Hill: Univ. of North Carolina Press, 1969); Pocock, *Machiavellian Moment*; Drew McCoy, *The Elusive Republic* (Chapel Hill: Univ. of North Carolina Press, 1980).

[200] For a typical account of this view, see Justice Johnson's opinion in *Ogden v. Saunders*, 25 U.S. (4 Wheat.) 122 (1819).

[201] See generally Steinfeld, *Rise of Free Labor*, 1–83.

[202] William Blackstone, *Commentaries on the Laws of England*, 125–36 (1765).

[203] See *The Case of Mary Clark, A Woman of Color*, 1 Blackf. 122 (Ind. 122).

[204] See statement of W. Hawley in *Slave Testimony: Two Centuries of Letters, Speeches, Interviews and Autobiographies*, ed. John Blassingame (Baton Rouge: Louisiana State Univ. Press, 1977), 1:394.

scarce resource.[205] Then too, in a land of opportunity it was always possible to believe the *New York Times*'s reassurances that "our paupers today, thanks to free labor are our yeomen and merchants of tomorrow."[206] Yet all these efforts of unpropertied workers to redefine themselves as free presupposed that freedom still ultimately depended on economic circumstance. The power to contract might be a means to material freedom or even a freedom-enhancing material asset, but it was not by itself an index of freedom. Former slaves insisted that full freedom required forty acres and a mule; "for all their glorification of labor," Lincoln's supporters "looked down upon those who labored for wages all their lives,"[207] and journeymen assumed that their chances of bettering themselves depended upon concerted action, not just individual talent and effort.

While the national economy became increasingly urban, industrial, concentrated, and stratified over the course of the nineteenth century, it was still natural for Americans coming of age before the Civil War to think of their country as a yeoman republic. The first substantive interpretations of the Fourteenth Amendment's Due Process Clause are found in the opinions of Lincoln appointees Swayne, Field, and Bradley, all born during the administrations of Jefferson and Madison. Their dissents in the *Slaughterhouse Cases*[208] understood the Civil War Amendments to preserve the "republic"[209] into which they had been born, by securing to its citizens the right to *use property productively.* Referring respectively to the Declaration of Independence and Blackstone, Field and Bradley objected to a New Orleans ordinance that required butchers to slaughter in a municipal slaughterhouse rather than on their own premises, reasoning that the "right to choose one's calling is an essential part of that liberty which it is the object of government to protect; and a calling, when chosen, is a man's property and right."[210] For self-employed proprietors of butcher shops it was literally true that "their occupation [was] their property."[211] The Republicans' faith that "the man who labored for another last year, this year labors for himself, and next year hires others to labor for him"[212] explains Field's belief that " 'the property which every man has in his own labor, as it is the original foundation of all other property, so it is the most sacred and inviolable.' "[213] This was the constitution of a republic of self-employed artisans, not unpropertied servants.

[205] See Robert Steinfeld, "The Philadelphia Cordwainers' Case of 1806: The Struggle over Alternative Legal Constructions of a Free Market in Labor," in *Labor Law in America: Historical and Critical Essays*, ed. Christopher Tomlins and Andrew King (Baltimore: Johns Hopkins Univ. Press, 1992), 20–43.

[206] Foner, *Free Soil, Free Labor*, 16.

[207] Ibid., 23.

[208] 83 U.S. (16 Wall.) 36 (1873).

[209] Ibid., 110 (Field, J., dissenting).

[210] Ibid., 116 (Bradley, J., dissenting).

[211] Ibid., 122 (Bradley, J., dissenting); see generally William Forbath, "The Ambiguities of Free Labor," *Wisconsin Law Review* 1985 (1985): 767.

[212] Foner, *Free Soil, Free Labor*, 30.

[213] *Slaughterhouse Cases*, 110 (Field, J., dissenting), quoting Adam Smith, *The Wealth of Nations*, book 1, ch. 10); *Butcher's Union Co. v. Crescent City Co.*, 111 U.S. 746, 757 (Field, J., concurring), quoting Smith, *The Wealth of Nations* (book 1, ch. 10).

In an 1887 case upholding a commercial regulation, the Court announced that "the privilege of pursuing an ordinary calling or trade, and of acquiring, holding and selling property, is an essential part of [the] rights of liberty and property, as guaranteed by the Fourteenth Amendment."[214] But the issue in this and other cases of the period was still the conflict between the productive use of property and the public power to police health, safety, and welfare where property, as the *Munn v. Illinois* majority said, was "affected with the public interest."[215]

But as these opinions were written, the American labor movement was realizing that a large-scale industrial economy offered wage laborers no future as self-employed artisans.[216] When the separation of labor and capital became more vivid in the social experience of most observers, the republican ideal of freedom as material independence proved unsustainable, though with polyvalent implications. To a labor leader, the demise of this ideal might suggest that free labor required collective ownership of large-scale enterprises; to a Progressive reformer, that labor required protective labor legislation; and to a Social Darwinist, that free labor consisted in unrestricted bargaining against a background of unequal talent and wealth.

Justice Brown's opinion for the seven-Justice majority in *Holden v. Hardy* reflected the second of these viewpoints. Brown did not view the right to contract as part of the "liberty" protected by the Due Process Clause, but as one policy for promoting property:

> As the possession of property, of which a person cannot be deprived, doubtless implies that such property may be acquired, it is safe to say that a state law which undertakes to deprive any class of persons of the general power to acquire property would also be obnoxious to the same provision. Indeed we may go a step further, and say that, as property can only be legally acquired as between living persons by contract, a general prohibition against entering into contracts with respect to property, or having as their valid object the acquisition of property, would be equally invalid.[217]

Here the right of contract is a mere instrument to the *acquisition* of property rather than itself a property right; and only a total deprivation of all instruments might infringe the right to property. Indeed, a legislature might conclude that it could best enhance the laborer's opportunity to acquire property by regulating the conditions under which he or she could alienate her labor.

By contrast, the Court viewed contracting by businesses as the *use* of property, that is, as the very thing protected by the Due Process Clause. Indeed, all the justices that joined the majority in *Holden* had participated in the Court's unanimous decision in *Allgeyer v. Louisiana*,[218] that a state could not prevent a shipper from purchasing insurance from an out-of-state insurer. *Allgeyer* held

---

[214] *Powell v. Pennsylvania*, 127 U.S. 678, 684 (1887).

[215] *Munn v. Illinois*, 94 U.S. 113 (1877); *Mugler v. Kansas*, 123 U.S. 623 (1887).

[216] Forbath, "The Ambiguities of Free Labor," 767.

[217] *Holden v. Hardy*, 391.

[218] 165 U.S. 578 (1897).

that "in the privilege of pursuing an ordinary calling or trade and of acquiring, holding and selling property must be embraced the right to make all proper contracts thereto."[219] But even here, economic context remained important, so that the contracting "proper" to the "acquiring" and "selling" of property might be very different.

It is only with *Lochner* that we find economic context effaced and the pursuit of property by penniless workers equated with the use of property by enterprising employers. At a point when few Americans still believed that the laborers of today were the employers of tomorrow, Peckham's *Lochner* opinion ascribed entrepreneurial status to all workers, reasoning that because "the general right to make a contract *in relation to his business* is part of the liberty of the individual protected by the Fourteenth Amendment (Allgeyer v. Louisiana) . . . the right to purchase or to sell labor is part of [that] liberty."[220]

To the *Lochner* majority, it was undoubtedly true, as Peller claims, that "a contract was a contract, whether for groceries, futures, or employment."[221] But not, as Peller continues, "because it was a universal form of association correlated with the transcendental subjectivity of the individual."[222] To the contrary, a contract for services was like a contract for goods *because services were like goods*: both were property and both were products of property. Anglo-American political thought had long attributed "subjectivity" to the property holder: the problem posed by "liberty of contract" is how unpropertied laborers could be assimilated into this category.

Perhaps *Lochner*, although a doctrinal innovation, was a cultural anachronism, reflecting a lingering faith in an agrarian and artisanal republic. Or perhaps the Court viewed laborers as transformed into loci of subjectivity by the magic of industrial labor discipline: perhaps they saw factory work as an edifying involvement with high technology.[223] Perhaps labor discipline dignified the employed worker, while the laborer out of doors and out of work could still be seen as violent, dissolute, or childlike.[224]

If many nineteenth-century Americans saw subjectivity as an achievement enabled by property or employment, we should be cautious in ascribing to the turn-of-the century Supreme Court the metaphysical assumptions that individual will was autonomous from economic context, and that economic context was not "affected with a public interest." The "yellow-dog" contract cases invited the Court to compare the public worth of competing private associations: the yellow-dog employment contract and the union. Not all contracting was equally valued.

---

[219] Ibid., 591.

[220] *Lochner v. New York.* 45, 53 (emphasis added).

[221] Peller, "Metaphysics," 1217.

[222] Ibid.

[223] See generally *Women at Work: The Transformation of Work and Community in Lowell, Massachusetts 1826–1860*, ed. Thomas Dublin (New York: Columbia Univ. Press, 1979).

[224] See generally Dianne Avery, "Images of Violence in Labor Jurisprudence 1894–1921," *Buffalo Law Review* 37 (1988): 1.

A century before *Holden* and *Lochner*, urban artisans had insisted that the right to bargain collectively was an important element of their material independence. Under the reasoning of *Holden v. Hardy*, like-minded legislatures, hoping to enhance workers' opportunity to acquire property, could preclude the worker from making yellow-dog contracts. Three years after *Lochner*, the Court rejected this argument in *Adair v. United States*.[225] Yet the Justices could not simply conclude that employment was a private matter immune from public regulation, because the employer's contractual freedom might require public power to operate against unruly workers. In a curious passage, the Court analogizes anti-yellow-dog statutes to the tort of enticement of a servant, suggesting that liberty of contract must be secured against both public and private interference.[226] Since the union and the yellow-dog employer could accuse each other of tortious interference with contract, the legal implementation of the abstract ideal of liberty of contract required a public choice as to which private associations deserved "liberty." In protecting the liberty of workers to contract with unions rather than with union busters, the Court implied, legislatures would make the wrong choice. The liberty, the privacy, the independence, the subjectivity of the worker were all better secured by association with the employer than by association with the union. This is not metaphysics, but social theory.

It may also be social theory rather than metaphysics that ultimately explains the *Lochner* opinion's assumption that bakers were "equal in intelligence and capacity to other men." Implicitly, the Court distinguished bakers from other classes of workers: sailors, who were, according to Justice Brown "deficient in that full and intelligent responsibility for their acts which is accredited to ordinary adults, . . . needing the protection of the law in the same sense which minors and wards were entitled to the protection of their parents and guardians";[227] miners, whose labor had sometimes been bound for life,[228] and whom the court had protected in *Holden v. Hardy*; and women, because "in the struggle for subsistence [woman] is not an equal competitor with her brother."[229]

Finally, even if there was in our history a brief doctrinal moment between the passing of the patriarchal employer and the rise of the paternalistic state, when all workers were represented as free and equal, we could not ascribe that equal status to metaphysical belief, without ignoring the possible role of racism. If over the course of the nineteenth century Americans began to de-emphasize the material and social constituents of individual freedom, that may in part have been because Americans were reluctant to extend material and social power to the slaves they had grudgingly resolved to free. Since *Lochner* is an interpretation of a Fourteenth Amendment passed to implement emancipation, perhaps race lay at

[225] 208 U.S. 161 (1908).

[226] Ibid., 173.

[227] 165 U.S. 287 (1897).

[228] David Brion Davis, *The Problem of Slavery in the Age of Revolution* (Ithaca: Cornell Univ. Press, 1975), 489–92.

[229] 208 U.S. 412 (1908).

the "root" of the Court's crabbed conception of liberty as the right to make and break labor contracts.

In fact, the history of abolitionist sentiment from the Revolution to the Civil War suggests that the controversy over slavery led White Americans to sharply differentiate free from unfree status and made it harder to view freedom as a quantitative category, varying with material independence.[230] In important ways, race and status were isomorphic concepts at the time of the Civil War. While the first stood for natural constraints on human freedom and the second for social constraints, both were asymmetrically distributed: only people of color were thought to suffer the natural constraints of race, whereas Whites were thought capable of transcending nature—they were raceless. Similarly, status defined the social position only of the dependent—the independent defined their own place in society through voluntary relations of contract.[231] If "liberty of contract" was characterized, as Peller argues, by such "vacuum-bounded categories" as freedom and dependence, is it utterly implausible to imagine that the sharply delineated categories of race inspired their structure?

As for the public-private distinction, it is well to remember that in the realm of race law this distinction was by no means self-evident or unspoken. To the contrary, since slavery had always been viewed as a domestic relation, and since the states had always been viewed as coequal sovereigns, the Reconstruction Congress and judiciary were inclined to assume that federal emancipation of the slaves would entail federal regulation of "private" relations but not necessarily supervision of the sovereign states.[232] It was only with the political collapse of Reconstruction that the judiciary, in a sense, had to hurriedly invent a public-private distinction in order to cabin the duties imposed on the federal government by the Civil War Amendments: hence, the state action limitation on the Fourteenth Amendment, precluding the federal government from guaranteeing equal protection or full citizenship by regulating private discrimination. In thus protecting private racial discrimination, the *Civil Rights Cases*, a generation before *Lochner*, linked free status to limits on public regulation of "private" contracting.[233]

Thus, the Court's treatment of bakers' disposition over their labor as all the property requisite to their freedom was a complex and contingent social judgment,

---

[230] Steinfeld, *Invention of Free Labor*, 122–146; Jonathan Glickstein, " 'Poverty Is Not Slavery': American Abolitionists and the Competitive Labor Market," in *Antislavery Reconsidered*, ed. Lewis Perry and Michael Fellman (Baton Rouge: Louisiana Stae Univ. Press, 1979), 195–218.

[231] Guyora Binder, "The Slavery of Emancipation," *Cardozo Law Review* 17 (1996): 2063.

[232] Robert Kaczorowski, "The Enforcement Provisions of the Civil Rights Act of 1866: A Legislative History in Light of *Runyon v. McCrary*," *Yale Law Journal* 98 (1988): 565; *United States v. Rhoades*, Fed. Case no. 16,151 (Circ. Ct. Dist. Ky., 1866) (Swayne, Cir. Just.) (upholding Civil Rights Act of 1866 as a Thirteenth Amendment statute); Kohl, "The Civil Rights Act of 1866, Its Hour Come Round at Last: *Jones v. Mayer Corp*," *Virginia Law Review* 55 (1968): 272; Jacobus ten Broek, *Equal under Law* (New York: Collier, 1965) (Abolitionist ideal of Full Protection as embodied in Equal Protection Clause implies protection against private depredations).

[233] 109 U.S. 3 (1883). "When a man has emerged from slavery . . . there must be some stage in the progress of his elevation when he takes the rank of mere citizen, and ceases to be the special favorite of the laws."

not an unthinking metaphysical assumption. It may have reflected historically specific beliefs about the social constituents of self-propriety and proper conduct, overlaying more deeply sedimented anxieties about race mixing and redistribution of land.

And yet even this contingent judgment did not by itself entail the result in *Lochner*. The decision against regulation depended not only on (1) a distinction between private property and property affected with the public interest, and (2) a view of bakers' labor as property, but also (3) a judgment that their labor was not affected with public interest. But Peller's "metaphysical" explanation of this last conclusion as entailed by the "priority of the public over the private" is fatally underdetermined.[234] The priority of public over private explains any decision against regulation but cannot distinguish *Lochner* from such decisions favoring regulation as *Munn v. Illinois*, *Holden v. Hardy*, and *Muller v. Oregon*. Peller asserts, without explanation, that the *Lochner* Court saw "the ultra-hazardous mining activity in *Holden v. Hardy*" as "qualitative[ly] different," from baking.[235] And yet all the Court says on this point is that baking "does not appear to be as healthy as some other trades, and is also vastly more healthy than others. . . . There must be more than the mere fact of the possible existence of some small amount of unhealthfulness."[236] This is a *quantitative* standard, albeit a more exacting one than the Court had adopted in *Holden v. Hardy* when it endorsed the "great expan[sion]" of labor regulation as a reasonable legislative response "to an enormous increase in the number of occupations which are dangerous, or so far detrimental to the health of employees as to demand special precautions for their well-being."[237] The majority's strained effort to distinguish *Holden v. Hardy* on the facts rather than overruling it outright may well have been necessary to the outcome of the case: *Lochner* was a 5–4 decision, depending on the votes of two members of the *Holden v. Hardy* majority, Justices Fuller and Brown. Is it plausible that their treatment of baking as "unaffected by the public interest" would have been unconscious and unambivalent?

If we recharacterize turn-of-the-century judicial thought as more social, contextual, flexible, and ambivalent than Peller's account would suggest, we get a more convincing account of its causal role in shaping social change and legal result. The two decades preceding *Lochner* were times of industrial confrontation, judicial activism, and social change, as well as doctrinal instability. William Forbath has recently suggested that while judges did not consistently strike down labor legislation and enjoin strikes during this period, they did both often enough to affect the strategic opportunities and ultimately the ideological aspirations and self-definitions of the labor movement. Labor abandoned such class-identified economic tactics as secondary boycotts and sympathy strikes and such class-identified political goals as securing the passage of social legislation, and it jettisoned its republi-

---

[234] Peller, "Metaphysics," 1212.
[235] Ibid.
[236] *Lochner v. New York*, 59.
[237] *Holden v. Hardy*, 391–92.

can critique of wage-labor as dependence: Samuel Gompers of the newly ascendant AFL claimed that the movement's "whole gospel ... is ... freedom of contract."[238] Thus, the judiciary dynamically reshaped the social as well as the doctrinal context of its own decisions. But if so, the supposedly uncontroversial metaphysical assumptions that, according to Peller, prepared the way for antilabor decisions could just as well be said to have followed in their train—a train that never let them rest at one station for long.

Far from being a thoughtless expression of unconscious metaphysical assumptions, *Lochner* was a negotiated exchange: between courts and labor unions, between precedent and innovation, between doctrinal categories and social visions, and between public and private power. It was strategic, it was contingent, it was contested; and, not only in the long run that separated the patriarchal master from the paternalistic state, but even in the short run that separated *Holden v. Hardy* from *Coppage v. Kansas*, it was ephemeral.

We have considered Peller's ambitious argument at length to illustrate the temptations placed in the path of even the most conscientious investigator by deconstruction's claims to oppose reductionism and totalization. The slogan that all readings are necessarily partial can become an excuse for ignoring available data, while the slogan that there is nothing outside of the text provides reassurance that any narrow and idiosyncratic selection of data will reflect the texture of the whole, disclosing traces of all that might have been included. By flattering its user that she has reckoned with the limits of her own account, the rhetoric of deconstruction paradoxically encourages her to narrow the domain of her data rather than her claims, so that any event she chooses to recount, however unique or contingent, becomes exemplary of the all-encompassing unity of "Western Metaphysics."

5.3 Deconstruction as Ethical Criticism

Introduction

This part explores the efforts of American feminists to use deconstruction as a source of ethical values for guiding critique and reform of law. Feminist legal theorists have seen deconstruction as useful for two related projects: (1) arguing that legal decision making should take into account previously ignored or subordinated points of view, such as those of women; and (2) refining—or refuting—a communitarian critique of liberalism that purports to articulate the viewpoint of women.

How does deconstruction support an argument for taking account of "excluded voices" in legal decision making? The deconstructive critique of totality implies that any representation of reality is incomplete or *reductive*. Accordingly, some feminist theorists reason, any description of the popular will or the general interest

---

[238] William Forbath, *Law and the Shaping of the American Labor Movement* (Cambridge: Harvard Univ. Press. 1991), 130–31.

will be reductive and could be improved by the inclusion of the voices of its constituent members. In addition, even where there is widespread agreement on normative principles, the phenomenon of iterability suggests that those principles will have a different meaning for every interpreter and will change meaning over time. Finally, that the meaningfulness of every concept depends upon what it purports to exclude suggests that majorities should preserve the capacity of minorities to articulate dissenting views. Thus, deconstruction strikes some feminist legal theorists as a mandate for such process values as tolerance, pluralism, participation, and dialogue. Further, deconstructive demonstrations of the inherent incompleteness of any rule system imply the inevitability of judicial discretion. Since judges are responsible for completing open-textured rule systems with some values, they should incorporate the ethical values endorsed by deconstruction in their decisions.

How does deconstruction contribute to articulating the "excluded voice" of women? Feminists have mainly looked to deconstruction as a "postmodern" corrective supplement to theorizing purporting to identify women's voice. An important example of such theorizing is cultural feminism, discussed in chapter 3. Cultural feminists attempt to develop distinctively feminist values from the language and experiences of women. A prominent example of such work is psychologist Carol Gilligan's effort to identify a distinctively female pattern of moral development.[239]

Cultural feminists have sought to derive a communitarian critique of the competitive, individualist, and instrumental ethos of liberalism from the nurturing experiences of many women. Influenced by Freudian psychology and Hegelian social theory, cultural feminists have attended to the disparate developmental experiences of men and women, critiquing both as frustrations of a drive for recognition that can only be realized in the mutuality of community. Although drawn to the values of care espoused by cultural feminism, deconstructive feminists have seen the cultural feminist account of women's experience and human drives as "essentialist" and have seen its ideal of community as dangerously "totalitarian." These theorists variously urge that women are not all the same, that their ethic of care and community has been imposed upon them, that dialogue can never be made completely inclusive, and that the communitarian desire for mutual recognition is really a desire to absorb and efface heteronomy. Here deconstruction is used not as a source of ethical values, but to raise epistemological questions about our ability to ascribe particular values to women.

Yet the opposition of deconstructive feminism to cultural feminism has its limits. While denying that the subjectivity of women is easily identified or interpreted, deconstructive feminists have remained committed to its moral relevance. Accordingly, they have joined cultural feminists in resisting the influential claim of Catherine MacKinnon that women's subjectivities are so determined by male

---

[239] Carol Gilligan, *In a Different Voice: Psychological Theory and Women's Development* (Cambridge: Harvard Univ. Press, 1982).

domination as not to be authentically their own. To some feminists, then, deconstruction suggests that the inevitable instability and indeterminacy of patriarchy leaves room for women to develop and elaborate a subjectivity of their own in the act of interpreting their confining roles. These feminists invoke deconstruction in support of a claim that women's experience is neither adequately represented by universalist models of humanity, nor dialectically deducible from those models by some simple operation of negation that would replace acquisitiveness with altruism, or independence with relatedness. The remainder of this chapter will assess these two feminist uses of deconstruction in law: the use of deconstruction to argue for the inclusion of the excluded voices of women and to correct cultural feminism's articulation of those voices.

As to the first use of deconstruction, we are sympathetic with the aspiration to achieve a participatory, pluralistic, and dialogic politics. That political deliberation will be richer if multiple viewpoints are represented seems obvious, as does the practical judgment that reforming institutions to enhance representation for vulnerable minorities contributes to this end. And who could object to tolerance? But we are skeptical that deconstruction adds much precision or appeal to these worthy aspirations. As we showed in part 5.1, Derridean deconstruction demonstrates the inevitability of reduction, representation, and mediation, and condemns the values of participation and authentic self-expression as naive, anti-intellectual, and dangerously sentimental. And unless selectively applied, "tolerance" is not a value at all, but a sentiment. The antipositivist recognition of the inevitability of normative discretion in interpreting and applying law is unexceptionable, but implicit in all pragmatist epistemology, whether or not affiliated with Derridean deconstruction.

As to the second use of deconstruction, we are sympathetic with the aspiration to a cultural feminism that recognizes women's cultural identities as diverse, contingent, and contested. Yet we are not persuaded that cultural feminism needs or gets nearly as much help from deconstruction as some deconstructive authors have claimed. The deconstructive critique of feminist and other communitarianisms reprises the sophistical tactics of Derrida's critique of Rousseau—it equates community with conformity and pragmatic generalization with essentialism. We suspect that cultural feminism can build a sufficiently complex and contingent vision of culture on its own foundations, without deconstructive correction. On the other hand, deconstructive feminism may exaggerate the contingency of gender roles, patriarchy, and other such cultural structures to the point that these dissolve into figments of imagination. We see roles as contingent on the actions and interpretive stratagems of companies of players, not individuals, and so identities are more a matter of negotiation than of interpretation. A world in which identities constrain individuals but are collectively chosen is a world in which identity is an important political issue. And it seems to us it is such a world that the enterprise of feminist theory must presuppose. If "the personal is the political," then who we are as persons is not just a matter of interpretation, but also a matter of social choice.

Deconstruction and the Jurisprudence
of Excluded Voices

In this section we will examine three works arguing that deconstruction mandates greater attention to the voices of groups traditionally excluded in legal decision making.

In "Expanding the Legal Vocabulary: The Challenge Posed by the Deconstruction and Defense of Law,"[240] Christine Desan offers deconstruction as the answer to a crisis of liberalism manifested by "the rise of the welfare state; the development of legal theories that balance individual interests against values such as group parity and public debate; court cases that mandate forced busing; the confusion that the issue of affirmative action inspires; [and] the retrenchment by Rawls of his theory of justice."[241] The root of this crisis, Desan assures us, is the insupportability of liberalism's premise of a social and epistemological world consisting of "autonomous subjects."

Desan takes as one symptom of this crisis the Critical Legal Studies critique of what she calls "objectification": "the elevation of subjective understandings to the status of objective standards." Objectification involves treating distributions of power as natural or given, rather than contingent on discretionary legal decision making. If the subject were understood to be inherently incomplete and dependent rather than autonomous, she reasons, no subjective viewpoint could ever be exalted as objectively true. Because of the epistemological limitations of the subject, Desan reasons, accurate representation of other subjectivities is impossible. Like Frug, Desan proceeds to base an argument for participatory democracy on the epistemological difficulty of representation. Yet cognizant of majoritarian democracy's threat to minority viewpoints, she also argues that democratic deliberation must especially heed traditionally excluded voices.

Desan illustrates this claim with a deconstructive critique of the communicative ethics of Frankfurt School critical theorist Jürgen Habermas. Although endorsing Habermas's identification of justice with universal participation in dialogue under conditions of equality, Desan objects to his assumption that under conditions of equality language can be a transparent medium. The aspiration to render language transparent, Desan reasons, allows for the possibility of objectification with its attendant domination. If language could simultaneously comprehend all subjective perspectives, a single speaker could claim such universality and thereby subordinate other speakers.

Desan endorses instead a Heideggerian view of language as always

> from an angle. While the angle enables our vision, it also limits it, defining our view and determining its highlights. . . . Speech . . . [becomes] a continual decision of what to reveal, thus also a selective interpretation that obscures what is not spoken. . . .

---

[240] Christine Desan, "Expanding the Legal Vocabulary: The Deconstruction and Defense of Law," *Yale Law Journal* 95 (1986): 969.

[241] Ibid., 984.

We therefore express different or undeniably "incommensurable," if not unrelated realities.[242]

Thus, objectification of one's own subjective viewpoint—with its attendant suppression of competing subjectivities—is not an error one can transcend by improving the conditions of discussion. Objectification of one's own viewpoint is implicit in any use of language.

Desan concludes that the inevitable partiality of all views implies an obligation to sometimes be silent and listen, and that "it is those whose situations are most different from our own who can illuminate most effectually our areas of blindness; therefore it is those who are most different whom we must be certain to include in our dialogue."[243] Desan also concludes that the inevitable subjectivity or partiality of language implies the inevitability of judicial discretion. Finally, if somewhat hyperbolically, Desan concludes that "an internal shift to an ideal of receptivity would make complacency and self-righteousness as distressing behaviors as we proclaim violence to be: all are barriers to real communication."[244] Her concrete proposals include the "humanizing" of the objects of public policy by requiring bureaucrats to meet face to face with those whose decisions they effect.

There are a number of related difficulties with this argument that are fairly typical of efforts to ground the authority of excluded voices in deconstruction. Deconstruction shares with structuralism an antihumanist critique of subjectivity. Yet the rhetoric of including excluded voices populates the cultural landscape with competing subjectivities and urges a transfer of authority from some to others. Hence, fusing this rhetoric with the deconstructive critique of subjectivity engenders an inescapable tension between viewing the subjectivity of the powerless as a source of authority to be venerated and viewing the subjectivity of the powerful as a source of embarrassment to be deconstructed.

If mediation is the condition of communication, and language the condition of subjectivity, Desan's fundamental concept of objectification seems inapt. The representations of others that we offer are not falsehoods, doing violence to their true subjectivity—they are part of a network of social recognition and mediation that makes subjectivity available to others. Thus, in representing others we do not automatically "objectify" them in the sense of reducing them to the status of objects or denying their freedom to make themselves. It matters a great deal to us *how* we are represented by others and what sorts of self-images society makes available to us. But it would be naive and sentimental to think that we could control our own image by precluding others from representing us at all. For one thing, we partly derive our own self-representations from culturally available characters and images. For another, we cannot hope to engage in politics without representing our own values or preferences, thereby inviting others to reinterpret them. For a third, we cannot hope to win esteem, avoid giving offense, or, in

[242] Ibid., 977.
[243] Ibid., 978.
[244] Ibid., 989.

short, live together, without finding out what others think of us. We cannot really want our self-images to be subject to our own control alone.

Although Desan endorses Heidegger's account of language, this account presents language as an enabling constraint—an order that forecloses other ways of ordering the world that might be better or worse for some purposes and some people. In this sense, language is inherently exclusive of possible social orders, possible cultures, possible identities, even possible personalities that different language might enable. But if language is inevitably exclusive, the fact of exclusion has no critical bite unless we judge the comparative value of the possibilities excluded. This suggests in turn that we can only argue coherently for the recognition of particular voices, not the indiscriminate inclusion of all possible voices. The best arguments for including excluded voices will be content- and context-specific.

So what are we to make of Desan's recommendation that we attend most to those voices that have been most excluded? However appealing this prescription, it does not follow from Desan's Heideggerian view of language. To the contrary, this view of language implies that the rhetoric of "excluded voices" is deeply misleading. The viewpoints excluded by any given ordering of the world are not "actual" refugee camps and barrios, but possible perspectives on those sites; and these perspectives, because of the reign of official truths, may not even be recognized or be available for expression by anyone in the society. The preclusion of possible perspectives is not necessarily the suppression of actual subjectivities. Nor can we be certain of our own locations: the "objects" we incompletely perceive include ourselves. If we are riven by contradiction, blind both to ourselves and to others, how do we know who is "most different" from us? Indeed, much poststructuralist criticism suggests that our principal purpose in ascribing exoticism to others is to achieve a stable and coherent representation of ourselves.[245] Indeed, Derrida criticizes Levinas's ethic of reverence for otherness or "alterity" on just these grounds.

The fashionably antihumanist way of putting this objection is to observe that the rhetoric of excluded voices sentimentalizes the oppressed, representing them as noble savages.[246] Thus, there is a persistent tension in Desan's argument between her antihumanist premises and her humane conclusions. Her calls for "real communication" and for "humanizing" government through face-to-face interaction therefore seem startlingly sentimental, given the constitutive importance for deconstruction of Derrida's polemic against favoring speech over writing and participation over representation.

One possible conclusion is that those bent on ethical application of deconstruction should heed Derrida and give up their merely "sentimental" attachment to the virtues of confession and conversation. Yet for many authors, a commitment to consciousness raising as a method of empirical research, "personal empowerment," and political mobilization is necessary to an identification with femi-

---

[245] E.g., Edward Said, *Orientalism* (New York: Vintage Books, 1978).

[246] This is Derrida's critique of Rousseau and Lévi-Strauss in *Of Grammatology*.

nism. If movements devoted to amplifying excluded voices inherently value authentic self-expression and direct communication, and if deconstruction is inherently skeptical about the value and even the possibility of these processes, the two enterprises seem antithetical.

Nevertheless, the next author we consider attempts a synthesis of feminism and deconstruction. In *The Philosophy of the Limit*, Drucilla Cornell offers "an ethical reading of what has come to be known as deconstruction."[247] She hopes to show that deconstruction yields normative implications by associating it with feminism. According to Cornell,

> Derrida's specific intervention is not simply to expose . . . the limit of logocentrism, but of the gender hierarchy as constituted in the era of the ego. . . . Thus it is not the case, as some political critics of Derrida have suggested, that there is no "social basis" to deconstruction if one means by social basis an appeal to how important relationships are constituted within a particular culture or historical period.[248]

The basic outlines of Cornell's strategy recall Desan's argument. Deconstruction's principles of iterability and textual infinity demonstrate the inherent incompleteness—the "*limits*"—of representation and thus the limited authority of any particular point of view. Deconstruction thereby reduces the relative authority of dominant views, increases the relative authority of subordinated views, and highlights the discretion of arbiters—such as judges—to choose between competing viewpoints. Yet Cornell adds several glosses on this basic reading of deconstruction as epistemological relativism, identifying it more persuasively with the themes of feminist critique and feminist practice.

First, Cornell puts a feminist spin on the deconstructive critique of dualism. Many of the hierarchically ordered dualisms Derrida regards as characteristic of Western metaphysics—meaning/sign, spirit/matter, reason/nature—may be seen as metaphoric extensions of mind/body dualism. And like many other feminists, Cornell sees mind/body dualism as a culturally embedded rationalization for gender hierarchy.

Next, she brings the deconstructive critique of mind/body dualism to bear on ethics, by stressing the mind/body dualism implicit in Kantian ethics. The Kantian imperative to subject desire to duty and follow a universalizable rule reflects an aspiration to subject the body to the rational control of the mind. Cornell follows Hegel and the Critical Theorists of the Frankfurt School in criticizing this aspiration to self-mastery.

From Hegel, Cornell draws a critique of Kant's aspiration to achieve individual autonomy by suppressing desire. Because self-development is achieved only by pursuing the desire for social recognition, the Kantian compulsion to purge the self of heteronomy yields neither freedom nor morality. Instead, individual freedom is a social achievement, and morality includes not just impersonal rules but interpersonal solidarity.

---

[247] Drucilla Cornell, *The Philosophy of the Limit* (New York: Routledge, 1992), ix.
[248] Ibid., 180.

From the Critical Theorist Theodor Adorno, Cornell draws a critique of the Kantian ideal of self-control as the manifestation of a desire to dominate, a desire easily transferred from one's self to others. The ideal of subjecting the body to a regime of reason ends up justifying male domination of women. Since a morality of rules mandates the subordination of the body, of feeling, and the women who are often taken to symbolize both, normative thought should not be organized around a search for universalizable conduct rules.

To the Kantian "morality" of impulse control, Cornell opposes Levinas's notion of "the ethical relation," which concerns not just conduct rules but also "the kind of person one must become in order to develop a nonviolative relationship to the Other."[249] An ethical reason for crediting or listening to the voices of others, then, would be to manifest the virtuous characteristics of humility and compassion rather than to inform oneself or to defer to the abstract rights of others. In invoking Levinas's ideal of the ethical relation, Cornell announces her ambition to link deconstruction to the relational ethic of care advocated by such cultural feminists as Carol Gilligan and embodied by the practice of consciousness raising.

Having identified ethics with respect for alterity, Cornell can argue that excluded voices have ethical rather than epistemological importance. While reading Derridean deconstruction as a relativist epistemology, Cornell reads that epistemological relativism, in turn, as an expression of Levinasian ethics. From this perspective, the errors that deconstructive readings reveal in texts are moral rather than metaphysical, failures of character rather than cognition. Thus, the moral of Derridean deconstruction is that every conceptual scheme is a limited or partial representation, a violently reductive interpretation of an infinite text. Drawing on Derrida's first "Force of Law" lecture, Cornell identifies deconstruction with protest against established legal institutions on the grounds that they are unfaithful to a transcendent ideal of justice. By invoking Levinas's concept of alterity, Cornell is able to identify this subversive perspective with movements of the oppressed. Thus, following Levinas, Cornell equates violence with such discursive practices as exclusion, reduction, and appropriation of the "Other." In this way, she rhetorically links the traces of meaning *inevitably* suppressed by *any* given interpretation to violently oppressed social groups. Interpretation becomes violence and interpretive possibilities figuratively become bloody corpses. From the merely logical inference that "the condition of delimiting a system as a system necessarily implies a beyond to the system,"[250] Cornell deduces the political-sounding conclusion that "the system, through the critical observer, is called to remember its own exclusions and prejudices."[251] Cornell identifies this critical observer as female.[252] Presumably, even the traces of meaning suppressed by *feminist* interpretations of reality are, figuratively speaking, women.

[249] Ibid., 13.
[250] Ibid., 142.
[251] Ibid., 149.
[252] Ibid., 117, 144.

In associating deconstruction with an ethic of "infinite respect for the other,"[253] Cornell eschews the conventional understanding of deconstruction as "trashing," or caustic, skeptical, unsympathetic reading. In one chapter she refigures deconstructive criticism as a constructive enterprise, as the work of the scavenger who redeems what has been discarded as trash by others. It is conventional, essentialist thought, she implies, that "trashes" what it excludes as inessential. Typically, what "logocentric" thought excludes as inessential is the concreteness and physical embodiment of its concepts. And because women are associated with embodiment, "logocentric" thought is also "phallogocentric." Deconstruction's attention to semiotic "difference" therefore implies an attention to the excluded voice of women in particular and more generally to bodily need and sensation.

By this point in the argument, Cornell has moved beyond any merely metaphoric characterization of discursive exclusion as violence: for Cornell, essentialist thought ignores or disguises real physical suffering. The voice that "phallogocentric" thought genders female and thereby silences is a cry of pain. The variously characterized targets of deconstruction—essentialism, logocentrism, the metaphysics of presence—suppress the authentic voice of suffering by interpreting it, by placing it in a transactional narrative of investment, sacrifice, exchange or progress. By juxtaposing suffering to a higher meaning, essentialism at once aestheticizes it and renders it inessential. Deconstruction disrupts such rationalizations of suffering by emphasizing "the disjuncture between meaning and being." Freed from its prison of reductive interpretation, "the oppressed thing—the object itself, the suffering, physical individual—bears witness to the failure of history to realize itself in the unity of subject and object."[254] Thus, the moral of a deconstructive reading is likely to be that "suffering, from the standpoint of the particular which endures it, is senseless. The only answer adequate to the suffering physical is the end to suffering, not a new version of the 'meaning' of what it has undergone."[255] By forcing us into unmediated confrontation with suffering, deconstruction "softens" us up for nonviolative relating to the Other: "our grasp of our existence as the suffering physical allows us to be soft. Goodness . . . is a form of tenderness."[256]

In sum, Cornell links deconstruction to feminism by means of a rhetoric that identifies together a sequence of dualisms opposing fallen institutions to transcendent ideals, law to justice, meaning to being, interpretation to suffering, reductive representation to excluded remains, rationalization to inarticulate cry, mind to body, masculine to feminine, and the powerful to the oppressed.

Cornell's prescriptive conclusions are predictable if somewhat vague. Respect for the Other turns out to mandate disapproval of, for example, apartheid.[257] Read as a theory about the necessary "limits" of language and authority, deconstruction

---

[253] Ibid., x.

[254] Ibid., 25–26.

[255] Ibid., 26.

[256] Ibid., 34.

[257] Ibid., 114; see also Jacques Derrida, "Racism's Last Word," in *Race, Writing and Difference*, ed. Henry Louis Gates (Chicago: Univ. of Chicago Press, 1986).

challenges any interpretation of legal sources as incomplete. Accordingly, the ideal of justice that deconstruction opposes to law is always internal to legal systems, rather than derived from some notion of natural law. Cornell reasons that in a democracy, where popular will is supposed to be sovereign, the views of numerical minorities and of the oppressed and the suffering are wrongly excluded from authoritative status. She offers the Ninth Amendment as an example of positive law that appeals to transcendent ideals. The "rights of the people" protected by the Ninth Amendment therefore refer to the "needs" of the underrepresented, such as the need of homosexuals for freedom of intimate association. Because no interpretation of legal authority can itself be authoritative, reasons Cornell, judgment is inherently discretionary: "Interpretation is transformation. Thus we need to remember that we are responsible, as we interpret, for the direction of that transformation."[258] Hence, legal decision makers have no excuse, no formal authorization, for ignoring the bodily suffering their decisions may cause. Abortion regulation, for example, should be consequentialist, taking into account the effects on women (but not fetuses?) of restricting abortion rights. In short, deconstruction as read by Cornell calls for a realist jurisprudence, in which painful facts speak directly to judges, unmediated by manipulable legal forms.

Even if Cornell's conventionally progressive recommendations are underdetermined by her argument, she should not be faulted for showing little interest in preempting smug indeterminacy critiques.[259] She rightly complains that "the recent debates on legal interpretation which have predominantly turned on linguistic intelligibility have focused on the wrong question."[260] Cornell's real aspiration is not to show that deconstruction yields determinate normative outcomes, but to show that it is both normatively engaged and sufficiently flexible to be compatible with the familiar normative project of feminism. This is the argument that merits serious consideration and critique.

In our view, however, this argument founders on the basic antagonism between Derrida's deconstruction of identity and any form of identity politics. Protecting feminism, as Cornell admits, entails treating femininity as a politically meaningful identity. "The feminine is not . . . merely a nominalist category. . . . [If] there is to be a feminism at all, we must rely on a feminine 'voice' and a feminine 'reality' that can be identified as such and correlated with the lives of actual women."[261]

---

[258] Cornell, *Philosophy of the Limit*, 115.

[259] Her lone effort to do so is less than convincing: "If a principle cannot give us one right answer, it can help us define what answers are wrong in the sense of incompatible with its rationale. For example, we might not all agree what the principle of reciprocal symmetry means, but we can rule out certain outcomes as incompatible with its realization. An example which Hegel himself often used is the legal rejection in modernity of all forms of indentured servitude." Ibid., 106 (emphasis and notes omitted). Numerous historical examples attest that indentured servitude is indeed compatible with modernity. See generally Steinfeld, *Invention of Free Labor*, and Robert Steinfeld, *The Coercion of Contract* (Cambridge: Cambridge Univ. Press, forthcoming 2000). Moreover, reciprocity is compatible with compulsory servitude so long as employees have a remedy of reinstatement for wrongful discharge—as do academics.

[260] Cornell, *Philosophy of the Limit*, 95.

[261] Drucilla Cornell, *Beyond Accommodation* (New York: Routledge, 1991), 3.

Hence, Cornell is constrained to reconcile deconstruction with this belief that women have a distinctive and shared point of view. Cornell's central strategy turns on associating Derrida with one of his most important targets, the pluralist ethics of Emmanuel Levinas. Yet the aspect of Levinas's thought to which Derrida objects, his ascription to the Other of an infinitely exotic or distinct identity, is hardly incidental to Levinas's pluralism.

Thus, Cornell's efforts to portray deconstruction as an ethic of respect for dissident viewpoints seem strained. Like Desan, Cornell ascribes to Derrida a relativist epistemology in which truth inheres in a diversity of discrete viewpoints. Yet Derrida's principles of iterability, trace, and textuality imply that there are no discrete viewpoints, since every position contains traces of its alternatives and opposites. Despite Derrida's argument in his second "Force of Law" lecture that apocalyptic appeals to the ideal of justice are dangerously totalitarian, Cornell characterizes deconstruction as "utopian."[262] She apparently accepts the first lecture, which purports to identify deconstruction with justice, and which was delivered to her own faculty, entirely at face value. She barely notices the second lecture that deconstructs the first,[263] and insofar as she mentions it, she reads it only as a repetition of the first lecture's utopian injunction that law not be identified with justice[264]—missing the more fundamental critique of justice itself as a violent and totalitarian aspiration.

Thus, in reinterpreting deconstruction as an ethic of respectful attention to excluded voices, Cornell is drawn into rhetorical formulations laden with the sentimentality and essentialist metaphysics that Derrida attacks, and with the narcissistic self-regard that Levinas would have us discard.

First, she consistently treats bodily experience—suffering—as existing, present, real, authentic, and complete, in need of no interpretation; while treating interpretation, representation, categorization, and the like as partial, derivative, artificial, and fallen. Yet the human experience of suffering is never wholly independent of the social processes of complaint and dispute resolution by which it may be recognized as suffering. Feeling is no more a private language than is thought.[265] This is not to deny commonsense notions that suffering is somatic and that violence is manifest when fist meets face. It is rather to accept commonsense notions as just that—notions validated by common sense, not private sensation. To recognize suffering often means not just identifying pain but recognizing its bearer as someone capable of feeling abandoned to that pain by others. Because suffering embraces not only physical pain but also the disappointment of hopes and expectations, and the violation of dignity, it has a narrative dimension. To recognize suffering is to emplot sensation within a moral drama framed by criteria of justice and responsibility. In these ways, suffering is conditioned by the possi-

[262] Ibid., 8.

[263] At the time of the first lecture, Cornell was a member of the Cardozo faculty. Only five of her twenty-two citations to "Force of Law" refer to the second lecture.

[264] Cornell, *Beyond Accommodation*, 156–68.

[265] See Miller, *Humiliation*, 53–129 (examining cultural dimensions of identifying violence and feeling).

bility of observation and interpretation as well as by sensation. To imply that suffering can simply be perceived and responded to without the mediation of reflection or convention is to indulge in sentimentality.

In fact, it is the sensibility of the witness rather than the sensation of the victim that is the focus of Cornell's deconstructive ethics. She sets out not to define the responsibilities of the participant in a "nonviolative" ethical relation, but to define "the kind of person one must become" in order to develop such a relationship. Deconstruction assists us in developing a virtuous capacity to feel compassion, humility, and respect. Hence, in Cornell's ethics, suffering becomes the occasion not for moral action, but for the gratifying experience of moral sentiments—it becomes in short an edifying aesthetic experience for its witnesses. Such an aesthetic appreciation of others' suffering seems at odds with Levinas's conception of the ethical relationship as nonexploitative.

Yet the aesthetic experience enabled by deconstruction may not even be the sympathetic appreciation of suffering, or the respectful acknowledgment of the other's difference. These are goals after which one strives, but unattainable ones. Recall Derrida's admonition that deconstruction is an impossible aspiration that can never be fully achieved. We can never expunge all trace of "violence" or "totalitarianism" from our representation of the other. At best we can maintain our vigilance, guard the other against our own appropriative or reductive impulses. Deconstruction therefore provides not an experience of sympathy, but an experience of striving towards sympathy by strenuously suppressing impure impulses. Thus, the inner experience that authenticates our claims to virtue is precisely the sanctimonious satisfactions of impulse control that tantalized Kant, and that Adorno condemned as sadistic. Read as an ethical philosophy, deconstruction urges us to bear witness not even to the suffering of others, but to our own refinements of conscience.

Justice and the Politics of Difference, by Iris Young, contains a more successful because more limited use of deconstruction in building an argument for the authority of excluded voices. Young is a political theorist whose principal aim is to reorient ethics around the goal of participatory democracy rather than distributive justice. Young sees deconstruction as useful in overcoming two obstacles to this agenda: the "ideal of impartiality" and the "distributive paradigm" in ethics.

Impartiality is contrary to the participatory ideal because it implies that normative commitment and political engagement are corrupting influences, so that affected parties must be excluded from rather than included in the process of social choice. Like Cornell, Young would substitute a relational, compassionate ethics for the abstract dispassionate ethics that has dominated neo-Kantian moral philosophy: "If . . . moral reason is dialogic, the product of discussion among differently situated subjects all of whom desire recognition and acknowledgment from the others, then there is no need for a universal point of view to pull people out of their egoism."[266] According to Young, the ideal of impartiality is hierarchical because it

---

[266] Iris Marion Young, *Justice and the Politics of Difference* (Princeton: Princeton Univ. Press, 1990), 106.

implies that just choice is choice by an elite of neutral experts. Because the ideal of impartiality is unattainable, its practical effect may be to elevate a particular viewpoint to elite status. And a particular danger is that the ideal of impartiality may rationalize gender hierarchy insofar as it supports a gendered division between realms of dispassionate, supposedly principled public decision making and supposedly irrational private decision making.

As for the distributive paradigm, it is contrary to the participatory ideal because it subordinates procedural to substantive justice. By measuring fairness in terms of the satisfaction of desires, the distributive paradigm takes desires as a given, thereby foreclosing claims that the culture that shapes desire is itself unjust. Hence, the distributive paradigm precludes claims that broader political participation in a given decision would justly alter the preferences of the participants. The ideal of impartiality and the distributive paradigm may work together to obscure the cultural implications of distributive decisions.

The ideal of impartiality is akin to the standard of objectivity criticized by Frug, Peller, and Desan and so is subject to the familiar skeptical critique:

> The ideal of impartiality in moral theory expresses a logic of identity that seeks to reduce differences to unity. The stances of detachment and dispassion that supposedly produce impartiality are attained only by abstracting from the particularities of situation, feeling, affiliation and point of view. These particularities still operate, however, in the context of action.[267]

While the reductionist "logic of identity" is implicit in the ideal of formal justice, Young also sees it in the distributive paradigm's emphasis on substance: "[The] Logic of Identity tends to conceptualize entities in terms of a substance rather than a process or relation; substance is the self-same entity that underlies change."[268] Both formal and substantive models of justice abstract decision making from the particularity of the claimant and her cultural context. Formal justice tells the claimant "we will hear you on condition that you pretend to be someone else," while substantive justice asks the claimant "how much will it take to shut you up?" Both conceptions of justice are antiparticipatory insofar as they imply third-party decision according to general standards, rather than participation by affected parties.

Generalization also abstracts a dispute from cultural and historical context. Thus, Young's version of the deconstructive critique of reduction invokes the traditional distinction between the social sciences as the study of general patterns of behavior and the humanities as the study of particular human products. By the "logic of identity," Young means the practice of classificatory judgment that Foucault describes as part of the "disciplinary" technology of the social sciences and the bureaucratic state. Young therefore sees deconstruction as part of a larger poststructuralist project of criticizing the bureaucratic and instrumental orientation of social science. In opposing literary theory to social science, however, she

---

[267] Ibid, 97.
[268] Ibid., 98.

invokes a Romantic understanding of the humanities as the study of particular subjectivities—an understanding that is also a target of deconstruction.

According to Young, the "logic of identity" is exclusive not merely in the sense of being hierarchical, but also in the sense of being intolerant and divisive:

> The logic of identity . . . inevitably . . . creates a distinction between inside and outside. Since each particular . . . has both similarities and differences with other particular[s] . . . the urge to bring them into unity . . . necessarily entails expelling some of the properties of the entities or situations. Because the totalizing movement always leaves a remainder . . . the logic of identity shoves difference into dichotomous hierarchical oppositions: essence/accident, good/bad, normal/deviant.[269]

Like Cornell, Young links this dualistic conceptual hierarchy to the oppression of groups. Yet she avoids reinscribing mind/body dualism by avoiding Cornell's reductive identification of oppression with physical suffering. Instead she develops a flexible and pluralistic conception of oppression as including not only violence but economic exploitation, social marginalization, psychic degradation, and cultural alienation. She shows that the ideal of impartiality makes anyone associated with the body more vulnerable to all of these forms of oppression. Young contends that in its modern disciplinary form, mind/body dualism takes the form of a visual orientation organized around the surveillance and inspection of bodies. According to Young, this consciousness designates the bodies of certain subordinated persons—women, people of color, the aged, and the infirm—as visual symbols of sexuality, violence, heteronomy, natural necessity, and death. In this way she concretely links patterns of authority and subordination to modern culture's "view" of the body. By contrast, Cornell's sentimental reduction of excluded voices to cries of physical suffering seems compatible with modern culture's symbolic confinement of oppression within the bodies of victims.

By recognizing the collective, cultural dimension of oppression and resistance, Young gives concrete political content to the plea for the inclusion of excluded voices. But in so doing, she develops a useful conception of cultural identity at odds with her nominal commitment to the deconstructive critique of identity.

A second form of oppression that Young links to mind/body dualism is psychic degradation or "powerlessness." Here Young has in mind the "Hidden Injuries of Class":[270] blue-collar workers' sense that they lack individuality, self-control, judgment, talent, and potential. One modern expression of mind/body dualism is a division of labor between task-definition and task-execution reflected in a class distinction between professional and nonprofessional employment. Thus, where deconstruction is sometimes seen as part of an attack on subjectivity, Young sees subjectivity as a human need that the just society would achieve for all. But she ignores the tension between this Marxist humanist critique of alienating work and the deconstructive critique of subjectivity. Psychological alienation seems an odd

---

[269] Ibid., 99.

[270] Richard Sennet and Jonathan Cobb, *The Hidden Injuries of Class* (New York: Vintage Books, 1972).

complaint for a deconstructive critic of the metaphysics of presence. If we can never be self-present, if we are inevitably self-estranged, how could we aspire to transcend alienation? One answer would read deconstruction as ascribing subjectivity to any participant in any culture who, as the reader of an inherently open, conflicted text, makes interpretive choices. Yet Young does not develop such a reading of deconstruction, perhaps because it would not be easily reconcilable with her view that the division of labor denies subjectivity to most.

Young's argument for an inclusive political dialogue is more persuasive than those offered by Cornell and Desan because it is a claim about democratic politics rather than knowledge. Her view is that rather than taking the subjectivities of discrete political actors as a given, politics is about the self-definition of political actors, and about the cultural settings which confer and recognize identities. Thus, for Young, the "distributive paradigm" misconceives politics as a technical problem of identifying and optimizing the interests of political actors. Accordingly, the epistemological problems of knowing subjectivities that follow from the distributive paradigm do not figure in her argument for dialogue. Instead, participation in dialogue is necessary for the social recognition and self-development that democratic citizenship presupposes. But precisely because Young's argument for the democratic participation of disempowered groups is a claim of justice rather than a claim that such participation is instrumental to social knowledge, it neither depends on, nor is hobbled by, deconstruction's epistemological skepticism.

Deconstruction, Cultural Feminism, and Women's Voice

A number of feminist authors have seen deconstruction as useful not only in enhancing the audibility and authority of excluded voices, but also in appreciating their diversity and complexity. Most centrally, feminists have argued that deconstruction corrects essentialist tendencies in the cultural feminist ethic of community and care. On this view, identifying feminism with altruism accepts the self-effacing role imposed upon women by romantic paternalism. A second charge deconstructive feminists have leveled at cultural feminism is that its purportedly feminine ethic of community and care is oppressively conformist and even "totalitarian." Yet it may be that much of the "essentialism" and "totalitarianism" that deconstructive readers find in cultural feminism is put there by deconstruction.

Consider an exemplary expression of cultural feminism, Jessica Benjamin's *The Bonds of Love*.[271] Benjamin elegantly synthesizes a wide array of influences. Like Adorno, she connects Hegel's critique of the Kantian ethic of independence and self-control with Marx's critique of alienation and Freud's psychology of ego development. The result is a critique of "domination" that associates the instrumental rationality of modern institutions with a sadistic, insecure person-

---

[271] Jessica Benjamin, *The Bonds of Love: Psychoanalysis, Feminism and the Problem of Domination* (New York: Pantheon, 1988).

ality type. To this she adds Nancy Chodorow's work on the gendering of ego development[272] and Carol Gilligan's work on the gendering of moral psychology[273] to show that the instrumentally rational personality, though obsessed with independence, depends upon and implies the presence of a second personality type: altruistic, self-effacing, even masochistic. The central drama of Benjamin's argument is a reinterpretation of Hegel's dialectic of master and slave. She recasts the master's futile effort to win recognition from the abject, dominated slave as the quest of the instrumentally rational personality to achieve ego differentiation through the control of its own impulses, of nature, and of "the Other." Because domination effaces everyone and everything from which the instrumentally rational personality might differentiate himself, this quest for differentiation through domination fails.

Benjamin postulates that when children are predominantly reared by one full-time parent, the parent-child relation can become the whole social world for the nurturing parent, whose identity then weakens. The child then quickly learns that one cannot make assertive demands of another without risking the other's disintegration, and so the child faces a dilemma: identify either with frustrated desire, or with needs that are met by others without being defined or asserted by oneself.

The first developmental route, often taken by males, involves isolation from and hostility towards others. Instead of learning from others, the instrumentally rational personality regulates himself and views others as either impediments to or implements for the satisfaction of desire. This posture towards the world is, however, self-defeating, because it is premised on the illusion that one can idenitfy one's own desires in isolation from others. Proceeding on the basis of such an illusion, people plan their lives in advance of experience, seeking rewards and accomplishments rather than relationships and experiences. A world of such isolated people—the world of the workplace and the marketplace—is not a world in which one can form associations that lead to social recognition and the healthy ego it enables. Nor is it a world in which one can engage in deliberative politics— the collective definition of the good. Instead politics is reduced to the planning of social life by policy "experts."

The second developmental route, often taken by females, involves passive dependence on others. This choice reflects an unwillingness to risk isolation either by subjecting the nurturing parent to insatiable demands or by withdrawing into the angry solipsism of instrumental rationality. The problem is that companionship is purchased at the price of an identity of one's own. People who adopt this approach may never develop the ability to differentiate their own needs, desires, or purposes from those of others. Thus, they are easily channeled into the "nurturing" role of full-time child rearing, which weakens their sense of independent

[272] Nancy Chodorow, *The Reproduction of Mothering: Psychoanalysis and the Sociology of Gender* (Berkeley: Univ. of California Press, 1978).

[273] Gilligan, *In a Difference Voice*.

identity still further and helps to reproduce instrumental rationality in their partners as well as in the next generation.

There is little in Benjamin's elegant argument that could be called "essentialist." Benjamin offers a genealogy of two interdependent roles, the assignment
and reproduction of which are highly contingent. For Benjamin, the assignment
of roles depends in large measure on individual choice; the reproduction of these
roles depends upon a web of circumstances that begins with the organization of
work and child care, but extends to the design of cities and policies concerning
public safety and national security. There is nothing natural or biologically predes-
tined about the gender roles Benjamin describes, nor does she romanticize the
"feminine" role. One might contest Benjamin's social theory, but any errors are
indeed errors of social theory and empirical observation, not of metaphysical
mystification.

Even where deconstructive feminists aim the charge of essentialism against a
more vulnerable target, it tends to fall wide of the mark. An illuminating example
is the charge of several deconstructive feminists that the essentialism of cultural
feminism caused a setback for women's equality in the highly publicized case of
EEOC v. Sears.[274] In that case feminist historian Rosalind Rosenberg persuaded
the Court that because of differences in the aspirations of men and women, the
underrepresentation of women in Sears's commission sales force was "consistent
with an absence of discrimination."[275] The Court questioned how many women
wanted commission sales work in light of testimony that women tended to find
it undesirably competitive and risky and to involve selling products usually purchased by male customers. Joan Scott, Joan Williams, and Zillah Eisenstein all
see the Court's use of gender stereotypes to blame women for their own lack of
opportunities as an indictment of cultural feminism.[276] Joan Williams, for example, argues that through the medium of Rosenberg, cultural feminism persuaded
the Court to change Title VII law, requiring for the first time that plaintiffs prove
that female potential employees were interested in particular work before statistical evidence of women's underrepresentation in a work force can establish a prima
facie case of sex discrimination.[277]

Yet the issue in the *Sears* case was not whether the underrepresentation of
women in Sears's work force resulted from discrimination, but whether it resulted
from discrimination *by Sears*. Rosenberg did not deny that the underrepresentation of women in commission sales was the product of discrimination—she simply denied that there was sufficient evidence to determine how much of that discrimination was attributable to Sears. In her affidavit, Rosenberg claimed:

[274] *E.E.O.C. v. Sears Roebuck Co.* 628 F. Supp. 1264 (N.D. Ill. 1986).

[275] Written rebuttal testimony of Dr. Rosalind Rosenberg, quoted in Zillah Eisenstein, *The Female Body and the Law* (Berkeley: Univ. of California Press, 1988), 112; see also *E.E.O.C. v. Sears* at 1315 ("differences in the number of men and women could exist without discrimination").

[276] Eisenstein, *The Female Body and the Law*, 110–4; Joan C. Williams, "Deconstructing Gender," *Michigan Law Review* 87 (1988): 797, 802–22; Joan Scott, "Deconstructing Equality-Versus-Differ-ence: Or the Uses of Post-Structuralist Theory for Feminism," *Feminist Studies* 14 (1988): 33.

[277] Williams, "Deconstructing Gender," 806–14.

I reject the temptation to blame employers for everything I do not like about the condition of women. Too many factors have shaped women's work force participation for such a monocausal view to be convincing. Among these factors are the restraints on women imposed by cultural norms and values and the socialization process that recreates generations of women many of whom share traditional notions about the meaning, requisites and responsibilities of womanhood, gender and femininity.[278]

Rosenberg does not deny that discrimination by Sears played *some* role in the gender disparity among commission salespersons. But the cases turned not on whether there might have been some discrimination, but rather on who bore the burden of proof. Before Rosalind Rosenberg ever testified, the Supreme Court had interpreted Title VII to require plaintiffs to prove that defendants (1) intentionally disfavored women in hiring because they were women, or (2) intentionally adopted a facially neutral hiring criterion or recruiting method that had an unfavorable impact on women. When claiming disparate impact, a plaintiff may establish a prima facie case of discrimination by showing a disparity between the female percentage of a labor market or applicant "pool" and the female percentage of those hired. Once a prima facie case has been made out, the burden shifts to the defendant to suggest some nondiscriminatory explanation for the disparity; if such an explanation is provided, the burden shifts back to the plaintiff to show that the disparity more likely resulted from discrimination than from the nondiscriminatory alternative.[279] The key decision of the district court was that because plaintiffs were not challenging any specific practice of defendants, but simply inferring from statistics that defendants must be doing something wrong, plaintiffs could not avail themselves of the disparate impact standard.[280] Absent an identifiable practice with disparate impact, plaintiffs had to show a pattern of intentional discrimination. This they could do either by combining a statistical disparity with proof of intentional discrimination in some cases (which plaintiffs did not attempt), or by showing that the statistical disparity was inconsistent with any explanation other than intentional discrimination by the defendant.

The problem with EEOC's case was not, as Williams alleges, that the persuasiveness of Rosenberg's testimony *changed* the evidentiary standard from one of disparate impact to one of intent. The problem was that EEOC's failure to plead a prima facie case of disparate impact prevented it from *availing itself* of that standard. Thus, Zillah Eisenstein is simply inaccurate when she writes, "the legal question at issue was whether discrimination was a plausible explanation for the statistical disparity between men's and women's positions in the company."[281] Because the plaintiffs failed to identify any practice producing that disparity, the legal question at issue was whether discrimination by defendant was the *only possible* explanation.

---

[278] Trial transcript quoted in Eisenstein, *The Female Body and the Law*, 111.

[279] *E.E.O.C. v. Sears* at 1281–82.

[280] Ibid., 1285.

[281] Eisenstein, *The Female Body and the Law*, 110.

Rosenberg's sin, if sin it was, is that she was willing to testify in a legal context in which acknowledging that men and women are often socialized differently could cost women employment opportunities. But this hardly implies that cultural feminism inherently restricts women's opportunities. The real problem may be that law is *too little* influenced by the cultural feminist view that men and women are often socialized into distinct roles. An antidiscrimination law that took this process into account would require that work be so designed as to reward the socially vital responsibilities of nurturance and the economically useful and personally fulfilling virtue of cooperation.[282] This would loosen the link between the distribution of gender roles and the distribution of wealth and privilege and might undermine the reproduction of gender roles. There is nothing essentialist in recognizing that nurturing and educating the young is a socially necessary function and that any vision of human fulfillment that is incompatible with this function of reproducing human capital must be exploitative.

Like the charge of essentialism, the charge that cultural feminism is totalitarian is hyperbolic. This charge is largely directed against cultural feminism's Hegelian aspiration to achieve a community based on mutual recognition. To deconstructive feminists such as Young and Cornell, the idea that individual identity is constituted and conferred by the recognition of others suppresses individuality and rationalizes coerced conformity. Individuals, they argue, cannot be totally circumscribed by their social contexts; their "difference" is not merely relational because their identities are iterable, or transportable to a new context of social relations.

Young offers a crude caricature of the Hegelian ideal of mutual recognition in developing a Derridean critique of the communitarianism of cultural feminist Seyla Benhabib. Young argues that "the ideal of community participates in what Derrida calls the metaphysics of presence . . . , a metaphysics that denies difference. The ideal of community presumes that subjects can understand one another as they understand themselves. It thus denies the difference between subjects."[283] Young points out that such a vision of community would be futile, since individuals are not transparently self-aware. We cannot understand others as ourselves if we do not understand ourselves.[284] But is the naive assumption that individuals are transparently self-aware inherent in the value of community? Young endorses Hegel's claim that others understand us better than we understand ourselves[285] but ignores its implication that we need relations with others in order to understand ourselves.[286] Thus community is created not by allowing the other to see us through our own eyes, but by allowing the other to see herself through our eyes.

[282] Christine A. Littleton, "Reconstructing Sexual Equality," 75 *California Law Review* (1987): 1279.
[283] Iris Marion Young, "The Ideal of Community and the Politics of Difference," *in Feminism/Post-Modernism* (Durham: Duke Univ. Press), 300, 302.
[284] Ibid., 310.
[285] Ibid., 309–11.
[286] Georg Wilhelm Friedrich Hegel, *The Phenomenology of Mind*, trans. James Black Baillie (New York: Harper & Row, 1967), 218–40.

In no way does the Hegelian dialectic of recognition deny the alterity of the other; to the contrary, its dynamism depends upon "difference."

Cornell also sees the Hegelian ideal of mutual recognition as totalitarian. According to Cornell, the idea that individual identity is socially conferred permits the Hegelian to pretend to recognize the Other while refusing to recognize her Otherness. Hegelian recognition is therefore another form of mastery. She ascribes such a critique to Derrida:

> For Derrida, Hegel remains a classic example of how the so-called recognition of identity through difference not only privileges identity over difference, but does so through the projection of the Other as only Other to me and, therefore, not truly other at all. For Derrida, the classic example in Hegel . . . is the ironic denial of Woman's otherness, her feminine specificity, in his very projection of her as the Other to Man.[287]

In Cornell's view, recognition is simply a form of appropriation reminiscent of colonial occupation: "Reason as a selection principle denies certain groups, peoples and nations 'actuality,' on the grounds that they are incidental to the narrative of reason in history. . . . In its worst form, Hegel's unifying spirit becomes a 'justification' for the imperialism of the West."[288]

But the concept of recognition attacked by Cornell bears little resemblance to Hegelian recognition as interpreted by cultural feminists like Benjamin. Benjamin presents recognition as a dynamic relationship that continuously transforms both participants. It is a mutual appropriation in which both terms are used up and something new arises in their place. Thus conceived, recognition does not lead to a static unity that dissolves the differences between people. To the contrary, it uses the differences between persons to continuously regenerate difference— change—within persons. As interpreted by Benjamin, then, Hegel's dialectic of recognition was a poststructuralist figure that anticipated Derrida's concept of iterability.

Cornell herself reiterates many of the themes of cultural feminism in *Beyond Accommodation: Ethical Feminism, Deconstruction and the Law*,[289] in which her antagonist is Catherine MacKinnon. MacKinnon has criticized cultural feminism on the grounds that patriarchy is so hegemonic that women's voices are entirely a product of male power.[290] Invoking Derrida, Cornell reasons that if all texts are indeterminate, internally contradictory, and self-subverting, so too is patriarchy. Following out the liberal individualist valences in Derrida, Cornell reasons that like any other culture, patriarchy presupposes a reader. This reader achieves something like an individual subjectivity in interpreting the indeterminate text of her culture. Hence, women are capable of fashioning insurgent values out of the materials of a thoroughly patriarchal culture.

[287] Cornell, *Philosophy of the Limit*, 171.

[288] Ibid., 21.

[289] Cornell, *Beyond Accommodation*.

[290] Conversation between Carol Gilligan and Catherine MacKinnon, in James McCormick Mitchell Lecture, "Feminist Discourse, Moral Values and the Law—A Conversation," *Buffalo Law Review* 34 (1985): 11.

This argument presents subjectivity as modal—a unique way of performing an iterable social role—rather than essential. To MacKinnon's slogan that feminism must be "unmodified," or relentlessly critical of women's conditions, Cornell responds that feminism is "always modified."[291] The Derridean principle of iterability means that nothing can be unmodified or unadulterated, including patriarchy. Hence, feminism is itself a modification or modal transformation of patriarchal culture.

Cornell's rhetorical strategy in both books is to use Derrida's deconstruction to create space for woman's voice within a structuralist account of gender domination. By these means she achieves a dynamic, contingent account of female identity that resembles the dialectical accounts offered by cultural feminists. While both Cornell and Benjamin develop a culturally contingent notion of individuality, however, there are crucial differences. For Benjamin, individuality is an achievement only of the just society and is not to be confused with the feminine virtues that, though undervalued, are aspects of a confining social role. For Cornell, by contrast, individuality is inevitable, either because it inheres in the act of reading texts, or because it inheres in the sensations of the body. On either account, the value of woman's voice consists in the authenticity of individual women's voices. The view that individuality is inevitable precludes any critique that, like Young's, charges a given society with maldistributing opportunities to develop individuality.

Notwithstanding the expected tensions between deconstructive and cultural feminism, the more striking point is their convergence. While purporting to refute or correct cultural feminism, deconstructive feminists arrive at an interpretation and indictment of instrumental culture quite similar to that offered by cultural feminism. And despite their reputation for "essentialism" and "totalization," cultural feminists seem to offer a conception of gender identity as contingent, as dynamic, as poststructuralist as any offered by deconstructive feminism. In sum, we incline to think that postmodern feminism learns much more from cultural feminism than from deconstruction, but we see it as a promising endeavor because of its attention to the contingent cultural setting of identity formation.

CONCLUSION

Deconstruction, as practiced by Jacques Derrida, combines three elements: a pragmatist epistemology of reading, a critical reading strategy consisting in the exposure of "traces" of metaphysical essentialism within any text, and a polemical attack on Romantic radicalism that associates it with totalitarianism. Thus, the politics of deconstruction is at odds with the democratic, communitarian, and anti-elitist values cherished by many of its American proponents. This does not prevent leftist American legal scholars from adopting Derrida's reading strategies, which can be used to criticize any text regardless of content. Yet they have used

[291] Cornell, *Beyond Accommodation*, 119.

these reading strategies in ways that seem inconsistent with both the epistemological premises and normative implications of deconstruction.

Critical legal scholars have often seen deconstruction through the lens of the debate over objectivity in interpretation. This has caused them to read Derrida's basically pragmatic rejection of metaphysical "essentialism" and epistemological foundationalism as a skeptical critique of interpretation. Yet skepticism presumes that epistemological foundations must be established for knowledge to be legitimate; pragmatism presumes that because such foundations cannot be established they cannot be necessary.

Feminist legal scholars have often seen the deconstructive notions of difference and iterability as useful in arguing for greater attention to the excluded voices of women and other subordinated groups. Yet the deconstructive critique of "presence" implies that exclusion, reduction, mediation, and representation are all inevitable; and that the ideals of full inclusion, unmediated communication, and authentic self-expression are sentimental myths. For Derrida this kind of sentimentality evokes fascist politics and the aesthetics of kitsch.

Thus, deconstructive criticism of law suffers from self-contradiction. Moreover, because it is aimed at the breathtakingly broad target of Western metaphysics, it has little interesting to say about law in particular. Deconstructive criticism of law views law as a language subject to semiotic analysis in the structuralist tradition, and views all language as literary language that subverts or deconstructs the structure that gives it meaning. Because it treats law as literary only in that law is a kind of language, deconstructive criticism cannot view law as having any distinctive cultural or political role that sets it apart from other social practices. Nor can it investigate how law generates meaning in different ways in different historical settings.

In our remaining chapter, we will develop a more promising version of the Law as Literature trope, one that treats law not as a semiotic process, but as a cultural practice of representing, contesting, and negotiating identities. The simultaneous appeal of the cultural feminist view that norms are rooted in cultural identities, and the poststructuralist view of such identities as contingent, raises interesting questions about legal disputes. To what extent do legal disputes presuppose shared identity, and to what extent do they involve contests between competing identities? If indeed identities are contingent on some process of collective choice, should we see normative disputes as settings in which such choices are made? Are these also the settings in which individuals claim or repudiate identities, donning selves like costumes? As we begin to conceive normative disputes in more dramaturgic terms, we can identify a new role for literary criticism of law. Rather than indulging skepticism or sentimentality, we can apply literary analysis to the drama of particular legal disputes and legal transformations, to better understand what is truly at stake. Whether we are bent on describing normative conflict or prescribing its solution, we will do better if we understand that it is the very identities of the participants that are at issue. If we do so, we may realize some of the unfulfilled promise of the literary criticism of law.

CHAPTER SIX

Cultural Criticism of Law

INTRODUCTION

A familiar view of law in modern society presumes that the coercive force of the state must be justified by consent: the consent of individuals to private arrangements or the consent of populations to public policies. Legal judgment, then, polices the disputed boundaries between public and private, mine and thine, consent and coercion. The fundamental operation of law is to identify legal persons, entitlements, and preferences; when law has identified all of these, it has fully represented society. On this view of law, authority is vested solely in human will, and it is the essentially mimetic task of law to reflect and enforce that will.

Much critical scholarship in law accepts the premise that law should mimic social will but then argues that law either does not or cannot do so. It is argued that the lines between public and private, mine and thine, and consent or coercion are arbitrary and cannot themselves be based in consent. Accordingly, it is the personal interests or contestable value judgments of officials, not the preferences of society, that resolve legal disputes. The only defense against this official discretion is a system of formal rules. Yet, the argument continues, these rules yield arbitrary results. By blinding legal decision makers to nuances of social context, rule formalism achieves results that popular will would reject as irrational; it distorts or ignores the preferences of affected parties and presents this indifference to its human consequences as a virtue.

This style of criticism courts the twin dangers of skepticism and sentimentalism. Criticism is egregiously skeptical when it treats practices as presumptively illegitimate unless they rest on a foundation of epistemological certainty. Since subjective judgment and reductive formalism are both useful tools of practical reasoning, they should not by themselves discredit legal decision making. Criticism is egregiously sentimental when it assumes that subjective judgment and reductive formalism, even if necessary to practical reasoning, are always inappropriate when applied to human beings. *How* human beings should be represented in social thought is a pressing moral question, but *whether* they should be represented is not. Criticism that can be dismissed as egregiously skeptical or sentimental ill serves the values that motivate it.

The dangers of skepticism and sentimentality are endemic to criticism that accepts the mimetic ideal of law as the accurate depiction of social will. It only makes sense to criticize law for inaccurately representing individual or collective preferences if preferences have a determinate character independent of their legal representations. A more sophisticated and less fragile critique recognizes that

social will may not be independent of its legal representation. Individual preferences depend upon socially conferred identities and socially distributed resources;
collective preferences depend on the method by which they are measured and the
order in which alternatives are posed. Because all of these conditions affecting
preferences are themselves influenced by law, law cannot simply reflect but must
also help compose society and its characters.

Thus, the legal representation of social will bears little resemblance to scientific
observation. It is more like the literary representation of such generic themes as
"the pastoral" and "the sublime," familiar myths such as Faust and Don Juan,
or stock characters such as Reynard the Fox and the hardboiled gumshoe. Like
preferences, none of these entities exists independent of its representations. These
representations are judged aesthetically rather than epistemologically: they are
judged according to the experience they enable rather than their truth to actual
experience. So too we can judge law aesthetically, according to the society it
forms, the identities it defines, the preferences it encourages, and the subjective
experience it enables. We can "read" and criticize law as part of the making of a
culture.

In this chapter we expound such a cultural criticism of law. In our view, critical
scholarship treats law as a dimension of culture insofar as it:

1. Views law as an arena for the performance and contestation of representations of self and as an influence on the roles and identities available to groups
and individuals in portraying themselves.

2. Interprets self-portrayal as a project that, whatever its instrumental pay-
offs, also has aesthetic and expressive import.

3. Treats the interests and preferences that motivate instrumental action as
dependent upon the identities actors assume.

The enterprise we propose would place legal critique roughly within the emergent interdisciplinary movement of cultural studies.[1] This movement has blurred
the boundaries between the humanities and the social sciences by viewing the
phenomena studied by political scientists, sociologists, economists, and historians
as social "texts" available for interpretation and criticism. It has also extended
the domain of ethnographic method from the study of traditional non-Western
societies to modern Western societies, thereby both expanding anthropology and
raising critical questions about the cultural assumptions that have confined it in
the past. A closely aligned movement in literary studies, "the New Historicism,"
has in essence made literary criticism an instrument of the ethnography or archaeology of modernity by treating literary texts as cultural artifacts.[2] But our proposal
is not just that legal phenomena be viewed as cultural artifacts or "social texts"

---

[1] Lawrence Grossberg, Cary Nelson, and Paula Treichler, eds., *Cultural Studies* (Princeton: Princeton Univ. Press, 1992).

[2] See generally Brook Thomas, *The New Historicism and Other Old-Fashioned Topics* (New York:
Routledge, 1991).

like any others. It is that legal forms and legal processes play a compositional role in modern culture—that cultural criticism must attend to the legal dimension of culture or remain superficial.

In this chapter we will consider examples of cultural representation in two sorts of legal settings. First we will review scholarship reading the representations of parties in a number of disputes: the Chicago Seven trial, the Klaus Barbie war crimes trial, trials of Catholics in seventeenth-century England, the appellate case of *Bowers v. Hardwick*, the Mashpee Indian lands trial, medieval Icelandic blood feuds, and violent street encounters that determine status in the underworld. These disputes take on expressive meaning for their participants against a background of legal and social norms regulating or recognizing statuses and identities. These norms enable actors to define themselves and one another, or to subvert those definitions.

Second, we will consider examples of the representation of character, credit, and value in commercial and financial law. The premise of this discussion is that commercial capitalism is not only a system of economics, but also a system of representation. The mobilization of resources for production depends upon the cultural work of representing them as commodities, while the disposition of what is produced depends upon the cultural work of constructing the characters who will make investment and consumption decisions. We will begin with ethnographies of exchange in a precommercial society and in a traditional society experiencing modernization. We will proceed through an account of the cultural conditions for the emergence of lending at interest and bankruptcy in early modern England, to a consideration of the cultural significance of the emergence of new forms of intangible property in nineteenth-century America. We will find that the legal forms of wealth and exchange mark the shifting, often contested boundaries between community and commerce, between intrinsic and instrumental worth.

These examples inform our conclusion that law neither reflects nor distorts a social world of subjects that exists independent of it. Instead law helps compose the social world: it is implicated both in degrading and commodifying once sacred spheres of cultural value and in making new values. Law, then, is best evaluated not for how well it represents us, but for who it enables us to become.

6.1 THEORETICAL SOURCES FOR CULTURAL CRITICISM OF LAW

We will begin by explicating a range of theoretical sources that can inform such a cultural criticism. These will include the anthropologist Clifford Geertz's account of the emerging phenomenon of interdisciplinarity in the humanities and social sciences; Nietzsche's account of self-development as an aesthetic project; Foucault's account of individual personality in modern society as a projection of institutional power; social theorist Pierre Bourdieu's accounts of practical action as a kind of cultural improvisation, and of aesthetic taste as the pursuit of "symbolic power"; and "New Historicist" Stephen Greenblatt's treatment of artistic creativity as an "exchange" of "energy" between the economic and symbolic orders. These fragments of theory converge on an understanding of modern social order as dependent on culture, of culture as centrally concerned with the representation of persons, populations, and institutions; and of the representation of persons, populations, and institutions as a way of illuminating social and moral values. With this view of culture in mind, we hope to "read" legal representations of society critically, but neither skeptically nor sentimentally.

Interdisciplinarity

That law can be read as a literary text is only a helpful claim if it tells us something about either law or literature that we did not otherwise know. Connecting disparate forms of discourse illuminates only when it enables new answers by bringing different questions into view.

Our general assumption is that fertile interdisciplinary study entails discomfiture. Hailing the "blurring" of generic lines between the social sciences and humanities, Clifford Geertz has argued that the application of the methods or premises of one discipline to another seems necessarily "discomposing":

> It is discomposing not only because who knows where it will all end, but because as the idiom of social explanation, its inflections and its imagery, changes, our sense of what constitutes such explanation, why we want it, and how it relates to other sorts of things we value changes as well. It is not just theory or method or subject matter that alters, but the whole point of the enterprise.[3]

Geertz notes that much social theory of behavior, formerly cast in causal, supposedly scientific terms, has recently been getting rewrought as game theory or dramaturgy: society is less a machine than "a serious game, a sidewalk drama, or a behavioral text."[4] The aggregations of human conduct that make up the world of the social scientist—class interests, efficient markets, and the like—are, to use the ubiquitous academic platitude, "cultural constructs" that inform social action as well as social research. In discerning patterns in social behavior or cultural practice, the scholar does not misapprehend them as irreducible constraints or irresistible forces of locomotion. For Geertz, they are neither the way the world really is, nor are they merely regulative fictions. Rather, they are collectively invented and reproduced contexts for assuming certain social roles. By focusing on how social actors conceive and model society, cultural analyses of society "replace the slide with the mirror," forcing social scientists to look back up the barrel of the microscope at themselves.

But if this sort of social-textual analysis discomfits the social scientist, it simultaneously frustrates the humanist who believes in willed or idealistic individual

---

[3] Clifford Geertz, *Local Knowledge: Further Essays in Interpretive Anthropology* (New York: Basic Books, 1983), 8.

[4] Ibid., 23.

conduct. Reinterpreted as role playing, the exercise of moral choice or aesthetic sensibility is reduced to involuntary participation in ritual, or cynical posing. As Geertz says in a passage particularly relevant to the Law and Literature enterprise, the reconstruction of standard explanations of behavior "sits rather poorly with traditional humanistic pieties."[5] As the foundational assumptions of one discipline become reconstructed according to the assumptions of another, the first discipline loses some of its gravity and independence. Gaming and aesthetic theories of behavior "conduce to a nervous and nervous-making style of interpretation . . . that mixes a strong sense of the formal orderliness of things with an equally strong sense of the radical arbitrariness of that order."[6] Thus, the interdisciplinary subversion of the dignity of the individual agent can come from disparate, seemingly incompatible sources. A structuralist reading of apparently rational economic behavior reinterprets it as role playing—possibly strategic but not, in any sense, straightforwardly instrumental. Conversely, a materialist account of the conditions of artistic production undermines the dignity of the artist precisely by portraying her as a rational utility maximizer—less an author than a copywriter, a shill.

The lesson of Geertzian interdisciplinarity is that Law and Literature scholarship ought to constitute an experiment in rebuilding the aesthetic in legal terms or the legal in aesthetic terms. It might show how literary apprehensions of social or pyschological reality borrow from the legal apprehension of social and psychological reality. Or it might show some symbiosis or conspiracy between the legal control of political energy and the cultural forms of imaginative meaning making we normally associate with the literary. Whatever the specific insights, the value of such research resides not in any confirmation of the power of a single method to subject an ever broader domain of data to a sovereign theory, but in an artful disjunction of method and data to illuminate a particular society's images of and beliefs about itself. In this way, interdisciplinary interrogation, in Geertz's terms, should not establish "interdisciplinary brotherhood" but offer instead a "conceptual wrench," or "a sea change in our notion not so much of what knowledge is but of what it is we want to know."[7]

As the "New Historicist" literary critic Stephen Greenblatt has said, literature normally functions within a culture in three ways: "as a manifestation of the concrete behavior of its particular author, as itself the expression of the codes by which behavior is shaped, and as a reflection upon those codes."[8] If literary criticism limits itself to the analysis of any one of these functions, it risks various forms of reductionism. A reading of the first sort might deteriorate into isolated literary biography. The second sort of reading can devolve into vulgar ideological "superstructure" analysis. The third risks a drift into extreme Arnoldian detachment, sacri-

---

[5] Ibid., 25.

[6] Ibid., 24–25.

[7] Ibid., 34.

[8] Stephen J. Greenblatt, *Renaissance Self-Fashioning: From More to Shakespeare* (Chicago: Univ. of Chicago Press, 1980), 4.

ficing a sense of art's concrete role in culture in the name of dry timeless verities. Greenblatt's alternative, which he calls a "more cultural or anthropological criticism,"[9] addresses all of these functions and rests on a few basic convictions:

> that men are born "unfinished animals," that the facts of life are less artless than they look, that particular cultures are inevitably drawn to a metaphorical grasp of reality, that anthropological interpretation must address itself less to the mechanics of customs and institutions than to the interpretive constructions the members of a society apply to their experiences.[10]

Thus, Greenblatt strives both to avoid effacing authorial inventiveness and to avoid idealizing that inventiveness as a quality discontinuous with practical social life. The author's inventiveness becomes an exemplar of the inventiveness immanent in much social interaction not ordinarily distinguished as "aesthetic." When we examine legal texts in this spirit,

> their significance for us is not that we may see through them to underlying and prior historical principles but rather that we may interpret the interplay of their symbolic structures with those perceivable in the careers of their authors and in the larger social world as constituting a single, complex process of self-fashioning and, through this interpretation, come closer to understanding how literary and social identities were formed in this culture. That is, we are able to achieve a concrete apprehension of the consequences for human expression—for the "I"—of a specific form of power, power at once localized in particular institutions—the court, the church, the colonial administration, the patriarchal family—and diffused in ideological structures of meaning, characteristic modes of expression, recurrent narrative patterns.[11]

The natural focus of such cultural criticism is imaginative literature, since "among artists the will to be the culture's voice—to create the abstract and brief chronicles of the time—is a commonplace." Nevertheless, Greenblatt notes that "the same will may extend beyond art."[12] Literature, then, "does not pretend to autonomy," because it is part of our everyday practice of representing and interpreting our social surroundings. This is true not only in the sense that the "construction" of a social situation requires inventiveness, but also in the sense that what we do not invent we appropriate from literary convention. Thus, we "read" our social surroundings with the help of familiar plots, characters, and sensibilities.

Self-Creation and Cultural Criticism

Many of the major theorists of culture who dwell in the world of postmodernism owe much to Nietzsche's philosophy, which joins together a hermeneutic ontology, a vitalist aesthetics, and a perfectionist ethics. We can start with Nietzsche's

---

[9] Ibid.
[10] Ibid.
[11] Ibid., 5–6.
[12] Ibid.

carefully hedged perspectivism, and his central argument that the world is sensibly viewed as a text subject to aesthetic interpretation.[13]

To describe the world as an interpreted text is not to say it has essential features that are hidden or distorted by human interpretation. Rather, according to Nietzsche's perspectivism, it is that by itself the world has no features at all, so that there is nothing to rightly or wrongly represent. The apparent world is not distinct from reality but is simply the world as it appears to any being who needs to survive in it and who must therefore arrange it selectively for her own purposes. Reality is not behind appearances—it is the total of those appearances. All perception is selective and aesthetic, and so to try to grasp everything is to grasp nothing.[14]

Perspectivism is not the same as relativism, which implies that multiple equally true claims can be made about the same object. Perspectives are not propositions or opinions about a reality that exists independent of them. Nietzsche insists that no particular point of view is epistemologically superior in the sense of affording those who occupy it a better picture of the world as it really is, but his position does not imply that all points of view are equally valuable.[15]

Perspectivism is not a stance of skeptical or aesthetic detachment. Perspectives cannot be adopted or discarded at will, but rather must make sense within a life. Thus, to develop a new interpretative perspective is no casual matter since it means living one's life differently. Perspectivism also differs from the ontological pluralism of modernism. An object can have many determinate characters and not be indeterminate. Though there cannot be a complete theory that explains everything, the world does have a distinct character at particular times in history because certain perspectives become dominant over others. The distribution of perspectives in a society and the relationships among them, at one time or over time, may have a distinct shape—at least from the perspective of a particular observer.

For Nietzsche, the phenomenon of human will is like all other things in the world—an interpretation. Subjectivity is merely the sum of its effects; it is not a given or an essence but is rather a fiction made out of the acts of one person, or many. In this sense, to ascribe causal will or motivation—to one's self, to other persons, to an institution or group—is to invent a literary character. Like a character in fiction or drama, a person is simply the sum of all the things she does or says. The character is related to each of her statements or actions not as substance to attribute but as whole to part. And the same is true for any person or institution to which we ascribe identity. Ascribing identity to the disparate acts of one or more persons means writing a narrative fiction, a "genealogy" that identifies a

[13] The interpretation of Nietzsche offered here draws especially on Alexander Nehamas, *Nietzsche: Life as Literature* (Cambridge: Harvard Univ. Press, 1985).

[14] "Facts are precisely what there is not, only interpretations." Ibid., 42 (quoting Friedrich Nietzsche, *The Will to Power*, trans. Walter Kaufmann and R. J. Hollingdale [New York: Vintage Books, 1968], 481).

[15] Nehamas, *Nietzsche: Life as Literature*, 3.

motivated character with origins and obligations, grievances and grudges, unfulfilled quests and unpaid debts.

Nietzsche called the practices and beliefs of our culture "interpretation" because every view of the world enables and is enabled by a particular kind of life and therefore presupposes and manifests particular values and interests. For Nietzsche, it is not that the world is indeterminate, but that it has a diversity of people who cannot all live by the same values. That a perspective is not just a way of seeing but a way of living implies that Nietzsche's perspectivism is not just an epistemology or ontology, but an ethics. Philosophy's goal is to help us become more self-conscious about our selectivity, more aware of the contingency of what we see on the way we live.[16] The point of this self-consciousness is to place in question not the truth of what we see, but the value of that way of seeing. If one comes to see one's own sensibility as impoverished or boorish, the appropriate response is to change the way one lives. Thus, the use of philosophy is not to escape the perspectival limits inherent in living, but to enhance our capacity to choose the limits we will live within, and our responsibility for that choice. It is this self-shaping capacity that Nietzsche refers to as "power."[17]

We may abdicate this power in a variety of ways. We may accept the naturalness of our world and repress awareness of our own interpretive activity. We may acknowledge the artifice in our world and become paralyzed by skepticism. We may acknowledge that our beliefs are necessarily subjective but treat them as self-justifying, as an expression of integrity or authenticity. We may treat our perspectives as an arbitrary matter of taste, incapable of justification, and lapse into complacent cynicism. Finally, we may be persuaded to deepen our sensibilities by philosophical argument, or be inspired to do so by exemplary works of art. But if we merely imitate the sensibility of the powerful philosopher or artist, we have not exercised our own self-shaping power. All of these responses weaken and demean us; but all are tempting because to self-consciously shape one's own perspective—to " 'give style' to one's character"[18]—is hard and painful work.

Much of the postmodernism and poststructuralism that derives from Nietzsche insists that just as we must challenge the assumption of a tangible world of objects that the human "subject" can examine, we must also challenge the even more basic assumption of a bounded and definable subject. As Alexander Nehamas notes, much thought after Nietzsche accepts this challenge, but in such a way as to underscore that the "aesthetic" project of making a consciousness for oneself is a thoroughly ethical act. For Nietzsche, aesthetics and ethics are aspects of the single enterprise of value making. All normative issues ultimately translate into

---

[16] In noting that certain ascetic ideals are present in the lives of "all the great, fruitful, inventive spirits," Nietzsche maintains that these people do not see these ideals as duties or virtues, but rather as "the most appropriate and natural conditions of their best existence." Ibid., 116 (quoting Friedrich Nietzsche, *On the Genealogy of Morals*, trans. Walter Kaufmann and R. J. Hollingdale [New York: Vintage Books, 1968], 8).

[17] E.g., Nehamas, *Nietzsche: Life as Literature*, 70–125.

[18] Ibid., 185–86; see Friedrich Nietzsche, *The Gay Science*, trans. Walter Kaufmann (New York: Random House, 1974), 290.

the question of how individuals compose themselves as subjects of their actions and experiences, a part of the more general material formation of humanity.

The quality and originality of sensibility individuals bring to the interpretation of their world is, for Nietzsche, an urgent ethical question. This gives literature and the other imaginative arts a special ethical and political significance. First, insofar as reading literature is interpretive activity, it is one occasion for expressing and developing an interpretive sensibility. In this respect reading literature is continuous with the rest of life. But literature and the other imaginative arts are also ethical models for living insofar as they manifest such virtues as originality, aesthetic value, self-discipline, and artistic integrity. The ethical reader is obliged to compose herself in such a way as to be open to the ethical lesson literature teaches. This entails a cognitive capacity to appreciate the virtues it manifests—an emotional capacity to be inspired to emulate them and the requisite imaginative capacity to emulate the work's originality rather than to merely imitate the work's sensibility. The cognitive capacity required of the ethical reader includes sufficient acculturation to appreciate how an author works within generic traditions, as well as the ways in which the author works with and on these traditions to articulate an original sensibility. The literary work's character in revising or criticizing its own cultural origins provides a model for normative inventiveness in the conduct of a life. Creating new values always means critically elaborating a culture, continuing a narrative fiction in a way that surprises us and yet so transforms our perceptions of what came before as to seem necessary and inevitable in retrospect.[19]

Nietzsche's location of the artistic sensibility and the artistic work within a larger culture gives his value theory a political dimension. But in approaching Nietzsche's politics we must avoid being misled by his celebration of "power." For Nietzsche, "power" was not a political term at all, but an ethical and aesthetic one. Nietzschean power is personal, not interpersonal. Ceding power to others is an ethical violation—in this Nietzsche anticipated and inspired the Sartrean critique of collaboration with authority. And it perverts power to render it political.

Nietzsche's own political ideas are bound up with his understanding of the contrast between classical and modern society. In classical Greece, a harmonious and homogeneous culture provided a structured path to collective participation in virtue. Public rhetoric and theater not only taught virtue but engaged the public in its ceremonial enactment. Tragedy, in particular, authoritatively expressed what it meant to be Athenian, so that it was able to establish the collective understanding necessary for deliberating about an authentically collective good. This shared understanding allowed political deliberation to refine and realize the capabilities not of the individual participants but of the polity itself.[20]

Tragedy used emotion to identify its audience with an exemplary self. The tragic hero is challenged by fate, but—with the vicarious participation of the

---

[19] Nehamas, *Nietzsche: Life as Literature*, 95–98, 111–13.
[20] Ibid., 42–43.

audience—nobly maintains a stable self in the face of suffering.[21] The shared public experience of contradiction evoked by tragedy, a contradiction not just of propositions but of feelings, was the source of its power to instruct, provoke, and ennoble. Nietzsche saw Socrates as the archenemy of this fertile antinomianism, bent on banishing the experience of contradiction to the realm of appearance and positing an invisible world of eternal verity in its place.[22] In Nietzsche's eyes, this disastrous separation of philosophy from poetry purported to relieve suffering by making "reality" an escape from the apparent world, yet it diminished human life by denying the validity of passion. Platonic idealism would spawn what was, for Nietzsche, the catastrophe of Christian world-denial, and start humanity down the slide from classical virtue to petty bourgeois respectability.

In modern society, Nietzsche maintained, the civic inculcation of virtue was no longer possible. The world was disenchanted, and authoritative cultural values could no longer keep or deserve the allegiance of the self-respecting. But the tragic consequence of this disenchantment was that the self could no longer gain stability through consensus and ritual. Thus, the dislocations attendant upon modernization not only imposed suffering but also stripped the self of its acculturated capacity to survive suffering. Liberalism collaborated in this spiritual atrocity, because in the name of neutrality and tolerance it abandoned the self to a realm of private taste insulated from any societal concern. Nor could political authoritarianism substitute for the lost cultural authority of virtue: Nietzsche rejected the power politics of Bismarck precisely because Bismarck used political means to secure nonpolitical ends and thus left the world in a state of dispirited disenchantment. Only art, not politics, could recover virtue in the wake of modernization.[23]

But the virtue attainable in modern society was a different kind of virtue. Modern virtue could not be the collective achievement of a culture defined by a shared sensibility. Instead virtue was the personal achievement of "power," and the creative artist was its paradigm. Yet the pursuit of artistic virtue still required a conducive culture—one with rich generic traditions, discerning audiences, and above all other ambitious artists. The cultural function of art was no longer the inculcation of an authoritative and collective identity but the provocation of others to fashion distinctive sensibilities of their own. The heroic figure of the artist replaced the tragic hero as icon of virtue, and the aspiration to re-create the culture replaced the aspiration to exemplify it.

The political dimension of Nietzsche's value theory lies in his concern for the cultural conditions of artistic creation and hence self-creation. While virtue was no longer common, the conditions of its exercise remained a common good. By developing and expressing a powerful sensibility one contributed to the common good, and by remaining indifferent to the self-demeaning complacency of others one detracted from it. In this sense, cultural criticism was a political obligation

---

[21] Ibid., 118–19.
[22] Ibid., 212–13.
[23] Ibid.

in modern society. The mutual provocation provided by artistic self-expression and cultural criticism was the modern equivalent of deliberative politics.

Although repulsed by authoritarianism, Nietzsche was unconcerned with the liberal problem of regulating the encounters of independent selves to minimize tyranny. From a Nietzschean perspective, this liberal project is pointless unless we have meaningful selves in the first place. The crucial question is not how to protect the self from invasion but how to strengthen the self's capacity to define and defend its own boundaries: not how we can preserve ourselves, but what kind of selves we ought to have.

Nietzsche's virtue-driven value theory may seem perfectionist, but the charge that he would have approved enslaving the many to produce one perfect work of art is a caricature. Nietzsche's concern was human virtue, not artistic merit—the art of living rather than the work of art. Whether human virtue is optimally distributed according to a principle of maximizing the average level of virtue in society, or the virtuousness of the most virtuous, or of the least virtuous, he neither said nor cared. Nietzsche was concerned with the "revaluation of all values," not their scaling and measurement.[24] The accounting questions that obsess welfare economists and theorists of justice, the debates over maximean, maximin, and maximax, would no doubt have struck Nietzsche as symptoms of a shopkeeper's morality.

Postmodern Social Theory: Discipline and Practice

Contemporary cultural criticism may be thought of as extending Nietzsche's perspectivism more fully into the social sphere, where we find collective acts of identity formation. Cultural history, then, focuses on the complex evolution of these social characters, viewing them as artistic creations that also provide highly pragmatic solutions to political and economic problems.

In *The Passions and the Interests*[25] the economist Albert Hirschman reviews how early capitalist society "invented" a new human figure: the rationally "interested" man whose preferences became the foundational elements of utilitarianism and capitalism. For Foucault, this interest-bearing person was the creature and instrument of a new disciplinary society. In *Discipline and Punish* Foucault identifies the new "human sciences" of the modern period as "disciplines" in that they discipline both the investigator and the object of investigation.[26] Disciplines are techniques of examining populations under controlled conditions that render them comparable, thereby defining them as objects not only of knowledge but also of

---

[24] Friedrich Nietzsche, *Ecce Homo*, in *Basic Writings of Nietzsche*, ed. and trans. Walter Kaufmann (New York: Modern Library, 1968), 782.

[25] Albert O. Hirschman, *The Passions and the Interests: Political Arguments for Capitalism before Its Triumph* (Princeton: Princeton Univ. Press, 1977).

[26] See Michel Foucault, *Discipline and Punish : The Birth of the Prison*, trans. Alan Sheridan (New York: Vintage Books, 1977); see also Michel Foucault, *The Order of Things: An Archaeology of the Human Sciences* (New York: Vintage Books, 1970), 344–45.

evaluation and regulation.[27] We can extend Hirschman by saying that to impose the instinct for preferences on people is to discipline them, if economically productive "interest" constrains the destructive passions. But "interest" solves another problem as well: interest is socially useful because it ensures predictable behavior. The predictable interests of others provide a determinate social environment within which to pursue one's own interests. Thus, interest solves an epistemological problem as well as an ethical one. If modern justifications for the exercise of power impose the need to measure the social world, the concept of interest gives us something to measure. In regulating behavior, interest provides the human sciences with those controlled conditions against which interests can be measured.

To the New Historicists, however, Foucault's "disciplinary" account of the "interested" subject leaves out the crucial dimension of what they call human "agency." In Foucault's view, power now does not exercise itself through individual human action or large state institutions, but is rather diffused through particular disciplinary mechanisms. Moreover, the disciplinary mechanisms create characters or social roles to which we now must aspire (the normal child, the healthy body, the stable and obedient mind) and other deviant personas we must vigilantly avoid. Foucault offers histories of the modes by which these social subjects have been made, by which we see the "fault lines" between the norms that define proper subjects and the deviations that are ruled out of order.

For Foucault, the individuality conferred on persons by disciplinary investigation is merely a bureaucratic text—a dossier, case history, or transcript. Recognizing themselves as objects of bureaucratic knowledge, persons interpret their own experience and measure their own worth according to the generic conventions of the human sciences. They author themselves only in the sense that they sign their names to scripted confessions. As Pauline Rosenau points out, postmodernists tend to view the human subject as a mere effigy, a "construct," a linguistic invention.[28] Foucault's discussion of power tends to omit any language of intention or purpose while anthropomorphizing power itself. We see local manifestations of power, but this power is never held or exercised by anyone in particular. We are encouraged to assume, though never told, that behind these manifestations lies a coherent force that transcends them.

By contrast to Foucault's disciplinary analysis, the New Historicist emphasizes the role of creativity in the fashioning of subjectivity. In a New Historicist analysis, individuals or groups typically deploy aesthetic skill in concocting a moti-

---

[27] See Foucault, *Discipline and Punish*, 135–41, 170–77. For Foucault's study of philology, biology, and political economy, see Foucault, *The Order of Things*. For his examination of psychology, see Foucault, *Discipline and Punish*; *The History of Sexuality*, trans. Robert Hurley (New York: Random House, 1978); and *Madness and Civilization: A History of Insanity in the Age of Reason*, trans. Richard Howard (New York: Random House, 1965). For his discussion of medicine, see Foucault, *The Birth of the Clinic: An Archaeology of Medical Perception*, trans. A. M. Sheridan (New York: Random House, 1973).

[28] Pauline Marie Rosenau, *Post-Modernism and the Social Sciences: Insights, Inroads, and Intrusions* (Princeton: Princeton Univ. Press, 1992), 42–43.

vated self, an identity. This character, though often treated as a fixed determinant, is in fact endlessly renegotiated to meet changing circumstance. A New Historicist approach to law would seek the act of express creation in what for the "human scientist"—the economist, the policy analyst—is the mere manifestation of fixed preferences.

A more elaborate theoretical foundation for this enterprise may be sought in the anthropology of Pierre Bourdieu,[29] who has tried to reincorporate human action into the field of social forces without reviving the notion of an "authentic" or presocial human subject. For Bourdieu, social practice is a generative, organizing scheme, an imprecise but systematic principle of selection and realization, tending, through steadily directed adjustments and corrections, to eliminate errors and to conserve even fortuitous successes.

The key to understanding human action for Bourdieu is the "habitus." The habitus consists of (1) a repertoire of "behaviors" and gestures developed as a result of either deliberate inculcation, imitation or random processes of trial and error; (2) dispositions to so behave in response to certain situations; (3) the ability to interpret situations as calling for such behaviors; (4) experience deploying these behaviors with more or less success in unfamiliar situations; (5) experience modifying such behaviors in unfamiliar situations; (6) a repertoire of goals the actor experiences as appropriate and attainable for someone like herself. The temporal urgency of action limits practice to this repertoire of familiar behaviors, ends, and strategies of adaptation. This means that there is an automatic quality even to such apparently reflective choices as undertaking a feasibility study, comparison shopping, checking the weather report, or sacrificing a rook.[30]

The habitus is the residue of an individual's experience through which she has absorbed the accumulated experience of many others.[31] Practice involves bringing it to bear on a current situation for which it may be ill-adapted: "Only in imaginary experience . . . does the social world take the form of a universe of possibles equally possible for any possible subject ."[32] Thus, the habitus represents an individual or "subjective" factor in the analysis of social action, but the individuality consists as much in a confining quirkiness as in any freedom of maneuver. For while the habitus enables some choice and creative adaptation it is also the repository of past socialization or "discipline."

That practical activity is organized by the habitus implies that practical intelligence may be very different from the calculating rationality that economic theory ascribes to actors. Indeed, Bourdieu argues that economic rationality should itself

[29] Pierre Bourdieu, *Outline of a Theory of Practice*, trans. Richard Nice (New York: Cambridge Univ. Press, 1977).

[30] Ibid., 72–95; Pierre Bourdieu, *The Logic of Practice*, trans. Richard Nice (Cambridge: Polity Press, 1990), 66–79.

[31] Bourdieu, *The Logic of Practice*, 72 (defining "habitus" as "systems of durable, transposable dispositions, structured structures predisposed to function as structuring structures") (internal citation omitted).

[32] Ibid., 64.

be seen as a habitus: a set of coping skills peculiar to certain social groups, arising only out of the requisite socializing experiences, and sustainable only in the requisite life-situation. As Bourdieu explains,

> Economic theory which acknowledges only the rational "responses" of an indeterminate, interchangeable agent to "potential opportunities" . . . converts the immanent law of the economy into a universal norm of proper economic behavior. In so doing, it conceals the fact that the "rational" habitus which is the precondition for appropriate economic behavior is the product of [a] particular economic condition, the one defined by the possession of the economic and cultural capital required in order to seize the "potential opportunities" theoretically available to all.[33]

Bourdieu's practical actor may pursue any number of ends. But if there is a common motivation driving individuals along the tracks laid by socialization, it is honor rather than greed. Thus, practical action is at base less reflective, more ritualistic, and more idealistic than rational choice models would suggest. In the right social milieu, however, the pursuit of esteem can certainly habituate actors to economic rationality.

Bourdieu's focus on the decision making of the practical actor gives him a more flexible model of social order than that offered by structuralists like Foucault. Since there is always a gap between the conditions under which the actor was habituated and the context calling for urgent practical action, social orders do not function smoothly. The actor is always, to some extent, in the position of a judge trying to apply archaic rules to novel circumstances. Moreover, because all participants in a social order are in the same position, no actor can ever be sure how other actors will respond to her stratagem: Practical actors are habituated to cope with this uncertainty, to expect variation in the responses of others and the judgments of observers as to which responses are socially appropriate.

The job of the critic, in understanding social practice, is not to "decode" its symbolism but to restore its practical necessity by relating it to the conditions of its genesis. That any choice can be accounted for retroactively does not mean perfect predictability, because even the strictest rituals leave room for strategies. Thus, social practice does not have the rulelike quality of a juridical code. Nevertheless customary norms can order and constrain practice because when one judges another she marshalls schemes of perception and appreciation more or less operative in the habitus of other participants in the practice.

Even where the agents' habitus are perfectly harmonized and apparently predictable, uncertainty as to outcome remains so long as the sequence of their reciprocal actions is incomplete. Bourdieu's model of the interaction that is structured but nevertheless colored with narrative uncertainty is the gift exchange.[34] Here the very conventions of the practice preclude an immediate and in-kind reciprocation of the gift, imposing on the recipient of a gift a perhaps unwanted discretion

---

[33] Ibid., 63–64.
[34] Ibid., 98–111, 126.

to choose the moment and currency of response.[35] This gives the practice of gift exchange a gamelike quality, in which the moves are "ruled" by strategy, not rule.[36] Bourdieu's image of a social practice, in which the application of rules unfolds over time as a process involving discretion and the possibility of subversion by multiple actors, is applicable to processes of legal decision.[37]

Indeed, Bourdieu is particularly interested in practices like law, where decision-making discretion is vested in office. By virtue of their office, particular decision-makers exercise a personal power that, because it is not reduceable to force or wealth, is "symbolic," that is, an effect of meaning. Official authority, in other words, marks a formal boundary within a culture, a sphere of power relatively autonomous from other spheres.[38] Because there exist such relatively autonomous spheres, governed by mechanisms capable of imposing their necessity on agents, those who are in a position to command these mechanisms are able to dispense with strategies aimed expressly and directly at domination. Strategies like law, aimed at formally regulating a field of practice, "transmute 'egoistic,' private, particular interests . . . into disinterested, publicly avowable interests."[39]

For Bourdieu, the role of law is to "symbolically consecrate . . . power relation[s] between groups and classes" by recording them in a form that anchors them securely to other power relations, eliminating the practical utility of perceiving them as contingent or contestable.[40] Agents bind each other into simultaneously enabling and confining roles that preclude the exhibition of naked self-interest by clothing it with the interests of office. Thus, the symbolic or "legitimating" role of law is to prettify or obscure domination with the veil of enchanted relationships. Of course, whether the authority of office will be recognized on a given occasion or resisted is always a matter of suspense—its exercise is always a bet. This means that authoritative decision makers have a strategic interest in conserving or enhancing their authority or "symbolic capital."[41]

Neither authority nor symbolic capital is confined to state officials. It is vested in professionals by virtue of training and state certification, and is vested less securely—because less formally—in persons of high social status. In a rigid caste society, the social status and symbolic authority of each person might be clear. But in more fluid societies, certainly in modern society, social status is always at risk and always negotiable. In bourgeois society, a struggle ensues to "distinguish" one's self as a subjectivity worthy of decision-making competence by virtue of superior knowledge, refinement of taste, or self-control. "Distinction" always places one at a distinct remove from her origins or interests. It informs personal identity with the qualities of office.[42]

---

[35] Ibid., 4–8, 98–111, 126, 171–74.

[36] Ibid., 6.

[37] Ibid., 98–111.

[38] Ibid., 41–42, 108–10, 238–39.

[39] Ibid., 40.

[40] Ibid., 188.

[41] Bourdieu, *Outline of a Theory of Practice*, 171.

[42] Ibid., 187–88.

A number of propositions are implicit in Bourdieu's analysis of "symbolic power" and "distinction." First, every social interaction has a competitive or strategic dimension. Every interaction takes place within a general contest over cultural authority. Second, the "disciplining" process in modern society does not mechanically form actors but engages their active, avid participation. The achievement of bourgeois subjectivity requires effort and luck. Third, the display of literacy, aesthetic refinement, and rhetorical skill are all means of staking a claim to "distinction," social status, and symbolic capital. The "literary" use of language therefore has a practical, power-enhancing dimension. Fourth, the exercise and conservation of power depend upon an aesthetic and dramaturgic activity of playing "characters" to an audience. Finally, the exercise of authority is conditioned on both the social criteria for its exercise and the discretionary application of those criteria by particular social actors. In this sense, conserving authority involves a "negotiation" or "exchange" of "symbolic capital" with norms, institutions, and individuals:[43]

> Linguistic exchange . . . is also an economic exchange which is established within a particular symbolic relation of power between a producer, endowed with a certain linguistic capital, and a consumer (or a market), and which is capable of procuring a certain material or symbolic profit. In other words, utterances are not only . . . signs to be understood and deciphered . . . ; they are also signs of wealth, intended to be evaluated and appreciated, and signs of authority to be believed and obeyed.[44]

Identifying a practical, strategic dimension of meaning in all aesthetic activity, and an aesthetic dimension in all practical action, brings power and culture, law and literature onto the same field of play.

New Historicism

The New Historicism is an intellectual movement that fulfills many of Geertz's criteria for cultural criticism.[45] It is historical in the mundane sense that it studies old cultures as well as contemporary ones. It is new in that it draws on both conventional historical dimensions—most obviously political and economic history—as well as more contemporary dimensions—such as social and ethnographic history. And it is relevant to Law as Literature in at least two senses: First, in apprehending cultural forces that cut across the normal dimensions, it sees individuals and groups in the virtually dramaturgic acts of suffering, exploiting, and renegotiating the identities and interests that channel their participation in political and economic life. Second, it entertains the possibility that any social or political document can be read not only instrumentally but also aestheti-

---

[43] Ibid., 171–83.

[44] Pierre Bourdieu, *Language and Symbolic Power*, ed. Gino Raymond and Matthew Adamson, trans. John B. Thompson (Cambridge: Polity Press, 1991), 66.

[45] Stephen Greenblatt, "Towards a Poetics of Culture," in H. Aram Veeser, ed., *The New Historicism* (New York: Routledge, 1989), 1–14; see also Thomas, *The New Historicism*, 3–23 (providing a brief introduction to the goals of New Historicism).

cally, as describing the cultural forces that underlie its production and as reinterpreting cultural forms and norms. Texts are both socially produced and socially productive.

Like any somewhat self-described new movement, the New Historicism has been prolix in its manifestos, but citing a few key principles is helpful. As explained by Greenblatt, the New Historicism assumes that every expressive act by an individual or group is embedded in a material network of practices; that every intellectual or political critique inevitably uses the very tools it condemns; that there is no substantial distinction between literary and nonliterary texts once they start circulating; that no discourse yields eternal truth or discovers eternal human nature; and that any critical method under capitalism participates in the economy it critiques. The New Historicism thus may often still use such formalist techniques as analyses of allusion, allegory, irony, and mimesis. But, contrary to the premise of the New Criticism, it seeks to dissolve literature back into historical complexity.[46]

The New Historicism offers an anthropology similar to Bourdieu's. For New Historicists, art is penetrated by its institutional context, ritual gestures, patterns of relation, and shared images of authority. Even though art is demarcated from ordinary utterances, the demarcation itself is a social event and signals not the effacement of the social but its absorption into the work.[47] Art's appeal to distant audiences does not signal its abstraction, but rather its incorporation of its social roots. Thus, art is the most fundamental trace of culture. Yet, at the same time, we best understand a culture by treating its supposedly nonartistic products as if they were art; that is, we read all social texts in the hope of finding the traces of their enabling social conditions, the traces that instrumental forces have failed to entirely efface.

Given these traces, the method of the New Historicist is to question the usual structures of history—whether linear, cyclical, or dialectical. Indeed, she sees not so much history as histories, full of heterogeneity, contradiction, fragmentation, and difference. The New Historicist writes a history at once messier and more inclusive than that supplied by nationalist historiography or modernization theory, finding throughout the course of a culture endless negotiations and trade-offs of cultural currency. The New Historicism is interested in the episodic, anecdotal, contingent, exotic, abjected, uncanny pieces of history—the ones that violate rules and laws of politics and social organization.[48] The New Historicists do not seek "raw" materials as does Lévi-Strauss:[49] They seek the "cooked" ones—the

---

[46] Greenblatt, "Towards a Poetics of Culture," 11; Hayden White, "New Historicism: A Comment," in Veeser, *The New Historicism*, 293–302.

[47] E.g., Stephen Greenblatt, *Shakespearian Negotiations: The Circulation of Social Energy in Renaissance England* (Berkeley: Univ. of California Preess, 1988), 4–5 (arguing that cultural and artistic practices are collectively produced in a society).

[48] Gerald Graff, "Co-optation," in Veeser, *The New Historicism*, 168–81.

[49] Claude Lévi-Strauss, *The Raw and the Cooked: Introduction to a Science of Mythology*, trans. John and Doreen Weightman (New York: Harper and Row, 1969), 1.

hidden cultural contrivances, not just the so-designated works of art but also related ceremonial practices that have been adduced ostensibly to illuminate works of art.

One reason why New Historicism can apply aesthetic criteria to things normally thought of as outside the realm of art is that it rejects any simple mimetic notion of art. Yet at the same time that it rejects mere mimesis, New Historicism rejects any new-critical view of the art work as self-sufficient. Rather, the New Historicism speaks of art, like all cultural forms, as a medium for negotiating and exchanging—a point at which one cultural practice intersects with another, borrowing its forms or attempting to ward off unwelcome appropriations or pressures. Art negotiates among "a class of creators, equipped with a communally shared and complex repertoire of conventions."[50] Thus, artists need a currency, a grammar and vocabulary of literary forms, operations, symbol systems, and stereotype characters. As Greenblatt notes in a list of "abjurations" for his style of criticism:

1. There can be no appeals to genius as the sole origin of the energies of great art.
2. There can be no motiveless creation.
3. There can be no transcendent or timeless or unchanging representation.
4. There can be no autonomous artifacts.
5. There can be no expression without an origin and an object, a from and a for.
6. There can be no art without social energy.
7. There can be no spontaneous generation of social energy.[51]

An artistic currency both draws on and contributes to the realms of religious ceremony, political argument, and economic transaction. For the New Historicist, there is no logical connection between a theory and its political consequences, or between any set of ideas and how they may be used in particular social contexts. The political valence of a theory does not inhere in the theory itself (or idea or text or practice) but is conjunctural. For our purposes—the application of such a critical method to law—this means both that the law's supposedly prosaic, instrumental process of weighing interests and defining entitlements is a contested social process of self-definition, and that the law's literary legibility in no way implies its refinement or transcendence of venality.

Because, almost by definition, its value turns so much on the specific topics to which it applies, we can say little more about such criticism in the abstract. But we can say something about how we might fruitfully develop cultural criticism of legal thought. An analysis of law as social text will suggest itself wherever we see legal thought as social thought. Inasmuch as jurisprudence was arguably a central tradition of Western social thought before the development of academic

---

[50] Ibid.
[51] Greenblatt, *Shakespearian Negotiations*, 12.

social science,[52] and inasmuch as progenitors of social science such as Madison, Bentham, and Lieber also profoundly influenced American legal development, and inasmuch as legal decision makers in twentieth-century America have come to see themselves primarily as policy analysts, social textualists will find themselves facing a crowded docket. In virtually any dispute, they are likely to find actors construing, deploying, enacting, enforcing, or resisting representations of society.

We now proceed to consider several readings of legal interactions as social texts. We will begin with a number of studies treating legal disputes as contests over how to represent society or its parts, expressive contests of meaning rather than instrumental contests over resources. The disputes in question take on expressive meaning for the participants against the background of bodies of law that influence or recognize character, status, and identity. The criminal law, for example, may determine guilt on the basis of assessments of the character or motives of an actor. The criminal law's purposes include the shaping of behavior not only by punishing and deterring wrongdoing, but also by educating the public about norms. The criminal law thereby operates to define the law-abiding as well as the criminal character. The civil law confers identity by determining who has standing to sue for a wrong, who is damaged by it, who is responsible for it. Traversing a social and moral terrain charged with legal meaning, individuals and groups can define themselves and one another by reference to legal norms. They can also attempt to challenge and subvert those definitions, and the norms that confer them. We will see actors pursuing these strategies in both criminal and civil trials, in constitutional litigation and political advocacy, and in such informal disputing behavior as the blood feud and the street confrontation.

6.2 CULTURAL READINGS OF DISPUTES

The Drama of Civil Rites

A relatively simple example of a reading of law as a dynamic of cultural representations concerns the criminal trial. What is at stake in a criminal trial? A literary criticism of law would find more than a conventional resolution of guilt or innocence. The criminal trial is as much a social ritual as a legal instrument, valuable in part because it can affirm many values at once. Indeed, the criminal trial is perhaps the central trope of law. The Legal Realist Thurman Arnold captured this idea in an essay in his aptly titled book *The Symbols of Government*:

> For most persons, the criminal trial overshadows all other ceremonies as a dramatization of the values of our spiritual government, representing the dignity of the State as an enforcer of law, and at the same time the dignity of the individual when he is an avowed

---

[52] E.g., Donald R. Kelley, *The Human Measure: Social Thought in the Western Legal Tradition* (Cambridge: Harvard Univ. Press, 1990), 252–75 (tracing how law was overpowered by philosophy and the social sciences in the nineteenth century).

opponent of the State, a dissenter, a radical, or even a criminal. So important is the criminal trial to the whole ideological structure of government that its disappearance in favor of an efficient and speedy way of accomplishing the incarceration of persons supposed to be dangerous to the social order, is always a sign of psychological instability of a people.[53]

If viewed functionally, the criminal trial, Arnold argues, is inherently a failure. He asserts that the rules of evidence are a woefully inefficient tool of investigation, the definitions of criminal responsibility rarely accord with sensible psychology, and the criminal sentence often fails to serve any social purpose.[54] But all this may be irrelevant since

> the only function which the criminal trial can perform is to express currently held ideals about crime and about trials. It can act as a brake against a popular hysteria which insists upon following any one of the ideals to its logical conclusion. . . . Obviously, therefore, the public administration of criminal justice is not a method of controlling crime. It is rather one of the problems which must be faced by those who desire to control crime. Without the drama of the criminal trial, it is difficult to imagine on just what institution we would hang our conflicting ideals of public morality.[55]

How can we "read" a trial to discover the social forms, rituals, and mechanisms of meaning that underlie its apparent function? How can a trial be a social text? One excellent example of such a cultural interpretation of a legal event appears in John Murray Cuddihy's jaunty book *The Ordeal of Civility*.[56] Cuddihy's overall theme is to note the not very coincidental fact that many major modernist thinkers were Jewish. He reinterprets the works of such figures as Freud, Marx, and Lévi-Strauss, not in the scientific terms in which they were written, but rather as an expression of Jewish subversive uprising against the demands of Anglo-Saxon civility.[57]

The general phenomenon of "Jewish theory" is really the spirit of misrule in the kingdom of Western thought. Whether it be Freud's id, Marx's proletariat, or Lévi-Strauss's Third World culture, the discovery of the Jewish theorist is the survival of that part of the human spirit that has resisted genteel acculturation. Thus, for each of these architects of modernism, the pain of passage from traditional society to modern, from the *Gemeinschaft* of the *shtetl* to the *Gesellschaft* of liberal society, lies not in its acknowledged costs—impersonality, loneliness, and the like—but in its supposed benefit—the dignity it confers upon the individual. The burden of this dignity is the ordeal of civility; the resentful response expressed in each of these spectacularly successful crashes of the lawn party of

[53] Thurman W. Arnold, *The Symbols of Government* (New Haven: Yale Univ. Press, 1935), 130.

[54] Ibid., 146.

[55] Ibid., 147–48.

[56] John Murray Cuddihy, *The Ordeal of Civility: Freud, Marx, Lévi-Strauss, and the Jewish Struggle with Modernity* (New York: Basic Books, 1974).

[57] Ibid., 3–14.

Western civilization is to violate decorum by exposing the soiled undergarments of civilization—its sexuality, materiality, savagery.

In that regard, one of Cuddihy's more bizarre chapters, "A Tale of Two Hoffmans: The Decorum Decision and the Bill of Rites,"[58] treats the defendants in the legendary Chicago Seven trial, especially Abbie Hoffman, as pursuing an analogous strategy of calculated embarrassment. In what amounts to a dramatization of Marx's essay on the Jewish question, Abbie Hoffman, by targeting Judge Julius Hoffman, placed Judaism on both sides of the civilization divide. Hairy, unkempt, accented, irrepressible, wise-cracking, shrugging, Yiddish-talking Abbie Hoffman broadly played the *shtetl*-dweller, just off the boat. Conspiratorially addressing Judge Hoffman as "Julie," he implicated the judge in the conspiracy for which he was being tried.[59] By calling public attention to Judge Hoffman's Jewishness, defendant Hoffman conveyed a multiple message.

First, the decorum of the courtroom, requiring each participant to portray himself as a universal citizen, was inauthentic, and thereby an illicit condition of his rights. Second, Judge Hoffman's effort to wear an Anglo-Saxon mask had failed. Third, his effort to mask himself was itself a humiliating confession of inadequacy and marginality rather than a display of dignity and importance. Judge Hoffman's devotion to decorum, and indeed to law, was just the craven assimilation of a self-hating Jew. Fourth, not only Judge Hoffman's efforts to police Defendant Hoffman's courtroom behavior, but the entire prosecution, was an effort to suppress the authenticity of the *shtetl* Jew and to mark his disruptive presence as un-American. Fifth, Judge Hoffman was not simply striving to "pass" but was actually collaborating in the persecution of his own people. In sum, Defendant Hoffman "argued" to Judge Hoffman that in stifling him, the judge was attempting to stifle his own authentic self. Meanwhile, the prosecution in what he believed to be his own courtroom was in fact the judge's own persecution.

For Cuddihy, the defendants turned their trial on conspiracy and riot charges into a wider debate on a general point of law: whether genteel decorum and bourgeois civility were constitutional conditions for the enjoyment of Anglo-Saxon civil liberties.[60] The Supreme Court had eliminated racial and wealth requirements for the enjoyment of civil rights, but was there a manners requirement as well? Is a trial really a ceremony in which citizens win their civil liberties at the price of a ritual of obeisance and fealty? Cuddihy suggests that the provocative, jesting actions of the Chicago Seven and of similar defendants in other 1960s era trials "aimed at demonstrating that every civil right has, as hidden proviso, a bourgeois rite, and that all civil rights are alienable with the nonperformance of civic rites."[61] The defendants had rightly perceived that the true social subtext of the trial was the affirmation of a certain type of political subject—the properly civil citizen who was the rightful owner of civil rights. Their "defense," therefore, took the

---

[58] Ibid., 189–202.
[59] Ibid., 194.
[60] Ibid., 196–97.
[61] Ibid., 199.

logically subversive form of refusing to adopt that social role, thus exposing the artificiality and superficiality of the state's and the court's notion of constitutional principle.

Later, at the trial of Bobby Seale and other Black Panthers, the judge demanded from the defendants an apology for misbehavior and a promise of good behavior as a condition of their remaining in the courtroom.[62] Codefendant David Hilliard later bragged "he had been crafty enough to outwit the system" by making the vow insincerely.[63] Cuddihy insists that the system had in fact outwitted the defendants, since it exacted from them precisely what it wanted—not true love and obedience, but mere ceremonial fealty. Hilliard mistakenly thought he had completed the act of deconstruction by co-opting the court's hypocrisy. Cuddihy believes that, in fact, this was not hypocrisy in any disturbing sense at all—it was honest aesthetic artifice.[64] The court happily accepted the proper "ceremonies of innocence" as the moral equivalent of civil identity. The court had subtly outnegotiated the subversives; the co-optation had been reversed.

Representing Nazism

Perhaps the paradigm of the legal proceeding in which the symbolic and expressive elements predominate over instrumental concerns is the war crimes trial.[65] Thus, the highly publicized 1987 trial in France of Nazi war criminal Klaus Barbie was presented to the public, by press and prosecution alike, as an edifying performance, an object of interpretation. Because the outcome was a foregone conclusion, the strategic courtroom advocacy we usually read as instrumental here organized itself into a contest over the cultural meaning of condemning an indefensible defendant whose trial seemed a scripted, sacrificial ritual.

Barbie's trial was an occasion for defining group identity. Representatives of various victim groups, authorized by French criminal procedure to participate in the prosecution, vied for martyr status.[66] Particularly charged was a debate between Jewish survivors and Resistance veterans over whether to interpret Nazism primarily as anti-Semitic genocide or as illiberal political repression.[67] Perhaps even more controversial were the efforts of Barbie's defense attorney, Jacques Vergès, to implicate the accusers in Barbie's crimes, portraying the Nazi occupation of France as a mere instance of imperialism. On this view, it was no more genocidal or repressive than France's colonization of Algeria, or Israel's occupation of the West Bank.[68] In this way, the Barbie trial, like the Chicago Seven trial, combined a reprise of the Jewish question with the New Left's theatrics of

[62] Ibid., 197.

[63] Ibid., 201.

[64] Ibid.

[65] This discussion is drawn from Guyora Binder, "Representing Nazism: Advocacy and Identity at the Trial of Klaus Barbie," *Yale Law Journal* 98 (1989): 1321.

[66] Ibid., 1339–55.

[67] Ibid., 1324–38.

[68] Ibid., 1355–62.

disruption. In exploiting the trial's opportunity to define themselves by opposition to Nazism, the victim groups ironically placed their identities *en prise*, hostage to Barbie's own account of the motives of his crimes.

How did Barbie's trial come to be staged as an edifying debate on the meaning of Nazism, and on the relative cultural identities of the French, the French left, and the Jews?

First, a global audience for such a performance was assembled by the news media, which portrayed Barbie as an emblematic Nazi who had deported Jewish children to death camps, murdered the left-wing Resistance leader Jean Moulin, and later served the repressive Bolivian regime that killed the chic revolutionary Che Guevara. Once captured, Barbie obligingly presented himself as an unrepentant Nazi, proclaiming continued devotion to his Nazi "ideals." Yet he invited interpretation of his actions by refusing to explain these ideals or even to appear in court.[69]

Second, in formulating Barbie's charges, the French judiciary invited competing representations of Nazism by making ideological motive an element of the charged offense. In order to circumvent French statutes of limitation and prohibitions on retroactive prosecution, the courts rooted "imprescriptible" liability for "crimes against humanity" in customary international law.[70] This reliance on international custom, however, provoked the defense argument that occupying powers have customarily committed atrocities. The courts attempted to distinguish Nazi from French colonial atrocities, opening a debate on the distinctive heinousness of Nazi atrocities. Careful to retain among the charged offenses not only Barbie's participation in genocide, but also his repression of the Resistance, the courts limited crimes against humanity to atrocities committed in the service of a "state practicing a policy of ideological hegemony." Accordingly, the prosecution was obliged to prove that Barbie's offenses were motivated by "the national socialist ideology."[71]

Because French procedure permits victims of a criminal offense representation at trial, victims competed for the role of Nazism's chief opponent, exemplifying the use of legal dispute as a setting for the aesthetic creation of identity. Yet the prosecution of Nazi ideology ascribes more coherence and integrity—more "identity"—to Nazi thoughts and practices than is probably warranted. The convergence of so many contending groups on the stratagem of defining themselves by contrast to Nazism reveals a contemporary crisis of cultural identity that transcends any particular group. The less confidence we feel in the coherence of our own purposes and principles, the greater the temptation to identify ourselves in contrast to a malignant ideology. Ironically, Nazism provided an identity for Germans only by ascribing a similarly malignant coherence of purpose to Jews. In representing ourselves as victims, we ascribe to the oppressor an enviable com-

[69] Ibid., 1324–28.
[70] Ibid., 1328–29.
[71] Ibid., 1337–39.

mitment and conviction that increasingly seems beyond the capacity of any morally sensitive person.[72]

This contemporary crisis of cultural identity was especially visible in two particular identity crises "in evidence" at the Barbie trial, those of post-Holocaust Judaism and post-Occupation France. The Holocaust destroyed the covenantal basis of Jewish theology in a divine promise of preservation and prosperity in return for fidelity. While orthodoxy had traditionally interpreted persecution and suffering as divine retribution for infidelity that could be redeemed by greater religious commitment, the devastation of the Holocaust seemed disproportionate even to the sin of modern secularism, and misdirected at the most traditional and faithful communities of Jews. The leading response to this covenantal crisis, enunciated at the trial by star prosecution witness Elie Wiesel, substitutes the memory of the Holocaust for fidelity to God as the fundamental commitment of Judaism, and substitutes the victims for God as the postwar Jew's covenantal partner. Yet this effort to derive a new Jewish identity from the martyrdom of traditional Jewry may be self-defeating insofar as it assimilates Judaism to Christianity.[73]

As the Holocaust for Judaism, so was the Occupation for France: the irreparable wound. The conflict it provoked between collaboration and resistance remained an internal war in which the battle lines could never be cleanly drawn. Yet the Occupation was also an integrative moment, fusing existentialist philosophy with Marxist politics to produce a left. Like postwar Jews, prewar existentialists were disillusioned theists in search of a civil religion. The resistance to fascism, however, provided the secular quest that could structure a moral universe. An impotent fringe before the war, the intellectual left found itself at war's end as the embodiment of a myth of universal resistance.[74] The difficulty was that this myth flew in the face of tacit knowledge that quiet collaboration had been ubiquitous. The price of the intellectual left's political power and cultural influence was collaboration in the lie that the Resistance had led a united France. The realization that they were now implicated in the very hypocrisy they opposed drove leftist intellectuals into a self-consuming critique that eventually repudiated the ideals of authenticity and moral autonomy that had originally inspired them. The structuralist pronouncements of the death of "Man" and "the Subject" were at once indictments of existentialism and extensions of its phobic obsessions with heteronomy and hypocrisy. Deconstructive critiques of languages and cultures as inherently incoherent reflected a further surrender to the inevitability of occupation.[75]

This context helps explain one of the great puzzles of the Barbie trial: how could Vergès, himself a Resistance veteran, visible in radical circles since the 1950s, defend a Nazi, the murderer of Jean Moulin and opponent of Che Guevara?

[72] Ibid., 1344–45.
[73] Ibid., 1345.
[74] Ibid., 1364–72.
[75] Ibid., 1355–64.

Part of the explanation lies in his shift away from a humanist conception of political advocacy as an effort to give voice to the authentic subjectivity of a dissident client. Vergès first achieved notoriety as a defender of Algerian revolutionaries and later defended Palestinians accused of terrorism. Both of these roles expressed a sympathy with the self-determination claims of dispossessed populations once fashionable with the French left. But with the emergence of the poststructuralist critiques of identity and authenticity, the ideal of self-determination seemed incoherent. A critique of colonialism could no longer be premised on the dignity of the colonized but had to focus on the hypocrisy of the colonist.

Vergès could defend a Nazi because he no longer accepted the responsibility, or even the possibility, of identifying with the personality and politics of his client. His was an effort not to defend a client, but to hijack the prosecution. The trial, Vergès contended, "is a kind of ritual. They mean, by spilling his blood, to do like they do when killing a goat, to exorcize some evil."[76] If the function of a scapegoat is to unify society by symbolically exorcizing violence, Vergès sought to "rupture" French society by forcing it to reintegrate Barbie.[77]

Vergès made deliberately ironic use of his role as defense attorney to accuse France of complicity in his clients' crime.[78] Where a conventional lawyer might have sought to deflect attention from evidence inculpating his client, Vergès offered several strained procedural arguments that served only to harp on evidence of Barbie's genocidal crimes that French authorities had long possessed and ignored. Another stratagem involved threatening to expose what he claimed was widespread collaboration with Barbie in the upper echelons of the Resistance. By threatening to undermine the trial's propaganda function, Vergès hoped to enhance the prospect that his technical objections to Barbie's prosecution would get a serious hearing. Moreover, by threatening scandalous revelations, Vergès drummed up an audience for his own propaganda message equating Nazism with colonialism.

Although represented by different parties at the Barbie trial, the identity crises of Judaism and of the French left are outgrowths of a common culture of despair that paralyzes moral choice in the wake of Nazi atrocities. Feeling their way in the darkness around the abyss of moral luck implied by the Holocaust, both traditions are reduced to immobility. Unfolding with bureaucratic inevitability, the Holocaust depended upon the action and inaction of millions of ordinary people. As a consequence, postwar society is permeated by an anxiety that any of its members might have participated, collaborated, or acquiesced under similar circumstances. Believing that all creeds define themselves by their antipathies, members of postwar society eschew commitment to any cause for fear of becoming complicit in future atrocities. And so, they conclude, the only relief from this moral paralysis rests in the recollection of Nazi crimes, because they constitute

---

[76] Ibid., 1356.
[77] Ibid., 1356–57.
[78] Ibid., 1357–59.

the only evil one can despise without fear of becoming a Nazi oneself. This was the cultural setting of the Barbie trial, a culture devoted to the contemplation of Nazi atrocity as an obscure but sacred text, a culture transcending and yet enabling all the cultural identities performed by its participants.[79]

Policing Religious and Sexual Identity

The legal scholar and literary historian Janet Halley has explored the complex interaction between the legal regulation of conduct and the legal regulation of identity in two widely disparate contexts: the policing of religion in Renaissance England, and the policing of sexual orientation in contemporary America. These examples primarily involve criminal law, but as various parties adapt to the terrain defined by criminal law, other "legal" arenas may be affected, including religious law, civil rights law, legislative advocacy, popular protest, individual self-presentation, and even self-perception.

In *Equivocation and the Legal Conflict over Religious Identity in Early Modern England*,[80] Halley examines how the strategy of equivocation developed by English Jesuits facing religious persecution reshaped the landscape of available religious identities for all concerned. All the while, both institutional parties to the dispute, the English state and the Jesuit order, insisted on the stability of religious identity.

Jesuits taught that Catholics could at once hide and inwardly reaffirm their religious faith without violating Catholic ethics. Jesuit priests were instructed to exploit the ambiguities of vocabulary and syntax so that they could be technically truthful to the English courts, while still avoiding answers that would condemn them:

> First, [a Jesuit] could use words having more than one common meaning—for example, declaring that a priest "lyeth not in my house," and meaning that he does not tell lies there. Second, he could give only one of several possible answers to a question—for instance, declaring that he came to a friend's house to have dinner and omitting to mention a purpose to celebrate mass as well. Third, he might exploit the ambiguities of hidden gestures, unclear pronoun reference, altered pronunciation—any addition to standard usage that would create an ambiguity.[81]

But the strategy of "mental reservation," of silently qualifying an answer, was the most threatening to English authorities:

---

[79] For further work on the problems of representing the Holocaust in history, literature, and law, see several recent essays by Lawrence Douglas: "Film as Witness: Screening *Nazi Concentration Camps* before the Nuremberg Trial," *Yale Law Journal* 105 (1995): 449; "The Memory of Judgment: The Law, the Holocaust, and Denial," in *History and Memory: Studies in Representation of the Past* 7 (1996): 100; "Wartime Lies: Securing the Holocaust in Law and Literature," *Yale Journal of Law and the Humanities* 7 (1995): 367.

[80] Janet E. Halley, "Equivocation and the Legal Conflict over Religious Identity in Early Modern England," *Yale Journal of Law and the Humanities* 3 (1991): 33.

[81] Ibid., 34–35.

For the Jesuits endorsed a form of response which gave the interpreter no indication of its possible ambiguities: a Catholic in England was allowed by this doctrine to make an audible statement that would mislead the hearer, and to add to it, silently, a modification (or *mental reservation*) that rendered the entire sentence true. For instance: "I did not see Father Gerard [*ut tibi dicam*] [i.e., in order to tell you about him]."[82]

As Halley notes, the strategy of mental reservation enabled Jesuits to maintain a secret but authentic Catholic identity, and it threatened the state precisely because it undermined the official policy of policing identity on the basis of religious affiliation. Civil order, notes Halley, was equated with transparent expression; accurate detection of identities was an important method of state policing. Catholics subverted the state by constructing private selves that could pass undetected.[83] To do so, they had to reject the state's assumption that language was transparently referential and inherently confessional. They treated language instead as "multivalent, unstable, and conventional," always in dialogue with an inner voice.[84]

The struggle between equivocation and referential clarity manifested itself in ordeals of civility. Thus, in the trials of Guy Fawkes and the other "Gunpowder" plotters, Attorney General Coke characterized the legal struggle as one over discourse: he accused the Catholics of subverting the language with dissimulation. The result was a trial over "tissues" of words,[85] where Fawkes insisted on his right to control the narrative of events, and Coke conceded his reciprocal entanglement by insisting that his version of the rebellion "will *appear* to be fact."[86]

In another trial, Anglican Dean Morton insisted that speech was always public, governed by law, and referential, while the Jesuit Parsons argued that internal speech was legally permissible and psychologically possible.[87] For Parsons, just as writing represents speech, speech represents inner mental propositions, and so a mental statement has the same status as a spoken one. Speech could be spoken without social intercourse and still be speech. Particularly when faced with illegitimate state authority, the speaker could retreat from society and speak only to himself.[88] Under such a view, however, privacy is not an impregnable shell, but "a social and legal relationship between the Catholic and his inquisitor."[89] Thus, a priest challenged to admit that his name was Peter could answer "no" (mentally reserving the full answer that he "was not Peter who was bound to reply to this judge"), because he viewed the judge as illegitimate.[90] Whether or not the priest is Peter, then, turns on his relationship to the legal authority with whom he speaks.

[82] Ibid., 35 (quoting *A Treatise of Equivocation*, ed. David Jardine [London: Longman, 1851]), 48–52.
[83] Ibid., 36.
[84] Ibid.
[85] Ibid., 39.
[86] Ibid.
[87] Ibid., 41–42.
[88] Ibid., 43.
[89] Ibid., 44 (emphasis omitted).
[90] Ibid.

By contrast, Morton held that "personal privacy is inviolable."[91] Underlying the inviolate self is a "constant conscience against which [the representational accuracy] of speech and writing can be tested."[92] The mind cannot honestly equivocate, because it cannot honestly misrepresent. A man knows his own mind before he proceeds to speak. He does not need speech to understand his own thoughts.

Morton suggests true speech is always public and relational, governed by law and custom, and all representation is subject to state control. The state has the power to interpret the meaning of the represented thought; the listener has the power to fix the speaker's identity. As Halley notes, this is, in effect, a battle over jurisdiction.[93] The state allows a private self, but controls all outward manifestations of selfhood. This is how the negotiation between competing notions of selfhood and conscience gets resolved. Thus, when an Irish grand jury refused to indict a Catholic who had obviously violated Anglican rules, the jurors were charged with perjury. The jurors equivocated in defense by saying that when they took the juror's oath, they did so with the reservation that they would not act against conscience, and further claimed that the deception was in the mind of the listener—the state. The court twisted the dialectic: since it was deceived, the speakers had lied.[94]

The mental reservation enabled one at once to avoid the sin of dissembling by silently confessing one's Catholicism, yet manage to dissemble by enacting the Catholic identity that one denied. Dissembling came to constitute the very Catholic identity it disguised because it traduced the Anglican effort to obliterate Catholicism. The result was Catholic religious identity reconstructed in Protestant terms, as a private and internal matter.[95] Yet the Jesuits would not go so far as to encourage or excuse participation in Anglican ritual, which they regarded as apostasy.[96] In this way they collaborated with their Anglican opponents in polarizing the field of religious identity.

Halley resists treating this struggle "deconstructively" as a clash between a repressive essentialism and the free play of textuality.[97] Such a glib reading leaves out the key element—a negotiation and reciprocity between the two sides over the common problem posed by the "church papists," who publicly partook in Anglican worship while silently considering themselves Catholics[98] and performing Catholic services at home.[99] Their actions were neither subversive nor civilly disobedient. They attended Anglican church not out of begrudging compliance with the penal law, but because they honestly valued church attendance. In doing so, church papists subverted both the Jesuit insistence on the formal

---

[91] Ibid., 46.
[92] Ibid.
[93] Ibid., 47.
[94] Ibid., 47–48.
[95] Ibid., 51.
[96] Ibid., 45.
[97] Ibid., 36.
[98] Ibid., 38.
[99] Ibid., 49–50.

manifestations that identified a Catholic and the Anglican insistence on a strict Anglican communion. In this way the church papists resisted the efforts of both Catholics and Anglicans to define the constitutive elements of religious identity, and they rejected the Manichaean dilemma imposed upon them by both sides. In their struggle to capture and identify this elusive group of church papists, Anglicans and Jesuits displayed a common insistence upon orthodoxy, even as they continuously revised the constituents of orthodoxy in response to one another's stratagems.

Much of Halley's other legal scholarship explores the similar fluidity of sexual orthodoxy and heresy in contemporary society. Her work on sexual orientation demonstrates how the regulation of sexual conduct and of sexual identity conditions, without completely determining, the identities that people develop, and how the strategic choices actors make reshape the law's categories and aims. According to Halley,

> debates about sexual orientation require all the players to participate in the construction of their own sexual orientation identities, and to make themselves available for interpretation along this register by others. In debating about sexual orientation, we do not just reflect or deliberate upon it and how it shall be used to effect redistribution of social goods: we also constitute it and enroll ourselves in it. . . . The role of law in constituting persons by providing a forum for their conflicts over who they shall be understood to be is deeply material, even though it involves not physical force but the more subtle dynamics of representation.[100]

In "The Politics of the Closet: Towards Equal Protection for Gay, Lesbian and Bisexual Identity,"[101] Halley provides a complex taxonomy of sexual identity in which persecution, secrecy, and publicity once again shape identity. The point of the piece is that homophobia discourages public advocacy of the interests of homosexuals. Halley urges heightened equal protection scrutiny of antihomosexual discrimination in the interest of correcting the political underrepresentation of homosexuals. In the course of developing her argument, Halley criticizes the view that sexual preference is immutable and the theory that suspect classification analysis must be contingent on the immutability of one's membership in a class.

Instead of insisting on the naturalness of sexual identity, Halley emphasizes the coercive influence on the formation of identity resulting from legal sanctions against homosexuality and legally backed social sanctions such as employment discrimination on the basis of sexual orientation. According to Halley, these sanctions have three significant effects. First, they reduce the number of people who identify as homosexual, by pressuring people not to manifest homoerotic feelings and by discouraging those who might otherwise choose to live as gay or lesbian for political or affectional reasons.[102] Second, they reduce the number of people

---

[100] Ibid. See also "Reasoning about Sodomy: Act and Identity in and after *Bowers v. Hardwick*," *Virginia Law Review* 33 (1993): 1729.

[101] Janet Halley, "The Politics of the Closet: Towards Equal Protection for Gay, Lesbian and Bisexual Identity," *U.C.L.A. Law Review* 36 (1989): 915.

[102] Ibid., 956–58.

who publicly support or ally with the political interests of gays and lesbians, by threatening these potential supporters with the burdens suffered by those to whom homosexuality is publicly ascribed, whether or not such people consider themselves homosexual.[103] Third, by intimidating most people into acquiescing in the default ascription of heterosexual identity, discriminatory sanctions turn the vast and potentially fluid margin between gay and straight into a vacant free-fire zone, a proverbial no-man's land.[104] Together, these three effects diminish the number of self-identifying homosexuals and make them more politically insular and discretely differentiated from the rest of the population than they need be. Hence, self-identifying homosexuals are inadequately represented by ordinary interest group politics and need the legal protection suspect classification status confers.

Halley acknowledges, but does not fully confront, one major difficulty. Given the inevitable shaping effect of law on social identity that Halley so well demonstrates, how can law's equally inevitable influence on political discourse be critiqued as undesirably coercive? Halley's social constructivist conception of identity seems to dictate that any argument for protecting the range of politico-sexual identities that antisodomy laws help suppress requires a substantive defense of the value of those identities.

Halley's "Reasoning about Sodomy"[105] offers a close reading of the *Bowers v. Hardwick*[106] opinions in light of the earlier development of the litigation. Halley highlights the struggle of the litigants and judges over the relationship between homosexual identity and the crime of "sodomy," generally defined in sexual-orientation-neutral terms. The Supreme Court's narrowing of the issue to the constitutionality, under the Due Process Clause, of punishing "homosexual sodomy" has been one of the most criticized aspects of the case.[107] Halley argues that the imperfect fit between the conduct proscribed by antisodomy statutes and homosexual identity paradoxically magnifies the effectiveness of antisodomy statutes in superordinating heterosexual identity. By threatening everyone with prosecution, regardless of his or her sexual orientation, antisodomy laws position heterosexual identity as a valuable but conditional privilege to avoid prosecution for technically criminal behavior. The conjunction of overbroad legal proscriptions and the contingency of enforcement on cultural identity creates a powerful symbiotic tension. The potential vulnerability of heterosexuals to prosecution enhances the cultural authority of heterosexuality even as it disempowers all those individuals who

---

[103] Ibid., 970–71.

[104] Ibid., 958–59.

[105] Halley, "Reasoning about Sodomy," 1721.

[106] 478 U.S. 186 (1986).

[107] See "Developments in the Law—Sexual Orientation and the Law," *Harvard Law Review* 102 (1989): 1508, 1523–25 (stating that the Supreme Court's reading of the privacy doctrine departed from precedent); Anne B. Goldstein, Comment, "History, Homosexuality, and Political Values: Searching for the Hidden Determinants of *Bowers v. Hardwick*," *Yale Law Journal* 97 (1988): 1073, 1081–91 (stating that the Court's ruling was based on Justices' misplaced historical views regarding homosexuality and privacy); Thomas B. Stoddard, "*Bowers v. Hardwick*: Precedent by Personal Predilection," *University of Chicago Law Review* 54 (1987): 648, 651–53 (arguing that the Court was wrong in reframing the case from sexual privacy into gay rights).

must vie for the uncertain protection of heterosexual status. Halley makes the even more surprising claim that the ambiguity of antisodomy prohibitions between the regulation of conduct and the regulation of identity enhances the cultural authority and stability of these prohibitions.[108] She identifies and resists the temptation to make the "naive deconstructive claim" that the "figural" instability of the *Hardwick* decision, or the more generally prevalent rhetoric on which it relies, "undermines . . . its claims to authority."[109] The indeterminate object of sexual regulation paradoxically legitimates it and magnifies its effect.

Litigating Tribal Identity

In *The Predicament of Culture*,[110] the intellectual historian James Clifford offers a "literary" rendering of a civil property trial over lands once owned by the Mashpee Indian tribe. In Clifford's analysis, the forms of legal procedure and the categories of legal entitlements can be read as an exercise in identifying how legal doctrine, ritual, strategic choice, and imagination interact to create group identity, tradition, and history. In an appreciative essay, Gerald Torres and Kathryn Milun develop Clifford's analysis into a normative argument for institutionalizing cultural diversity as a means of enriching what we might call the media of self-expression.[111]

In this case, tribal affiliation is the identity in controversy.[112] The difficulty in defining the characteristics of a tribe in Indian law implicates the wider problem of group identity—the relationship between tribe, nation, ethnic group, and culture. As the Indian witnesses in the Mashpee trial are questioned about their identification with the purported tribal group, we see how their effort to identify themselves requires them to negotiate a topography of identity not entirely within their control.[113] At the same time, the effort to claim and conserve what the larger society will respect as "tradition" requires its invention and adaptation. The tribe's interests do not derive so much from tradition but from a shared project of constructing what society will recognize as a tradition.

The ultimate issue in *Mashpee Tribe v. New Seabury Corp.*[114] was whether land had been unlawfully conveyed from the Mashpee tribe to non-Indians in the nineteenth century. Specifically, the alienation of land had not taken place by treaty, which is the sole means permitted by the Indian Non-intercourse Act of 1790.[115] The decisive question, however, was the preliminary one of legal stand-

---

[108] Halley, "Reasoning about Sodomy," 1770–72.

[109] Ibid., 1747–48.

[110] James Clifford, *The Predicament of Culture: Twentieth-Century Ethnography, Literature, and Art* (Cambridge: Harvard Univ. Press, 1988), 277–346.

[111] Gerald Torres and Kathryn Milun, "Translating *Yonnondio* by Precedent and Evidence: The Mashpee Indian Case," *Duke Law Journal* (1990): 625, 656–58.

[112] Clifford, *Predicament of Culture*, 277, 288–99.

[113] E.g., ibid., 281, 286, 291–93, 310–12 (giving testimonies of various witnesses).

[114] 427 F. Supp. 899 (D. Mass. 1978).

[115] Torres and Milun, "Translating *Yonnondio*," 663 n. 25 (citing relevant provision of the Non-Intercourse Act).

ing: whether an entity existed called the Mashpee tribe that could be a party to a lawsuit.[116] Of course, to own land or enjoy rights to land, one must be a person, natural or legal. The Mashpee trial raised the historically embedded question of how a group whose members' economic, religious, and political lives partially overlap can identify a common denominator that is sufficiently coherent and compelling to win recognition as a legal person. For the Indians and for their expert witnesses in anthropology, the overlap is best captured as a shifting coalition of relations, changing over time, and varying in emphasis. The law, however, imposes criteria of continuity and coherence that seem procrustean in the face of anthropology and history.[117]

The disjunction between legal identity and ethnographic identity provoked this exasperated plaint from the trial judge:

> I am seriously considering striking all of the definitions given by all of the experts of a Tribe and all of their opinions as to whether or not the inhabitants of Mashpee at any time could constitute a Tribe. I let it all in on the theory that there was a professionally accepted definition of Tribe within these various disciplines.
>
> It is becoming more and more apparent that each definition is highly subjective and idiosyncratic and generated for a particular purpose not necessarily having anything to do with the Non-Intercourse Act of 1790.[118]

The judge ultimately instructed the jury to determine whether the Mashpee were a tribe by the legal criteria enunciated by the Supreme Court in a 1901 case also having nothing to do with the Non-Intercourse Act: "By a 'tribe' we understand a body of Indians of the same or a similar race, united in a community under one leadership or government, and inhabiting a particular though sometimes ill-defined territory."[119] Thus, as Torres and Milun note, the judge assimilated indigenous peoples into a sort of late Victorian model of the sovereign nation-state that requires racial purity, political hierarchy, and (relative) territorial stability.[120] Crucially, the judge also instructed the jury that if, at any point in the last two centuries, the Mashpee did not meet these criteria, they could never subsequently recover tribal status.[121]

The trial was essentially a conflict between two narratives of Indian history. The opposing sides held different images of tribal status, or, more generally, disparate notions of culture and social identity. The jury did not have the option of devising an equitable compromise between these visions but could only endorse one or the other. In this sense, the law follows the logic of literacy, of the historical

---

[116] Clifford, *Predicament of Culture*, 278 (as opposed to, e.g., the Passamaquoddy and Penobscot tribes).

[117] Ibid., 277–80.

[118] *Mashpee Tribe v. New Seabury Corp.*, 427 F. Supp.

[119] *Montoya v. United States*, 180 U.S. 261, 266 (1901); Record in *Mashpee Tribe v. New Seabury Corp.* 592 F.2d 575 (1st Cir. 1978).

[120] Torres and Milun, "Translating *Yonnondio*," 634.

[121] Clifford, *Predicament of Culture*, 333–34.

archive, rather than the logic of changing collective memory; the shifting oral history of Mashpee had to be set in documentary stone.

The plaintiffs' experts were anthropologists relying on field work to define the concept of "tribe," while the defendants relied more on the historians' tool of written documentation. One anthropologist witness proffered five criteria for the definition of a tribe: "a group of Indians, members by birth or ascription, 'a kinship network,' a clear consciousness of kind—'we' versus 'they,' a territory or homeland, and political leadership."[122] He described how powwows, although sometimes catering to outsiders and tourists, also serve social, spiritual, and educational functions that are sacred and private. Another witness rejected any such sharp doctrinal definition of tribe, portraying instead a field of family resemblances and local histories as reference points.[123] When the flexibility of this witness's definition was denounced for its vagueness, the witness responded that the more formalistic definitions presume distinctions among categories— religious, political, etc.—that are antipathetic to Indian thinking.[124] Thus, the "Indian" definition of a tribe is a perfect example of Greenblattian negotiation. As the witness put it, "What you are talking about is a group of people who know where they are. They may have to respond to outside pressures and adopt political structures, religious structures, or economic structures to deal with out- side society."[125]

Conversely, the defendants relied on written history to develop categorical definitions of what constituted a tribe. The defense purported to show that the so- called Mashpee tribe was not a distinct tribe at all, but in fact a loose composite of refugees from several other tribes and ethnic groups. Indeed, it was noted, English pilgrims had helped create the artificial society called Mashpee out of charity, establishing a "South Sea Indian Plantation" as a refuge for Indians from a variety of tribes who had converted to Christianity.[126] The Christian conversion itself, of course, undercut any claim of cultural continuity for the tribe, as Chris- tian ritual replaced traditional powwows and other "pagan" rites.[127] In the defen- dants' view, then, any Mashpee claim to land had to rest on a "written deed and on English law rather than on any aboriginal sovereignty."[128]

The defense supported their claim that the Mashpee had moved from sover- eignty to legal and cultural assimilation by citing several historical events. First, after an appeal to King George III and a series of legislative acts, the Mashpee won the right to become an incorporated town in 1870.[129] As the area became commercial between 1870 and 1920, tribal governance almost completely disap- peared, because Indians were too busy becoming "individual citizen-farmers,

[122] Ibid., 319.
[123] Ibid., 322–23.
[124] Ibid., 324.
[125] Ibid., 323.
[126] Ibid., 294–95.
[127] Ibid., 295.
[128] Ibid., 295–96.
[129] Ibid., 296.

workers, and businessmen."[130] Moreover, the Indian inhabitants of Mashpee not only fought with the colonists against the British in the Revolutionary War, but sided with Whites in wars against other Indians. Furthermore, the defendants argued, the Mashpee Indians intermarried widely with other Indians and with Blacks and thus sacrificed cultural integrity in the name of expansion or assimilation.[131] Finally, in the defendants' view, few current residents who claimed Indian heritage knew much about Indian ritual and tradition, and, to learn about them, those few actually had to travel to Western reservations or to take Native American Studies classes in college.[132]

The plaintiffs told a very different story: acknowledging that many of the members of the putative Mashpee tribe were refugees from other groups, they argued that what had created refugee status was "precisely" the devastation wrought on tribal integrity by contact with Whites.[133] But rather than merely insisting that the Mashpees constituted a tribe according to conventional notions, the plaintiffs argued even more forcefully that the conception of a tribe as a stable sovereign nation is a Western concept required by the rigid categories of Western lawmaking.[134] The Mashpee Indians could be viewed as sharing a coherent culture so long as the criteria of coherence could remain fluid.

On the religion issue, the plaintiffs insisted that although many Indians had become Baptists, their conversion was consistent with the general pattern of fluid identity and specifically incorporated Indian traditions and beliefs. In addition, Indian preachers retained a powerful role within the Indian Christian church, often conducting bilingual services, and turning their churches into an arm of Indian culture that resisted outside influence. The plaintiffs argued that the Mashpee decision to fight with the colonists against other Indians was partly a matter of sheer survival and partly the perfectly conventional act of one tribe fighting another. The plaintiffs also argued that intermarriage in no way defeats tribal identity so long as the shifting nature of group identity is recognized.[135] As Clifford notes,

> Mashpee was a refuge for misfits, refugees, and marginal groups. At certain times a natural alliance against dominant white society formed between the town's Indian "survivors" and newly freed blacks. The crucial issue is whether the core Indian community absorbed the outsiders or were themselves absorbed in the Indian melting pot.[136]

The plaintiffs argued that they resisted Western schemes of land tenure and town governance for as long as they could.[137] The South Sea Indian leaders recognized that some formal structure for land titles such as town status was necessary to save their lands from White aggression. In 1834 they adopted "modified planta-

---

[130] Ibid., 300.
[131] Ibid., 296–97.
[132] Ibid., 309, 313–14, 316.
[133] Ibid., 302–7.
[134] Ibid.
[135] Ibid., 303–6.
[136] Ibid., 306.
[137] Ibid., 303–5.

tion status," roughly akin to reservation status, as a way of keeping collective control over land and immigration while maintaining contact with White society.[138] Moreover, "continuing entailments on land sales outside the community guaranteed a flexible nineteenth-century tribalism."[139] In addition, land allotments accorded with traditional Indian patterns of land use. What to the white man may have been indicia of political immaturity may have been to the Mashpee a rejection of formal township status in the name of Indian citizenship; it may have been prudent, however, to explain their position to the Massachusetts legislature in terms of progress towards conventional citizenship and proprietorship. The Mashpee claimed that only a small and unusually assimilated minority of the tribe's members had voted for disentailment, and they were essentially coerced into doing so as the condition of their political enfranchisement.[140]

Furthermore, the plaintiffs attributed the demise of tribal self-rule in the late nineteenth century to the coercive policies of the Bureau of Indian Affairs.[141] Moreover, they questioned the assumption that tribal decision making had disappeared, noting that this assumption was based on the Western custom of embodying political decisions in written records, as opposed to the Indian oral tradition.[142] Finally, the plaintiffs noted that the Mashpee remained a powerful and coherent influence in local politics through church and town government. While many tribes sought recognition from a newly sympathetic Bureau of Indian Affairs in the 1930s, for example, the Mashpee did not have to, since an Indian majority controlled the town government.[143]

For the plaintiffs, the Mashpee's story was one of coercion, adaptation, and survival. For the defendants, it was a perversely congratulatory story of successful assimilation into American pluralism. In fact, the history of the Mashpee is one of stops and starts—assertions of political independence, attempts to establish tribal identity within the new structure, assimilation of other marginal groups into that structure, choices between state or federal protection and political independence, and negotiation through the maze of both coercion and enticement by White society. As Clifford puts it, "their history was a series of cultural and political transactions, not all-or-nothing conversions or resistances. Indians in Mashpee lived and acted between cultures in a series of ad hoc engagements."[144]

Several of the plaintiffs' witnesses were people who moved casually, and sometimes invisibly, between Indian and non-Indian life. They might live in Mashpee and work in Boston;[145] they might be involved in tribal affairs, but then spin

---

[138] Ibid., 308.

[139] Ibid.

[140] Ibid., 298–300, 305, 307–8.

[141] Ibid., 309.

[142] Ibid., 309–10 (stating that "traditional myths and stories were told around kitchen tables").

[143] Ibid., 300–301, 308–9.

[144] Ibid., 342.

[145] Ibid., 311. Russell Peters's testimony revealed that although living in Mashpee, he worked in Boston.

off separately to administer business considered to be inconsistent with Indian culture.[146] Did that prove or disprove the coherence of the Indian identity?

Witnesses were questioned as to how often they participated in native dances[147] or wore regalia.[148] Teachers of Indian culture were asked why their students needed any education in being Indian if they were inherently Indian.[149] The witnesses' and anthropologists' response, of course, was that the defendants were imposing a Procrustean notion of tribal identity. A defense witness said that though he called himself a Wampanoag Indian, he was referring to his Indian ancestry and not to any tribal affiliation. Indeed, he acknowledged, without any concession on the legal issue, that he could not define "tribe."[150] The fetish over tribal purity was, psychologically, the problem of the Caucasian defendants. Unfortunately it became the plaintiff's legal problem.

Clifford argues that the Mashpee have survived as a coherent people precisely because they have not conformed to White categories.[151] Continuity is required by hybrid identity, but continuity is at war with coherence. Indeed, Clifford argues, the jury instructions, requiring that both continuity and coherence of tribal status be established as independent elements, were essentially self-contradictory. Indian politics was informal, not hierarchical; in order to file a suit in 1976, the Mashpee formed the Mashpee Wampanoag Tribal Council, Inc. to serve as the tribe's legal arm.[152] In effect, the tribe paid obeisance to legal form by creating a legal identity for the purpose of asserting its natural and continuous identity; it followed civil rites to assert bourgeois rights. Torres and Milun point out the paradox: "The law does not permit the Mashpee's story to be particularized and still be legally intelligible."[153] Yet Clifford suggests that the need to assert identity for the purpose of the lawsuit had a continuing "feedback" effect on the tribe, since it probably revived the movement for tribal independence.[154] The lawsuit is part of the story of the tribe's adaptation, not simply an alien imposition. Moreover, Clifford argues, in helping to shape the Mashpee's current identity, the lawsuit altered not just the perception, but the reality of their past—a reality that is never finally settled:

> Interpreting the direction or meaning of the historical "record" always depends on present possibilities. When the future is open, so is the meaning of the past. Did Indian religion or tribal institutions disappear in the late nineteenth century? Or did they go

---

[146] Ibid., 293. In his testimony, John Peters was asked about the several businesses in which he had been involved. Peters "comment[ed] that the art of making money is probably inconsistent with being an Indian," but said that all Mashpee Indians do it. See also ibid., 311 (quoting the testimony of Russell Peters, who indicated that "no self-respecting tribe would become incorporated").

[147] Ibid., 301.

[148] E.g., ibid., 283.

[149] Ibid., 313–15.

[150] Ibid., 330.

[151] Ibid. 336–43.

[152] Ibid., 310.

[153] Torres and Milun, "Translating *Yonnondio*," 630.

[154] Clifford, *Predicament of Culture*, 341–43.

underground? In a present context of serious revival they went underground; otherwise they disappeared. No continuous narrative or clear outcome accounts for Mashpee's deeply contested identity and direction. Nor can a single development weave together the branching paths of its past, the dead ends and hesitations that, with a newly conceived future, suddenly become prefigurations.[155]

At the end of the evidence, the jury deliberated on whether the proprietors of Mashpee constituted a tribe on six specific dates between 1790 and 1976. The jury came up with an inconsistent—and therefore mildly subversive—answer that amounted to a full legal loss for the plaintiffs. Asked to apply consistent criteria of tribal existence over two centuries of intense change and disruption, the jury found that the Indians had become a tribe in the 1830s but had ceased to be one by the 1860s.[156]

The lesson of Mashpee may be that culture itself is a Western concept or that the Indian version of it cannot meet the test of having essential features. A "community reckoning itself among possible futures is not a finite archive."[157] As Clifford asks, "What if identity is conceived not as a boundary to be maintained but as a nexus of relations and transactions actively engaging a subject?"[158] In Clifford's estimation, tribal identity had no "sine qua non," but rather was the "contingent mix of elements" the Indians contemplated as they conceived themselves as a culture.[159] When a group "negotiates" its identity, it persists and patches itself together; it can lose "a central organ" and remain alive.[160] Language, land, blood, leadership, religion—any of these specific elements can be replaced: "Metaphors of continuity and 'survival' do not account for complex historical processes of appropriation, compromise, subversion, masking, invention, and revival. . . . The Indians at Mashpee made and remade themselves through specific alliances, negotiations, and struggles."[161]

Clifford depicts Mashpee culture as being created by the Indians from available cultural materials, and yet carrying on independent of their wills and haunting them with a sense of belonging, loyalty, and duty they could not always trace with historical or logical rigor. Their "interest" consisted of the qualities and consequences of their cultural identity, including owning the land in question, even if the purpose of ownership was to reaffirm that otherwise fragile identity. It may be that the plaintiffs, having lost control of town government, needed common land to perpetuate the viability of an Indian identity. And it may be, as Clifford suggests, that they wanted to maintain an Indian identity not so as to occupy it, but to live in the cultural space between that identity and the conventional white world.[162] In the end, Torres and Milun endorse the plaintiffs' land

---

[155] Ibid., 343.
[156] Ibid., 333–36.
[157] Ibid., 325.
[158] Ibid., 344.
[159] Ibid., 323.
[160] Ibid., 338.
[161] Ibid., 338–39.
[162] Ibid., 342.

claim not on the basis of its historic authenticity, but in order to preserve the diversity of identities by reference to which individuals can fashion a self.[163]

Thus, they prefer the plaintiffs' narrative of resistance and survival to the defendants' narrative of assimilation on the aesthetic ground that it enriches the expressive possibilities of culture. The difficulty that Torres and Milun duck is the same one finessed by Halley. To demand tolerance for an identity one is powerless to change is to make an appeal for compassion; but to demand the opportunity to fashion an identity one could live without is to make a more difficult and dangerous appeal for approval. Once the case for protecting minority cultures is made in aesthetic rather than mimetic terms, it must suffer the aesthetic judgment of the majority.

Disputing Intent and Status in a Stateless Society

In *Bloodtaking and Peacemaking: Feud, Law and Society in Saga Iceland,*[164] William Miller offers an account of the linked cultural processes of law-creation and dispute resolution in medieval Iceland. While the sources he relies on—the revenge sagas—are conventionally viewed as "literary" rather than "legal," Miller reads them as social and political documents, as keys to the code of social action. Though he conveys an infectious enthusiasm for these sources, Miller takes an approach that is frankly more archaeological than appreciative. While he considers the authorial intentions of the anonymous scribes of the sagas, his real interest lies in the motives of the social actors depicted in the stories. Thus, Miller incorporates both the New Critical rejection of authorial subjectivity and the poststructuralist tendency to read a text largely for the traces of other texts. And here, most significantly, those other "texts" are not literary at all, but the structures of social action—the dimensions of wrong, redress, honor, and household obligation that render action meaningful. Within these traces, however, Miller reestablishes human powers of action and imaginative invention. Thus, his readings are self-consciously literary in the way we recommend: it is the aesthetic of social action he is after, the artistry of jurisgenesis by ordinary people in a stateless society in which the Nietzschean obligation to define and defend identity cannot be fobbed off onto the bureaucratic state.

Though Miller emphasizes the artificiality of distinguishing between law and other social norms, he demonstrates that even purely legal texts can be illuminated by a literary apprehension.[165] Iceland had many remarkably detailed legal rules. One quoted text prescribes the proper methods for removing buried bones when a church is moved, including rules governing personnel, time of day, divisions of labor, and consecrating rituals to be performed by priests.[166] From such sources,

---

[163] Torres and Milun, "Translating *Yonnondio*," 655–58.

[164] William Ian Miller, *Bloodtaking and Peacemaking: Feud, Law, and Society in Saga Iceland* (Chicago: Univ. of Chicago Press, 1990).

[165] E.g., ibid., 222–32 (explaining how law can be analyzed from a literary perspective).

[166] Ibid., 222–23.

Miller infers that Icelandic law looks as if it were "abstracted from specific cases rather than deduced from disembodied principle," and that, on the whole, the extent of detail suggests a highly oversanctioned society, one in which fines were assessed even for leaving portions of a meadow unmowed.[167]

In Miller's view, Icelandic law is of such elaborate complexity as to suggest a sheer pleasure in law's formulation for its own sake. Law so permeated the society that it became the subject matter for children's games,[168] and funeral services included a trial to assign ghosts homes to free up space for living souls and un-haunt houses.[169] The Law Rock and the Lawspeaker were central symbols of unity and continuity.[170] In one sense, law suppressed violence, since there were so many legal claims that could function as channels for belligerence; aggressive counter-claiming could take the place of fighting.[171] But the beginning of a lawsuit was as fraught with menace as an actual violent attack.[172] Disputing was also a form of sociability in that legal actions were freely transferable, and part of a legal claim included showing the ability to muster potential supporters.[173] Power, legal entitlement, and reputation were exchangeable currencies.

While the sagas are works of imaginative literature, they presuppose legal norms and procedures, types of legal claims and strategies, and culturally plausi-ble motives for invoking law and for obeying or flouting legal norms. They give us a taxonomy of legal statuses and an inventory of behaviors appropriate or inappropriate to each. While the sagas may thus serve as archaeological data, part of what they reveal about the system of disputing is its expressive possibilities—the resonances of meaning, the complexities of feeling, the sheer strategic inven-tiveness it enabled. To Miller it matters little whether these expressive possibilities were realized by actual disputants or merely imagined by tale tellers—they are part of the culture to be reconstructed.

Consider Miller's rendering of the short saga "Thorstein the Staffstruck," set in 990 and written down around 1250.[174] Here is the basic plot: the old man Thorarin is a poor farmer dependent on his sturdy son Thorstein. Thorstein has a fight with Thord, servant of a rich farmer Bjarni. The dispute starts out as a horse fight, but then Thord strikes Thorstein. The story is ambiguous as to whether the blow was intentional or not, and this ambiguity soon becomes critical. Thorstein retreats quietly, but his father later goads him into seeking redress. He again confronts Thord, questions what his mental state with respect to the blow had been, and then strikes him dead. Bjarni is then goaded into counterrevenge by,

---

[167] Ibid., 223.

[168] Ibid., 227

[169] Ibid.

[170] Ibid., 18–19, 226–28. The Lawspeaker had a seat on the court of legislation. It was the Law-speaker's responsibility, when asked, to tell people what the law was. Ibid., 18. The Law Rock was the place at which publication of a lawsuit was made and legal proceedings occurred. Ibid., 227.

[171] Ibid., 233.

[172] Ibid., 234.

[173] Ibid., 239–43.

[174] Ibid., 52–58. The following synopsis in the text is culled from these pages.

among others, his servants Thorhall and Thorvald. Ironically, he sends these two to attack Thorstein, who kills them, as expected. But then Bjarni's wife prods him to seek revenge personally. Bjarni demurs at first, saying that to kill Thorstein would simply render old Thorarin dependent on him, but finally he goes off to win revenge. Bjarni and Thorstein confront each other, but then engage in a strange balletlike pretense of fighting. Each avoids killing the other, and Thorstein resolves the conflict by agreeing to become Bjarni's servant.

The story is about honor, revenge, negotiation, and compensation. The preliminary questions are why Thord struck Thorstein and what sort of compensation must follow; in addition, Thorstein has killed three of Bjarni's men and may have to compensate him. Hence, we enter a dizzyingly chaotic market where the currencies are honor and revenge. In a section of his essay aptly titled "The Politics of Accident,"[175] Miller reveals that Thord's mental state was linked to the mode of recompense. We normally think of mental state as an historical event taking place inside one person's head, provable by inferences from behavior and words. But in the Icelandic "social market," where the key and scarce commodity is honor, a past mental state is a function of subsequent social agreement.[176] Thorstein must interpret the blow to determine whether there is a wrong to avenge.

Thorstein is initially willing to treat the blow as an accident. When the two servants denounce Thorstein with the offensive name Staffstruck, however, they recharacterize the blow as an insult, in effect imputing their own malice to Thord.[177] Thord likewise resists the characterization of his actions as an accident, thereby daring the initially diffident Thorstein to press his case. Public displays of forbearance needed to be cleverly orchestrated not to seem degrading to the injured party, given the ability of the injurer and others to recharacterize claimed accidents as intentional attacks.[178]

Icelandic legal culture disdained accident claims by the injured party; indeed, both sides were dishonored when a claim of accident was lodged. When the injured party raised the accident interpretation, it meant that he would prefer to drop the claim—a sign of weakness. When the wrongdoer raised accident as a defense, however, he had to offer compensation. To acknowledge responsibility and pay compensation implied that the injurer acted out of fear of the victim. Yet refusal to compensate meant that the wrong then had to be prosecuted, if at all, as intentional. Thus, both parties faced pressure to retroactively confer intentionality on the aggressor's acts. But the decision whether to so confer intentionality was a communal one turning on the relative popularity of the parties, their social status, and the course of their dealings with each other or with other members of the community.[179]

---

[175] Ibid.

[176] Ibid., 66. Harmful bumbling was actionable, however, if it was witnessed by five neighbors and if compensation was not paid quickly. In such a case, if the bungler did not pay, he could then be punished as an outlaw.

[177] Ibid., 63.

[178] Ibid., 64.

[179] Ibid., 63–67.

Thus, ironically, to be the victim of accident meant dishonor as well as misfortune, but dishonor would fall on the wrongdoer as well. Only children, women, and the elderly had accidents. "Real men" struck deliberate blows. Consequently, so long as the burden of construction fell on the wrongdoer, the event would not be viewed as an accident at law. A master could intervene for his servant and concede that the servant's action was an accident and pay compensation, but that approach raised a whole set of questions about the social situation. In this case, no settlement was offered because Bjarni was more prestigious than Thornstein, and a breach of relations with poor, low-status people did not threaten social stability.[180]

A conventional legal scholar might study this story to determine the criteria for establishing mental state and the resulting rules governing compensation. Miller, however, demonstrates that any inference of such rules depends on a construction of actors' intentions, which remain perpetually susceptible to social reinterpretation. "Accident" is not a category of human action but an interpretive stratagem; its meaning is not descriptive but performative. In reading the legal culture of medieval Iceland to grasp the aesthetic of its legal relations, Miller's key discovery has been that the "facts" of intention and wrongdoing are a matter of creative—and coercive—interpretation that serves to confirm or alter social relations.

Bjarni's failure to seize Thorstein and put him to death brings shame on Bjarni's household.[181] Bjarni's ambivalence about exercising his legal rights is a humiliating admission that he does not sufficiently value social obligation. Moreover, it is precisely his own heroic past that underscores this failure; in effect, Bjarni is a victim of his self-created social identity.[182] Thus, when he suffers the insults of his own servants, he must have them killed to redress the insult he has brought on himself. Bjarni and Thorstein must then negotiate the demands of honor to achieve the desired settlement. They undergo a ritualized ballet of threatened physical violence and actual rhetorical finesse; their battle is a social dialogue, alternating insult and deference to establish stable reciprocal identities.[183] This is not to say that their encounter is so ritualized as to be scripted. It is, notes Miller, a game played for keeps in which the outcome is uncertain. They have common interests, but they must pick their way with utmost care to realize them. As Bourdieu observes,

> Any really objective analysis of the exchange of gifts, words, [or] challenges . . . must allow for the fact that each of these inaugural acts may misfire, and that it receives its meaning, in any case, from the response it triggers off, even if the response is a failure to reply that retrospectively removes its intended meaning.[184]

---

[180] Ibid., 66–68.

[181] Ibid., 69–70.

[182] Bjarni's reactions are complicated by frequent reminders of his reputation as a "kin killer," having killed his mother's brother. Ibid., 70.

[183] Ibid., 73–74.

[184] Bourdieu, *Outline of a Theory of Practice*, 5.

It is not in Bjarni's interest to take on Thorstein and his father as dependents. He has learned what a bother a servant can be, since a man of honor must defend his servants against even the consequences of their own misdeeds. But to kill Thorstein is to inherit responsibility for the elderly Thorarin, with no accrual of honor since Thorstein is the lesser man. Indeed, it is somewhat demeaning for Bjarni to contend with Thorstein; yet he must do something to satisfy social demands. Nor can he accept Thorstein's deference unless it equals or exceeds the value of the lives of the three servants he has lost.[185]

For his part, Thorstein gains a temporary increment of honor by fighting with Bjarni but can afford neither to lose nor to win. To lose is to die, while to win is to face punishment as a murderer. The social distance between them is such that honor will never accrue to Thorstein. Thorstein's only hope is to show enough mettle that Bjarni can afford to spare him, without so insulting Bjarni that Bjarni is obligated to kill him after all. He survives, with some measure of honor, at the price of his freedom and his father's land. As for Thorstein's decrepit father, Bjarni must contrive a claim against him to allow the proud old man to accede, under the appearance of duress, to the settlement already achieved.[186]

The story is fraught with Hegelian paradox: Bjarni cannot retain his honored status if he treats his retainers as worthless instruments. He must reciprocate their deference with at least the limited recognition that protection implies. The competition for recognition forces Bjarni and Thorstein into unwanted conflict, but it also dictates that neither can achieve his purpose by killing or even dishonoring the other. In addition to these social theoretical implications, the saga is significant as a political allegory: it renders the loss of freedom and the advent of feudalism as a tragic but inevitable bargain. A large part of Miller's achievement lies in his demonstration that the setting for this bargain is far from a state of nature.

Violence as Self-fashioning

In the cultural landscape of the sagas, law and honor are fundamentally harmonious values, and "private" violence can serve both. But in modern society, where the state holds the proverbial monopoly on legitimate force, honor becomes a potentially subversive value that law struggles to suppress. A perverse consequence is that the hope of staking a claim to honor can motivate violations of the law. The social conditions for the communal recognition of honor may have disappeared, but the framework of legal norms offers a medium in which the disaffected can carve their own sagas. As the Chicago Seven trial demonstrated, the imposition of bourgeois civility generates its own perverse incentives to transgress in the pursuit of transcendence.

Thus, the materialist psychology of incentives and deterrent threats that informs not just penology but criminal law doctrine may be thought to miss an entire

---

[185] Miller, *Bloodtaking and Peacemaking*, 75.
[186] Ibid., 72–75.

dimension of aesthetic meaning in criminal action, a delusional realm partly idio-syncratic and partly subcultural in which the desperate acts of small-time chisel-lers live in legend, a fantasy world pocked with real bullets. If we attend to this dimension of violent crime, we can read it as an artistic practice of "self-fashion-ing" that defies the instrumental logic of deterrence analysis and transcends the Procrustean psychology of mens rea analysis.

In one of his essays of New Historicist criticism, Stephen Greenblatt discovers the advent of the phenomenon of "self-fashioning" in Renaissance culture.[187] Greenblatt perceives in early Renaissance England a change in the intellectual, social, psychological, and aesthetic structures that govern the generation of social and cultural identities, an increased self-consciousness about fashioning identity as an artistic process. That process is complex and dialectical, evincing a new stress on the "executive power of the will," but also a sustained assault on the will; a new social mobility, but also a new assertion of power by both family and state to determine social movement; a heightened awareness of alternative modes of social, theological, and psychological organization, but also a new dedication to control of those modes and destruction of alternatives. This process is, of course, viewed with suspicion by Christianity. For Greenblatt, to have a coherent identity, in Renaissance terms, entails several elements: "a sense of personal order, a characteristic mode of address, a structure of bounded desires."[188]

The process of self-fashioning applies to the practices of parents and teachers, elite manners, hypocrisy and deception, ceremony, and self-representation. It thus blurs the distinction between literature and social life, crossing boundaries be-tween the creation of literary characters, the shaping of identity, the experience of being molded by forces outside one's control, and attempts to fashion other selves. Greenblatt's is, in a sense, a Nietzschean vision of the individual in the state of self-construction.[189]

Sociologist Jack Katz's remarkable study *Seductions of Crime* has exposed some contemporary criminality as an expression of this kind of self-fashioning.[190] The "text" for Katz is the inner and outer behavior of the criminal, as recorded in Katz's interviews and observations, and as captured, and misrecognized and reconstructed, by legal categories. Katz reviews a wide variety of criminal artists-in-the-self-making: the "righteous slaughterer" who kills out of a sense of moral justification even where no law recognizes the defense; the petty shoplifter who acts out a sensual fantasy of "sneaky thrills." But perhaps the key social identity discovered by Katz to underlie and somewhat escape our formal legal definitions is the type of the "badass."

The paradigmatic "badass" role captures the young man who is "tough, not easily influenced, highly impressionable, or anxious about the opinions that others

[187] Greenblatt, *Renaissance Self-Fashioning*.

[188] Ibid., 1.

[189] Ibid., 1–9.

[190] Jack Katz, *Seductions of Crime: Moral and Sensual Atttractions in Doing Evil* (New York: Basic Books, 1988).

hold of him . . . not morally malleable." The badass perpetually constructs alien aspects of his self and continually scripts conduct hostile to civilization. His guiding theme is "Not only I am I not here for you, but I affirmatively come from a place that is unreachable by your world."[191] As Katz notes, "meaning" is vital. When the criminal "means" it, he exhibits a transcendent will. It would be superficial to view his violence as gratuitous. Rather, it backs up his meaning without any utilitarian analysis, since his public self is not to be adjusted to contingent circumstances. But the badass's stance is more complex when it requires interaction to make sure his desires have been conveyed, and his regular roughhousing rituals are deflections of normal impulses towards social caring. In his clothing and his walking styles, he exhibits a negative moral capability in the form of a distinctive sensuality—he wants to make clear that at any arbitrarily chosen moment he might suddenly thrust chaos into the world.

Thus, the badass's guiding purpose is not so much to threaten particular violence but rather to show that he "means" it, and so he must distinguish himself from imitators who do not "mean" it. Moreover, the specifics of his "meaning" must be elusive, in order to reinforce his awesome, ominous presence. The badass alone controls the boundary between rationality and irrationality and lets the world know that he is not beholden to make this meaning intelligible to others by clarifying the distinction. He must control the whole social construction of meaning. The badass's menacing stare forces the capitulation of downcast eyes, which only invites further aggression. If he catches the eye of another, he challenges with the question "Whattchalookinat?" If the other answers "nothing," the badass responds, "You calling me nothing?" He refuses fiction and manipulates literal interpretation; he thus forces his power of meaning making on others simply in order to establish that he can do so.[192]

A collective version of the badass's individual construction of identity is the phenomenon of the "street elite," which expresses itself through the rituals of street fighting. As Katz shows, for gangs, violence has constructive power to transform their principles of association from symptoms of childhood to standards of glory; they make a metaphor of sovereignty respected by peers and feared by society; they sustain their claim of elite status in an aura of dread. In the arena of the school, for example, the gang member's goal is not to take on and conquer formal terms of rational authority, but to prove it absurd and pathetic—to humili-

---

[191] Ibid., 80.

[192] Ibid., 110–12. Like Miller's Icelandic commercial artists of interpretation, Katz's street toughs engage in reciprocal acts of social definition, in ceremonies of debt negotiation in which two clever people attempt to con each other by putting on a "front." T asks G for a loan, but then G makes a demand on T, claiming a need for money to buy food for his family. Ironically, neither really needs the money, but each constructs himself as a poor person and risks the consequent humiliation in order to derive a sense of control and transcendence through the art of conning. G fended off T by refusing his call for brotherly support—showing he had transcended the need for petty affection. He had to show he did not need anyone's help in the world. As one example of negotiation, truck robberies turn into embezzlement though ritualized bribery of the drivers. The victim is insinuated into the robber's networks of illicit relations and becomes an accomplice against the truckowner.

ate authority, not to overthrow it. As for gang leadership, the great leaders lead
by aesthetic, not physical prowess. They are the most successful at expressing
and reinforcing the ruling symbolism of the gang.[193]

In Katz's chapter "Doing Stick-Up,"[194] the most "professional" robbers create
elaborate symbols that attest to rational utilitarian justifications for their professionalism: they are cold calculators, out for money, willing to achieve their ends
by any means necessary. Yet the overall shape of their lives is self-destructively
irrational. Not only do they compulsively risk violent resistance and apprehension, they compulsively squander the gains for which they took the risk, on gam-
bling, on binges of drink, drugs, and sex, on lavish gifts and opulent display. Even
on the job, irrationality lies at the heart of their work, leading them to kill at the
slightest provocation. Of course, robbers who kill resisting victims might be
viewed as rational, but why do not more robbers of resisters who have little money
just run away? After all, the robber has engaged in little planning investment and
hence has little sunk cost; moreover, much resistance that provokes killing is not
very physically threatening. The answer, for Katz, is that the robber mainly exhibits a commitment to being a hard man. The stickup man lives in a zone of great
suspense as to whether his will will be obeyed. Successful robbers commit their
crimes as part of a general life of illicit activity and within the persona of the
hardman; donning and living by this persona is the only way to finesse the suspense and fear they normally experience. Acting like a hardman requires blotting
out a lot of stimuli, including fear. It leads to many irrational decisions but nevertheless fulfills a rationality that Katz calls "trans-situational." It is the price of the
persona that transcends the chaos of a disordered life on the social margins.

The "hardmen" fulfill some existential need by creating situations that limit
their control, and within those artificial boundaries they appear to meet high standards of rationality. In short, they script dramas full of exogenous limits on their
action in order to demonstrate or test their ability to sustain personal integrity in
the face of an (artificially) recalcitrant universe. The aesthetic aspect of the act
is apparent in the tendency of robbers to formally characterize their actions by
announcing, "This is a robbery!" They achieve a subjective moral advantage
through this declaration of aesthetic control.[195] They announce that they will stick
to their plan beyond any reason and thereby exhibit an existential power of resilience in response to the buffetings of fate—all of which fate is entirely self-
created. Thus, much robbery is really aesthetic recreational violence. It punctuates
a life structured as perpetually open to illicit action. Each moment must be suf-
fused with deviant salience. Thus, in this aesthetic sense, the causes of crime are
constructed by the offenders themselves—as lures and pressures they experience
as exogenous. One motive to dissipate the proceeds of one crime is to regenerate
the need to commit the next. These lives may have the structure of addiction

[193] Ibid., 114–63.
[194] Ibid., 164–94.
[195] Ibid., 164–69.

even with no substance abuse. Chaos is produced so it can be transcendentally controlled. Being "bad" is fundamentally not a matter of acting criminally or immorally, or even acting with physical aggression, but something that is more precisely defined with a morally charged, spatial metaphor: charting out a big space in public interactions and claiming to be able to fill it.

What if any policy implications might flow from Katz's reading of crimes as Nietzschean aesthetic projects? Perhaps little more than the caveat that the causal chain linking incentives to crimes is incalculably more twisted than conventional criminology imagines. A cultural reading of crime might provoke us to rethink the criminal law's libertarian emphasis on the actor's wrongful intentions at the moment of acting, and to focus blame instead on the character and persona from which the wrongful act seems to flow unreflectively. Thus, we may want to broaden our inquiry into the actor's responsibility for the character he has become, for the aesthetic project he is embarked upon.[196] But if a cultural analysis of criminal violence may sometimes expand responsibility by broadening the temporal inquiry, it may undermine the utilitarian case for punishment. If violence is an aesthetic project of defining one's self by contrast to officially enforced norms of civility, it will not easily be commodified and reduced to the logic of price. An effective crime policy may not be a law enforcement strategy at all, but a cultural strategy. On the other hand, the perverse inventiveness of the criminal countercultures Katz uncovers should discourage any confidence that the state can dictate the identities its stratagems engender.

6.3 CULTURAL READINGS OF CAPITALISM

Negotiating and Representing Value, Credit, and Character

Our examples of cultural criticism of law have suggested that legal disputes can be read as social texts that reflect the role of legal norms in the art of composing identities. In the remainder of this chapter, we consider how to read the legal forms shaping transactions in modern capitalism as essentially aesthetic instruments by which people or groups try to redeem their sense of social identity from its material origins. Our thesis is that the legal categories of modern capitalism regard economic transactions as expressions of unexaminable preferences to be regulated, balanced, constrained, negotiated with, and respected, but that an examination of the legal forms by which these preferences are recognized, and the doctrines by which they are regulated, reveals that economic actors seek to establish morally satisfying social identities as part of their career projects. Our analysis focuses on the legally recognizable forms of wealth and the legally recognizable character types of wealth holders. These two typologies blend to some extent as idealist projections of social forms and identities and can best be read as aesthetic

---

[196] See Kyron Huigens, "Virtue and Inculpation," *Harvard Law Review* 108 (1995): 1423 (presenting an example of this characterological conception of culpability).

creations designed to modify, justify, and even redeem the "purer" desire for wealth that is assumed to underlie them. We offer currency as the general metaphor for legal constructions of worth that enable individuals or groups to transcend their origins and trade away their cultural liabilities.

Capitalism is not just a system of economics and politics, it is a system of representation in which symbolic forms retain vast power over those who use or create them. Money itself becomes a cultural force, independent of the will of market actors; the aesthetics of the market thus control the actors in the market. At the same time, the ideal of an absolutely free market is itself a myth. Not only are modern markets created by the state definition and protection of entitlements, but they depend upon the sustenance of a social and cultural order that constitutes and encumbers market actors, an order threatened by unrestricted alienability.

Thus, according to Karl Polanyi, the free market unregulated by society or government is a happy fiction.[197] In the history of commerce, markets were always channeled by regulation, custom, and ceremony so as to protect culture from degradation. Under the guild system, for example, "the relations of master, journeyman and apprentice; the terms of craft; the number of apprentices; the wages of the workers, were all regulated by the custom and rule of the guild and the town."[198] The mercantile system simply served to make these rules uniform throughout England. Mercantilism insisted on commercialization as a national policy, but confined it not only within national boundaries, but also within certain sectors of the economy. A prerequisite to the pursuit of this policy was the development of the merchant as a social type and social class—the carving out of a cultural space for commerce.

Polanyi describes the evolution of industrial capitalism in cultural rather than technological terms. He views capitalism as an expansion of the economic functions of the commercial sector that changed the ways in which society was articulated and represented. With the purchase of heavy equipment and the erection of factories,

> Industrial production ceased to be an accessory of commerce organized by the merchant as a buying and selling proposition; it now involved long term investment with corresponding risks. Unless the continuance of production was reasonably assured such a risk was not bearable.
>
> But the more complicated industrial production became the more numerous were the elements of industry the supply of which had to be safeguarded. Three of these, of course, were of outstanding importance: labor, land and money. In a commercial society their supply could be organized in one way only: by being made available for purchase. Hence, they would have to be organized for sale on the market—in other words, as commodities.[199]

---

[197] Karl Polanyi, *The Great Transformation: The Political and Economic Origins of Our Time* (Boston: Beacon Press, 1957), 68–76.
[198] Ibid., 70.
[199] Ibid., 75.

Before industrialization, land and labor were at least partially protected from commodification. But more significantly, they were conceived as stable components of a social order rather than economic assets.[200] To reconceive them involved an effort of the figurative imagination because, as Polanyi puts it,

> Labor, land and money are obviously not commodities; the postulate that anything that is bought and sold must have been produced for sale is emphatically untrue in regard to them. . . . Labor is only another name for a human activity which goes with life itself, which in its turn is not produced for sale but for entirely different reasons, nor can that activity be detached from the rest of life, be stored or mobilized; land is only another name for nature, which is not produced by man; actual money, finally, is merely a token of purchasing power which, as a rule, is not produced at all, but comes into being through the mechanism of banking or state finance. None of them is produced for sale. The commodity description of labor, land, and money is entirely fictitious.[201]

Needless to say, organizing markets in the "fictive" commodities of labor, land, and money required law to identify and define saleable interests in each. This technical work was facilitated by the cultural work of fashioning new social types. This cultural work included the creation of the banker and broker as fictive producers and the wage worker as fictive product, and the reconstruction of the social types of gentleman and peasant so as to render them detachable from the land. Yet Polanyi argues that the representation of humanity, nature, and purchasing power as fully alienable commodities could never become a reality because of the catastrophic social consequences:

> To allow the market mechanism to be the sole director of the fate of human beings and their natural environment, indeed, even of the amount and use of purchasing power, would result in the demolition of society. . . . In disposing of a man's labor power the system would, incidentally, dispose of the physical, psychological, and moral entity "man" attached to that tag. Robbed of the protective covering of cultural institutions, human beings would perish from the effects of social exposure; they would die as the victims of acute social dislocation through vice, perversion, crime, and starvation. Nature would be reduced to its elements, neighborhoods and landscapes defiled, rivers polluted, military safety jeopardized, the power to produce food and raw materials destroyed. Finally, the market administration of purchasing power would periodically liquidate business enterprise, for shortages and surfeits of money would prove as disastrous to business as floods and droughts in primitive society. . . . No society could stand the effects of such a system of crude fictions even for the shortest stretch of time unless its human and natural substance as well as its business organization was protected against the ravages of this satanic mill.[202]

Polanyi's key thesis is that the origin of the cataclysms of this century lies in the "utopian endeavor of economic liberalism" to create the self-regulating market

[200] Ibid., 68–71.
[201] Ibid., 72.
[202] Ibid., 73.

system he deems inimical to social existence.[203] For Polanyi, the nineteenth century saw a virtual revolution in the history of human society—a commitment to gain as an explicit justification of everyday behavior.[204] In this regard, Polanyi views Max Weber as the first great protestor against the effort to efface the social grounding of economic systems. For Polanyi, as for Weber, humans act to sustain their social relationships more than to safeguard their interest in material goods.[205] Humans' greatest assets are their social claims, and material goods serve largely to secure that end.

In this sense, the processes of production and distribution are linked to social interests rather than economic interests. For Polanyi, as for Foucault, the real engine of the Industrial Revolution was behavioral psychology, not mechanical engineering.[206] Factory legislation and social laws were required to protect industrial man from the implications of the commodity fiction; land laws and agrarian tariffs to protect natural resources; and central banking and monetary regulations to prevent capitalism from killing itself through the congenital disease of overproduction.[207] The disembedding of production from the traditional social order undermined a host of cultural identities, but it did not free the economy from the demands of culture. The "demolition" of traditional society provoked the organization of new identities, especially the nationalisms that mobilized support for social welfare policies, protectionism, and public works. It also loosed the genies of fascism and militarization.[208]

Thus, a key task of Law and Literature scholarship might be to read economic transactions and legal forms for the tropes and fictions that enable the formation and perpetuation of a commercial society and culture. We begin with two "ethnographic" examples. The first, Miller's rendition of exchange in medieval Iceland, provides a picture of the culturally embedded economy of a precommercial society.[209] The second, Michael Taussig's *The Devil and Commodity Fetishism in South America*, depicts a peasant culture's representation of the commodification process as a self-alienating transaction with the devil.[210]

The Aesthetics of Exchange in Medieval Iceland

When property gets conveyed in the medieval Icelandic sagas, the legal characterization of a transfer varies between dispute and voluntary exchange, depending on the status and identity "constructions" of the parties. This was a world in which

---

[203] Ibid., 29.
[204] Ibid., 30.
[205] Ibid., 45–46.
[206] Ibid., 40–42.
[207] Ibid., 202–4.
[208] Ibid., 29–30.
[209] Miller, *Bloodtaking and Peacemaking*, 77–109.
[210] Michael T. Taussig, *The Devil and Commodity Fetishism in South America* (Chapel Hill: Univ. of North Carolina Press, 1980).

exchanges were at once ceremonial and strategic, designed to alter or confirm a social relation rather than serve any strictly economic purpose. Each mode of exchange had its own rules and vocabulary. The buy-sell relationship was viewed as a one-shot exchange with strangers or foreigners with whom one expected no continuing relation. To offer or request such a transaction was to declare one's indifference to, or possibly one's social distance in rank from, the other. A gift was different, because it gave the recipient time and room to characterize the transfer. It demanded some reciprocation in deference to the giver, but the response was left to the recipient's discretion. Indeed, narrative suspense was a constitutive feature of gift exchange.

Gifts had to be repaid, but such repayments were fraught with difficulties. If one repaid too quickly or precisely, or in the impersonal currency of money, one transformed the gift into a sale or, worse, spurned it altogether. Thus, gift recipients were burdened by an obligation they could not discharge immediately or without risk. In a sense, the obligation could never be fully discharged, for the only equivalent response to a gift is another gift. Paradoxically, the response had to be imprecise, incommensurable, excessive, somehow unequal to count as a gift. The very discharge of the obligation conserved the imbalance, the indebtedness, and the tense ordeal of sociability initiated by the first gift.[211]

Some of Miller's most interesting stories involve extra-market transfers that remained open for social interpretation even after the transfer. In an exemplary vignette, one Ospak raids the house of farmer Alf and then says of the goods, "They were not given, they were not paid to me, nor were they sold either."[212] To say they were not paid is to say that they did not represent compensation for some past grievance. But neither were they stolen, in Icelandic legal terms, since the taking was overt. Rather, this taking was what the Icelandics called a ran or raid— a "open, hostile taking."[213] A ran put a severe strain on the scheme of social definitions—it resembled a gift in that it admitted reciprocity, but it was the prior possessor who had to make the response and it was the raider who won the prestige.[214] In such a market of symbols, the corrective justice of the blood feud becomes hard to distinguish from the allocative efficiency of commercial exchange. Most crucially, in a market in which honor was the critical commodity, the social definition of the mode of transfer was more controversial than the price.[215]

The types of transaction in medieval Iceland included "gift-exchange, compensation awards, raids," and "transfers in consideration of marriage."[216] These cate-

---

[211] Miller, *Bloodtaking and Peacemaking*, 80–84.

[212] Ibid., 77.

[213] Ibid.

[214] Ibid., 83.

[215] Ibid., 77–81. Interestingly, dealings in land were more complex, because the impossibility of equivalent reciprocation for the conveyance of land threatened the receiving party with long-term subordination to the giver. Prospective recipients therefore often tried to shift the classification of a land-gift to a sale or expropriation category so that they could avoid dependence. Ibid., 107–8.

[216] Ibid., 78.

gories proved crucial tools of social interpretation because the Icelanders lacked regular commercial markets; thus, all exchanges were ad hoc and were continually subjected to flexible interpretation.[217] If food was consumed at the possessor's farm or if the visitor openly removed the host's horse or cloak after sharing a meal, the transfer was deemed a gift. On the other hand, if the visitor took away unused food or provisions, or took swords or horses without having shared a meal, the parties then had to negotiate a definition of the transaction—it could have been a gift, a purchase, a raid, or a payment for a wrong.[218] Moreover, retroactive definitions of the transaction could change over time. Thus, in one story, one Eldgrim approached one Thorleik and asked to buy some studhorses. Thorleik said that the horses were not for sale, and Eldgrim treated this refusal as an arrogant act that virtually invited him to perform a ran. Once the ran was threatened, however, Thorleik agreed to negotiate the terms of combat; once Eldgrim's "offer" was reconstrued as a threat, the parties could proceed on the basis of mutual hostility.[219]

In another story,[220] one Gunnar runs short of food and offers to buy hay from one Otkel. Otkel refuses to sell or to give. Gunnar chooses not to perform a ran and instead proposes to buy a slave. Later Gunnar's wife orders the slave to steal food from Otkel. Gunnar discovers the theft and offers to compensate Otkel. Otkel refuses any settlement and summons Gunnar's wife for the theft and Gunnar for illicit use of the property. Otkel is abandoned by supporters at court; Gunnar is granted self-judgment and absolves himself of liability. The price on Otkel's refusal is not the issue. Rather, the motivation is social—the parties fence between hostility and civility, and among idioms of gift, sale, and raid.

Otkel's "refusal to sell or give" became for Gunnar "a challenge to take forcefully."[221] There was no such thing as a choice of atomized isolation. Once Gunnar initiated, Otkel had to choose a response. He did not want a sale but knew that any refusal to sell could lead to a raid; at the same time, Otkel did not want to make a gift because it made him dependent on Gunnar's later definition. On the other hand, Otkel might have refused to sell precisely because he interpreted Gunnar's offer as an obnoxious threat of raid, or perhaps as an implicit claim of a difference in their social status. Equals did not engage in buy-sell relations, and Otkel might have wanted to claim equality.[222] Gunnar's wife's theft was like a ran because it was public; she thereby put the onus of defining the relationship back on Otkel.[223] Gunnar offered to resolve this issue by adjudication through witnesses, but Otkel was afraid his prestige was too weak to survive such adjudication. Gunnar then offered Otkel the chance to determine the proper compensation;

---

[217] Ibid., 77–84.
[218] Ibid., 80–81.
[219] Ibid., 101–4.
[220] Ibid., 84–93.
[221] Ibid., 88.
[222] Ibid., 91.
[223] Ibid., 89.

being at Gunnar's behest, however, this suggestion was actually an insult to Otkel.[224] Thus, a party's resistance to sale exposed him to the danger of subjecting his selfhood to the market forces of prestige-currency and social interpretation.

Soul Selling and Commodification in Colombia

In *The Devil and Commodity Fetishism in South America*, Michael Taussig draws on the Marxist notion of commodity fetishism, Polanyi's concept of fictive commodities, and Weber's classic study of religion and capitalism to read the industrialization of peasant societies less as a process of disenchantment than as a totemic struggle of competing spirit worlds.[225] For Taussig, the cultural problem confronting agricultural entrepreneurs in developing societies is aptly stated by Marshall Sahlins:

> Induced to raise a cash crop, [peasants] would not react "appropriately" to market changes: as they were interested mainly in acquiring specific items of consumption, they produced that much less when crop prices rose, and that much more when prices fell off. And the introduction of new tools or plants that increased the productivity of indigenous labor might only then shorten the period of necessary work, the gains absorbed rather by an expansion of rest than of output. . . . Traditional domestic production . . . is production of use values, definite in its aim, so discontinuous in its activity.[226]

As Weber argued, this eminently commonsensical attitude can only be overcome by a "long and arduous process of education," culminating in the acceptance of accumulation as a "calling."[227] The aim of this process is the inculcation of a new perception of time as continuous, measurable, fungible, cumulable, and exchangeable. Measured in time, labor becomes intelligible as a fungible fictive commodity, analogous in form and function to money.[228] The inculcation of such a new metaphysics may require or engender a new religious experience or a repopulation of the spirit world.[229] Once peasant laborers come to experience work as time, they can make themselves reliably available to employers. By the magic of the contract, the narrative suspense surrounding gift exchange is eliminated, and it becomes possible to secure the future availability of the factors of production.

In one of the milieus Taussig studies, the sugar plantations of the Cauca Valley in Colombia, the alien legal forms of currency and the wage contract were appropriated by the peasantry as metaphors. These forms represented the spiritual dialectic of disenchantment and re-enchantment, dispossession and possession that attends the coming of capitalism.

---

[224] Ibid., 90–91.

[225] Taussig, *Devil and Commodity Fetishism*, 3–38.

[226] Ibid., 20–21, quoting Marshall Sahlins, *Stone Age Economics* (Chicago: Aldine Atherton, 1972).

[227] Max Weber, *The Protestant Ethic and the Spirit of Capitalism*, trans. Talcott Parsons (New York: Scribner's, 1958), 62.

[228] Ibid., 48–50 (citing Benjamin Franklin).

[229] Ibid., 155–83.

The residents of the Cauca Valley were the descendants of emancipated slaves and the inheritors of a syncretistic religious tradition that integrated African animist elements into a Catholicism that had traditionally vilified such animism as devil worship.[230] Taking advantage of political instability, many former slaves were able to establish themselves in the nineteenth century as allodial or collective farmers by squatting on land, driving out masters, or farming and gathering on undeveloped land.[231] A lengthy struggle ensued to force these ex-slaves and their descendants into wage labor on plantations, by rounding them up, driving them off the land and fencing it, charging them rent in cash or labor, or destroying their crops. For a century after abolition, the peasant farmers of the Cauca Valley continued to see these stratagems as attempts to restore slavery.[232]

In the twentieth century, peasant farming came under new pressures. Population increases resulted in the subdivision of plots. Development loans enabled the large haciendas to purchase peasant lands and encouraged the remaining peasant farmers to shift from subsistence farming and gathering to cash crop monoculture. The resulting indebtedness and dependence on fluctuating prices drove many more peasants into wage labor.[233] The decline of subsistence farming also eroded communal patterns of work and consumption. By the time of Taussig's research in the 1970s, few peasants were able to support themselves on their own land. Most families combined peasant farming with wage labor on the plantations. They described wage labor as more lucrative, but intensive to the point of destroying their health. Wage labor also subjected them to a level of supervision that remained identified with slavery.[234]

Taussig invokes this context of social and economic change in explaining two dangerous occult rituals said to prevail within the community. The first was a rite of self-commodification leading to diabolical possession:

> According to a belief that is widespread among the peasants of this region, male plantation workers sometimes make secret contracts with the devil in order to increase productivity, and hence their wage. Furthermore, it is believed that the individual who makes the contract is likely to die prematurely and in great pain. While alive, he is but a puppet in the hands of the devil, and the money obtained from such a contract is barren. It cannot serve as productive capital but has to be spent immediately on what are considered to be luxury consumer items, such as fine clothes, liquor, butter, and so on. To invest this money to produce more money—that is, to use it as capital—is to invite ruin. If one buys or rents some land, the land will not produce. If one buys a piglet to fatten for market, the animal will sicken and die. In addition, it is said that the sugarcane thus cut will not regrow. The root will die and the plantation land will not produce until exorcized, plowed over, and replanted.[235]

---

[230] Taussig, *Devil and Commodity Fetishism*, 65.
[231] Ibid., 46–51.
[232] Ibid., 49–50, 55–56.
[233] Ibid., 70.
[234] Ibid., 83–85.
[235] Ibid., 94.

Even though the ritual was ascribed only to the most productive and best remunerated wage workers, reports of the ritual gave voice to a critique of the entire system of wage work as demeaning, self-alienating, unhealthful, and encouraging of selfishness.[236] Beyond that, the notion that the devil's seed is barren expressed a perception that cash crop monoculture, both on and off the plantations, undermined the economic viability of peasant farming and the social ties it sustained. This critique was also expressed in anthropomorphic representations of both sugarcane and money as diabolical forces.[237] Taussig evokes a long tradition in the Cauca Valley of political broadsides against the plantation owners portraying sugarcane as an evil spirit bent on enslavement.[238] But he also reports widespread belief in, and anxiety about, the ritual of baptizing money, according to which

[t]he godparent-to-be conceals a peso note in his or her hand during the baptism of [a] child by the Catholic priest. The peso bill is thus believed to be baptized instead of the child. When this now baptized bill enters into general monetary circulation, it is believed that the bill will continually return to its owner, with interest, enriching the owner and impoverishing the other parties to the deals transacted by the owner of the bill. The owner is now the god-parent of the peso bill. The child remains unbaptized, which if known to the parents or anybody else would be a cause of great concern since the child's soul is denied supernatural legitimacy. . . . This practice is heavily penalized by the church and the government.[239]

The baptized bill would receive the name of the child, and its godparent could summon the bill by name. Taussig repeats accounts of baptized bills making off with contents of cash registers and reports that payment with such a bill was a criminal offense. Anxiety about the dangers of baptized bills reflected fears of capital investment and commercial exchange as con games, enriching capitalists at others' expense. The surreptitious appropriation of the baby's soul and name indicates that the perceived threat of capital was not solely economic; it also critiques economic investment as the perversion of a natural principle of growth symbolized by the child and realized in peasant agriculture.[240]

Taussig resists a reading of these rituals as quaint and prerational superstitions. For one thing, he argues, they pithily express real dynamics of impoverishment, dislocation, and dehumanization that accompany economic modernization. By contrast, he argues, these losses are unremarked and unaccounted for in the discourse of an established market society.[241] To the peasants of the Cauca Valley, the notion that the accumulation and investment of capital enhances social welfare was a myth belied by their own experience. Instead, it reflected a perverse fetish-

---

[236] Ibid., 96, 98, 101, 103.
[237] Ibid., 93–94.
[238] Ibid.
[239] Ibid., 126.
[240] Ibid., 126–29.
[241] Ibid., 134–35.

ism of commodities and currency.[242] At the moment of economic modernization, we find not rationality triumphing over superstition, but contending mythologies reading one another.

Interest, Credit, and Character in Renaissance England

The early Renaissance development of the legal regulation of economics is a happy opportunity for Whiggish historians to describe the triumph of rational market economics over the forces of feudal superstition and narrow-mindedness. A society that viewed land as the only moral form of wealth, that denounced creditors as sinful usurers, borrowers as desperate failures, and the international trade and money market as a conspiracy of illusionists, learned that trade, abstract money, and pump-priming credit were the true sources of prosperity. Two closely related areas of legal regulation might well undergird this history: usury law and bankruptcy law. There is, of course, a great deal of truth to this Whiggish story, but its happy tale of microeconomic enlightenment ignores the huge expenditure of moral and aesthetic capital necessary to achieve this economic and legal transformation. Traces of this expenditure are legible in the evolution of the new cultural forms of merchant vocation, moneylending at interest, currency, and credit. Thus, what follows is a "literary" reading of a transitional era in English commerical law. This reading treats technical legal developments as entwined with the creation of a type of social character who can be viewed not just as an economic stereotype but as a dramaturgic model capturing the moral norms and tensions of a society that needed a new concept of the self to accompany an emerging capitalist system.

Consider the following excerpt from the 1624 English usury law:

> Whereas at this time there is a very great abatement in the value of land, and other the merchandize, wares and commodities of this kingdom . . ., and whereas divers subjects of this kingdom, as well the gentry as merchants, farmers and tradesmen, both for their urgent and necessary occasions for the following their trades, maintenance of their flocks and employments, have borrowed, and do borrow divers sums of money, wares, merchandizes and other commodities . . . but by reason of said general fall and abatement of the value of land, and the prices of the said merchandize, wares and commodities, and interest in loan continuing at so high a rate as ten pounds in the hundred pounds for a year, doth not only make men unable to pay their debts, and continue the maintenance of trade, but their debts daily increasing, they are enforced to sell their lands and flocks at very low rates, to forsake the use of merchandize and trade, and to give over their leases and farms, and so become unprofitable members of the commonwealth. . . .
>
> Be it therefore enacted. . . . That no persons shall . . . upon any contract . . . take directly or indirectly, for loan of any monies, wares, merchandize or other commodities whatsoever, above the value of eight pounds a year for the forebearance of one

---

[242] Ibid., 138–39.

hundred pounds a year, and so after that rate for a greater or lesser sum, or for a longer or shorter time. . . .

And be it further enacted . . . That all and every scrivener and scriveners, broker and brokers, solicitor and solicitors, driver and drivers of bargains for contracts, which shall . . . take or receive, directly or indirectly, any sum or sums of money, or other reward or taking for brocage, soliciting, driving or procuring the loan or forebearing of any sum or sums of money, over or above the rate or value of five shillings for the loan or forebearing of one hundred pounds for a year . . . shall forfeit for every such offence twenty pounds, and shall have imprisonment for half a year.

Provided, That no words in this law shall be construed or expounded to allow the practice of usury in point of religion or conscience.[243]

The story can begin with a bit of etymology. No word in the history of commerce is more important and complex than "interest." Early in the history of Renaissance usury law, the notion emerges that interest and usury are not the same thing. Usury is sinful and rapacious. Interest, on the other hand, can suggest relational generosity, willingness to bear burdens while enjoying benefits, and the legitimate parallel development of personal and social wealth. Its etymology is obscure: the word is a form of an impersonal infinitive meaning something like "it makes a difference, it matters, it concerns"—though literally it might mean "to exist among."[244] It is associated with both advantage, in the commonest connotation and harm, and disadvantage, in the Old French sense of damages. The closest thing to a general denotation may be a relation of being objectively concerned in something. It suggests both self-interest and sharing, a state of being generously concerned and yet also self-concerned.

Even in the late sixteenth century, when England still theoretically forbade all profits on loans, court and church law distinguished *interesse* from *usura*. *Interesse* represented the damages a creditor could obtain for the harm caused by the debtor's failure to repay—sometimes even damages representing the loss of investment opportunity. By contrast, *usura* represented any pre-arranged profit or any pre-arranged liquidated damages. Under legal *interesse*, the measure of compensation was *id quod interest*, the difference between the creditor's position in consequence of the debtor's laches and the position that might reasonably have been anticipated as the direct consequence of the debtor's fulfillment of his obligation. The compensation was permissible under the canon law only when it could be shown that such loss had really arisen (*damnum emergens*). At a later period, *lucrum cessans*—loss of profit through inability to reinvest—was also included as legitimate. Perhaps the key to usury, in Aquinian terms, was that the lender had no right to arrange profit on the loan if he in no way arranged to share the risk of the lender's activities; otherwise, he was gratuitously profiting from the debtor's labors, the supposed true source of the debtor's anticipated profits. Thus, medieval theology assumed—in a way ironically consistent with Marxism—that the legitimate source of profit was human labor, not the mere use of money.

---

[243] *Statutes*, 21 Jac.I. ch.17, 1624.
[244] *Oxford English Dictionary*, 2d ed., s.v. "usury," 1099–1100.

The history of usury details countless legal maneuvers and restructuring devices by which lenders evaded the usury laws—most often by reconceiving the loan as a rental or mortgage on land or an annuity.[245] As late as Shakespeare's time the courts and Church were still insisting, at least in their explicit generalizations, that prearranged profit on loans was always illegal, regardless of whether or not the lending was "biting"—that is, cruel and exploitative to the debtor.[246] Yet parallel developments in theology and market economics had begun to yield a new conception of the difference between interest and usury.[247] Whereas older law had described certain loans at interest as per usurious—as presumptively evidencing social mala fides—a new, more Protestant approach made no presumption of usurious intent, at least for loans up to a certain statutory rate of interest. If the state argued that a loan at or under such a rate was usurious, it would have to prove illegal intent—no easy task, since it was not the duty or power of secular authority to look into the hearts of men. By the 1550s two distinct positions had emerged in Continental theology and law and had begun to affect English thought. One was an "objectivist" position—holding illegal and immoral any lending with a guaranteed return more than the value of the loan. The other was a "subjectivist" or "nominalist" position—holding that there was no reliable external measure of the morality of a loan.[248]

In the legislative battles that led to the 1571 and then the 1624 usury laws, these two views contended and were negotiated.[249] Legal change was slow and erratic, but the law of usurious lending eventually came to reflect a compromise between these two competing perspectives. These legal developments were accompanied by the emergence of new social imagery appropriate to the new character type of the legitimate money merchant. This was a figure who was morally selective in his lending, following natural equity as well as contractual law. He never took interest from paupers; he never profited more from the loan than the borrower did. Moreover, he deliberately made some interest-free loans to poor debtors (whom he often forgave), he respected the statutory rate of maximum interest, and he always consulted the public good.[250]

Lawrence Stone offers an interesting view of the social character of the lending class in the late Elizabethan Era.[251] This class or group lies at the transition between merchants and bureaucratic officeholders, on the one hand, and landed

---

[245] Charles P. Kindleberger, *A Financial History of Western Europe*, 2d ed. (New York: Oxford Univ. Press, 2 1993), 41–42.

[246] Joyce Oldam Appleby, *Economic Thought and Ideology in Seventeenth Century England* (Princeton: Princeton Univ. Press, 1980), 67–68.

[247] Kindleberger, *Financial History of Western Europe*, 41.

[248] Benjamin Nelson, *The Idea of Usury: From Tribal Brotherhood to Universal Otherhood*, 2d ed. (Chicago: Univ. of Chicago Press, 1969), 73–108.

[249] Ibid.; Thomas Wilson, *A Discourse upon Usury*, 2d ed. (London: F. Cass, 1962), 155–69.

[250] Appleby, *Economic Thought and Ideology*, 67–71.

[251] Lawrence Stone, *The Crisis of the Aristocracy 1558–1641* (Oxford: Clarendon Press, 1965).

gentry or aristocracy on the other.[252] As progressively more wealth flowed into the merchant class at the turn of the seventeenth century, the merchants and artisans tried to absorb and sustain aristocratic values.[253] Where possible they tried to convert their money to land, not just for security but also for status: living off rents was dignified, while living off earned professional income was not.[254] The transition between land ownership and liquid mercantile capital became easier with the advent of equity of redemption and the possibility of nonpossessory land mortgages.

Relatively few moneylenders were specialists—most did it as a by-product of their profession or social standing—lending first to kin or neighbor and then to arm's-length parties. Indeed, even the clergy—who had more liquid assets than most—came to lend to their own congregation. The best legal deterrent to violation of commercial laws was some sort of social opprobrium.[255] "Credit" remained a key concept, reflecting reputation, honesty, and solvency, and as merchants found it increasingly feasible and profitable to lend at interest, the merchant character counterbalanced this questionable activity with charitable giving.[256] Stone notes that the huge majority of charitable giving in this era came from the mercantile, not the gentry, class. The prototypical merchant lived well enough to give off signs of success—but not ostentatiously—thus reconciling the Protestant desiderata of thrift and prosperity, and he felt under some duty to be visibly open-handed with his money. As one family inscription said, "What they spent, that they lent." Ironically, merchants were peculiarly able to donate large sums, because they were more likely to be childless—living in cities meant their children faced greater mortality from disease—and in any event rarely felt the need to sustain family dynasties. Stone suggests that charity was a psychic compensation for the "social impoverishment" caused by the vicious competition of the mercantile market.

The new legislation focused on creating a model character of the properly interested moneylender, rather than drawing a line between specific good and bad actions. No one loan on its face could be determined to be usurious or not; the context—the character of the lender—was decisive. Thus, freedom of religious conscience became aligned with new premises of market economics. Indeed, historians of this period now interpret the original restrictions on loans at interest as aimed at suppressing an emerging Renaissance humanist definition of selfhood, a self free to fashion itself into a new social identity. In this regard, moneylenders were viewed as evil in part because they violated the natural boundaries of class and status—they were social climbers trying to fashion themselves into higher-status figures. By contrast, the new Protestant economics and theology of lending authorized commercial actors to transform economic into social capital.

[252] Ibid., 6–9, 23–25, 28.
[253] Ibid., 23.
[254] Ibid., 24.
[255] Ibid., 233; Appleby, *Economic Thought and Ideology*, 69–70.
[256] Stone, *Crisis of the Aristocracy*, 233–48.

The result was a statutory and judicial construction that was as much a charter for proper character development as an economic regulation. Thus, in his book *The Passions and the Interests*,[257] Albert Hirschman reviews how early capitalist society needed to "invent" a new human figure: the very person of "interests." When the medieval chivalric code and Christian ethical theology weakened in the face of the discoveries and intellectual innovations of the Renaissance, the concern of political and intellectual leaders for an instrument of social constraint turned to secular sources. Hirschman describes how we then invented the rationally "interested" man. This character was the offspring of four intellectual developments: the lament that passions might be checked only by other passions, not reason or faith; the contrast drawn in political theory between the rational pursuit of state interest and the short-sighted impulsiveness attending princely motives of honor; the increasing identification of "interest" with avarice; and finally, the emerging sense that relative to the lust for power and glory, greed was a benign form of selfishness. These four shifts in moral psychology enabled a new model of governance as neither the internal restraint of virtue nor the external constraint of coercion, but the manipulation of greed. The man of property remained the model citizen, no longer on the republican assumption that wealth ensured incorruptible independence, but on the contrary trope that read wealth as vulnerability and unheroic timidity. The man of interest was the new human type whose preferences then became the foundational elements of utilitarianism and capitalism. As Hirschman stresses, the rational pursuit of self-interest was celebrated as a form of political governance and moral self-governance before being hailed as an engine of growth. To be "interested" came to be seen as a form of sociability: to have a stake in or take an interest in others' affairs. To have interests might equally connote commercial or philanthropic ventures. Eventually it would describe George Eliot's pseudo-literate rural gentry coping with their social irrelevance by taking a fashionable "interest" in reform.

The history of bankruptcy law affords a direct parallel and more richly documented example of the collective creation of a cultural identity for a social character—the virtuous merchant.[258] As with the cultural advent of the good moneylender, early bankruptcy law invites a reading in cultural and aesthetic terms as dramaturgy. English society conceives a character type to express its ambivalence about early capitalist economics, and the character becomes enriched by social imagery and related legal regulation—it plays to type. But the character takes on a life of its own, adapts to and in turn changes the commercial circumstances in which it was conceived. Eventually it helps induce changes in the law of bankruptcy that justify themselves on the basis of a new conception of the merchant character type.

[257] Hirschman, *The Passions and the Interests*.

[258] Robert Weisberg, "Commercial Morality, the Merchant Character, and the History of the Voidable Preference," *Stanford Law Review* 39 (1986): 3, 13–55.

The first English bankruptcy statute, in 1543, premised its aggressive regulation of absconding debtors on certain social observations:

> Where divers and soondry persones craftelye obteyning into theyre handes greate sub-staunce of other mennes goods doo sodenlie flee to partes unknowne or kepe theyre houses, not mynding to paie or restore to any of theyre creditours theyre debts and dueties, but at theyre own willes and pleasures consume the substaunce obteyned by credite of other men, for theyre owne pleasure and delicate lyving, againste all reasone equity and good conscience.[259]

Early bankruptcy law was a purely punitive device that assumed that most debtors were elusive absconders—often typed as devious Jews or Lombards. Its purpose was to give brute power to creditors to arrest the flight of the debtor and dismember his estate.

The stereotypical debtor himself was elusive and insidious, a devious merchant who bought and sold goods but neither produced nor consumed them.[260] The merchant was stereotyped as a pretender, using other men's assets to create an appearance of wealth without substance. He was a middleman who manipulated the market by trading on the abstract value of goods rather than either introducing materiality into commerce or using materiality for economic productivity. Accordingly, early bankruptcy law tried to constrain and target its punitive force by applying itself only to merchant debtors who neither produced nor consumed goods. The so-called trader rule of the early Renaissance bankruptcy laws delineated this category of characters. An Elizabethan version had defined a potential bankrupt as "a merchant or any other person using or exercising the trade of merchandize by way of bargaining, exchange, rechange, bartry, chevisance, or otherwise, in gross or by retail, . . . or seeking his or her trade of living by buying and selling."[261]

Underlying the law was the image of the merchant as the sly manipulator, the exploiter of smoke and mirrors. He operated in the spectral and corruptible world of credit, reputation, and rumor that stood in stark contrast to the tangible concreteness of farming and artisanal production. Although the emerging capitalist economy depended for its solvency and liquidity on these abstract market machinations, it also harbored deep moral ambivalence about them. The Renaissance playwright Thomas Dekker offered typical imagery of the merchant debtor, the "Politick Bankrupt":

> a Harpy that lookes smoothly, a Hyena that enchants subtilly, a Mermaid that sings sweetly, and a Cameleon, that can put himselfe into all colours. . . . He wind[e]s himselfe up into the height of rich mens favors, till he grow himselfe, and when he sees that they dare build upon his credit, knowing the ground to be good, he takes upon him the condition of an Asse, to any man that will loade him with gold; and useth his credit like

---

[259] Ibid., 21, quoting *Statutes*, 34 and 35 Hen. 8, ch. 4, 1542–43.
[260] Ibid., 13–16.
[261] Ibid., 22, quoting *Statutes*, 13 Eliz. ch. 7, 1570.

a Ship freighted with all sorts of Merchandise by ventrous pilots; for after he hath gotten into his hands so much of other mens goods or money, as will fill him to the upper deck, away he sayles with it, and politickly runnes himselfe on ground, to make the world beeleve he had sufferd shipwrack.[262]

Hence, the merchant is the embodiment of social paranoia about a capitalist world in which abstract representation of value becomes both an economic necessity and a moral and epistemological threat.

What the history of commercial law then shows, however, is the emergence of a counterperception, or a newly conceived identity for the merchant.[263] English law and culture by the seventeenth century began to treat credit and commerce, however abstract, as ethereal and spiritual bonds among people and nations, the solvent of brotherhood and the glue of international harmony. Abstract money, which had been viewed as an elusive and insidious falsehood, was rationalized as a sort of symbolic force of nature, not an object of devious manipulation. The English economy demanded credit to unloose its resources to run the military. Thus, credit was not only desirable but inevitable, a sort of predestination that transcended human agency, and the merchant was its oracle:

> All the possessions [of commercial societies] consist[ed] of scattered and secret securities, a few warehouses, and passive and active debts, whose true owners are to some extent unknown, since no one knows which of them are paid and which of them are owing. . . . The wealthy merchant, trader, banker, etc. will always be a member of a republic. In whatever place he may live, he will always enjoy the immunity which is inherent in the scattered and unknown character of his property, all one can see of which is the place where business in it is transacted. It would be useless for the authorities to try to force him to fulfill the duties of a subject; they are obliged, in order to induce him to fit in with their plans, to treat him as a master, and to make it worth his while to contribute voluntarily to the public revenue.[264]

If the "moral problem of credit lay with the image of the merchant as a creature of pure interest, unconstrained by traditional standards of religious virtue or social responsibility, the solution had to be in a justifying ideology of self-interest" as itself virtuous.[265] Mercantile self-interest ensured predictability and enhanced reasonable reliance. This was the "le doux commerce"—an international utopia of mutual dependence.[266] The very elusiveness of credit capital shows it not to be morally barren, but a communal, public good. The fragile arm's-length commercial links of the mercantile world are the links of a new utopia. Here is some of the new, positive imagery of credit:

---

[262] Ibid., 14, quoting Thomas Dekker, *The Seven Deadly Sinnes of London* 16 (London, 1606), 16.

[263] Ibid., 16–21.

[264] Ibid., 18, quoting Quesnay and Mirabeau, extract from *Rural Philosophy*, quoted in Hirschman, *The Passions and the Interests*, 94–95.

[265] Weisberg, "Commercial Morality," 18–19.

[266] Ibid.

Of all beings that have existence only in the minds of men, nothing is more fantastical and nice than credit; it is never to be forced; it hangs upon opinion; it depends upon our passions of hope and fear; it comes many times unsought for, and often goes away without reason; and when once lost, it is hardly to be recovered. . . . It very much resembles . . . fame and reputation.[267]

The new, affirmative figure of the merchant was a Weberian Protestant ethical hero whose greed was really a calling, whose self-interest was indeed a counterweight to other passions. This new notion of the merchant character entailed a new aesthetic apprehension of the nature of economic and social life:

[Divine providence] has not willed for everything that is needed for life to be found in the same spot. It has dispersed its gifts so that men would trade together and so that mutual need which they have to help one another would establish ties of friendship among them. This continuous exchange of all the comforts of life constitutes commerce and this commerce makes for all the gentleness of life.[268]

The merchant was the hero of international concord—he blurred boundaries, and softened military characters:

While the farmer, employed in the separate cultivation of land, considers only his own individual profit; while the landed gentleman seeks only to procure a revenue sufficient for the supply of his wants, and is often unmindful of his own interests as well as of every other; the merchant, though he never overlooks his private advantage, is accustomed to connect his own gain with that of his brethren, and is, therefore, always ready to join with those of the same profession, in soliciting the aid of government, and in promoting general measures for the benefit of their trade.[269]

English law and culture had created a new, inverted identity for the merchant: Now he was not sly and manipulative, but weak in a sense in which all humans subject to the vagaries of fate and the market could identify with. By the end of the seventeenth century the absconding charlatan had become the sympathy-invoking hero of the economy, the passive figure who suffered the accidents of the natural and economic world in order to enhance the movement of capital.

The very factors that made the trader a suspicious character also made him a sympathetic one. Gerard de Malynes depicts the merchant as the least willful of creatures. Far from conniving to evade the rules of bankruptcy law, the merchant helplessly falls prey to them because of the "mutability and inconstancy" of commercial life:

---

[267] Ibid., 20, quoting Charles Davenant, "An Essay upon the Probable Methods of Making People Gainers in the Balance of Trade," reprinted in *The Political and Commercial Works of Charles D'Avenant*, ed. Charles Whitworth (London, 1771), 2:275.

[268] Weisberg, "Commercial Morality," 19 n.53, quoting Jacques Savary, *Le Parfait Negociant* (Lyon, 1701), 1.

[269] Weisberg, "Commercial Morality," 19 n.54, quoting William Lehmann, *John Millar of Glasgow, 1735–1801* (Cambridge: Cambridge Univ. Press, 1960), 339.

For to be rich and to become poor, or to be poor and to become rich, is a matter inherent to a Merchants estate, and as it were a continual and successive course of the volubility of variable, blind fortune. . . . For it hapneth many times, that Merchants having taken up money at interest to augment their trade, and thereby doing good to their Prince and Countrey, shall receive some unexpected losses by wars on land, or Embargo's or restraints of Princes upon the seas, of their ships and goods, or by having sold their goods and merchandises at home at long days of payment . . . having their best means in remote places. . . . For some rich men . . . are so tied to the Clog of their wealth, that upon the least rumours of troubles and accidents happening to their debtors, they become suspicious of these mens estates, and fearing to become losers, are so inquisitive of their debtors means, to the great hurt and impairing of Merchants credit and reputation, that thereby they are driven into a streight on a sudden, and so overthrowe them (unawares many times) to their own hindrance and loss.[270]

Later, Daniel Defoe put it as follows:

Some disasters may befall a tradesman, which it was not possible he should foresee; as fire, floods of weather, thieves, and many such; and in those cases the disaster is visible, the plea is open, . . . the man can have no blame. A prodigious tide from the sea, join'd with a great fresh or flood in the river Dee, destroy'd the new wharf below the Roodee at West Chester, and tore down the merchants warehouses there, and drove away not only all the goods, but even the buildings . . . if . . . the poor tradesman was ruin'd by the loss of goods on that occasion, the creditors would see reason in it that they should every one take a share in the loss; the tradesman was not to blame.[271]

When, in the 1705 Statute of Anne, the right of discharge was added to the law, it ratified this more positive image of the merchant and influenced construction of the trader rule. The discharge rule made it tolerable (though not quite yet very desirable) for a debtor to be the subject of a bankruptcy proceeding. As a result, the trader rule faced a new counterpressure to expand to include deserving debtors. The state of being a bankrupt debtor changed from a reprehensible crime to a sympathetic commercial crisis. Only traders suffered losses by accident—others lost through prodigality. A trader's capital is uncertain and invisible—a reversal of the earlier epistemological problem. The uglier implications—rumor, illusion, collusion—were the corruption of the mercantile condition, not an inherent part of it.[272]

Representing Wealth and Worth in American Law

The question of what money represents has complex sociological, religious, philosophical, and even literary roots. Literary Critic Marc Shell recounts that the Holy Grail was the original exotic artifact, symbolizing divinity, kingship, and wealth

---

[270] Weisberg, "Commercial Morality," 26, quoting Gerard Malynes, *Lex Mercatoria* 156 (1686).

[271] Weisberg, "Commercial Morality," 28, quoting Daniel Defoe, *The Complete English Tradesman* (London, 1726), 91–92, 209.

[272] Weisberg, "Commercial Morality," 30–32.

in medieval Europe. Like money, it was a pure floating signifier. Thus, empty of meaning, it could be the vessel of meaning, a perfect symbol of the union of the real and ideal, the earthly and the divine. The earliest Grail sellers lived in trading centers, and the Grail was the heart of the notion of both literary and financial symbolism that promised both wealth through credit economics and redemption for a dying aristocracy.[273]

Shell also notes the long tradition of literary fascination with money as symbolic representation.[274] This fascination arises from the puzzling symbolic ambiguities entailed in inscribing meaning into a piece of dull metal or into a piece of "worthless" paper. For example, "when the inscription disappears from the surface of a coin, is the remaining ingot still money?" Or when "the ingot itself disappears leaving nothing but the inscription," is this remainder still money?[275]

A coin may be both sign and intrinsically valuable, but paper money is all symbol.[276] Credit money further widens the gulf between the symbolic value of money and any underlying commodities.[277] Thus, with increasingly widespread use of credit, paper, and negotiable instruments, the critical significance of money to culture became enriched.[278] *Faust*'s "Paper Money" scene is Goethe's critique of idealist philosophy.[279] Washington Irving was fascinated by the relationship between monetary inscriptions and "mere words." Commenting on inflation during a 1720 paper money experiment, Irving said, "promissory notes, interchanged between scheming individuals, are liberally discounted at the banks, which became so many mints to coin words into cash; and as the supply of words is inexhaustible, it may readily be supposed what a vast amount of promissory capital is soon in circulation."[280]

As we have seen, some New Historicists portray art as a social and economic "product" that strives mightily to efface its grounding in economics. The histori-

---

[273] Marc Shell, *Money, Language, and Thought: Literary and Philosophical Economies from the Medieval to the Modern Era* (Berkeley: Univ. of California Press, 1982), 40: "The grail was the sign of an age not only of impoverished aristocrats who, like the [sinner]/fisher king, seemed to await redemption, but also of a new merchant class, which greeted graceful mercy and money . . . as its special emblems." The royal merchant hero became a character type to replace older heroes, and the divine store sought by Grail heroes was replaced by alien property sought by merchants. Cf. ibid., 45–46.

[274] Ibid., 27–46.

[275] Ibid., 15. "This relationship of sign or symbol (the inscription) to substance (the ingot) is the heart of the aesthetic version of the paper money debate."

[276] Ibid., 19: "While a coin may be both symbol (as inscription or type) and commodity (as metallic ingot), paper is virtually all symbolic."

[277] Ibid: "As Marx argues, credit money (the extreme form of paper money) divorces the name entirely from what it is supposed to represent and so seems to allow an idealist transcendence, or conceptual annihilation of commodities."

[278] Ibid., 18: "With the advent of paper money certain analogies, such as 'paper is to gold as word is to meaning,' came to exemplify and inform logically the discourse about language."

[279] Ibid., 102: "The Paper Money Scene is part of a critique of the idealist philosophy that operates without material guarantees or substantial securities."

[280] Ibid., 19 n.39, quoting Washington Irving, "The Great Mississippi Bubble: A Time of Unexampled Prosperity," in Washington Irving, *The Crayon Papers* 38 (New York: T. Y. Crowell, 1883), 38.

cist critic challenges this aesthetic, seeking to redistribute the tools of critical power. A central theme of the New Historicism, then, is the dissolution of the division between the economic and the aesthetic, the alienated and the authentic, the subjectivity of the consumer or investor and that of the Romantic artist. Thus, New Historicists argue, the inner sensibility celebrated by nineteenth-century literature is also the private sphere of bourgeois life, furnished with the consumer goods that drove the Industrial Revolution.

Charlotte Gilman's "The Yellow Wallpaper," for example, describes the effort to make oneself into a site of both production and consumption—to be "self-actualized" into the market:[281]

> Dreiser didn't so much approve or disapprove of capitalism; he desired pretty women in little tan jackets with mother-of-pearl buttons, and he feared becoming a bum on the streets of New York. These fears and desires were themselves made available by consumer capitalism, partly because a capitalist economy made it possible for lower-class women to wear nice clothes and for middle-class men to lose their jobs, but more importantly because the logic of capitalism linked the loss of those jobs to a failure of self-representation and linked the desirability of those women to the possibility of mimesis.[282]

Capitalism thus creates objects of desire and then the subjects that desire them.[283] Writing, like money, is an ineffable blend of the material and the ideal, and thus depicts the internal drama of characters seeking to situate themselves in a market culture.[284] The artist and market actor both seek to fulfill the roles depicted in their own self-representations.[285]

A brief excursus on the Marxist notion of the fetishism of commodities is useful here.[286] The critical Marxist seeks to avoid the "voluntarist" error of reducing the functional requisites of capitalism to the preferences of powerful capitalist actors.[287] Thus, law may exhibit power independent of or in opposition to the will of individual capitalists or even the capitalist "class" and yet at the same time also articulate the systemic requirements of capitalism. The key example of such relative autonomy is the formal equality of status afforded equally to workers and capitalists in a liberal state, and manifested in a host of civil rights and liberties. Since this equal status is undermined in practice by the inequalities of political, economic, and cultural power associated with class, it is merely formal.[288] How-

---

[281] Walter Benn Michaels, *The Gold Standard and the Logic of Naturalism* (Berkeley: Univ. of California Press, 1987), 13 (describing Charlotte Perkins Gilman, "The Yellow Wallpaper," in *The Charlotte Perkins Gilman Reader*, ed. Ann J. Lane, [New York: Pantheon Books, 1980]).

[282] Ibid., 19.

[283] Ibid., 20.

[284] Cf. ibid., 21. Writing is "neither material nor ideal. . . . And the drama of this internal division . . . is an urgent artistic concern in the period between the Civil War and World War I."

[285] Ibid., 26–28.

[286] Isaac D. Balbus, "Commodity Form and Legal Form: An Essay on the 'Relative Autonomy' of the Law," *Law and Society Review* 11 (1977): 571, 574 (defining the fetishism of commodities).

[287] Ibid., 572–73.

[288] Ibid., 577–81.

ever, it sets limits on the power and privilege of capitalists and is, in this sense, autonomous from their will. The relative autonomy of this "legal form" from the will of actors results from what Balbus calls a "homology" between the legal form and the commodity form.[289]

At the political level, individuals are "homologized" into the abstract identity of equal "citizens" in order to make political and economic representation of their "interests" possible. Indeed, humans become their "interests," ceasing to act like social beings, but instead merely inviting commodity-like negotiations with others' interests. The homology between commodity form and legal form threatens to become identity when we encounter anthropomorphized enterprises, legal persons that are also negotiable property interests. Individuals and inanimate enterprises then become mutually commensurable and negotiable on the plain of interests.

The development of American legal forms in the nineteenth century is largely about the evolution of a right of negotiability as a means of abstracting money from tangible property or from individual market transactions and assignments. Money became a more abstracted symbol that could float above property and contracts, though it could always be reduced to those things when necessary. For Morton Horwitz, the abstraction of property and contract into money had a "shattering effect" on contract law.[290] Legislatures resisted the negotiability of private money out of fear of losing control of the money supply. Thus, law in a capitalist society controlled the meaning of social and contractual relations by controlling the ability of inscriptions of debt and value to float free of their origins, to achieve transcendent abstraction.[291] But there is a more complex story to tell about the rise of commercial formalism in American law and economics, a story that oddly parallels the development of the merchant character in England.

TRANSCENDENTAL COMMERCE

It may be hard to imagine two nineteenth-century philosophers as different as Marx and Emerson. Yet Emerson was, in his own way, equally fascinated by the relation of money, commodity, symbol, and value.[292] In imagining labor as a form of idealist endeavor, Emerson asserted that in paying for labor we should be paying for the knowledge and virtue of the laborer. In any society past the minimal barter stage, we must do so through symbols of currency that can translate knowledge and virtue into wealth and credit. Though these symbols become somewhat abstract and are therefore subject to counterfeiting, the Marxist warns us of the dangers of fetishism and alienated labor; Emerson reminds us that we need commodification to capture dynamic process in stable form. Ironically, the

---

[289] Ibid., 584–86.

[290] Morton J. Horwitz, *The Transformation of American Law, 1780–1860* (Cambridge: Harvard Univ. Press, 1977), 147.

[291] Ibid., 212–16.

[292] Howard Horwitz, *By the Law of Nature: Form and Value in Nineteenth-Century America* (New York: Oxford Univ. Press, 1991), 74–76.

Emersonian idealist does not denounce commodification as much as the materialist Marxist does.

For Emerson, to denounce commodification is to implicitly make a very questionable claim for the transparency of symbolism that denies the key dynamic quality of symbols. It is to assume a rigid relation between symbol and reality, rather than to accept the endless exchange of energy between the world of symbols and the processes they represent. Commerce is not the degradation of virtue but the medium of virtue. Economic complexity and conflict may indicate that humans unfortunately misperceive value in exchange, but that does not make exchange itself immoral. For Emerson economic forms border on the sacramental.

PROTECTIONISM

An explicit legal example of the "application" of transcendentalism to legal doctrine is offered by Howard Horwitz in his boldly imaginative book *By The Law of Nature*. Horwitz offers the initially improbable idea that commercial regulation in the form of trade protectionism can be read as an aspect of American Transcendentalist literature.[293] This notion finds strong support in Polanyi's argument that one of the most underrated forms of social legislation in the nineteenth century was the use of a national currency.[294] According to this view, the original thinkers of economic liberalism considered national imprints on currency meaningless, since they viewed money as a pure medium of exchange. Yet governments, recognizing money as a political tool and a purchasing asset, turned monetary nationalism into a major form of social protectionism, which, according to Polanyi, was even more important than labor legislation, social security, or land use controls.[295]

As Horwitz argues, both protectionism and Transcendentalism sought to reform the internal economy (national and individual) to perfect American character so that property could become an instrument to higher ends.[296] What protectionism protected was the individual and the nation from the volatility of markets. It encouraged the kind of self-reliance that harmonized with universal will, as opposed to purely free trade that promoted a vulgar variant of individualism, selfishness. Protectionism was to enlarge citizens' consciousness of their interdependence with capital, labor, farmers, and merchants. Free trade, on the other hand, was viewed as a false, negative freedom, in which the merchant essentially enslaves individual labor to foreign commercial intermediaries and degrades men into machines. Under protectionism, one can flexibly choose the market in which one competes. And by protecting the home market, protectionism would lead to a perfecting of world markets and ultimately render itself unnecessary. The good commercial character would become a universal.

---

[293] Ibid., 57.
[294] Polanyi, *The Great Transformation*, 24–25.
[295] Ibid., 231–32.
[296] Howard Horwitz, *By the Law of Nature*, 57–61.

NATURAL MONEY

Walter Benn Michaels's view of money in the nineteenth century captures its haunting quality and its role as a currency of identity. For Michaels, capitalism creates both its objects and its subjects; it creates the desires for the commodities it creates. Money has both value and no value, as it is both a real thing and a representation, and bourgeois art endlessly plays on this relationship.[297] Like money, bourgeois art is neither ideal nor material; that is, it is not ideal insofar as it has cash value, and it is not material insofar as its value is a function of its meaning. After all, a representation can be sold many times at once and in different places. In Michaels's critical history, the goal of Naturalist literature was to end representation—to capture the thing itself, and so the rhetoric of money as representation helps us appreciate the moral aesthetics of certain legal forms.[298] Some forms of practical writing are avowedly part of the market. While more refined types purport to transcend vulgar market effects or origins, all writing is indeed ultimately part of commerce. Michaels shows through the example of the Naturalists how literature is indeed part of the market.[299]

A perfectly representative character for Michaels is Frank Cowperwood, of Dreiser's *The Financier.* For Cowperwood, the actual commodities he could acquire were not real enough because they were not mental enough. Money could flout ordinary conceptions of identity, "producing its own harvests and determining the value of products whose worth it was intended only to symbolize."[300]

The characters in Naturalist novels look to the storehouse of legal forms to produce those representations of wealth that can help them forestall the self-destructive dangers of capitalist logic—excessive production or excessive consumption—to create an everlasting identity for themselves. Money and corporate form provide continuity of personal identity. The person needs a permanent impersonal form, and the impersonal form needs a personal identity, so the person takes on the role of owner or guardian of the fortune.

Michaels traces the parallel worries of writers and legal scholars as to whether a corporation is "real" and notes the non sequitur that reality is somehow associated with personhood.[301] A corporation, however artificial and different from a natural person, can be as "real" as an artificial lake.[302] As Michaels notes, the early finance capitalists, like Dreiser himself, were less concerned with the distinction between the infinite "verbal" and the finite "physical" than we might have supposed.[303] Rather, these early financiers were more disposed to see the infinite power of language not as a threat to capitalism but as an essential part of its

---

[297] Michaels, *Gold Standard*, 156–59.

[298] Ibid., 156–61.

[299] Ibid., 137–80.

[300] Ibid., 68.

[301] Ibid., 188–206.

[302] Ibid., 203.

[303] Ibid., 200–213.

technology. It is the purpose of artificial legal bodies to immortalize desires and to govern and express interests.

Capitalists like Cowperwood produce legal forms like the futures contract, the corporation, and the trust to arrest the volatile dynamism of the market. In the untrammeled market, commerce can destroy itself by overproducing, ironically flouting human intentions. The human endeavor to produce leads to unintended panics, and nature replaces work as a force of the economy. Art, of course, is supposed to reflect timeless truth and beauty that escape the market. Capitalists like Cowperwood express this hope by converting art into a form of wealth that they hope merely to accumulate, not sell. The perverse result is that art becomes too much like a commodity, dependent on acceptance for value. Lacking absolute value, it ends up looking just like money.

Thus, as Michaels plays out the dizzying permutations of the real and the represented, avarice is just another form of aesthetic retreat that strives but fails to escape the market. Does one want money to have the unused power to buy? Does one buy for the pleasure of buying, not owning? The spendthrift enjoys buying nothing, while the miser wants to stay out of the market by using money to buy money. If the value of gold depends on its scarcity, then it depends on the value it would have if it were not money. Those who love the inherent value-beauty of gold treat its value as aesthetic, as representational. We do not desire things in themselves—we want representations, or, more perversely, we want real things that look like representations. Art is neither merely formal nor an illusionistic image of something else. It marks the potential discrepancy between material and identity, the discrepancy that makes money, painting, and people possible. As Michaels says, misers love gold because to them it represents money.[304]

The relevance of this literary history to law is that the advent of a money culture inspires legal and aesthetic efforts to create forms that express and contain the dynamic forces of market capitalism. Rather than see such forms as the negotiable instrument as suppressing the true social relations underlying economic transactions,[305] a literary approach to these forms sees them as more complex aesthetic vehicles. Ideological and legal battles over money are bizarre, because the legal actors fail to realize that the conditions under which these conflicts occur really create the subjects of the conflicts. It may be a perverse fallacy that economies can be subjects and have desires, but it is a fallacy that makes an economy possible and accommodates our tendency to view natural objects as if they were human. For Michaels, souls living under capitalism know what they do and why they do it, but not the effect of what they do. These souls cannot comprehend the connection between individual acts and the whole economy. Personification of the economy, and smaller personifications of economic forces in legal forms, are efforts to ease the anguish of this uncertainty.

---

[304] For Michaels's inquiry into the historical perception of currency, see ibid., 139–46.

[305] Morton Horwitz, *Transformation of American Law, 1780–1860*, 231.

THE CORPORATION

For Michaels, the corporation represents the eternal capitalist life, the form of commerce that transcends the vagaries of commerce.[306] A corporation is usually viewed as "a fictitious artificial person composed of natural persons, created by the state, existing only in contemplation of law, invisible, soulless, immortal."[307] What is fictitious is the attribution to corporations of personhood, and yet this fiction may be intrinsic to the prevailing concept of person, which, in turn, implicitly explains the acts of individuals by reference to such mysterious spectral entities as the will or the soul. Since the corporation is imaginary, it is easy to impute human desire or other qualities to it, and this imputation, in turn, reflects the way we imagine ourselves. Likewise, people, at least as commercial actors, may be constructed corporate fictions.

The corporation is a figure of ravenous desire, conceived as a mere agent of distribution but ending up as the great consumer of value. It is the answer to the wonderful question of capitalism that Michaels poses: How do rich people who seem to have all that a person could want manage to keep on wanting?[308] A person has to have a limited body and hence a limited appetite, but the corporation can transcend these limits. Just as the corporation, saviorlike, takes upon itself the liability of its investors, it also takes on their desires and keeps them safe from satiation.[309] And if a corporation has no essential personality, we are wholly free to impute to it anything we want. This is the ironic essence of literary Naturalism, reducing both things and persons to personifications of supposedly biological or material forces.[310] Capitalism, like nature, has a weird purposiveness. The same human mind that can create an epic poem by conceiving and depicting the great monstrous purposive forces of physical and human nature can conceive of the corporation as the formal embodiment of such forces.

THE MONOPOLY TRUST

So long, however, as the corporation enjoyed and suffered the legal rights and responsibilities of a "person," it was subject to attack under antimonopoly laws because it was seen as a willful market agent. Howard Horwitz uses aesthetic criteria to "read" the monopoly trust, a bizarre late-nineteenth-century legal instrument, as the solution to this legal (and cultural) problem.[311]

According to Horwitz the trust form was designed to circumvent laws that prohibited interstate ownership, and to bring order to competitive chaos through vertical and horizontal integration. Corporate directors nominally abdicated con-

---

[306] Michaels, *Gold Standard*, 202–13.

[307] Arthur W. Machen Jr., "Corporate Personality," *Harvard Law Review* 24 (1911): 253, 265 (noting that the entity that is personified by the corporate fiction is itself no fiction).

[308] Michaels, *Gold Standard*, 205–6.

[309] Ibid., 187–88.

[310] Ibid., 200–203.

[311] Howard Horwitz, *By the Law of Nature*, 171–91.

trol to trustees, and turned stockholders' shares into trust certificates. Thus, the trustees ran the businesses, not the shareholders nor their agents, the directors. The trust represented a "decapitation of the corporation," a viciously clever device to erase any traces of individual agency or will in commercial transactions so as to evade conventional legal responsibility for illegal business practices. As such, the trust went much further than the corporation in dissolving the individualist ego into a higher spirit that is both the end of and the apotheosis of American individualism. The trust transgressed and at the same time enhanced individualism.[312]

Horwitz asks the intriguing question: What is the relationship between the monopoly trust and transcendentalism? Was the first John D. Rockefeller a transcendentalist? Was he the Emersonian man? Was Frank Cowperwood, the hero of Dreiser's *The Financier*, the Nietzschean man?[313] Horwitz draws on Emersonian aesthetics to help us understand how the "robber barons" of that era altered the corporate entity in a manner that reflected the nineteenth-century American cultural struggle over the role of individualism.[314] The great irony of the big corporation was that it crushed the individual under the weight of abstract commercial power while also reflecting the triumph of voluntarism and of a disembodied will freed from the constraining particularity of the empirical individual or social group.[315]

If we believe that individual will is the original and only proper ground for moral judgment, then the character of the trust threatens that belief. Dreiser's Cowperwood says, "A man . . . must never be an agent . . . acting for himself or others"[316] because to represent is to introduce the possibility of misrepresenting. The trust enables the superman to appear to be the mere medium of transcendental forces.

In that sense, corporate practice and literary practice are "affiliated cultural formations." For all their differences, Emerson and Rockefeller use the same logic: "the morality of action is justified by the transcendence of personal agency. Emersonian self-reliance, epitomized in the famous transparent eyeball figure, seeks virtue and self-perfection in self-eradication," and "the financier's immorality was obscured in the shadow of the institution he spawned."[317]

The key to Rockefeller's success was his skill in getting confidential information—his skill was not occult, but highly strategic.[318] For Emerson's visionary compact between mind and nature, self and other, the harmony is never a balanced negotiation but an endless exchange and appropriation.[319] The poet's integrative faculty draws the concrete into the public and the universal. Rockefeller's faculty

[312] Ibid., 182–83.
[313] Ibid., 171–72.
[314] Ibid., 181–86.
[315] Ibid., 172.
[316] Thedore Dreiser, *The Financier* (New York: Harper, 1912), 44.
[317] Howard Horwitz, *By the Law of Nature*, 172.
[318] Michaels, *Gold Standard*, 173–74.
[319] Ibid., 174.

is the subtle eye for collecting information. But it is a rapacious and imperialistic mind that does the integrating. Mere commodities take on universal, transcendent significance when purified through the self, and visible form is no longer essence. As in politics, purporting to merely be the medium through which plural wills or a collective will speaks may merely sublimate the most arrogant expression of power. This is consonant with Darwinian notions of capitalism, such as Carnegie's view that there is a "special talent" intrinsic to the self and independent of material circumstances that causes wealth.[320]

Through the monopoly trust, the corporation gave up "mean egotism" and agency to an "autotelic" figure.[321] Commercial exchanges were no longer interest-driven transactions but traces of natural market forces merely represented in the passive medium of the trusteeship. In this ironic separation of ownership and control, the trust was an invisible nonentity; it had no legal form and filed no reports. It could not be found because it was pure illusion and elusion. The trustees claimed not to be agents of real principals, but rather the "actualizers" of market forces.[322] No formal traces of agency were ever left. No contracts were drawn, but parallel transactions occurred in natural harmony. The trust was "sheer form." It "did nothing."[323] It was dressed up in utopian justifications as an ideal universal democracy, blurring the public and private. Ida Tarbell said of Rockefeller what Emerson said of the universal merchant: "His body is in one spot, but his eyes are turned to all regions of the world."[324]

THE FAMILY TRUSTEE

A final example of the cultural aesthetics of legal form is a logical extension of the monopoly trust—the family trustee or fiduciary. As described by the sociologist George Marcus, a fiduciary is a catalytic character who converts interests into disinterestedness.[325] He is a negotiator among social and cultural norms, economic forces, and wealth. The fiduciary serving as a trustee for family wealth translates the rapacious and often conflicting self-interests of the heirs of a patriarchal financial dynasty into a rational collective unit, one whose collective interest in self-perpetuation requires transcendence over the individual interests of the members. By means of the family trust, individual rapacity, the force of selfish agency, is transformed into the self-less, transcendent interest of the family. At the same time, the warmth, loyalty, commitment, and sentiments of family life are transformed into a cold, impersonal monolith. The cultural instrument to achieve this negotiation is a legal form—the family trust in its various guises. A fiduciary is the perfect figure of the person who transcends interests by effacing his own

---

[320] Ibid., 179.

[321] Howard Horwitz, *By the Law of Nature*, 184.

[322] Ibid.

[323] Ibid., 189.

[324] Ibid.

[325] George E. Marcus with Peter Dobkin Hall, *Lives in Trust: The Fortunes of Dynastic Families in Late Twentieth-Century America* (Boulder: Westview Press, 1992), 71–72.

agency. He acts for and in the interests of others. In so doing he also purifies those interests by embodying them in the person of a disinterested fiduciary.

The trust is a form of social discipline of capitalist energy: while the classic story of modernization sees labor as undergoing discipline to be able to participate in rationalized production processes, the trust form performs the same role for capital itself.[326] Capital especially requires discipline when the children of the great patriarchal estates become sufficiently tempted by anomic consumption interests to threaten dissolution of the estate. As the family ages into patrician and noblesse oblige status it also becomes weak, such that it must create a transcendent, controlling emblem of itself to ensure cohesion and reputation. The phenomenon of the dynasty is an aberration in a democratic culture and yet, as an icon of upward mobility, an object of veneration in a culture no less devoted to opportunity. The dynasty's emblematic qualities come not from the individual commitments of heirs to their common lineage, but from the law and work of fiduciaries. Insofar as the dynasty is an emblem of upward mobility it represents individual opportunity that, because of its multigenerationality, holds forth the promise of an endless future of ever-greater wealth and achievement. No matter how lowly and humble, any individual can aspire to eventual transcendence through his posterity, since there is no formal boundary of blood and lineage restricting entry into the American aristocracy.

One specific type of trustee, which Marcus calls the insider-outsider, is a very refined sort of cultural-legal artist. He is close enough to the family to occasionally consult on familial disputes, but the family understands that he must maintain neutrality and distance if he is to help the family negotiate its self-transcendence. This fiduciary injects the dynastic interest into diffuse, volatile family relations and monitors the linkages of family and property through their gradual, anticipated decoupling. A good trustee monitors the dynamic processes of money transformation into an apparently static form that allows the holders of the wealth to appear as passive beneficiaries.[327] Under capitalism, fiduciaries are especially vital because wealth is a dynamic abstraction and depends on "a coordinating human intermediary to perform these transformations."[328] The trustee is thus a subtle director for this social drama. "The fiduciary," Marcus claims, "is interested in money and values as abstractions within the conventions of investment institutions";[329] for the family members, he is a legal specialist carrying out plans, explaining their rights and duties by translating events into a legal calculus, sometimes demystifing the reified nature of family wealth—sometimes re-reifying it to prevent members from dismembering the corpus. As he performs the technical tasks of fending off taxes and regulations, the trustee helps construct the family's wealth for different purposes, using alternative images or abstract forms to serve various needs.

---

[326] Ibid., 54–56.
[327] Ibid., 72.
[328] Ibid., 57.
[329] Ibid., 72.

For Marcus, the disinterested fiduciary can act for those who are interested yet remain above suspicion himself, since his stewardship is not of any individual interest, but of the family as a whole. Ironically, the technical servant of the family is also the morally superior preacher to it, performing the tasks that members cannot do themselves and often would, individually, prefer not to see done at all. The fiduciary is "rational" in a complex way: he carries out and embodies the rational self-interest of the family but must synthesize it out of the possibly irrational appetites of the individual members. Thus, he is an artist of legal forms and cultural norms, whose working material is the conceptual currency of law and business.[330]

In its quest for a noble cultural identity, the family projects an ideal representation of itself and then subordinates itself to that representation. The fiduciary was both the creator and protector of that representation, thus saving the family from itself. The foundation became a superior fiduciary product; institutional donations replaced individual merchants' donations. As a result, American philanthropy came to depend on the beneficiaries of the patriarchal donors, the people whose "job" was to enjoy rather than to consume capital.[331] This group includes charitable institutions that receive money and spend it according to fiduciary norms. Of course, this often means cultural institutions—such as museums, universities, and libraries—so that we bring aesthetic transcendence full circle. Beyond these trusted managers of philanthropic capital stand the brigades of cultural service workers they support—the artists, authors, musicians, curators, librarians, and academics who complete the cultural laundering and embroidery of capital.[332]

Organized dynasties dissolve after a few generations, but their enduring legacy is a fiduciary-managed trust of patrimonial capital. In the effort to create a timeless entity, the trust must circumvent such explicitly time-bound laws as the rule against perpetuities—hence the notion of the perpetual charitable foundation, the permanent agent of disinterestedness. The trustee-artist finesses the tension between the demands of money management and the dynamics of family sentiment, though his actions are likely to constrain and distort the latter to serve the former.[333]

The family does not pressure the fiduciary to resolve family disputes—indeed, the family may even recruit ad hoc consultants for that job: "The transcendence of the fiduciary is thus mutually sustained by the fiduciary and those he serves."[334] The fiduciary might be partly independent of the family, but his own life is at the edge between the two forces he balances.

As Georg Simmel noted in *The Philosophy of Money,* "The ideal purpose of money, as well as of the law, is to be a measure of things without being measured

[330] Ibid., 62–70.
[331] Ibid., 58–59.
[332] Ibid., 69.
[333] Ibid., 57–59
[334] Ibid., 69.

itself, a purpose that can be realized fully only by an endless development."[335] Hence, the fiduciary is a "human incarnation of the abstract functioning of law and money,"[336] the authoritative interpreter in a legal and capitalist idiom of a rich family's constitution and development, seen by family members themselves less rationally and holistically. The trust is a reified phenomenon replacing patriarchal authority. Family members "trust" not family feelings but cold abstraction. The fiduciary helps interpret family life without exposing itself to interpretation beyond the mere affirmation of its authority. Thus, in capitalism, a form of lineage and dynasty finds strength in a mechanism defined by a rationality that is "alien to the mix of sentiment and self-interest which we think motivates family relations."[337]

An interesting aspect of the fiduciary profession is that it is anthropologically self-conscious, using such revealing criteria to describe itself as "disinterestedness, stewardship, and rationality."[338] The profession assumes that social relations are driven by self-interest, and that families are odd mixtures of competition and cooperation. Family loyalty always comes dynamically mixed with individual greed. The job of the trustee is to harness and balance those energies, but also to offer the world—and the family itself—a better interpretation of these family dynamics.

The family's capital and identity achieve ultimate transcendence of interest with the foundation of a philanthropic trust for the support of the arts or the disinterested pursuit of knowledge.[339] To preserve itself accumulated capital must work itself free of interestedness, so that the abstraction of legal form proves to be a logic of transcendence as well as commodification—a double movement of alienation of the material from the human and of the anthropomorphosis and apotheosis of the material. The accumulation of capital is accompanied by a constant effort of the imagination, reconstructing an always ephemeral region of the sacred, temporarily just beyond the bounds of commodification, but always on the verge of profanation and obsolescence.

POSTMODERNISM AND COMMERCIAL FORM

The Emersonian view of commercial form finds a fascinating echo in contemporary critical theory. Postmodernist scholars like David Harvey have discerned that poststructuralist form is exemplified by the contemporary commodification of money, reduced to (or exalted to) electronic international blips that defy normal constraints of space and time.[340] Money symbolism, in the pop culture criticism

---

[335] Georg Simmel, *The Philosophy of Money*, trans. Tom Bottomore and David Frisby (London: Routledge and Kegan Paul, 1978), 511; see also Marcus, *Lives in Trust*, 70.

[336] Ibid.

[337] Ibid.

[338] Ibid., 71.

[339] Ibid., 69.

[340] David Harvey, *The Condition of Postmodernity: An Inquiry into the Origins of Cultural Change* (Oxford: Blackwell, 1989), 63–64.

of this era, became the art of the 1990s. "Swap" transactions[341] and electronic manipulations of the Eurodollar market[342] have become the abstract impressionism of contemporary commerce. Indeed, if there were deconstructionists writing for the *Wall Street Journal*, they would say that we cannot control our representations because they end up implicating all the other representations of which they are a network. In a postmodernist culture of symbolic inflation, all styles at once are on display, a circulation of diverse and contradictory cultural elites. We are suffering, implies Harvey, a crisis of representation, a readjustment of our sense of time and space in politics, economics, and culture. A whole issue of the literary journal *Diacritics* addressed how crises in representation are simultaneously aesthetic and financial.[343]

Marx called money the lubricant of community, but money has become the "real" community of international relations, the International Monetary Fund the institutional embodiment of globalization that the United Nations pretends to be. To perform the commodity function, money must be replaced by symbols of itself—in credit instruments. If, in a Marxist view, the bourgeoisie cannot survive without endless revolutions in the technology of commodification, without sped-up turnover time and liquidity of capital, to exacerbate the insecurity and so maintain the availability of workers, capitalist money production must be in an endless state of revolution. Now we can say that money is truly fictitious capital—all investment is a credit bet on either production not yet realized or others' misperception of the value of what has been or will be realized. Possibility masquerades as currency. Thus, to the postmodernist cultural critic, economic policy is cultural policy. But government policy therefore has to control the fluid and open spaces of money markets—to contest within its borders the effects of widespread individualism and ephemerality, and to carve out islands of fantasy amid the tempests of currency—since if currency is the only medium of self-expression, there can no longer be any self-interest to pursue.

Postmodernist pronouncements of the death of subjectivity to the contrary, we are probably far from such a predicament. The particular representations of subjectivity most recently venerated will follow the inevitable logic of commodification and profanation, but they will be replaced by others. The work of culture in market society is not the preservation of existing identities from alienation. It is the imaginative work of constantly fashioning new identities and new institutional forms that briefly embody them before turning into "pods." For better or worse, the very rapidity of commodification remarked by postmodernists engenders a corresponding speed up in cultural innovation. Legal disputing, transacting, enacting, and planning are implicated in that constant, Sisyphean effort of imagination. It follows that the literary dimension of law is not lost in some remote

[341] See, e.g., Henry T. C. Hu, "Swaps, the Modern Process of Financial Innovation and the Vulnerability of a Regulatory Paradigm," *University of Pennsylvania Law Review* (1989): 333, 336.

[342] Harvey, *Condition of Postmodernity*, 163–64.

[343] See generally *Diacritics*, summer 1988 (reviewing various articles on economics and real property).

Arcadian past when politics was virtue, when work was craft, when exchange was fraternity. Instead the literary imagination is inherent in the law of modern society, simply because law is both the means by which we continuously refashion society and one of the media in which we represent and critique what we have fashioned.

Does law's participation in the work of "humanizing" the market make law inherently redemptive? Yes, so long as we understand redemption as an aspect of the functioning of a market economy rather than an escape from it—a balm for civilization's discontents rather than a cure. The cultural redemption of capitalism, like the abatement of pollution and the disposal of waste, paradoxically conserves the conditions of its own necessity. To identify law as redemptive in this sense is to portray it less as an antidote to alienation than as a co-dependent.

But the imaginative work of law involves much more than the cosmetic ornamentation of market society. The fictions and figures of law are the very architecture of not only the diverse markets, but all the other institutions that compose society. These institutions have no necessary pattern or purpose to which culture must conform.[344] The institutions we establish, the roles those institutions constitute, the dramas of dispute and transaction those roles enable, the institutional changes those dramas bring about—these are neither constraints on culture nor causes of culture. They are culture itself.

CONCLUSION

It follows that reading and criticizing the fictions, figures, and stratagems of law is indispensable to cultural criticism. George Marcus and Michael Fischer have observed that twentieth-century cultural criticism has typically taken one of two forms: "First, at its most philosophical, cultural critique has posed as an epistemological critique of analytic reason . . . grounded in the sociology of knowledge. . . . The effect of this style of cultural critique is demystification."[345] While noting that demystification has been an aim of Nietzschean, Marxist, and Weberian cultural critique, Marcus and Fischer add that epistemological criticism is most recently associated with poststructuralist semiotics. A second style of cultural criticism, also drawing on Nietzsche, Marx, and Weber, has emphasized the "Romantic" critique of modernization: "It worries about the fullness and authenticity of modern life and idealizes the satisfactions of communal experience. Behind the growth

[344] For example, while Polanyi, Balbus, and Taussig argue that the formation of "capitalism" involves inculcating belief in fictive commodities, one may equally portray the analytic category of "capitalism" itself as an imaginative construct, since its three defining features—commodity production, capital accumulation, and free labor—have no necessary connection or determinate meaning. See Roberto Mangabeira Unger, *Social Theory: Its Situation and Its Task* 101–19 (1987) (describing the difficulty in determining the key concepts of capitalism); Guyora Binder, "What's Left?" *Texas Law Review* 69 (1991): 2002–8.

[345] George E. Marcus and Michael M. J. Fischer, *Anthropology as Cultural Critique: An Experimental Moment in the Human Sciences* 114 (Chicago: Univ. of Chicago Press, 1986).

of the market, bureaucracies, large corporations, and professional social services, it sees a decline of community and of . . . individual self-worth."[346] Victims of their own success, both of these forms of cultural criticism have lost their capacity to shock or inform: "as rhetorical strategies they have become exhausted."[347] It is now understood that the particular enchantments of traditional society are lost forever, and that they have been replaced not by transparent rationality, but by other enchantments. Accordingly, we have argued throughout this book that criticism is no longer well served by the familiar rhetorical attitudes of skepticism and sentimentality. But there is a third model of cultural critique derivable from the classic critics of modernity, Nietzsche especially. The aim of such criticism is not to recover virtues of the heroic age but to fashion new ones. Thus conceived, the cultural criticism of law is part of the work—at once political and aesthetic— of choosing what kind of culture we hope to have and what kind of identities we hope to foster.

[346] Ibid.
[347] Ibid., 115.